South African Economic Policy under Democracy

South African Economic Policy under Democracy

Edited by Janine Aron, Brian Kahn, and Geeta Kingdon

OXFORD
UNIVERSITY PRESS

Great Clarendon Street, Oxford OX2 6DP

Oxford University Press is a department of the University of Oxford.
It furthers the University's objective of excellence in research, scholarship,
and education by publishing worldwide in

Oxford New York

Auckland Cape Town Dar es Salaam Hong Kong Karachi
Kuala Lumpur Madrid Melbourne Mexico City Nairobi
New Delhi Shanghai Taipei Toronto

With offices in

Argentina Austria Brazil Chile Czech Republic France Greece
Guatemala Hungary Italy Japan Poland Portugal Singapore
South Korea Switzerland Thailand Turkey Ukraine Vietnam

Oxford is a registered trade mark of Oxford University Press
in the UK and in certain other countries

Published in the United States
by Oxford University Press Inc., New York

© Janine Aron and Brian Kahn, 2009

The moral rights of the authors have been asserted
Database right Oxford University Press (marker)

First edition published 2009

All rights reserved. No part of this publication may be reproduced,
stored in a retrieval system, or transmitted, in any form or by any means,
without the prior permission in writing of Oxford University Press,
or as expressly permitted by law, or under terms agreed with the appropriate
reprographics rights organization. Enquiries concerning reproduction
outside the scope of the above should be sent to the Rights Department,
Oxford University Press, at the address above

You must not circulate this book in any other binding or cover
and you must impose the same condition on any acquirer

British Library Cataloguing in Publication Data

Data available

Library of Congress Cataloging in Publication Data

Data available

Typeset by SPI Publisher Services, Pondicherry, India
Printed in Great Britain
on acidfree paper by CPI Antony Rowe, Chippenham, Wiltshire

ISBN 978-0-19-955146-0

1 3 5 7 9 10 8 6 4 2

Music and Economics

The editorial royalties from the sale of this book will be donated to the Buskaid Trust, a musical charity dependent on private donations, which supports a music school in Diepkloof, Soweto, dedicated to teaching stringed instruments to local township children <http://www.buskaid.org.za>. The charity was established by professional viola player, Rosemary Nalden, in 1992 and the Buskaid Music School subsequently opened in 1997. Ten years on it has 70 children attending its music school, its own workshop for repairing instruments, an 'in-house' teacher-training programme, and a string ensemble that has toured internationally, most recently performing at the Proms in Britain in 2007 with the English Baroque Soloists. Buskaid has recorded classical music CDs, and music in South Africa's rich tradition, such as its own Kwela arrangements.

This charity, and others like it, could form the seed for greater access for disadvantaged children in South Africa to a musical education. Inspiration for the democratic access to music education comes from the pioneering scheme in Venezuela, the National System of Youth and Children's Orchestras of Venezuela—known popularly as *el sistema*. Founded in 1967 by the economist and musician, Jose Antonio Abreu, *el sistema*, now state-funded, offers free instruments and musical training, and, like Buskaid, promotes responsibility, teamwork, community, and work ethic through the joy and achievement of orchestral playing. Currently 250,000 children benefit, with 15,000 music teachers, and 600 orchestras throughout Venezuela, including the famous Simon Bolivar Youth Orchestra. The current annual cost to the Venezuelan state is about £15 m, equivalent to 0.04 of one percent of South Africa's 2007/8 government expenditure. Britain, Scotland, and the county of Los Angeles recently adopted the methods of *el sistema* in pilot projects, to provide underprivileged children with a sense of purpose and aspiration.

This book recognizes the importance of beneficial social networks, and of the commitment of state funding to long-term educational and social projects for the disadvantaged.

Janine Aron
September, 2008

Contents

	List of Contributors	ix
1.	South African Economic Policy under Democracy: Overview and Prospects *Janine Aron, Brian Kahn, and Geeta Kingdon*	1
2.	Accounting for South Africa's Growth Revival after 1994 *Stan Du Plessis and Ben Smit*	28
3.	The Development of Transparent and Effective Monetary and Exchange Rate Policy *Janine Aron and John Muellbauer*	58
4.	Transforming Fiscal Governance *Tania Ajam and Janine Aron*	92
5.	Capital Flows, Financial Markets, and the External Balance Sheet *Jonathan Leape and Lynne Thomas*	118
6.	Trade Policy in South Africa *Lawrence Edwards, Rashad Cassim, and Dirk van Seventer*	151
7.	Capital Formation in South Africa *Johannes W. Fedderke*	182
8.	The Evolution and Impact of Industrial and Competition Policies *Anthony Black and Simon Roberts*	211
9.	The Macroeconomic Impact of AIDS and ART *Ben Smit and Linette Ellis*	244
10.	A Long-run Perspective on Contemporary Poverty and Inequality Dynamics *Murray Leibbrandt, Ingrid Woolard, and Christopher Woolard*	270

Contents

11. Unemployment: South Africa's Achilles' Heel
    Geeta Kingdon and John Knight   300

12. The Persistence of Inequalities in Education
    Servaas van der Berg   327

    Index   355

List of Contributors

Tania Ajam AFREC (Pty) Ltd, Suite 228, Private Bag X18, Rondebosch 7701, South Africa

Janine Aron CSAE, Department of Economics, Manor Road Building, Manor Road, Oxford OX1 3UQ

Anthony Black School of Economics, University of Cape Town, Private Bag, Rondebosch 7701, South Africa

Rashad Cassim Statistics South Africa, Private Bag x44, Pretoria 0001, South Africa

Stan Du Plessis Department of Economics, University of Stellenbosch, Private Bag X1, Matieland 7602, South Africa

Lawrence Edwards School of Economics, University of Cape Town, Private Bag Rondebosch 7701, South Africa

Linette Ellis Bureau for Economic Research, Private Bag X5050, Stellenbosch 7599, South Africa

Johannes W. Fedderke School of Economics, University of Cape Town, Private Bag Rondebosch 7701, South Africa

Brian Kahn South African Reserve Bank, P.O. Box 427, Pretoria, 0001, South Africa

Geeta Kingdon Institute of Education, University of London, 20 Bedford Way, London WC1H 0AL

John Knight CSAE, Department of Economics, Manor Road Building, Manor Road, Oxford OX1 3UQ

Jonathan Leape CREFSA, London School of Economics, Houghton Street, London WC2A 2AE

Murray Leibbrandt School of Economics, University of Cape Town, Private Bag Rondebosch 7701, South Africa

John Muellbauer Nuffield College, Oxford OX1 1NF

List of Contributors

Simon Roberts Competition Commission, P. Bag X23, Lynnwood Ridge 0040, South Africa

Ben Smit Department of Economics, University of Stellenbosch, Private Bag X1, Matieland 7602, South Africa

Lynne Thomas CREFSA, London School of Economics, Houghton Street, London WC2A 2AE

Servaas van der Berg Department of Economics, University of Stellenbosch, Private Bag X1, Matieland 7602, South Africa

Dirk van Seventer TIPS, PO Box 11214, Hatfield, Pretoria 0028, South Africa

Christopher Woolard SALDRU, 1 University Avenue, University of Cape Town, Private Bag X3, Rondebosch 7701, South Africa

Ingrid Woolard SALDRU, 1 University Avenue, University of Cape Town, Private Bag X3, Rondebosch 7701, South Africa

1

South African Economic Policy under Democracy: Overview and Prospects

Janine Aron, Brian Kahn, and Geeta Kingdon

1. Introduction: Economic legacy and the transition[1]

The transition to democracy in South Africa (SA) in 1994 brought great promise for the future. It enfranchised millions of citizens, altered the implicit 'social contract', and created expectations of progress in social and economic well-being and reduced inequality. The economy emerged from economic and political isolation in the early 1990s. The apartheid-era policies and consequent international sanctions on trade and investment had biased economic policies in an inward-looking direction, and created significant distortions which stunted the growth potential of the economy. The country's reintegration with the rest of the world brought hope of increased trade and restored capital flows. Aided by international integration, sound macroeconomic policies were expected to bring fiscal and monetary stability, helping to foster economic growth and support redistribution. In particular, it was hoped that employment opportunities would increase, and that both the access to, and quality of, education and health would improve, further helping to alleviate poverty.

However, the social and economic legacy of the apartheid era presented significant policy challenges. SA's re-entry into the global environment required

---

[1] Acknowledgements: Janine Aron acknowledges funding support from the Economic and Social Research Council, U.K. (grant RES-000–22–2066). Janine Aron and Brian Kahn are grateful for comments and interaction when writing this introduction from Stan Du Plessis, Gavin Keeton, John Knight, Jonathan Leape, Murray Leibbrandt, John Page, Francis Teal, and especially John Muellbauer. The views represented here are those of the authors alone, not of the institutions to which they are affiliated.

restructuring of the economy in order to become competitive, inevitably resulting in short-run adjustment costs. Yet these came at a time of heightened expectations for redressing past imbalances. The initial conditions were inauspicious for a rapid turnaround in economic growth. Not only had the economy experienced a long-term real growth decline relative to a selected group of market economies (see Figure 2.2), but had fallen further behind in the productive employment of capital and labour. The labour market was segmented along racial lines, and blacks were mainly unskilled. Combined with high unemployment rates, the low wages meant that poverty was widespread. The distributions of income and wealth were highly unequal, with the income Gini coefficient of around 0.7, one of the highest in the world. Such extreme inequality raises the risk of social instability, and potentially the risk premium for capital through possible future redistributive taxes and transfer payments (Aron and Muellbauer, 2005). The distribution of land was also highly skewed as a result of restrictions on property ownership by blacks, and forced removals. Despite a healthy banking sector, most blacks lacked access to banking services, and restrictions on home ownership deprived most blacks of the necessary collateral for mortgage and other borrowing.

The duality of the economy extended to the education and health systems. The attainment and quality of education varied greatly between racial groups (see Chapter 12). In particular, access to quality education by blacks was restricted, and the black education system was extremely poor. Teacher training suffered similarly. Since 1976, education had been an important locus of the struggle against apartheid under the slogan: 'no education before liberation', and many schools had become essentially dysfunctional. Further, access to good health facilities was largely restricted to whites. Demographic factors such as high fertility rates (see Figure 2.3, Chapter 2) and high levels of urbanization, following the repeal of laws preventing permanent migration to the cities, placed pressure on the labour markets, as well as on service delivery at the local level. The need for provision of public services to those previously excluded suggested a long-term effort with associated economic costs.

The protracted period of sanctions from the late 1970s also led to a distorted economy. The lack of access to foreign capital due to financial and investment sanctions constrained economic growth. Exchange controls were an important part of the regulatory environment, and also contributed to the development of large conglomerates, mainly originating in the mining sector. Lack of foreign opportunities meant that these conglomerates grew into areas which were not necessarily their core competence resulting in inefficiencies and constraining domestic competition (see Chapter 8). Trade sanctions exacerbated the prevalent protectionist tendencies. Manufacturing therefore developed as highly protected and uncompetitive, despite half-hearted attempts to stimulate manufactured exports in the 1980s.

Introduction

On the macroeconomic front, fiscal policy had been relatively disciplined, but deteriorated seriously towards the end of the apartheid era. The inherited fiscal position after apartheid was unsustainable, with a large and growing domestic debt and budget deficit (the latter reaching nearly 8 per cent of GDP by 1992/3). Fiscal governance lacked transparency and accountability, and intergovernmental relations were dysfunctional with over-complex provincial and municipal structures (see Chapter 4). Government expenditure had also long been skewed in favour of whites. Monetary policy was highly variable with volatile interest rates; and real interest rates were negative during part of the 1970s and 1980s. Together with restricted skills development and racial policies in employment, this helped distort production towards greater capital intensity.

Ironically, certain strengths also emerged from the dual economy. The drive to self-sufficiency under sanctions led to parts of the infrastructure, particularly those serving the white community, being well developed. These included transport and roads, communications, electricity generation, and pockets of technology, such as Sasol, the chemical giant, which developed from the apartheid state's strategic objective to reduce dependence on imported oil. Parts of the education system, especially white schools and universities, were of good quality. Importantly, the financial sector was also relatively highly developed, sophisticated and well regulated, including a deep domestic bond market and a well capitalized equity market.

By 2008, the SA economy looked very different to that in 1994. International relations in credit and foreign currency markets and in trade had been normalized, restoring sovereign reputation and credibility and reflected in improved international credit ratings. Real growth rates of around 5 per cent were achieved and investment had begun to rise. Macroeconomic stability, in the form of fiscal balance, declining public debt and relatively low inflation, was the norm; and the economy was more open, competitive, and liberalized. The structure of the economy had also changed: the tertiary sector expanded relative to the rest of the economy, in particular financial services, while the shares of manufacturing, mining, and agriculture declined substantially. Social welfare expenditure had increased significantly, despite prudent fiscal policies, as had expenditures on education, health, housing, and basic infrastructure provision. Current account surpluses, a necessity under financial sanctions during the latter period of the apartheid era, were replaced by current account deficits in excess of 7 per cent of GDP, though still relatively easily funded by foreign inflows.

However, apart from the stabilizing achievements of fiscal policy and monetary policy in a more open economy, the policy record, particularly on the supply side of the economy, has been less than impressive. Implicitly this has been recognized in the government's Accelerated and Shared Growth Initiative for SA (AsgiSA, 2006). A major growth constraint listed is 'the cost, efficiency and capacity of the national logistics system', resulting in part from backlogs in infrastructure investment. To a degree these are from past curbs on government expenditure, as well as industrial and regulatory policies and regulation. The record has also been poor in reducing unemployment. Though declining moderately in recent years, it remains very high at 36 per cent in 2007, on the 'broad' measure (23 per cent on the 'narrow' measure). Human capital is critical to employment prospects, but the performance of the education system has been disappointing, despite greatly increased expenditure and broadening of access. The quality of the workforce has also been affected by the AIDs pandemic, and the poor provision of other services affecting well-being and performance, such as housing and health. Finally, while poverty has fallen since 2000, mainly due to increased fiscal transfers, high aggregate inequality and inequality within each race group have persisted.

This volume explores many of the above issues in detail, though of necessity it is selective in its coverage.

2. The evolution of economic policy thinking

The philosophy of economic policy in SA had it roots in the so-called Pact government which came into power in 1924, representing a coalition of white labour and local capital. Successive governments, culminating in the Nationalist government in 1948, focused economic policy on the preservation and promotion of white interests. Racist and repressive policies and legislation by an interventionist state helped to fashion an economic structure based on minerals and cheap black labour. Mining and much of the manufacturing sector were in private hands, but the government was directly involved in manufacturing in several instances, including ISCOR (iron and steel), Sasol (oil from coal), and ARMSCOR military equipment. Infrastructure too was largely a government monopoly, with Transnet responsible for rail, ports, and pipelines, and Eskom for electricity. While mining was relatively unregulated, the manufacturing sector was subject to import substitution policies and protective barriers against imports; and agriculture was tightly controlled through a plethora of agricultural marketing boards and price controls.

During the 1970s, there were some attempts to liberalize the economy in line with international trends, and to reduce the role of the state in the economy as the limits of import substitution policies were recognized. Various commissions appointed during the 1970s focused on export promotion (Reynders Commission, 1972); the liberalization of the financial sector and monetary policy (De Kock Commission, 1978, 1985); labour legislation (the Wiehahn Commission, 1979); and the utilization of manpower (the Riekert Commission, 1979). Nattrass (1988) has argued that these commissions, which promoted an

Introduction

enhanced role for the private sector in the economy and a greater emphasis on free markets, signalled a major ideological shift in economic thinking.

While some privatization and deregulation occurred in the 1980s, the intensification of trade and financial sanctions against SA curtailed any remaining appetite for liberalization. For example, exchange rate liberalization was reversed (see Chapter 3) when a debt standstill was declared in 1985, after Chase Manhattan Bank refused to roll over the government's short-term foreign debt and other banks followed suit. Monetary policy was then dominated by balance of payments concerns and tighter trade policy was used to curtail demand at a time when export promotion was difficult if not impossible. Despite the privatization of ISCOR and Sasol, other state enterprises such as Eskom and ARMSCOR remained firmly under the control of the state.

The ban on the ANC was lifted in 1990. While the exiled ANC had no formal plan for economic change, there were concerns that should it assume power, economic policy might take a strongly socialist turn, including the nationalization of key industries. Nationalization was a cornerstone of the Freedom Charter adopted by the ANC in 1955. Yet the fall of communism under autocratic regimes in the early 1990s provided a strong demonstration of the inadequacy of such policies, and ultimately, the outcome in SA confounded the sceptics. Waldmeier (1998, in Chapter 14) provides an interesting account of what she terms the ANC's 'crash course in reality', through economic consensus building in the years preceding democratic elections: among SA's sophisticated union leadership, local and foreign business leaders, international and domestic politicians, and representatives of SA's financial institutions. Debates at the time had contrasted strategies of growth-through-redistribution and redistribution-through-growth. Yet even prior to the multi-party interim government of late 1993, the then Finance Minister, Keys, revealed to the ANC the deteriorated state of the nation's finances they would inherit. Less than 10 per cent of the budget was available for the redistributive goals, after servicing a mountainous debt and current expenditures on wages and salaries. Moreover, domestic savings were perilously low and insufficient for investment needs. This required the resumption of sustainable foreign inflows, that had all but ceased under apartheid.

These factors helped shape policies. The new ANC government, while endorsing redistributive objectives and overcoming the racial legacies of apartheid, placed emphasis on first creating a stable macroeconomic framework through monetary and fiscal prudence and restructuring the economy in a now more open economic environment (see section 3). They sought to increase competitiveness through industrial policy and competition policy initiatives, and attracting increased foreign investment as a stimulus to growth. Hirsch (2005) characterizes ANC policy as being framed within a social democratic approach to social reform, with the state providing a positive environment for high levels of private sector investment. Moreover, the ANC's long experience in exile head-quartered in Zambia, may have influenced their view as regards multilateral assistance. Hirsch writes: 'the ANC did not wish to entrust international financial institutions or international banks with the country's future' (Hirsch, 2005, p. 3).

The ANC recognized that successful economic policy was subject to constraints laid down by the international system. An export-oriented economy based on private sector investment would be acceptable to the international trading and financial system. Since coming into power, the ANC has moved consistently in the direction of responsible monetary and fiscal policies. Liberalization began with enthusiasm: the pace of trade liberalization was quite marked initially, privatization initiatives were begun, and financial sector liberalization was extensive, particularly the lifting of controls on foreign investment. However this trend did not continue unchecked or extend to all sectors. Trade liberalization has slowed and is no longer seen as a priority (see Chapter 6), but rather has been subordinated to industrial policy. Exchange control liberalization on residents has been very gradual. Privatization is no longer seen as central to policy; regulatory red tape, such as pertaining to mineral rights in the mining sector, has resulted in a stifling of private investment in that sector; and labour laws have been strengthened rather than liberalized. There appears to have been a reversion towards more state intervention or state direction in the economy.

3. International reintegration, macro-stability, and the reduction of uncertainty

In the early years of the new ANC government, much attention was given to achieving macroeconomic stability. Inevitably this led to criticisms that the government was emphasizing stabilization rather than growth. Yet for a country with an elevated risk premium, macroeconomic stabilization was essential, particularly given the deteriorated fiscal position under apartheid.

The initial economic policy view of government was contained in the Reconstruction and Development Programme (RDP) White Paper of 1994. The bulk of the macroeconomic proposals in the RDP were focused on stabilization policies, with the assumption that higher levels of investment, particularly foreign investment, would be encouraged by the commitment to macroeconomic stability, thereby promoting growth. This was reinforced by the Growth, Equality, and Redistribution (GEAR) framework adopted in June 1996 which aimed to raise international credibility by clarifying the objectives of macro-policy, after the exchange rate crisis in early 1996 (see Chapter 3). It was also reacting to the recent publication of economic strategy proposals by the trade union movement (Cosatu, 1996) and a business foundation (South Africa Foundation, 1996).

Introduction

Fiscal prudence, tax reform, and increased transparency of administration, a reorientation of spending to the social sector, and longer-term expenditure planning, were hallmarks of both the RDP and the GEAR plans. The well-articulated fiscal objectives of these plans were entrenched in the 1996 Constitution[2], and subsequent legislation addressed the many constitutional imperatives, including the restructuring of key organizations such as the (re-named) South African Revenue Services (SARS).

Both plans sought to cut the budget deficit through fiscal consolidation, improved debt management, and more efficient tax collection. A more realistic fiscal position was also seen as facilitating the sustainability of the RDP over time. Both plans aimed to decrease the government dissaving that was contributing to the nation's abysmal domestic savings rate, and hence the dependence on 'foreign savings' in the form of volatile capital inflows to fund investment. Both plans, though within the constraints of consolidation, aimed to substitute investment for consumption expenditure (e.g. on infrastructure), and to alter the composition of spending from military expenditure and debt service towards social expenditure, such as health, pensions and grants, housing, and education. These spending and redistribution goals aimed to address the pervasive supply-side constraints on medium-term economic growth

By contrast with the detailed fiscal policy objectives, there was a rather cursory treatment of monetary policy in the RDP plan. After 1994, monetary policy continued to be governed by the South African Reserve Bank Act (No 90 of 1989), detailing the powers and functions of the central bank. But little emphasis was given to improving the transparency of monetary policy. An important step forward was the constitutional granting of instrument independence to the central bank in setting monetary policy under the Act. Yet the plans and the Interim and Final Constitutions expressed the monetary policy objectives differently, and until mid 1996 there was no clear prioritization amongst these objectives (see Chapter 3).

GEAR interpreted the long-term monetary policy objective as keeping the real effective exchange rate at a competitive level, inflation low and real interest rates positive, but monetary policy continued to lack a transparent and credible target by which to hold the central bank accountable.[3] The consequence was further uncertainty regarding the goals of monetary policy, until the new and transparent system of inflation targeting was introduced in 2000 (see Chapter 3).

---

[2] An Interim Constitution was adopted in 1994 and the Final Constitution in December 1996.

[3] The monetary target guidelines upon which the SARB was purportedly firmly basing its anti-inflation strategy (Stals, 1996), worked poorly, if at all, in the context of liberalized domestic financial markets.

Chapters 3 and 4 argue that the macro-stabilization aims of the RDP and GEAR were in large measure achieved, and under the testing conditions of globalizing through trade reform and capital account liberalization. These developments, since 1994, are discussed in the next two sections.

3.1. Transparent and predictable fiscal, monetary, and exchange rate policies

Systematic risk was lowered by the post-1994 political dispensation, and it was entrenched by the fiscal policies adopted since 1994 and by monetary policies, primarily after 1999 under inflation targeting. The fiscal–monetary policy mix has created an environment of macroeconomic stability conducive to greater investment and long-term growth, lowering sovereign risk, uncertainty, and the real (tax-adjusted) user cost of capital. This has been reflected in the improvement in international credit ratings, sustained portfolio capital inflows, and in the rise in domestic investment in recent years (see Chapters 2, 5, and 7). A key feature of both fiscal and monetary policy (the latter only since 2000) has been the improved transparency, accountability, and predictability of policy-making under the new government.

3.1.1. FISCAL POLICY

Central to the government's macroeconomic stabilization was fiscal policy. The debate in the early 1990s was between those who favoured high deficits in the interests of increasing social expenditures as opposed to those who were more concerned with the nature of the government budget constraint and not to 'crowd out' private investment. The latter saw fiscal restraint as necessary to avoid fiscal dominance (i.e. the subordination of monetary policy to arbitrary fiscal policy) and the loss of international credibility.

Ajam and Aron (Chapter 4) argue that the government addressed both aspects, by reprioritizing and restructuring the government accounts, reducing the budget deficit through increased efficiency in expenditure and revenue collection. Constitutionally based reforms raised fiscal transparency and accountability at national, provincial, and municipal spheres of government, and greater predictability was created through multi-year budgeting. An extensive tax reform was successfully implemented and more efficient tax collection through the independent revenue authority SARS expanded the revenue base. The efficiency gains allowed the reduction in individual and corporate taxes and considerable personal tax relief, although the overall tax burden remained relatively unchanged. However, in the transition, fiscal policy remained relatively pro-cyclical, apart from the operation of automatic stabilizers, and much of the stabilization required fell to monetary policy. By the mid 2000s small budget surpluses were being achieved, and fiscal policy became more counter-cyclical (see Chapter 4).

Introduction

Reorienting spending away from defence and subsidies, with a lower and more sustainable debt burden through improved debt management, has permitted greater priority for social spending, especially on education, health, and social welfare. However, deep concerns remain about the quality of education, health, housing, and other provincial service delivery outputs and about their impact on poverty reduction and the progressive realization of socio-economic rights. Disappointing micro-service delivery in social expenditure is in part due to capacity or skills constraints rather than inadequate fiscal allocations (Ajam and Aron, 2007), and for education, (see Chapter 12). The difficulty in holding provincial governments accountable for delivery, given the loss of revenue raising powers and limited budgetary discretion in a more centralized fiscal system, has motivated a policy review on the structure and functions of provincial and local government (see Chapter 4).

Moreover, the public capital constraint is only belatedly receiving extensive policy attention, e.g. significant expansions were planned in the 2005 budget, 40 per cent of which was for Eskom and Transnet. However, the long-term decline in infrastructure investment and capital stock, with real investment per capita falling by 72 per cent from 1976 to 2002 (Bogetić and Fedderke, 2006), should have been addressed earlier (on electricity, see below in section 5.4). In line with international evidence, infrastructure in SA has been found to influence growth, with electricity capacity having the greatest and most robust impact (see Chapter 7).

3.1.2. MONETARY AND EXCHANGE RATE POLICY

Aron and Muellbauer in Chapter 3 contrast the two monetary regimes operating from 1994. During 1994–9 monetary policy still focused at times on the exchange rate, resulting in a high degree of interest rate volatility. Exchange rate weakness in 1996 and 1998 elicited aggressive interest rate responses from the SARB, including significant forward market intervention to influence the exchange rate. In consequence, the net open foreign currency position[4] was US\$23 billion by 1998, implying a large negative net international reserve position, with substantial costs accruing to the fiscus.

The adoption of inflation targeting was announced by the Minister of Finance, Trevor Manuel, in February 2000. Inflation fell from double-digit levels in the 1990s to well within the 3–6 per cent target range from late 2003. It then remained at relatively low levels, though in April 2007, it breached the upper end of the inflation target range following strong and persistent increases in global food and energy prices. The new monetary framework has

---

[4] The net open foreign exchange position (NOFP) refers to the accumulation by the South African Reserve Bank of foreign currency obligations through forward market intervention that were far in excess of its net international foreign currency reserves.

seen several improvements with evolving institutional design. Quantitative indices measuring central bank transparency, reveal a substantial rise in transparency between 1994 and 2007, a result robust to the use of different weights in the indices (see Chapter 3). There is now far more information by which to hold the central bank accountable. The evidence also suggests monetary policy is more easily predictable by the financial markets since the inception of inflation targeting, helping to reduce uncertainty and encourage investment. Moreover, tax-adjusted real interest rates are measured as relatively similar to comparable emerging market countries and have not been excessively high.

With the introduction of inflation targeting, the exchange rate ceased to be a policy objective, although the consistent accumulation of foreign reserves has had some impact on the exchange rate. A significant achievement, that helped reduce sovereign risk, was the elimination in early 2004 of the net oversold forward position accumulated under the previous monetary policy regimes. There is now full transparency about the forward market position. Largely as a result of the closing out of the forward book and the accumulation of foreign exchange reserves, which exceeded US$30 billion by the end of 2007, the exchange rate has become less of a 'one-way bet' and less volatile, thus helping to reduce inflation and interest rate volatility. Monetary policy decisions taken in response to sizeable external and domestic shocks under inflation targeting have also improved relative to the preceding framework: Chapter 3 contrasts the steady handling of the 2001 exchange rate shock with the policy responses during the 1998 exchange rate shock.

Real exchange rate volatility has been lower in SA during 2003–7 than in most emerging market inflation targeting countries on both short-term and longer-term volatility measures (see Chapter 3). This begins to address one of the constraints to growth identified in the government's most recent growth initiative, AsgiSA (2006) (and see section 5.7 below). Nevertheless the rand continues to be affected by changes in global risk aversion, changes in perceptions of SA-specific risk and by commodity price movements. There is also some concern about the perceived risk from a widening deficit on the current account of the balance of payments that, with an increased growth momentum in the 2000s, averaged 7.3 per cent of GDP by 2007. The deficit was driven initially by higher consumption expenditure, but later by a strong investment surge, particularly related to infrastructural investment (see Chapter 7). The financial markets have regarded the deficit as reflecting underlying risk and macroeconomic vulnerability, particularly since it is financed largely through portfolio flows rather than through more stable long-term FDI flows.

However, Leape and Thomas in Chapter 5 argue that the low levels of FDI reflect the relatively highly developed nature of SA's domestic financial markets which facilitates portfolio investment as an alternative to direct investment. While the pattern of investment in the bond market reflects high frequency trading, portfolio equity inflows have been relatively stable and long term in nature. Others have also argued that FDI does not necessarily result in net inflows, as FDI can be financed domestically (in part) and flows are often hedged (Hausmann and Fernández-Arias, 2001, and Fernández-Arias and Hausmann, 2001).

3.2. Global reintegration: trade policy, capital markets, and debt

SA's re-entry into the global economy coincided with the global liberalization of trade and capital movements. World trade was opening following various rounds of the GATT and the WTO, to which SA was readmitted in 1994. Financial flows were also liberalized and the IMF encouraged countries, including emerging markets, to move towards full capital account convertibility. The Asian and related currency crises from 1997, however, prompted a more cautious approach to financial openness. SA followed suit during the 1990s with significant trade and capital account reforms.

A recurring theme in this volume is the impact of increased openness on improving growth. Central to the liberalization drive, and an important part of the GEAR programme, was rapid trade liberalization in the 1990s, characterized by shifts away from quantitative restrictions and subsidies and a substantial decline in the level of nominal and effective protection (see Chapter 6). SA can now be classified as an only moderately protected economy with protection higher than in Chile, Indonesia, Malaysia, and Mauritius, but lower than in Brazil, Thailand, Egypt, and India. The empirical evidence reviewed by Edwards et al. in Chapter 6 finds trade reform has had a beneficial effect on trade flows, on productivity and on prices in SA industries. The net employment effects are mixed, although the results suggest that there has been some restructuring of employment away from import competing sectors towards export oriented sectors.

However, no further progress on Most Favoured Nation (MFN) rates has been made since 2000. Despite some simplification, the tariff structure remains complex and nominal and effective protection is high in some sectors. Also, an anti-export bias remains with a deleterious effect primarily on non-commodity manufacturing. Tariff reviews are now being conducted on a case-by-case basis, which is administratively burdensome and has the danger of being obstructed by industry lobby groups. It would appear that tariff reform is no longer a government priority. AsgiSA does not identify trade policy as a key instrument. Currently the thrust of trade policy has moved towards actively pursuing trade reform through preferential trade agreements.

Leape and Thomas in Chapter 5 show that in liberalizing exchange control restrictions on capital flows, the government has followed differentiated policies towards residents and non-residents. By March 1995, virtually all capital flow restrictions on non-residents were ended with the abolition of the financial rand, which had operated in a dual exchange rate mechanism with the commercial rand (see also Chapter 3). Capital inflows increased substantially, dominated by portfolio equity investment. Chapter 5 argues that the gradual approach to reform of exchange controls on residents reflects the priority given to macroeconomic stabilization and financial sector development. Institutional investors have been the main conduit for international diversification by individuals, and there has been a move in the direction of prudential regulation of foreign exposure rather than direct controls.

Experience with controls showed that they were not fully effective in insulating the economy from volatile capital flows. Increasing emphasis has therefore been placed on the development of the domestic bond market and maintaining a low level of government external debt as a means of reducing exposure to external shocks. In 2004, government debt denominated in foreign currencies amounted to 6 per cent of GDP, compared to an average of 45 per cent for selected upper-middle-income economies in Latin America. The government's foreign debt strategy has focused on providing a benchmark for credit ratings in international markets for other SA borrowers, as well as lengthening the maturity structure of foreign-currency debt.

4. Trends in inequality and poverty

Poverty and inequality reductions were endorsed as prominent policy goals in the RDP and in GEAR. The newly enfranchised in 1994 suffered high levels of poverty and manifest inequality in relation to the white minority group. Long-term trends in income inequality from 1917 to 1995 demonstrate that average real incomes rose for all race groups but that income gaps by race persisted (see Chapter 10). From the 1970s aggregate income dynamics were increasingly driven by the dynamics within the African group as the relative size of this group as a share of the total population increased over time and as inequality within this group increased rapidly. Nonetheless, when total inequality is decomposed into between race-group and within race-group portions, the between-group component in SA has always been larger than available international comparators, a stark marker of apartheid-driven inequality. Inequality remains high by international standards, and both aggregate inequality and inequality within each race group continued to increase through the 1990s and into the 2000s. These findings on inequality are corroborated by the work of other researchers.

Poverty trends over the democratic period are more contentious. Poverty rose between 1996 and 2001, measured using census data and two different poverty lines ($2 per day and R250 per month in 1996 values). While this finding is corroborated with Income and Expenditure Survey data by several authors for 1995–2000, others find that the number of individuals below the poverty line was stable over this period, though the depth of poverty, as measured by the average income of the poor relative to the poverty line, increased. There is consensus that poverty has fallen since 2000, partly due to fiscal redistribution through an expansion of social grants, especially the state old age pension and the child support grant. The latter grant has been particularly important in the last six years (see also Chapter 4).

Two key factors driving poverty reduction are employment and remuneration behaviour in the labour market, and the fiscal transfers from of the state for poverty alleviation via transfers. Leibbrandt et al. in Chapter 10 examine these, using census and a variety of household survey datasets over a long period, covering pre- and post-apartheid eras. They pay particular attention to the changing contributions to inequality, of wage income and state transfer income coming into households. Income derived from the labour market dominates the distribution of aggregate household income. A decomposition analysis shows that its role in the inequality in household income is the result of both unequal wages/earnings and the large number of households with no access to labour market earnings. For the African group particularly, joblessness is an important contributor to total earnings inequality across households. The operation of the labour market—and high and rising unemployment—has complicated the alleviation of poverty and inequality for the post-apartheid government (see also Chapter 11). Demographic changes raising the African share of the population (now 80 per cent) suggest that race-based redistribution will become a progressively less important route to equality than addressing the sources of increasing *within* race-group inequality.

Future poverty could also be reduced through further increases in grants and in social expenditures to improve living conditions, targeted at the poor; and assistance targeted at the unemployed. However, given the massive post-2000 roll-out of social expenditures, further expansion has to confront the issue of fiscal sustainability (see concerns raised in Chapter 4), and the potential disincentive effects of such grants. Another route is via policies to promote access to labour income in an expanded public works programme (see sections 5.2 and 5.7).

5. The longer-term concerns: growth and the reduction of unemployment

A stable macroeconomic environment is an essential precondition for growth, and ultimately redistribution. However, in itself it is not a growth 'strategy'. An important focus of this volume is on economic growth and its long-term determinants in SA.

The demise of the apartheid government ensued in part because of a realization within the ruling Nationalist Party government that the economy was doomed to a cycle of low and declining growth as a result of trade and financial sanctions. The initially poor growth performance after 1994 is partly explained by the necessary restructuring of a highly protected economy: jobs were created in some sectors, but lost in others particularly in the second half of the 1990s (see Chapter 6). However, the past decade has been a relative success story: growth performance has improved, as has its stability; and investment has begun to rise. Comparing the period from 1981q1 to the final month of the Nationalist Party government, with the period under the ANC until 2007q4, the annualized real growth rate rose substantially from 1.1 to 3.6 per cent; growth volatility halved from 3.2 to 1.5 per cent;[5] and real per capita growth rose from 1.3 to 2 per cent. Growth has also improved under the present regime, especially when measured from late 1999, after the 1998 currency crisis with its punitive interest rate rises: from 2000 to 2007. The real growth rate averaged 4.3 per cent, and averaged 5.1 per cent in 2004–7. But while there has been a recovery, SA remains outside the set of fastest growing countries.

Economic performance remains well below that required to meet the pressing social developmental goals, and there has consequently been much emphasis on growth under the Government's 2006 AsgiSA plan. To address the problems of persistent unemployment and poverty, the target is to raise the permanent growth rate of the economy to average 4.5 per cent until 2009 and 6 per cent between 2010 and 2014, to be achieved partly through raising the investment ratio to 25 per cent of GDP. The restructuring seems to have borne fruit. Studies undertaken by the South African Reserve Bank (2006) and the International Monetary Fund (2007) suggest that estimated potential output growth has increased from between 2.25 to 3 per cent during 1995–2001 (Arora and Bhundia, 2003) to between 4 and 4.5 per cent by 2006. The Reserve Bank study indicated that under various infrastructural expenditure scenarios, potential output growth could increase to as much as 6.9 per cent (see also Chapter 2).

The factors behind the renewed growth and investment are elucidated in the next two sections. These underline the gains from reforms toward greater macro-stability, and a more open and globally integrated economy, both largely accomplished by the end of the first decade after democratic elections. However, a growth and investment strategy rests mainly on *longer-term* determinants, including well-functioning labour markets and appropriate labour legislation, sufficient and smoothly functioning infrastructure, high quality education and skills training, a healthy workforce, appropriate industrial policies, and effective competition policies. These factors are also considered in more detail below.

---

[5] This uses the absolute value measure described in Chapter 3, Table 3.1.

Introduction

5.1. Accounting for growth: relative roles of total factor productivity, investment, and labour

Du Plessis and Smit (Chapter 2) use growth accounting methods to try to disentangle the underlying factors behind the growth revival. The relative contributions of capital, labour, and total factor productivity (TFP) to growth are calculated using a range of assumptions for the share of labour. The method unfortunately is sensitive to the poor quality of the SA employment data, e.g. by excluding significant sectors from the underlying survey, the employment data used to proxy the labour input are unreliable (see also section 5.2). The result is that labour's contribution to growth tends to be understated and that of the residual, or TFP, overstated, even where informal sector employment is included.

In common with earlier studies, the authors find the pattern of growth in SA has switched from being based mainly on factor accumulation, to one based on the efficiency gains or innovation encapsulated by TFP growth. TFP growth accounts for at least half of the economic recovery in growth since 1994, contrasting with its negative contribution in the previous decade under apartheid. The contribution of capital to growth appears modest but slightly higher after 1994 than in the preceding decade, while that of labour remained positive but actually fell after 1994. Analysis of sectoral developments produces similar results, with the contribution of TFP growth most pronounced in the secondary and tertiary sectors.

The authors examine a range of empirical evidence for SA to explain their findings of the observed relative contributions of productivity, capital, and employment growth. Their analysis suggests that openness to trade and capital flows, reduced uncertainty and lower interest rates mainly explain SA's growth and investment recovery since 1994. The lower user cost of capital, and reduced systemic and sectoral uncertainty, are largely due to the fiscal and monetary policies of the new government (see Chapters 3 and 4), and this underlines the importance of sustaining the macro-stability gains. The findings of Edwards et al. in Chapter 6 confirm that trade liberalization improved aggregate productivity growth and export growth, and helped to diversify the composition of exports. They argue there are further gains to be reaped from tariff simplification and a unilateral phase-down in tariff rates. Many questions remain unresolved in the empirical literature on SA's lacklustre employment growth, discussed below. Greater openness and factor pricing again appear to have been relevant. However, although exports became a source of employment, increased import penetration induced a decline in the positive net trade effect over time.

5.2. Unemployment and labour markets

Lock of access to earned income is by far the most important factor behind poverty and income inequality in SA. The increase in expectations among the citizenry at the time of transition was probably greatest in the area of employment. Democratic SA inherited one of the highest rates of unemployment in the world, but in the first decade after emancipation, unemployment worsened further before starting to improve after 2003. On the 'broad' measure, unemployment rate rose from 29 to 42 per cent between 1995 and 2003, but then fell to 36 per cent by 2007. On the official 'narrow' measure, it rose from 17 to 28 per cent in the same period, and then fell to 23 per cent by 2007. Such rates represent mass economic hardship and the waste of human resources, and perpetuate high crime rates.

Kingdon and Knight in Chapter 11 analyse unemployment and its rise in the post-apartheid period. The analysis is complicated by poor labour market data, flawed by definitional, sampling, and coverage problems, and limited comparability over time (see Klasen and Woolard, 1999). It is thus hazardous to make categorical statements about labour market changes over time, though the risk is somewhat reduced taking a longer-term view compared with year-on-year changes. Using household survey data from 1995 to 2007, the authors evaluate the role of labour legislation, the government's labour market policies and the knowledge gaps about the functioning of the labour market in explaining unemployment. They find the rise in unemployment up to the early 2000s is mainly attributable to slow economic growth and a sharp increase in labour force participation. The rapid divergence in the supply of and demand for labour placed a burden of adjustment on the labour market that would have strained even the most flexible of labour markets. In practice, major parts of the SA labour market are inflexible, resulting in rising unemployment in this period.

The authors argue the fall in unemployment between 2003 and 2007 was due partly to faster growth in employment (with elevated economic growth), but also to the far slower growth of the adult population and labour force compared say to 1995–2003, likely explained by the spread of HIV/AIDS (see Chapter 10). To this extent, only limited comfort can be drawn from the recent reductions in unemployment rate. Substantial in-migration from Zimbabwe (some estimates put a lower bound at about 1 million), probably not recorded in the household surveys or even in the population censuses, is expected to have reduced the incomes of informal sector workers and raised the unemployment rate. The potential for further in-migration of unskilled labour from SADC countries is problematic.

Labour market inflexibility via the effects of labour legislation is a key to the *persistence* of high unemployment in the post-apartheid period (Chapter 11). The ANC government strengthened pro-worker labour legislation in its first 5 years, reducing employers' powers over pay and working conditions and making hiring and firing more costly. The system of labour market governance embodied in legislation such as the Labour Relations Act of 1995, the Basic Conditions of Employment Act of 1997, and the Employment Equity

Act of 1999 is arguably less appropriate in SA's conditions of unemployment and extreme labour market segmentation than in a fully employed economy. The measurement of the potential ill-effects of labour legislation is difficult, and well-established research results on this question are not yet available. However, many employers complain about constraints such as the legal and procedural requirements with respect to hiring and firing of workers, the extent of union power to raise wages[6] or disrupt production, the extension of bargaining agreements, and the 'hassle factor' arising from the labour relations legislation. This can result in hiring fewer workers, substituting capital for labour, diverting managerial resources from the main task, out-sourcing of non-core activities, depressing business optimism and discouraging investment. Well-intentioned labour laws can thus have unfortunate unintended labour market consequences. The danger is that in protecting the rights of formal sector workers, the interests may be harmed of the growing number of informal sector poor and the unemployed poor. The inflexibilities of the labour market may then exacerbate not only income inequalities but also the underlying problem of inadequate employment creation.

Another aspect of 'inflexibility' concerns a lack of linkage between the skills of those in the unemployment pool and the investment that is driving growth. Skills training has become a central plank of labour market policy in SA, for instance through the creation of Sector Education Training Authorities (SETAs) and the 'grant-levy' training system that they operate. Evidence suggests that many employers either do not perceive the need to train at the lower skill levels or that the current grant-levy scheme is not sufficiently attractive to them (Kingdon and Knight, 2007: 837–9). To impact on poverty, it may be necessary to create tax incentives for firms to invest in technology intensive in the use of relatively unskilled labour and upgrading low level skills.

The implication is that sustained economic growth will support the generation of new employment and continued reductions in the unemployment rate, especially if the balance of growth favours sectors most intensive in unskilled labour usage (e.g. agriculture, mining, small scale services, and some manufacturing). The government has also introduced public works programmes (see section 5.7 below). Together with skill development programmes, these may create employment or merely redistribute it. Again there are no rigorous studies that examine their effectiveness in SA, though well-conducted evaluation would assist policy design, especially given the expansion of active labour market policies under AsgiSA.

---

[6] Kingdon and Knight (2006) also find the union wage premium increased between 1993 and 1999, suggesting that union wages are more insulated than are non-union wages from downward market pressures due to changes in labour supply.

5.3. Investment and infrastructure

Some of the impetus of the stronger growth trend has come from higher investment. This improvement was driven in part by the resumption in public sector infrastructural investment after 2003. As argued by Fedderke in Chapter 7, infrastructure investment has an important impact on TFP: positive productivity gains are achieved through lowering transport costs, and improving access to export markets. Private sector investment growth has been significant, and aggregate annual expenditure on fixed investment measured 16.4 per cent of GDP on average during 1994 to 2007 (and exceeded 20 per cent of GDP in 2007). However, despite the improvement under the ANC government, the investment ratio remains low by international standards, and by the AsgiSA target.

The evidence in Chapter 7 suggests that investment in SA has mainly been driven by rates of return and reduced uncertainty due to improved institutions. Raising the net rate of return on investment remains an important means of stimulating investment in fixed capital stock. Therefore the focus of macroeconomic policy in promoting price stability through fiscal discipline and a relatively successful inflation targeting policy framework has contributed to the improved investment climate. Moreover, the greater transparency and accountability of the institutions of macro-policy, and the medium-term policy frameworks they have adopted (see Chapters 3 and 4), have enhanced the predictability and credibility of policy, reducing economic uncertainty. Other factors include lower company taxes and increased openness, which have allowed for more foreign investment.

Nevertheless there are some concerns. Uncertainty plays a fundamental role in investment decisions, and uncertainty measures in SA appear to be bound into wider institutional contexts, covering property rights, crime, human capital investment, as well as the stability of the political system (see Chapter 7). The risk premium, as reflected in long-term bonds, has indeed declined significantly; nevertheless, it is volatile, and still high relative to developed countries. Given a widening gap between investment and domestic saving, the risk premium is likely to be of continued importance in influencing the compensating foreign inflows.

A further concern relates to the importance of market structure as a determinant of investment. Pricing power in the economy has been reduced somewhat through trade liberalization and the opening of the economy (see Chapter 6; and Aron and Muellbauer, 2007). Also, as discussed in Chapter 8, there has been a more proactive competition policy. Nevertheless, despite a decline in market concentration, some evidence suggests continued barriers to entry in SA manufacturing and sustained monopolistic pricing power that may constrain investment growth.

Finally, the composition of investment has attracted comment. Frankel et al. (2006) argue that much of the recent investment has been in non-tradable sectors

Introduction

such as real estate and finance, exacerbating the expanding current account imbalance. However, this categorization may be misleading because of complementarities between tradable and non-tradable investment, e.g. where construction activities feed into infrastructure rather than house-building and offices. Mining investment has declined, despite the commodity boom since 2002/3. This is linked to infrastructural bottlenecks and regulatory uncertainties due to delays in finalizing the new Mineral and Petroleum Resources Royalty Bill of 2008. Exchange rate expectations, given the appreciated rand during 2003–6, may also have played a part.

5.4. Industrial policy and competition

Despite attempts to diversify toward a broader-based industrial structure driven by international competitiveness, SA's industry remains predominantly resource-based. Prior to the democratic transition, manufacturing was protected, concentrated, and dominated by highly capital intensive sectors, many with a link to SA's mining and resources base. Strategic concerns of the apartheid government, such as defence and liquid fuels, and the needs of the resource extraction and processing industries, were extensively nurtured via interventionist state policies.

Diversification, especially by an expansion of manufacturing, was seen by the ANC government as a potential source of new exports and employment growth. Yet resource-based, heavy manufacturing industries have remained the strongest performers while non-traditional manufactured exports (with the exception of automotive products) and labour intensive sectors have performed relatively poorly. Black and Roberts in Chapter 8 argue this is a result of path dependency, where the strongest have continued to thrive. Ironically, given the stated goals for industrial policy, post-apartheid policies have in many cases reinforced the resource-based ventures through selective taxation and credit policies. The authors argue that despite a raft of measures aimed at supporting manufacturing, industrial policy after 1994 has proved unfocused, with a negligible impact in shaping the economy's desired development path.

Emphasis was also placed on trade liberalization to create a more competitive economy, but the authors argue when examining heterogeneous sectors that this mainly reinforced existing patterns of specialization. Despite extensive trade liberalization, the barriers to entry in concentrated sectors and substantial transport costs have encouraged monopolistic pricing, anti-competitive mark-ups, and collusive behaviour in various sub-sectors of industry. This has also inhibited industrial development, and is illustrated by case studies for the steel, chemicals, and food products sectors in Chapter 8.

Regulation and competition policy have not helped to overcome the problems. The regulation of utilities has paid insufficient attention to the conditions and incentives governing price-setting and other decision-making by large corporations, whether privatized or state-owned. In telecommunications and electricity—both key intermediate inputs into industry—the continued monopolistic pricing has favoured capital and energy intensive industrial activities. Flaws in the restructuring programme for electricity resulted in under-investment in generation and maintenance, and distorted prices. The price of electricity was far too low for profitable investment, deterring new private sector entrants. The institutional structure was also inappropriate, with Eskom responsible for both electricity distribution and most generation, a relationship that would inevitably favour its own generation at the expense of new entrants to the grid. The consequences, which have included power outages in early 2008 that caused the mines to shut down for 2 weeks, reverberated internationally as foreign investors noted the emergence of electricity supply constraints in mining and manufacturing production, affecting the growth outlook.

The record on competition policy is mixed: while competition policy has had some success in evaluating mergers, it has not been effective against anti-competitive behaviour by large or dominant firms. Chapter 8 argues for industrial policies to play a stronger complementary role alongside competition policy in addressing barriers to entry and encouraging competitive dynamism. This would entail flexibility and coordination on the part of government, to provide appropriate incentives to firms. Given the planned spending on infrastructure announced by government (see Chapters 2, 4, and 7) such considerations appear paramount.

5.5. The persistence of poor educational outcomes

Education is an important factor in obtaining well-remunerated employment, given the economy-level shifts in demand towards more skilled labour. Improving black education is also crucial to reducing the racial unemployment and earnings gap (see Chapter 11). The democratic government introduced major revisions to apartheid education policies and greatly increased resources for formerly non-white schools. The reforms were intended to influence access and quality, and to redress the sharp racial differences in educational outcomes. The reforms have been credited with promoting equity in education and with more equitably distributing public expenditure on education. Van der Berg in Chapter 12, however, explains that though race gaps in quantitative educational measures such as average years of education have substantially fallen over the period, quality differentials remain large.

Despite massive resource shifts to black schools in the post-apartheid period, overall learning achievement levels (as measured by matriculation pass rates) did not improve and the mainly black schools—which constitute the majority of schools—continue to have extremely low pass rates with high variability.

Moreover, the percentage of teenagers taking higher level mathematics at high school has been falling, measured since 1994. Chapter 12 investigates why equality of schooling outcomes has proven elusive despite greatly increased resources. It confirms the findings of the international literature that input-based policies are not effective in improving quality of schooling. But it raises the policy question: what can the government do to improve teacher quality/effort and student learning achievement levels?

Regressions of matriculation pass rates using school level data show that racial composition of a school remains a major explanatory factor after controlling for students' socio-economic background and school inputs. Since the remarkable differentials in learning levels amongst black schools cannot be accounted for mainly by differences in socio-economic background or teaching resources, this points to the importance of school management, a problem of x-inefficiency rather than allocative inefficiency. This suggests a shift from reallocating resources amongst schools—an equity imperative in the initial post-apartheid period—to improving the functioning of poor schools, for greater equity of outcomes.

There are further policy avenues for improving quality of education, based on international research: performance-related pay, to motivate higher teacher effort; training (the high proportion) of teachers teaching mathematics and science to secondary classes, but who themselves have only secondary qualifications in these subjects; increasing the accountability of schools either via public private partnership arrangements (e.g. a voucher system) and/or by providing parents information about school performance and enabling school choice. Teacher unions have watered down the principle of performance-based pay that the government has tried to introduce. The new pay deal (the Occupation Specific Dispensation, implemented in 2008) is thus unlikely to have a major effect on teacher performance in practice. The teacher unions also opposed the provisions of recent education reform that included some of the elements above. Thus, the political feasibility of rational policies is an important concern. Potential policies include better utilization of existing resources, increased attention to non-personnel expenditure (the overwhelming proportion of post-apartheid resource increases in education has gone to teachers as higher salaries), and regularly generating learning achievement data to inform both policy-makers and parents, thus reducing information asymmetries and fostering school accountability.

5.6. The impact of AIDS on growth

The spread of the HIV/AIDS epidemic is one of the most significant developments since the political transition in 1994. From 0.1 per cent of the population in 1990, HIV prevalence in SA increased to 11.2 per cent in 2007, or more than 5 million infected individuals. The consequences of the mortality and morbidity associated with HIV/AIDS include sharp declines in life expectancy, living standards, and productivity (with implications for economic growth) as well as increases in the number of orphans. The government's response to the epidemic has been highly controversial and internationally criticized (for an account, see Nattrass, 2004). After years of inhumane and irrational prevarication, when the epidemic was allowed to take a firm hold, the government eventually succumbed to public pressure and announced a large-scale anti-retroviral treatment (ART) programme in August 2003 (Nattrass, 2007). The government now aims belatedly under the National Strategy Plan, 2007–11 to reduce the incidence of new HIV infections by 50 per cent in 2011, and provide access to treatment, care, and support to 80 per cent of sufferers.

Smit and Ellis in Chapter 9 analyse the macroeconomic effects of the HIV/AIDS epidemic for 2000–20, and, for the first time, the likely impact of the ART programme. Their considerations include the effect of slower population and labour force growth on production and expenditure; costs to companies providing medical aid and death benefits; the costs of absenteeism, lost experience and skills, higher recruitment and training costs, and lower labour productivity; and health and welfare spending by the government.

Unfortunately, of the numerous modelling assumptions made, some are untestable or have to be based on inadequate evidence. The economic costs also depend on the nature of the model employed: short-run macro-econometric models capturing the effects of AIDS on labour supply and the demand for health care show a relatively mild impact; medium-term CGE models and long-run models, that also consider the effect of AIDS on human capital formation, find more severe economic effects. Their analysis using various scenarios in the former type of model, finds an average lowering of GDP growth by 0.5 percentage points per annum for 2000–20, compared to a scenario without HIV/AIDS. The provision of ART with a 50 per cent uptake, however, reduces this impact by a fifth. Even if the nature of the model used may understate the costs of past policy errors towards HIV/AIDS, and the human suffering is not factored into these models, the results underscore the imperative for prevention and treatment of HIV and AIDS in SA.

5.7. AsgiSA

The growth response to the 1996 GEAR plan appeared to be lacklustre by the late 1990s. Chapter 3 argues this was linked to serious policy mistakes in dealing with periodic currency crises. In 1998, prime borrowing rates rose to around 25 per cent, damaging growth and investor confidence. Growth picked up under the new monetary policy regime, but the government was concerned that the nature of growth was unbalanced: firstly it was based on strong commodity prices, capital inflows and consumer demand; secondly, the benefits of growth were not widely spread, with a third of the population

Introduction

not benefiting directly from economic growth. Moreover, the government had adopted the ANC's 2004 manifesto with core objectives to halve poverty and unemployment by 2014.

This prompted the Government's AsgiSA plan, which was formally adopted in 2006. The plan arose out of consultations with a range of stakeholders, and ultimately followed the 'binding constraints' approach of Hausmann et al. (2008). This seeks to identify the main constraints to growth, focusing policy on their alleviation. Constraints were identified through consultation rather than a quantitative economic study. Few in number, they were pervasive in the economy: the volatility and level of the currency; cost, efficiency and capacity of the national logistics system; shortage of suitably skilled labour; barriers to entry, limits to competition and limited new investment opportunities; the regulatory environment, especially for the burden on small and medium business; and deficiencies in state organization, capacity, and leadership.

It is early to assess the success of AsgiSA and it is unclear to what extent recent improvements can be ascribed to the initiative. The main progress has been made in recent infrastructure investment (AsgiSA Annual Report, 2007), with significantly increased budget allocations (see also Chapters 7 and 8). Progress in other areas has been less clear to date, and the Annual Report alludes to the limited scale of impacts of current programmes, particularly with respect to second-economy initiatives. The main employment generation component of AsgiSA is expanded public works programmes. However, a major evaluation of past programmes in SA concluded their impact was limited because they failed to take the majority of households even temporarily out of poverty (see McCord, 2004). The National Industrial Policy framework released at the end of 2006 identified business process outsourcing, tourism, and biofuels as sectors for special priority attention, but the biofuels strategy has been delayed.

In support of the AsgiSA initiative, the National Treasury commissioned a study by a so-called International Panel, under the chairmanship of Ricardo Hausmann. The focus of their diagnostic was on the tradable goods sector which has grown the least of all sectors and suffered the biggest employment losses. The Panel produced 21 policy recommendations in May 2008. As in the original AsgiSA document, the level and volatility of the real exchange rate were implicated in the sluggishness of manufacturing. The proposal is that 'more attention be given' to the level and stability of the real exchange rate within the inflation targeting framework, which would require intervention by the SARB. Yet the extent of this purported overvaluation of the currency and the suggested appropriate level of the equilibrium real exchange is not directly addressed. Nor is it clear how real exchange rate stability can be brought about without jeopardizing the primacy of monetary policy (see discussion in Chapter 3), particularly given large movements in commodity prices to which the real exchange rate is notably responsive. They suggest the remaining capital controls should be eliminated which could lower the real exchange rate. However, the scale of pent-up demand for foreign assets may be less than anticipated (see Chapter 5). To lower interest rates, they recommend greater fiscal support: a larger contribution from government to national savings is suggested (a budget surplus, of 1–2 per cent of GDP for 2008), and countercyclical fiscal policy. However, the conclusion to Chapter 3 also emphasizes the imperative for raising household savings.

Trade policy is also identified as having retarded the tradable goods sector: as noted in Chapter 6, trade policy has been subordinated to industrial policy. The Panel proposes further liberalizing input tariffs, and simplification of the tariff structure. The Panel also highlighted labour market constraints, an issue *not* identified by AsgiSA, though both emphasize skills shortages and the increasing lack of skills at the top end. Labour market policy proposals include a wage subsidy to encourage employment of young people and encouraging high-skilled immigration. Black economic empowerment (BEE) is considered to have constrained growth, and greater flexibility is suggested in its implementation, for instance eliminating the equity participation requirement for new firms, and providing better information regarding BEE.

Industrial policy proposals are somewhat *dirigiste*, but there is no evidence that the state will better be able to take the lead than the private sector (see Chapter 8). Given the identified information externalities and coordination failures, their recommendations give a core role to the Industrial Development Corporation in financing and identifying new products, processes and zones, with a strong oversight role proposed for the Department of Trade and Industry. They also suggest a pro-active competition policy to reduce barriers to entry. The study neglected the mining sector: yet there has been a commodity boom and the mining sector has not been able to take full advantage because of regulatory bottlenecks in government, and transport infrastructural constraints.

Whether the Panel's recommendations will be acted on as a whole is unclear. The current rhetoric is for a move to the left in economic policy, and there has been mixed reaction from ANC circles. There is considerable opposition to a larger fiscal surplus, but there is support for a monetary policy that implies lower interest rates and a weaker rand. However, this is not a 'pick and choose what you like' proposal. The argument for a looser monetary policy and lower interest rates is predicated on a very tight fiscal policy to help prevent inflation and to maintain a depreciated real exchange rate.

6. Conclusion and prospects

The SA economy has come a long way since the demise of apartheid. There have been significant successes, particularly on the macro-economic front,

Introduction

but the many challenges highlighted in the chapters of this volume remain. To some extent, SA is now at a crossroads. By late 2007, threats to sustained growth appeared in the form of a general global slowdown; domestic political developments which signalled a possible move towards more populist policies; and the emergence of electricity supply constraints which had direct impacts on mining and manufacturing production and affected international investor sentiment. The changes in leadership at the ANC's conference in Polokwane during December, 2007, and the shift in the locus of power within the alliance suggest that there could be a change in the direction of economic policy. Fears have been expressed that the hard-won stability gains created on the monetary and fiscal policy front could be undermined. Arguably, the enviable fiscal position now provides far more scope for fiscal laxity than in the immediate post-1994 period. However, the constraints applied to domestic policy by the international environment are as pertinent today as they were in 1994 when the ANC first came to power.

The slow pace of growth was a cause for concern in the 1990s. Growth has improved since 2000, and the investment ratio to GDP has increased to a creditable 21 per cent, though in the face of a low savings rate, pressure is evident in the expanding deficit of the current account of the balance of payments. A benign view of the widening deficit would argue that from an inter-temporal perspective, deficits at these levels are sustainable because they are providing for future growth and higher exports. This also implies that the financing of the deficit would be dependent on continued positive growth prospects rather than on traditional interest parity. Whereas investment in infrastructure could reduce future bottlenecks for export growth and make the current account deficit sustainable, SA's reliance on portfolio capital inflows means that it is vulnerable to reversals even for reasons that may not be SA specific, such as generalized risk aversion. On the other hand, meeting the large projected infrastructural demands of the economy may itself place pressure on the fiscus, interest rates and the balance of payments (Chapter 7). The global financial crisis in 2008, and worsening terms of trade for SA, make the outlook for continued capital flows less favourable. The threat of policy reversals may also impact negatively on capital flows. Significant shifts in the external balance sheet towards predominantly rand-based liabilities make SA better-placed to manage such shocks; while evidence of 'home bias' and the shift to prudential regulation of foreign exposures suggests that risks associated with destabilizing resident outflows have also been greatly reduced (see Chapter 5). Ultimately, however, the economy will have to rely on increasing domestic savings (see Chapter 3), which, given the inequalities of income and wealth may be difficult.

Solving SA's unemployment problem remains a key challenge. Part of the answer lies in structural labour market reforms. Probably of even greater importance is sustaining high levels of economic growth in a more diversified, competitive and labour intensive economy. This will require measures to increase TFP growth, structural reforms to ensure greater competitiveness in the economy, as well as a continued focus on infrastructure expenditure to reduce bottlenecks, particularly with respect to electricity and the transport infrastructure. At the same time, social policy interventions are crucial for longer-term growth, including improved service delivery in education, housing, health and AIDS prevention and treatment, to support well-being and a healthy labour force. It is vital that the government deal with failures in the educational system, which continue despite the large increase in resources, if they are to avoid perpetuating the present problem of low skills with joblessness. Increased employment opportunities and effective social policy interventions are the key to reducing poverty in SA and eventually bringing about a decline in inequality. This is best achieved in an environment of sustainable growth and macroeconomic stability.

References

Ajam, T. and J. Aron. 2007. 'Fiscal Renaissance in a Democratic South Africa'. *Journal of African Economies* 16(5): 745–1, Oxford University Press.

Aron, J. and J. Muellbauer. 2005. 'Monetary Policy, Macro-Stability and Growth: South Africa's Recent Experience and Lessons'. *World Economics*: 6(4): 123–47.

——2007. 'Inflation Dynamics and Trade Openness'. Centre for Economic Policy Research, London, *Working Paper Series*, no. 6346. Available at <http://www.cepr.org>.

Arora, V. and A. Bhundia. 2003. 'Potential Output and Total Factor Productivity Growth in Post-Apartheid South Africa'. *Working Paper* WP 03/178 (September).

AsgiSA (Accelerated and Shared Growth Initiative for South Africa). 2006. *Annual Report*. Republic of South Africa: The Presidency.

——2007. *Annual Report*. Republic of South Africa: The Presidency.

Bogetić, Ž. and J. W. Fedderke. 2006. 'Forecasting Investment Needs in South Africa's Electricity and Telecom Sectors'. *South African Journal of Economics* 74(3): 530–56.

Cosatu (Congress of South African Trade Unions). 1996. *Social Equity and Job Creation: The Key to a Stable Future*. Johannesburg: Cosatu.

De Kock Commission. 1978. De Kock, G. *Commission of Inquiry into the Monetary System and Monetary Policy in South Africa, Interim Report*. Pretoria: Government Printer.

——1985. De Kock, G., *Commission of Inquiry into the Monetary System and Monetary Policy in South Africa, Final Report*. Pretoria: Government Printer.

Fernández-Arias, E. and R. Hausmann. 2001. 'Capital Inflows and Crisis: Does the Mix Matter?' In Jorge Braga de Macedo and Enrique V. Iglesias (eds.) *Foreign Direct Investment Versus Other Flows to Latin America*. Paris: Inter-American Development Bank and OECD.

Frankel, J., B. Smit, and F. Sturzenegger. 2006. 'South Africa: Macroeconomic Challenges after a Decade of Success'. *CID Working Paper*, no. 133 (September).

Hausmann, R. and E. Fernández-Arias. 2001. 'Foreign Direct Investment: Good Cholesterol?' In Jorge Braga de Macedo and Enrique V. Iglesias (eds.), *Foreign Direct*

Investment Versus Other Flows to Latin America. Paris: Inter-American Development Bank and OECD.

Hausmann, R., D. Rodrik, and A. Velasco. 2008. 'Growth Diagnostics'. In J. Stiglitz and N. Serra (eds.) *The Washington Consensus Reconsidered: Towards a New Global Governance*. Oxford: Oxford University Press.

Hirsch, A. 2005. *Season of Hope: Economic Reform under Mandela and Mbeki*. Pietermaritzburg: University of Kwazulu Natal Press and International Development Research Centre.

International Monetary Fund. 2007. *South Africa: IMF Country Report no 07/274* (August). Washington DC.

Kingdon, G. and J. Knight. 2006. 'How Flexible are Wages in Response to Local Unemployment in South Africa?', *Industrial and Labor Relations Review*, 59(3): 471–95.

—— 2007. 'Unemployment in South Africa, 1995–2003: Causes, Problems and Policies', *Journal of African Economies*, 16(3): 813–48.

Klasen, S. and I. Woolard. 1999. 'Levels, Trends, and Consistency of Employment and Unemployment Figures in South Africa'. *Development Southern Africa* 16: 3–36.

McCord, A. 2004. 'Policy Expectations and Programme Reality: The Poverty Reduction and Labour Market Impact of Two Public Works Programmes in South Africa'. *ESAU Working Paper*, no. 8. London: Overseas Development Institute.

Nattrass, J. 1988. *The South African Economy: Its Growth and Change*. Cape Town: Oxford University Press.

Nattrass, N. 2004. *The Moral Economy of AIDS in South Africa*. Cambridge: Cambridge University Press.

—— 2007. *Mortal Combat: AIDS Denialism and the Struggle for Antiretrovirals in South Africa*. Pietermaritzburg: University of KwaZulu-Natal Press.

Reynders Commission (Republic of South Africa) 1972. *Commission of Inquiry into the Export Trade of the Republic of South Africa*, RP69/72. Pretoria: Government Printer, 1972

Riekert Commission (Republic of South Africa) 1979. *Report of the Commission of Inquiry Into Legislation Affecting Utilisation of Manpower*. RP32/1979. Pretoria: Government Printer.

South Africa Foundation. 1996. *Growth For All: An Economic Strategy for South Africa*. Johannesburg: South Africa Foundation.

South African Reserve Bank. 2006 (May). *Monetary Policy Review*. Pretoria: South African Reserve Bank.

Stals, C. 1996. 'The Challenges for Monetary Policy'. Address to the 19th Annual Investment Conference, Frankel Pollak (Pty) Limited, Johannesburg (20 February 1996).

Waldmeier, P. 1998. *Anatomy of a Miracle*. London: Penguin.

Wiehahn Commission (Republic of South Africa) 1979. *Report of the Commission of Inquiry into Labour Legislation*, RP47/1979. Pretoria: Government Printer

2

Accounting for South Africa's Growth Revival after 1994

Stan Du Plessis and Ben Smit

1. Introduction[1]

The peaceful political transition in 1994 fuelled expectations of a turnaround from the economic decline under apartheid. In the preceding decade, trade and financial sanctions and internal political opposition to the apartheid government contributed to the weakest ten-year growth performance since the Second World War. The removal of these constraints was widely expected to transform the economy, and many argued that rising prosperity was also needed to sustain the political transition (e.g., De Wet, 1995). The years since 1994 have seen an improved growth performance, though initially modest on average, both by international standards and those of South Africa's own history.

This chapter sets out to describe, identify underlying factors, and seek explanations for South Africa's economic recovery since 1994. The chapter begins in section 2 with a description of the trends in aggregate and sectoral growth, highlighting areas responsible for the growth revival. The initial conditions for an economic recovery are evaluated using local and comparable international data in section 3, and growth accounting methods are applied to distinguish the relative contributions of capital, labour, and total factor productivity to the growth revival at the aggregate, sectoral, and sub-sectoral (for manufacturing) levels. The chapter contributes to the existing literature in two ways. A broader range of measures than used in previous studies is considered for the contribution of labour at the aggregate level in the growth accounting exercise, and it uses data of a more recent vintage. The chapter also contributes an analysis of sectoral developments since 1997.

---

[1] Acknowledgements: This chapter is a revised and extended version of Du Plessis and Smit (2007). The authors are grateful for comments from Janine Aron, Johannes Fedderke, Brian Kahn, John Muellbauer, and two anonymous referees.

In section 4, the potential causes for the relative contribution of capital, labour, and productivity are discussed with reference to South African and international literature. However, the South African literature is mainly based on earlier samples of data (overlapping at best for a few years with the period since 1994), and many of the causes that evidently operated earlier may not help to explain more recent trends. Three factors which operated earlier appear also to have been important recently in promoting South Africa's growth recovery. These are openness to trade and capital flows (Chapters 5 and 6 this volume), lower interest rates and the reduced uncertainty associated with stable macroeconomic policies (Chapters 3 and 4 this volume), and a successful political transition. A conclusion and consideration of prospects for growth follow in section 5.

2. Trends in economic growth since 1994

The performance of the South African economy has fluctuated considerably in the post-war era, and particularly since the early 1980s. Figure 2.1 shows the level of real per capita GDP and the real GDP growth rate from 1960 to the third quarter of 2007. Notable is the decline in real per capita GDP since 1981, and its subsequent revival since 1995. South Africa's real economic growth rate averaged 3.2 per cent (1.2 per cent in per capita terms) during 1995–2004, a substantial improvement on the 0.8 per cent average growth rate (–1.3 per cent in per capita terms) during 1985–94. Although this was a welcome improvement, South Africa's growth remained relatively low by world standards.[2]

The improved growth performance has gathered pace: the average growth rate for the first five years after 1994 was 2.6 per cent, 3.6 per cent in the following five years to 2004, and more than 5 per cent from 2005 to 2007 with forecasters optimistic that the growth rate will remain above 4 per cent (on average) for the next few years (e.g., Laubscher, 2006). It is, however, difficult to identify this performance with a change in the long-run growth potential of the economy, as the recovery has coincided with the longest post-war upswing of the South African business cycle.

The behaviour of the components of overall GDP reveals some noteworthy characteristics of the pattern of growth in the past two decades. The sectoral distribution of total production during 1984–2007 is presented in Table 2.1, both as ratios to nominal GDP and in terms of average real growth rates.

The most striking feature is the sustained rise of the tertiary sector relative to the rest of the economy, accounting for a more than proportionate

---

[2] In the decade following 1994, the regional per capita GDP growth rates for sub-Saharan Africa and Latin America were 1.1 per cent and 0.8 per cent respectively, while South Asia (with 3.7 per cent) and East Asia (with 6.2 per cent) did considerably better (Rodrik, 2006: 2).

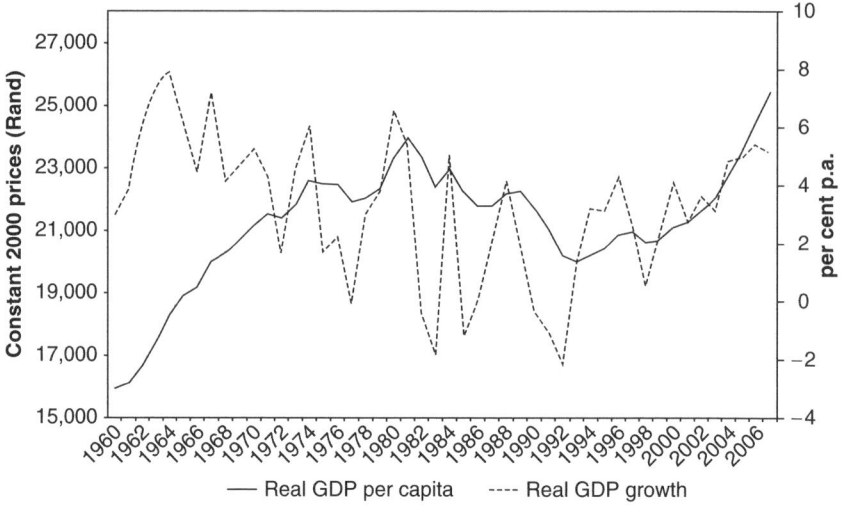

Figure 2.1. Real GDP per capita and growth of real GDP
Source: Quarterly Bulletin, South African Reserve Bank

share (78 per cent) of GDP growth since 1994, as it had done in the preceding decade (94 per cent of GDP growth between 1985 and 1994). The fastest growing individual sub-sectors from 1994 to 2007, were 'transport, storage, and communication' and 'financial intermediation, insurance, real estate, and business services' in the tertiary sector and 'construction' in the secondary sector. The construction sub-sector has experienced spectacular growth at more than 15 per cent per annum on average from 2005 until 2007. Meanwhile, the manufacturing sector contributed less than proportionately to growth in both decades, but especially in the decade before 1994, when its share of GDP declined from 23 to 20.9 per cent between 1984 and 1994. Manufacturing grew at 3.2 per cent from 1994 to 2007 but still declined as a proportion of total output. The primary sector (at an average growth rate of 0.3 per cent) provided the smallest contribution to the growth revival from 1994 to 2007—the mining and quarrying share of GDP declined from 12.7 per cent in 1984 to 7.7 per cent in 2007 and 'agriculture, forestry, and fishing' fell from 4.8 to 3.2 per cent.

Investment trends in the South African economy over the last two decades are shown in Table 2.2, including the average growth rates of investment, and the division of investment by type of organization, asset, and economic activity. Expenditure on fixed investment improved sharply during 1995–2007 compared to the previous ten years. Nevertheless, fixed capital formation as a percentage of GDP remained low by international standards and also relative to what is required for sustained high real GDP and employment growth rates

Table 2.1. Sectoral distribution of production

	Ratio to nominal GDP/%				Average annual real change/%	
	1984	1994	2004	2007	1985–94	1995–2007
Primary sector	17.5	11.9	10.3	10.9	0.5	0.3
—Agriculture, forestry and fishing	4.8	4.6	3.2	3.2	3.9	0.8
—Mining and quarrying	12.7	7.3	7.1	7.7	−0.6	0.2
Secondary sector	30.5	27.7	23.7	23.6	−0.03	3.5
—Manufacturing	23.0	20.9	19.0	18.2	−0.1	3.2
—Electricity, gas and water	3.7	3.6	2.3	2.5	4.0	2.0
—Construction (contractors)	3.7	3.1	2.4	2.9	−2.6	6.2
Tertiary sector	52.0	60.4	66.0	65.5	1.4	4.3
—Wholesale and retail trade, catering and accommodation	11.6	14.2	14.0	13.9	−0.1	4.8
—Transport, storage and communication	9.0	8.7	9.8	9.0	1.6	6.5
—Financial intermediation, insurance, real estate, and business services	13.1	16.0	20.8	22.2	1.8	5.7
—Community, social and personal services	18.3	21.5	21.4	20.5	2.0	1.8
GDP at basic prices	100	100	100	100	0.9	3.7

Source: Quarterly Bulletin, South African Reserve Bank

for much of the period from 1995 to 2007, though it rose sharply from a level of 15.2 per cent of GDP in 2004 to 20.6 per cent in 2007.

Notable too is the sharp increase of private investment expenditure in total investment expenditure, contrasting with the declining share of government investment expenditure, though this trend seems to have bottomed out since 2005. Further, investment in machinery and equipment was not only the largest category of investment by type of asset but also amongst the most rapidly growing over the decade following 1994. Classified by type of economic activity, the largest categories are fixed investment in the financial sector (25 per cent in 2007) and the manufacturing sector (20.2 per cent in 2007). A number of sectors have experienced double-digit investment rates from 2005 to 2007.

International capital flows are of great importance for the South African economy due to a long-standing mismatch between domestic saving and domestic investment. In Chapter 5, Figure 5.2 illustrates the improvements in overall flows, mainly contributed to by the growth in portfolio investment after the sanctions era, though the level of foreign direct investment rose sharply from a low base. The turnaround from capital outflows (1985–94) to capital inflows (1994–2007) implied that foreign savings (defined as capital

Table 2.2. Gross fixed capital formation

	Ratio to Total Fixed Investment/%				Average annual real change/%	
	1984	1994	2004	2007	1985–94	1995–2007
Investment by type of organization						
—General government	23.2	15.5	15.5	12.9	−5.5	4.1
—Public corporations	18.2	11.5	11.0	13.6	−6.0	10.1
—Private	58.6	72.9	73.5	73.5	−0.1	7.2
Investment by type of asset						
—Residential buildings	15.0	10.3	10.2	11.7	−5.1	6.4
—Non-residential buildings	13.0	12.2	10.1	9.5	−2.0	3.3
—Construction works	17.3	14.3	14.9	18.6	−3.5	7.5
—Transport equipment	10.8	15.0	13.8	14.3	−2.7	9.3
—Machinery and other equipment	41.2	44.2	47.0	43.4	−0.5	7.5
Investment by kind of economic activity						
—Agriculture, forestry and fishing	3.6	4.0	3.2	2.1	−1.4	1.6
—Mining and quarrying	10.2	9.0	7.9	8.9	−2.0	7.3
—Manufacturing	18.8	23.3	20.7	20.2	0.1	6.4
—Electricity, gas and water	16.4	7.5	5.2	6.5	−9.5	7.0
—Construction (contractors)	1.5	1.1	1.9	1.6	−5.6	10.9
—Wholesale and retail, trade, catering and accommodation	6.2	6.4	7.2	7.6	−1.9	8.5
—Transport, storage and communication	10.1	11.1	13.5	14.9	−2.3	11.6
—Financial intermediation, insurance, real estate and business services	21.3	23.4	24.6	25	−1.7	7.3
—Community, social and personal services	11.9	14.1	15.8	3.35	0.2	5.3
	Ratio to GDP/%				Average annual real change/%	
Gross fixed capital formation	24.0	15.2	16.2	20.6	−2.3	6.9

Source: Quarterly Bulletin, South African Reserve Bank

flows plus the change in foreign reserves) swung from a negative 2.5 per cent of GDP in 1985–94 to a positive 2.4 per cent in 1995–2004.

3. Untangling South Africa's economic growth since 1994

Having described the key trends in aggregate and sectoral growth in South Africa, this section employs a growth accounting methodology to identify the underlying factors of the growth recovery, using recent aggregate and sectoral data. It begins with an examination of the initial conditions in some underlying growth factors in the early 1990s.

3.1. Initial conditions

South Africa had, at one time, possessed not only the potential for catch-up growth but had to an extent realized that potential. By 1900 the economy had developed sufficiently for it to be a likely member of the international 'convergence club', in the reckoning of Dowrick and DeLong (2005). Although on an international comparison the average per capita growth rate was unspectacular during 1913–29, it accelerated to an impressive 3.8 per cent between 1929 and 1950. During this period, South Africa's per capita growth was amongst the fastest in the developing world and far higher than in the leading industrialized economies. However, throughout the post-war era South Africa's per capita economic growth was unimpressive relative to the international sample used, and the economy gradually left the 'convergence club' (Dowrick and DeLong, 2005).

The long-run relative decline of South Africa's growth performance is demonstrated in Figure 2.2, a box plot of the per capita GDP for the countries in a comparative sample relative to USA per capita GDP, for the periods indicated.[3] Three trends stand out in this chart. First, there are only two intervals on this graph during which South Africa gained both against the USA and relative to the peer group, i.e. a modest gain between 1970 and 1980, and a more substantial gain between 1913 and 1950. Second, South African per capita GDP stagnated relative to the USA since the fifties and has declined since 1980. Third, the international peer group gained against the USA during the fifties and sixties, so that South Africa's per capita GDP fell back within the international group even while it kept pace with the USA.

In addition to the long-term pattern of economic growth, proxies for the development of human capital, the fertility rate, access to public services, income inequality, the export share in GDP, and the share of manufactured goods within exports provide further information about the initial conditions for economic recovery in South Africa by 1994. Figure 2.3 compares the initial conditions for South Africa along these dimensions with the median value for a peer group of developing countries in 1994.

The male and female literacy radii show the adult literacy rate for both sexes as a percentage of the total population, and the radii for primary and

---

[3] To judge the trajectory of the South African economy leading up to 1994 a counterfactual experience is required and an international comparison is one way of creating such a counterfactual. To that end we combined the groups selected by two leading sources on the comparative economic performance of the South African economy, i.e. Moll (1991) and Feinstein (2005). Both authors collected a set of market economies that were broadly comparable at the start of the First World War.

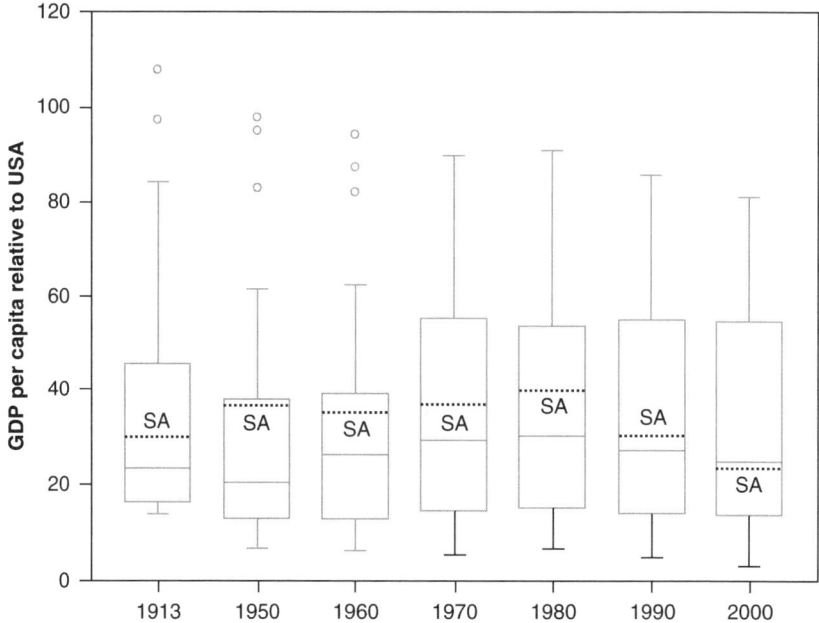

Figure 2.2. Relative historical performance of the South African economy in GDP per capita

Source: Calculated using data from Penn World Table version 6.1 (Heston, Summers, and Aten, 2002; and Maddison 2002). The data set was constructed by combining the groups suggested by Feinstein (2005) and Moll (1991). There was considerable overlap between these two authors, and extending the Feinstein (2005) selection by 3 countries (Sri Lanka, Turkey, and Venezuela) gave the union of the two sets. A data appendix is available on request from the authors.

Note: The box plot is of standard construction (see for example, Hamilton, 1996) and shows the middle 50 per cent of the data inside each box, the median as the solid line within each box and the outliers as dots beyond the whiskers (which mark a distance of 1.5 times the inter-quartile range above the third quartile and below the first quartile). Each box shows the distribution of GDP per capita relative to the USA for the sample countries for the particular year shown on the x-axis. The dotted line shows the position of SA within the distribution for each of the years.

secondary school enrolment show the percentage of the school age population enrolled at these school levels. While only the male literacy rate amongst the education radii show South Africa in an unfavourable light against the group by 1994, the South African scores on all these measures hide very considerable variation between (racial) groups. Also the South African male literacy rates were substantially lower (at 82 per cent) than those countries in the dataset closest to South Africa in terms of per capita income in 1994, namely Argentina (96 per cent), Mexico (92 per cent), and Venezuela (92 per cent).

The educational legacy of apartheid was not only lower educational attainment for the black and coloured groups, but also a between-group

Accounting for South Africa's Growth Revival after 1994

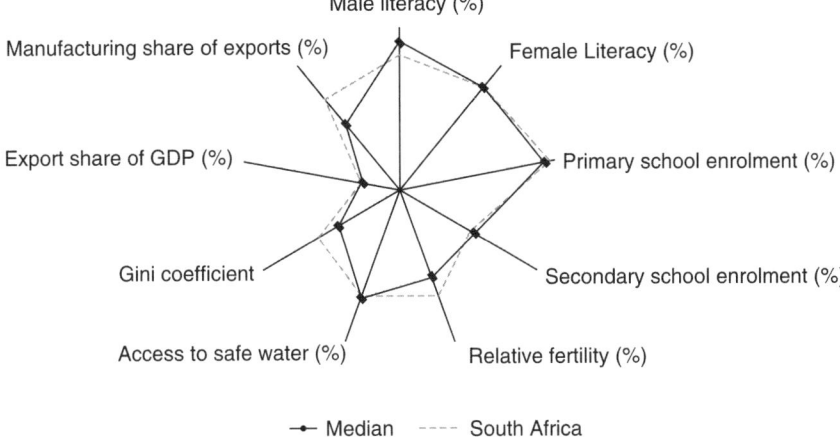

Figure 2.3. Initial conditions measured by social and economic indicators

Source: Calculated using data from World Development reports (1995; 1996; 1998; 2001). The peer group is the same group of 33 countries used in Figure 2.2 less those countries which were unambiguously developed countries by 1994. This left a group of 21 developing countries in the control group: Algeria, Argentina, Brazil, Chile, Columbia, Egypt, Ghana, Indonesia, Korea (South), Malaysia, Mexico, Morocco, Nigeria, Pakistan, Peru, Philippines, South Africa, Sri Lanka, Thailand, Turkey, and Venezuela.

Note: All of the conditions were assessed in 1995, with the exception of fertility (1994) the export share of GDP (1994), the manufacturing share of exports (1995) and the Gini coefficients which are mostly based on censuses from 1994 to 1996. The data for each item is scaled from 1 to 100 along the relevant radius. A data appendix is available on request from the authors.

quality gap. For example, in the year 2000, 55.6 per cent of all matriculants passed their higher grade mathematics exam, while only 15.3 per cent of black pupils passed the same exam (van der Berg in Chapter 12 this volume). Furthermore, the average pass rates hide the acute problem of poor quality education in South Africa. On the Southern and Eastern African Consortium for Monitoring Educational Quality (SACMEQ) comparative test of reading and mathematics for grade six learners, South African learners ranked on average eighth and ninth out of fourteen countries for reading and mathematics respectively (Chapter 12 this volume). The relatively poor performance in mathematics is especially disconcerting given the important synergies between mathematical ability in human capital and productivity (see section 4.1 below).

The relative fertility radius in Figure 2.3 shows the total fertility rate for each country as a proportion of the fertility rate in Nigeria (the highest in the peer group at 5.6). At the time of its political transformation, South Africa still had a higher fertility rate than the median for the peer group (as well as notably larger than the sub-group of Argentina, Mexico, and Venezuela). This added to the demographic pressure in the labour market (where labour market participation expanded dramatically, see section 4.3 below), and in the poor rural regions.

Inequality in South Africa at the time of the political transition is shown along the Gini coefficient radius in Figure 2.3: South Africa and Brazil had the most unequal income distributions in this sample by the mid nineties. However, severe inequality does not distinguish South Africa from the comparable group of countries in terms of GDP per capita, for example, Argentina, Mexico, and Venezuela. Such extreme inequality raises the risk of social instability or, as Aron and Muellbauer (2005) observe, could raise the risk premium for capital through the need for future redistributive taxes and transfer payments.

The provision of public services in South Africa, as proxied by the 70 per cent of the population with access to safe water in 1995, though similar to that of Brazil (72 per cent), fell short of the similar provision in Mexico (83 per cent) and Venezuela (79 per cent), even if the relevant radius in Figure 2.3 suggests that the South African situation was typical for the peer group.

Finally, the proportion of exports to GDP and the manufacturing share of exports radii in Figure 2.3 show that the South African economy was not out of step with the peer group. Furthermore, South Africa had a much higher export share than Argentina or Mexico (though not Venezuela). Rodrik (2006) has also observed this relatively favourable position for exports in the early nineties, finding the comparison between South Africa and Malaysia in 1988 suggestive of comparably promising export potential.

With the exception of the export share, the conditions for a rapid turnaround in economic growth were inauspicious in 1994. Not only had the economy long been in relative (and ultimately absolute) decline, but had fallen further behind in the productive employment of capital and labour. The attainment and quality of education varied greatly between racial groups, and the same racial variation lay behind the unfavourably large fertility rate by 1994. The Gini income coefficient and a proxy for the provision of public services suggested a level of inequality likely to present a continuous future economic burden, and possibly to pose a social and economic threat to South Africa's longer-term stability.

3.2 Growth accounting

South Africa's economic growth over the past ten years can be analysed by means of growth accounting, where a first step is to identify the relative contributions of the major factors of production, capital and labour, and of overall productivity. Such an exercise focuses on the proximate, rather than the fundamental causes of growth but provides a means of allocating observed total output growth between the changes in factor inputs and total factor productivity (TFP).

The growth accounting exercise follows standard methodology (Barro, 1999; Bosworth and Collins, 2003). A constant return to scale production function is assumed:

$$Y = AK^\alpha (LH)^{1-\alpha} \tag{1}$$

where Y is total output, K is capital stock, L is employment, H is average human capital measure and A is total factor productivity (TFP). The output elasticity of capital is given by α, and the output elasticity of labour by (1–α).

The growth rate in output can then be decomposed into components associated with factor accumulation and TFP. Differentiating the equation above with respect to time (assuming a Hicks neutral technology) and dividing by Y, yields:

$$\frac{\dot{Y}}{Y} = \frac{\dot{A}}{A} + \alpha\left(\frac{\dot{K}}{K}\right) + (1-\alpha)\left(\frac{\dot{LH}}{LH}\right) \tag{2}$$

Assuming perfect competition, α and 1 – α can be estimated respectively by the share of capital and of labour in total income. The growth rate of TFP (i.e. $\frac{\dot{A}}{A}$) can then be derived, given time series data on Y, K, and LH.

In decomposing South Africa's economic growth performance over the past ten years three alternative measures of the labour factor, LH, are utilized. The first assumes no contribution of changes in average human capital, i.e. H = 1.0 in equation (1) above. The second measures changes in average human capital on the basis of the average years of schooling of the South African labour force, i.e. H = $(1.07)^S$, where S = average years of schooling and seven per cent return to schooling is assumed for each year (Bosworth and Collins, 2003). The third disaggregates employment into three categories of skills levels (highly skilled, skilled, and semi- and unskilled), each weighted with its respective shares in the total wage bill (Fedderke, 2002). The relevant data are presented in Table 2.3.[4]

Table 2.4 shows the results of the growth accounting exercise and reveals the important role of multifactor productivity in South Africa's economic growth performance over the past two decades. In the ten years after 1994, productivity growth was the major factor in the growth revival,[5] which contrasts sharply with the negative contribution to growth by productivity in the preceding ten years. The contribution of capital to growth, though modest, was slightly higher after 1994 than in the preceding decade. Labour's contribution declined across the two periods, though it remained positive. Labour's contribution is higher in rows 3 to

---

[4] Labour market time series in South Africa should be used with caution. Both the institutional environment of the labour market and data collection methods have changed significantly over time (Banerjee et al., 2006). To the extent that the informal sector is underestimated in the labour series but captured in output, growth accounting risks overstating the contribution of TFP growth. Unlike with the Labour Force Survey data (see, Burger and Yu, 2006), however, it is not possible to determine whether the Quantec data used here systematically over- or understate employment.

[5] South Africa's TFP growth was also relatively high by world standards. Bosworth and Collins (2003) found that during 1990–2000, total factor productivity for the world economy (measured by 84 countries) increased by 0.8 per cent per annum. The comparable number for the 19 African countries in the study was –0.5 per cent.

Table 2.3. Factors of production and income shares

	1985–94	1995–2004
	Average annual change (%)	
Fixed capital stock (2000 prices)	1.01	1.37
Employment (total)[a]	1.14	1.13
—Highly skilled[b]	4.03 (50.7)	2.07 (49.8)
—Skilled[b]	1.85 (34.6)	1.82 (34.7)
—Semi- and unskilled[b]	0.23 (14.7)	0.37 (15.4)
	1.8	0.9
	Average share in Total Income	
Wage income share[c]	0.57	0.54
Capital income share[c]	0.43	0.46

The figures in brackets represent average wage bill shares.
[a] Formal and informal sector employment as estimated by Quantec Research on the basis of the Survey of Employment and Earnings (P0271), the Survey of Employment Earnings (P0275), and the Labour Force Survey (P0210).
[b] Based on the 2000 Census.
[c] Based on national accounts statistics as published by the SARB.

Table 2.4. Sources of output growth in South Africa: 1985–2004

Human capital treatment	Period	Real annual output growth	Capital contribution	Labour contribution	Total factor productivity
		%	Average in percentage points		
No provision for human capital	1985–94	0.8	0.45	0.63	−0.28
	1995–2004	3.1	0.62	0.62	1.86
Human capital based on average years of schooling	1985–94	0.8	0.45	1.11	−0.76
	1995–2004	3.1	0.62	0.88	1.60
Human capital represented by 3 skills levels	1985–94	0.8	0.45	1.49	−1.14
	1995–2004	3.1	0.62	0.95	1.53

Source: Authors' calculations using data in Table 3.

6 of Table 2.4, suggesting that improvements in average human capital during this period had a positive, though modest, impact on growth (see also, Fedderke, 2002).

Recent studies on South Africa's growth performance, Fedderke (2002) and Arora (2005), have also highlighted the sharp turnaround in the contribution of multifactor productivity (Table 2.5).

Additional information on the proximate causes of South Africa's growth revival may be gained by applying a growth accounting exercise at the sectoral and sub-sectoral levels. The results are given for the main sectors of the economy in Table 2.6 and for the manufacturing sub-sectors in Table 2.7.[6]

The following broad conclusions are reached from a sectoral decomposition of South Africa's growth performance over the past two decades: (i) that multifactor productivity dominated capital and labour as positive proximate causes of the growth revival in the decade since 1994; (ii) while capital also contributed positively since 1994, the growth rate of the labour input (in the formal sector) declined (except for two of the tertiary sub-sectors: wholesale and retail trade and financial intermediation); and (iii) the contribution of multifactor productivity was most pronounced in the secondary and tertiary sectors. The positive contribution by TFP in manufacturing since 1994 contrasts with the negative contribution by TFP during the nineties found by Fedderke (2002). Since Fedderke's (2002) sample for the nineties did not run beyond 1997, the contrasting results suggest that the contribution of TFP growth to the growth revival gathered strength as the decade from 1995 unfolded. Finally capital accumulation contributed most to growth in the construction and services sectors.

4. The evolution of capital, labour, and productivity

In this section we combine lessons from the growth literature on South Africa with empirical evidence to identify likely explanations for the relative contributions of investment and labour and productivity to growth in South

Table 2.5. Recent studies on the sources of output growth in South Africa

Study	Period	Real annual output growth	Capital contribution	Labour contribution	Total factor productivity
		%	Average in percentage points		
Arora (2005)	1980–94	1.2	0.8	0.7	−0.4
	1995–2003	2.9	0.7	0.9	1.3
Fedderke (2002)	1970s	3.21	2.54	1.17	−0.49
	1980s	2.20	1.24	0.62	0.34
	1990s	0.94	0.44	−0.58	1.07

---

[6] An important caveat is that the results at the three-digit sub-sectoral level should be interpreted with care. The derivation of three-digit data from data compiled at the two-digit level, using the infrequently updated input-output data available for South Africa, risks missing sectoral shifts and hence could misrepresent the contribution of the various factors (Fedderke, 2002).

Table 2.6. Sources of output growth in South Africa: Sectoral: 1985–2004

	Real annual output growth		Capital contribution		Labour contribution		Total factor productivity	
	%		Average in percentage points					
Period	1985–94	1995–2004	1985–94	1995–2004	1985–94	1995–2004	1985–94	1995–2004
Primary sector	0.47	0.31	0.51	0.32	−0.43	−0.75	0.39	0.74
—Agriculture, forestry and fishing	3.89	0.44	−1.38	−0.18	−0.04	−0.35	2.55	0.61
—Mining and quarrying	−0.58	0.26	1.45	0.50	−1.07	−1.37	−0.96	1.13
Secondary sector	−0.03	2.73	0.21	0.31	−0.50	−1.22	0.26	3.64
—Manufacturing	−0.1	2.78	0.49	0.7	−0.47	−0.67	−0.12	2.75
—Electricity, gas and water	3.95	1.61	−0.29	−0.86	−1.55	−0.92	5.79	3.39
—Construction (contractors)	−2.64	3.48	−0.83	1.65	−0.36	−3.44	−1.45	−1.61
Tertiary sector	1.41	3.79	0.54	0.72	0.24	0.97	0.64	2.10
—Wholesale and retail trade, catering and accommodation	−0.11	4.3	0.48	1.07	0.27	1.18	−0.86	2.05
—Transport, storage and communication	1.58	6.85	0.09	0.97	2.8	−1.6	4.29	7.48
—Financial intermediation, insurance, real estate and business services	1.77	5.16	0.76	0.76	4.11	3.26	−3.10	1.14

Source: Data from Quantec.

Africa from 1995 to 2004. Unfortunately, the sample post-1994 may overlap at best for a few years (and sometimes not at all) with the samples previously used to examine the various drivers of economic growth. Thus, it is necessary to assume that the systematic relationships driving capital, labour, and productivity have not changed fundamentally between the estimated sample and period under consideration.

4.1. Explaining TFP growth

TFP growth accounts for the bulk of the growth in South Africa. To identify the factors influencing TFP it is necessary to give theoretical content to TFP growth. It might have resulted from spill-overs associated with capital investment (Romer, 1986), or spill-overs associated with investment in human

Table 2.7. Sources of output growth in South Africa: Manufacturing sub-sectors: 1985–2004

Period	Real annual output growth %		Capital contribution		Labour contribution		Total factor productivity	
			Average in percentage points					
	1985–94	1995–2004	1985–94	1995–2004	1985–94	1995–2004	1985–94	1995–2004
Food, beverages and tobacco	−0.01	0.86	1.05	0.12	−0.24	−1.28	−0.82	2.02
Textiles, clothing and leather	−1.89	0.54	−0.60	−0.15	−1.20	−1.59	−0.09	2.28
Wood and paper; publishing and printing	0.54	1.34	−0.91	1.20	0.20	−0.05	1.25	0.19
Petroleum	1.06	5.36	1.02	0.80	0.24	0.12	−0.20	4.44
Other non-metallic mineral products	−0.49	0.41	−1.17	−0.03	−0.06	−1.80	0.74	2.24
Metals, metal products, machinery and equipment	−2.29	3.44	0.58	0.56	−1.49	−0.46	−1.38	3.34
Electrical machinery and apparatus	−0.33	2.95	−0.82	−0.51	−0.87	−3.72	1.36	7.18
Radio, TV, instruments, watches and clocks	1.83	−1.22	−0.71	0.80	1.73	−0.58	0.81	−1.44
Transport equipment	−2.80	4.72	1.58	2.32	−1.36	0.12	−2.02	2.28
Furniture and other equipment	7.97	1.98	2.05	3.90	1.03	0.28	4.89	−2.20

Source: Data from Quantec.

capital (Lucas, 1988), or from explicit investment in research and development, often called Schumpeterian TFP growth (Fedderke, 2005).

Fedderke (2006) proposed an econometric test for the relative importance of the two types of spill-over effects on TFP growth and the presence of Schumpeterian effects, using a panel data set for South African manufacturing sectors, 1970 to 1997. The study used a dynamic panel model with TFP as the dependent variable and a range of explanatory variables, including growth in the capital stock for Romer-type spill-overs and human capital proxies for Lucas-type spill-overs. No evidence was found for Romer-type spill-overs and only modest evidence of Lucas-type spill-overs, associated with human capital proxies such as the proportion of matriculants taking mathematics and science and the proportion of university degrees awarded in the natural, engineering, and mathematical sciences. There was evidence of Schumpeterian effects, notably a positive effect from research and development (R&D), and from proxies of human capital investment, that measured the 'quality' as opposed to the 'quantity' of human capital.

Fedderke (2005) has identified the 'core determinants' of South Africa's TFP growth as a combination of factors determining the quality of human capital development and R&D activity. This is a strong interpretation of the results given that they were derived with data for the manufacturing sector alone (representing only 20 per cent of GDP). Generalizing these results to the entire economy is particularly difficult since, on Fedderke's own calculation, the contribution of TFP to growth at the sectoral level was negative for manufacturing in the nineties while positive in services, mining and agriculture (Fedderke, 2002).[7] These 'core determinants' showed marked declines in the quality of education and in R&D activity up to the democratic transition (Fedderke et al., 2003a); and van der Berg (see Chapter 12) finds the decline has continued through 2001 for the quality of human capital development. Thus, these 'core determinants' may not account for the rise in TFP growth observed across many sectors in the economy since 1994.

The renewed interest in potential Schumpeterian effects on TFP growth has led to a reconsideration[8] of the potential relationship between competition and innovation, previously studied by, for example, Scherer (1967). While the theoretical literature (e.g. Dixit and Stiglitz, 1977) suggests that competition might depress innovation[9], the empirical literature (e.g. Nickell, 1996) has found evidence of a positive relationship between competition and innovation. Aghion et al. (2005) offer a new model predicting an inverted U-shape for the relationship between innovation and competition, consistent both with their own empirical evidence (from a panel of listed UK firms in 1973–94) and the positive relationships found by empirical studies based on linear regression models.[10] This prediction has been confirmed for manufacturing firms in South Africa by Aghion et al. (2006).

---

[7] These results for manufacturing using data up to 1997 are not found for 1995–2004, see above.

[8] Recent international papers include those by Nickell (1996), Blundell et al. (1999) and Aghion et al. (2005).

[9] The negative relationship between competition and innovation is also consistent with the endogenous growth models of, for example, Romer (1990) and Aghion and Howitt (1992), where competition reduces innovation by lowering monopolistic rents. However, as Nickell (1996) observes, the theoretical literature also contains models predicting a positive effect for competition on innovation, by sharpening the incentives for managers, by increasing the response of profitability to managerial effort or by encouraging greater effort by workers who share in rents.

[10] The peak of the inverted-U (in terms of the measure of competitiveness) lies close to the median in the sample of Aghion et al. (2005). With a median of 0.95 (where 1 means perfect competition), these data would yield a positive linear relationship between the measure of competitiveness and innovation.

The potential impact of product market imperfections has recently received attention in the South African literature (see also Chapter 8 below). Fedderke et al. (2007) quantified the extent of competition in a panel of three-digit South African manufacturing industries, using the technique of Roeger (1995) to calculate mark-ups of price over marginal cost. They control for potential determinants of the mark-up (e.g. the business cycle, import and export penetration, market structure, and industry competitiveness), and they use the dynamic heterogeneous panel estimation technique of Pesaran et al. (1999) to allow for heterogeneity between sectors. The study finds that mark-ups are substantially higher in South African manufacturing industries than in comparable US industries, despite the greater likelihood of competitive pressure from foreign firms in South Africa. These results are robust to the inclusion of various control variables and of intermediate inputs in the calculation of marginal cost. An important further result is that lower mark-ups are associated with industries more open to international trade, see below.

Aghion et al. (2006) build on these results with further data sets and a larger international sample. They used three data sets[11] (two at the industry level and one at the firm level) to calculate price–cost margins[12] and labour productivity over time and across industries. They confirm the finding of Fedderke et al. (2007), that competition (measured by the absence of pricing power) is both weak in South African manufacturing industries on an international comparison, and that it has remained persistently weak (despite evidence of increased competition for part of the nineties, a trend since apparently reversed). They also find evidence of a positive and economically meaningful relationship between increased competition and labour productivity growth in South African manufacturing industries. This result, however, cannot be an important explanation for the relative increase in TFP growth at the aggregate and sectoral levels in South Africa since 1994. Their measures of pricing power remain persistently high over a period in which TFP growth increased markedly as a contributor to GDP growth.

However, the important finding by Fedderke et al. (2007), that openness to international trade is associated with industries where mark-ups are lower, does potentially offer a partial explanation for the rise in TFP growth. Indeed, using a consistent set of tariff data for 1988–2004, Edwards (2005) finds significant

---

[11] These data sets are: (i) an industry-level panel data set for South Africa and 1,000 other countries since the sixties from the UNIDO (United Nations Industrial Development Organization) International Industry Statistics 2004 database; (ii) an industry-level panel data set at the three-digit level for 1970–2004 from South Africa's TIPS (Trade and Industrial Policy Strategies) data base and (iii) a firm-level panel since the early 1980s for listed companies in South Africa and 55 other countries from Worldscope.

[12] Aghion et al. (2006) confirmed the robustness of their results with two different measures of the price–cost margin and one direct measure of the mark-up.

reductions in the level of nominal and effective protection in South Africa during the 1990s, a finding robust to sensitivity tests. Edwards and Lawrence (2006) also report evidence of effective liberalization at the aggregate and sectoral level in South Africa since the late 1980s. Another channel whereby openness might enhance TFP growth is through the direct transfer of technology, either as information, or embodied in traded goods. Arora and Bhundia (2003) suggest their evidence is consistent with this channel, using South Africa's trade ratio[13] as an aggregate measure of openness in a time series model to explain TFP growth (as one of two (weakly exogenous) factors). Jonsson and Subramanian (2001) report even stronger results, attributing 90 per cent of TFP growth in South Africa during 1990 to 1997 to increased openness to trade.[14] However, Arora and Bhundia (2003) also suggested a second explanatory factor, namely investment in machinery and equipment, that we explore further below.

4.2. Explaining capital accumulation

Even though the long-run convergence of the economy depends on TFP and the latter has lately accounted for a larger proportion of economic growth in South Africa, capital retains a prominent position in any comprehensive account of economic growth in South Africa (for example, Fedderke, 2005). In Robert Chirinko's (1993) review of the literature on the empirical modelling of business investment spending he identified three important research areas: 'financial structure and liquidity constraints'; 'additional dynamics', especially the connection between irreversibility and uncertainty; and 'an expanded view of the firm and investment decisions'. The South African contributions to the literature on investment are summarized under these three headings.

4.2.1. FINANCIAL STRUCTURE AND LIQUIDITY CONSTRAINTS

An important topic in models of investment expenditure in the South African literature of the last decade is whether the financial structure and/or credit factors have been an important constraint, despite the fairly high degree of

---

[13] South Africa's trade ratio was 49.2 per cent in 1984, declined to 42 per cent by 1994 and rose to 53.9 per cent by 2004 (*Quarterly Bulletin*, South African Reserve Bank).

[14] These authors identified four channels in the endogenous growth literature along which potentially positive effects for trade liberalization on TFP growth might operate, namely:

(i) to employ a larger variety of intermediate goods and capital equipment which could enhance the productivity of its other resources; (ii) to acquire technology developed worldwide, especially in the form of embodied capital goods; (iii) to increase the variety of products produced and consumed; and (iv) to improve the efficiency with which resources are used, which can help to change market structures and reduce markups, thereby imparting dynamic efficiency benefits.

(Jonsson and Subramanian, 2001: 198–9).

financial sector development for an emerging market economy (Demirguc-Kunt and Levine, 2001; Aron and Muellbauer, 2005).

Du Toit and Moolman (2004) used a time series model (for 1970–2000) of a modified neoclassical investment function to incorporate a constraint on the internal and external sources for finance. Their model, driven by the short-run impact of low saving, precarious external reserves and a high user cost of capital, under-predicted actual investment post-1994 (Du Toit and Moolman, 2004: figure 3). However, the user cost of capital has since declined (Aron and Muellbauer, 2005) and external reserves have risen strongly, the combination of which is consistent with the rise in aggregate investment expenditure reported in Table 2.2.

Fedderke (2004) proposed a model in the Dixit and Pindyck (1994) tradition to incorporate adjustment costs and both sectoral and systemic uncertainty as its main features. He also included a proxy for credit rationing—the ratio of gross operating surplus to total fixed capital stock—in a model estimated on a panel of three-digit manufacturing sectors for 1970–97. The credit variable did not prove significant in the model.

Investment expenditure has also been modelled as part of a system of equations with investment expenditure and real GDP growth amongst the jointly endogenous variables. Kularatne (2002) offers two models in this tradition for South African growth and investment. He finds a significant contribution from two financial sector variables to GDP growth: the ratio of private credit extension to GDP and a measure of stock market liquidity; however, these operate only indirectly via the investment rate. Kularatne (2002) and Fedderke (2005) both suggest that the absence of a direct impact on GDP growth is consistent with credit rationing. However, the same evidence is also consistent with many alternative hypotheses, including model misspecification (Kularatne, 2002).

In summary, there is no consensus yet on the influence of financial sector or liquidity constraints on investment expenditure in South Africa. The literature, except for Kularatne (2002), does not support strong statements about the role of the financial sector in the pattern of investment expenditure since 1994.

In contrast, several papers have found a significant role for the user cost of capital in explaining investment expenditure at various levels of aggregation in South Africa. By implication the real interest rate, the rate of depreciation and the corporate tax rate become relevant explanatory factors for capital accumulation. Fedderke et al. (2001b) suggested from their evidence that the user cost of capital had been an important constraint on investment in South Africa during the seventies, but had become less so over time. This is consistent with Aron and Muellbauer's (2005) calculation of the tax-adjusted real market interest rate for South Africa post-2000, comparing favourably with a sample of industrialized and developing countries, and supporting their claim that inflation targeting has not entailed debilitating high real interest rates.

4.2.2. UNCERTAINTY AND IRREVERSIBILITY

Following Dixit and Pindyck's (1994) influential contribution, the explicit modelling of uncertainty has become a feature of empirical investment functions. Adding the restrictive assumption of irreversibility to the assumption of uncertainty leads this kind of model to predict that higher uncertainty will lower investment expenditure, even under risk neutrality. However, a less restrictive assumption of downward sloping demand curves yields the same prediction when combined with uncertainty (Nickell, 1978). The empirical literature provides broad support for the hypothesis that uncertainty lowers investment internationally (Aron and Muellbauer, 2005). Fedderke argues in Chapter 7 that the Dixit and Pindyck model matches the South African investment experience closely.

Consistent with the international literature, Bleaney (1994), Fielding (1997), and Fedderke (2004) all report significant adverse effects for uncertainty on investment expenditure. Aron and Muellbauer (2005) also list systemic risk factors that have declined since 1994, including: closing the forward book, the adoption of inflation targeting, the recovery of economic growth, and prudent fiscal policy.[15] Based on the evidence of the South African literature an overall decline in systematic risk would have contributed to a rise in investment expenditure.

4.2.3. AN EXPANDED VIEW OF THE FIRM AND ITS INVESTMENT DECISION

A third plank in Chirinko's research agenda is to see the investment decision in the context of the many other decisions taken continuously by firms (Chirinko, 1993: 1904). The South African literature has advanced in this direction over the last decade, in a number of respects.

Firstly, there has been an expanded use of simultaneous equation models. Kularatne (2002) demonstrated joint endogeneity between growth, investment and liquidity, Mariotti (2002) also exploited the joint endogeneity between growth and investment to trace the impact of certain macroeconomic policy outcomes on growth, and most recently, Fedderke and Luiz (2005) have built a theoretical case, supported with econometric evidence, for the joint endogeneity of investment and political instability in South Africa.

Secondly, the interaction between the labour market and investment decisions has been examined. Fedderke (2004) considered the effect of human capital on the formation of physical capital. His result suggests a complemen-

---

[15] However, they suggest also factors that might have increased systemic risk since 1994, such as fears of the future protection of property rights and of future taxation, high crime rates, high HIV/AIDS incidence and inflexible labour markets.

tarity between human capital and investment in physical capital in the manufacturing sector; which has important policy implications given the dominant role of the public sector in education in South Africa.

In the third place, a burgeoning literature has considered the interaction between private and public investment. There might be important crowding-in or crowding-out effects for public investment in physical capital, and both the composition and size of public sector investment are relevant. If public investment is large relative to the tax base, the resulting debt burden and likelihood of either rising future taxes or future financial instability might depress investment expenditure. In contrast, public investment projects that lower transactions costs for private business, or solve public-goods-type problems, might show a complementary effect on private investment. Agénor's (2004) summary of the empirical literature for developing countries provides broad support for the complementarity thesis on public investment. Both Fielding (1997) and Fedderke (2000) found evidence of crowding in by public investment in South Africa.

More recent studies focus on a type of capital often financed by the public sector in South Africa, namely infrastructure. Fedderke and Luiz (2005) demonstrate a feedback relationship between GDP growth and infrastructure investment from a newly constructed database measuring the stock of infrastructure over time. Much stronger evidence is reported by Fedderke et al. (2006) that infrastructure investment might lead output growth in South Africa. Both a direct impact for infrastructure on growth, and an indirect channel via higher private sector investment in productive capital were found. These results are important given the slowdown in infrastructure investment in South Africa since the seventies which has seen the country fall behind other middle income countries along a number of infrastructure dimensions (Bogetic and Fedderke, 2005). Moreover, investment in public infrastructure has continued to decline since 1994. The evidence suggests this may have acted as a drag on growth. This conclusion is reinforced by evidence of a positive relationship between infrastructure and TFP in the country's manufacturing industries (Fedderke and Bogetic, 2006).

Finally, various studies have examined the influence of international capital flows in South Africa. For example, Fedderke and Liu (2002) argued with the support of time series evidence for 1960–95 that net capital flows to South Africa had been adversely affected by political risk and (temporarily) by financial liberalization (see Chapter 5).

In summary, the empirical literature on investment expenditure in South Africa suggests that the recovery in investment since 1994 could be attributed to a combination of the following factors: lower systemic risk, lower user cost of capital and by an increased inflow of foreign capital, which has been associated with lower risk and macroeconomic policy prudence. Lower corporate taxes and institutional protection for property rights have also been associated with improved FDI.

4.3. Explaining employment growth

Explaining employment behaviour in the South African economy in the period since 1994 is no simple matter. Not only is there little consensus in the literature on the potential causes of employment growth, but, as pointed out above, the quality of statistics on employment, unemployment, and other labour market characteristics has generally been found wanting (Standing et al., 1996; Klasen and Woolard, 1999). A comparative assessment of empirical analyses on the causes of employment growth is complicated by problems with interpreting the statistics. For example, earlier analyses of employment using formal sector statistics, suggest that South Africa experienced 'jobless' growth in the 1990s, while recent analyses adjusting for informal employment give a more positive picture of employment generation (Bhorat and Oosthuizen, 2005; Burger and Woolard, 2005). In discussing the possible determinants of employment the following are considered: output growth, wages and trade liberalization, and a number of others are noted.

The standard potential determinants of employment in a market economy include output growth and (real) wages. South Africa's output growth since 1994 has been insufficient to support a rate of employment growth that can address the growing unemployment problem (for a detailed analysis of unemployment in the post-apartheid period, see Chapter 11). Fedderke et al. (2001b: 498) have observed that 'economic growth in South Africa has been poor at generating additional employment ever since the 1970s'. Indeed, some of the earlier research (e.g., Loots, 1998) suggested that the employment elasticity of output growth (at least with respect to formal sector employment) was in a secular decline. But this, too, has been disputed, and more recent research, e.g., Bhorat and Oosthuizen (2005), argues that employment growth at least kept pace with the growth of the working age population since the late 1990s.

The impact of real wages on employment has been considered in a number of studies, generally indicating that labour demand in South Africa is relatively wage elastic. Fallon and Lucas (1998), for example, estimated a wage elasticity of employment of −0.71 and Nattrass (2000: 84) refers to estimates ranging from −0.66 to −0.85. Fedderke et al. (2003b) found even higher wage elasticities of −1.97 in manufacturing, and elasticities for unskilled labour in the formal labour market ranging from −2.00 to −2.23. Consequently, if real wages had increased substantially since 1994, this could (at least partly) explain the relatively slow employment growth. As Fedderke (2005: 22) notes: 'labour mispricing continues to be an important factor in South Africa's poor track record of job creation'. Unfortunately the evidence on real wages remains complex. For example, Kingdon and Knight (Chapter 11) report declining earnings on average for all types of workers, though earnings increased for workers in the large-scale formal sector. Banerjee et al. (2006) and Burger and

Yu (2006),[16] in turn, suggest that real wages were largely stagnant during this period.

Trade liberalization, often associated with improved economic growth and employment performance (e.g., Dollar and Kraay, 2002), has been identified as limiting South Africa's employment growth in the 1990s, particularly for unskilled labour. A strong proponent of this view is Nattrass (2000), who identifies competition from low wage, labour intensive exporting countries and the shift to capital- and skill-intensive productive sectors under the impact of globalization, as important factors restraining employment growth. Barker (2003: 186) concurs that employment has fallen due to a relative increase in demand for skilled workers (and a decrease in the demand for unskilled labour) with the drive to increased productivity by South African firms aiming to improve their international competitive position. He also emphasizes the increase in the capital- and skill intensity of production of the natural resource-based products that feature strongly in South Africa's export mix.

However, the proposition that trade liberalization has impacted negatively on unskilled employment in South Africa has also been challenged. Edwards (2001) offers two counter arguments, first that factors other than trade liberalization may have been responsible for sectoral shifts away from unskilled labour (e.g. changes in domestic demand, labour regulations, and relative wages); and second, the creation of employment in export-producing firms. Finally, Fedderke et al.(2003b) show that trade liberalization has resulted in a positive impact on labour demand but that the associated technological changes have been labour-saving.

Other factors which might have constrained employment growth (but remaining controversial in the literature) fall into three groups. The first covers labour market institutions: for example, labour market inflexibility due to the relatively strong position of labour unions in South Africa and new labour legislation enacted after 1994 (Barker, 2003; Burger and Woolard, 2005); and the mismatch between the required skills levels and the labour force and employment (Burger and Woolard, 2005; Pauw et al., 2006). A second group of factors is sectoral, including concerns over a perceived increase in the capital intensity of production (Bhorat and Oosthuizen, 2005; Pauw et al., 2006), increased concentration in the manufacturing sector (Fedderke and Szalontai, 2003) and sectoral changes in demand, i.e. from mining and agriculture to services (Bhorat and Oosthuizen, 2005; Banerjee et al., 2006). The final group reflects the labour market impact of the high prevalence of HIV/AIDS in South Africa (Arndt and Lewis, 2000; Laubscher, Smit, and Visagie, 2001).

In summary, although the empirical literature on South Africa's lacklustre employment growth has considered several possible determinants to explain

---

[16] However, it should be noted that real wages (of especially unskilled labour) increased substantially in the ten years prior to 1994, raising the level of real wages.

this outcome, many questions remain unresolved. It is clear, however, that the increasing openness of the economy and factor pricing (for real wages) have played an important role since 1994 (as they have for capital and productivity).

4.4. Conclusion: Prospects for future growth

Having unpacked and examined the various contributing factors to economic growth in South African since 1994 we are now in a position to reassemble the message from the constituent parts. Compared with a peer group of countries the initial conditions for a dramatic growth recovery in South Africa were inauspicious in 1994. The economy had been in relative decline for decades while the legacy of apartheid was particularly evident in a very high level of income inequality (with the associated risks of punitive taxes or social unrest) and in the highly unequal and poor quality of education across the different population groups. Meanwhile demographic factors (e.g. a relatively high fertility rate) placed pressure on the labour market.

The 3.2 per cent average real growth for the first ten years after 1994 represented a clear improvement on the previous decade though it was still low by international standards. Total factor productivity growth accounts for 50 per cent or more (depending on the assumptions used in the growth accounting) of South Africa's economic recovery since 1994. With very few exceptions this aggregate level result also holds at the level of sectors and the (manufacturing) sub-sectors in the South African economy. While it is difficult to account for this recovery in productivity growth, the most compelling evidence reported here finds the economy's increasing openness to international trade to be the leading cause of rising productivity locally. Authors such as Jonsson and Subramanian (2001) explained this by appeal to the endogenous growth literature, but Fedderke et al. (2007) added evidence that this effect might be working through increased competition at the sectoral level. It remains for future research to examine through which channels trade openness has encouraged productivity growth in South Africa since 1995.

Trade openness and openness to international capital flows, are also important factors explaining the revival of investment expenditure as a contributing factor to growth after 1994. Other factors that have been associated with higher investment rates in South Africa, such as a lower user cost of capital and lower systemic and sectoral uncertainty, are also consistent with the modest recovery in investment. Factor prices and increased openness also feature strongly in the labour market literature, and in attempts to explain the lacklustre performance of employment growth since 1994. In contrast with investment, where the factor price has been declining, the suspected high level of real wages has a role, as well as the nuanced effect of trade liberalization on labour demand.

In summary, the evidence offered here suggests that openness to trade and capital flows, lower uncertainty and lower interest rates mainly explain South Africa's growth recovery since 1994. There are important policy implications. The lower systematic risk associated with the post-1994 political dispensation has economic as well as social value, and the orthodox macroeconomic policies of this period have lowered overall risk and the user cost of capital (see Chapters 3 and 4). Finally, increasing openness to trade and capital flows has been key to the economic recovery, which suggests possible gains from further steps in this direction (see Chapter 6).

Since 2004, there has been a sharp increase in growth, averaging above 5 per cent during 2004–2007. This rise in growth has shifted upward growth forecasts too, for example the Bureau for Economic Research's 3-year forecast increased from 2.9 per cent in 2003 to 5.0 per cent in 2007, while that of the National Treasury rose from 3.7 per cent in 2003 to 4.9 per cent in 2007 (BER, 2003; BER, 2007; National Treasury, 2003; National Treasury, 2007). While the economy was growing more rapidly since 2004 the South African Government formulated a new growth initiative in response to the improved, but still modest, growth of the preceding decade and with a view towards sustained real growth of 6 per cent per annum. The Accelerated and Shared Growth Initiative (ASGISA), as this initiative became known, focuses on relaxing certain binding constraints on growth. The National Treasury also obtained the services of an international panel of economists to help diagnose these constraints and to suggest appropriate policy interventions. This group under the leadership of Ricardo Hausmann—also called the International Panel—released its final report in May 2008 with a summary of their various analytical papers and 21 policy recommendations.[17]

A central analytical result of the International Panel's research is the claim that the higher growth since 2004 'does not appear to be externally sustainable' (Hausmann, 2008: 2) and the likely range for potential GDP growth rate is between 3 per cent and 4.5 per cent due to this and other constraints (Du Plessis, Smit, and Sturzenegger 2008). This claim is consistent with the following evidence: the observation that economic growth has largely been driven by domestic demand, leading to a widening current account deficit that reached 7.3 per cent of GDP in 2007; that the growth in domestic demand has been driven by investment in non-tradables (such as real estate and finance) and by expenditure on consumer durables (Frankel et al., 2007); and that export growth and investment in the tradable goods sector have been lacklustre, despite the very favourable terms of trade shock from rising commodity prices over the same period (Edwards and Lawrence, 2006).

---

[17] Links to the research undertaken by the International Panel is available on the website of the National Treasury <www.treasury.gov.za> accessed 22 Sept. 2008.

To the concerns over the external sustainability of the presently higher growth the International Panel added concerns that infrastructure bottlenecks and especially a skills shortage are important domestic growth constraints (Hausmann, 2008). The electricity crisis of early 2008 is a striking example with far-reaching consequences: Starting in November 2007 a series of blackouts and planned load-shedding by the government owned electricity company, ESKOM, culminated in a crisis during January 2008. At the root thereof (see also Chapter 8) lay mismanagement of coal stocks by ESKOM, inadequate generating capacity (due to a deficient expansion plan and poor maintenance of existing capacity), a failure to allow the emergence of private sector cogeneration and exports to neighbouring countries in excess of ESKOM's contractual obligations (NERSA, 2008: 38–9). In the first quarter of 2008 the short term cost of this crisis could be seen in the GDP data where growth had slowed rapidly on aggregate and where value added declined by 22 per cent in mining, the sector affected most severely by the crisis. In the long term the costs will mount as supply will remain inadequate for years to come—ESKOM has already fallen a year behind on its new build programme (NERSA, 2008: 38)—and electricity prices are likely to rise considerably.

The International Panel's analysis is plausible: the widening current account deficit and the composition of the demand reflected in that deficit suggests that growth above 5 per cent is externally unsustainable, given present constraints. It remains to consider how these constraints are likely to evolve over the coming years.

The government has embarked on a large infrastructure investment programme to alleviate the bottlenecks in the logistical system. Indeed this is a central plank of the ASGISA strategy. But the pay-off of to these projects is long term and during construction they add to the external burden by widening the gap between planned investment and domestic savings. The external imbalance of South Africa's growth trajectory is likely to remain a concern and expose the economy to the risk of a disruptive financial market shock originating in the international financial markets. The trajectory for planned investment and the reality of low domestic savings offers little hope that the current account deficit will close rapidly. There has not been any sign of a rapid rise in household savings. Larger public sector savings would off-set this imbalance somewhat and it is for this reason that the International Panel recommended a fiscal surplus of at least 1 to 2 per cent of GDP but sensitive to the economic cycle. Government has already adopted a structural budget balance as a guidepost to prevent pro-cyclical fiscal policy, but there has been no indication that Government will raise the budget surplus systematically as recommended by the International Panel. It is even less likely that the now rising faction of the ANC under the leadership of Jacob Zuma will move in that direction on assuming power in 2009.

In contrast with the expected progress in infrastructure there is little prospect of relieving the skills constraint in the medium term. The national education system, though comparatively well funded, is failing to deliver, especially when the evaluation considers the quality of education. The prospects are not much better over the medium term: while reforms in the school system are expected to yield some improvement in the quality of education over time, this will take many years to filter through to the labour market. For the foreseeable future then, a lack of skills is likely to hold back economic growth.

We have come full-circle with this analysis of the post-1994 growth experience and the medium term prospects for growth in South Africa. The historical analysis of South Africa's economic growth revival after the country's political transition in 1994 provided ample evidence of the central role played by the opening up of the economy to international trade and capital flows. Looking ahead, the international integration of the economy is again likely to prove a crucial part of the growth experience, but now acting as a constraint on a pattern of growth that has become unsustainable externally. Without a rise in domestic savings or a revival in the export sector, the International Panel's estimate of potential GDP growth in the range of 3 to 4.5 per cent is a compelling estimate of average economic growth in South Africa over the medium term.

References

Agénor, P. R. (2004). *The Economics of Adjustment and Growth* (2nd edition). Cambridge, Mass., Harvard University Press.

Aghion, P. and P. Howitt (1992). 'A Model of Growth through Creative Destruction'. *Econometrica*, 60(2): 323–351.

Aghion, P., N. Bloom, R. Blundell, R. Griffith and P. Howitt (2005). 'Competition and Innovation: An Inverted-U relationship'. *Quarterly Journal of Economics*, 120(2): 701–28.

Aghion, P., M. Braun and J. W. Fedderke (2006). 'Competition and Productivity Growth in South Africa'. *CID Working Paper*, no. 132, August 2006. Cambridge, Mass.

Arndt, C. and J. D. Lewis (2000). 'The Macro Implications of HIV/AIDS in South Africa: A Preliminary Assessment'. *South African Journal of Economics*, 68(5): 856–87.

Aron, J. and J. Muellbauer (2005). 'Monetary Policy, Macro-stability and Growth'. *World Economics*, 6(4): 123–47.

Arora, V. (2005). Economic growth in Post-apartheid South Africa: A Growth Accounting Analysis. In: M. Nowak and L. A. Ricci (eds.), *Post-Apartheid South Africa: The First Ten Years*. Washington: IMF publications services.

Arora, V. and A. Bhundia (2003). Potential Output and Total Factor Productivity Growth in Post-Apartheid South Africa. *IMF working paper*: WP/03/178. Washington.

Banerjee, A., S. Galiani, J. Levinsohn and I. Woolard (2006). Why has Unemployment Risen in the New South Africa. *CID Working Paper*, no. 134. Boston, Mass.

Barker, F. S. (2003). *The South African Labour Market* (4th edition). Pretoria: Van Schaik Publishers.

Barro, R. J. (1999). 'Notes on Growth Accounting'. *Journal of Economic Growth*, 4(2): 119–37.
BER (2003). *Economic Outlook*, (October). Stellenbosch: Bureau for Economic Research at the University of Stellenbosch.
—— (2007) *Economic Outlook*, (October). Stellenbosch: Bureau for Economic Research at the University of Stellenbosch.
Bhorat, H. and M. Oosthuizen (2005). 'The Post-Apartheid South African Labour Market'. Development *Policy Research Unit Working Paper*, no. 13. Cape Town.
Bleaney, M. F. (1994). 'Political uncertainty and private investment in South Africa'. *South African Journal of Economics*, 62(3): 188–97.
Blundell, R., R. Griffith and J. Van Reenen (1999). 'Market Share, Market Value and Innovation in a Panel of British Manufacturing Firms'. *Review of Economic Studies*, 66: 529–54.
Bogetic, Z. and J. W. Fedderke (2006). 'International Benchmarking of South Africa's Infrastructure Performance'. *Journal of Development Perspectives*, 2: 7–31.
Bosworth, B. and S. M. Collins (2003). 'The Empirics of Growth: An Update'. *Brookings Papers on Economic Activity*, 2003(2): 113–79.
Burger, R. P. and I. Woolard (2005). 'The State of the Labour Market in South Africa after the First Decade of Democracy'. Cape Town, *Centre for Social Science Research Working Paper*, no. 13.
Burger, R. P. and D. Yu (2006). 'Wage Trends in Post-Apartheid South Africa : Constructing an Earnings-series from Household Survey Data'. *Stellenbosch Working Paper*, no. WP10/2006. Stellenbosch.
Chirinko, R. S. (1993). 'Business Fixed Investment Spending: Modelling Strategies, Empirical Results and Policy Implications'. *Journal of Economic Literature*, 31 (December): 1875–911.
De Wet, G. L. (1995). 'The Prognosis for Growth and Development in South Africa'. *South African Journal of Economics*, 63(4): 473–88.
Demirguc-Kunt, A. and R. Levine (2001). *Financial Structure and Economic Growth: A Cross Country Comparison of Banks, Markets and Development*. Boston, Mass.: The MIT Press.
Dixit, A. K. and R. S. Pindyck (1994). *Investment under uncertainty*. Princeton, NJ: Princeton University Press.
Dixit, A. K. and J. E. Stiglitz (1977). 'Monopolistic Competition and Optimum Product Diversity'. *American Economic Review*, 67: 297–308.
Dollar, D. and A. Kraay (2002). 'Growth is Good for the Poor'. *Journal of Economic Growth*, 7(3): 195–225.
Dowrick, S. and J. B. DeLong (2005). 'Globalisation and Convergence'. In: J. Williamson (eds.), *Globalization in historical perspective*. Chicago: University of Chicago Press.
Du Plessis, S. and B. Smit (2007). 'South Africa's Growth Revival after 1994'. *Journal of African Economies*, 16(5): 668–704.
Du Plessis, S.A., B.W., Smit, and F. Sturzenegger (2008) 'Identifying Aggregate Supply and Demand Shocks in South Africa', *Journal of African Economies*, (forthcoming).
Du Toit, C. and E. Moolman (2004). 'A Neoclassical Investment Function of the South African Economy'. *Economic Modelling*, 21(4): 647–60.
Edwards, L. (2001). 'Globalization and the Skills Bias of Occupational Employment in South Africa'. *South African Journal of Economics*, 69(1): 40–71.
—— (2005). 'Has South Africa Liberalised Its Trade?' *South African Journal of Economics*, 73(4): 754–75.

Edwards, L. and R. Lawrence (2006). 'South African Trade Policy Matters: Trade Performance and Trade Policy'. *CID Working Paper, no.* 135, October 2006. Cambridge, Mass.

Fallon, P. and R. Lucas (1998). 'South African Labour Markets: Adjustment and Inequalities'. *Informal Discussion Papers on Aspects of the Economy of South Africa*. Washington, World Bank.

Fedderke, J. W. (2000). Investment in Fixed Capital Stock: the South African Manufacturing Industry 1970–97. *ERSA working paper*, 16. Johannesburg: University of Witwatersrand

—— (2002). 'The Structure of Growth in the South African Economy: Factor Accumulation and Total Factor Productivity Growth 1970–1997'. *South African Journal of Economics*, 70(4): 612–46.

—— (2004). 'Investment in fixed capital stock: testing for the impact of sectoral and systematic uncertainty'. *Oxford Bulletin of Economics and Statistics*, 66(2): 165–87.

—— (2005). 'South Africa: Sources and Constraints of Long-Term Growth, 1970–2000'. *World Bank Paper Series*, no. 94. Washington.

—— (2006). 'Technology, Human Capital and Growth: Evidence from a Middle Income Country Case Study Applying Dynamic Heterogeneous Panel Analysis'. In: South African Reserve Bank, Banco de Mexico and The People's Bank of China (eds.), *Economic Growth*. Proceedings of a G20 seminar held in Pretoria, South Africa, on 4–5 August 2005.

Fedderke, J. W. and Z. Bogetic (2006). 'Infrastructure and Growth in South Africa: Direct and Indirect Productivity Impacts of 19 Infrastructure Measures'. *World Bank Policy Research Paper* 3989. Washington.

Fedderke, J. W. and W. Liu (2002). 'Modelling the Determinants of Capital Flows and Capital Flight: With an Application to South African Data from 1960 to 1995'. *Economic Modelling*, 19(3): 419–44.

Fedderke, J. W. and J. Luiz (2005). 'The political economy of institutions, stability and investment: a simultaneous equation approach in an emerging economy—The case of South Africa'. Cape Town, Mimeograph University of Cape Town.

Fedderke, J. W. and G. Szalontai (2003). Industry Concentration in South African Manufacturing: Trends and Consequences, 1972–1996. *ERSA Working Paper*, no. 23. Cape Town.

Fedderke, J. W., R. H. J. de Kadt, and J. M. Luiz (2001a). 'Indicators Of Political Liberty, Property Rights, and Political Instability in South Africa'. *International Review of Law and Economics*, 21: 103–24.

Fedderke, J. W., J. S. Kayemba, D. W. Henderson, M. Mariotti, and P. Vaze (2001b). 'Changing Factor Market Conditions in South Africa: the Capital Market—A Sectoral Description of the Period 1970–1997'. *Development Southern Africa*, 18(4): 493–511.

Fedderke, J. W., R. de Kadt, and J. Luiz (2003a). 'A Capstone Tertiary Educational System: Inefficiency Duplication and Inequity in South Africa's Tertiary Education System, 1910–93'. *Cambridge Journal of Economics*, 27(3): 377–400.

Fedderke, J. W., Y. Shin, and P. Vaze (2003b). 'Trade and Labour Usage: And Examination of the South African Manufacturing Industry. *ERSA Working Paper*, no. 15. Cape Town.

Fedderke, J. W., P. Perkins, and J. Luiz (2006). 'Infrastructural Investment in Long-Run Economic Growth: South Africa 1875–2001'. *World Development*, 34: 1037–59.

Fedderke, J. W., C. Kularatne, and M. Mariotti (2007). 'Mark-up Pricing in South African Industry'. *Journal of African Economies*, 16(1): 28–69.

Feinstein, C. H. (2005). *An Economic History of South Africa: Conquest, Discrimination and Development*. Cambridge: Cambridge University Press.

Fielding, D. (1997). 'Aggregate Investment in South Africa: A Model with Implications for Political Reform'. *Oxford Bulletin of Economics and Statistics*, 59(3): 349–69.

Frankel, J., B. Smit and F. Sturzenegger (2007). 'South Africa: Macroeconomic challenges after a decade of success'. *CID Working Paper*, no. 133. Boston, Mass.

Hamilton, L. (1996). *Data analysis for social scientists*. New York: Duxbury Press.

Hausmann, R., (2008). *Final Recommendations of the International Panel on Growth*. Pretoria: National Treasury.

Heston, A., R. Summers, and B. Aten (2002). *Penn World Table, version 6.1*. Center for International Comparisons at the University of Pennsylvania.

Jonsson, G. and A. Subramanian (2001). 'Dynamic Gains from Trade: Evidence from South Africa'. *IMF Staff Papers*, 48(1): 197–224.

Klasen, S. and I. Woolard (1999). 'Levels, Trends and Consistency of Employment and Unemployment Figures in South Africa'. *Development Southern Africa*, 16(1): 3–16.

Kularatne, C. (2002). 'An Examination of the Impact of Financial Deepening on Long-Run Economic Growth: An Application of a Vecm Structure to a Middle-Income Country Context'. *South African Journal of Economics*, 70(4): 647–87.

Laubscher, P. (2006). *Economic Prospects*, 21(4). Stellenbosch: Bureau for Economic Research.

Laubscher, P., B. W. Smit, and L. Visagie (2001). The Macroeconomic Impact of HIV/AIDS in South Africa. Stellenbosch, Bureau for Economic Research, *Research Note* No, 10.

Loots, E. (1998). 'Job Creation and Economic Growth'. *South African Journal of Economics*, 66(3): 319–36.

Lucas, R. J. (1988). 'On the mechanics of economic development'. *Journal of Monetary Economics*, 22(3): 3–42.

Maddison, A. (2002). The World Economy: a Millennial Perspective. Paris, OECD.

Mariotti, M. (2002). 'An Examination of the Impact of Economic Policy on Long-Run Economic Growth: an Application of a Vecm Structure to a Middle-Income Country Context'. *South African Journal of Economics*, 70(4): 688–725.

Moll, T. (1991). 'Did the Apartheid Economy "Fail"?' *Journal of Southern African Studies*, 17(2): 271–91.

National Treasury (2003). *Medium Term Budget Policy Statement*, November 2003. Pretoria: National Treasury.

—— (2007). *Medium Term Budget Policy Statement*, October 2007. Pretoria: National Treasury.

Nattrass, N. (2000). 'The Debate About Unemployment in the 1990s'. *Journal for Studies in Economics and Econometrics*, 24(3): 73–89.

NERSA, (2008). 'Inquiry Into the National Electricity Supply Shortage and Load Shedding Reported by the Energy Regulator', 12 May 2008. Pretoria: National Energy Regulator of South Africa.

Nickell, S. (1978). *The Investment Decision of Firms*. Cambridge: Cambridge University Press.

——(1996). 'Competition and Corporate Performance'. *Journal of Political Economy*, 104(4): 724–46.

Pauw, K., M. Oosthuizen, and C. van der Westhuizen (2006). 'Graduate Unemployment in the Face of Skills Shortages: A Labour Market Paradox'. *Development Policy Research Unit Working Paper*, no. 0/114. Cape Town.

Pesaran, M. H., Y. Shin, and R. P. Smith (1999). 'Pooled Mean Group Estimation of Dynamic Heterogeneous Panels'. *Journal of the American Statistical Association*, 94: 621–34.

Rodrik, D. (2006). 'Understanding South Africa's Economic Puzzles'. *CID Working Paper*, no. 130, August 2006. Cambridge, Mass.

Roeger, W. (1995). 'Can Imperfect Competition Explain the Difference between Primal and Dual Productivity Measures? Estimates for US Manufacturing'. *Journal of Political Economy*, 103: 316–30.

Romer, P. M. (1986). 'Increasing Returns and Long-Run Growth'. *Journal of Political Economy*, 94: 1002–37.

——(1990). 'Endogenous Technological Change'. *Journal of Political Economy*, 98: s71–s102.

Scherer, F. (1967). 'Market Structure and the Employment of Scientists and Engineers'. *American Economic Review*, 57: 524–31.

Standing, G., J. Sender and J. Weeks (1996). 'Restructuring the Labour Market: The South African Challenge'. Geneva. An ILO Review.

World Bank (1995). *World Development Report 1995. Workers in an Integrating World*. Oxford: Oxford University Press.

——(1996). *World Development Report. From Plan to Market*. Oxford: Oxford University Press.

——(1998). *World Development Report. Knowledge for Development*. Oxford: Oxford University Press.

——(2001). *World Development Report 2000/2001. Attacking Poverty*. Oxford: Oxford University Press.

3

The Development of Transparent and Effective Monetary and Exchange Rate Policy

Janine Aron and John Muellbauer

1. Introduction[1]

A stable and predictable framework for macro-policy is an important precondition for investment and growth of employment and income. In this chapter, we examine the monetary policy legacy of the last decade. We argue that the inflation targeting framework introduced in February 2000, see van der Merwe (2004), improved the credibility and effectiveness of macroeconomic policy. The criticism the new framework has received is largely misconceived. Moreover, the fiscal consolidation, and improved transparency and predictability of fiscal policy, have supported monetary policy (see Chapter 4).

Figure 3.1 shows the growth, inflation, and interest rate record for South Africa (SA) since 1990. From 2000, the record shows a marked improvement, despite the nominal exchange rate shock in the last quarter of 2001, which together with regional grain price rises, raised inflation in 2002–3. The moderate interest rate responses to the 2001 currency depreciation and regional food price inflation, and to global food and energy price rises in 2007–8, contrast favourably with the aggressive rate rises in the 1997–8 currency depreciation, and misguided currency market interventions, that incurred great costs to the public finances and in growth foregone. In Table 3.1, we compare some macroeconomic aggregates and their volatility[2] by the period of office

---

[1] Acknowledgements: This chapter is a revised and extended version of Aron and Muellbauer (2007a). The authors acknowledge funding support from the Economic and Social Research Council, U.K. (grant RES-000-22-2066). We are grateful for comments from two anonymous referees and Brian Kahn, as well as to many others acknowledged in the above paper.

[2] This measure is defined as the absolute value of the difference in annual percentage rates of change between a variable in the current quarter and its rate of change four quarters ago.

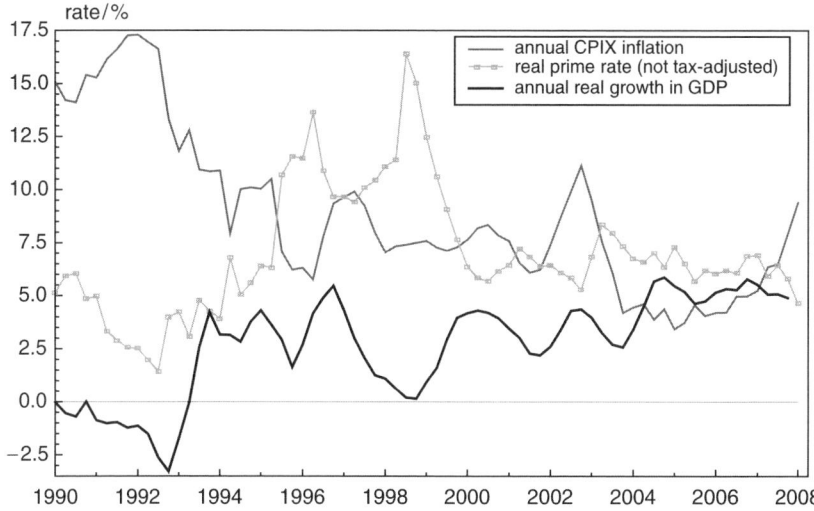

Figure 3.1. Real growth, CPIX inflation and the real prime interest rate

Sources: The prime rate is from IFS (International Monetary Fund). Real GDP, seasonally adjusted, is from the SARB's *Quarterly Bulletin*. The CPIX measure is our constructed (seasonally unadjusted) measure for metropolitan and urban areas (Aron and Muellbauer, 2004), spliced in February 2000 (when targeting began) to the seasonally unadjusted CPIX measure, obtained from *Statistics South Africa*. Changes are annual percentage changes measured over four quarters.

of central bank governor and the government in power. This yields four distinct phases: De Kock (National Party), Stals (National Party), Stals (ANC), and Mboweni (ANC), the last of these largely coinciding with the move to inflation targeting.

Under Governor Mboweni there has been a decline in nominal currency depreciation, in nominal interest rates, and in inflation, though interest rates have risen since mid 2006 and double-digit inflation returned in March 2008 under global pressures. Both growth and per capita GDP growth have improved significantly, particularly compared to the substantial declines in output per head under De Kock and in the first Stals period. The volatility of output growth and of real interest rates has declined under Mboweni. Real interest rates on average are lower than under the second Stals period, but substantially higher than under De Kock and in the first Stals period. The volatility of changes in nominal interest rates and in CPI inflation[3] are, however, higher than in the second Stals period, given larger exchange rate and food and energy price shocks.

What interpretation to put on these comparisons is far from obvious. There has been much international debate about the causes of the 'great moderation':

---

[3] The volatility of inflation measured by the consumer expenditure deflator, which excludes interest rates and which we use to approximate the targeted CPIX given the absence of data before 1994, was lower under Mboweni (see Table 1).

Table 3.1. Overview of macro-aggregates by regime of central bank governor

Party	National Party government		ANC government	
Governor Regime	De Kock 1981q1–1989q2	Stals 1989q3–1994q1	Stals 1994q2–1999q2	Mboweni 1999q3–2007q4
Macro-variable	Average	Average	Average	Average
Nominal effective exchange rate change (%)	–11.0	–5.7	–9.0	–2.5
NEER (level) volatility	0.16	0.06	0.11	0.12
Real effective exchange rate change (%)	–1.4	2.5	–3.6	1.1
REER (level) volatility	0.12	0.03	0.07	0.09
Inflation rate (CPI, %)	14.7	13.3	8.0	5.2
Inflation rate (CPI) volatility	2.5	2.2	2.4	3.6
Inflation rate (CPD, %)	14.9	14.6	8.1	6.0
Inflation rate (CPD) volatility	2.7	2.4	2.5	1.8
Inflation rate (CPIX, %)	—	—	—	6.3
Inflation rate (CPIX) volatility	—	—	—	1.7
Nominal interest rate (%)	17.1	19.0	19.2	13.3
Nominal interest rate volatility	4.4	1.7	1.7	2.4
Real interest rate (%)	2.2	4.4	11.2	7.4
Real interest rate volatility	5.7	1.6	2.9	2.2
Growth rate (%)	1.8	–0.2	2.6	4.2
Growth rate volatility	3.7	2.4	1.7	1.4
Growth rate per capita (%)	–0.6	–2.6	0.5	3.1

Sources: SARB's *Quarterly Bulletin* and (IFS) International Monetary Fund.

Notes:

1. Governor De Kock began his tenure on 1 January 1981; Governor Stals on 8 August 1989; and Governor Mboweni on 7 August, 1999.
2. Changes are annual percentage changes measured over four quarters.
3. The volatility measures are defined as follows: e.g. for inflation, *the absolute value* of the annual percentage change in inflation less annual percentage change in inflation one year ago. This measure places less emphasis on outliers than the conventional standard deviation.
4. Unlike the CPI, the CPIX (for 'metropolitan and urban areas') contains no interest rate component, but it is available from 1994 only, and is policy relevant from 2000. The consumer price deflator (CPD) also contains no interest rate component and is officially available throughout the sample. The real prime is thus defined using CPD to approximate the CPIX, and is *not* tax-adjusted. For comparison, see Figure 3.1 for the real prime rate defined using our constructed CPIX (Aron and Muellbauer, 2004), and see Figure 3.4 for the tax-adjusted SA real treasury bill rate defined using our constructed CPIX.
5. Nominal (NEER) and real (REER) effective exchange rates are the latest measure excluding Zimbabwe, spliced in 1990 to the preceding measure, which included Zimbabwe.

that is, the decline in inflation, inflation volatility, and output volatility observed across the industrialized world since the early 1980s, see Bernanke (2004). We will argue that the new monetary policy regime has enabled SA to participate in these global trends, despite major exchange rate shocks.

Transparent and Effective Monetary and Exchange Rate Policy

The outline of the chapter is as follows. In section 2, we review the design and operational framework of monetary policy. Section 3 assesses the view of the South African Reserve Bank (SARB) on monetary policy transmission in the light of our previous research on SA. In section 4, the transparency, credibility, and predictability of monetary policy is examined. In section 5, regime shifts in exchange rate policy are discussed. In section 6, the performance of the SARB is considered, via its forecasting performance, its monetary policy decisions taken in response to external and domestic shocks, and the level of its real interest rates. Section 7 concludes and considers future challenges and prospects under inflation targeting.

2. The design and operational framework of monetary policy

There have been three broad monetary policy regimes since the 1960s. The first regime was a *liquid asset ratio-based system* with quantitative controls on interest rates and credit, and operated until the early 1980s. A range of reforms enacted from the early 1980s toward a *cash reserves-based system* followed the recommendations of the De Kock Commission Reports (1978, 1985). After gradual technical changes on assets requirements, and a redefinition of the role of the discount rate, this second regime was in full operation by mid 1985 (see Gidlow, 1995a,b). Pre-announced monetary target ranges, which by then had already been abandoned by the UK and USA, were used from 1986 for a broad definition of money (M3) (details in Aron and Muellbauer, 2002a). Any usefulness of these targets was sharply diminished by extensive financial liberalization beginning in the 1980s, and a more open capital account from 1995. From 1990, the targets were supplemented by an eclectic set of indicators, including the exchange rate, asset prices, output gap, balance of payments, wage settlements, credit growth, and the fiscal stance (Stals, 1997). Such indicators probably played a role in earlier years, but the weights applied to them were not revealed. Policy was very opaque in this period,[4] and this diminished the accountability of the SARB.

The adoption of an inflation targeting regime in 2000 aimed to enhance policy transparency, accountability and predictability. The system has seen several improvements with evolving institutional design since 2000 (see Du Plessis, 2002; Van der Merwe, 2004). Interest rate policy is determined by a Monetary Policy Committee (MPC),[5] see Table 3.2. The target range for

---

[4] Aron and Muellbauer (2002a) apply an extension of the Taylor Rule model (Taylor, 1993) to try to estimate the weights applied to different policy objectives in the interest rate rule during 1986–97.

[5] The structure of the MPC has changed since its formation in October 1999, as have the frequency of its meetings. In 2007, it comprised seven SARB officials, chaired by the governor, and meeting six times per year as of 2004. By the South African Reserve Bank Act (No. 90 of 1989, and subsequent amendments), only the governor and deputy governors can vote on monetary policy matters; however, in practice, decisions are made by 'consensus'.

Table 3.2. MPC meetings and interest rate decisions

MPC meeting	Repo rate/%	Prime rate/%	MPC meeting	Repo rate/%	Prime rate/%	MPC meeting	Repo rate/%	Prime rate/%
13 Oct. 1999	~12.31	15.5	14 Mar. 2002	**11.5**	**15**	13 Oct. 2005	7	10.5
24 Nov. 1999[A]	~12	15.5	13 Jun. 2002	**12.5**	**16**	8 Dec. 2005	7	10.5
13 Jan. 2000[B]	**11.75**	**14.5**	12 Sep. 2002	**13.5**	**17**	2 Feb. 2006	7	10.5
2 Mar. 2000[C]	~11.75	14.5	20 Nov. 2002	13.5	17	13 Apr. 2006	7	10.5
6 Apr. 2000	~11.75	14.5	20 Mar. 2003	13.5	17	8 Jun. 2006	**7.5**	**11**
19 May 2000	~11.75	14.5	12 Jun. 2003	**12**	**15.5**	3 Aug. 2006	**8**	**11.5**
15 Jun. 2000	~11.75	14.5	14 Aug. 2003	**11**	**14.5**	12 Oct. 2006	**8.5**	**12**
11 Aug. 2000	~11.75	14.5	10 Sep. 2003[D]	**10**	**13.5**	7 Dec. 2006	**9**	**12.5**
21 Sep. 2000	~11.75	14.5	16 Oct. 2003	**8.5**	**12**	15 Feb. 2007	9	12.5
16 Oct. 2000[D]	**12**	14.5	11 Dec. 2003	**8**	**11.5**	12 Apr. 2007	9	12.5
16 Nov. 2000	12	14.5	26 Feb. 2004	8	11.5	7 Jun. 2007	**9.5**	**13**
19 Jan. 2001	12	14.5	22 Apr. 2004	8	11.5	16 Aug. 2007	**10**	**13.5**
16 Mar. 2001	12	14.5	10 Jun. 2004	8	11.5	11 Oct. 2007	**10.5**	**14**
25 Apr. 2001	12	14.5	12 Aug. 2004	**7.5**	**11**	6 Dec. 2007	11	14.5
14 Jun. 2001	**11**	**13.75**	1 Oct. 2004	7.5	11	31 Jan. 2008	11	14.5
26 Jul. 2001	11	**13.5**	9 Dec. 2004	7.5	11	10 Apr. 2008	**11.5**	**15**
4 Sep. 2001[E]	**10**	**13**	10 Feb. 2005	7.5	11	12 Jun. 2008	**12**	**15.5**
20 Sep. 2001	**9.5**	13	14 Apr. 2005	**7**	**10.5**	14 Aug. 2008	N/A	
15 Nov. 2001	9.5	13	9 Jun. 2005	7	10.5	9 Oct. 2008	N/A	
15 Jan. 2002[D]	**10.5**	**14**	11 Aug. 2005	7	10.5	11 Dec. 2008	N/A	

Sources: MPC statements, SARB website; *Quarterly Bulletin,* SARB; IFS, International Monetary Fund.
Notes:
 1. Prime rates are end of month, repo effective the next day, '~' refers to the characterization of the rate as 'at or around' in the MPC statement.
 2. A= Fixed repo rate; B= Discontinued fix; C= Postponed meeting replacing scheduled 22 Feb. 2000 meeting; D=Special meeting; E=Technical change (the rate change on 4 Sep. 2001 was reported in the SARB's *Quarterly Bulletin.*).
 3. Dates at which interest rates were *changed* are highlighted in bold (only these are reported in the *Quarterly Bulletin*).

inflation is set by the National Treasury after consultation with the SARB. Currently, the inflation target aims to achieve a rate of increase in the overall consumer price index excluding the mortgage interest cost (the so-called CPIX),[6] of between 3 and 6 per cent per year.[7]

As a small open economy, SA is subject to exogenous shocks, which affect inflation. A supply side shock such as a sudden rise in oil prices or a drought affecting food prices may cause a movement away from the target, but over which monetary policy has little influence in the first instance. Monetary policy can be expected to react to 'second round effects', and apparent changes induced in inflationary expectations. Several early versions of an 'escape' clause were designed to create more transparency about the discretion the central bank must use in these circumstances. In November 2003, the SARB in consultation with the National Treasury revised the 'escape' clause for more flexibility and clarity, repackaging it as a forward-looking 'explanation clause' (for details on these escape and explanation clauses, see Aron and Muellbauer, 2007a).

Amongst other requirements, the shift to inflation targeting demands good forecasting models of inflation and clarity on the mechanisms of monetary transmission (Leiderman and Svensson, 1995). The emphasis of the modelling activities in the SARB has shifted away from the maintenance of a single large-scale macroeconomic model towards a more compact or core model, supplemented by various other models. This is also in line with the international trend of using a 'suite of models' approach (Smal et al., 2007). The process of interest rate setting[8] can now broadly be described by Svensson's recommended moderate policy of flexible and forward-looking[9] inflation targeting (Svensson et al., 2002), so coping reasonably well with supply shocks. Inflation is not controlled at the shortest possible horizon by aggressive and volatile

---

[6] The mortgage interest cost measures mortgage-related housing costs in the CPI. Raising interest rates to counter inflationary pressures also raises the interest cost component of measured inflation. Unless excluded, this could provoke a further tightening of monetary policy.

[7] The inflation target announced in February, 2000, was specified as an average rate of increase in CPIX of 3–6 per cent per annum for the calendar year 2002. This was revised in October 2001 to 3–6 per cent for 2003 and 3–5 per cent for 2004 and 2005; in October 2002, to 3–6 per cent for 2004 and 3–5 per cent for 2005; and in February 2003, the target range for 2005 was increased from 3–5 per cent to 3–6 per cent. The unfortunate requirement that CPIX be within the target range on average over the calendar year was altered only in November 2003, to a continuous target of 3–6 per cent beyond 2006. The rectification of this design fault potentially reduces the interest rate volatility from a progressively shortening target horizon.

[8] In operational terms, the repurchase or 'repo' interest rate is market-determined in tenders of liquidity through repurchase transactions.

[9] The SARB appeared to practice a stricter version of inflation targeting in the early years. Partly this may have been to establish initial inflation credibility, by placing a higher weight on inflation stabilization in the early years, when expectations were heavily backward-looking, creating much persistence in inflation. More recently the SARB appears to have moved toward a more flexible approach, facilitated by the institutional changes in November 2003.

policy, with often volatile interest rates, but rather at a longer horizon of two to three years. The flexible approach aims also to stabilize the business cycle and hence the output gap. In the short term, inflation may well deviate, and sometimes significantly, from the target.

3. Assessment of the SARB's view of monetary policy transmission

The latest SARB view of the monetary policy transmission mechanism is cogently summarized in a flow chart in the *Monetary Policy Review* (May 2004). This is thoroughly informed by recent literature, such as Bean et al. (2002). It emphasizes the asset price channel via bonds, equities, the exchange rate, and property prices and notes that 'the role of expectations of economic agents in determining the impact of monetary policy changes is difficult to restrict to a particular channel'.

This view is an advance on the flow chart presented by Smal and de Jager (2001: chart 1, p.5), that restricted the role for inflationary expectations to influence only wages, while the only influence on these expectations was money and credit. Evidence suggests wage setting in SA is quite backward-looking (Aron et al., 2003). Wages appear to be unaffected by information less than two quarters old and there is no role for expectations proxies, including forecasts of inflation rates and exchange rate changes derived from econometric models. These empirical results point to wage settlements as a major source of inflation inertia in SA. The implication is that bringing inflation down helps keep inflation down. However, one would expect more moderate wage settlements where the policy framework had succeeded also in reducing inflation volatility.

Neither of the SARB reviews of monetary policy transmission mentions the cost channel, see Barth and Ramey (2001), whereby higher interest rates may raise the cost of capital for firms and households and who may try to pass these costs on. For instance, with a weight of 10.32 per cent on the mortgage interest rate in headline CPI during 2002–8, workers' wage demands could increase with higher interest rates.

Our research on wages also finds evidence of another asset price channel sometimes omitted in discussions of monetary transmission: rising house prices[10] have a positive effect on wage settlements two quarters later and with an average lag of four quarters. Since interest rates have strong effects on house prices, this is one route by which higher rates *reduce* inflation.

---

[10] House prices have no role in the CPI so that finding such a role in the wage equation suggests workers perceive housing costs as part of their budget.

The *Monetary Policy Review* (May 2004) emphasizes the credit channel of monetary policy transmission. SA resembles the UK in that mortgage rates are primarily floating rates, rapidly responsive to movements in the repurchase or 'repo' rate; owner-occupation in the formal sector, financed by mortgage debt, is high; lenders can readily access the housing collateral of borrowers in payment default; and loan to value ratios are high. Moreover, through flexible mortgages, homeowners can readily borrow more when the value of their housing equity rises. This is in sharp contrast to much of continental Europe, Italy being the polar opposite in terms of access to credit (Muellbauer, 2007).

In SA and the UK, rising house prices expand collateral for consumer borrowing, with large effects on consumer spending (see Aoki et al., 2002). Aron and Muellbauer (2000; 2009) estimated a long-run propensity to spend for SA out of housing wealth[11] of between 7 and 10 per cent. This currently implies that a 10 per cent rise in real house prices would raise consumption by 0.6–0.9 per cent. Given the rapid transmission from the repo rate to the mortgage bond rate, and strong effects from the latter onto house prices and so housing wealth and consumption, it is not surprising to find powerful monetary policy transmission. Understanding the mechanics of the household part of the channel, of which the housing wealth element is only a part, can suggest other offsetting or stabilizing policy interventions (see section 7).

It is often said that monetary policy has no effect on output in the long-run. However, a large body of economic theory suggests that high uncertainty impedes investment, and empirical evidence finds a negative link from inflation volatility to growth (e.g., Judson and Orphanides, 1996; Aron and Muellbauer, 2005). The SARB in its communications could do more to embed the case for their monetary policy regime that aims to reduce uncertainty, because of the long-run growth and welfare benefits.

4. Transparency, predictability, and credibility of monetary policy

4.1. Transparency

Greater transparency of policy not only facilitates accountability, but may also influence the effectiveness of monetary policy. Theoretical and empirical evidence on central bank transparency, defined as the disclosure of information about monetary policy, has recently been surveyed by Geraats (2002). Eijffinger and Geraats (2006) outline a framework to assess the

---

[11] Housing wealth and other liquid and illiquid wealth measures were constructed in Aron and Muellbauer (2006) and Aron et al. (2006; 2008). Housing wealth is measured as the real stock of housing multiplied by the real house price index. In the short-run, as the stock changes slowly, housing wealth can be approximated by the level of real house prices. It could, however, represent consumer confidence as well as wealth or collateral.

different channels of transparency, organized by political, economic, procedural, policy, and operational categories of central banking. Objective information disclosure by central banks is used to score the five channels of transparency, creating a total transparency index, and is applied to nine OECD countries.[12] In Aron and Muellbauer (2007b, Table 1 and Appendix survey), similar central bank transparency indexes are calculated for the SARB for two years: under Governor Mboweni in 2007; and in 1994 under his predecessor, Governor Stals; and these are contrasted with OECD results from Eijffinger and Geraats (2006) for 2002.

Central bank transparency in SA has improved greatly under inflation targeting, from a score of five in 1994, to ten in 2007 (out of a possible fifteen), using the equal weighting of categories as assumed by Eijffinger and Geraats (2006). This improvement is robust to two different weighting schemes, one suggested by Ian Plenderleith, formerly of the MPCs of the SARB and the Bank of England (assigning zero weights to the publication of minutes and voting records by the MPC and to disclosing an explicit policy inclination after MPC meetings), and the other derived by us from a weighting system used by Mahadeva and Sterne (2000). The score for the SARB may improve further as the institutional design of the system matures. The Bank of England and Reserve Bank of New Zealand, in targeting systems with much accumulated experience, have overall scores in 2002 of thirteen and fourteen, respectively. The Reserve Bank of Australia's overall score of nine in 2002 is below that of the SARB.

The survey results suggest transparency on the Geraats equal weighted index could be improved by: publishing more detailed economic forecasts and annual[13] evaluations of forecast errors; publishing (non-attributed) minutes of MPC meetings; giving a more detailed assessment of future economic conditions in the MPC's monetary policy statement; and giving an explicit future policy inclination in MPC statements. Currently, forecasts are based on the constant interest rate assumption. It is argued that scenarios with a forecast interest path, as pioneered in New Zealand, would serve to meet the objective of enhancing predictability of future interest rate policy (Svensson, 2001; Svensson et al., 2002). However, Goodhart (2005) argues that if an MPC's non-*constant* forecast were to be published, it might be regarded by the public as more of a *commitment* than an uncertain forecast; and it might influence the private sector's forecasts by more than its own uncertainty warranted (see also Morris and Shin, 2004).

---

[12] There are three questions for each of the five aspects of transparency, with equal weight and a maximum score of one. Scores were assigned by surveying available information on websites and in published government and central bank documents. The five sub-indexes, each based on the respective three questions, were summed to obtain an overall index.

[13] Recently an analysis of forecast errors from 2000 up to 2005 was published in a working paper, Smal et al., (2007).

4.2. Credibility

In principle, examining the evolution of inflation expectations before and after the adoption of inflation targeting could indicate whether there has been convergence to the target—or equivalently, whether monetary policy is credible to agents. Aron and Muellbauer (2007b) examine inflation expectations data from an ongoing survey by the Bureau of Economic Research (Kershoff, 2000). Households, trade unions, businesses, and financial analysts are asked for their expectations of average CPIX and average CPI inflation for the current and following calendar years. Thus the expectations horizon *shortens* for each consecutive quarterly survey in the year. Examining expectations for the *same* quarter for each year to achieve a constant horizon, reveals that expectations have come within the target range, despite the exchange rate shock of 2001–2. This is encouraging evidence for monetary policy credibility. The different agents' expectations have converged on the analysts' arguably better-informed view. For the analysts, the difference between the expected inflation rate and the historical rate was initially negative, as inflation expectations declined relative to past experience, and then tended to zero, with both inflation and inflation expectations stabilizing at similar, lower levels. For business and the trades unions, the difference between the expected inflation rate and the historical rate has fluctuated around zero, consistent with their taking the historical rate as a guide to the future rate, or being slow learners following the analysts.

4.3. Predictability

More predictable interest rates signal that the central bank's policy rule is well understood, and there is little asymmetric information between the central bank and the private sector. A simple assessment of the predictability of interest rates is given by comparing one, two, and three month ahead forecasts of the end of quarter prime rate with the realized prime (as a proxy for the repo rate), using monthly Reuters data on analysts' interest rate forecasts, beginning in 2000.[14] We found the predictions have a maximum error of about 1.25 per cent, and usually far less (Aron and Muellbauer, 2007b). The shift in market rates due to interest rate decisions by the central bank is termed the 'surprise factor', where a large shift indicates the market has not fully anticipated the decision. While the surprise has been greater for SA than some other targeting countries (such as Australia, New Zealand, Norway, and the UK, see Bernhardsen and Kloster (2002: 55)), this can be attributed to the larger size of repo rate adjustment, reflecting a higher and more volatile inflation rate

---

[14] The Reuters data are unfortunately somewhat noisy being based on a small sample of analysts.

in SA. Absolute values of prime rate forecasts for the end of each quarter and the spread between maximum and minimum forecasts, scaled by the median, both show a slight declining trend, from the second quarter of 2001. The evidence is consistent with the new inflation targeting framework being largely embodied in expectations by 2001.

This is confirmed by our study of the forward market's forecasting errors of changes in the repo rate, Aron and Muellbauer (2007b) which broadly follows the analysis of Swanson (2006). We use daily data on forward rate interest agreements (FRAs)[15] at several horizons to measure the forecasting error $e_{i,t}$ from the following regression:

$$\Delta r_{i,t} = \alpha_i + \beta_i \Delta R_t + e_{i,t}$$

The dependent variable is the change in the repo rate since the previous meeting, and the regressor is the change in the FRA rate from the day after the previous meeting to the day before the current meeting. The estimated betas are close to 1 with t-ratios of 7 or more, and R-squared of at least 0.5, suggesting that the forward market anticipated repo rate changes well, and from the very beginning of explicit inflation targeting in 2000.[16] Indeed, one of the remarkable features of the new regime concerns the muted impact of the large currency (SA rand) depreciation at the end of 2001 on interest rate expectations, and on interest rates. The absolute values of the forecasting errors show an insignificant downward trend from 2000, that is only weakly consistent with further learning about the operation of the new system. This remained true when controlling for recent macroeconomic volatility[17] and the recent volatility of the repo rate.

5. Regime shifts in exchange rate policy

SA's exchange rate policy has largely mirrored—though lagged—the dominant international exchange rate regimes, and the episodes are summarized in Table 3.3. Policy has evolved as follows: from a range of fixed rate episodes in the 1970s (including a separate inflexible 'securities' rand for use

---

[15] A Forward Rate Agreement (FRA) is an agreement between two parties to set future borrowing rates in advance. We use the data on 3-month agreements at horizons of four, five, and six months.

[16] A previous study, Ballim and Moolman (2005), runs the above regression in reverse, to measure the market's response to policy rate changes throughout the interest rate spectrum, interpreting evidence of greater anticipation as indicating improved monetary policy transparency. However, their residuals do not have a clear forecast error interpretation. See also a similar study in Aron and Muellbauer (2007a).

[17] Macroeconomic volatility was measured from the residuals of a parsimonious five-equation monthly VAR in differences for the logs of the consumer price index, wholesale price index, the exchange rate, the Dollar gold price, and industrial production.

Transparent and Effective Monetary and Exchange Rate Policy

Table 3.3. Regime Changes in the South African Foreign Exchange Market

Episode	Dates	Exchange Rate Regime
1	1961q1–1971q2	Pegged to fixed £
2	1971q3–1974q2	Pegged in episodes to floating $ or £
3	1974q3–1975q2	'Controlled Independent Float': devaluations every few weeks
4	1975q3–1979q1	Fixed regime: pegged to the $
5	1979q2–1982q4	Dual foreign exchange system: controlled floating commercial rand and floating financial rand
6	1983q1–1985q3	Unification to a controlled floating rand
7	1985q4–1995q1	Return to the dual system
8	1995q2–1999q4	Unification to a controlled floating rand
9	2000q1–	Freely floating rand under inflation targeting

Sources: Detailed parity changes as reported in Aron et al. (2000).
Notes:
1. Note that during episodes 1–4, a securities (or 'switch') rand was operative for the purchase of South African securities by non-residents, but not transferable between non-residents. This was replaced by the more flexible financial rand in episode 5.

of non-residents); through to managed floats from mid 1979 to 1999, where a dual exchange rate system embodying a more flexible 'financial' rand[18] for non-residents was operative for all but about eight years of this period insulating the 'commercial rand'; and thereafter to a freely floating unified exchange rate under inflation targeting. There was little access to international finance in the sanctions era after 1976, especially after 1985, except for some trade finance; but after the 1994 elections capital flows increased strongly. Flows, and particularly short-term flows, further accelerated with the effective lifting of exchange controls on non-residents in March 1995, when the dual exchange rate regime was finally successfully unified.

By contrast with the sudden lifting of controls on non-resident flows (with the exception of the 'blocked rands' of emigrants until recently[19]), controls were retained for residents and only gradually dismantled, and hence continued partly to insulate the unified exchange rate. Chronological details can be found in Chapter 5, and Leape and Thomas characterize the process

---

[18] The intended impact of the financial rand was to break the direct link between domestic and foreign interest rates, as well as to insulate the capital account from certain categories of capital flows. The financial rand applied to most non-resident portfolio and direct investment. All other transactions, including all current account transaction (as well as repatriation of profits, interest and dividends) were channelled through the official or commercial rand market. Foreign loans, including trade credits, were also transacted at commercial rand rates.

[19] Until 2003, there was an estimated R20-billion's worth of blocked rands in SA, capital held in the country in terms of existing exchange control regulations; since February 2003, this capital can be repatriated subject to a levy.

as avoiding large and potentially destabilizing capital flight in a transitional period.

From the time of adoption of a managed floating rate in a dual system in 1979, the SARB actively intervened in both spot and forward foreign exchange markets (e.g. during the gold boom of the early 1980s, see Kahn, 1992[20]), although was limited by low levels of reserves. After August 1989, the SARB actively sought to stabilize the real effective exchange rate, partly out of concern for the international competitiveness of SA's manufacturing exports (Aron et al., 2000). The apparent aim was to prevent excessive real appreciation of the rand when the currency was tending to appreciate in nominal terms. Moreover, during 1988–94, exchange rate and monetary policies were dedicated to ensuring a current account surplus to finance the capital outflows resulting from the debt rescheduling agreements.There was, however, no *explicit* official policy to stabilize the real exchange rate, and the official stance of a *de jure* freely floating rate continued beyond 1994.

The change from negligible capital inflows to substantial inflows after 1994 (for given domestic capital and trade controls), implied a transition to a new 'permanent' or long-run equilibrium level of inflows (Aron and Elbadawi, 1999). This *structural* shift in the size of sustainable flows required adjustment via a 'permanently' more appreciated real exchange rate (unless offset by liberalization of exchange controls on residents). However, in practice, the initial appreciation was strongly resisted through considerable intervention. At the same time domestic exchange controls, the release of which could have limited the appreciation, were retained. In section 6.2 we contrast unfavourably the handling of external shocks under the two regimes; by Stals under monetary targeting with an opaque monetary rule, and by Mboweni under inflation targeting and a transparent monetary rule. Both faced the classic policy trade-off under an open capital account between an independent monetary policy and an exchange rate 'target' (e.g. Obstfeld, 1996). Policy actions during 1994 to 1998 were often highly questionable. However, under inflation targeting, the exchange rate genuinely floats[21] or it would compromise the credibility of independent monetary policy. SA weathered the exchange rate shock in 2001, without the recourse to excessive interest rate rises or costly intervention of the earlier period.

A significant achievement has been the elimination by February 2004 of the net open foreign exchange position (NOFP),[22] accumulated under

---

[20] Smoothing the real rand price of gold during 1979 to 1988 led to a highly variable real exchange rate which cushioned the gold mining industry from terms of trade fluctuations, but had a negative impact on the manufacturing export sector.

[21] The question of profitable intervention to accumulate foreign exchange reserves through short-term smoothing, as in another targeting country Australia, is returned to in the conclusions

[22] It is now called the International Liquidity Position (ILP).

Transparent and Effective Monetary and Exchange Rate Policy

previous monetary policy regimes, and especially under Stals during 1993–8. Due to low foreign exchange reserves, intervention mainly occurred through the forward market, largely through foreign exchange swaps with authorized foreign exchange dealers (Kahn and Leape, 1996). The NOFP is the uncovered part of the oversold forward book, that is, SA's forward purchases of US dollars less its forward sales of US$, plus SA's net international reserves (including gold). Figure 3.2 shows the NOFP, expressed in rands as a percentage of GDP, in negative territory from 1985 and reaching a low of (minus) US$23 billion in 1998. The downward swings coincide with intervention episodes in 1994–8. The forward book losses proved very costly to the fiscus. Since the 1998 debacle, full transparency has been instituted about the forward market position. The closure of the forward book and the accumulation of foreign exchange reserves, which exceeded US$30 billion by the end of 2007, has reduced sovereign risk and hence exchange rate volatility.

The real and nominal effective exchange rate movements under floating regimes from 1980 are shown in Figure 3.3. Real appreciation from high commodity prices occurred before 1985, around 1987, and after 2001; and sharp depreciations were seen during the debt crisis of 1985, the home-grown currency crisis in 1996 and contagious currency crises in 1997 and 1998, and the exchange rate shock of 2001. Despite the preponderance of recent shocks, average nominal depreciation under Mboweni was lower than in preceding governor regimes, whereas average real appreciation for the same period contrasts with a substantial average real depreciation in the second Stals period, from 1994:2

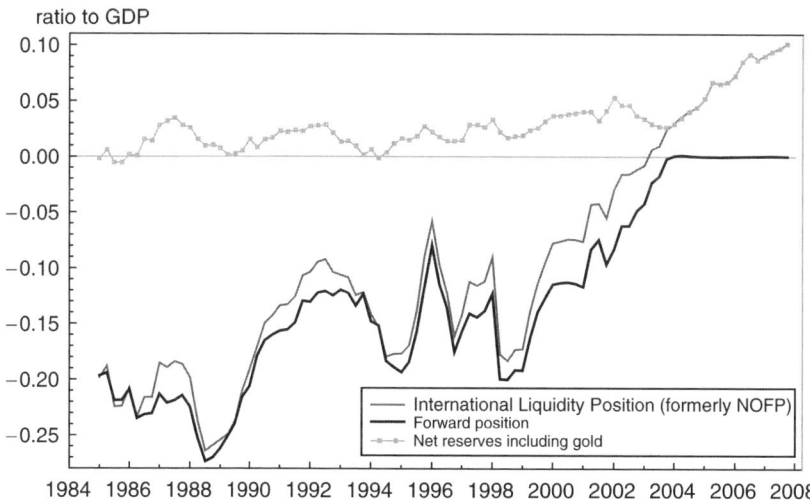

Figure 3.2. Foreign exchange reserves and international liquidity position of the SARB
Sources: South African Reserve Bank.

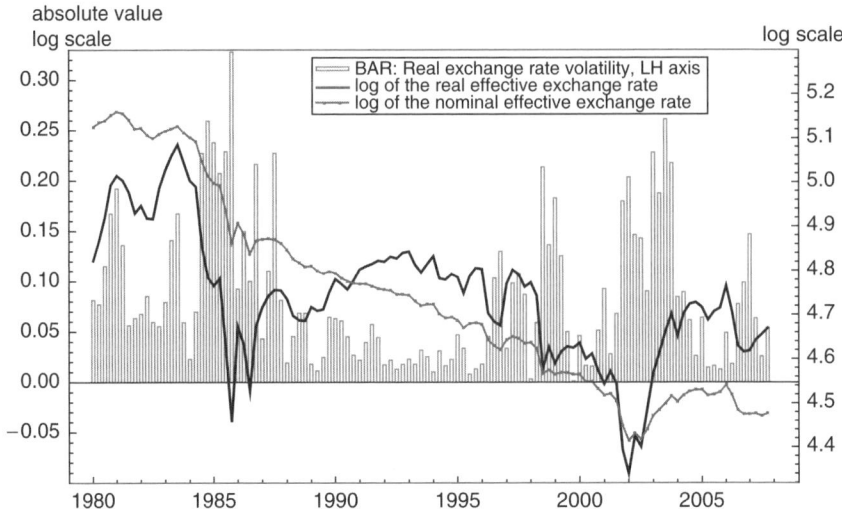

Figure 3.3. Exchange rates and volatility

Sources: The nominal and real effective exchange rates (in logs) are average measures excluding Zimbabwe, spliced in 1990 to the preceding measure, which included Zimbabwe, all from the *Quarterly Bulletin* of the SARB. The volatility measure is defined in Table 1.

to 1999q2 (Table 3.1). The figure also illustrates quarterly real exchange rate volatility, employing the same definition of volatility utilized in Table 3.1 that captures short-term volatility. It contrasts with a standard deviation measure of the *level* of the log real exchange rate that focuses on deviations from the period mean. Real exchange rate volatility has been relatively high on the short-term measure since 1999q3, a little higher than in the preceding Stals period, but not as high as under De Kock (Table 3.1). Comparing SA's real exchange rate volatility with all emerging market inflation targeting countries finds more short-term real exchange rate volatility than the others for 1999–2007; but less long-term volatility on the standard deviation measure than Australia and comparable though higher long-term volatility than the rest. From 2004 to 2007 (i.e. after the closure of the NOFP), SA has had lower volatility than all bar Australia on both measures, and comparable values to Australia.

6. The performance of monetary policy

6.1. Evaluating the forecast errors of the SARB

The SARB's suite of models comprises a core model, a small-scale model, vector autoregressive models, Phillips-curve models and a monthly disaggregated forecasting model (van der Merwe, 2004). Smal et al. (2007) provide estimates

Transparent and Effective Monetary and Exchange Rate Policy

of the key equations of the core model. Only inflation forecasts are published,[23] in the form of fan-charts (e.g. none of output). The past forecast errors of these models are not annually evaluated, and this lowers the SARB's *economic* transparency score (section 4). We have attempted a crude analysis of the SARB's forecast errors using the fan-charts.[24] Table 3.4 shows the size of errors both one year ahead and two years ahead for each of the fan-charts.

Table 3.4 shows positive *one year ahead* forecast errors (column 5) for forecast dates between 2001q1 and 2002q2, negative errors for forecast dates between 2002q4 and 2005a3 and positive errors thereafter. The *two year ahead* forecasts errors (last column) are positive for forecast dates from 2000q3 to 2001q3, negative for forecasts made between 2002q2 and 2004q4 and positive for forecasts made thereafter.

Table 3.4. Simple evaluation of SARB forecast errors

Date of MPR publication	Date of forecast	Forecast: 1 year ahead	Actual: 1 year ahead	Forecast error	Forecast: 2 years ahead	Actual: 2 years ahead	Forecast error
May. 2008	2007q4	7.9	N/A	N/A	6.0	N/A	N/A
Nov. 2007	2007q2	6.0	11.0	5.0	5.4	N/A	N/A
May. 2007	2007q1	5.9	9.4	3.5	5.2	N/A	N/A
Nov. 2006	2006q2	6.0	6.3	0.3	5.5	11.0	6.5
May. 2006	2006q1	5	6.3	1.3	4.7	9.4	4.7
Nov. 2005	2005q3	5.7	5.0	−0.7	5.3	6.5	1.2
May. 2005	2004q4	4.8	4	−0.8	5.0	4.6	−0.4
Nov. 2004	2004q2	4.8	3.7	−1.3	5.6	4.1	−1.5
May 2004	2003q4	5.9	4.4	−1.5	5.7	4	−1.4
Oct. 2003	2003q2	4.5	4.7	0.2	5.1	3.7	−1.6
Mar. 2003	2002q4	5.7	4.2	−1.6	5.7	4.4	−1.3
Oct. 2002	2002q2	6.4	7.6	1.2	5.2	4.7	−0.5
Apr. 2002	2001q3	8.1	10.2	2.1	5.3	6.1	0.8
Oct. 2001	2001q1	5.9	7.0	1.1	6.0	9.6	3.6
Mar. 2001	2000q3	6.5	5.6	−0.9	5.2	10.2	5.0

Sources: One and two year ahead forecasts read off the fancharts, *Monetary Policy Review*, SARB; actual data from the SARB's *Quarterly Bulletin* (four quarter changes, %). The SARB forecast errors are the difference between the two.

Notes:
 1. Actual inflation is the quarterly average of monthly CPIX data, at annual rates.
 2. Where data are not yet available, this is indicated by N/A.

---

[23] Forecasts are conditional: but private sector economists have complained about the lack of information on the assumptions (e.g. of oil prices, the exchange rate, and degree of pass-through).

[24] The central forecasts are not published in numerical form, and we have estimated them from the pictures. The forecasts refer to the four-quarter inflation rate at specific dates, one and two years ahead. Ehlers and Smal (2006) have favourably compared the forecast performance from the core model with those from other sources for the period 2000–5, e.g. Reuters (see Smal et al., 2007).

Thus, actual inflation tended to be higher than forecast from 2002 to mid-2003,as no-one could have forecast the extent of the collapse of the rand at the end of 2001 and of the rise in maize prices. SARB forecasts overestimated the speed with which the inflation was to fall after the exchange rate and food price shocks[25]. Inflation then tended to be little lower than forecast until the end of 2006,probably because of the unexpected strength of the rand, and moderate global inflation,despite some rises in oil prices. Some of the over-estimate of forecast inflation (negative error) based on quartely data up to 2002q4 was surely due to *Statistics South Africa's* overestimate of actual inflation of 1.4 per cent for CPIX for 2002q4[26].

Further rises in oil and food and other commodity prices, which became dramatic in 2007–8, then led to large under-forecasts of inflation, of the order of 5 percent per annum[27]. However, the inflation which tended to peak in the third quarter of 2008 has been under-forecast in virtually all countries. one contributing local factor for SA was the weakening in the exchange rate after the electricity power shortages began to affect the output of mining and industry.

6.2. How has monetary policy reacted to external and domestic shocks?

6.2.1. THE STALS ANC ERA: 1994Q2–1999Q1

Probably the most important factor impeding growth after 1994 was high real interest rates (Aron and Muellbauer, 2002b). Capital inflows increased markedly after the elections from a low base following a decade of financial sanctions. Aron and Elbadawi (1999) argue that the SARB had dual policy objectives from April 1994 until the first currency crisis in February 1996. These were to contain inflation through an interest rate policy based on explicit monetary targets; and to stabilize the nominal exchange rate by preventing appreciation of the currency.[28] Despite large and persistent currency

---

[25] Interestingly, Aron and Muellbauer (2009) find evidence in an equation for producer prices that rises in raw food prices are passed on faster than reductions, consistent with the delayed fall in inflation.

[26] Up to 1999, rental data used in constructing housing costs in CPI and CPIX came from the October household survey. Following the discontinuation of this survey, *Statistics South Africa* made the assumption that the average nominal increases in rent recorded in 1999 also applied in all subsequent years (34.5 per cent). In practice, rent increases were far smaller, as evidenced by private sector data sources. After the rent measurement error was discovered, *Statistics South Africa* had to revise CPI and CPIX inflation downwards substantially (discussed in what follows). Stopford's revelation of the overstatement of inflation in *Statistics South Africa's* data was first made public in April 2003 (Stopford, 2003).

[27] Our research highlights the special role of raw food prices in the inflation process in SA, see Aron et al. (2003) and Aron and Muellbauer (2009). This channel is omitted from the SARB's core model. Given that in September, 2007, the 12-month inflation rate for the PPI for agriculture, forestry and fishing was running at 22 per cent, more of the rise in CPIX inflation should have been predictable in November 2007.

[28] Subsidiary goals were to withdraw from the forward foreign exchange market, and to accumulate foreign reserves (Stals, August 1994).

interventions, the SARB claimed the rand was floating and that intervention was solely to smooth temporary and reversible short-term fluctuations (Stals, 1995). However, during the 21 months from the elections, the nominal bilateral rand/dollar exchange rate moved by no more than 2 per cent from R3.65 per dollar, while in April 1995 to January 1996, the range was even narrower, moving in an 'implicit' band of R3.65±1 per cent per dollar. The steady bilateral rate in the face of huge net capital inflows was viewed by many investors as an implicit, 'one-sided' nominal target (e.g. Union Bank of Switzerland, 1996).

With an open capital account and persistent capital flows, a policy trade-off can arise where sustaining an exchange rate 'target' occurs at the expense of higher inflation, higher interest rates and eventually reduced output (e.g. Obstfeld, 1996). In SA, sterilization of the effects of the reserve accumulation began only late in 1994, and substantial unsterilized intervention in the market occurred at the expense of monetary targets (Stals, 1995). Private sector credit grew strongly, and money growth deviated from target growth zones with persistent overshooting from 1994 onwards. Monetary policy was tightened considerably, attracting even more inflows.

The exchange rate intervention was unsustainable. Foreign investors anticipated a relaxation of domestic exchange controls at the Budget in early March, 1996, to help combat the appreciation.[29] A currency crisis was well underway by mid February, and the bilateral rand had depreciated 20 per cent by late April. The SARB intervened massively to defend the currency, and of a net cumulative intervention of US$5.3 billion (mid February to the end of April), about US$3.5 billion occurred via the forward market (Kahn and Leape, 1996).

Later crises occurred in October 1996, November 1997, and April 1998, triggered largely by contagion effects from the Asian crisis and declining prices of gold and other exported metals. The prime rate rose to 20.25 per cent after the first crisis, and remained at that level until the end of 1997, falling to 18.25 per cent just prior to the April, 1998 crisis, when it rose as high as 25.5 per cent. With inflation averaging just over 6 per cent in 1998, this implied very high real interest rates (Figure 3.1). Heavy intervention in the forward market drove the NOFP from negative US$12 billion to negative US$23 billion between April and August 1998—a change equivalent to about 8 per cent of GDP—but had little success in stemming the fall of the rand (Figure 3.2). By contrast with the SARB, the Australian Reserve Bank left interest rates unchanged, believing that with slow pass-through from the exchange rate to consumer prices, and with the deflationary terms of trade and demand shocks, no rise in interest rates was necessary. The Australian economy passed through this period with

---

[29] In the event, the intended decontrol package was put on hold until July 1997.

inflation and growth little affected—in contrast to SA, which suffered a serious decline in growth. Caballero et al. (2005) have drawn a similar unfavourable contrast between Chile's sharp rise in interest rates in 1998 and Australian policy.

6.2.2. INFLATION TARGETING UNDER MBOWENI: 1999Q3–2008Q1

Mboweni's Governorship began in mid 1999, and inflation targeting in February 2000. There followed an eighteen month period of stasis in nominal interest rates (Table 3.2) and relative stability in real interest rates (Figure 3.1). The variable repo rate announced at around 12 per cent in the first MPC meeting in October 1999 was still around this level in May 2001 (Table 3.2). The 25 basis point rise in an unscheduled meeting of October 2000 was a steady response to the anticipated second round effects of external shocks.[30] The static monetary policy stance presumably aimed to stabilize inflationary expectations in the early stages of the targeting regime, in the face of sharply rising international oil prices from early 1999 (rising from US$10 to over US$30 a barrel by September 2000), and rising international interest rates. The targeted CPIX rose modestly with food and other transport-dependent components. The exchange rate reversed its past year's appreciating trend after February 2000 (which had helped to reduce the NOFP from around negative US$21 billion in March 1999 to negative US$10 billion by April 2000).

The first really challenging episode to face the MPC from the inception of inflation targeting was the sharp depreciation that began in 2001q4. Given the available information, their interest rate responses in the aftermath are hard to fault. As the *Monetary Policy Review,* October 2001 explains, by July 2001, annual CPIX inflation had come down close to the 6 per cent top of the target range, and was expected to fall below that level by 2002. Indeed based on quarterly averages, the annual CPIX measure of inflation had fallen to 5.9 per cent in 2001q2, within the target range. There were signs of deflationary forces in declining oil and other commodity prices and in foreign producer price indices. The US economy suffered a sharp slowdown,[31] and global stock markets and economic activity also declined. Short-term interest rates in industrial countries fell sharply, most dramatically in the USA; and further falls had occurred after the 11 September attacks in New York. The repo rate in SA was consequently reduced by 100 basis points in June 2001, by 100 basis points on the 4 September (a technical adjustment leaving

---

[30] There was no impact on the prime rate, as for cost reasons the commercial banks generally do not act on 25 basis point changes.
[31] The NBER business cycle dating committee later declared that March 2001 marked the beginning of a technical recession.

market rates unchanged), and by a further 50 basis points on 20 September to 9.5 per cent. However, given the concomitant fall in rates abroad, the foreign interest differential did not narrow.

However, between 1 September and 31 December 2001, the currency depreciated by 42 per cent against the US dollar. This was a substantial set-back for the long-term aim of progressively reducing the inflation rate in SA. Much has been written about the causes of this episode, including the voluminous report of the Myburgh Commission (2002). However, to put the episode into perspective, on quarterly averages of the nominal effective exchange rate, the quarterly depreciation rate was 20 per cent in 2001q4, and 11 per cent in 2002q1. One can obtain estimates of what part of these depreciations can be regarded as unexplained shocks from differenced vector autoregressive (VAR) models.[32] The results suggest that as little as 11 of the 20 per cent depreciation in 2001q4 and as little as 3 of the 11 per cent in 2002q1 (i.e. about half of the depreciation over two quarters) cannot be explained in terms of standard variables including gold price changes, foreign inflation, interest rates, domestic inflation rates, and the output gap.

Our own interpretation of the unexplained shock in 2001 agrees with many financial market participants giving evidence to the Myburgh Commission, who put the main emphasis on two factors. The first is the market perception that the well-signalled intention of the SARB to shrink the NOFP had created the impression of a 'one-way bet' in terms of currency depreciation. The second is the perceived tightening of foreign exchange regulations in October 2001, which resulted in a sharp reduction in liquidity in the foreign exchange market. In thin markets, volatility is likely to increase, and with the perception of the 'one-way bet', this took the form of a sharp fall in the value of the rand. Evidence for the liquidity reduction comes in two forms. First, there was a sharp rise in buy–sell spreads in the forward market after the tightening of regulations was announced. Second, on the SARB's own evidence, higher foreign exchange volatility had, in the past, almost always been associated with higher trading volumes. However, volumes shrank in October to December 2001, signalling a liquidity problem.[33]

---

[32] We estimated VAR models on quarterly data, consisting of eight variables: oil price or gold price inflation, the output gap, exchange rate change, import price inflation, PPI inflation, CPI inflation, short-term interest rate, and money growth. The reduced form residuals from the VAR are orthogonalized using a Cholesky decomposition to identify the structural shocks, where the variables are in the order given above (see also, McCarthy, 2000). With such rich specifications, there is some risk of over-fitting, which may under-estimate the size of unexplained shocks.

[33] Bhundia and Ricci (2005) place more weight on nominal shocks, citing 'the acceleration of money supply growth from around mid-2001' as a potential source of such shocks (p. 166). However, the money stock data were distorted by the restructuring of De Beers and the Anglo American Corporation, while amongst other factors, private sector liquidity preference increased through greater precautionary and speculative demand for money as a response to uncertainty (*Quarterly Bulletin*, March 2002: 38–9).

We now examine the inflationary implications of these shocks. CPIX inflation was 6.2 per cent in 2001q4, and peaked at 11.1 per cent in 2002q4, a rise of 4.9 percentage points. Estimates of pass-through from exchange rate shocks to CPIX in our VAR models, suggest that less than half this rise can be attributed directly to the exchange rate shocks. Another important reason for the rise in inflation was the rise in food prices, led by maize prices, cogently explained in the *Monetary Policy Review* (April 2002: 8–10). Regional droughts, the farming crisis in Zimbabwe and the switch to higher import parity prices with regional excess demand were the main factors, which were then exacerbated by the fall in the rand. CPIX inflation excluding food prices would have been more than 2 percentage points lower in the second half of 2002 than with food prices included. However, this difference is likely to understate the contribution of food prices to the rise in inflation.[34]

A third significant factor in the rise in inflation, even when subsequently corrected was *Statistics South Africa*'s rent measurement error, due to the upward bias in inflation perceptions it created (*Monetary Policy Review*, November 2003: 2–3). In May 2003, *Statistics South Africa* revised down the twelve-month CPI and CPIX inflation rates for March 2003, by 2.3 and 1.9 percentage points respectively. The annual CPIX and CPI inflation rates for 2002q4 were revised down by 1.4 percentage points, for 2002q3 down by 0.9 percentage points, and for 2002q2 down by 0.6 percentage points (using quarterly average data).[35] Thus, averaging for the four quarters 2002q2 to 2003q1, CPIX inflation was overstated by around 1.2 percentage points and CPI inflation by a little more. It is likely that price setters and wage negotiators used the upward biased inflation data in making their decisions, so contributing to higher inflation.

The contrast of this episode with the interest rate response to exchange rate depreciation in 1998 under Stals is striking. The MPC raised the repo rate from 9.5 to 10.5 per cent at a special meeting in January, 2002, a very moderate response to the turmoil on the foreign exchange market, and to 11.5 per cent in March, 12.5 per cent in June and 13.5 per cent in September, a level then sustained until June 2003. To assess the monetary policy stance, the SARB's one-year ahead inflation forecasts (Table 3.4) can be subtracted from then current repo rate, giving the real repo rate as 5.5 per cent in March 2001, 3.6 in October 2001, 3.4 in April 2002, 7.1 in October 2002, 7.8 in March 2003, and 4.0 per cent in October 2003. This suggests that policy was tightest from about mid 2002 to mid 2003.

Real GDP growth averaged over 3.5 per cent per annum from the second half of 1999 to the end of 2002, despite recessionary world economic conditions.

---

[34] This is due to neglecting the effect of higher food prices on other prices and on inflationary expectations.

[35] The source for these figures is the SARB *Quarterly Bulletin* (March and June 2003).

During 2003, growth slowed sharply, partly for global economic reasons with the imminent invasion of Iraq, and partly because real interest rates were held at relatively high levels in the second half of 2002 and the first half of 2003. Keeping the repo rate at 13.5 per cent from September 2002 to February 2003 seems understandable in view of the inflation surge that peaked in October 2002 at 14.3 per cent for on CPI and 12.7 per cent for CPIX (in 12 month rates on the erroneous inflation data).

The March 2003 decision to maintain the rate unchanged at 13.5 per cent is harder to understand, however, in view of the tightening of policy it implied (a higher real interest rate of 7.8 per cent, see above). There had indeed been publicity around recently announced increases in administered prices, and there had been large public sector wage increases in 2002q3. On the other hand, the effective exchange rate had strongly recovered over six months, mainly due to sustained increases in commodity prices; inflation had already fallen; and the SARB had recently become aware of a likely overstatement in the inflation data, though not of its precise magnitude. Further, the uncertainty concerning the Iraq war had made the world economic outlook hard to predict (*Monetary Policy Review*, April 2003: 22), but would have been expected to depress activity. Another source of uncertainty concerned unit labour costs data: it later emerged that changes in the employment survey in September 2002 had made these figures suspect.[36]

The first cut of 150 basis points occurred only on 12 June 2003, after the CPIX overstatement of 1.9 per cent announced on 30 May (Table 3.2). As the extent of the slowdown in growth and inflation became apparent, and given further currency appreciation, further cuts then followed rapidly: 100 basis points in each of August and September; 150 basis points in October and 50 basis points in December. In 2004, the repo rate was held at 8 per cent, until an unexpected 50 basis points cut occurred in August, despite gently rising short-term rates in the USA and some other industrial countries. The following three MPC meetings in 2004 maintained this rate, and it averaged about 7 per cent in the following year.

Criticism of the SARB's initially slow reaction in the first half of 2003 is overshadowed by the resource cost to SA of *Statistics South Africa's* data errors. The average overstatement of inflation for the four quarters from 2002q2 to 2003q1 was 1.2 percentage points for CPIX and a little more for CPI. Given forward-looking inflation targeting, we believe that interest rates were likely kept at least 1 percentage point higher for at least four quarters than if the

---

[36] Unit labour costs were estimated at an 11.1 per cent annual change for non-agricultural sector for 2002q3 (later revised down to 8.9 per cent). For the manufacturing sector, the annual increase in unit labour costs to 2002q3 was estimated at only 1.1 per cent, later revised down to an incredible minus 2.3 per cent (see SARB *Quarterly Bulletin*).

errors had not occurred.[37] Our work on forecasting real GDP for SA (Aron and Muellbauer, 2002b) suggests that a one percentage point rise in real interest rates lowers GDP by around 0.25 per cent four to eight quarters later. The cost in output to the economy of these errors could therefore plausibly have been as high as 0.25 per cent of one year's GDP.

In June 2006, the MPC began an extended tightening cycle, which saw the repo rate rise from 7 per cent in May 2006 to per cent by June 2008 reduced to 11.5 per cent in December. Initially rates rose to dampen domestic inflationary pressures and later to counter the second-round inflationary effects of supply shocks coming from global food and energy prices and from the rise in domestic electricity prices. The experience of electricity power cuts beginning in January 2007 became more intense in the winter of 2007-8, suggesting a downward revision of SA's capacity to produce, and hence a greater need to curtail domestic demand. A case could be made that this, combined with inflation in raw food prices, and the negative exchange rate reaction to the power supply problems, might have warranted a somewhat more aggressive monetary tightening than the rise in the repo rate from 9 per cent in May 2007 to 11.5 per cent in April 2008. However, as criticism of inflation targeting has mounted round the world under the pressure of imported inflation, some critics have argued just the opposite. It is clear that in 2008 the MPC faced the second really challenging set of circumstances since inflation targeting began.[38]

6.3. Are real interest rates too high under inflation targeting?

Critics of the monetary policy framework in SA argue that it has resulted in real interest rates being kept too high, with a consequent cost in growth and high unemployment. Our objection to this view has been discussed elsewhere (Aron and Muellbauer, 2005). We summarize the main points here.

Power (2004) has argued that *equity finance* in SA is inordinately expensive and constrains growth. Given assumptions about the size of the equity

---

[37] There are two main steps in the argument. The first assumes that the inflation error resulted in an overestimate of the forecast inflation rate, partly because of inflation persistence via wage and price formation, and partly because of commonly used intercept adjustment used by forecasters when previous forecasts are seriously off track, as was clearly believed (based on erroneous data) to be the case in early 2003. The second step assumes that the SARB 'leant against the wind' by raising the repo rate by more than forecast inflation. Thus, even if the 1.2 percentage point inflation error averaged over a year resulted in a smaller upward bias of say 0.8 percentage points in the forecast inflation rate, this could easily translate into a repo rate higher by 1 percentage point or more.

[38] The intensification of the global financial and economic crisis in the latter part of 2008 engulfed all primary commodity producers, triggering large exchange rate depreciations, including in SA. The MPC had to balance the currency depreciation in the context of high inflation and the large current account deficit, against the collapse of global inflation and weakening economic activity.

premium relative to government bonds, he puts this down to high bond yields, blaming the aggressive application of inflation targeting. There are serious problems with his argument and his proposed alternative monetary framework of exchange rate targeting.

First, bank finance is an important alternative to equity finance[39] and tax-adjusted real borrowing rates have been moderate. The relevant borrowing rate for companies is the *real* and *after-tax* rate, as interest payments by companies are tax-deductible (Jansen, 2004). In Figure 4.4 we compare SA's quarterly tax-adjusted[40] real interest rates for the last eight years with those of the USA, UK, Australia, Chile, and Brazil. Contrary to the view of critics, SA's *real* domestic tax-adjusted cost of borrowing to companies compares relatively well with competitors. For instance, SA's tax-adjusted real rates largely lie below Chile's and are below Australia's in every year except for 2001; they are substantially below Brazil's rates (except in 2003, though bank margins are so high in Brazil that bank lending rates always exceed SA's); and they lie below those of the UK, except in 2003 and 2004, but usually exceed those of the US, where real policy rates were negative in the aftermath of the 2001 recession and the events of 9/11.

Another perspective on comparative real interest rates is given by an open economy view of the drivers of real rate differentials of government bonds. These are relevant for Power's argument about equity finance, and because they influence the cost of corporate bond finance. These bond yield differentials have fallen since the late 1990s in SA, but not as far as expected by 2005. The question is why and whether monetary policy is to blame. The real bond rate differential between SA, and, say, the USA, is given by the expected real depreciation of the rand against the dollar, plus a risk premium. The risk premium reflects real exchange rate uncertainty (a combination of nominal exchange rate and relative inflation uncertainty), global risk appetite (i.e. the willingness of global investors to invest in emerging market assets), political uncertainty and administrative restrictions, for example, on capital flows (Kahn and Farrell, 2002). Quantitative and qualitative information can help elucidate the factors behind high real bond rates in SA.

One element in the risk premium, abstracting from real exchange rate uncertainty, is sovereign risk, the market's perception of the probability of

---

[39] In each year of the last decade new equity finance accounted for less than 4 per cent of the funding of industrial companies on the Johannesburg Stock Exchange (Jansen, 2004). Debt, including trade credit, made up 40–50 per cent of funding, with retained earnings accounting for around 40 per cent. The situation is similar in the UK and other major economies.

[40] Tax adjustment uses the KPMG surveys of corporate tax rates to 2007. For SA, the corporate tax rate applicable to companies was 30 per cent (29 per cent since 2006). However, there is an additional 'Secondary Tax on Companies' at the rate of 12.5 per cent on any net dividends declared, and if a company distributes 100 per cent of its retained earnings as a dividend, then an effective tax rate of 36.9 per cent currently applies. For international comparability, T-bill rates or their nearest equivalent have been chosen. The interest rates at which companies can borrow are typically higher by 2 or more per cent in every country.

default by the SA government on its foreign-denominated bonds. It is measured by the spread between SA foreign-denominated government bonds (e.g. the 2017 US dollar denominated bond, first issued in 1997) and those of foreign governments (e.g. the US government) over comparable duration. Sovereign risk spreads narrowed for SA, as for most emerging markets, approaching their previous lows achieved in 1997–8 in 2005, but have risen sharply in 2008.

Quantitative work by Ahmed et al. (2005) on the determinants of SA's sovereign spread suggests the main factors driving the spread had moved in the right direction by 2005: the forward book had been retired; global risk appetite had fallen to historic lows; the state of the public finances and the relative growth record had improved; the time to maturity of the 2017 bond had fallen; and the exchange rate had appreciated with the commodity price boom. Thus, the spread should have narrowed further, but had not, even by 2007, despite *sustained* improvement in most of these factors.

While the measured factors show unambiguous links to sovereign risk, there are slowly evolving, hard-to-measure factors that could be accounting for the failure of the spread to narrow further. Some were mentioned in evidence to the Myburgh Commission (2002), such as SA's attitude to the political and economic disaster that has befallen Zimbabwe. Rises in sovereign risk in 2007–8 to levels last seen in 2002, are linked to uncertainty over the political succession and concern over electricity supply problems and the associated loss in SA's reputation for good government. Inflation targeting cannot conceivably have increased either sovereign risk or real exchange rate risk.[41] If anything, the increased clarity and transparency of monetary policy, combined with sound fiscal policies (Chapter 4), should have reduced both kinds of risk and so benefited business investment. Business investment is likely also to be influenced by structural aspects over which monetary policy has no direct influence, including the high costs of hiring and firing, the crime rate, and the costs of the redistribution, which is gradually compensating for the tragic legacy from the Apartheid years of exclusion of black South Africans from economic life.

---

[41] Grandes et al. (2003, 2005) calculate the currency premium—that part of the one year interest rate differential with the USA not due to sovereign risk, for rand-denominated bonds of one year maturity, as 728 basis points over 2000–2. Their empirical study on the determinants of the currency premium suggests retirement of the NOFP has reduced the currency premium; building up foreign exchange reserves reduces the risk of speculative attacks; and that inflation targeting with the target being met reduces the premium. However, they do not explicitly mention the most obvious reason for the 728 basis points premium—the inflation differential between SA and the USA. Their empirical work is flawed by this and other problems, including finding that the most significant variables explaining the one year premium have the opposite sign of that predicted by their theory.

Transparent and Effective Monetary and Exchange Rate Policy

7. Conclusion and forward-looking assessment

This chapter provides evidence to show that under SA's inflation targeting monetary policy regime, central bank transparency, credibility and predictability have improved markedly, also providing benchmarks by which to hold the SARB fully accountable (for the first time) for its interest rate decisions. There have been important gains in the performance of monetary policy. Average inflation is lower on all measures, and is less volatile for CPI measures that exclude the nominal interest rate, than in preceding regimes back to 1980 (e.g. CPD in Table 3.1). Given the larger exchange rate and food and energy price shocks under targeting, the volatility of changes in nominal interest rates has risen, reflected in more volatile CPI inflation. Despite large shocks, real after-tax interest rates have been low and fairly stable compared to other countries since 2000 (Figure 3.4). It is a creditable achievement that output volatility has declined, with a strong improvement in the growth rate and per capita growth rate since 2002.

There is currently a lively international debate about the merits of inflation targeting in the light of the pressures from imported inflation driven by global

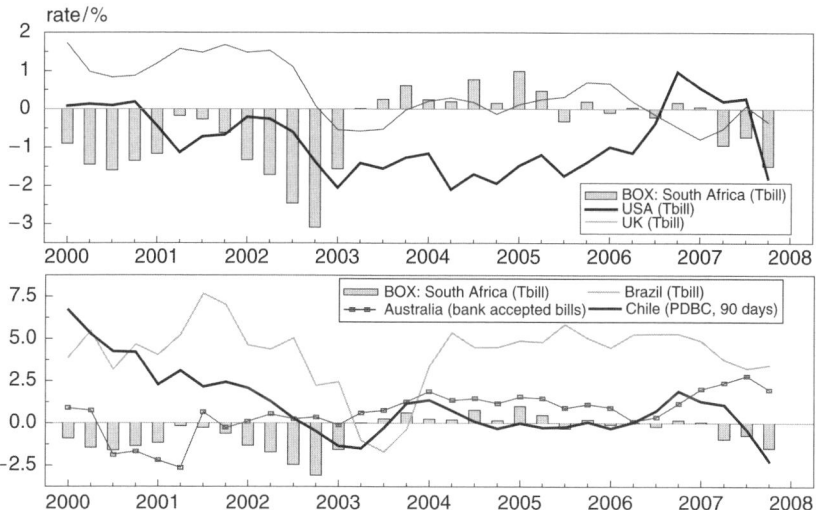

Figure 3.4. Comparative real tax-adjusted market interest rates

Sources: Treasury bill rates (NOMi, 60c) and the consumer price index (CPI, 64) are from the International Monetary Fund, International Financial Statistics (IFS). The South African CPI measure used is the targeted CPIX (metropolitan and urban) from the South African Reserve Bank. In the absence of Treasury bill rates, we used the Bank accepted Bills, 90 days, from the Reserve Bank of Australia; and the Interest Rate on Central Bank Discountable Promissory Notes (PDBC), 90 days, from the Banco Central de Chile. Tax adjustment uses the KPMG annual survey of effective corporate tax rates—denoted 'tax', after scaling by 100 below.

Notes: 1. Real interest rates are defined as follows: $REALi_t = 100((1+\frac{(1-tax)NOMi_t}{100})\frac{CPI_{t-4}}{CPI_t} - 1)$

energy and food prices since 2007. Our view is that the flexible inflation targeting regime is capable of handling these pressures and the extension of such monetary policies to the major developing countries of Asia would have done much to reduce the global inflation problem. Inflation targeting in SA takes account of output in its models, and while external shocks in 2008 fuelling inflation need to be reacted to for their second round effects, the system is flexible enough to allow a gradual path back to the target range without excessive rate rises (see discussion on escape clauses in Aron and Muellbauer, 2007a).

Mistakes have been made, but on a far smaller scale than before 2000. We have contrasted unfavourably the poor management of external shocks in 1998, with the steady handling under inflation targeting of the 2001 exchange rate shock. The exchange rate genuinely floats under the targeting regime and can play the stabilizing role suggested by traditional open-economy models (Caballero et al., 2005). With SA's low foreign debt and a large shift in the proportion of foreign liabilities denominated in rand (doubling since the early 1990s to almost 80 per cent by 2007, see Chapter 5), SA has fewer reasons to have a 'fear of floating' than many emerging market countries (Calvo and Reinhart, 2002). It is likely that the exchange rate pass-through to domestic prices has fallen in recent years, following international trends (Campa and Goldberg, 2005), further mitigating any fear of floating.

The forward book position has been transparent since 1999, and a significant achievement has been the closure by February, 2004 of the net open foreign exchange position or NOFP, accumulated under previous monetary policy regimes, especially during 1993–8 (Figure 3.2), and expensive to the fiscus. The SARB has since been able to accumulate a respectable level of foreign exchange reserves, potentially for reducing short-term exchange rate instability.[42] These changes have reduced SA's sovereign risk and exchange rate volatility, further helping to lower inflation and interest rate volatility.

Notably, since the closure of the NOFP, we find real exchange rate volatility in SA has fallen below that in emerging market inflation targeting countries, bar Australia, but is comparable to Australia. The Accelerated and Shared Growth Initiative for SA (ASGISA) implicated the level and volatility of the real exchange rate in the poor performance of the manufacturing sector; and the International Panel appointed by the National Treasury proposes that more attention be given to the level and stability of the real exchange rate, which would require intervention by the SARB (see Chapter 1, section 4.7). However, they do not specify the size of the putative overvaluation of the currency,[43]

---

[42] The inflation-targeting Australian Reserve Bank is a successful example of the strategy of temporary ironing out of exchange rate fluctuations which has made profits (Becker and Sinclair, 2004) by intervening only at extremes of the exchange rate to stabilize the rate, but not to influence it persistently in any direction.

[43] What earlier looked like a long-term appreciation of the exchange rate through a persistent 'super-commodity' price cycle, sustained by growing demand in China and other Asian economies for its commodities, has now clearly collapsed.

nor do they offer a solution to Obstfeld's dilemma for a credible and independent monetary policy in an open economy (Obstfeld, 1996). Moreover, the evidence for exchange rate volatility impeding trade is tenuous at best (Tenreyro, 2007).

We consider that there is widespread misunderstanding of the role of the SARB and of inflation targeting in particular. The role of the SARB is not to stoke up inflationary demand through inappropriately low interest rates—this will not serve the interest of long-term growth. Nor is it to jeopardize its hard-won credibility through attempting to influence the economy in a *sustained* way while simultaneously purporting to have an inflation target as a primary objective. This has already failed under the preceding monetary regime in SA and multiple times elsewhere. Several chapters in this book (e.g. Chapters 2 and 7) have highlighted the important role that *medium-term* macro-policy stability has played in SA, via the gains from inflation targeting and supportive fiscal policy, in reducing real interest rates, volatility and uncertainty and thus helping restore investment and growth. However, many of the key drivers of growth are more deep-seated in nature, such as industrial policy (Chapter 8), infrastructure investment (Chapters 7 and 8) and education and health (Chapters 9, 11, and 12). There is no quick fix through monetary and exchange rate policy to SA's growth and employment problems while such long-term factors remain problematic. Finally, inflation hurts the poor most: they are the least able to raise incomes and have least access to savings, credit, and other 'buffers' to cushion them from inflation shocks. They are likely to be amongst the biggest beneficiaries of a less volatile inflation environment. The SARB would do well to consolidate its popular support by articulating clearly its concerns for the well-being of the mass of the population and explaining how its policies help the poor.

However well monetary policy is run, it is only one policy arena relevant for determining macroeconomic outcomes (Svensson, 2001; Svensson et al., 2002). SA currently has an unbalanced economy posing difficult challenges for monetary policy-makers, and more could be done to consolidate the gains from macro-stability with complementary policies. Despite sustained high commodity prices, SA had a current account deficit that reached over 7 per cent of GDP in 2007 and 2008, mainly driven by investment in non-tradables[44] such as real estate and finance and by expenditure on consumer durables (Chapter 2). SA become vulnerable to a reversal of foreign inflows that had financed this deficit until the global financial crisis of the latter part of 2008.

The dependence on foreign inflows is due to the abysmal levels of saving in SA, which have fallen further under democracy (Chapter 7). Government

---

[44] In 2007–8 it has been driven by oil imports which have risen in value; and also capital goods imports, as a result of investment in infrastructure. Where construction activities feed into infrastructure rather than house-building and offices, these are clearly complementary goods.

saving in recent years has helped (more is being recommended, see Chapter 2), but it is imperative to raise household and corporate saving, and reduce property speculation and excessive consumer spending via the acquisition of debt. Micro-measures can encourage this, but paramount is attention to the regulation of credit markets where South Africa's record is good, and imposition of stabilizing property taxes. Such measures would also protect SA's financial stability.

Economic activity in SA is very responsive to short-term interest rates. One reason is the efficiency of its financial and legal systems, making its credit markets among the most liberal in the world. The other reason is the floating rate nature of much private debt, which exposes households and businesses to interest rate fluctuations. The floating rate nature of debt is partly the result of historically volatile inflation and interest rates. As volatility subsides with credible monetary policy, the private sector may be more willing to offer longer-term debt contracts. There may be a role for government to aid in this process via financial regulation, greater transparency, and improving information for borrowers.

A paradox of the success of inflation targeting is that it may have exacerbated rising household debt, and hence contributed to higher house prices and lower saving. Faith in the lower volatility of inflation, interest rates and output raised desired debt to income ratios further (though the global economic crisis of 2008 is likely to have reversed this trend). Easy acquisition of debt has fuelled consumption at the expense of personal saving, thus constraining the domestic funds potentially available for corporate investment. Falling nominal interest rates between 2002 and 2005, more affordable mortgages and ease of remortgaging contributed to the rise in mortgage debt and in house prices.[45] More valuable housing collateral itself promoted borrowing and spending. The inflationary consequences are well understood[46] via the output gap, a worsening current account balance and hence a depreciating exchange rate (unless other factors strengthen the exchange rate). The risks for financial stability have been well demonstrated by the UK and US experience in 2007–8. The potential trade-off for interest rate policy poses serious dilemmas for the MPC.

Well-designed property and land taxes are ideally placed to meet growth and distribution objectives as well as stabilizing the economy (Muellbauer, 2005). Large real house price rises have disturbing implications for the distribution of resources between young households and those households already owning homes, and between poorer and more affluent households. Given

---

[45] The recent peak in annual growth in house prices of 35.5 per cent occurred in September 2004 (*Quarterly Bulletin*, March 2006).

[46] The Bank of England's MPC has been struggling with related dilemmas for much of the last decade.

SA's extremes of wealth inequality, a progressive and transparent property tax would moderate rises in house prices and keep housing more affordable for the young and the less well off, and tap the wealth of the most affluent without much effect on their incentives to engage in economic activity (Aron and Muellbauer, 2005).

Another area for complementary policy initiatives concerns management of what looked like a terms of trade 'super-cycle', with sustained high commodity prices. From the point of view of employment creation, SA's terms of trade gains in recent years have been partly offset by real exchange rate appreciation in 2004–6 and oil price increases, which has constrained the growth of manufacturing. Rodrik (2006) argues that manufacturing growth is less skill dependent than other sectors and therefore an important contributor to employment creation. Chile appears to have been able to limit its currency appreciation by keeping commodity export earnings offshore and encouraging foreign investors to externalize dividends to prevent commodity related appreciation from devastating other areas of export growth. Norway's limiting damage to manufacturing through potential 'Dutch disease' by using a stabilization fund, is another excellent example. In both cases, state ownership of (and/or the taxes from) private sector resource extracting companies have generated large revenues which have been partly invested in a diverse range of off-shore assets. Such a stabilization or sovereign wealth fund should help stabilize the real exchange rate and government spending during economic down-turns, when funds can be repatriated.

Finally, the *quality* of data available to the SARB and to the Treasury has important implications for outcomes. Estimates of unit labour costs, productivity growth and employment growth for SA have long been highly unreliable (Chapter 11), creating much greater uncertainty about basic economic trends than faced by other major central banks. Poor data quality is particularly unfortunate in view of the reliance on modeling under the targeting framework. Modern time series models require two or more decades of reliable data to achieve robust results. Historical data errors continue to affect modeling attempts in the future, resulting in a long-lasting deterioration in the quality of future models, forecasts, and policy deliberations.

Another instance concerns CPI data (see Aron and Muellbauer, 2004), where there is no publicly available technical handbook describing the methodology of construction of indices, despite the issuance of index-liked bonds; where availability of historical data is limited; and where there are some conceptual problems in data construction. An important reason for volatile interest rates and why controlling inflation in SA is costly in lost output lies in the construction of the headline CPI, with its large interest cost component. Interest rate rises probably have to be *larger* to have enough of a negative impact on expenditure to offset their headline inflation-increasing effect. Countries where CPI used to include mortgage costs, e.g. the USA, Australia, and New Zealand, have shifted to a definition of homeowners' costs based on imputed rents. Imputed rents are based on rental market observations and respond only gradually to interest rate. We have long argued in various papers for a switch to the imputed rent basis for SA.[47] It would then make much sense for the SARB to base monetary policy on a *single* new headline CPI as its target, and avoid the confusion to wage negotiators of choosing between CPI and CPIX, and the risk that trade unions will demand compensation for whichever of the two has risen more.

References

Ahmed, F., V Arora, and L. Ricci. 2005. 'Sovereign Spreads in South Africa'. In M. Grandes and N. Pinaud (eds.), *Reducing Capital Cost in Southern Africa*, Development Centre Studies, OECD, ch. 4.

Aoki, K, J. Proudman, and G. Vlieghe. 2002. 'Houses as Collateral: Has the Link between House Prices and Consumption in the U.K. Changed?' *Economic Policy Review*, 8(1): 163–77. Federal Reserve Bank of New York.

Aron, J. and J. Muellbauer. 2009. 'Monetary Policy and Inflation Modeling in a More Open Economy in South Africa'. In Gill Hammond, Ravi Kanbur, and Eswar Prasad (eds.), *New Monetary Policy Frameworks for Emerging Markets: Coping with the Challenges of Financial Globalization*, Bank of England/Edward Elgar (forthcoming).

—— 2009. 'Wealth, Credit Conditions and Consumption in SA'. *CEPR Working Paper* (forthcoming)

—— 2007a. 'Review of Monetary Policy in South Africa since 1994'. *Journal of African Economies* (Oxford University Press) 16(5): 705–44.

—— 2007b. 'Transparency, Credibility and Predictability of Monetary Policy in South Africa', paper presented at the Bank of England/Cornell University workshop on 'New developments in monetary policy in emerging market economies', Bank of England, 17–18 July 2007.

—— 2006. 'Estimates of Household Sector Wealth for South Africa, 1970–2003'. *Review of Income and Wealth*, 52(2): 285–308.

—— 2005. 'Monetary Policy, Macro-Stability and Growth: South Africa's Recent Experience and Lessons'. *World Economics*, 6(4): 123–47.

—— 2004. 'Construction of CPIX Data for Forecasting and Modelling in South Africa'. *South African Journal of Economics*, 72(5): 1–30.

—— 2002a. 'Estimating Monetary Policy Rules for South Africa'. In Norman Loayza and Klaus Schmidt-Hebbel (eds.), *Monetary Policy: Rules and Transmission Mechanisms*, Series on Central Banking, Analysis and Economic Policies, vol. 4, Central Bank of Chile, pp. 427–75.

---

[47] It is important that the switch comes at a neutral point in the interest rate cycle. While completing this chapter, *Statistic South Africa* announced it will implement an inputed rent measure, when rebasing CPI in January 2009. The National Treasury announced in November that this is to be the SARB's new inflation target. Unfortunately, the switch will therefore take place at almost the exact peak of interest rates, as in the US in 1983, distorting the medium term inflation picture.

—— 2002b. 'Interest Rate Effects on Output: Evidence from a Gdp Forecasting Model for South Africa'. *IMF Staff Papers* 49 (November): 185–213.

—— 2000. 'Personal and Corporate Saving in South Africa', *World Bank Economic Review*, 14(3): 509–44.

Aron, J., J. Muellbauer, and J. Prinsloo. 2008. 'Estimating the Balance Sheet of the Personal Sector in an Emerging Market Country: SA, 1975–2005'. Ch. 10 in James B. Davies (ed.), *Personal Wealth from a Global Perspective*, UNU-WIDER Studies in Development Economics, Oxford University Press, pp. 196–223.

Aron, J., J. Muellbauer, and J. Prinsloo. 2006. 'Estimating Household-Sector Wealth in South Africa'. *Quarterly Bulletin* (June): 61–72. South African Reserve Bank.

Aron, J., J. Muellbauer, and B. Smit. 2003. 'Understanding the Inflation Process in South Africa'. *Keynote Address*, Eighth Annual Conference on Econometric Modelling for Africa, Stellenbosch University, South Africa, July. Available at <http://www.csae.ox.ac.uk>: 'The SA Macroeconomic Research Programme'.

Aron, J., I. Elbadawi, and B. Kahn. 2000. 'Real and Monetary Determinants of the Real Exchange Rate in South Africa'. In I. Elbadawi and T. Hartzenberg (eds.), *Development Issues in South Africa*, London: MacMillan, ch. 8.

Ballim, G. and E. Moolman. 2005. 'Testing the Potency and Transparency of the South African Reserve Bank's Inflation Targeting Policy'. Hardcover, Standard Bank, South Africa.

Barth, M. and V. Ramey. 2001. 'The Cost Channel of Monetary Transmission'. *NBER Macroeconomics Annual*, 16: 199–240.

Bean, C., J. Larsen, and K. Nikolov. 2002. 'Financial Frictions and the Monetary Transmission Mechanism: Theory, Evidence and Policy Implications'. *Working Paper*, no. 113, European Central Bank.

Becker, C. and M. Sinclair. 2004. 'Profitability of Reserve Bank Foreign Exchange Operations: Twenty Years After The Float'. *Research Discussion Paper* 2004-06 (September), Economic Research Department, Reserve Bank of Australia.

Bernanke, B. 2004. 'The Great Moderation'. Remarks by Mr Ben S. Bernanke, Member of the Board of Governors of the US Federal Reserve System, at the meetings of the Eastern Economic Association, Washington DC, 20 February 2004. Federal Reserve Website.

Bernhardsen, T. and A. Kloster. 2002. 'Transparency and Predictability in Monetary Policy'. Bank of Norway *Economic Bulletin* q2: 45–57.

Bhundia, A. and L. Ricci. 2005. 'The Rand Crises of 1998 and 2001: What Have We Learned?' In Nowak, M. and L. Ricci (eds.), *Post-Apartheid South Africa,* International Monetary Fund.

Caballero, R., K. Cowan, and J. Kearns. 2005. 'Fear of Sudden Stops: Lessons from Australia and Chile'. *Journal of Economic Policy Reform*, 8(2): 313–54.

Calvo, G. and C. Reinhart. 2002. 'Fear of Floating'. *Quarterly Journal of Economics*, 117(2): 379–408.

Campa, Jose Manuel, and Linda S. Goldberg. 2005. 'Exchange Rate Pass-Through into Import Prices'. *Review of Economics and Statistics*, 87(4): 379–690.

De Kock, G. 1978. Commission of Inquiry into the Monetary System and Monetary Policy in South Africa, *Interim Report*. Pretoria: Government Printer.

—— 1985. Commission of Inquiry into the Monetary System and Monetary Policy in South Africa, *Final Report*. Pretoria: Government Printer.

Du Plessis, S. A. 2002. 'Evaluating the SARB's Inflation Target'. *South African Journal of Economics* 70(6): 982–1007.

Ehlers, R. and M. M. Smal. 2006. 'The Accuracy of the South African Reserve Bank Inflation Forecast'. *Report to the Monetary Policy Committee of the South African Reserve Bank* (April). Pretoria..

Eijffinger, S. and P. Geraats. 2006. 'How Transparent Are Central Banks?' *European Journal of Political Economy*, 22(1): 1–21.

Geraats, P. 2002. 'Central Bank Transparency'. *Economic Journal* 112: F532–F565.

Gidlow, R.M. 1995a. *South African Reserve Bank Monetary Policies under Dr. T.W. de Jongh, 1967–80*. The South African Reserve Bank.

—— 1995b. *South African Reserve Bank Monetary Policies under Dr. Gerhard de Kock, 1981–89*. The South African Reserve Bank.

Goodhart, C.A.E. 2005. 'The Interest rate Conditioning Assumption'. Prepared for the John Flemming Memorial Conference, 9–10 September 2005, Nuffield College.

Grandes, M., M. Peter, and N. Pinaud. 2003. 'The Currency Premium and Local-Currency Denominated Debt Costs in South Africa'. *Working Paper*, no. 230, OECD.

—— 2005. 'The Currency Premium and Local-Currency Denominated Debt Costs in South Africa'. In M. Grandes and N. Pinaud (eds) *Reducing Capital Cost in Southern Africa*, Development Centre Studies, OECD, ch. 3.

Jansen, Z. 2004. 'Note on the Funding Structure of Non-Financial Companies, 1990–2003'. *Quarterly Bulletin*, South African Reserve Bank (June): 61–6.

Judson, R. and A. Orphanides. 1996. 'Inflation, Volatility and Growth'. *FEDS Paper*, no. 96-19 (May). Federal Reserve Board.

Kahn, B. 1992. 'South African Exchange Rate Policy, 1979–1991'. *Research Paper*, no. 7, Centre for the Study of the South African Economy and International Finance, London School of Economics.

Kahn, B. and G. Farrell. 2002. 'South African Real Interest Rates in Comparative Perspective: Theory and Evidence'. *Occasional Paper, no. 17* (September), South African Reserve Bank.

Kahn, B. and J. Leape. 1996. 'Managing the Rand's Depreciation: The Role of Intervention'. *Quarterly Review*, Centre for Research into Economics and Finance in Southern Africa, London School of Economics (April): 2–13.

Kershoff, G.. 2000. 'Conducting Inflation Expectation Surveys in South Africa'. Mimeo (October), Bureau for Economic Research, Department of Economics, University of Stellenbosch: Stellenbosch. Available at <http://www.ber.sun.ac.za/forecasts.htm>.

Leiderman, L., and L. E. O. Svensson. 1995. *Inflation Targets*. London: Centre for Economic Policy Research.

Mahadeva, L. and G. Sterne. 2000. (eds) *Monetary Frameworks in a Global Context*. Routledge.

McCarthy, J. 2000. 'Pass-Through of Exchange Rates and Import Prices to Domestic Inflation in Some Industrialized Economies'. Federal Reserve Bank of New York *Staff Report* 111.

Morris, S. and H. Shin. 2004. 'Coordination risk and the price of debt'. *European Economic Review* 48: 133–53.

Muellbauer, J. 2007. 'Housing, Credit and Consumer Expenditure'. *Housing, Housing Finance, and Monetary Policy*, A Symposium Sponsored by the Federal Reserve Bank of Kansas City, Jackson Hole, Wyoming, 30 August –1 September 2007. Published: Federal Reserve Bank of Kansas City, pp 267–334.

—— 2005. 'Property Taxation and the Economy after the Barker Review'. *Economic Journal* 115(502): C99–C117.

Myburgh Commission. 2002. Commission of Inquiry Into the Rapid Depreciation of the Exchange Rate of the Rand and Related Matter: Final Report (30 June).

Obstfeld, M. 1996. 'Models of currency Crises with Self-fulfilling Features'. *European Economic Review*, 40: 1037–47.

Power, M. 2004. 'Why is the Cost of Capital so High in South Africa? What is SA Inc. Doing About It?' OECD conference 'How to Reduce Debt Costs in Southern Africa', Johannesburg 25–26 March 2004.

Rodrik, D. 2006. 'Understanding South Africa's Economic Puzzles'. Cambridge, Mass., *CID Working Paper*, no. 130, August.

Roley, V. V. and H. G. Sellon, Jr. 1995. *Monetary Policy Actions and Long-Term Interest Rates*. Federal Reserve Bank of Kansas City.

Smal, M. M. and S. de Jager. 2001. 'The Monetary Transmission Mechanism in South Africa'. *Occasional Paper* No 16, September, South African Reserve Bank.

Smal, M. M., C. Pretorius, and N. Ehlers. 2007. 'The Core Forecasting Model of the South African Reserve Bank'. *Working Paper* WP/07/02, June.

Stals, C. 1997. 'Effect of the Changing Financial Environment on Monetary Policy in South Africa'. Address to the Annual Dinner of the Economic Society of South Africa, Pretoria Branch, 15 May.

—— 1995. 'Monetary Policy in South Africa'. Address to the Second South African Economy, Investment and Trade Conference, London, October 17.

—— 1994. 'Governor's Address'. Pretoria: South African Reserve Bank (August 23).

Stopford, J. 2003. 'Inaccurate Statistics a Threat to the Economy'. Business Day (Johannesburg), South Africa, April 23.

Svensson, L. 2001. 'Independent Review of the Operation of Monetary Policy in New Zealand: Report to the Minister of Finance'. February. Available at <www.princeton.edu/~svensson>.

Svensson, L., K. Houg, A. Berg, H. Solheim, and E. Steigum. 2002. 'An Independent Review of Monetary Policy and Institutions in Norway'. (September) *Norges Bank Watch*. Centre for Monetary Economics, BI Norwegian School of Management.

Swanson, E. T. 2006. 'Have Increases in Federal Reserve Transparency Improved Private Sector Interest Rate Forecasts?' *Journal of Money, Credit, and Banking* 38(3): 791–820.

Taylor, J. 1993. 'Discretion versus Policy Rules in Practice'. *Carnegie-Rochester Conference on Public Policy*, 39: 195–214.

Tenreyro, S. 2007. 'On the trade impact of nominal exchange rate volatility'. *Journal of Development Economics*, 82(2): 485–508.

Union Bank of Switzerland, *Economic Research Note*, 13 February 1996.

van der Merwe, E. 2004. 'Inflation targeting in South Africa'. *Occasional Paper*, no. 19, July, South African Reserve Bank.

4
Transforming Fiscal Governance

Tania Ajam and Janine Aron

1. Introduction[1]

South Africa under democracy inherited a highly unequal wealth and income distribution and a legacy of decades-long discriminatory provision in public health, education, and infrastructure across population groups. The African National Congress government assumed office in April 1994 amid great uncertainty about its ability to maintain the rule of law and resist unsustainable policies in the face of populist pressures. While dealing with the aftermath of the apartheid era, it embarked simultaneously on a socio-economic transformation project in the spirit of the new Constitution. Inherited fiscal conditions presented a rather bleak picture. There had been some moves towards broadening the tax base, but nevertheless, aggregate fiscal discipline was weak. Escalating government expenditure coupled with weak revenue collection had created burgeoning deficits, raising concerns about sustainability and the spectre of a debt trap. Allocative efficiency at a macro level had begun to improve even in the apartheid era, with shifts towards increased social spending (van der Berg, 2001). However, allocation in sectors such as health and education left much to be desired. Operational efficiency was particularly weak in the homelands and under-serviced Black areas. On the whole, fiscal governance was bedevilled by a lack of transparency and accountability.

South Africa—as a small, open economy—has also had to respond to the uncertainty and volatility of globalization, and this has curtailed fiscal policy discretion (Abedian, 1998; Calitz, 2000). Globalization has created pressures to reform fiscal policy institutions and budgetary systems, and also for policy convergence, including deficit reduction, tax reform to broaden the tax base

---

[1] Acknowledgements: This chapter is a revised and extended version of Ajam and Aron (2007). Janine Aron acknowledges funding support from the Economic and Social Research Council, U.K. (grant RES-000-22-2066). We are grateful for comments from Estian Calitz (Stellenbosch University), John Muellbauer (Oxford University), and an anonymous referee.

(while lowering marginal rates), and the restructuring of public sector enterprises. Deviant fiscal behaviour, seen as a signal of unsound economic fundamentals, could be penalized by adverse foreign capital flows.

This chapter reviews the policies and outcomes of South Africa's fiscal reform since 1994, and explores the main challenges it has raised. Despite the initial conditions, the South African government has achieved a remarkable turnaround in the fiscal position (see also Horton, 2005). In section 2, the improved governance of fiscal policy with its base in constitutional provisions is discussed. The key fiscal reforms since 1994 are summarized in section 3. The performance of national fiscal policy is examined in section 4, by means of the trends of the main budget indicators, measures of the cyclically adjusted fiscal stance, a comparison of budget projections and actual outcomes, the management and sustainability of debt, and, finally, the contribution of fiscal policy to South Africa's improved macroeconomic stability. Section 5 explores the implications of the vertical fiscal imbalance created by a combination of highly centralized revenue raising powers and increased decentralization of expenditure responsibility to sub-national governments. Section 6 concludes.

2. Improved governance of fiscal policy

In South Africa, unlike many other countries, the ideals of good fiscal governance are constitutionally entrenched. The adoption of South Africa's first Constitution in 1996[2] precipitated a paradigm shift in public policy and a restructuring of the public sector. The Constitution required that budget processes of all three spheres of government promote transparency, accountability, and effective financial management (ss. 215–17). Legislation was mandated to characterize the form of these budgets and when they were tabled. Parliament was granted powers to exercise more effective oversight over budget formulation and implementation (ss. 55 and 77), and even to amend Money Bills. During the apartheid era, Parliament's role was merely to 'rubber stamp' the budget.

Prior to the 1996 Constitution, the system of fiscal governance in South Africa was highly fragmented, and the wholly inadequate oversight mechanisms resulted in great inefficiencies. There were several distinct budgets in the old dispensation, including those of four provincial administrations and ten homelands (comprising four notionally 'independent states' and six notionally 'self-governing' territories). These separate public services had thus to be merged, consolidated and rationalized, while avoiding breakdown in service delivery. The adoption of the Constitution precipitated a complete

---

[2] An Interim Constitution was adopted in 1994 and the Final Constitution in 1996.

restructuring into a unitary state with three spheres of government: national, 9 provincial governments, and 283 local municipalities (down from 784 in the apartheid era). The Constitution exerted three major influences on the nascent fiscal arrangements of the democratic South Africa: the impetus towards budget and financial management reform; the creation of a fiscally decentralized system of intergovernmental fiscal relations; and the introduction of justiciable socio-economic rights.

The Constitution required the establishment of a National Treasury to apply recognized accounting practices, classifications, and norms to ensure transparency and expenditure control in each sphere of government, and when financing the deficit through increased public debt (s. 216). Procurement at each level was expected to be 'fair, equitable, transparent, competitive and cost-effective'—though preferential allocation in some cases was allowed for.[3] The National Assembly of the Parliament was charged with providing mechanisms to enforce oversight for greater accountability (c. 4) and oversight over budget formulation and implementation. For greater provincial expenditure control, provision was made for halting for up to four months the transfer of national funds to provinces in breach of legislation, pending parliamentary approval and a report from the Auditor General.

The emerging intergovernmental fiscal system was influenced by the constitutional requirements for expenditure assignment, revenue raising powers and intergovernmental grants, and borrowing powers. Compared to provincial administrations in the apartheid state, under the Constitution the provinces have been assigned greater responsibilities for the delivery of goods and services, either individually or jointly with national government and/or local governments. For instance, with shared responsibility (e.g. in primary and secondary education and health), the national government sets policy but implementation occurs at a sub-national level. However, revenue raising powers under the Constitution have remained highly centralized. The most productive taxes, such as VAT, personal, and corporate income tax, are reserved for national government. Provincial governments collect very little own revenue (s. 228) and the income raised within the province typically amounts to less than 5 per cent of the provincial budget. The Financial and Fiscal Commission, an independent body established in terms of the Constitution,[4] is required to make recommendations to Parliament on equitable allocations to national, provincial, and local government from nationally collected revenues in line with their expenditure responsibilities and functions. Given that the provincial

---

[3] These include policies that restrict tendering for contracts to achieve targets for black empowerment or affirmative action employment.

[4] In the 1996 Constitution, the mandate of the Financial and Fiscal Commission is given in s. 220, while the later Financial and Fiscal Commission Act of 1998 explains the organization's structure and functions.

governments and municipalities have limited borrowing powers,[5] they are highly dependent on their share of nationally collected revenue to finance the implementation of their constitutionally assigned functions.

The separation of policy and financing (at national level) and implementation (at provincial level) potentially promotes unfunded mandates and complex coordination problems. This important issue is discussed in section 5. Local governments are endowed with more substantial fiscal capacity, being entitled by the Constitution to impose rates on property and surcharges on fees for services provided by or on behalf of the municipality (e.g. for electricity or sewerage). Prior to 1994, many municipalities were in financially precarious positions, were badly managed with dysfunctional systems, and did not engage with the communities they were supposed to serve. However, while the 1996 Constitution sketched a new vision of developmental local government (c. 7), and local government has since been in a continual state of transformation, there is little evidence of general improvement.

Most other constitutions confer only civil and political rights upon their citizens. The South African Constitution also confers justiciable socio-economic rights to be realized within the available resources of the state. The Bill of Rights (ss. 7 through 39) details the obligations of the state to ensure progressive realization of the right to housing (s. 26), the right to health care, food, water, and social security (s. 27), and the right to education (s. 29).

3. Fiscal reforms since 1994

Fiscal reform initiatives were first articulated through government macro-economic programmes, the Reconstruction and Development Programme (RDP), launched in January 1994, and the Growth Employment and Redistribution (GEAR) strategy of June 1996. Fiscal prudence, tax reform, and increased transparency of administration, a reorientation of spending to social sector spending, and longer-term expenditure planning were hallmarks of both the RDP and the GEAR plans. The fiscal reform strategy has been remarkably consistent over time, and can be roughly broken down into three broad areas: budget and financial management reform; the creation of the intergovernmental fiscal system; and tax policy and administration reforms.

The budget and financial management reform imperatives of the 1996 Constitution were given substance by the Public Finance Management Act of 1999, initiating the move from an input-oriented expenditure control system towards a more performance-oriented system. The Act formally established the

---

[5] Loans may be made raised only to finance capital expenditure and not for current expenditure. No national government guarantee is available in respect of sub-national claims.

National Treasury, amalgamating the former departments of Finance and State Expenditure. As pointed out by Siebrits and Calitz (2004), the 1999 Act does not prescribe numerical fiscal rules, but emphasizes 'regular financial reporting, sound internal expenditure controls, independent audit and supervision of control systems, improved accounting standards and training of financial managers, and greater emphasis on outputs and performance monitoring'. In 2003, the Municipal Finance Management Act extended such budget reforms to local government.

The quality, timeliness, and comprehensiveness of fiscal data have much improved since 1994. Fiscal data are regularly published in the *Budget Review* and the *Intergovernmental Fiscal Reviews*. The introduction of the *Medium Term Budget Policy Statement* (MTBPS) from December 1997 has improved debt and cash management strategies. Published annually, the MTBPS states the government's aggregate revenue and expenditure intentions over the next three years, as well as indicative figures on the division of revenue among provincial governments. Multi-year budgeting, also used in the UK, had its genesis in the 1999 Act, realized through the Medium-Term Expenditure Framework (MTEF) in 1998/9, providing three-year rolling budgets for the national and provincial governments in March, and underlying macroeconomic projections. Since 1999, the budget has been tabled before the start of the financial year. A new budget and reporting format was introduced in 2004, aligned with the International Public Sector Accounting Standards issued by the International Federation of Accountants, and based on a new standard chart of accounts (National Treasury, 2004: p. vii).

Significant milestones in the evolution of intergovernmental fiscal relations have included the creation of the Budget Council in 1996, an intergovernmental forum presiding over the revenue sharing process;[6] establishing formula-based revenue sharing,[7] based on recommendations by the Financial and Fiscal Commission; and promulgation of the Intergovernmental Fiscal Relations Act of 1997 that introduced predictability and transparency into the intergovernmental budget process.

Tax policy and administration reforms have greatly contributed to broadening the tax base and enhancing revenue collection efficiency. Shortly after the 1994 elections, the Katz Commission was appointed to investigate comprehensive administrative and tax reforms, producing eventually nine reports. Foremost from an organizational point of view was the creation of an autonomous revenue service to be known as the South African Revenue Service (SARS),

---

[6] The Budget Council, formalized in the Intergovernmental Fiscal Relations Act of 1997, consists of the National Minister of Finance and his nine provincial counterparts. The Financial and Fiscal Commission attends Budget Council meetings as an observer.

[7] The formula based revenue sharing mechanism initially applied only to provincial governments, but was extended to local governments in 1998/9.

combining the Inland Revenue and Customs and Excise departments. SARS raised audit capability through the introduction of computerized systems, enhanced capacity to investigate and prosecute tax evaders, and improved debt recovery procedures. At the same time discriminatory tax legislation was reviewed to further eliminate gender and racial discrimination, and to ensure compliance with constitutional provisions on the right to privacy and administrative justice. Some of the tax reforms made between 1994 and 1999 include the granting of tax amnesties, the introduction of tax relief for low- and middle-income taxpayers and the reduction of the number of income tax brackets. Reforms were made to fringe benefit taxation and the taxation of Trusts. Company tax rates and the secondary tax on companies (STC, introduced in 1993/4) were reduced, and there was a significant fall in ad valorem excise tax rates. A tax on retirement funds was introduced in 1996; and in 2000, a capital gains tax was introduced. Tax incentives were introduced for a limited period in the form of a Tax Holiday Scheme and accelerated depreciation allowances. In due course transfer pricing and thin capitalization provisions were incorporated in the Income Tax Act. Several double tax treaties with foreign jurisdictions were concluded, and there was also a move from source to residence-based taxation.

4. Performance of national fiscal policy

South Africa since 1994 has not adopted legislated constraints on fiscal variables for the national government (i.e. fixed fiscal targets), or numerical rules in the manner of monetary policy (see Chapter 2). The rationale behind fiscal rules which pre-commit to certain policies is that they, in principle, trade-off reduced policy-setting freedom and flexibility for greater self-discipline and fiscal credibility. Fiscal rules cannot substitute for authentic government commitment to fiscal discipline, since they can relatively easily be circumvented, ignored or abandoned (Kopits and Symansky, 1998). Siebrits and Calitz (2004) characterize the fiscal regimes used in South Africa as 'target-guided discretion' during 1994 to 1998, and 'transparency-based discretion' thereafter, with an underlying strong commitment to fiscal prudence. They argue that the flexible nature of these regimes has proved beneficial in a volatile external environment of currency crises, political democratization and strong popular pressure for more expansionary policies. Moreover, the limited discretion of fiscal policy has not lost credibility to the Treasury, given its consistent fiscal discipline in practice.

4.1. Trends of the main budget indicators

A feature of fiscal policy from 1994 is that the authorities maintained a fairly tight overall fiscal position, despite political pressures or constitutional commitments for some degree of expansion, and while operating in a not always favourable external environment. At a national level, the considerable fiscal consolidation has been sustained through a mix of expenditure cuts and revenue gains—especially from income taxes, and improved administration. Given that provincial governments have negligible own revenue sources, the emphasis there was more on expenditure control, especially in the wake of provincial overspending in 1997/8, discussed in section 5. Consolidation has been supported by the reforms outlined in section 3. In consequence, there has been a significant reduction in the budget deficit, and an improved primary balance, reflecting more sustainable debt management (Figure 4.1).

Early in 1994, the future government had launched the Reconstruction and Development Programme (RDP), which emphasized fiscal adjustment. Shortly after the election success of 1994, the government announced a targeted reduction in the budget deficit of 2.5 per cent of GDP over five years, constant revenues as a share of GDP and cuts in non-interest expenditure. During the early phase of adjustment under the RDP, the fiscal authorities established credibility by meeting deficit targets (Table 4.1). The budget deficit which averaged 4.3 per cent in the decade to 1992/3, and was 7.3 per cent of GDP in 1992/3, fell to 5.6 per cent of GDP in 1993/4, declining further in the subsequent three fiscal years to 5 per cent of GDP in 1996/7. The primary balance achieved a surplus in 1994/5 that was thereafter sustained. Revenue increased from 21.9 to

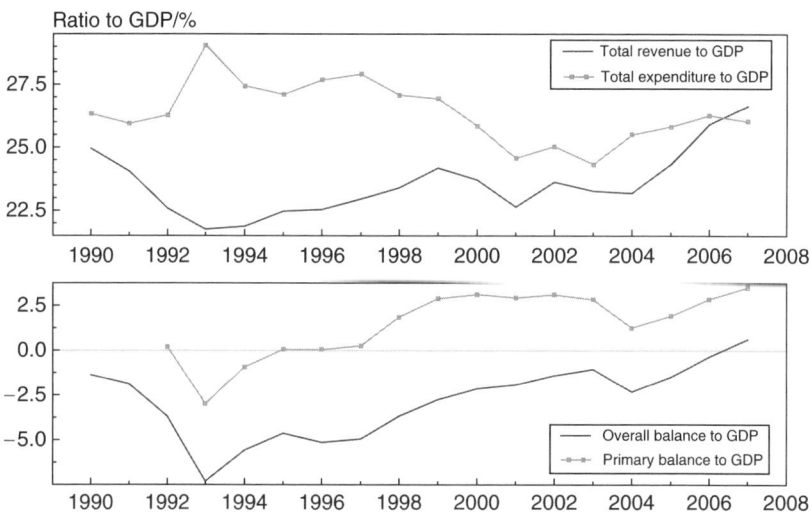

Figure 4.1. Conventional and primary balances as a percentage of GDP, fiscal years from 1989/90 to 2006/7

Source: South African Reserve Bank, *Quarterly Bulletin*, various issues.

Note: The fiscal year ends in March, and hence, the year 2007 would refer to 2006/7.

23 per cent of GDP from 1993/4 to 1996/7, facilitated by the establishment of SARS. Corporate income tax was cut to 35 per cent in 1995, and the dividend tax reduced by half. Non-interest expenditure was essentially constant, averaging 22.6 per cent of GDP across these years, with expenditure cuts mainly targeting the wage bill, subsidies, and some areas of capital spending. Poor management, however, saw significant provincial expenditure overspending and provincial borrowing had subsequently to be suspended in 1998/9.

Fiscal reform and consolidation continued with the introduction of the Growth Employment and Redistribution (GEAR) strategy in June 1996, which aimed for a 3 per cent of GDP deficit target within four years, and a revenue ceiling of 25 per cent of GDP. The first two budgets after GEAR first cut the wage bill, and a year later limited civil service wage rises and strengthened management in the provincial and municipal governments. Provincial performance improved and registered a surplus in 1998/9, and together with revenue gains under SARS, the deficit target was easily met in 1998/9. The deficit fell to 3.7 per cent in 1997/8 and then to 2.8 per cent in 1998/9, with the primary surplus reaching 3.1 per cent of GDP in 1999/2000 (Table 4.1). Revenue had climbed to 24.2 per cent of GDP by 1998/9, while non-interest expenditure fell to 21.3 per cent of GDP. The MTEF was also introduced in 1998/9, allowing multi-year budgeting.

The institutional reforms governing revenue collection and expenditure management bore fruit in the following fiscal years from 1999/2000, the latter strengthened by the passing of the Public Finance Management Act in 1999 (section 2). By 2002/3, the deficit had fallen to its lowest level since the start of reforms, of 1.1 per cent of GDP. Debt management improvements and lower interest rates brought sustained savings on debt service, that were redeployed to social and some capital expenditure, bringing the primary surplus to 1.3 per cent of GDP by 2003/4. The ceiling for revenue to GDP of 25 per cent continued to be observed until 2005/6. Expenditure cuts continued to focus on the wage bill, with cuts in civil service employment phased in from 1998 on. The corporate income tax rate was lowered further to 30 per cent and a capital gains tax was introduced. Worldwide income came under the personal income taxation net, but tax rates were lowered and thresholds adjusted. In the 2003/4 budget and the following two budgets, a larger deficit of 3.1 per cent was projected, with plans for increased social sector spending (including the provision of HIV/AIDS drugs) and capital spending. In the event, the actual deficits were far lower, at 2.3 per cent, 1.5 per cent and only 0.4 per cent of GDP, respectively, partly due to poor capacity in provincial administrations resulting in unspent funds. The budget balance was in surplus by 2006/7 (though a small deficit of 1.5 per cent had been targeted for the fiscal year, Table 4.1). The MTEF projections for 2008/9, while targeting surpluses, continue to signal the government's intention to maintain a more expansionary stance, with declining planned surpluses from 2007/8 to 2009/10.

Table 4.1. Fiscal indicators and cyclically adjusted fiscal estimates (in per cent of GDP)

	1992/3	1993/4	1994/5	1995/6	1996/7	1997/8	1998/9	1999/2000	2000/1	2001/2	2002/3	2003/4	2004/5	2005/6	2006/7
Main budget indicators															
Revenue	21.8	21.9	22.5	22.5	23.0	23.4	24.2	23.7	22.6	23.6	23.3	23.2	24.7	26.0	26.6
Expenditure	29.1	27.4	27.1	27.7	27.9	27.1	26.9	25.8	24.6	25.0	24.3	25.5	25.8	26.3	26.0
Non-interest expenditure	24.7	22.8	22.4	22.5	22.7	21.5	21.3	20.6	19.7	20.5	20.4	21.0	22.4	23.1	23.1
Interest	4.3	4.6	4.7	5.2	5.2	5.5	5.6	5.3	4.9	4.5	3.9	3.6	3.4	3.2	2.9
Balance	−7.3	−5.6	−4.6	−5.1	−5.0	−3.7	−2.8	−2.1	−1.9	−1.4	−1.1	−2.3	−1.5	−0.4	+0.6
Primary balance	−3.0	−0.9	+0.1	0.0	0.3	1.9	2.9	3.1	2.9	3.1	2.8	1.3	1.9	2.9	3.5
Nominal GDP (R billions)	381	443	497	564	636	700	757	837	952	1050	1198	1289	1480	1586	1807
Deviations from budget targets															
Balance							0.4	0.9	0.5	1.0	0.8	0.0	1.4	2.7	2.1
Primary balance							0.5	0.6	0.5	0.9	0.8	−0.4	1.3	2.5	2.1
Revenue							0.7	0.8	0.5	1.4	1.1	−0.4	1.4	2.6	1.9
Non-interest expenditure							0.2	0.2	0.1	0.5	0.4	0.0	0.1	0.1	−0.2
Measuring fiscal stance															
Potential/actual GDP	1.030	1.018	1.003	1.000	0.980	0.988	1.009	1.004	0.995	1.003	1.000	1.011	1.003	1.001	0.995
Fiscal stance	5.3	3.5	2.8	2.9	3.1	1.3	−0.1	−0.3	0.1	−0.2	0.1	1.5	1.0	0.05	−0.5
Revenue stance	0.9	0.8	0.2	0.1	−0.3	−0.8	−1.5	−1.1	0.0	−1.0	−0.5	−0.5	−1.7	−3.3	−4.0
Non-interest expend. stance	4.4	2.8	2.7	2.8	3.4	2.1	1.4	0.8	0.1	0.7	0.8	2.0	2.6	3.3	3.5
Fiscal impulse		−1.8	−0.7	0.1	0.2	−1.7	−1.4	−0.2	0.4	−0.3	0.3	1.4	−0.5	−0.9	−0.5
Revenue impulse		−0.1	−0.6	−0.1	−0.4	−0.4	−0.8	0.5	1.1	−1.0	0.4	0.1	−1.1	−1.6	−0.7
Non-interest expend. impulse		−1.7	−0.1	0.1	0.6	−1.3	−0.6	−0.6	−0.7	0.7	0.0	1.3	0.6	0.7	0.2

Source: Calculations using data from South African Reserve Bank, *Quarterly Bulletin*

The tax reforms have markedly improved the effectiveness of tax collection and revenue sources have diversified (Table 4.2). The broadening of the tax base has permitted considerable tax relief since 1995, of which 85 per cent comprised personal income tax relief. The declining importance of taxes on international trade and transactions as a source of revenue reflects the government's trade liberalization policies. Value Added Tax (VAT) accounted for roughly a quarter of total gross tax revenues from 1986/7 to 2004/5. Personal income tax has declined from an average of 41 per cent to 34 per cent of total gross tax revenue, between the periods 1993/4 to 1999/2000 and 1999/2000 to 2005/6. Concomitantly, a greater share was taken by company taxation, and two relatively new taxes, the secondary tax on companies (introduced in 1993/4) and the tax on retirement funds. The period was also characterized by increases in the number of user charges (e.g. toll road fees, hospital fees, and other direct payments for benefits received). Calitz and Siebrits (2003) have noted the redistributive thrust of these charges.

4.2. Cyclically adjusted fiscal measures

To estimate the fiscal stance purely as a result of discretionary fiscal policy, a correction can be made for cyclical economic factors that may have affected revenue and expenditure. For instance, in periods where output exceeds *potential* or trend output (that is, where the output gap is positive), there will be an enhanced tax take from the increased output and possibly reduced expenditures on social benefits due to greater demand in the economy, resulting in an overall contraction of the budget deficit. A simple way to adjust fiscal estimates cyclically is to employ a measure of the output gap to adjust revenue and expenditure values relative to GDP to the amounts needed to maintain revenue and expenditure at the level of a neutral or base year, that is, a year when potential and actual output approximately coincided. Subtracting these neutral levels of revenue and expenditure from actual levels of revenue and expenditure, gives the revenue stance and expenditure stance, from which the fiscal stance can be calculated.

We update the exercise of Horton (2005), estimating potential output for South Africa using a Hodrick Prescott filter, but choosing the fiscal year 2000/1 as the reference year when the output gap was close to zero.[8] The fiscal stance, shown in Table 4.1, is calculated as the difference between the revenue stance and the (non-interest) expenditure stance, or the *primary* balance relative to

---

[8] Horton's choice of the base year 1998/9, though the output gap was close to zero, is perhaps less plausible than 2000/1, given the very high interest rates experienced that year following an exchange rate crisis, and that induced the lowest real annual growth rate in a decade. In 2000/1, the output gap was also close to zero, but more normal macroeconomic conditions prevailed. Further, the new data from the benchmarking and rebasing of the National Accounts (December 2004) are used here, and revised budgetary data.

Table 4.2. The changing composition of revenue sources

	Persons & Individuals	Companies	Secondary Tax on companies	Tax on retirement funds[b]	Taxes on Property[c]	VAT[d]	Taxes on International Trade	Fuel Levy[f]	Other Taxes[g]
Average contribution of revenue sources to total main budget tax revenue/%									
1986/7–1993/4[a]	34.3	19.7	0.1	0.0	1.6	25.1	5.5	6.5	7.2
1993/4–1999/2000[a]	41.0	12.1	1.1	1.5	1.7	24.7	7.2	4.1	6.6
1999/2000–2005/6	33.7	18.4	2.3	1.9	2.1	25.9	5.3	3.6	6.7
2005/6–2008/9[h]	29.7	20.8	3.0	0.5	2.2	28.4	4.3	5.1	6.1
Average annual nominal growth rates of revenue source/%									
1986/7–1993/4[a]	20.1	4.1	—	—	14.5	15.9	46.9	12.7	14.8
1993/4–1999/2000[a]	14.7	10.5	23.8	27.6	16.8	11.3	10.5	4.4	9.9
1999/2000–2005/6	6.6	26.2	24.7	-2.8	19.6	15.5	2.6	18.7	14.1
2005/6–2008/9[h]	10.4	11.0	11.2	-14.6	4.9	10.9	15.3	13.1	3.1
Average annual real growth rates of revenue source/%									
1999/2000–2005/6	0.13	18.6	17.2	-8.7	12.3	8.6	-3.6	11.5	7.3
2005/6–2008/9[h]	5.6	6.2	6.39	-18.3	0.37	6.1	10.3	8.2	-1.4

Source: Calculations were based on National Treasury, *Budget Review* (2006) and other *Budget Reviews*. Real annual growth rates were obtained using CPIX deflator (2000 = 100). CPIX projections for the MTEF period were based on *Budget Review* (2005: 12).

Notes:
[a] Figures prior to 1995/6 include collections by the former TBVC states (so called Independent Hondards) and self-governing territories.
[b] Average annual growth rates for retirement funds tax introduced in 1996/7 is from 1996/7 to 1999/2000.
[c] Taxes on property includes donations tax, estate duty, marketable securities tax and transfer duties.
[d] Including sales duty, replaced by general sales tax in July 1978, and value added tax in Sept. 1991
[e] Includes customs duties, import surcharges, diamond export duties, miscellaneous customs and excise income, as well as ordinary levy collections.
[f] Including the former fuel levy directed to Regional Services Councils and the levy allocated to the National Road Fund for the period 1983/4 to 1986/7.
[g] Including various levies, mining leases and ownership, cinematographic tax and other special levies, the skills development levy, specific and ad valorem taxes, and stamp duties and fees.
[h] Medium-Term Expenditure Framework (MTEF) period.

its neutral value.[9] The annual change in the fiscal stance is termed the fiscal impulse, and it reveals whether policy tightened (negative impulse) or loosened (positive impulse). The revenue or expenditure impulses can reveal the sources of the policy change. Table 4.1 and Figure 4.2 suggest that discretionary policy was tightened from 1992/3, with the fiscal stance rather positive at the outset, but falling to zero by 1998/9 from a combination of expenditure cuts and revenue gains by 1998/9. Sharp expenditure cuts are shown by the negative expenditure impulse for 1993/4 and 1997/8, when the fiscal impulse was strongly negative, and moderate cuts ensued in the following three years. In 1998/99, the impact of the establishment of SARS and associated reforms is apparent in a supportive negative revenue impulse, and significant negative revenue impulses are also seen in 2001/2, 2004/5, and 2005/6. The rise in budgeted social and investment spending after 2001/2 loosens the fiscal stance, despite the revenue gains (Figure 4.2).

Comparing the output gap with the fiscal impulse (Figure 4.2) suggests that before about 2002/3, policy under democracy had been largely pro-cyclical

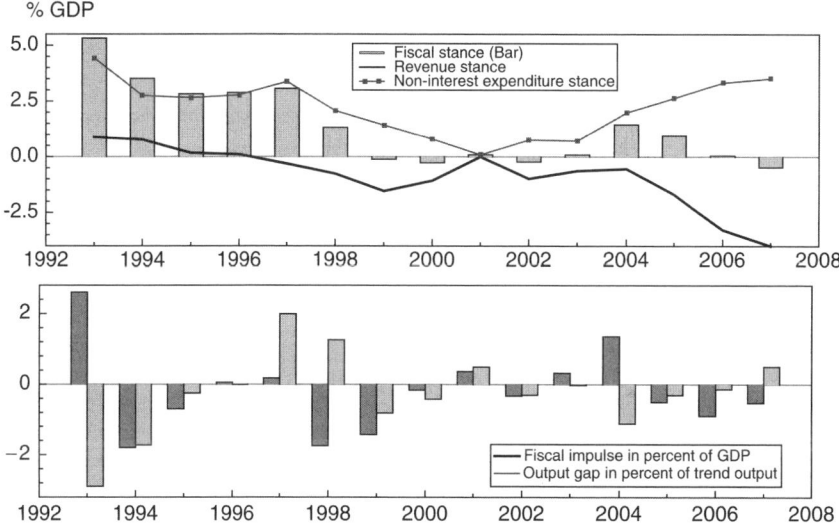

Figure 4.2. Fiscal impulse and the output gap, fiscal years from 1992/3 to 2006/7
Source: Calculations using data from South African Reserve Bank, *Quarterly Bulletin*.
Note: For details of calculations, see Table 4.1 and associated text.
The fiscal year ends in March, and hence, the year 2007 would refer to 2006/7.

[9] The assumptions for the calculation of neutral values are that neutral revenue grows at the rate of GDP, while neutral non-interest expenditure grows at the rate of trend GDP (as in Horton, 2005). One would expect revenue to fluctuate with GDP, but expenditure to move more smoothly, since a social benefits system is not developed in South Africa (social expenditures are planned in advance for means-tested or age-threshold groups).

(with the exception of 1997/8). For instance, when actual output was less than potential output (the output gap was negative), the fiscal impulse was also negative. Thus, when there was excess capacity in the economy, fiscal policy continued to be consolidated in the early years. Policy has become more counter-cyclical in the most recent years, when it relaxed with excess capacity in 2003/4 and was tightened in 2006/7 when the output gap was positive. Three years have experienced a fiscal stimulus since 1999/2000.

An alternative approach to distinguish discretionary and cyclical fiscal policy, by the estimation of structural balance indicators, has been executed by two sets of authors for different periods and assumptions, Horton (2005) and Swanepoel and Schoeman (2003). Horton's results confirm the above findings of discretionary tightening to 1999/2000 (with the exception of 1996/7), and loosening thereafter, especially in 2003/4. Swanepoel and Schoeman (2003) concur that fiscal discretionary policies were frequently procyclical, including fiscal consolidation during a period of slower economic growth from 1993 to 1999.

The degree of fiscal discipline is remarkable in the light of theories of public expenditure, such as the Meltzer–Richard hypothesis which posits that, in countries with highly unequal income distribution, the extension of voting rights to lower-income groups is likely to increase the growth of redistributive public expenditure (Meltzer and Richard, 1981). Black et al. (2005: 97–8) point to two factors that help explain the restraint: some redistribution had already occurred prior to 1994; and post-1994 reforms achieved a reallocation of spending without significant increases in government's overall expenditure share. The signalling effect for global capital flows alluded to earlier may also have contributed to the fiscal restraint.

4.3. Budget projections and actual outcomes

The deviations of actual revenue, non-interest expenditure and balance measures from budget targets, as a percentage of GDP, are also shown in Table 4.1. Actual expenditures have usually been close to planned limits, or in some cases have undershot limits. In 2003/4 despite intentions to increase spending, actual expenditure was below budgeted, indicating lack of spending capacity. By contrast, even when revenue projections were revised upwards in the budgets, these were outstripped by actual collections. The windfall tax revenue gain in 2001/2 translated directly into personal income tax relief the following year. In 2003/4, tax collections fell below budgeted estimates, attributable to lower company profits and customs receipts in an environment of muted economic growth. In 2004/5 and especially in 2005/6, actual revenues again exceeded estimates, indicating that diminishing returns to tax reform had not yet set in. The result has been stronger balance and primary balance outturns than budgeted, that in recent years have amounted to over 1 per cent of GDP. Factors causing deviations include fluctuations in the business cycle and periods of both overspending and underspending by provincial governments; but the main cause of deviations are over-conservative revenue projections, particularly of corporate income tax after 1999.

4.4. Debt management and sustainability

The net borrowing requirement of the main budget is obtained by subtracting extraordinary transfers from the deficit on the main budget and adding extraordinary receipts.[10] The net borrowing requirement is financed through changes in domestic and foreign loan liabilities, and changes in cash and other balances. The consolidation of the fiscal position has helped reduce domestic debt from 46 to 25 per cent of GDP between 1997/8 and 2006/7 (Figure 4.3), and debt service has correspondingly fallen from 6 to just below 3 per cent of GDP. Foreign debt remains a small proportion of overall debt, at just under 5 per cent of GDP in 2006/7, up from about 1 per cent of GDP in 1993/4. Foreign debt rose to nearly 8 per cent of GDP in 2001/2, reflecting increased borrowing (at longer maturities) and the effects of the rand depreciation. Debt management has focused on extending the maturities of foreign debt and

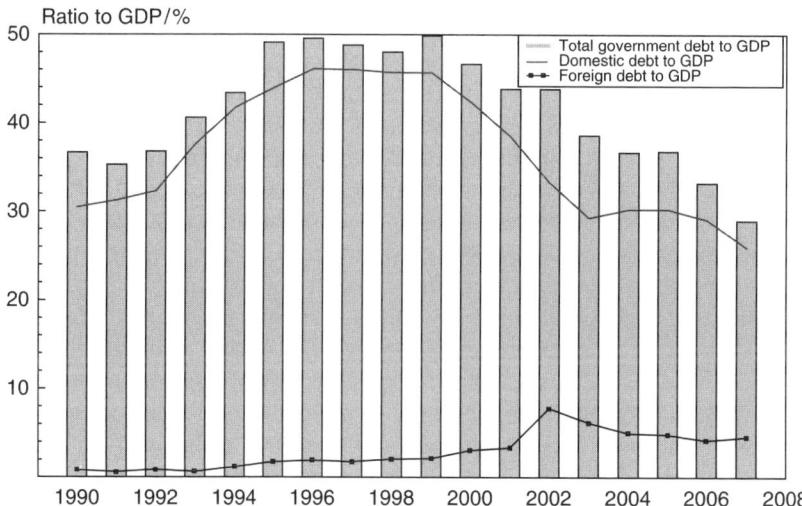

Figure 4.3. Debt indicators, fiscal years from 1989/90 to 2006/7

Source: South African Reserve Bank, *Quarterly Bulletin*, various issues.

Note: The fiscal year ends in March, and hence, the year 2007 would refer to 2006/7.

[10] Extraordinary transfers include premiums received on destination bonds in switch auctions. Extraordinary receipts include proceeds of sale of state assets and strategic supplies, as well as 'book profit' on domestic government bond buy-backs and source bonds issued in source auctions.

domestic debt, consolidating debt instruments and introducing inflation-indexed bonds. Increased diversification and an improved term structure of debt have contributed to reduced fiscal risk.

Horton (2005) under a range of cautious assumptions,[11] projects debt forward from 2004, and examines the dynamics under a variety of short-term shocks. The shocks include a fall in growth, substantial real depreciation of the exchange rate, increase of the debt stock, and a worsening of the primary balance. He finds the projected debt is moderate and sustainable over the next decade from 2004.

4.5. The contribution of fiscal policy to South Africa's improved macroeconomic stability

South Africa's growth performance has improved: real economic growth rate averaged 3.6 per cent (2.0 per cent per capita) during 1994q2–2007, versus 1.1 per cent (−1.2 per cent per capita) during the last apartheid decade, 1984–1994q1, and has averaged 5.1 per cent (4.2 per cent per capita) from 2004 to 2007. However, these averages remain low by world and by South Africa's own historical standards (see Chapter 2). The combination of tight fiscal policy, and misguided monetary policy (see Chapter 3—particularly during 1998 to 1999 when nominal interest rates reached a peak of over 25 per cent)—may have contributed to depressing growth rates. However, the Finance Minister's decision for the central bank to adopt inflation targeting from early 2000 under a new Governor greatly improved the transparency, credibility and predictability of monetary policy (Aron and Muellbauer, 2007). With better management of interest rates under inflation targeting and reduced volatility, perceived currency and sovereign credit risks have declined, tax-adjusted real interest rates have been far lower, and annual consumer price inflation fell from high double-digit figures in the 1990s to well within the 3 to 6 per cent target range by late 2003.[12] The fiscal consolidation and improved transparency and predictability of fiscal policy have supported monetary policy: the improved coordination of fiscal and monetary policy is a further strength of post apartheid reform. Fiscal constraint has also helped to bolster national savings, as household saving has fallen sharply. A case could be made that growth could have been more severely compromised had the inherited fiscal threat not been neutralized first, under the difficult conditions of currency volatility and low investor confidence.

---

[11] The assumptions include revenue remaining below 25 per cent of GDP, extra expenditure of 0.1–0.2 per cent of GDP for health (HIV/AIDS treatment), but other non-interest expenditure to remain constant, growth at around 3 per cent per annum, a constant real effective exchange rate and interest rates declining slightly in the medium-term.

[12] From the second quarter of 2007, under pressure from imported oil price and food price inflation, the target was breached (see Chapter 3 for discussion).

The fiscal–monetary policy mix has created an environment of macroeconomic stability conducive to future growth (Aron and Muellbauer, 2005). Empirical evidence suggests that investment in South Africa is substantially driven by uncertainty (see Chapters 2 and 7). This is true for private sector physical capital augmentation, for portfolio capital flows, and for foreign direct investment (Fielding 2000; Fedderke and Liu, 2002; Fedderke, 2004; Fedderke and Romm, 2005). With the improvement of the investment climate through the greater systemic stability of South Africa, and improved policy credibility and transparency, lower business costs have promoted investment in all three dimensions. However, while a more efficient tax burden may have promoted private sector participation in the economy, with low inflation there has been a further shift in effective taxation from the personal to the corporate sector,[13] and effective corporate tax rates remain high by the standards of comparable emerging market countries (Aron and Muellbauer, 2005).

Unfortunately, the public capital constraint is only belatedly receiving extensive policy attention (e.g. significant expansions were planned in the 2005 budget).[14] In line with international evidence, infrastructure in South Africa has been found to influence growth (e.g., Perkins et al., 2005), with electricity capacity having the greatest and most robust impact. Yet there has been a long-term decline in infrastructure investment and capital stock, with real investment per capita falling by 72 per cent from 1976 to 2002 (Bogetić and Fedderke, 2006), that should have been addressed earlier (for further discussion, see Chapter 7). In the case of low-quality education and training, another important long-term constraint on growth, van der Berg (Chapter 12) suggests that fiscal allocation is only part of the solution to these ills.[15] The issue is not the quantum of education expenditure (this is South Africa's single largest non-interest government expenditure item and it spends much more than its developing country counterparts), but effectiveness and efficiency.

---

[13] Corporations can deduct interest on debt from taxable profits, while households cannot deduct such interest from taxable income, and interest rates have fallen with lower inflation.

[14] Most basic service infrastructure is implemented by provincial and local government. The financing for such infrastructure comes from national department budgets which are transferred to the sub-national governments in the form of conditional grants in the Division of Revenue Act. Investment in electricity generation, infrastructure, and ports are all national competences, where there has been under-investment.

[15] Reduced disparities in funding allocation appear not to have reduced the variability of educational outcomes across provinces. Van der Berg finds that large differentials in performance among black schools cannot be attributed to socio-economic background or teaching resources, but rather to school management and the functioning of the schooling system. He concludes that additional fiscal resources on their own can only make a limited contribution to enhancing educational outcomes.

5. Fiscal decentralization

The highly centralized nature of revenue raising powers in South Africa, with increased decentralization of expenditure responsibility, has created a vertical fiscal imbalance. The provincial governments face significant expenditure mandates, but have restricted own financial resources. Provincial governments are highly dependent on the 'equitable share' grant, regulated by s. 214 of the Constitution, to finance the implementation of their constitutionally assigned functions. After deducting interest obligations and other statutory payments from total tax collected by SARS and other revenues, the balance is 'equitably' split up among the three spheres of government. The provinces also receive conditional grants which they have to earmark for pre-specified purposes, such as health, infrastructure, housing, and social development. Equitable share allocations and conditional grants comprised roughly 96 per cent of all provincial revenue in 2003/4. The share of overall nationally collected revenue for national government fell from over 42 per cent in 1989/9 to around 37 per cent by 2005/6 for national government, while rising for provincial and especially local government. This increase in revenue for sub-national governments helped to finance their increased expenditure responsibilities.

The fiscal federalism literature suggests that such a mismatch between revenue and expenditure powers could potentially weaken accountability at the margin and lead to soft budget constraints at sub-national levels, possibly even creating disincentives for raising resources at the national level (Shah, 1994). Conventionally, it is suggested that the assignment of spending responsibility should precede the division of tax powers. However, Rao and Singh (1999) suggest the choice between assigning tax powers and providing transfers to sub-national governments to finance their services, depends upon the trade-off between the additional efficiency loss due to sub-national taxation and efficiency gains from cost-efficient spending by them (plus considerations of regional equity). In Australia, Breton (1996) and Groenewegen (1979) argue that vertical fiscal imbalances in fiscal federal arrangements reflect rational economic motives, as the 'high coordination costs' of administering income tax and some other taxation have required 'high concentration' of powers. Similarly, Momoniat (2002), one of the architects of the South African fiscal system, suggests that the design, though departing from the conventional prescripts of fiscal federalism theory, has been advantageous. He argues for the maximization of the revenue potential of existing revenue sources, and phasing in devolved additional taxation powers only after effective expenditure controls and efficient revenue collection procedures are firmly in place. The risk of moral hazard could then be contained with a strict no-bail out approach by the government, backed by a policy of not guaranteeing sub-national loans or deficits.

The provincial governments, in aggregate, were substantially in deficit from 1996/7, which reverted to a surplus from 1998/9 to 2001/2 (Figure 4.4). That all provincial governments were affected to a greater or lesser extent has suggested systemic problems in the intergovernmental system. Under-budgeting has been cited as the main reason for these deficits rather than over-spending (Department of Finance, 1998:13). The lion's share of provincial budgets is devoted to personnel related expenditures, linked to delivery of labour intensive health and education services, while roughly one third is on social development. This introduces rigidity to provincial budgets, since social security benefits are set nationally and provinces have very little control over salaries. In 1996/7, the employment of teachers and health personnel was expanded with improved remuneration, as provincial governments started addressing backlogs in these two areas. Health and education costs rose by 26 and 31 per cent, respectively, from 1995/6 to 1996/7. An inherited incremental budgeting system, based on the previous year's budgeted figures rather than actual figures, resulted in the budgeted personnel[16] increases falling well below increases in actual expenditure. The situation was compounded by bad financial management systems and lack of effective internal controls. Budget 'gaming'

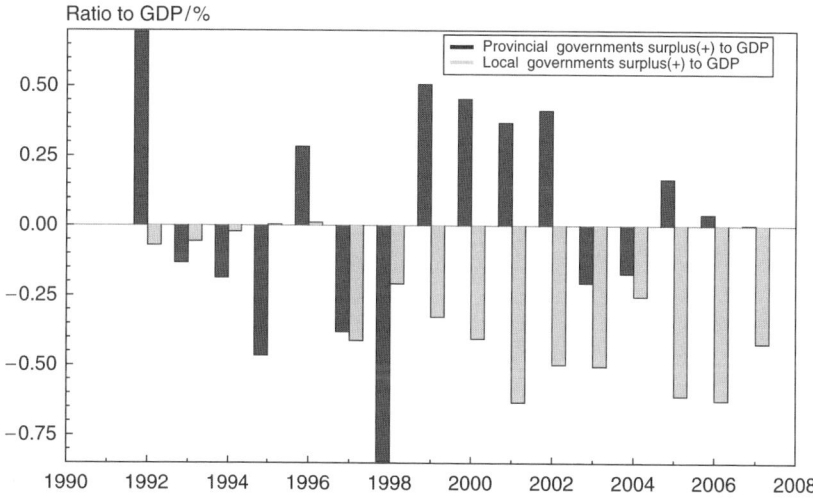

Figure 4.4. Provincial and local governments' deficits and surpluses, fiscal years from 1991/2 to 2006/7

Source: South African Reserve Bank, *Quarterly Bulletin,* various issues.

Note: The fiscal year ends in March, and hence, the year 2007 would refer to 2006/7.

---

[16] Not all civil servants from the ex-homelands had unique identity numbers or were on the government payroll system. In addition, 'ghost' workers were rife.

may also have occurred, where provinces deliberately under-budgeted in the hope of receiving a bail-out from national government.

National government eventually did intervene in terms of s. 100[17] of the Constitution, in response to this overspending episode. The two most affected provinces (the Eastern Cape and KwaZulu-Natal) were bailed out and further funds were distributed to all the provincial governments. There were fears that this would lead to a softening of the provincial governments' budget constraints; however, the bail outs were conditional on improvements in financial management and an undertaking by the affected provinces to run budget surpluses in 1998/9 to repay their debt. This took considerable political will, given the fact that KwaZulu-Natal and the Eastern Cape are two of the poorest provinces in South Africa, with a significant social backlog. A further payment was allocated to provincial governments in the 1998/9 adjustments budget, conditional on their agreement to implement debt repayment schedules.

The surpluses in 1999/2000 and in 2000/1 were not solely a response to debt repayment obligations. They also reflected an inability to spend budget allocations, with the binding constraint not being purely financial, but rather one of management capacity, especially in relation to capital projects.[18] The fiscal constriction coupled with an inability to spend effectively, impacted on service delivery in the Eastern Cape and KwaZulu-Natal between 1995/6 and 2000/1. Significantly lower growth rates resulted for social development expenditure and education in these two provinces, by comparison with other historically disadvantaged provinces, such as Limpopo, Mpumalanga, and the North West.[19]

A conditional grant for spending on social grants arrears in the 2002/3 financial year was transferred at the end of the 2001/2 fiscal year. When this is netted out, the 2001/2 surplus declines significantly. In 2002/3 and 2003/4, provincial governments again ran deficits (Figure 4.4). The 2002/3 deficits

---

[17] This allows national government to intervene when a provincial government fails to meet an executive obligation. The Eastern Cape government had failed to make welfare payments, triggering constitutional court challenges, and had failed to pay creditors.

[18] This inability to spend resulted in rollovers, for instance, with some 71 per cent of housing funds rolled over in 1995/6, 20 per cent in 2000/1 and 12 per cent in 2001/2 (National Treasury, 2003: 163). Although 1,614,512 houses had been built by the end of 2003/4 (National Treasury, 2004: 125), the rate of delivery has been insufficient to meet a housing backlog estimated at 2,406,747 units using Census 2001 data (National Treasury, 2003: 127).

[19] The horizontal division of the total provincial share to the individual provinces (and of the total local government share to individual municipalities) is effected by means of a formula. The formula is updated to reflect new census data, typically phased in over time in order to avoid undermining the predictability of provincial budgets. This primarily demographically driven formula is highly redistributive. Between 1998/9 and 2003/4, of the nine new provinces, the Northern Cape's share has remained fairly constant, the Western Cape and Eastern Cape shares have declined, and the shares of the more populous Gauteng, KwaZulu-Natal, and Limpopo have increased.

were planned and budgeted for, funded from the cash balances available to provincial governments after debt payments (National Treasury, 2003: 15). The deficits were also driven by increases in transfers, in particular, the child support grant. Of the combined provincial deficit in 2003/4, just over half was due to over-expenditure on social security grants, which had grown at an annualized rate of over 40 per cent (National Treasury, 2004: 158). The following three fiscal years again saw provincial surpluses.

The pressures of social grants on provincial budgets, and the potential for efficiency gains through increased economies of scale, saw responsibility for the payment of social grants re-assigned to a single national agency (the South African Social Security Agency) in April 2006. The new configuration is more closely aligned to fiscal federalism theory, which recommends that distribution functions be located at the national level (Musgrave and Musgrave, 1989). 'Social services' jointly consume the bulk of non-interest consolidated national and provincial expenditure, averaging just below 60 per cent of total expenditure. SA has a substantial system of state-provided social assistance, exceptional compared with many other middle-income countries (Chapter 10; Agüero et al., 2007; Case and Deaton, 1998). While education and health expenditure have fallen as a percentage of non-interest expenditure between 1997/8 and 2006/7 (remaining fairly constant in real terms), social welfare expenditure, which includes means-tested child support grants, disability grants and universal old age grants, is expected to increase to 18.5 per cent of non-interest expenditure in the MTEF period, from a low of 14 per cent in 1997/8. This would make it the second largest category after education spending.

Social security grant beneficiaries have increased rapidly, from 5.8 million in 2003 to 11.9 million in 2007 (National Treasury, 2007a). While old-age pension beneficiaries have only increased at an average annual growth rate of 2 per cent, the safety net for children beneficiaries under 14 years old has been progressively widened over this period. Child support grant beneficiaries rose from 2.6 million in 2003 to 7.8 million in 2007, with an annual average growth rate of 31.6 per cent. The foster care grant and the care dependency grant grew annually at an average growth rate of 28.7 per cent and 15.6 per cent, respectively (National Treasury, 2007a). Research has indicated that this unprecedented expansion in income support has been well targeted; for instance, Agüero et al. (2007) have found robust evidence that these targeted unconditional payments have bolstered early childhood nutrition as measured by child height-for-age, and they also present evidence for the likely beneficial long-term raised earnings based on these short-term transfers (see also Chapter 10). Large increases in entitlement spending may, however, tend to create fiscal rigidities, be politically irreversible and reduce fiscal discretion during business cycle downturns.

The government has committed to further social security and retirement financing reform. Currently under consideration is a mandatory contributory earnings-related savings and social insurance framework, accompanied by a wage subsidy for those with incomes below the personal income tax threshold (National Treasury, 2007b). This would provide basic retirement, death and disability benefits, and would bridge the currently existing gap between social assistance grant arrangement, which caters for the poorest of the poor, and the tax-incentivized private pensions sector, catering for formal sector employees.

What implications do these outcomes hold for the political economy of South Africa and the balance of power between the provincial and federal levels of government? The bottom line is that while South Africa has done well in stabilizing the macro-economy, the microeconomic objectives still require concerted focus. There have been considerable achievements in reprioritization of expenditures from defence and subsidies towards health, education, and social development accompanied by improvements in access to public services. However, deep concerns remain about the quality of education, health, housing, and other provincial service delivery outputs and about their impact on poverty reduction and the progressive realization of socio-economic rights (see Ajam and Aron, 2007; and Chapter 12).

The creation of the provincial governments was not driven by economic motives, but primarily political motives. There is now concern about the future of provincial governments, especially those that are not performing adequately. Hunter and Ajam (2007) contend that while there may be political or social motivations for maintaining the provincial governments in their current incarnation, there is no cogent fiscal or financial rationale. The static and dynamic allocative efficiency enhancements suggested by fiscal federalism theory can be achieved when a province has sufficient discretion over its budget to allow it to be responsive to regional priorities, and it should be held accountable by its electorate for its decisions. The lack of meaningful revenue raising powers and limited budgetary discretion (e.g. through increasing conditionality of grants, nationally imposed norms and standards for service delivery and centrally bargained wage settlements) means that it is difficult to hold provincial governments accountable in practice.

6. Conclusion

South Africa has overcome adverse initial conditions and achieved a remarkable fiscal transformation since 1994 through adopting durable, credible and well-coordinated reforms, outlined in earlier sections of this paper. Constitutionally-based reforms have rendered policy at all levels of government more transparent and accountable, and more predictable through multi-year budgeting. Expenditure restraint was exercised initially while the tax system was comprehensively overhauled, promoting a more durable adjustment (Mackenzie et al., 1997). The composition of the fiscal adjustments, containing personnel related expenditures, subsidies, and transfers while actually lowering both company and personal tax rates, have further enhanced the credibility and likely durability of the reform (Alesina et al., 1998; Alesina and Ardagna, 1998).

Allsopp and Vines (2005) maintain there is an active role for fiscal policy in flexible inflation targeting regimes in setting the policy mix and in managing shocks and imbalances. The fiscal–monetary policy mix in South Africa has created an environment of macroeconomic stability conducive to future growth. Inflation targeting was successfully introduced and the restrained fiscal stance and improved debt management has helped support a low inflation monetary policy (Chapter 3). Lower and more predictable inflation and interest rates have helped contain business costs, while greater fiscal and monetary policy credibility and transparency has reduced uncertainty in the economy. South Africa's international economic standing has been enhanced, evidenced by reduced sovereign risk spreads and improved debt ratings.

The undoubted macro-stability gains contrast sharply with poor delivery at the micro-economic level. The fiscal strategy underpinning the GEAR macro-programme was based on two major objectives. The first was a deficit reduction strategy. The second pillar was the budget reform programme to strengthen redistribution. The underlying rationale seems to have been that even though the quantum of expenditure would decline, this would be offset by the enhanced equity, efficiency, and effectiveness in the way these resources were used. While the former objective has been attained, the latter has, at best, only been partially achieved. International reform experience cautions that the benefits of budget reforms such as the medium term expenditure framework, performance-based budgeting and accruals only manifest themselves over an eight to ten year horizon. The sheer magnitude of the budget reform project was probably underestimated by the incoming government, both because the degree and scope of dysfunction in the inherited apartheid fiscal machinery could not have been fully ascertained then, and given the magnitude of the economic development problems facing South Africa. The timing and synchronization of the costs and benefits of these two strategies has also proved problematic. Deficit reduction created immediate, concentrated costs to society, with its (uncertain) benefits only to be realized in the future. There were also substantial set-up costs associated with the budget reform, and thereafter, incremental maintenance costs.

Poor micro-service delivery in social expenditure, and the difficulty in holding provincial governments accountable given the loss of revenue raising powers and limited budgetary discretion in a more centralized fiscal system, has motivated a policy review on the structure and functions of provincial and local government.[20] One set of proposals involves retaining provincial governments, albeit in an altered form. One suggestion is to amalgamate provincial governments (e.g. Northern Cape and Western Cape; or Mpumalanga, Gauteng, and Limpopo back into the old 'Transvaal'). An alternative is to disestablish provincial legislatures, turning provincial governments back into administrative arms only. Unfortunately, the creation of the nine provincial legislatures created political rents for governing party elected members who could not get onto the national party list, and resistance could be expected from this vested-interest group. A further option would be changing the basis for political representation in provinces. Instead of their being elected directly on a proportional representation basis, they could rather be appointed or elected from each of the local governments in the province. Van Ryneveld (2007) suggests that it may be appropriate to leave social services (such as education and health) to the provincial governments and devolve built-environment services (such as transport and infrastructure) to local government. If further responsibility of financing social services were devolved to municipalities, poor municipalities would find themselves in the predicament of greater need because of greater poverty but simultaneously lower revenue capability as a result of low levels of economic activity. Provision of basic services (water, sanitation, etc.) will have to continue to be grant funded in the interests of equity. A second set of proposals involves eliminating provincial governments completely in favour of a more powerful local government sphere. However, there are also serious concerns about the ability of the local sphere (especially district municipalities) to deliver. This has prompted recommendations that the role of district municipalities be redefined to a more limited focus, mainly on coordination, bulk supply of services to local municipalities, and support of weaker local municipalities, or be abolished completely resulting a single tier local government structure.

The hard-won sustainability of fiscal policy might still be threatened in the future. Reduced revenue collection windfalls from tax reform coupled with fiscal risk from the existing social security entitlements will have to be carefully managed. The government's recent focus on the cyclically-adjusted budget balance as a measure of fiscal stance is an attempt to take into account the temporary nature of revenue gains as a result of high commodity prices. Recent surpluses on the conventional balance budget (2008/9) provide the fiscal room for stabilization in response to deteriorating trade conditions or increased financial risk.

---

[20] Department of Local and Provincial Government, 2007, expected to culminate in a White Paper in 2008.

However, mediocre improvements in the quality and scope of actual service delivery and the continuing dearth of management capacity for delivery, in a context of an increasing number of households, the ravages of HIV/AIDS, improvements in economic growth insufficient to substantially lower unemployment and persisting poverty, inequality and deprivation, could mean the government will face increasing pressure to extend existing cash-based entitlements. Lobbying in recent years for the proposed introduction of a universal Basic Income Grant is a case in point. Political sustainability of policies is at least as important as fiscal sustainability. Further, a long-term decline in infrastructure investment and capital stock is only belatedly receiving attention. The challenge for South Africa is to increase social and infrastructure expenditure at a sustainable rate and to enhance the quality of service delivery, to avoid undermining the impressive fiscal stability gains at the macroeconomic level.

References

Abedian, I. (1998) 'Fiscal Policy and Economic Growth', in I. Abedian and B. Standish (eds.) *Economic Growth in South Africa: Selected Policy Issues*, Cape Town: Oxford University Press.

Agüero, J. M., M. R. Carter and I. Woolard. (2007). 'The Impact of Unconditional Cash Transfers on Nutrition: the South African Child Support Grant', International Poverty Centre, *Working Paper* no 39, September.

Ajam, T. and J. Aron (2007) 'Fiscal Renaissance in a Democratic South Africa', *Journal of African Economies*, 16(5): 745–81.

Alesina, A. and S. Ardagna (1998) 'Tales of Fiscal Adjustment', *Economic Policy*, 27 (October): 487–546.

Alesina, A., R. Perotti, and J. Tavares (1998) 'The Political Economy of Fiscal Adjustments', *Brookings Papers on Economic Activity*, 1: 197–266.

Allsopp, C. and D. Vines, (2005) 'The Macroeconomic Role of Fiscal Policy', *Oxford Review of Economic Policy*, 21(4):485–508.

Aron, J. and J. Muellbauer (2007) 'Transparency, Credibility and Predictability of Monetary Policy in South Africa', paper presented at the Bank of England/Cornell University workshop on New Developments in Monetary Policy in Emerging Market Economies, Bank of England, 17–18 July 2007.

Aron, J. and J. Muellbauer (2005) 'Monetary Policy, Macro-Stability and Growth: South Africa's Recent Experience and Lessons', *World Economics*, 6(4): 123–47.

Black, P., K. Siebrits, and T. van der Merwe (2005) 'Public Expenditure and Growth', in Black, Calitz and Associates (eds.) *Public Economics*, 3rd edn, Oxford University Press.

Bogetić, Z. and J. W. Fedderke (2006) 'Forecasting Investment Needs In South Africa's Electricity And Telecom Sectors', *South African Journal of Economics*, 74(3): 557–74.

Breton, A. (1996) *Competitive Governments: An Economic Theory of Politics and Public Finance*, Toronto: Cambridge University Press.

Calitz, E. (2000) 'Fiscal Implications of the Economic Globalisation of South Africa', *South African Journal of Economics*, 68(4): 564–606.

Calitz, E. and K. Siebrits (2003) 'Fiscal Policy in the 1990s', *South African Journal of Economic History*, 18(1&2): 50–75.

Case, A. and A. Deaton (1998) 'Large Cash Transfers to the Elderly in South Africa', *Economic Journal*, 108: 1330—61.

Department of Finance (1997) *Budget Review 1997*, Pretoria: Government Printers.

—— (1998) *Budget Review 1998*, Pretoria: Government Printers.

Fedderke, J. W. (2004) 'Investment in Fixed Capital Stock: Testing for the Impact of Sectoral and Systematic Uncertainty', *Oxford Bulletin of Economics and Statistics*, 66(2): 165–87.

Fedderke, J. W. and W. Liu (2002) 'Modelling the Determinants of Capital Flows and Capital Flight: With an Application to South African Data from 1960 to 1995', *Economic Modelling*, 19(3): 419–44.

Fedderke, J. W. and A. T. Romm (2005) 'Growth Impact and Determinants of Foreign Direct Investment into South Africa, 1956–2003', *Economic Modelling*, 23(5): 738–60.

Fielding, D. (2000) 'Investment under Credit Rationing and Uncertainty: Evidence from South Africa', *Journal of African Economies*, 9(2): 189–212.

Groenewegen, P. D. (1979) 'Federalism', in A. Patience and B. Head (eds.) *From Whitlam to Fraser*, Melbourne: Oxford University Press.

Horton, M. 2005. 'Role of Fiscal Policy in Stabilization and Poverty Alleviation', in N. Nowak and L. Ricci (eds.) *Post-Apartheid South Africa*, International Monetary Fund, ch. 2.

Hunter, R. and T. Ajam (2007) 'Theme Paper on Provincial Government Finance', Unpublished research paper commissioned by the Department of Provincial and Local Government as part of its Policy Review on Provincial and Local Government.

Kopits, G. and S. Symansky (1998) 'Fiscal Policy Rules', *IMF Occasional Paper* 162, Washington D.C.: International Monetary Fund.

Mackenzie, G. A., W. H. Orsmond, and P. Gerson (1997) 'The Composition of Fiscal Adjustment and Growth: Lessons from Fiscal Reforms in Eight Economies', *IMF Occasional Paper* 149, Washington, D.C.: International Monetary Fund.

Meltzer, A. H. and S. F. Richard (1981) 'A Rational Theory of the Size of Government', *Journal of Political Economy*, 89(5): 914–27.

Momoniat, I. (2002) 'Fiscal Decentralisation in South Africa: A Practitioner's Perspective', Mimeo, National Treasury, South Africa.

Musgrave, R. A. and P. B. Musgrave (1989) *Public Finance in Theory and Practice*, 5th edn. New York: McGraw-Hill.

National Treasury (2003) *Intergovernmental Fiscal Review*, Pretoria: Government Printers.

—— (2004) *Budget Review 2004*, Pretoria: Government Printers.

—— (2005) *Budget Review 2005*, Pretoria: Government Printers.

—— (2006) *Budget Review 2006*, Pretoria: Government Printers

—— (2007a) *Budget Review 2007*, Pretoria: Government Printers.

—— (2007b) *Medium Term Budget Policy Statement 2007*, Pretoria: Government Printers.

Perkins, P., J. W. Fedderke, and J. Luiz (2005) 'An Analysis of Economic Infrastructure Investment in South Africa', *South African Journal of Economics*, 73(2): 211–28.

Rao, M. G. and N. Singh (1999) 'The Assignment of Taxes and Expenditures in India', *CREDPR Working Paper*, March, 1999, Economics Department, University of California Santa Cruz.

Shah, A. (1994) 'The Reform of Intergovernmental Fiscal Relations in Developing and Emerging Market Economies', *Policy and Research Series* 23, World Bank, Washington DC.

Siebrits, F. K. and E. Calitz (2004) 'Should South Africa Adopt Numerical Rules', *South African Journal of Economics*, 72(4): 759–70.

Swanepoel, J. A. and N. J. Schoeman (2003) 'Countercyclical Fiscal Policy in South Africa: Role and Impact of Automatic Fiscal Stabilisers', *South African Journal of Economic and Management Studies*, 6(4): 802–22.

van der Berg, S. (2001) 'Trends in Racial Fiscal Incidence in South Africa', *South African Journal of Economics*, 69(2): 243–68.

van der Berg, S. (2007) 'Apartheid's Enduring Legacy: Inequalities in Education', *Journal of African Economies*, 16(5): 849–80.

van Ryneveld, P. (2007) 'Review of Local Government Finance', Unpublished research paper commissioned by the Department of Provincial and Local Government as part of its Policy Review on Provincial and Local Government.

5
Capital Flows, Financial Markets, and the External Balance Sheet

Jonathan Leape and Lynne Thomas

1. Introduction[1]

Following the political transition in 1994, the South African government implemented major policy reforms to facilitate foreign capital inflows while also gradually permitting increased capital outflows by South African residents. The result has been a transformation in the external position, with net foreign investment helping to alleviate the constraints implied by low levels of domestic savings (Figure 5.1). Changes in the level and composition of capital inflows have been an important feature of the economic policy environment, both in terms of supporting strategies for increasing economic growth and in managing the impact of external shocks.

In this chapter, we examine the volume and composition of capital flows in South Africa, distinguishing between net flows of foreign (non-resident) capital and net flows of domestic (resident) capital. Two key themes of the chapter are the response of investors to capital account liberalization and the role of domestic capital markets in influencing the composition of flows. We begin in section 2 with an assessment of exchange control reform in South Africa, emphasizing the gradual nature of the liberalization strategy and the priority given to macroeconomic and financial sector stability.

Section 3 examines the composition of foreign capital inflows, in particular the high levels of inward portfolio investment supported by developed

---

[1] Acknowledgements: This chapter draws on a three-year research programme on capital flows, financial regulation and tax policy, funded by the South African National Treasury. The authors are grateful to Ismail Momoniat at National Treasury for initiating the research and to Jonathan Dixon and Olano Makhubela for valuable discussions. The authors also thank Janine Aron and Brian Kahn for comments; and the South African Reserve Bank for assistance with data. The views expressed are those of the authors.

local capital markets. A distinction is made between short-term trading by non-residents in the local bond market and investment in the South African equity market which has provided a comparatively long-term form of external financing. Building on this analysis, we assess whether South Africa is underweight or overweight in emerging market equity portfolios relative to international benchmarks based on market size and GDP and draw conclusions for future investment flows. Foreign direct investment (FDI) has been low relative to portfolio investment in South Africa and also relative to the average across middle-income economies. While other studies have focused on the low level of FDI and areas for improvement in the investment environment, our analysis emphasizes the large, relatively long-term portfolio equity investment supported by South Africa's developed financial markets. One implication is that strategies to attract foreign investment should take into account both types of flows.

Section 4 focuses on outward investment by South African residents in the form of institutional investors, companies and individuals. Drawing on the discussion of exchange control reform, we show that holdings of foreign assets have increased substantially since 1995 and that much of this increase has occurred as a result of the liberalization of institutional investment. We examine the presence of home bias in equity portfolios across selected countries and find that South Africa is broadly in line with international experience; moreover, remaining exchange controls are not a convincing sole explanation for the apparent preference for domestic equities in the case of South Africa, suggesting that there are other limits to capital outflows.

Section 5 concludes with an assessment of the implications of the changes in the financial account since 1994 for the external balance sheet and for macroeconomic policy.

2. Exchange control liberalization

The political transition in the early 1990s triggered a series of policy changes aimed at normalizing South Africa's external position.

The reform strategy gave priority to the elimination of restrictions on foreign investors. The first step was the final resolution of the foreign debt standstill, a moratorium on the repayment of foreign loans imposed by the South African government during the crisis of 1985, when foreign credit lines to South Africa were withdrawn. A further step was taken in late 1994, with the acquisition of credit ratings from the principal international rating agencies and the issue of a US$750 million global bond by the government, marking South Africa's re-entry into international capital markets. This was followed by the abolition, in March 1995, of the financial rand, the dual exchange rate

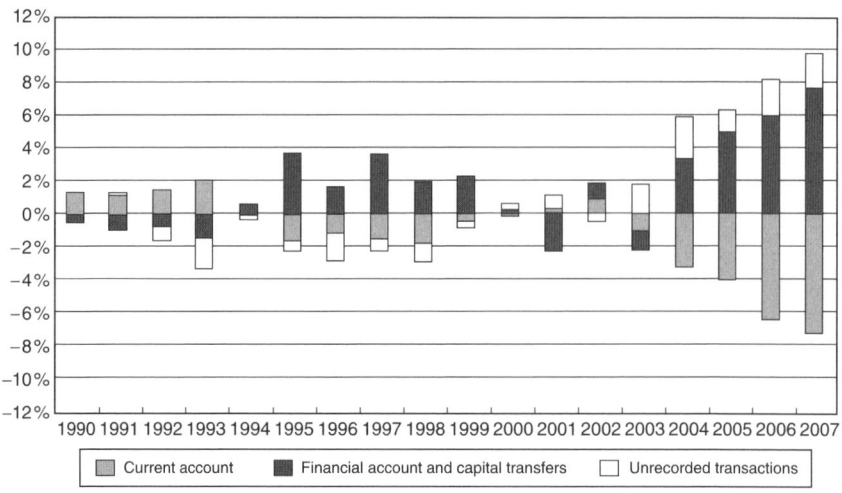

Figure 5.1. Balance of payments, per cent of GDP
Source: Calculated from *Quarterly Bulletin*, March 2008 dataset, South African Reserve Bank.

mechanism that had been in place since 1961 (apart from a brief interlude in 1983–5). The removal of the dual exchange rate regime marked the end of virtually all exchange control restrictions on non-residents.

With respect to residents, South Africa has followed a gradual approach to the liberalization of exchange controls, mainly in the form of phased increases in allowances for foreign investments by institutional investors (retirement funds, long-term insurers, collective investment schemes, and investment managers), companies, and individuals. Liberalization has been particularly significant for institutional investors. Their dominant position in personal savings combined with existing supervisory controls makes institutional investors a natural conduit for international diversification without risk of illegal capital flight and tax evasion, while their large, mostly rand-denominated domestic liabilities create a natural limit to their demand for foreign assets.[2] Macroeconomic stabilization and financial sector development have taken precedence over the rapid elimination of controls in order to create the conditions for an orderly process of foreign diversification by domestic investors, with limited risks to financial stability. The importance of sequencing and

---

[2] Some level of foreign investment is, of course, desirable for institutional investors from the perspective of the diversification of investment risk. International diversification may also be desirable in the context where pensioners consume imported goods and services (e.g., Davis, 2002).

coordination of capital account liberalization and financial sector development has been emphasized in international debates (for instance, Ishii and Habermeier, 2002). Moreover, some international studies suggest that certain types of capital controls may still have a useful role in macroeconomic management (for instance, Williamson et al., 2003; and Kaplan and Rodrik, 2001), although there is no consensus in this area (for instance, Forbes, 2005, explores the costs imposed by capital controls).[3]

2.1. External reform in South Africa

One distinguishing feature of external reform in South Africa has been the priority given to minimizing market and macroeconomic disruption. This has been reflected in three aspects of the reform strategy. Firstly, virtually all reforms have been implemented gradually, in contrast to the 'big bang' strategies pursued in some other emerging market countries. This approach minimized the volume of funds affected at any point in time, and hence the impact on key prices (especially the exchange rate), while also enabling the government to implement a flexible strategy for reform, responding to private sector reactions and changing economic circumstances. A second, related aspect has been management of private sector expectations in the lead up to changes. This was most evident in the preparations for the elimination of the dual exchange rate mechanism in 1994–5, when official and unofficial announcements, combined with foreign exchange intervention, led to a gradually narrowing spread between the financial rand and the commercial rand, limiting the scope for speculative positions that might otherwise have derailed reform. Finally, attention has been given to establishing appropriate fiscal and regulatory frameworks before reforms are implemented, e.g., by tightening the fiscal position after 1994, by formalizing government guarantee arrangements in 1997 and by strengthening supervision of financial institutions over the period. Gradualism has produced internal and external criticism about the slow pace of reform, but it has also avoided policy reversals—even during the currency crises in 1996, 1998, and 2001.

Another distinguishing feature of foreign exchange reforms in South Africa has been the sharply different strategies pursued with respect to resident and non-resident investors, as noted above. This divergent treatment of residents and non-residents has had implications for the role of exchange controls in macroeconomic management. In Chile, for example, variable deposit requirements were imposed on all foreign credits to strengthen the authorities' ability

---

[3] International evidence on the economic impact of controls is rather mixed not least because there are substantial measurement problems in defining and analysing controls (Eichengreen, 2001).

to manage the impact of capital inflows on domestic liquidity and aggregate demand. In South Africa, however, efforts to manage the impact of capital flows on domestic liquidity have been limited to manipulation of the controls on residents and largely restricted to the timing of reforms. Periods of capital inflows have often been characterized by significant reforms to the remaining exchange controls on residents, while periods of instability and capital outflows have usually been characterized by a much slower pace of reform.

Finally, the reform strategy pursued by South Africa has recognized that exchange controls have historically performed a variety of regulatory functions, many of which continue to be important in a post-exchange control environment. This has contributed to the gradualist reform strategy, as emphasis has been given to identifying where alternative regulatory instruments are required and to ensuring a smooth transition to the new regulatory regime. These considerations have been most salient in the reform of exchange controls on institutional investors, where a shift to prudential regulation of foreign exposure has been implemented over an extended period. A more general concern that has run through the reform process is the continuing need for effective regulatory instruments for macroeconomic risk management. The frequency of international financial crises and, more broadly, the volatile external environment facing emerging economies have demonstrated the potentially destabilizing effects of cross-border capital flows. For this reason, while restrictions on cross-border transactions, and the associated market distortions, have been reduced, South Africa has retained a degree of regulatory control.

In common with international experience, exchange controls have not been fully effective in preventing capital outflows. An exchange control and tax amnesty introduced in 2003–4 resulted in R68.6 billion in foreign assets being declared, equivalent to around 12 per cent of South Africa's total private foreign assets at the end of 2003. While attempts to estimate the magnitude of capital flight have produced markedly different results (see, for example, Kahn, 1991; Smit and Mocke, 1991; and Fedderke and Liu, 2002), it is clear that illegal flows have, historically, represented an important channel for resident outflows.

2.2. A chronology of reforms

Up until 1995, South African residents had limited (legal) options for international diversification given the extensive exchange control regime. South African companies could obtain permission to invest abroad; approval depended on national interests and the use of foreign funding was encouraged. Shareholdings in domestic companies with foreign investments—'rand hedge' shares—provided the main legal channel for acquiring international exposure for South African institutions and individuals in the presence of strict exchange controls.

Capital Flows, Financial Markets, and the External Balance Sheet

As shown in Table 5.1, exchange control reform created a series of new channels for international investment by residents. Foreign asset allowances for the large institutional investor sector were introduced, first through asset swaps with foreign investors and later with no requirements for matching inward investment; the final shift from exchange controls to prudential regulation of foreign investment was announced in 2008. Private individuals were permitted to invest an increasing amount of funds directly abroad, as well as through domestic institutional investors. The exchange control regime for corporate FDI was liberalized, with increasing flexibility in the use of domestic capital in financing approved outward investments and an expanded definition of FDI in terms of the ownership threshold. As explored in section 4, another important factor has been the re-domiciling of a number of large South African multinationals, which has provided an additional channel for international diversification.

While the reforms undertaken to date have eliminated the most distortionary aspects of exchange controls, some constraints remain with implications for potential future outflows. The 'blocked rand' system, which limited emigrants' ability to expatriate their South African capital, has been liberalized but retains a limit (in line with private individuals), above which outflows are subject to an exit tax. Resident individuals remain subject to a variety of minor controls on cross-border transactions, most of which are intended to support the limit on outward investment. Restrictions have also been retained on companies' passive (portfolio) investments. New limits for banks' foreign asset holdings were first announced in 2005, with further reforms set out in 2008, suggesting that portfolio adjustments in that sector may now occur.

While the reform of exchange controls thus remains incomplete in certain respects, the dominant forms of investment have now been substantially or wholly liberalized. As explored in section 4, the available evidence suggests that most of the adjustment to exchange control reform has now taken place.

3. Foreign investment in South Africa

Portfolio investment has dominated net foreign (non-resident) capital inflows into South Africa for most of the period since 1994 (Figure 5.2).[4] Inflows of FDI capital have been comparatively low, although there have been periods of

---

[4] Foreign investment has three broad categories, as defined in the IMF *Balance of Payments Manual* (5th edn, 1993). *Foreign direct investment* (FDI) consists of net flows of equity and other capital from foreign investors with a significant degree of influence or control of the local enterprise, typically involving an ownership stake of 10 per cent or more or other means of influence. *Portfolio investment* consists of investment in debt and equity securities (other than FDI). *Other investment* consists of residual flows that are not captured as FDI or portfolio investment, including loans, trade credit, currency and deposits, and other liabilities.

Table 5.1. Summary of major exchange control liberalizations for South African residents

1. South African institutional investors

1995: Asset swap mechanism allows institutions to exchange up to 5 per cent of total assets for foreign assets in approved arrangements with foreign counterparties. Institutions include retirement funds, long-term insurers, and collective investment scheme (CIS) companies, extended to approved investment managers in **1997**.

1996: Foreign asset limit increases to 10 per cent through asset swaps or a cash flow allowance of 3 per cent of the net inflow of funds, extended with a further cash flow allowance of 2 per cent for equity investment in SADC countries in **1997**.

1998: Foreign asset limit increases to 15 per cent, with cash flow allowance of 10 per cent (in SADC) and 5 per cent (in rest of world).

2000: Foreign asset limit for CIS companies increases to 20 per cent. Cash flow allowance equalised at 10 per cent.

2001: Asset swap mechanism is removed; cash flow allowances are maintained in 2001 but not renewed in **2002**.

2003: Foreign investment is permitted up to existing limits without asset swap or cash flow restrictions but subject to application. New reporting requirements are introduced in a shift towards prudential regulation.

2004: An additional allowance of 5 per cent of assets is introduced for investment in locally-listed African securities, extended to all portfolio investment in Africa in **2006**.

2005: Foreign asset limit for CIS companies and investment managers increases to 25 per cent.

2008: Final shift to prudential regulation of foreign exposure is announced. Foreign asset limits increase to 20 per cent for retirement funds and the underwritten policies of long-term insurers and 30 per cent for CIS companies, investment managers and the investment-linked policies of long-term insurers, with further work on final limits taking place in 2008. The pre-application process is replaced with a reporting system.

2. South African private individuals

1997: Foreign investment allowance enables individuals to invest up to R200,000 abroad, subject to tax compliance, with associated allowances for travel and other expenditures. Investment allowance increases to R400,000 in **1998**, R500,000 in **1999**, and R750,000 in **2000**.

2003: A joint exchange control and tax amnesty is announced; R68.6 billion of foreign assets is declared under this initiative. The allowance for emigrants to take funds out of South Africa is equalised with the individual investment allowance; amounts above this can be transferred subject to a 10 per cent levy and exiting schedule. This applies to both new emigrants and emigrants with blocked assets.

2006: Investment allowance increases to R2 million, following completion of amnesty process. The allowance remains at this level as of **2008**, with a streamlined allowance of R500,000 for travel, gifts, maintenance etc.

3. South African companies: FDI

1997: Allowances permit the use of domestic funds in financing approved FDI: R50 million for investment in SADC; R30 million for investment in the rest of the world (up from R20 million in **1996**). Companies are permitted to raise foreign funding on the strength of the domestic balance sheet.

1998: Allowances for the use of domestic funds increase to R250 million (SADC) and R50 million (rest of world)

2000: The use of domestic funds is extended to cover: (i) 10 per cent of investment where total cost exceeds the R50 million and R250 million limits; (ii) repayment of 10 per cent of foreign debt raised to finance FDI.

2001: Investment allowances increase to R750 million (Africa) and R500 million (rest of the world).

2002: Investment allowance increases to R2 billion for investment in Africa.

2003:	Investment allowance increases to R1 billion for investment outside Africa. Use of the allowances is extended to financing approved expansions of existing investments. Repatriated earnings from foreign subsidiaries may be used for subsequent approved investment without limit.
2004:	Allowance for funding the excess cost of approved investment increases to 20 per cent of cost above the R2 billion or R1 billion limit. Allowance for repayment of foreign loans increases to the greater of R1 billion per investment (R2 billion for Africa) or 20 per cent of total loan capital (February).
	Limits on financing new FDI are removed; the approval process continues to apply. Earnings from foreign subsidiaries may be retained or transferred offshore for any purpose (October).
2006:	Requirement for *majority* ownership of FDI (ownership share of more than 50 per cent) is reduced to a threshold of 25 per cent for investments in Africa.
2007:	Ownership threshold for FDI outside of Africa is reduced to 25 per cent.
2008:	Approval process for FDI is removed for company transactions amounting to less than R50 million per year. Ownership threshold for FDI is further reduced to the acquisition of 10 per cent of voting rights.

4. Other liberalizations

1996:	The allowance for local borrowing by foreign-owned companies is increased to 100 per cent of shareholder investment. This is further increased in **2004** to 300 per cent.
2004:	Foreign firms are permitted to list on the JSE and BESA, with additional institutional allowances (as above) to support listings by African companies, institutions and governments. Resident investment in these securities is limited initially to institutional investors and private individuals but extended to companies, trusts, partnerships and banks in **2008**.
2005:	South African banks are permitted to hold foreign assets of up to 40 per cent of domestic regulatory capital as part of shift to prudential regulation of foreign exposure. In **2008**, a further announcement is made of the intention to simplify the regulation of foreign exposure for banks, within a macro-prudential limit of 40 per cent of liabilities.
2007:	JSE receives permission to establish a rand currency futures market. Participation in this market without restriction is extended to companies, trusts, partnerships and banks in **2008**.

Source: National Treasury *Budget Review*, *Budget Speech*, and *Medium-Term Budget Policy Statement*, various years <www.treasury.gov.za>; South African Reserve Bank, *Exchange Control Manual* <www.reservebank.co.za>

Note: The complexity of exchange controls and the liberalization process means that this summary is necessarily selective and concise, rather than comprehensive. Dates reflect the timing of announcements.

substantial inflows with several large transactions. Net flows of other investment have generally been smaller than portfolio investment, although this form of investment increased in 2005–2007.[5] The higher share of portfolio investment relative to FDI contrasts with the experience in other developing and emerging market economies: between 1994 and 2002, FDI accounted for 30 per cent of capital inflows in South Africa, compared to just over 70 per cent for emerging economies with similar risk characteristics (Ahmed et al., 2005).

---

[5] Various editions of the Reserve Bank *Quarterly Bulletin* between 2006 and 2007 highlight the role of loans and non-resident deposits with South African banks in driving these flows.

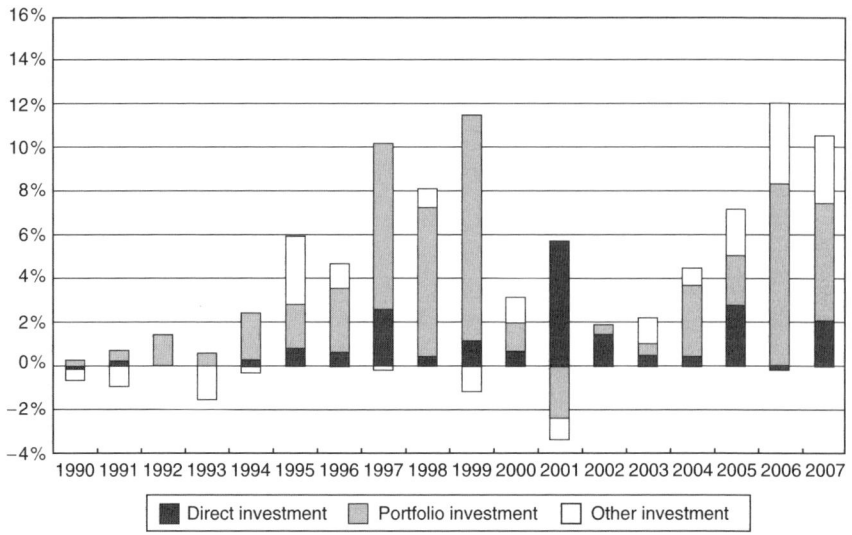

Figure 5.2. Composition of net inflows of foreign capital, per cent of GDP
Source: Calculated from *Quarterly Bulletin*, March 2008 dataset, South African Reserve Bank.
Note: Direct investment, portfolio investment, and other investment are defined in the main text.

The international literature on capital flows has explored the role of various factors in determining the mix of FDI, portfolio and other forms of flows, including financial market and associated institutional development, exchange rate policies, capital controls, and international interest rates.[6] There have also been several studies examining the determinants and composition of capital flows to South Africa.

Fedderke and Liu (2002) confirm the impact of political risk on capital flows and flight from South Africa between 1960 and 1995, as well as the expected role of favourable growth prospects and improved (relative) returns in attracting capital inflows. Wesso (2001) examines quarterly total net capital flows (liabilities and assets) in South Africa between 1991 and 2000 and identifies positive impacts for stronger growth and increased (relative) returns, and negative effects for higher inflation and government deficits. These studies highlight the importance of measures to support political and macroeconomic stability, although structural changes in the period since 1995 suggest that an updated analysis of the determinants and composition of capital flows would

---

[6] See, for example, Ahmed et al. (2005), Goldstein and Razin (2005), Albuquerque (2003), Hausmann and Fernández-Arias (2000), Montiel and Reinhart (1999), Taylor and Sarno (1997).

be useful, as well as a distinction between the factors influencing net inflows by non-residents and net outflows by residents.

Ahmed et al. (2005) examine capital flows to developing countries between 1975 and 2002. They distinguish between common determinants of FDI and portfolio investment, such as growth, the quality of institutions, and international interest rates, and determinants specific to particular types of capital flows. Factors found to influence FDI include: trade openness and better infrastructure (positive); export surrender requirements, inflation and exchange rate volatility (negative). Factors specific to portfolio investment include the level of financial market development. Compared to countries with similar risk characteristics, South Africa is found to have had lower values for growth, trade openness, infrastructure, and institutional quality, and higher exchange rate volatility, over the period 1994 to 2002. Arvanitis (2005) presents similar findings for South Africa relating to growth, trade openness, and infrastructure, together with weaker labour quality and possibly taxation, as part of the explanation for lower levels of FDI but there remain significant unidentified effects. Using annual data for 1962 to 1996, Fedderke and Romm (2006) identify rates of return, market size, property rights, political stability, corporate taxation, wage costs, and the impact of openness to imports versus exports as determinants of FDI in South Africa.

This section of the chapter adds to these previous studies of foreign capital inflows in South Africa by examining the composition of portfolio investment and role of foreign investors in domestic capital markets over the period 1994 to 2007, while highlighting the implications of well-developed capital markets for the volume and share of FDI flows.

3.1. Foreign portfolio investment in South Africa

While South Africa's developed capital markets have facilitated the high volumes of portfolio investment shown in Figure 5.2, transactions in the equity and bond markets have differed sharply. For international investors, the equity market has been a vehicle for long-term emerging market investment, while the bond market has provided a platform for short-term interest rate and exchange rate positions.

3.1.1. FOREIGN INVESTMENT IN SOUTH AFRICAN EQUITIES

The domestic equity market in South Africa is much larger than the average for middle-income economies. At the end of 2006, the total market capitalization of securities traded on the JSE was equivalent to 290 per cent of GDP; of this, we estimate that around 168 per cent of GDP represented the listed equity of domestic companies.[7] In comparison, the average market capitalization in middle-income economies was just 80 per cent of GDP. The equity market in South Africa is also reasonably liquid compared to middle-income averages, especially in terms of the annual value of trade on the exchange.[8] The size and liquidity of the market is reinforced by a sound institutional framework for the protection of investors.[9]

Net equity investment surged between 1997 and 1999 and it is particularly striking that high volumes of equity investment continued throughout the emerging market financial crises in 1997 and 1998. During this period, the asset swap mechanism with domestic institutional investors permitted foreign investors to acquire large blocks of South African assets (see section 2). This first surge therefore reflects portfolio rebalancing by both residents and non-residents, although demand for South African assets outstripped the supply available through asset swaps at this time: total portfolio inflows *net* of portfolio outflows by residents averaged 4.5 per cent of GDP a year between 1997 and 1999.

The high share of portfolio investment in total capital flows follows in part from the developed nature of the local equity market. Other related aspects of South Africa's economic transformation since 1994 have also been important in determining the volume of flows. Figure 5.3 illustrates portfolio investment in equity securities, as measured in the balance of payments statistics, together with net non-resident purchases of shares on the JSE. Most portfolio investment takes the form of trade on the JSE; other transactions include international share placements and local transactions not conducted through the JSE. As noted in section 2, the financial rand mechanism was abolished in March 1995, representing a one-off liberalization of exchange controls for non-resident investors. A further factor in this period was the inclusion of South Africa in international emerging market equity indices,[10] contributing to new

---

[7] For consistency we exclude companies that are classified as non-resident in the balance of payments statistics from this measure of domestic equities traded on the JSE. Non-resident companies include large former South African multinationals that moved domicile and primary listing to the UK in the late 1990s: Anglo American, Billiton (now BHP Billiton), Old Mutual, and South African Breweries (now SABMiller), among others. We also exclude other securities traded on the exchange, such as derivatives. Data on market capitalization and the largest listed companies are published by the JSE in its *Annual Report* 2006 (pp. 50–52).

[8] The reported value of shares traded in South Africa in 2006 was equivalent to 123 per cent of GDP, compared to 39 per cent on average across middle-income economies. The turnover ratio in South Africa increased from less than 10 per cent in the mid 1990s to 50 per cent in 2006, compared to 73 per cent in middle-income economies. Data on market capitalization and liquidity are from *World Development Indicators*, World Bank.

[9] For example, South Africa scored 8 out of 10 in the strength of investor protection index compiled by the World Bank/International Finance Corporation *Doing Business*, compared to an average for the OECD of 6 (data for 2008 from <http://www.doingbusiness.org/>).

[10] South Africa was included in the IFC (now S&P/IFC) and MSCI emerging market indices in 1995, representing a substantial new addition in terms of weighting.

Capital Flows, Financial Markets, and the External Balance Sheet

interest in the South African market from international investors using these indices as benchmarks for asset allocation and investment performance.

Inflows dropped sharply in 2001–3, although the very large outflow recorded in 2001 was heavily influenced by the one-off restructuring of the corporate relationship between Anglo American plc and De Beers, which involved the buyout of minority shareholders in De Beers, with associated large transactions recorded on both the assets and liabilities sides of the financial account.[11] While domestic factors contributed to increased uncertainty, a broader decline in emerging market investment was an relevant influence in this period. In 2001–2, portfolio equity investment in developing countries was at its lowest level in US dollar terms since the early-1990s,[12] reflecting a more general decline in investor confidence in both developed and emerging equity markets.

Equity investment in South Africa recovered in 2004–5 and then surged early in 2006 to its highest level relative to GDP since 1999. Rising commodity prices, increased global liquidity and prospects for stronger growth in this period contributed to these high levels of inflows but equity inflows fell back towards the end of 2007 following the crisis in global credit markets.

While flows of equity investment have varied over time, net outflows were recorded in only four (of 52) quarters between 1995 and 2007, as shown in Figure 5.3. This points to a relatively stable and long-term accumulation of equity investment, reflected in the increased foreign ownership of listed equity in South Africa. In 1995, the stock of non-resident portfolio equity investment amounted to 5 per cent of the market capitalization of domestic companies listed on the JSE; this increased to an average of around 20 per cent between 2000 and 2006 (as a per cent of GDP, the stock increased from 8 per cent in 1995 to 34 per cent in 2006). The long-term nature of this investment is also apparent if we compare the stock of non-resident portfolio equity investment with the turnover implied by the gross purchases and sales of shares by non-residents on the JSE: this suggests an average holding period of just over thirteen months between 1997 and 2006. The sustained increase in foreign investment in South African companies evident in both the stock and flow data contrasts with the more volatile pattern of non-resident investment in the domestic bond market, as discussed below.

3.1.2. FOREIGN INVESTMENT IN SOUTH AFRICAN BONDS

The pattern of bond investment is shown in Figure 5.4, which compares the balance of payments data on total non-resident investment in debt securities

---

[11] Net portfolio outflows by non-residents in the second quarter of 2001 amounted to 2.7 per cent of GDP, while inward FDI by non-residents was 5.2 per cent. On the assets side, the repatriation of direct investment capital amounted to 4.2 per cent of GDP and the outflow of portfolio investment by residents was 3.7 per cent.

[12] Data on capital inflows to developing countries are from *Global Development Finance*, World Bank.

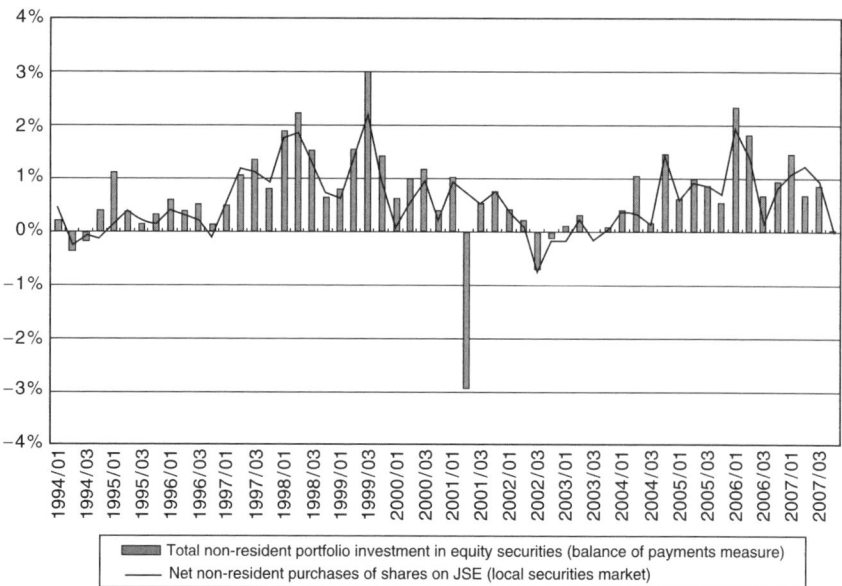

Figure 5.3. Foreign portfolio investment: equity securities, quarterly as per cent of annualized GDP

Source: Portfolio equity investment from *Balance of Payments Statistics*, International Monetary Fund; net non-resident purchases on JSE and GDP from *Quarterly Bulletin*, South African Reserve Bank.

with data on net non-resident outright purchases of domestic bonds on the Bond Exchange (BESA). In addition to non-resident trade in domestic debt, the balance of payments series includes flows associated with the issue and repayment of international bonds by South African entities. Following the political transition in 1994, the government developed a track record for borrowing in international bond markets, achieving a longer maturity profile for foreign-currency debt and providing a benchmark for other South African borrowers. This represented another aspect of South Africa's reintegration into global capital markets. The focus in this section, however, is on non-resident investment in the domestic (rand-denominated) bond market. The developed domestic bond market has enabled South Africa to maintain a low level of external debt and to avoid the associated vulnerabilities to shocks that have affected many developing countries.[13] In 2004, government debt denominated in foreign currencies amounted to 6 per cent of GDP,[14] compared to an

---

[13] Kahn (2005) discusses the development of domestic bond markets in the context of reducing external vulnerabilities in developing countries.

[14] We include foreign loans of the central bank in this measure of government debt for greater consistency with the measure used in Cowan et al. (2006).

average of 45 per cent for selected upper middle income economies in Latin America reported in Cowan et al. (2006).

Since 1997, the data on non-resident purchases and sales of bonds on BESA distinguishes between two types of transactions: *outright* purchases and sales of bonds and *repurchase* transactions.[15] While foreign investors can combine outright purchases with repurchase transactions to take interest rate positions (as an alternative to transactions in financial derivatives such as swaps and forward rate agreements), only outright transactions are classified as portfolio investment in the balance of payments statistics. Repurchase transactions are classified as collateralized loans and therefore as other investment in the balance of payments (an example of how offsetting transactions may appear under different headings of the financial account).

The volatile pattern of net inflows and outflows of portfolio investment in debt securities (Figure 5.4) has contrasted with the more stable equity investment. There have been periods of substantial net outflows of debt capital,

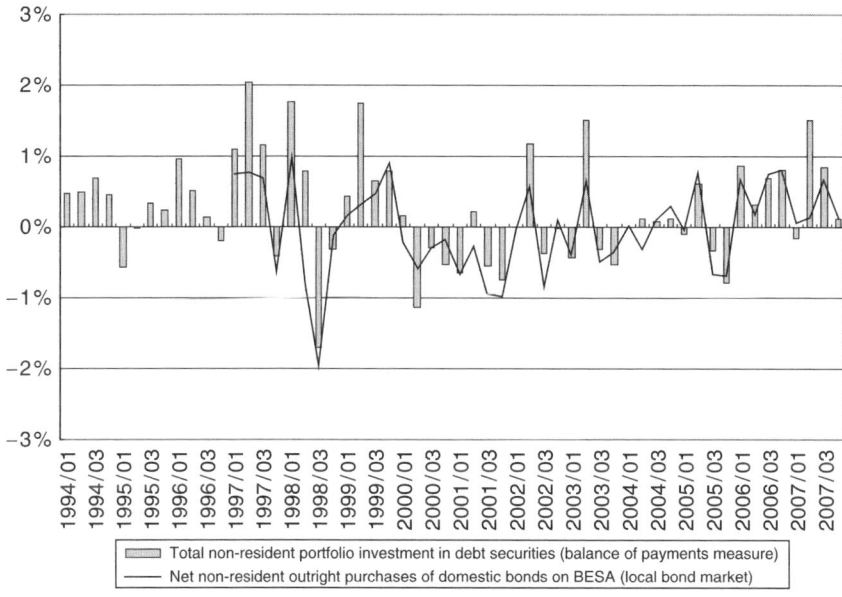

Figure 5.4. Foreign portfolio investment: debt securities, quarterly as per cent of annualized GDP

Source: Portfolio investment in debt securities from *Balance of Payments Statistics*, International Monetary Fund; net non-resident purchases on BESA and GDP from *Quarterly Bulletin*, South African Reserve Bank.

[15] Repurchase transactions are defined as arrangements involving the sale of securities with a commitment to repurchase the same or similar securities at a specified price and date (IMF, 1993).

especially between 2000 and 2005, although these may not always have translated into a net overall outflow of capital from South Africa as investors may switch from bonds to other local instruments such as equity or bank deposits. Moreover, this form of investment was more sensitive to the emerging market crises of the late 1990s than equity flows. The net outflows in the fourth quarter of 1997 coincided with the spread of the Asia crisis and the outflows recorded in the second half of 1998 followed continuing contagion and the emergence of the debt crisis in Russia.

Non-resident trade in the bond market has increased substantially relative to that in equities. While much of the overall volume of non-resident transactions in the domestic bond market is associated with repurchase arrangements, gross *outright* purchases and sales of bonds were on average more than 2.5 times the size of gross equity purchases and sales between 1999 and 2003 and remained more than 50 per cent larger than gross equity trade even with the substantial increase in the value of equity transactions between 2004 and 2007. The liquid domestic bond market provides opportunities for a rapid turnover of positions by foreign investors. For the market as a whole, the value of annual purchases on BESA was around 20 times market capitalization between 2000 and 2006. For non-residents, annual purchases amounted to 36 times the value of their holdings, with about one-third of the transactions taking the form of outright purchases and two-thirds repurchase transactions.

The disparity between gross and net purchases and sales in the bond market by non-residents suggests a pattern of high frequency trading driven by (and contributing to) short-term price fluctuations.[16] Although much of this short-term trade is in the form of repurchase transactions, even outright trade in bonds has a much higher turnover rate than equity. A comparison of gross outright purchases and sales by non-residents on the Bond Exchange with the stock of rand-denominated bonds held by non-residents suggests an estimated holding period of bonds of just over one month on average between 1999 and 2006, compared to almost fourteen months for equity in this period.

3.2. Is South Africa underweighted in emerging market equity portfolios?

Following on from the long-term increase in equity investment identified above, in this section we examine whether the share of foreign portfolio equity investment received by South Africa is in line with that predicted by broad benchmarks for the composition of an emerging equity market portfolio. We use cross-country data on foreign-owned portfolio equity securities

---

[16] Non-resident annual *gross* purchases and sales of bonds were on average equivalent to 123.5 and 123.9 per cent of GDP between 2000 and 2007, with a *net* overall sale of 0.4 per cent of GDP. By contrast, annual *gross* purchases and sales of equity averaged 20.4 per cent and 18.2 per cent of GDP, with a *net* overall purchase of 2.2 per cent.

from the IMF *Coordinated Portfolio Investment Survey 2005* (CPIS) to estimate the total stock of foreign equity investment in emerging economies and the share of investment in each of the host emerging economies.[17]

The first comparison is to a benchmark portfolio based on the market capitalization and liquidity of shares available in emerging equity markets, drawing on the composition of the Standard and Poor's (S&P) Emerging Market indices. We use the country (or market) weights of the S&P/IFC Global Composite emerging market index (S&P/IFCG Index) as the underlying benchmark for emerging market equity investment. The country weights in the index are based on float-adjusted market capitalization of selected stocks and reflect the most actively traded domestic companies in each market.[18] At the end of 2005, the S&P/IFCG Index included equities from thirty-two emerging markets. However, we exclude four markets where there are apparent gaps in the CPIS coverage of foreign equity investment and therefore adjust the S&P/IFCG country weights to reflect the subset of twenty-eight markets.[19]

Figure 5.5 compares the allocation of foreign equity investment across the ten largest host emerging economies against the weighted benchmark described above. The gap between the actual share of equity investment and the benchmark share provides an indication of whether foreign investors as a whole are underweight or overweight in a particular emerging market. Emerging market investors are underweight in South African equities relative to this benchmark. The gap between actual investment and benchmark investment was 2.3 percentage points in 2005 (actual share of 6.2 per cent versus benchmark of 8.5 per cent); in other words, foreign investors were 28 per cent underweight.

A similar finding emerges if the related S&P/IFC Investable Composite index (S&P/IFCI Index) is used to derive the benchmark composition of emerging market investment. The S&P/IFCI Index takes into account restrictions on foreign investment in individual stocks and has additional conditions for inclusion of individual stocks based on market capitalization and liquidity (Standard and Poor's, 2006a). Once practical openness to foreign investment

---

[17] The CPIS data on portfolio investment in the host economy are compiled by national statistical agencies in the source economy drawing on a common set of definitions, with 72 countries contributing data on foreign asset holdings to the 2005 survey. Data and methodological information are available from the CPIS page on the IMF website.

[18] The S&P/IFCG country indices have a target of 70 to 80 per cent of the total market capitalization of listed shares. Float-adjusted market capitalization reflects the market capitalization available to portfolio investors, adjusting for strategic and related holdings (Standard and Poor's, 2006a). The country composition of the market capitalization of the index is reported in the Standard and Poor's *Global Stock Markets Factbook 2006*.

[19] The markets included in the analysis are: Argentina, Brazil, Chile, China, Colombia, Czech Republic, Egypt, Hungary, India, Indonesia, Israel, Jordan, Korea, Malaysia, Mexico, Morocco, Pakistan, Peru, Philippines, Poland, Russia, South Africa, Sri Lanka, Taiwan, Thailand, Turkey, Venezuela, Zimbabwe.

is taken into account, South Africa appears more underweighted (not shown here): the actual share of investment of 6.2 per cent compares to the weight in the S&P/IFCI Index of 10.0 per cent at end-2005.

While South Africa appears underweighted in emerging market equity portfolios given the size of the local equity market, it receives comparatively high levels of portfolio equity investment relative to the size of the economy. This is shown in Figure 5.5, which also compares the share of foreign equity investment to a GDP-based benchmark[20] for the largest host emerging economies at the end of 2005. Against this benchmark, foreign equity investors *overweight* South Africa: the actual share of foreign equity investment of 6.2 per cent is substantially higher than its GDP share of 2.6 per cent. These seemingly contradictory results reflect the fact that domestic equity market capitalization relative to GDP is high in South Africa. The large and reasonably liquid securities market has allowed South Africa to attract more portfolio investment than the size of the economy would otherwise suggest. As argued earlier, this has supported the dominance of portfolio investment in capital inflows.

The sustainability of the external position depends, in part, on the prospects for further inflows of portfolio equity investment. After the one-off portfolio rebalancing in response to reintegration that occurred in the second half of the 1990s, portfolio investment flows now vary with emerging market flows generally. Although South Africa's underweighting by foreign investors relative to the size of the equity market may be primarily a reflection of the high ratio of market capitalization to GDP in South Africa, it may also reflect some adverse perceptions of domestic risks. A step increase in the *share* of investment capital allocated to South Africa would thus depend both on prospects for relatively rapid growth and on favourable perceptions of the domestic economy and investment environment. At the same time, it is clear that the *level* of foreign investment in emerging markets will continue to be determined by global savings, risk preferences and perceptions, evidenced both in recent surges in flows (2006) and slumps following external shocks (late 2007 and 2008).

3.3. Is foreign direct investment too low?

Figure 5.2 shows that inflows of FDI capital in South Africa did increase after 1994 but have remained relatively low compared to portfolio investment inflows. Between 1994 and 2007, average annual FDI as a percentage of GDP was 1.4 per cent, compared to 2.9 per cent (to 2005) in middle-income economies.[21] The pattern of FDI flows to South Africa since 1994 can be generally

---

[20] Here, benchmark country weights are calculated as the share of local GDP in total GDP across the same twenty-eight emerging market economies. Data are from *World Development Indicators*, World Bank and national sources for Taiwan.

[21] Data on middle-income economies from *World Development Indicators*, World Bank.

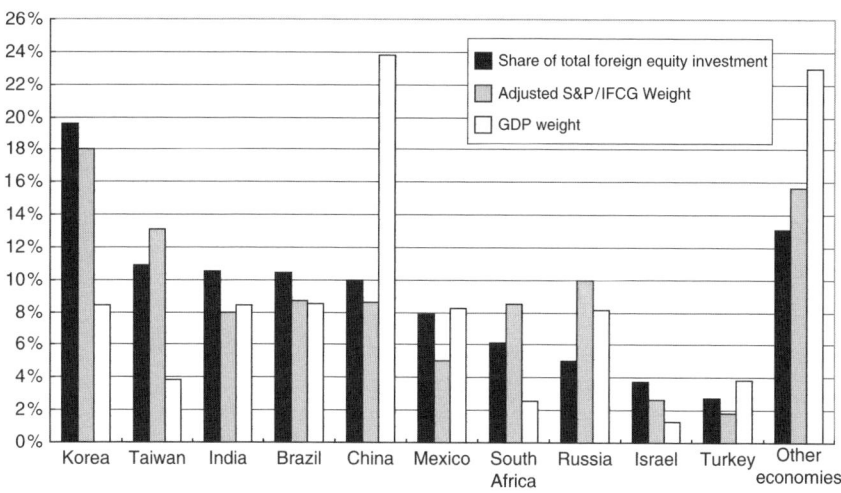

Figure 5.5. Foreign equity investment in emerging economies (stock), end-2005

Source: Shares of foreign equity investment in emerging economies are calculated from the IMF *Coordinated Portfolio Investment Survey 2005*. Benchmark weights based on equity market size are calculated from the country weights in the S&P/IFCG Index from *Global Stock Markets Factbook 2006*, Standard and Poor's. GDP weights are calculated from the *World Development Indicators*, World Bank and from the Central Bank of Taiwan. See text for details and countries covered.

Note: For the market size comparison, investors are 'underweight' when the black bar is lower than the grey bar and 'overweight' when the black bar is higher than the grey bar.
For the GDP comparison, investors are 'underweight' when the black bar is lower than the white bar and 'overweight' when the black bar is higher than the white bar.

characterized as relatively low volumes interrupted by occasional large transactions.[22]

Despite low average volumes of FDI capital flows, alternative indicators of foreign investment suggest that multinationals are active across a wide range of sectors in South Africa. Thomas et al. (2005) examine the sources and sectoral composition of foreign direct investment in South Africa using the database compiled by the BusinessMap Foundation between 1994 and 2004. The database captures public announcements of the value of investment by foreign companies or foreign-owned enterprises in South Africa. The study finds that, although foreign investment has tended to be concentrated in the automobile and mining sectors, there is evidence that South Africa has attracted

---

[22] Large FDI transactions include the partial privatization of Telkom in 1997, the acquisition of De Beers shares from minority shareholders as part of the restructuring of Anglo American and De Beers in 2001, and the partial acquisition of ABSA by Barclays Bank in 2005. Net FDI inflows increased during 2007, including several large private equity acquisitions; it is, however, too soon to predict whether this increase is likely to be sustained especially in the context of the shock to global credit markets late in 2007.

foreign interest across a fairly diverse range of industries. Based on the *stock* of FDI reported by the South African Reserve Bank at the end of 2006, 40 per cent of liabilities were in the mining sector, with 27 per cent each in the manufacturing sector and the financial and business services sector (see also Arvanitis, 2005).

Evidence on the total *stock* of FDI in South Africa also supports the view that the role of foreign investors in the economy is significant. South Africa has built on the historical presence of foreign firms, although the era of sanctions and disinvestment saw the stock of FDI decline relative to the size of the economy: from an average of 29 per cent of GDP between 1960 and 1979 to just 9 per cent by the end of 1993. Moreover, the internationalization of some of the largest South African multinationals in the late 1990s has added significantly to foreign ownership in the economy.[23] By the end of 2006, the stock of FDI in South Africa was equivalent to 35 per cent of GDP. While there is substantial variation across countries in this measure, South Africa is broadly in line with the overall ratio for developing countries estimated by UNCTAD for 2005.[24]

The value of the stock of FDI in South Africa, coupled with the presence of foreign firms across diverse industrial sectors, suggest that the recent history of FDI capital flows, as recorded in the balance of payments, may understate the level of activity of foreign-owned enterprises in the economy.

3.3.1. FINANCIAL MARKETS AND THE MIX OF FDI AND PORTFOLIO INVESTMENT

As discussed above, recent studies of FDI in South Africa have focused on the low level of FDI inflows. However, the presence of comparatively developed financial markets in South Africa suggests that the role of external capital in supporting growth and development may be somewhat different than in countries with less-developed markets. One potential explanation for low levels of FDI flows is that they are, in part, a reflection of well-developed capital markets and related institutional structures that promote transparency and investor protection. For instance, Hausmann and Fernández-Arias (2000) suggest that a high share of FDI in total capital inflows may reflect negatively on the domestic economy, indicating high transaction costs that prevent other forms of entry and linkages. Goldstein and Razin (2005) develop a model in which investors with liquidity needs seek investments with less asymmetric information and hence prefer portfolio investment, where available, to FDI.

---

[23] The re-domiciling of Anglo American, Billiton, Old Mutual, and South African Breweries in the UK in the late 1990s has resulted in an increasingly international shareholder base for these companies. Foreign ownership of the local enterprises of these multinationals has risen substantially, reinforcing the classification of these parent companies as foreign owners.

[24] *World Investment Report* 2006, UNCTAD.

Capital Flows, Financial Markets, and the External Balance Sheet

These results suggest that a low share of FDI in total capital inflows may be less an indication of significant barriers to FDI and more a reflection of the broader investment opportunities provided by developed capital markets.

A related factor is that well-developed domestic markets can also leverage investment by foreign-owned enterprises.[25] The local financial system provides a source of financing for foreign firms, facilitating hedging of local exposures. In addition, established domestic firms provide a pool of investment partners for foreign firms.[26] The large equity market, together with the associated information and legal infrastructure, provides a range of potential targets for full or partial acquisitions. Indeed, a large proportion of new foreign investment in South Africa is in the form of acquisitions (Gelb and Black, 2004; Thomas et al., 2005).[27] Opportunities for domestic financial markets to support foreign investment have further increased with exchange control reform: since 2004, foreign firms have been permitted to list in the local equity and bond markets and the allowance for the use of local financing by foreign-owned firms is now 300 per cent of shareholder investment (Table 5.1).

Further empirical work in this area would help to clarify the role of local financial markets and domestic firms in facilitating investment by foreign firms in South Africa. Other related research questions concern the implications of the composition of capital flows for the impact of external shocks and spillover effects on the real economy.

4. Outward investment by South African residents

In this section, we consider capital outflows and holdings of foreign assets by South African investors. The analysis focuses on the response to capital account liberalization since 1995, with a particular emphasis on foreign portfolio investment by South African residents.

As discussed in section 2, the government has followed a gradual approach to the liberalization of exchange controls on residents, mainly in the form of phased increases in allowances for different forms of capital outflows. These reforms have largely determined the pattern of capital outflows over the period, as shown in Figure 5.6. Portfolio investment has been the main conduit for long-term capital outflows, dominating total outflows between 1996

---

[25] See, for instance, Lehmann et al. (2004) and Hausmann and Fernández-Arias (2000).
[26] Along similar lines, Alfaro et al. (2006) explore how domestic financial markets support FDI spillovers in the form of backward linkages.
[27] Thomas et al. (2005) report on the composition of 392 inward investments by companies from the European Union between 1994 and 2004 as captured in the BusinessMap Foundation FDI database: 34 per cent were acquisitions, 32 per cent were greenfield or joint venture investments, 25 per cent represented expansions of foreign-owned enterprises, with the remaining announcements reflecting a more general interest in investing in the country.

and 2002. These flows were driven by a rebalancing of domestic portfolios following the introduction of foreign asset allowances for institutional investors. Direct investment by South African companies has shown only a small rise relative to the early 1990s, despite considerable progress on exchange control reform.[28] Nevertheless, the international profile of South African companies has increased in this period, especially in the rest of Africa (for instance, DBSA and NEPAD, 2003).[29] Moreover, some of the largest South African multinationals pursued internationalization strategies through re-domiciling in the late 1990s.[30] Other investment includes foreign loans, trade credit, foreign currency and deposits, and residual assets not classified as direct or portfolio investment. These flows have often been large due, in part, to the role of the local banking sector in absorbing foreign currency inflows.

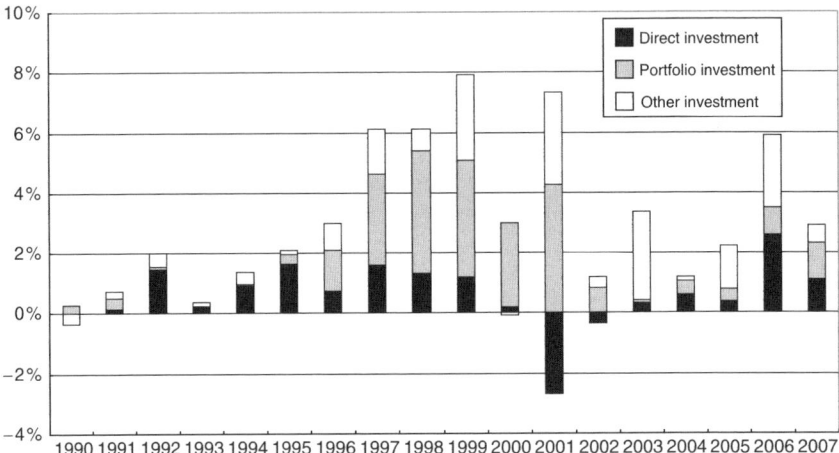

Figure 5.6. Composition of net outflows of domestic capital, per cent of GDP

Source: Calculated from *Quarterly Bulletin*, March 2008 dataset, South African Reserve Bank.

Note: Direct investment, portfolio investment, and other investment are defined in the main text. Net outflows are shown as a positive number. The opposite convention holds in the balance of payments data.

---

[28] The large outflow recorded in 2006 is associated with a single transaction in the telecommunications sector. The large *inflow* in 2001 (i.e., a repatriation of domestic capital) reflects the unwinding of the cross shareholding between De Beers and Anglo American plc, with related large transactions elsewhere on the financial account, as noted elsewhere.

[29] The strategy on exchange control reform has reflected a strong policy preference for encouraging South African investment in the rest of Africa.

[30] Billiton (now BHP Billiton) established its primary listing and domicile in the UK in 1997, followed by Anglo American, Old Mutual and South African Breweries (now SABMiller) in 1999 and Dimension Data in 2000. Investec established a dual-listed structure in 2002, moving the primary listing of its international assets to the UK. These companies continue to have secondary listings on the JSE.

4.1. Trends in foreign diversification: FDI versus portfolio investment

Before 1995, South African residents had limited options for international diversification. However, South African companies were able to invest abroad under certain conditions and, at the end of 1995, the stock of FDI assets owned by South African companies amounted to 16 per cent of GDP. The ratio for Australia and Canada at this time was broadly similar at 14 per cent and 20 per cent, respectively. Shareholdings in domestic companies with foreign direct investments thus provided the main legal conduit for international diversification by South African individual and institutional investors. As noted in section 2, illegal outflows had also been important historically, as exchange controls were less than fully effective in preventing capital outflows.

Exchange control reform from 1995 onwards created new channels for international diversification, as discussed above. Foreign asset allowances for the large institutional investor sector were introduced; private individuals were permitted to invest an increasing amount of funds directly abroad, as well as through domestic institutions; and the exchange control regime for corporate FDI was substantially liberalized. Furthermore, the re-domiciling of South African multinationals in the late 1990s (noted above) created a new conduit for increasing foreign exposure for South African investors via secondary listings on the JSE.

Figure 5.7 shows the change in portfolio and FDI foreign asset holdings over the period.[31] The grey bar reflects holdings of foreign equity and debt securities by individuals, including indirect exposure gained via the investments of domestic institutional investors. This is estimated as the sum of portfolio debt and equity securities held by the private non-banking sector,[32] as reported in the South African Reserve Bank *Quarterly Bulletin*. The black bar reflects holdings of FDI assets by individuals via shareholdings in South African companies with foreign investments (including holdings via domestic institutional investors). Since some shareholders in domestic companies are non-residents, part of the FDI assets of the domestic corporate sector will be indirectly owned by non-resident shareholders. We therefore adjust the reported value of FDI assets in the *Quarterly Bulletin* for the estimated claims of non-residents.

---

[31] This is not intended as a complete picture of foreign asset holdings of individuals, for instance it would not include holdings of international bank deposits.

[32] In general, the private non-banking sector includes institutional investors, non-financial companies and individuals. However, we expect the series on portfolio investment to be dominated by institutional investors as the holdings of individuals are likely to be small relative to the assets under management by institutions and non-financial companies are only able to undertake direct investment.

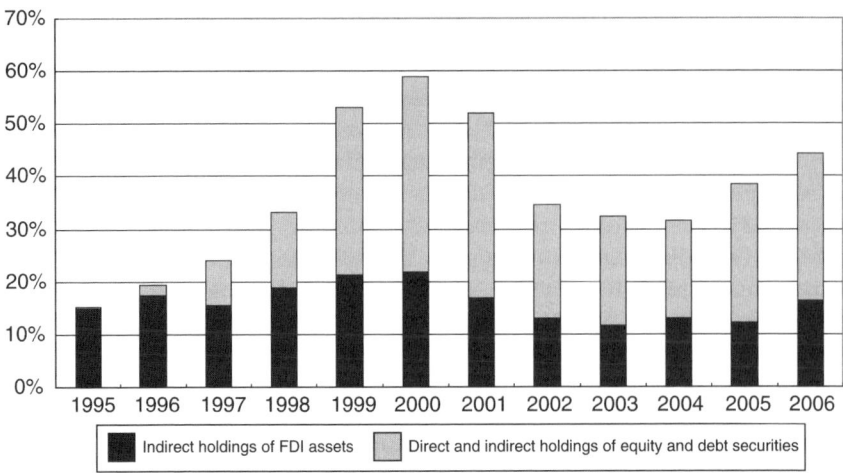

Figure 5.7. Estimated holdings of foreign assets by South Africans (stock), per cent of GDP
Source: Calculated from data in *Quarterly Bulletin*, March 2008 dataset, South African Reserve Bank with market capitalization from the World Federation of Exchanges and the JSE. See text for details.

The most striking aspect of Figure 5.7 is the surge in portfolio investment that followed the liberalization of controls on institutional investors; this was reinforced by the impact of re-domiciling of South African multinationals in 1999.[33] The increase in outward FDI was much more muted but this is not surprising given that there were already significant levels of FDI assets in 1995. Overall, foreign asset holdings of South African residents rose from just 15 per cent of GDP in 1995 to a peak of 59 per cent in 2000 before falling and then rising again to 44 per cent in 2006. However, valuation effects have an important impact on this trend: for instance, the value of foreign assets between 2001 and 2004 reflected in part the depreciation and appreciation of the rand. The experience in South Africa appears to reflect both 'catch-up' in response to exchange control reform as well as a more general increase in international demand for foreign assets as a feature of globalization. For instance, similar upward trends in foreign asset holdings are evident in the resource-based economies of Australia and Canada, although diversification via portfolio investment has occurred over a longer period in these more developed coun-

---

[33] Re-domiciling meant that South African shareholdings in these companies were now classified as foreign assets in the international investment position data (Walters and Prinsloo, 2002).

tries. Chile has also demonstrated rapid international diversification since the mid 1990s, with regulatory reforms supporting a higher level of foreign investment.[34]

An important issue for the sustainability of the external position is whether portfolio rebalancing by South African investors remains unfinished—implying a continued pent-up demand for foreign assets—or is now substantially complete. The next section explores this issue drawing on the international literature on home bias in investment portfolios.

4.2. Is there home bias in South African equity portfolios?

One of the key features of cross-border portfolio investment that has emerged from the literature is an observed tendency for investors to hold high proportions of domestic assets despite the potential gains in terms of risk diversification offered by foreign assets, i.e., 'home bias'. In this section, we assess the degree of home bias in South Africa and selected comparator countries. The analysis focuses on equity securities, which account for over 90 per cent of South Africa's total stock of foreign portfolio assets.

Figure 5.8 shows the estimated composition of portfolio equity holdings in 2005 for South African residents together with a group of comparators. Comparator countries were selected using thresholds for the size of local equity markets and holdings of foreign assets, in order to limit the comparison to countries with reasonably well-developed markets.[35] Holdings of foreign equities are from the IMF *Coordinated Portfolio Investment Survey* (CPIS). Holdings of domestic equities are estimated as the residual of market capitalization of domestic listed companies[36] less non-resident investment in domestic equities,

---

[34] For Australia, the equivalent measure of foreign asset holdings rose from 20 per cent of GDP in 1995 to 41 per cent in 2003. For Canada, foreign asset holdings increased from 30 per cent of GDP in 1995 to 51 per cent in 2005. For Chile, foreign asset holdings increased from 7 per cent in 1997 to 45 per cent in 2005; foreign asset limits for pension funds have steadily increased in Chile from just two per cent in 1992 to 30 per cent by 2002 (Roldos, 2004). The comparison is calculated using data from the *Balance of Payments Statistics* and *International Financial Statistics*, International Monetary Fund and *World Development Indicators*, World Bank.

[35] The thresholds are at least 25 per cent of GDP for the size of the local equity market and foreign asset holdings of at least 5 per cent of GDP. These thresholds are rather arbitrary but generally exclude countries where foreign diversification appears to be very limited. We also remove a small number of countries with large international fund management centres, where reported holdings of foreign equities are exceptionally large relative to GDP or where inward portfolio investment exceeds local market capitalization. Finally, we exclude Euro Area economies because the common currency means that the definition of foreign assets is not straightforward.

[36] For comparator countries, market capitalization data are from the *World Development Indicators*, World Bank. For South Africa, market capitalization data from the JSE are used in order to estimate the market capitalization of domestic listed companies, excluding listed companies classified as non-resident in the portfolio investment data and other categories of securities traded on the exchange.

also derived from the CPIS.[37] An important caveat in the estimate of holdings of domestic equity is that international market capitalization data will include strategic/controlling investments by both residents and non-residents, which strictly should not be classified as portfolio investment. Our estimate of holdings of domestic equities will therefore be biased upwards due to the inclusion of (resident and non-resident) controlling investments in domestic listed firms. The presence of controlling shareholders implies there will be an inherent home bias in analyses of portfolio allocation relative to the world market portfolio (Kho et al., 2006; Dahlquist et al., 2003).[38]

In all of the countries shown, investors hold more than half of the portfolio in domestic equities, most much more than half. However, there is considerable heterogeneity across these countries, with foreign asset holdings ranging from less than 20 per cent of the estimated portfolio in Israel, Japan, Argentina, Chile, Australia, the USA, and South Africa to more than 40 per cent of the portfolio in New Zealand, Norway, and Sweden. At the end of 2005, an estimated 18 per cent of the South African equity portfolio was in foreign assets, compared to an average of 27 per cent across the group of nineteen countries. Foreign diversification for South Africa is thus somewhat below the average across this selected group but does not appear to be out of line with international practice given the heterogeneity across countries. Furthermore, the foreign asset share in South Africa has been slightly diluted by a more rapid increase in the estimated value of domestic equities since 2001 (the earliest date for which CPIS data are available for this international comparison). The average share of foreign assets in the equity portfolio between 2001 and 2005 was 21 per cent for South Africa, more in line with the cross-country average of 25 per cent.

The extensive international literature on home bias has examined various possible explanations, although there is no particular consensus and the empirical evidence has mostly focused on developed countries. Some studies have questioned how much of the bias can be explained by the role of domestic assets in hedging domestic risks and by the transaction costs of international investment, while others have explored the potential contribution of information asymmetries and behavioural factors. Another strand has suggested that concentrated corporate ownership structures and governance factors may also limit international shareholdings.[39]

The presence of exchange controls on residents in South Africa is one potential explanation for the high share of domestic assets in the portfolio shown in

---

[37] A similar approach is used in Fidora et al., 2006.

[38] We test the implications of this bias for South Africa by comparing results obtained using an estimated free float adjustment of market capitalization based on the FTSE/JSE Index (drawing on information provided on the JSE website). The adjustment implies that the share of foreign equities in the total equity portfolio rises by 5.3 percentage points (from 18.4 per cent to 23.8 per cent) in 2005, suggesting a non-negligible effect.

[39] Some examples from this literature include French and Poterba (1991), Tesar and Werner (1995), Lewis (1999), Dahlquist et al. (2003), Faruqee et al. (2004), Kho et al. (2006).

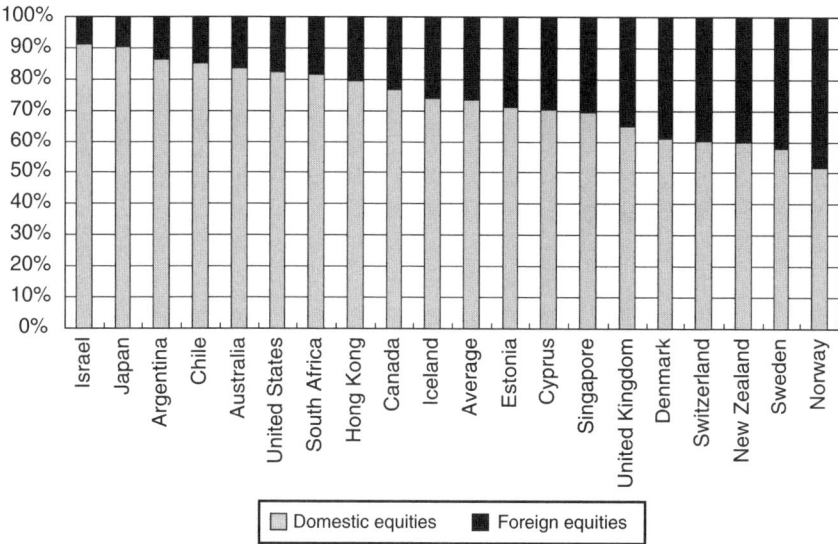

Figure 5.8. Estimated composition of equity portfolios: domestic versus foreign assets, end-2005

Source: Calculated from data in the IMF *Coordinated Portfolio Investment Survey 2005*, *World Development Indicators*, World Bank and the JSE. See text for details.

Figure 5.8. While prudential regulation and capital controls are not generally important explanations for home bias in developed countries, their impact could have been greater in South Africa given that foreign asset limits have been in place for institutional investors, which manage a large fraction of personal savings.[40]

Foreign portfolio investments held by the private non-banking sector amounted to R404 billion at the end of 2005, including both debt and equity securities, largely reflecting the foreign asset holdings of institutional investors. Total assets of institutional investors at this time amounted to around R2,514 billion.[41] This implies that across the institutional investor sector as

---

[40] Institutional investors are the main conduit for portfolio equity investment. Private individuals can transfer funds abroad directly subject to a limit but can also invest in foreign assets via domestic institutions. Non-financial companies and banks, too, face foreign investment restrictions.

[41] Data are from the South African Reserve Bank *Quarterly Bulletin*. The figure for total assets of institutional investors is the sum of total assets of long-term insurers, official pension funds, private self-administered pension and provident funds and unit trusts (collective investment schemes). No data on the total assets managed by other registered investment managers is available, although funds managed on behalf of private individuals will be small relative to pension and insurance assets.

a whole, foreign assets represented at most around 16 per cent of total assets under management in 2005. The ratio for 2006 was similar; we use the data for 2005 here for consistency with Figure 5.8.

This measure of foreign assets includes all securities issued by non-resident entities, including non-resident equities traded on the JSE. This is a relevant point because it means that former South African multinationals listed on the JSE (Anglo American, BHP Billiton plc, SABMiller and Old Mutual) are classified as foreign assets in the international investment position (see Walters and Prinsloo, 2002). These companies are amongst the largest on the JSE and hence form an important part of institutional investors' portfolios. However, these JSE-listings have continued to be classified as domestic assets for exchange control purposes and as such do not count towards the foreign asset limits for institutional investors. It follows that a significant fraction of the estimated foreign exposure of 16 per cent is likely to be accounted for by locally-traded securities that do not count towards the foreign asset limit.

The implication is that holdings of other foreign assets must be significantly below the exchange control limits across a large fraction of the institutional investor sector. At the end of 2005, these limits stood at 15 per cent for retirement funds and long-term insurers and 25 percent for collective investment scheme companies and other investment managers (Table 5.1 describes more recent reforms to these limits). This point is further demonstrated in Leape and Thomas (2008) with alternative data on the asset allocations of institutional investors: using the narrower exchange control definition of foreign assets, we show that foreign assets amounted to around 10 per cent of total institutional assets at March 2008.

This evidence suggests that home bias in South African portfolios is not solely the result of exchange controls.[42] The factors driving portfolio allocation by institutional investors in South Africa are a useful subject for further research. One implication for the longer-term is that an underlying preference for domestic assets may work to limit outflows in a post-exchange control environment, especially in the context where insurance companies and retirement funds remain subject to some form of prudential portfolio regulations (see section 2). That said, institutional investors are large by international standards, with assets of around 175 per cent of GDP at the end of 2006. Earlier data for 2001 show that, within the OECD, only Switzerland, the USA, UK, Netherlands, and Sweden had a higher ratio of institutional assets to GDP than South Africa

---

[42] Transaction costs associated with exchange control compliance may have distorted foreign investment decisions. This could work in two ways, however: applications to use foreign allowances may have been discouraged if transaction costs are high but institutions may also have been reluctant to sell foreign assets and bring capital back to South Africa in response to changing market conditions where application processes for future foreign investments have administrative costs. The removal of the application process announced in March 2008 should eliminate these transaction costs.

Capital Flows, Financial Markets, and the External Balance Sheet

(OECD, 2003). Small changes in institutions' desired foreign exposure could therefore continue to have a large impact on net capital flows in the future.

5. Concluding comments

South Africa's external position has been transformed since 1994. The government has undertaken a series of policy reforms aimed at normalizing the foreign exchange market and international financial relations. South Africa's sovereign credit ratings have improved over time in response to these reforms and to macroeconomic stabilization and a stronger external position. Capital inflows have increased substantially, dominated by portfolio equity investment. In parallel, the strategy of gradual removal of restrictions on outward investment by South African residents has enabled significant portfolio diversification while avoiding large and potentially destabilizing capital outflows.

Integration into global capital markets has had a profound impact on South Africa's external capital structure. As shown in Figure 5.9, South Africa's foreign assets have increased almost fourfold, as a per cent of GDP, since 1994. Much of the increase is due to the sharp rise in portfolio equity investment, which now accounts for more than a third of foreign assets. Other investment has also risen, driven partly by the rise in foreign reserves (shown separately in Figure 5.9). These increases have been mirrored by a sharp decline in the share of direct investment assets—which have remained largely unchanged as a per cent of GDP. Foreign liabilities have also increased, although less sharply as shown in Figure 5.10. The rise in liabilities is the result of substantial increases in direct investment and portfolio equity investment liabilities, which have resulted in a large shift in the proportion of foreign liabilities denominated in rand: direct investment, portfolio equity investment, and portfolio rand-denominated debt accounted for about half of total foreign liabilities in the mid 1990s but increased to around 80 per cent of liabilities by the end of 2006.[43]

The transformation of the external balance sheet has had implications for macroeconomic policy. It has helped South Africa to sustain a shift to a more free-floating exchange rate—abandoning the activist foreign exchange intervention strategy that prevailed through the late 1990s—and thereby supported the shift in monetary policy to an inflation targeting regime in 2000 (Chapter 3). The rise in rand-based liabilities and in foreign currency (reserve) assets has also enhanced South Africa's ability to sustain current account deficits, by reducing the likelihood of a sudden stop in capital inflows as well as that of a

---

[43] The re-domiciling of South African multinationals in 1999 led to a large one-off increase in FDI liabilities (Figure 5.10) and in portfolio equity assets (Figure 5.9). The asset and liability figures also reflect valuation effects, notably as a result of exchange rate changes.

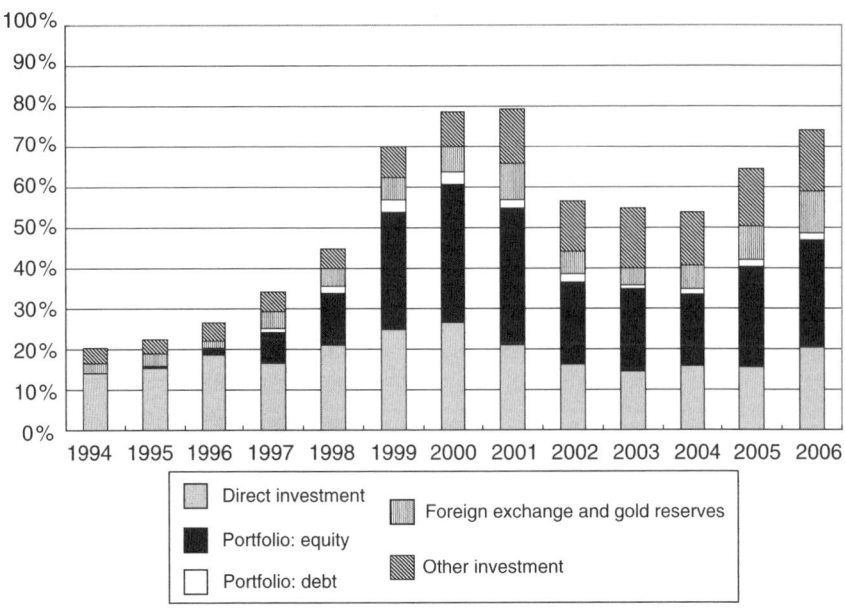

Figure 5.9. Composition of foreign assets (stock), per cent of GDP
Source: Calculated from *Quarterly Bulletin*, March 2008 dataset, South African Reserve Bank.

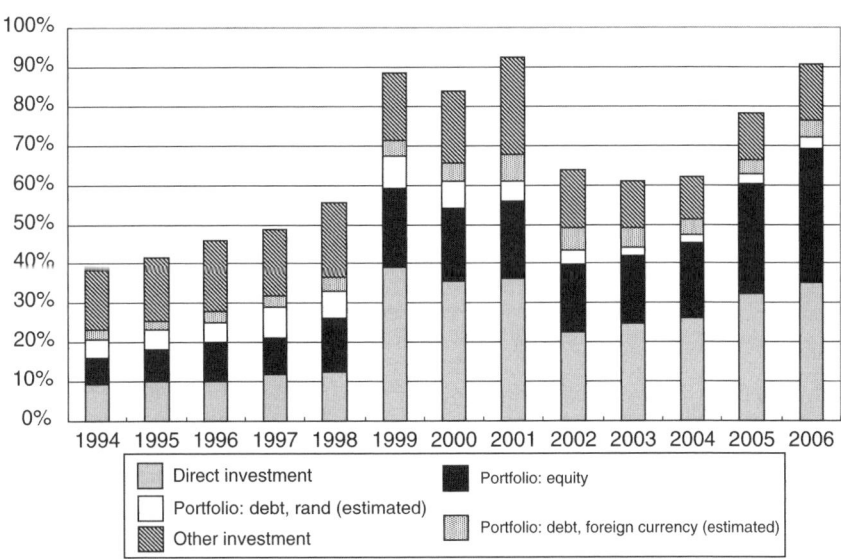

Figure 5.10. Composition of foreign liabilities (stock), per cent of GDP
Source: Calculated from *Quarterly Bulletin*, March 2008 dataset, South African Reserve Bank.

sharp macroeconomic adjustment should a sudden stop occur. While a sudden stop in inflows would have inevitable adverse consequences for growth, the shifts in the external balance sheet mean that South Africa is better-placed to manage such shocks.[44] Although the impact of a sudden flight of domestic capital is likely to be less than that of a sudden stop, our analysis, which differentiates between inflows of foreign capital and outflows of domestic capital, highlights the need to assess both risks.[45]

As discussed in section 3, the sustainability of higher current account deficits will depend critically on factors influencing South Africa's weighting by international investors, including growth prospects and risk, as well as on those affecting the overall level of emerging market investment, including international trends in savings and risk preferences. While these risk factors affect South African investors, too, the substantial portfolio re-balancing undertaken in the late 1990s together with evidence of home bias and the shift to prudential regulation of foreign exposures, discussed in section 4, suggests that the macroeconomic risks associated with destabilizing resident outflows have now been greatly reduced.

The composition of capital flows and the external balance sheet has important implications for the management of macroeconomic risk in South Africa, especially in light of the large current account deficits that have accompanied stronger economic growth. As demonstrated by the simultaneous shocks resulting from the international credit crisis and the sharp rise in food prices in 2007–8, policy responses to capital flows must be considered as part of a broader framework for reducing vulnerability to external shocks as well as limiting their impact, especially on the poor. This framework should encompass the traditional tools of macroeconomic management—fiscal, monetary, and exchange rate policy—and also trade and industrial policy in encouraging the diversification of production and exports, social policy in the creation of effective safety nets to protect the poor, and financial sector policy in supporting efficient and liquid markets and sound institutions.

---

[44] The literature demonstrates that sudden stops are fairly common events in emerging economies and their short-term macroeconomic impact can involve sharp adjustments in the current account, a combination of loss of reserves, exchange rate depreciation, and increased interest rates; and a fall in growth, which may be severe. Various structural and policy factors have been found to influence the scale of impact and speed of recovery: greater openness to trade, floating exchange rate regimes, and low dollarization of liabilities have been associated with greater resilience to shocks (for example, Calvo et al., 2004, 2008; Frankel and Cavallo, 2004; Guidotti et al., 2004). Frankel et al. (2006) highlight large current account deficits as a key vulnerability for South Africa but find that other external fundamentals are mainly encouraging. They argue for further improvements to support South Africa's ability to manage these risks.

[45] Rothenburg and Warnock (2006) distinguish between episodes of sudden stops in foreign capital inflows and sudden flight by domestic investors in emerging economies and find that true sudden stops are accompanied by a greater macroeconomic impact.

References

Ahmed, F., R. Arezki, and N. Funke (2005), 'The Composition of Capital Flows: Is South Africa Different?', *Working Paper* WP/05/40, International Monetary Fund.

Albuquerque, R. (2003), 'The Composition of International Capital Flows: Risk Sharing Through Foreign Direct Investment', *Journal of International Economics*, 61: 353–83.

Alfaro, L., A. Chanda, S. Kalemli-Ozcan, and S. Sayek (2006), 'How Does Foreign Direct Investment Promote Economic Growth? Exploring the Effects of Financial Markets on Linkages', *Working Paper* 12522, National Bureau of Economic Research.

Arvanitis, A. (2005), 'Foreign Direct Investment in South Africa: Why Has It Been So Low?', in Nowak, M. and L. A. Ricci (eds), *Post-Apartheid South Africa: The First Ten Years*, International Monetary Fund.

Calvo, G. A., A. Izquierdo, and L. F. Mejía (2008), 'Systemic Sudden Stops: The Relevance of Balance-Sheet Effects and Financial Integration', *NBER Working Paper* 14026, National Bureau of Economic Research.

—— (2004), 'On the Empirics of Sudden Stops: The Relevance of Balance-Sheet Effects', *NBER Working Paper* 10520, National Bureau of Economic Research.

Cowan, K., E. Levy-Yeyati, U. Panizza, and F. Sturzenegger (2006), 'Sovereign Debt in the Americas: New Data and Stylized Facts', *Working Paper* #577, Research Department, Inter-American Development Bank.

Dahlquist, M., L. Pinkowitz, R. Stulz and R. Williamson (2003), 'Corporate Governance and the Home Bias', *Journal of Financial and Quantitative Analysis*, 38(1), 87–110.

Davis, E. P. (2002), 'Pension Fund Management and International Investment—A Global Perspective', Discussion Paper PI- 0206, The Pensions Institute, Cass Business School.

DBSA and NEPAD (2003), *Financing Africa's Development: Enhancing the Role of Private Finance*, Development Report 2003, Development Bank of Southern Africa and NEPAD

Eichengreen, B. (2001) 'Capital Account Liberalization: What Do Cross-Country Studies Tell Us?', *The World Bank Economic Review*, 15(3), 341–65.

Faruqee, H., S. Li, and I. K. Yan (2004), 'The Determinants of International Portfolio Holdings and Home Bias', *IMF Working Paper* WP/04/34, International Monetary Fund.

Fedderke, J. W. and W. Liu (2002), 'Modelling The Determinants of Capital Flows and Capital Flight: With an Application to South African Data from 1960 to 1995', *Economic Modelling*, 19:419–44.

Fedderke, J. W. and A. T. Romm (2006), 'Growth Impact and Determinants of Foreign Direct Investment into South Africa, 1956-2003', *Economic Modelling*, 23: 738–60.

Fidora, M., M. Fratzscher, and C. Thimann (2006), 'Home Bias in Global Bond and Equity Markets: The Role of Real Exchange Rate Volatility', *Working Paper Series*, no. 685, European Central Bank.

Forbes, K. J. (2005), 'The Microeconomic Evidence on Capital Controls: No Free Lunch', *NBER Working Paper 11372*, National Bureau of Economic Research.

Frankel, J. A. and E. A. Cavallo (2004), 'Does Openness to Trade Make Countries More Vulnerable to Sudden Stops, Or Less? Using Gravity to Establish Causality', *NBER Working Paper* 10957, National Bureau of Economic Research.

Frankel, J., B. Smit, and F. Sturzenegger (2006), 'South Africa: Macroeconomic Challenges after a Decade of Success', *Working Paper* No 133, Center for International Development, Harvard University.

French, K. R. and J. M. Poterba (1991), 'Investor Diversification and International Equity Markets', *American Economic Review*, 81(2): 222–6.

Gelb, S. and A. Black (2004), 'Foreign Direct Investment in South Africa', in Estrin, S. and K. Meyer (eds), *Investment Strategies in Emerging Markets*, Cheltenham, UK: Edward Elgar.

Goldstein, I. and A. Razin (2005), 'An Information-Based Trade-off between Foreign Direct Investment and Foreign Portfolio Investment', *NBER Working Paper* 11757, National Bureau of Economic Research.

Guidotti, P. E., F. Sturzenegger and A. Villar (2004), 'On the Consequences of Sudden Stops', *Economia*, (Spring): 171–214.

Hausmann, R. and E. Fernández-Arias (2000), 'Foreign Direct Investment: Good Cholesterol?', *Working Paper* #417, Research Department, Inter-American Development Bank.

Ishii, S. and K. Habermeier (2002), 'Capital Account Liberalization and Financial Sector Stability', *Occasional Paper* 211, International Monetary Fund.

Kahn, B. (2005), '"Original Sin" and Bond Market Development in Sub-Saharan Africa', in Teunissen, J. J. and A. Akkerman (eds.), *Africa in the World Economy: The National, Regional and International Challenges*, The Hague, Netherlands: FONDAD.

—— (1991), 'Capital flight and exchange controls in South Africa', *Research Paper, no. 4*, Centre for the Study of the South African Economy and International Finance, London School of Economics.

Kaplan, E. and D. Rodrik (2001), 'Did the Malaysian Capital Controls Work?', *NBER Working Paper* 8142, National Bureau of Economic Research.

Kho, B.-C., R. M. Stulz, and F. E. Warnock (2006), 'Financial Globalization, Governance and the Evolution of Home Bias', *NBER Working Paper* W12389, National Bureau of Economic Research.

Leape, J. and L. Thomas (2008), 'Prudential regulation of foreign exposure for institutional investors in South Africa', *Research Paper*, Centre for Research into Economics and Finance in Southern Africa, London School of Economics.

Lehmann, A., S. Sayek, and H. G. Kang (2004), 'Multinational Affiliates and Local Financial Markets', *IMF Working Paper* WP/04/107, International Monetary Fund.

Lewis, K. (1999), 'Trying to Explain Home Bias in Equities and Consumption', *Journal of Economic Literature*, 37: 571–608.

Montiel, P. and C. Reinhart (1999), 'Do capital controls and macroeconomic policy influence the volume and composition of capital flows? Evidence from the 1990s', *Journal of International Money and Finance*, 18(4).

OECD (2003), *Institutional Investors: Statistical Yearbook* 2003.

Roldos, J. E. (2004), 'Pension Reform, Investment Restrictions and Capital Markets', *Policy Discussion Paper* PDP/04/4, International Monetary Fund.

Rothenberg, A. D. and F. E. Warnock (2006), 'Sudden Flight and True Sudden Stops', *NBER Working Paper* 12726, National Bureau of Economic Research.

Smit, B. W. and B. A. Mocke (1991), 'Capital Flight from South Africa: Magnitudes and Causes', *South African Journal of Economics*, 59(2): 101–17.

Standard and Poor's (2006a), *S&P Emerging Market Indices: Index Methodology*, December 2006.

—— (2006b) *Global Stock Market Factbook 2006*.

Taylor, M. P. and L. Sarno (1997), 'Capital Flows to Developing Countries: Long and Short-Term Determinants', *The World Bank Economic Review*, 11(3): 451–70.

Tesar, L. L. and I. M. Werner (1995), 'Home Bias and High Turnover', *Journal of International Money and Finance*, 14(4): 467–92.

Thomas, L. and J. Leape, with M. Hanouch and R. Rumney (2005), 'Foreign Direct Investment in South Africa: The Initial Impact of the Trade, Development and Cooperation Agreement between South Africa and the European Union', *Occasional Paper, no.* 1, Regional Trade Facilitation Programme, Imani Development (International)/UK Department for International Development.

Walters, S. S. and J. W. Prinsloo (2002), 'The Impact of Offshore Listings on the South African Economy', *Quarterly Bulletin*, South African Reserve Bank, September.

Williamson, J., S. Griffith-Jones, and R. Gottschalk (2003), 'Should Capital Controls Have a Place in the Future International Monetary System?', *Research Paper*, Institute of Development Studies.

Wesso, G. R. (2001), 'The Dynamics of Capital Flows in South Africa: An Empirical Investigation', *Quarterly Bulletin*, South African Reserve Bank, June.

6
Trade Policy in South Africa

Lawrence Edwards, Rashad Cassim, and Dirk van Seventer

1. Introduction[1]

The democratic election of the new government in 1994 coincided with an important shift in South Africa's development strategy; from export promotion with import controls to greater openness through tariff liberalization. Despite some fears to the contrary, the new government agreed to an ambitious programme of tariff liberalization as part of its offer in the GATT (General Agreement on Tariffs and Trade) Uruguay round (Bell, 1997). The government also concluded free trade agreements (FTAs) with the European Union (EU) and the Southern Africa Development Community (SADC) and more modest trade agreements with MERCOSUR[2] and the European Free Trade Association (EFTA) states.

These reforms led to a substantial simplification and rationalization of the South African tariff structure[3] (Jenkins et al., 1997; Edwards, 2005). The number of tariff lines fell from over 12,000 at the beginning of the 1990s to 6,500 in 2006. Non *ad valorem* tariff rates, which were used frequently in the early 1990s, were replaced with *ad valorem* rates. Export subsidies, import surcharges and non-tariff barriers were phased out.

While there is general agreement that these reforms reduced average nominal protection, whether this translated into reduced effective protection at the sectoral level remains contentious. This chapter evaluates South Africa's trade policy under democracy, and critically reviews the burgeoning empirical

---

[1] Acknowledgements: The authors are grateful for comments from Janine Aron and Brian Kahn.

[2] Mercado Commun del Cono Sur (Southern Common Market). Argentina, Brazil, Paraguay, Uruguay, and Venezuela are full members.

[3] South Africa is part of the Southern African Customs Union which includes Botswana, Lesotho, Namibia, and Swaziland. Industrial and trade policy has essentially been conducted by South Africa throughout the history of the Union. Reference is therefore generally made to South Africa rather than SACU when discussing trade and industrial policy.

studies of the effects of trade reform on trade flows, growth, employment, poverty, productivity, and inflation. Drawing on these reflections, the chapter contributes to the policy debate on further reform of the trade regime, again on the policy agenda given the recent launch of the Department of Trade and Industry's National Industrial Policy Framework (NIPF). Furthermore, South Africa presents a good case study of the effects of trade liberalization in a middle-income economy, and can therefore offer important lessons.

Several conclusions can be drawn from the chapter. South Africa made considerable progress in reducing 'most favoured nation' (MFN) tariff rates which fell from 17.9 per cent in 1994 to 9.6 per cent in 2000. Effective protection and the anti-export bias also fell during this period, although some industries still retain effective protection rates in excess of 40 per cent. These trends place South Africa in line with other middle-income economies in terms of the reduction in protection and the final level of protection. Since 2000, there has been no further progress in reducing MFN tariff rates. Rather, tariff liberalization has been pursued, albeit modestly, through preferential trade agreements, primarily with the EU and SADC.

The empirical evidence reviewed here suggests that trade reform has positively influenced trade flows; has stimulated aggregate productivity growth; and has significantly reduced the mean wholesale price inflation rate as well as the exchange rate pass-through into wholesale prices. The effect of trade reform on employment has not been fully resolved. An important shortcoming in all this research is the lack of firm-level analysis of the effects of trade liberalization.

Despite past progress in reducing tariffs, scope remains for further tariff reform. The current tariff structure remains complex relative to other middle-income economies as measured by the coefficient of variation, the number of tariff bands, and the number of domestic spikes (Edwards and Lawrence, 2007). Nominal and effective protection rates remain high for many sectors, particularly those producing final consumer goods. There are also opportunities for liberalization of trade in services, which remain relatively protected.

The political and economic will for further comprehensive trade reform by government, however, seems not very strong. Comprehensive tariff reform is not emphasized in the government's current growth and trade initiatives. Rather, tariff determination is to be conducted on a case-by-case basis and guided by a more active industrial policy that aims to facilitate industrial diversification.

We argue in this chapter that such a piecemeal approach may well turn out to be counterproductive. In addition to being an administratively burdensome process, there is a strong possibility that tariff reform will be obstructed by industry lobby groups. A more comprehensive reform strategy needs to be considered, whereby government commits itself to tariff simplification and a unilateral phase-down in tariff rates.

Trade Policy in South Africa

The chapter is made up of three main sections. Section 2 reviews the process of trade reform in South Africa since the 1970s, with a particular focus on multilateral and preferential trade reform since 1994. Section 3 then evaluates the extent to which trade reform since 1994 has reduced nominal protection, effective protection and the anti-export bias. This is followed in section 4 by a review of the empirical literature analysing the impact of trade liberalization and openness on the South African economy. The chapter concludes with an assessment of the scope for further trade reform.

2. Trade reform in South Africa from the 1970s

2.1. From import substitution industrialization to export promotion

Prior to the 1970s, South Africa's trade and industrial policies were aimed primarily at encouraging import substitution industrialization. These policies are comprehensively described by Jenkins et al. (1997) and Bell (1993). Trade policy began to change in the 1970s in response to a decline in the contribution of import substitution policies towards growth (Fallon and Pereira de Silva, 1994), a continued dependence on gold as a source of foreign exchange and diminished export pessimism brought about by rapid export-led growth in some of the newly industrialized countries of South East Asia (Jenkins et al., 1997). A chronology of the subsequent reforms is presented in Table 6.1.

Reforms began with the relaxation of quantitative restrictions (QRs) and the introduction of an Export Development Assistance scheme in 1972, which was then reinforced in 1978 (Bell, 1993; 1997). Although tariff increases compensated for the relaxation of QRs, these were not fully compensatory resulting in a net decline in protection (Bell, 1993; 1997). Nevertheless, the trade regime remained protectionist as the incentives introduced were an attempt to redress some of the anti-export bias rather than shift the economy towards export orientated growth (Jenkins et al., 1997: 7). Attempts to increase manufacturing exports were also offset by the appreciation of the rand during the early 1980s in response to the rise in the gold price.

The replacement of QRs with tariffs continued during the 1980s and the share of import value subject to QRs fell from 77 per cent to 23 per cent between 1983 and 1985 and then to below 15 per cent in 1992. The period, however, was characterized by intermittent use of import surcharges in response to balance of payments crises. They were first used from 1977 to 1979 in response to the virtual cessation of capital inflows after the Soweto riots in 1976 (Aron and Muellbauer, 2007). Surcharges were reintroduced from 1982 to 1983, and then again in 1985 after a severe sovereign debt crisis ensued following the 'Rubicon speech' of the

Table 6.1. Chronology of trade liberalization from the early 1970s

1972–6	The 'Reynders Commission of Inquiry' in 1972 emphasized the need to diversify into non-gold exports through export promotion methods.
	Export Development Assistance scheme introduced.
	Substitution of tariffs for Quantitative Restrictions (QRs) resulting in net decline in protection (Bell, 1997).
1979–80	Rise in gold price resulting in the appreciation of rand.
1980	Reinforced system of export incentives.
1983–5	Proportion of value of imports subject to QRs falls from 77 per cent to 23 per cent over the period.
	Relaxation of import permits by switching from a positive list to a negative list.
	Real depreciation of rand.
1985–92	Proportion of tariff items subject to QRs falls from 28 per cent in 1985 to less than 15 per cent in 1992.
September 1985	Introduction of 10 per cent import surcharge on all imported goods not bound by GATT.
August 1988	Differential surcharge rates applied to luxury goods (60 per cent), capital goods (10 per cent), motor vehicles (20 per cent) and intermediate goods (10 per cent).
	Increased applications for *ad valorem* and formula duties by businesses (Bell, 1993)
1989	'Structural adjustment programmes' involving a system of duty free imports for exports implemented for motor vehicles and textiles and clothing.
1990	General Export Incentive Scheme (GEIS) introduced. Provides a tax free financial export subsidy to exporters based on the value of exports, degree of processing and local content of the exported product.
1990–1	Reduction of import surcharges to 40 per cent, 5 per cent, 15 per cent and 5 per cent for luxury, capital, motor vehicles and intermediate goods, respectively.
23 June 1994	Import surcharges abolished for Capital and Intermediate goods.
1 October 1995	Remaining import surcharges abolished.
1994	South Africa's GATT offer during Uruguay Round:
	About 98 per cent of all tariff lines are to be bound at the Harmonized System (HS) eight-digit level as against 18 per cent before the round
	Reduction in the number of tariff rates to six: 0 per cent, 5 per cent, 10 per cent, 15 per cent, 20 per cent and 30 per cent
	Rationalization of the over 12,000 tariff lines
	Tariffication of QRs on agricultural products
	Special provisions (extensions of the adjustment period and raised maximum tariff rates) for textile, clothing and motor vehicle industries granted.
	Decision taken to phase out GEIS.
	Adoption of anti-dumping and countervailing duties legislation
1995	Payments under GEIS becomes taxable, range of eligible products reduced.
1994–7	Deregulation of agricultural marketing and control boards established under the Agricultural Marketing Act of 1968. Import control on agricultural products removed.
1996	New Tariff Rationalization Process (TRP) formulated: Tariff lines and peaks to be reduced, Formula and Specific duties to be converted into *ad valorem* rates, Imports that have no 'suitable substitutes' to be duty free, *ad valorem* rates of 30 per cent on final products, 20 per cent on intermediate goods and 10 per cent on primary goods are generally not to be exceeded.
	GEIS limited to fully manufacturing goods, although the local content requirement for the maximum subsidy is reduced from 75 per cent to 65 per cent.

August 1996	Signing of the SADC Free Trade Protocol (implemented in September 2000)
1 July 1997	Termination of export subsidies provided under GEIS.
1 January 2000	Implementation of SA-EU Trade, Development and Cooperation Agreement (TDCA)
2000	Preferential access to USA for some products under African Growth and Opportunity Act (AGOA)
21 October 2002	2002 SACU Agreement introduces a new institutional structure; a dispute settlement mechanism; the requirement to have common policies on industrial development, agriculture, competition, and unfair trade practices; and a new system regarding the common revenue pool and sharing formula (WTO, 2003: viii)
December 2004	Preferential Trade Agreement signed between SACU and MERCOSUR
2006	Preferential Trade Agreement signed between SACU and the European Free Trade Association (EFTA) states.
January 2007	Imposition of quotas on imports of clothing and textiles from China

Source: Updated account based on Edwards (2005).

then President, P. W Botha.[4] Differential surcharge rates on luxury goods (60 per cent), capital goods (10 per cent), motor vehicles (20 per cent) and intermediate goods (10 per cent) replaced the uniform 10 per cent rate in August 1988. These had a substantial impact on the overall level of protection, for example raising collection duties from just under 6 per cent to 11 per cent in 1990.

In addition, there was an increase in the application by and award of protection to businesses in the form of *ad valorem* and formula duties[5] in response to the economic downturn (Bell, 1993: 9). The result was a period of rising protection in the late 1980s (Holden, 1992) and an increasingly complex tariff structure compared to a range of developing countries (Belli et al., 1993). The protective regime was compounded by the imposition of trade and investment sanctions—first by Sweden in 1979 and then from 1985/6 by the remaining Nordic countries, six members of the Commonwealth Group of nations, the members of the European Community and the USA (Evenett, 2002). The industrial policy landscape was then increasingly shaped by strategic interventions to reduce the dependence of South Africa on imports of products such as liquid fuels.[6]

---

[4] The debt crisis, where South Africa suspended capital and interest payments on foreign debt, arose from a combination of various factors. Firstly, the collapse in the gold price in the early 1980s reduced the foreign currency value of South Africa's main export. Secondly, political instability and the imposition of the state of emergency in July 1985 led to an outflow of capital and a refusal by foreign banks to renew their short-term loans. Finally, failure by President Botha to introduce anticipated reforms to the apartheid system, in what is known as his 'Rubicon Speech' on 15 August 1985, was followed by a sharp depreciation of the currency and the imposition of trade and financial sanctions by many countries.

[5] Formula duties, which set a price floor for imports, were frequently used as an instrument to prevent dumping.

[6] These initiatives included the commissioning of a gas-to-liquid plant (Mossgas) to exploit the natural gas fields on the Southern Cape coast in 1987 and continued investments in synthetic fuel plants to produce liquefied petroleum gas from coal by the South African Coal, Oil and Gas Corporation (Sasol).

The early 1990s were characterized by a much stronger export promotion drive. The implementation of 'structural adjustment programmes' involving a system of duty free imports for exported goods of the motor vehicle, clothing and textile industries in 1989 was shortly followed in 1990 by direct export subsidies for manufactured goods under the General Export Incentive Scheme (GEIS) (Table 6.1). Import surcharges were also gradually reduced and finally eliminated by 1995, and further efforts were made to reduce quantitative restrictions. While these measures reduced protection, an anti-export bias still existed in a majority of the manufacturing sectors (Belli et al., 1993), and little emphasis was placed on reducing the level and complexity of nominal tariff protection.

2.2. Tariff liberalization under the WTO agreement

The year 1994 signalled an important shift in South Africa's development strategy, from export promotion with import controls to greater openness through tariff liberalization. This shift is most strongly reflected in South Africa's commitment in the GATT Uruguay Round to bind 98 per cent of all tariff lines, rationalize the over 12,000 tariff lines and replace quantitative restrictions on agricultural products with tariffs (Table 6.1). In addition, South Africa offered to reduce the number of tariff categories to six at rates ranging from 0 to 30 per cent with any discretionary changes to the system being disallowed.

Trade reform was accompanied by a number of domestic policies, including the new macroeconomic policy, 'Growth, Employment, and Redistribution' (GEAR) that aimed, in part, to transform South Africa into a 'competitive, outward orientated economy' (Republic of South Africa, 1996). Government also finally deregulated the agricultural marketing and control boards, including import controls on agricultural products, established under the Agricultural Marketing Act of 1968.

These policies initiated a process of tariff reform unprecedented in South Africa's history. As shown in Table 6.2, the number of tariff lines fell from over 12,000 at the beginning of the 1990s to 6,500 by 2006. Progress was also made in improving the transparency of the tariff structure with the replacement of specific, mixed, compound, and formula duties[7] with *ad valorem* duties. The share of *ad valorem* rates in all tariff rates rose from 69 per cent in 1994 to 97 per cent in 2006. Finally, non-tariff measures were phased out, particularly those relating to agricultural and processed food products. In all cases, the bulk of South Africa's tariff reform took place prior to 2000 and only limited reductions and rationalizations took place subsequently.

---

[7] Anti-dumping and countervailing duty legislation was adopted to replace the need for these types of duties.

Trade Policy in South Africa

Table 6.2. Structure of MFN tariffs of SACU, 1990–2006

	1994	2000 MFN	2006 MFN	2006 EU	2006 SADC
1. Number of tariff lines	11231	7868	6420	6420	6420
2. Share ad valorem (per cent)	69	75	97	97	99
3. Number of tariff bands	770	214	100	95	9
ad valorem	31	38	38	37	6
Other	739	176	62	58	3
4. Duty-free tariff lines (% all lines)	26.1	44.4	53	66	99
5. Domestic tariff 'spikes' (% all lines)[a]	3.7	4.8	8.8	14	0.49
6. International tariff 'spikes' (% all lines)[b]	43.5	35.2	21.2	8.8	0.2
7. Coefficient of variation[c]	1.1	1.2	1.4	1.6	16
8. 'Nuisance' applied rates (% all lines)[d]	1.5	1.2	1.3	0.8	0
9. Simple average	17.9	12.8	8.2	4.8	0.1
10. Weighted average	15.7	8.1	7.4	7.9	0.0
11. Bound tariffs		96.4	96.6		

Source: Edwards (2005), updated with the 2006 tariff schedule obtained from South African Revenue Services.
Notes:
   a. Calculations are based on tariff schedules including *ad valorem* equivalents. SACU refers to Southern African Customs Union.
   b. Domestic tariff spikes are defined as those exceeding three times the overall simple average applied rate. For 2002 and 2006 these are presented separately for each trade agreement.
   c. International tariff spikes are defined as those exceeding 15 per cent.
   d. Coefficient of variation is calculated as the standard deviation divided by the overall simple average.
   e. Nuisance rates are those greater than zero, but less than or equal to 2 per cent.

2.3. Preferential trade agreements

In addition to multilateral trade reform, the government has pursued a dual track of concluding new regional and bilateral free trade agreements and re-negotiating the terms of the existing Southern African Customs Union (SACU). The focus on preferential trade agreements has to a large extent defined trade policy since 2000. In this section, we explore these agreements in more detail.

2.3.1. THE SOUTHERN AFRICAN CUSTOMS UNION

SACU is one of the oldest customs unions in the world and was established in 1910. Historically, South Africa unilaterally set the tariffs in accordance with its own industrial policies, but as compensation, the customs revenue was disproportionately allocated to the other SACU members. The introduction of the 2002 SACU Agreement altered the modus operandi of the customs union by creating new institutional structures to administer tariff policy. Other changes included a dispute settlement mechanism; the requirement to have common policies on industrial development, agriculture, competition, and unfair trade practices; and a new system regarding the common revenue pool and sharing formula (WTO, 2003: p. viii). The agreement democratized the decision-making process, allowing the BLNS countries (Botswana, Lesotho, Namibia, and Swaziland) a greater say in the setting of tariffs.

These reforms have resulted in a number of unintended consequences that may inhibit cross-border trade and tariff reform. Under the new revenue sharing formula the customs pool is allocated according to each country's share of total intra-SACU trade, excluding re-exports. SACU economies are now required to monitor trade flows and have the undesirable incentive to inflate such data so as to increase their revenue shares. Estimates of BLNS trade with South Africa, for example, are shown to vary by up to 60 per cent (Flatters and Stern, 2006).

The formula has also perpetuated a dependency on customs revenue as a source of government revenue in many of the BLNS economies. Customs revenue currently accounts for over 50 per cent of total revenue for Lesotho and Swaziland, 41 per cent for Namibia, 20 per cent for Botswana and less than 4 per cent for South Africa (Flatters and Stern, 2006). This dependence on revenue creates perverse incentives for trade policy. BLNS countries may, for example, be less willing to tolerate reductions in common external tariffs if this leads to large reductions in customs revenue. South Africa has the incentive to make extensive use of rebates as the benefits are captured by domestic firms, but the costs in terms of revenue reductions are disproportionately borne by the BLNS countries (Flatters and Stern, 2006). Finally, the formula inhibits new accessions as this may lead to revenue dilution for existing members.

Reform of the revenue sharing formula may be a necessary step if the SACU members are to pursue further tariff reform in a pro-active manner within the institutional framework set up by the 2002 SACU Agreement.

2.3.2. RECENT PREFERENTIAL TRADE AGREEMENTS

Preferential trade agreements have become the central thrust of South Africa's current trade policy (Table 6.1). South Africa concluded comprehensive free trade agreements with the EU and SADC. These came into effect in 2000. The government has also signed a commitment to extend the SADC FTA to a customs union by 2010, a common market by 2015 and a monetary union in 2016.

More recently, preferential trade agreements have been concluded with MERCOSUR (signed in December 2004) and EFTA (mid 2006). Negotiations on a free trade agreement between SACU and the USA commenced in 2003, but disagreement on the inclusion of 'new generation items (services, intellectual property, government procurement and investment) led to a collapse in the negotiations in 2006. In the future, the government aims to enter bilateral trade agreements with India and China.

Various factors govern South Africa's interest in securing preferential trade agreements with different regions and countries. These agreements are seen as a mechanism to complement multilateral agreements through securing market access and reflect a strong mercantilist ethos amongst bureaucrats in the ministry of trade and industry (Cassim, 2007; DTI, 2007: 42). This is most clearly indicated in the DTI's (1997: 42) stated objective of bilateral agreements, namely 'to achieve substantial market access for manufactured and agricultural goods and leverage export-oriented investment'. Interest in the FTA with the EU was also driven by the desire to send out a positive signal to investors about South Africa's commitment to trade reform and to address broader development issues including aid and support for industry. Hence the name: 'Trade, Development and Cooperation Agreement' (TDCA).

A central feature of the free trade agreements with the EU and SADC is the asymmetrical implementation of tariff reductions. The EU agreed to liberalize at a faster pace (3 years compared to 12 for South Africa), and with a broader coverage (95 per cent of all imports as compared with 86 per cent for South Africa). Average South African tariffs are to be phased down from 8.8 per cent in 1999 to 4.9 per cent in 2012, although they are to remain relatively high (above 10 per cent) on certain sectors including clothing, vehicles, footwear, and processed food. This nevertheless represents a significant differential in protection for many sectors compared to current MFN rates (see later).

As far as the SADC FTA is concerned, South Africa is subject to more rapid liberalization reforms and a set of 'general offers', while other members are permitted to make 'differential offers'. From South Africa's perspective, the phasing-in of this agreement is scheduled to occur over an 8 year period, while other SADC countries are given a 12 year phase-down period upon accession and it is expected that by 2012, 98 per cent of the SADC region's trade will be subject to zero tariffs (Cassim and Zarenda, 2004). The SADC FTA has already resulted in the elimination by SACU of almost all tariffs on SADC imports four years after accession (Table 6.2), while SADC tariffs imposed on SACU exports have started to decline from 2007. Despite the reduction in SACU tariffs, SADC imports still appear to be restricted by stringent rules of origin (Flatters, 2002).

3. Has the level of protection fallen in the South African economy?

The question whether the simplification of the tariff structure shown in Table 6.2 is associated with substantial reductions in the level of protection in South Africa has received considerable attention (Fedderke and Vase, 2001; Rangasamy and Harmse, 2003; van Seventer, 2001; Cassim, 2003; Edwards, 2005). In this section we investigate the extent to which the shift in trade regime reduced nominal protection, effective protection, and the anti-export bias, using sectoral level data.

3.1. Nominal protection

Nominal protection is commonly measured using collection rates (the ratio of collection duty to import value) and simple or weighted average scheduled tariff rates. A cursory review of the aggregate collection rates for South Africa suggests only moderate tariff reductions, unless the elimination of import surcharges is included. Total collection rates, inclusive of surcharges, fell sharply from 10.5 per cent in 1990 to 4 per cent in 2000, but 5 percentage points of this decline can be attributed to the elimination of surcharges.

The collection rates, however, are an incomplete measure of tariff protection in South Africa. They underestimate protection where tariffs are prohibitively high and do not adequately reflect the effect of quota protection, although apart from some agricultural and food products, these had largely been eliminated by 1994. Collection rates are also biased downwards by various duty drawbacks and rebates on offer to exporters and some domestic industries. The bias is extensive, especially for motor vehicles because of large rebates under the Motor Industry Development Programme and clothing and textiles under the Duty Credit Certificate System (Kaplan, 2003).[8] An alternative measure of protection is the average tariff rate derived from the tariff schedules. Edwards (2005) has constructed detailed tariff schedules for South Africa from 1988 to 2004 using data published in the South African government gazettes. These data, updated to 2006 using data obtained from the South African Revenue Services, are used to calculate the import weighted average tariff rates by sector presented in Table 6.3.[9]

Looking at the level of tariffs over time, it is clear that a considerable reduction in nominal protection was achieved during the 1990s. The import weighted average tariff for manufacturing dropped from 19.9 per cent in 1994 to 9.6 per cent in 2000, with the elimination of surcharges accounting for 2 percentage points of this decline. The decline in protection during the 1990s was comprehensive and the import weighted average tariff fell in all aggregate sectors presented in Table 6.3. Relatively large declines in protection, equiva-

---

[8] For example, tariff rates on clothing and vehicles were in excess of 100 per cent in the early 1990s, yet the collection rates in 1994 for motor vehicles and clothing were only 10 per cent and 33 per cent, respectively (Edwards, 2005). The collection rates for these sectors by 1998 were no lower, despite reductions in the scheduled tariff rates.

[9] Scheduled tariff rates have their own problems. The average is sensitive to the choice of weights and to the calculation of tariff equivalents for non-ad valorem rates. Unit values for 1994 and 2000 were found to be highly erratic and the collection rate is used to calculate the tariff equivalent for these years, while import unit values were used to calculate tariff equivalents for 2006.

Table 6.3. Import weighted average protection by sector

Industry [SIC]	1994 MFN + surcharges	1994 MFN	2000 MFN	2006 MFN	EU	SADC	Total
Total	**17.6**	**15.7**	**8.1**	**7.4**	**7.9**	**0.0**	**7.3**
Agriculture, forestry & fishing [1]	6.5	5.5	8.1	3.8	1.7	0.0	2.9
Coal mining [21]	0.0	0.0	0.0	0.0	0.0	0.0	0.0
Gold & uranium [23]	10.0	10.0	0.0	0.0	0.0	0.0	0.0
Other mining [22/24/25/29]	0.2	0.2	0.0	0.0	0.0	0.0	0.0
Manufacturing [3]	**19.9**	**17.9**	**9.6**	**9.8**	**8.0**	**0.1**	**8.9**
Food [301–4]	19.0	16.6	11.1	11.3	8.2	0.0	10.5
Beverages [305]	14.2	9.1	12.1	5.4	1.9	0.0	2.7
Tobacco [306]	44.4	40.4	25.7	33.7	16.9	0.0	19.0
Textiles [311–12]	32.6	30.0	23.7	19.8	8.6	0.0	16.8
Wearing apparel [313–15]	76.6	67.6	49.9	38.1	18.4	0.0	35.6
Leather & leather products [316]	18.6	14.5	14.7	21.2	12.4	0.0	19.9
Footwear [317]	56.1	43.0	31.0	29.8	22.4	0.0	29.2
Wood & wood products [321–2]	4.9	4.2	3.2	6.4	1.3	0.0	4.4
Paper & paper products [323]	9.0	8.7	8.2	8.8	1.9	0.0	4.5
Printing & publishing [324–6]	11.7	8.7	1.3	1.6	0.7	0.0	1.0
Coke & refined petroleum [331–3]	30.8	30.8	1.8	0.2	1.0	0.0	0.4
Basic chemicals [334]	6.3	6.3	1.8	2.4	0.8	0.0	1.8
Other chemicals [335–6]	9.0	7.2	2.6	2.7	1.8	0.0	2.2
Rubber products [337]	20.1	18.6	17.5	17.1	9.6	0.0	14.0
Plastic products [338]	22.0	19.5	12.6	14.1	9.5	0.0	12.1
Glass & glass products [341]	16.6	10.7	8.3	8.3	4.6	0.0	6.9
Non-metallic minerals [342]	13.8	11.2	5.3	8.4	3.4	0.0	6.2
Basic iron & steel [351]	7.7	7.1	3.5	3.1	0.0	0.0	1.8
Basic non-ferrous metals [352]	6.3	6.0	0.8	0.6	1.1	0.0	0.5
Metal products [353–5]	16.5	13.4	6.7	8.8	3.9	0.0	6.6
Machinery & equipment [356–9]	4.7	2.7	1.1	1.6	0.4	0.0	1.0
Electrical machinery [361–6]	11.0	8.7	5.9	6.6	3.6	0.0	5.1
Communication equipment [371–3]	16.0	11.5	2.7	3.0	0.2	0.0	1.9
Professional & scientific [374–6]	4.7	1.5	0.5	0.1	0.1	0.0	0.1
Motor vehicles [381–3]	67.0	66.6	34.2	25.9	26.5	5.3	26.2
Other transport equipment [384–7]	2.2	1.0	0.2	0.5	0.1	0.0	0.3
Furniture [391]	27.6	21.7	19.4	19.4	13.1	0.0	16.6
Other manufacturing [392–3]	18.3	11.9	4.9	4.7	1.9	0.0	3.5

(Continued)

Table 6.3. (Continued)

Industry [SIC]	1994 MFN + surcharges	1994 MFN	2000 MFN	2006 MFN	2006 EU	2006 SADC	2006 Total
Broad Economic Classification							
Capital goods	14.8	1.6	2.6	1.3	0.3		2.0
Consumption goods	19.9	12.8	17.2	3.6	0.0		12.7
Intermediate goods	8.4	7.7	5.1	7.6	0.0		5.6
Passenger vehicles	99.9	46.0	30.3	31.9	15.0		31.2
Goods not elsewhere specified	3.4	0.0	0.0	0.0	0.0		0.0

Source: Own calculations using raw data from Edwards (2005).
Notes: For formula duties and mixed duties in 1994 and 2000, the collection rate was used where it exceeded the *ad valorem* component. The collection rate was also used as the *ad valorem* equivalent of specific duties in 1994 and 2000. In 2000 the upper bound *ad valorem* rate in the mixed duty was used for clothing and textiles. If the mean value is used, the average tariff for clothing falls to 42.4 and for textiles to 19.2. In 2006, *ad valorem* equivalents were based on import unit values calculated using value and volume data at the HS eight-digit level.

lent to a 10 per cent or more reduction in price, were experienced in clothing, footwear, motor vehicle, coke products, other manufacturing and communication equipment between 1994 and 2000. Average protection rates nevertheless remained in excess of 20 per cent for many of these sectors (leather, textiles, motor vehicles, clothing, footwear, and tobacco).

For many of these sectors, reductions in tariffs proceeded at a faster pace than was required under South Africa's offer to the WTO, reflecting significant unilateral trade liberalization (Bell, 1997). In addition, South Africa unilaterally reduced the GATT agreed 12-year adjustment period and maximum tariff level of 45 per cent for textiles and clothing to an 8-year phase-down period and a 40 per cent terminal tariff. Similarly, tariffs on motor vehicles and automotive components fell faster than the phase-down specially negotiated in GATT.

Since 2000, little further progress has been made in reducing MFN rates and the import weighted average tariff on manufacturing at around 9.8 per cent in 2006 was roughly equivalent to that of 2000. MFN reform from 2000 has been limited to some rationalization and simplification of tariffs lines for clothing and textile products in 2004 and a decline in average tariffs on motor vehicles from 34.2 per cent in 2000 to 26 per cent in 2006. More progress has been made in reducing average tariffs on EU and SADC imports, which fell to 8 per cent and 0.1 per cent for manufactured goods in 2006, respectively (Table 6.3). At the sectoral level, tariff protection on SADC imports fell to zero for almost all sectors except motor vehicles where an average tariff of 5.3 per cent is still applied. For the EU, average tariffs also fell in most sectors, the main exception being motor vehicles where tariffs did not fall relative to MFN rates. Since products from the motor vehicles sector account for a high proportion of imports from the EU, this has resulted in only a moderate decline in aggregate protection on imports of EU goods.[10]

These trends place South Africa in line with the experience of other middle-income economies. The current level of protection in South Africa measured as 7.3 per cent is slightly lower than other middle-income countries (8.3 per cent), but is higher than the average for high-income OECD countries (3.4 per cent).[11] The extent to which tariffs have fallen is also roughly equivalent to other middle-income economies. Tariff protection in South Africa fell from 15.7 per cent to 7.3 per cent (7.3 per cent decline) between 1994 and 2006, which is similar to the decline from 15.3 per cent to 8.3 per cent (6 per cent decline) for the average lower-middle-income economies over the same period.[12]

3.2. Effective protection[13]

Whether the declines in nominal tariffs translated into lower effective rates of protection (ERP) is contested, as typified in the debate between Fedderke and Vase (2001: 447) and Rangasamy and Harmse (2003: 721). The controversy stems from conflicting methodologies and data sources and the studies are not directly comparable (Edwards, 2005).

Table 6.4 follows Edwards and Lawrence (2008) and reports estimates of the effective rates of protection for manufacturing, including various aggregates for groups of industries labelled as Commodity and Non-Commodity manufacturing. Commodity manufacturing covers sectors that have a high share of primary commodity inputs in their value (see categories in the notes to Table 6.4). The aggregate measures of protection are calculated using 1990 trade shares and industry estimates of ERP obtained from Edwards (2005) and updated to 2006. The advantage of these ERP estimates, as opposed to other studies, is that they are based on a comparable set of scheduled tariff rates for South Africa, including preferential rates for EU and SADC, at the HS eight-digit level over the period 1988–2003.

---

[10] The import weighted average protection for all products is actually higher for the EU (7.9 per cent) than MFN countries (7.4 per cent) in 2006. This reflects the relatively low proportion of primary products with low tariffs that are imported from the EU. The large volumes of vehicles imported free of duty from the EU under the Motor Industry Development Programme will also bias import weighted average protection measures upwards.

[11] Average tariff data for middle-income and OECD countries obtained from World Bank (http://go.worldbank.org/LGOXFTV550). See also Edwards (2005) for a comparative analysis of tariff liberalization in South Africa.

[12] Change in tariff is calculated as $(T_{2006}-T_{1994})/(1+T_{1994})$, where T represents tariff and the subscript refers to the year.

[13] Effective protection measures the protection on value added and is calculated as $ERP_j = \left(T_j - \sum_i a_{ij}T_i\right) / \left(1 - \sum_i a_{ij}\right)$ where T_j is the tariff on outputs, T_i is the tariff on inputs and a_{ij} is the quantity of intermediate input i used in the production of one unit of j. Lower tariffs on final goods reduce effective protection, while lower tariffs on intermediate inputs raise effective protection. The net effect of liberalization on effective protection therefore depends on the decline in final tariffs relative to tariffs on inputs. This debate to some extent continues earlier deliberations on trade liberalization in the 1980s (Bell, 1993; Holden, 1992).

Table 6.4. Effective protection rates, export taxes and the anti-export bias

	1994	1996	1998	2000	2002	2006
Effective Rate of protection (ERP) (%)						
All Goods	35.0	22.0	16.5	12.9	10.9	9.5
Manufacturing	41.6	26.2	19.6	15.3	13.0	11.4
Non-Commodity Manufacturing	43.9	28.3	21.9	16.1	13.6	11.8
Commodity Manufacturing	35.3	20.5	13.5	13.2	11.5	10.1
Implicit Export taxes (xtax) (%)						
All Goods	14.3	10.3	8.0	8.0	6.9	5.6
Manufacturing	28.1	19.9	15.5	15.5	13.4	10.8
Non-Commodity Manufacturing	48.3	37.0	29.9	26.0	22.4	17.9
Commodity Manufacturing	18.4	11.6	8.5	10.5	9.1	7.3
Anti-Export Bias (AEB)						
All Goods	1.6	1.4	1.3	1.2	1.2	1.2
Manufacturing	2.0	1.6	1.4	1.4	1.3	1.2
Non-Commodity Manufacturing	2.8	2.0	1.7	1.6	1.5	1.4
Commodity Manufacturing	1.7	1.4	1.2	1.3	1.2	1.2

Source: Adapted from Edwards and Lawrence (forthcoming 2008) and Edwards (2005) and updated to 2006 using tariff data obtained from the South African Revenue Services.

Notes: Commodity manufacturing includes coke and refined petroleum, food, tobacco, iron and steel, other manufacturing, non-metallic minerals, wood and wood products, basic chemicals, and basic nonferrous metals. Primary commodities constitute more than 10 per cent of the value of output for these industries, as calculated using the 2000 Supply Use table for South Africa. Surcharges are included in 1994 estimates. Xtax values are aggregated using 1990 export values and ERP values are aggregated using 1990 import values.

The data indicate that there has been a considerable reduction in effective protection during the 1990s, but, as in the case of nominal protection, progress has slowed since 2000. Average effective protection for all traded goods fell sharply from a high of 35 per cent in 1994 to 12.9 per cent in 1999 and then only moderately to 9.5 per cent in 2006 as MFN reform stagnated. Declines in ERP were experienced for Commodity Manufacturing and Non-Commodity Manufacturing, although wide variations in the level and decline in protection are found at the sectoral level (Edwards, 2005). Particularly strong declines in protection were experienced in textiles, wearing apparel, footwear and communication equipment. Despite this, textiles, wearing apparel, and footwear still remain amongst the top five most protected sectors with ERP exceeding 40 per cent (Edwards, 2005).

3.3. Anti-export bias

Tariffs affect export performance in two ways. Firstly, tariffs raise the price of intermediate inputs and therefore reduce the profitability of export production. Secondly, nominal tariffs raise the relative return to production for the domestic market causing firms to shift production out of the export market and into the domestic market. Anti-export bias measures aim to capture these impacts.

Edwards and Lawrence (2008) measure these effects using two indicators. The extent to which tariffs on inputs are a tax on exports is calculated by dividing the input share weighted average tariffs by value added in world prices.[14] This is shown in Table 6.4 under the heading xtax. The second effect, the increased profitability of production for the domestic market, is captured by the effective rate of protection. The anti-export bias of production, which measures the profitability of production for the domestic market relative to the export market, is then calculated as (1 + ERP) / (1 − xtax). Values of the anti-export bias in excess of 1 indicate relatively high returns in the domestic market compared to the export market.

Tariff liberalization during the 1990s was effective in reducing the anti-export bias. In 1994 domestic production was roughly 60 per cent more profitable than production for the export market (Table 6.4). By 2000 this had fallen to 20 per cent, after which there were no further reductions. More interesting are the reductions in the anti-export bias within manufacturing. During the early 1990s, the tariff structure was particularly detrimental to exports of Non-Commodity Manufacturing (Edwards and Lawrence, 2008). This reflects a greater reliance by such firms on manufacturing inputs subject to input tariffs. In 1994, estimated export taxes on Non-Commodity Manufacturing (48 per cent) were more than twice those on Commodity Manufacturing exports. Table 6.4 shows that this resulted in an anti export bias of 2.8, which far exceeded the 1.7 for Commodity Manufacturing.

Over the next twelve years, trade liberalization substantially reduced the anti-export bias, both by lowering the tax on inputs and effective protection. What is striking, though, is that the impact of liberalization in reducing xtax for Non-Commodity Manufacturing has been significantly larger than the impact on Commodity Manufacturing. Under the assumption of perfect pass-through of tariffs to domestic prices, the effect of these reductions is equivalent to an improvement in export profitability of 58 per cent for Non-Commodity Manufacturing, compared to 14 per cent for Commodity Manufacturing (Edwards and Lawrence, 2008). As a consequence, Non-Commodity Manufacturing experienced a larger decline in the anti-export bias, from 2.8 to 1.4, than the reduction for Commodity Manufacturing, from 1.7 to 1.2. Nonetheless, although significant liberalization has taken place, it still appears to be the case that South Africa's trade policy hinders its export performance overall.

These estimates do not take into account the phasing out in 1995 of export subsidies provided by the General Export Incentive Scheme and the imple-

---

[14] $xtax_j = \sum_i a_{ij} T_i \Big/ \Big(1 - \sum_i a_{ij}\Big)$ where T_i is the tariff on inputs and a_{ij} is the quantity of intermediate input i used in the production of one unit of j. Improvements in export profitability are calculated as $(xtax_{t0} - xtax_{t1})/(1 - xtax_{t0})$ where $t1$ refers to the final period and $t0$ refers to the initial period.

mentation of various compensatory supply-side export promoting schemes (WTO, 1998). The decline in the anti-export bias is shown to be significantly lower once these effects are included (Tsikata, 1999; Edwards, 2005). On the other hand, export incentives for the motor industry under the Motor Industry Development Programme (MIDP) and clothing and textiles under the Duty Credit Certificate Programme are also not included, which would enhance the trends shown in Table 6.4. The effect of the change in export bias on these sectors has to our knowledge not been investigated at a micro level. As will be noted later, this is an area for further analysis.

4. Empirical evidence of the impact of openness on the South African economy

The substantial tariff liberalization experienced from the early 1990s makes South Africa a potentially interesting case for a study of the economic effects of trade liberalization. Such research in South Africa has been inhibited by various factors. Tariff liberalization coincided with the election of a new government and the implementation of other policy reforms covering the labour market, the macro economy, social welfare payments, and industry. Isolating the effects of trade liberalization from these other policy changes is difficult.

Attempts to measure trade policy are fraught with measurement problems for observable components (such as tariffs), and by the presence of difficult to quantify components of policy (such as quotas and a range of other non-tariff barriers); see Aron and Muellbauer (2007) for a recent survey of the literature. For instance, the detailed tariff database constructed by Edwards (2005) provides consistent estimates of protection in South Africa from 1988, but does not measure protection from non-tariff barriers and possibly under-estimates protection from specific tariffs and formula duties used extensively in the 1990s.

Finally, firm-level data, particularly of a panel nature, is absent in South Africa and firm level responses to liberalization are therefore not easily explored (see similar comments in the conclusion to Chapter 7). Much of the empirical analysis on the impact of openness on the South African economy has therefore utilized aggregate or industry level data combined with various proxies for the liberalization period.

Nevertheless, some insights into the effects of openness on the South African economy can be drawn from the available empirical literature. This section reviews this literature, focusing on the effect of trade liberalization on trade volumes, employment, productivity growth, inflation, and prices.

4.1. Trade volumes

Tariff liberalization is expected to be closely correlated with changes in trade flows. To assess this graphically, Figure 6.1 presents indices (2000 = 100) of the real volume of imports, non-gold exports, and the inverse of the tariff collection rate. What is noticeable is that increased growth in the volume of imports and exports in the early 1990s corresponded with tariff reductions, the elimination of surcharges and the removal of trade sanctions. Also of interest is that import volumes stagnated during the 1970s and 1980s, a period of declining investment and output growth, but also of increasing protection in the form of surcharges. This casual examination (without controlling for other factors) suggests that import volumes are reasonably responsive to changes in tariff protection.

More rigorous conditional relationships have been estimated. Although most empirical estimates of the determinants of import volumes in South Africa do not include direct measures of tariff protection (Bahmani-Oskooee and Niroomand, 1998; Senhadji, 1997; Gumede, 2000), the effect of protection is indirectly captured through the import price which is inclusive of tariffs. Estimated aggregate import price elasticities range from –0.53 (Bahmani-Oskooee and Niroomand, 1998) to –1.04 (Senhadji, 1997), suggesting that aggregate import volumes respond positively to lower import prices brought about by tariff liberalization.[15]

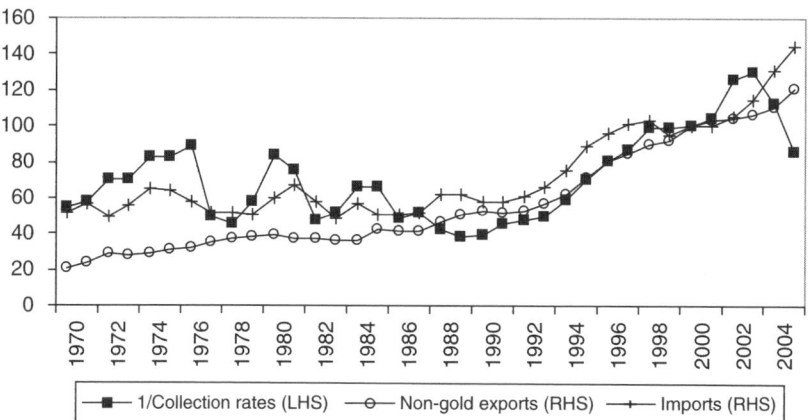

Figure 6.1. South African trade flows and tariff protection (2000 = 100)
Source: SARB *Quarterly Bulletin*.

Note: The measure of tariff protection is based on import duty collection rates and is calculated as the value of import duties collected (including surcharges) divided by the value of imports (in nominal terms). All trade flows are measured in real values.

---

[15] Senhadji (1997) uses the Hanson Fully-Modified estimator with annual data over 1960 to 1993. Bahmani-Oskooee and Niroomand (1998) also use annual data over a similar period (1962 to 1992), but use Johansen's cointegration technique. The pass-through of tariffs to import prices during the 1990s is estimated at 85 per cent by Rangasamy (2003). Together with the import price elasticties, this implies an elasticity of import demand with respect to tariffs of –0.55 to –0.88.

Edwards and Lawrence (2008) update these studies using cointegration analysis with quarterly data from 1962 through 2004. They include a measure of tariff protection, using collection duties, in the import demand function and control for the effect of domestic income and import prices relative to domestic producer prices. They do not, however, control for the effect of trade sanctions imposed between 1986 and 1992/3. Their estimates indicate a long-run import price elasticity of –0.98 when using the South African Reserve Bank import price index (RB5035L) and an elasticity of –0.32 for the tariff variable. Using these elasticities, they then calculate that tariff liberalization accounted for approximately 50 per cent of growth in import volumes during the 1990s, with the remainder largely due to a recovery in gross domestic expenditure (elasticity of approximately 1.3).

Their results, however, are sensitive to the choice of import price index. A higher import price elasticity (–1.72) is estimated in the working paper of Edwards and Lawrence (2006) when using the imported producer price index (RB7049N), but in this case the coefficient on collection duties is insignificant. Nevertheless, the results are consistent in that import volumes are found to respond positively to lower import prices, in part brought about through tariff liberalization. The evidence therefore suggests that liberalization has played an important role in boosting import volumes from the early 1990s.

Looking at export volumes in Figure 6.1, it is evident that non-gold exports stagnated during the early 1980s, increased in the mid 1980s, and then accelerated from 1992. Edwards and Lawrence (2008) argue that a significant portion of export growth from 1990 can be attributed to reductions in the anti-export bias from trade liberalization. Using a panel of forty-four manufacturing sectors over the period 1990–2002, they estimate with a static fixed effects estimator, the relationship between exports as a share of gross output and various indicators of tariff protection. Other control variables (time dummies which capture time specific effects common to all sectors, the sectoral capital labour ratio, the sectoral share of skilled labour in employment, and a proxy for export profitability, namely the nominal effective exchange rate divided by producer prices) are also included.

They find that increases in the nominal tariff, effective rate of protection and export tax have a statistically significant negative impact on export orientation in manufacturing.[16] The results, however, are driven by Non-Commodity manufactures and the estimated function performs poorly when applied to Commodity manufactures. Non-Commodity manufactures are found to be particularly responsive to tariffs on inputs (xtax) with an estimated elasticity

---

[16] Tsikata (1999) finds consistent results using a standard export function (where growth in export volumes is regressed on the change in the log values of the real effective exchange rate, capacity utilization and foreign income), for aggregate manufacturing over the period 1970–96. A one per cent reduction in collection rates is estimated to improve aggregate manufacturing exports by 0.86 per cent in the long run.

of –3.3. The estimated elasticities for nominal tariffs and effective protection rates are –0.9 and –0.3, respectively. The 'transparency' of the tariff structure, as measured by the share of tariff lines with *ad valorem* rates, is also an important determinant of export performance of Non-Commodities (elasticity of 0.75), but comes in with the wrong sign for Commodities. Liberalization and simplification of the tariff structure from the 1990s therefore appears to have stimulated manufacturing exports, but has not affected all sectors equally.

The improved export growth identified by Edwards and Lawrence (2008) could also have arisen from improved foreign market access as foreign economies removed trade barriers and ended trade sanctions from 1992, although some of these effects will have been captured by the time dummies included in their analysis. A comprehensive analysis of the effect of sanctions is provided by Evenett (2002), who uses a gravity model over the period 1978 to 1999 to estimate the effect of sanctions on South African exports to Nordic countries (Denmark, Sweden, and Norway), some European Community members (Italy, France, and Great Britain), Japan and the USA. He finds that sanctions by the European Community and the USA reduced South African exports by 27 per cent and 34 per cent, respectively. No consistent negative effects were found for Japan and Nordic countries in the different estimations. More interestingly, he finds that the removal of sanctions did not lead to a full recovery of exports, particularly to the USA, implying that the adverse consequences of sanctions are sustained long after their removal.

In conclusion, the empirical evidence suggests that the evolution of South African trade flows has been strongly influenced by domestic as well as foreign barriers to trade.

4.2. Employment

As documented in Chapter 11 in this volume, a major consequence of insufficient employment growth in the post-apartheid period has been a rise in unemployment. The contribution of the increased openness of the South Africa towards employment in this period has been explored in detail. The relationship, however, remains inconclusive. Most studies analysing the sources of change in employment and production in South Africa do not use direct measures of tariff protection in their analysis. The empirical applications also draw on different empirical methodologies, some of which lack clear theoretical grounding (see Edwards (2006) for a review).

Fedderke et al. (2003) is one of the few studies to estimate a theoretically consistent relationship between openness and factor returns in South Africa. Their approach is based on the Stolper–Samuelson theorem which states that a rise in the relative price of a sector, raises the real and relative return of the factor used intensively in that sector. For example, a rise in the price of capital-intensive goods relative to labour-intensive goods reduces wages relative to the return to capital.

The empirical application of this theorem is explained in detail in Leamer (1996) and Feenstra and Hanson (1999). In essence this approach estimates the zero profit relationship:

$$\hat{p}_{it}^{est} = \sum_{j=1}^{M} \theta_{ijt}\, \hat{w}_j + \varepsilon_{it},$$

where θijt denotes the cost share of factor j in industry i and $\hat{p}_{it}^{est}$ denotes an estimate of the percentage change in output price due to trade liberalization and technological change, amongst other variables. The estimated variables $\hat{w}_j$ denote factor returns that are consistent with or, in the terminology used in the literature, are 'mandated' by output price changes under the assumption of zero profits across all sectors. The estimated coefficients are therefore essentially predictions of wages that are consistent with the zero-profit conditions of the Stolper-Samuelson theorem. They are not estimates of the effect of trade on actual wages.

Fedderke et al. (2003) use dynamic heterogeneous panel estimation techniques to estimate returns to labour and capital 'mandated' by openness (ratio of exports and imports to output), effective protection, industry concentration and expenditure on Research and Development. The database consists of twenty-two South African manufacturing sectors and covers the period 1970 to 1997. They find that trade liberalization and openness induced relative price changes that increased the returns to labour relative to capital in South African manufacturing industries. In contrast technological progress is estimated to have negatively affected the return to labour relative to capital.

Unfortunately, their results provide limited insight into the effect of trade liberalization from 1994 on labour. Their estimate of the effect of openness on factor payments is based on the entire sample period (1970–97). Trade flows (Figure 6.1) and measures of openness fluctuated considerably throughout this period and their results do not necessarily reflect the effect of increased openness from the 1990s. The estimated positive effect of liberalization on wages for labour is based on changes in effective rates of protection between 1988 and 1997, which covers some of the liberalization period. However, the effective protection rates are based on collection duties and under-estimate the decline in protection of important labour-intensive sectors such as clothing, footwear, and textiles where duty rebates are extensively used (Edwards, 2005). The implication is that they under-estimate the negative effect of liberalization on labour.

Alternative estimates for the equivalent set of manufacturing sectors using scheduled rates over the period 1994 to 2003 are provided by Edwards (2006). These results show that tariff protection fell relatively sharply in sectors using semi-skilled and unskilled labour intensively. According to his regressions, liberalization 'mandated' a real wage decrease of 19 per cent for labour, compared to a zero change in return for capital. Unskilled labour was the most adversely affected with a 'mandated' decrease in real wages of 37 per cent. These decreases are consistent with the decline in real earnings from wage employment from 1995–2003 shown in Chapter 11 in this volume.

The analysis of employment in South African manufacturing by Rodrik (2006) also yields results contrary to those of Fedderke et al. (2003). Rodrik (2006) calculates that the relative price of manufacturing (value added price index of manufacturing divided by the GDP deflator), adjusted for total factor productivity growth, fell by 30 per cent from the late 1970s to 2004. Using a panel of eight 1-digit sectors over the 1980–2004 period, he estimates that the decline in relative prices of manufacturing is the predominant cause of the fall in manufacturing employment from 1994–2004. The results are directly contrary to those of Fedderke et al. (2003) where relative price shifts raised the demand for labour.

Rodrik (2006) also presents additional fixed effect estimates (twenty-eight manufacturing sectors, 1970–2004) and aggregate estimates using OLS (1980–2004) to show that import penetration is an important source (up to a quarter) of the decline in the relative price of manufacturing. By implication, import penetration through its effect on the relative price of manufacturing, has had a negative impact on employment since 1994.

The main shortcoming of Rodrik's (2006) analysis is that the 'bulk' (83.5 per cent) of the decline in the relative price of manufacturing, and therefore the associated decrease in employment, can be attributed to an unexplained time trend. Further, the direct fixed effect estimates of the determinants of employment in manufacturing suggest that rising export orientation from the 1990s will have partially offset the negative effect of import penetration on employment. The results of these price studies therefore remain inconclusive and are sensitive to the choice of tariff measure, the estimation technique and the time period covered.

Alternative studies (Edwards, 2001a, 2001b, 2006; Dunne and Edwards, 2007; Jenkins, 2008) analyse the factor content of trade flows and then infer the impact of trade on employment or wages. Key limitations of these studies are that the methodology used lacks a clear theoretical grounding (Leamer, 2000) and that they do not estimate the direct link between changes in factor content and trade liberalization. The results are nevertheless informative. Drawing from Dunne and Edwards (2007), Figure 6.2 presents a decomposition of the sources of employment growth in manufacturing from 1970 into Final Demand, Exports, Import Penetration, and Technology.[17]

---

[17] The method can be described as follows: Gross output (X) is expressed as $X = dD + E$, where d is the ratio of domestically produced goods to total demand, D is total demand (inclusive of imports) and E is exports. This relationship can be decomposed into changes in demand (ΔD), export expansion (ΔE) and import penetration (ΔdD) as follows: $\Delta X = d\Delta D + \Delta dD + \Delta E$. The limitations of these decomposition approaches are widely documented (Baldwin, 1995; Leamer, 2000). In particular, the various sources of employment growth are not independent of each other.

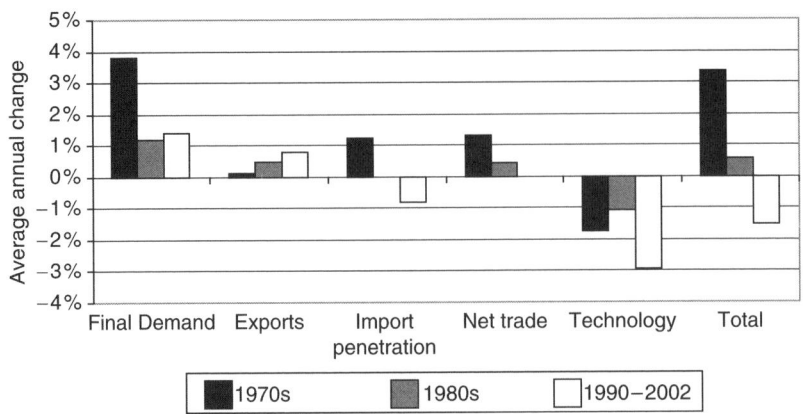

Figure 6.2. Sources of employment growth in manufacturing, 1970–2002
Source: Dunne and Edwards (2007).

Changes in employment from trade flows broadly follow changes in the trade policy regime. During the 1970s, import substitution was an important source of growth in manufacturing employment (1.2 per cent per annum) and exceeded the contribution of export expansion (0.1 per cent per annum). Its influence declined over the following two decades as industrial policy shifted away from import substitution industrialization, and import penetration increased. In contrast, exports became a more important source of employment, although this failed to offset the fall in employment from rising import penetration.

Manufacturing employment fell sharply from 1990 to 2002, but trade flows appear to play a relatively minor role in this decline. Growth in exports raised employment, but this was completely offset by rising import penetration. The net direct effect of trade flows on employment was therefore close to zero. The aggregate results hide important sectoral changes in the composition of trade. Jobs were created through export growth within the natural resource-based and chemical sectors, but these gains were offset by increased import penetration within labour-intensive sectors such as clothing, footwear, and leather products (Edwards, 2006; Dunne and Edwards, 2007). The overall conclusion, however, is that trade flows are not the dominant source of the decline in manufacturing employment from 1990 to 2002.

What appears to be the dominant source of change in demand for labour in all periods, particularly the 1990s, is technological change. As shown in Figure 6.2, improvements in productivity reduced employment by close to 3 per cent per annum between 1990 and 2002. A problem is that technological change could itself be related to liberalization as firms adopt new technologies or restructure production in response to increased international competition. Adrian Wood (1994) terms this 'defensive innovation'. There is some evidence of trade-induced technological change, and we interrogate this relationship in more depth in the following section. Nevertheless, the net impact of trade on labour in South Africa from the early 1990s remains uncertain.

4.3. Productivity

Openness to trade can stimulate productivity growth through enhanced competitive pressures, access to new technology embodied in imported inputs, access to a wider range of complementary intermediate inputs and scale economies as export firms expand. Various studies have evaluated the effect of trade flows on productivity growth in South Africa (Belli et al., 1993; Jonsson and Subramanian, 2001; Arora and Bhundia, 2003; Fedderke, 2006) and form part of the broader literature on growth in South Africa presented in Chapter 2. Jonsson and Subramanian (2001), for example, estimate the long-run relationship between openness (measured as the ratio of the sum of real imports and real exports to real GDP) and total factor productivity growth, using cointegration analysis over the period 1971–97. They estimate that a 10 percentage point increase in openness is associated with an increase in total factor productivity (TFP) by about 5 per cent in the long run.

Panel data estimates yield consistent results with the above. Fedderke (2006) employs the Pooled Mean Group estimator to evaluate the determinants of TFP growth using 22 South African manufacturing sectors over the period 1970 to 1997. He finds that a 10 per cent improvement in the ratio of net exports (exports minus imports) to GDP raises TFP growth by 1 per cent in the long run. Jenkins (2008) also uses a panel data set consisting of 28 manufacturing industries from 1980–2001, but, unlike the above studies, estimates the separate effects of exports and imports on productivity using a labour demand equation specified in first differences. Import penetration is found to be negatively associated with productivity growth in most estimates with an elasticity ranging from –0.04 to –0.08. Export orientation is more sensitive to the inclusion of industry and time fixed effects and is significant and negative in only half the estimates with an elasticity of approximately –0.02. Using these results, Jenkins (2008) estimates that increased trade indirectly reduced employment in manufacturing by 81,000 to 117,000 from 1990 to 2001.

A severe limitation of these studies is that openness is itself an outcome variable and is influenced by numerous variables in addition to trade policy. Particularly problematic is that trade flows are influenced by productivity growth leading to potentially severe endogeneity bias in the above estimates.

Several studies therefore have included direct measures of trade policy in their analysis. Jonsson and Subramanian (2001) also use cross-section analysis to investigate how variations in TFP growth across twenty-four different South Africa manufacturing sectors are related to tariff reductions during the period

1990–4 and 1994–8. A 1 percentage point decline in their tariff variable (1+tariff) is estimated to raise the TFP growth rate by 0.43 to 0.74 percentage points, although the effect diminishes with larger declines in tariff rates. Harding and Rattsø (2005) estimate a barrier model of productivity growth using a panel of 28 South African manufacturing industries over the period 1970–2003. Unfortunately, data availability meant that aggregate collection rates and not sectoral level protection measures are used as their main barrier to technological adoption. Their results suggest that 70 per cent of aggregate productivity improvement in the post sanction period (1993–2003) is explained by liberalization. Lower tariffs also enhance the spillover of foreign technology to the domestic market.

The empirical evidence points to a strong positive effect of increased openness and trade liberalization on productivity growth in South African manufacturing. However, the mechanism through which this occurs requires further interrogation. There is very little analysis of the effect of liberalization on productivity at the firm level, largely as a result of the lack of firm-level panel data. The improvement in productivity found in the aggregate analyses possibly reflects changes in the composition of production as inefficient firms are driven out of the market and not necessarily enhanced productivity within existing firms. Aggregate productivity improvements may also be driven by increases in the scale of production by the remaining firms. Without firm level data over time, the firm level sources of aggregate productivity growth will remain unknown.

4.4. Prices

A further area of research is the impact of trade and tariff liberalization on inflation and pricing power in the South African economy. Aron and Muellbauer (2007) develop an innovative openness measure that aims to capture measurable trade policy and hard-to-measure non-tariff barriers. Using quarterly models from 1979 to 2005, they find that increased openness has significantly reduced the mean wholesale price inflation rate and find some evidence for a reduced exchange rate pass-through into wholesale prices. Lower price inflation from liberalization should be most beneficial to low income consumers who spend a higher proportion of their income on traded products compared to high income consumers who also consume services (Daniels and Edwards, 2007), although this depends on the extent to which lower wholesale prices are passed through to final consumers. The reduced exchange rate pass-through effect also insulates consumers from an exchange rate depreciation, but, also means that they benefit more slowly from lower prices when the exchange rate appreciates. The importance of accounting for openness in inflation models is underlined by recent work by Aron and Muellbauer (forthcoming 2009) who demonstrate how the South African Reserve Bank's own producer price inflation equation in its published core model can be significantly improved by including either their above time-series openness measure or more conventional measures.

Related studies evaluate the effect of trade and trade liberalization on mark-up pricing. Fedderke et al. (2007) and Edwards and van de Winkel (2005) estimate the mark-up pricing relationship using industry panel data for South African manufacturing over the periods 1970–96 and 1970–2002, respectively. They both find that import penetration reduces mark-up pricing in South African industries in the long-run, but this relationship could arise because relatively efficient industries are more profitable and thus better able to compete against potential imports. Additional fixed effect panel estimates by Edwards and van de Winkel (2005) using direct tariff measures for twenty-eight manufacturing industries over the period 1988–2002 show a negative association between effective and nominal tariff protection and mark-ups.

The results are therefore consistent with the view that liberalization and increased openness from the 1990s reduced inflation and mark-up pricing in South Africa. However, a number of caveats remain. The relatively slow adjustment of output prices to increased openness found by Aron and Muellbauer (2007) implies that in the short run mark-ups may actually rise before the longer-term effects of increased competition feed through. The studies referred to here also only explore the relationships at the aggregate or industry level and pricing behaviour at the firm level remains unexplored.

4.5. Other research

The partial equilibrium analyses discussed so far have been complemented by general equilibrium analyses, which allow for a range of macroeconomic, industry and household feedback effects to be modelled explicitly. Thurlow (2007) uses a recursive dynamic general equilibrium and microsimulation model to assess the effects of trade liberalization on growth, employment and poverty in South Africa from 1993 to 2003. His model consists of 39 sectors/commodities, 3 geographic regions, and 240 aggregate households. The effect of trade liberalization via productivity growth is also modelled using the aggregate tariff-productivity elasticity estimated by Jonsson and Subramanian (2001). The unique sectoral productivity responses to liberalization are therefore not captured.

He finds that trade liberalization, measured as a decline in the sectoral collection rate, raised expenditure for all individuals on average and hence reduced poverty. These gains work primarily through productivity improvements: gains from tariff liberalization alone were small, but positive. Important sectoral effects from liberalization are also shown. Employment in manufacturing declined, but was more than offset by increases in the private services sector. Moreover, trade reforms contributed to the rising capital and skill-intensity of production which increased income inequality.

5. Conclusion and assessment of scope for further trade reform

The empirical evidence reviewed suggests that trade liberalization and increased openness has had a beneficial effect on trade flows, on productivity and on prices in South African industries. The net employment effects are mixed, although the results suggest that there has been some restructuring of employment away from import competing sectors towards export oriented sectors.

What implications for future trade reform can be drawn from this review? Despite reductions in protection from 1990, scope remains for further tariff reductions and tariff simplification. The SACU tariff structure is relatively complex compared to other middle-income countries when measured by the coefficient of variation, the number of tariff bands, and the number of domestic spikes (Edwards and Lawrence, 2007). As of 2006, there were still thirty-eight different *ad valorem* rates and sixty-two different specific and mixed duties applied to MFN countries. This far exceeds the six proposed in 1994. Finally, as shown in this chapter, nominal and effective protection remains high, both on consumer goods and key production inputs.

South Africa is participating in the Doha round of the WTO and if an agreement is reached, this is likely to lead to further reductions in MFN tariffs. However, unilateral liberalization of MFN tariffs can be pursued to speed up the process of reform. South Africa can also play a more active role in the liberalizing trade in services. Services trade currently accounts for approximately 17 per cent of total South African trade. South African service firms are particularly active in Africa in the banking, retail, telecommunication, construction, and restaurant sectors (Stern and Khumalo, 2007). Similarly, foreign involvement in South Africa has increased, particularly in telecommunications, airlines, and banking.

Although South Africa has made commitments of some form or another to about half of all the services sectors under the General Agreement on Trade in Services (GATS) negotiations (Steuart, 2005), protection on services trade remains high. Estimates of the 'tariff' equivalent of services restrictions by Hoekman (1995) indicate that South African 'tariffs' approach the most restrictive benchmark countries in the internationally more protected sectors including transport related services, life insurance, basic telephony, and education. South Africa appears more progressive in sectors where tariff equivalents are low internationally (Stern and Khumalo, 2007). The empirical evidence, although scarce, suggests that together with other regulatory policies, liberalization forms a key policy instrument available to government to enhance competition in South African services sectors (Hodge, 2001). Further research on the liberalization of services in South Africa is urgently required.

Comprehensive and unilateral trade reform is not currently on the government's agenda. Tariff reform is not prioritized in the government's current growth initiative, the Accelerated and Shared Growth Initiative of South Africa (ASGISA), which was launched in 2006 (Republic of South Africa, 2006). The policy document expresses a desire to diversify out of primary product exports, but the role of trade policy in achieving this outcome is not clearly outlined.

The National Industrial Policy Framework, which outlines the Department of Trade and Industry's (DTI) vision of a future industrial policy, touches on trade policy, but does not consider comprehensive trade policy reform as central to their vision. A critical review of the tariff structure is to be undertaken, focusing particularly on tariffs on intermediate inputs. Bilateral and regional trade agreements are to be the central thrust of South Africa's trade policy. These are to be used in a strategic manner that does not necessarily require a free trade agreement and will focus strongly on enhancing foreign market access.

In all cases 'tariff determinations will be conducted on a case-by-case basis, taking into account the specific circumstances of the sector involved' (DTI, 2007). A key objective is that trade reform is to be sequenced with industrial policy to facilitate industrial diversification (Mpalhwa, 2007). This emphasis on the sequencing of trade policy with industrial policy on a case-by-case and country-by-country basis, as opposed to comprehensive multilateral or unilateral liberalization, arises from concerns by policy makers that further unilateral and across-the-board liberalization would foster specialization in resource-based sectors and weaken South Africa's bargaining leverage in bilateral and multilateral trade negotiation (DTI, 2007; Mpahlwa, 2007).

This view runs counter to some of the evidence presented above which suggests that liberalization has resulted in considerable dynamic gains to the economy in the form of productivity growth and trade performance, including diversification of exports. There are some additional concerns with the approach to trade reform to be followed by the DTI. The administrative burden and information requirement to set tariffs for over 6,000 product lines is immense. The process also requires consensus by all SACU members who have different levels of capacity to investigate product level tariff proposals and have very different industrial development needs. Asymmetries in information between business and government also make the tariff setting process vulnerable to capture by industries. South Africa has a long history of effective lobbying by industries for tariff increases.[18] The mechanisms to insulate government from this lobbying have not been clearly outlined in the NIPF.

---

[18] Industry capture was evident in the numerous tariff changes implemented in the late 1980s by the Board of Trade and Tariffs (Bell, 1993) and the 1990s when organized industries were effective in lobbying for tariff increases in the face of rising import penetration (Casale and Holden, 2002). More recently, the implementation of quotas on imports of clothing and textile products from China reflects the outcome of intense lobbying by labour, in particular the South African Clothing and Textile Workers Union (Edwards and Morris, 2007).

One mechanism suggested by Edwards and Lawrence (2007) is to consider an approach that dramatically simplifies the current structure, by using a few, or even just a single tariff rate. Exceptions for industrial policy purposes or safeguard purposes could be granted, subject of course to rigorous cost-benefit analysis. But, as deviations from the norm, these tariff exceptions could only be temporarily applied. Such a system would be easier to administer, reduce smuggling and false invoicing, provide some insulation from industry lobby groups, and send a clear signal to investors and industries as to the priority of the protected sectors for industrial development.

Finally, the emphasis on reform through preferential trade agreements needs to be scrutinized. The presence of several preferential trade agreements are, at one level, useful in as far as they reduce the costs of trade diversion and serve as an alternative to trade liberalization driven through the WTO. The costs also need to be considered. Preferential trade agreements can raise the complexity and opaqueness of the tariff schedule and therefore dilute the incentives for efficient resource allocation. Sensitive products are also easily excluded from the bilateral agreements leading to sustained tariff peaks. The different rules of origin and tariff phase-downs of each agreement also compound the complexity of doing business in industries that are integrated into the global supply chain.

A more comprehensive reform strategy, whereby government commits itself to tariff simplification and possibly a unilateral phase-down in tariff rates, needs to be considered.

References

Arora, V. and A. Bhundia (2003) 'Potential Output and Total Factor Productivity Growth in Post-Apartheid South Africa', *IMF Working Paper* WP/03/178, Washington, D.C.: International Monetary Fund.

Aron, J. and J. Muellbauer (2007) 'Inflation dynamics and trade openness', Centre for Economic Policy Research, London, *Working Paper Series*, no. 6346. Available from http://www.cepr.org>.

——(2009) 'Monetary Policy and Inflation Modeling in a More Open Economy in South Africa', in G. Hammond, R. Kanbur, and E. Prasad (eds.), *New Monetary Policy Frameworks for Emerging Markets: Coping with the Challenges of Financial Globalization*, Bank of England/Edward Elgar (forthcoming).

Bahmani-Oskooee, M. and F. Niroomand (1998) 'Long-run Price Elasticities and the Marshall-Lerner condition revisted', *Economic Letters*, 61(1): 101–9.

Baldwin, R. E. (1995) 'The Effect of Trade and Foreign Direct Investment on Employment and Relative Wages', *National Bureau of Economic Research Working Paper*, no. 5037, Cambridge, Mass.

Bell, T. (1993) 'Should South Africa Further Liberalise its Foreign Trade?', in M. Lipton and C. Simkins (eds.), *State and Market in Post Apartheid South Africa*, Johannesburg: Witwatersrand University Press.

—— (1997) 'Trade Policy', in J. Michie and V. Padyachee (eds.), *The Political Economy of South Africa's Transition*, London: Dryden Press.

Belli, P., M. Finger, and A. Ballivian (1993) 'South Africa: A Review of Trade Policies', *World Bank Informal Discussion Papers on Aspects of the South African Economy*, no. 4, The Southern Africa Department, The World Bank.

Casale, D. and M. Holden (2002) 'Endogenous Protection in a Trade Liberalizing Economy: The Case of South Africa', *Contemporary Economic Policy*, 20(4): 479–89.

Cassim, R. (2003) 'The Pace, Nature and Impact of Trade Policy in South Africa in the 1990s', *South African Journal of Economic History*, 18(1): 76–95.

—— (2007) 'Mainstreaming Trade into South Africa's National Development Strategy', *African Trade Policy Research Centre Working Paper* 51, United Nations Economic Commission for Africa.

Cassim, R. and H. Zarenda (2004) 'South Africa's Trade Policy Paradigm—Evolution or Involution', in E. Sidiropoulos (ed.), *South Africa's Foreign Policy: 1994–2004*, South African Institute of International Affairs, Wits University.

Daniels, R. and L. Edwards (2007) 'The Benefit-Incidence of Tariff Liberalisation in South Africa', *Journal for Studies in Economics and Econometrics*, 31(2): 69–88.

Dunne, P. and L. Edwards (2007) 'Trade, Enterprise Production and Employment', *Journal for Studies in Economics and Econometrics*, 31(2): 49–68.

Department of Trade and Industry (DTI) (2007) *National Industrial Policy Framework*, Pretoria.

Edwards, L. (2001a) 'Globalisation and the Skill Bias of Occupational Employment in South Africa', *South African Journal of Economics*, 69(1): 40–71.

—— (2001b) 'Trade and the Structure of South African Production, 1984–97', *Development Southern Africa*, 18(4): 471–91.

—— (2005) 'Has South Africa Liberalised its Trade?' *South African Journal of Economics*, 74(4): 754–75.

—— (2006) 'Trade Liberalisation and Labour Demand in South Africa during the 1990s', in H. Bhorat and R. Kanbur (eds.), *Poverty and Policy in the Post-Apartheid South Africa*, Pretoria: Human Science Research Council Press.

Edwards, L. and R. Z. Lawrence (2006) 'South African Trade Policy Matters: Trade Performance and Trade Policy', *National Bureau of Economic Research Working Paper*, no. 12760, Cambridge, Mass.

—— (2007) 'SACU Tariff Policies: Where should they go from here?' Report prepared for the South African National Treasury as part of the National Treasury/Harvard Growth Project.

—— (2008) 'South African Trade Policy Matters: Trade Performance and Trade Policy', forthcoming in *Economics of Transition*, 16(4): 585–608.

Edwards, L. and M. Morris (2007) 'Undressing the Numbers: The Effect of Import Quotas on Clothing and Textile Employment', *Journal of Development Perspectives*, 2(2): 121–40.

Edwards, L. and T. van de Winkel (2005) 'The Market Disciplining Effects of Trade Liberalisation and regional Import Penetration on Manufacturing in South Africa', *Trade and Industry Strategies Working Paper*, 1–2005.

Evenett, S. (2002) 'The Impact of Economic Sanctions on South African exports', *Scottish Journal of Political Economy*, 49(5): 557–73.

Fallon, P. and L. Pereira de Silva (1994) 'Economic Impact of Economic Sanctions in South African Export Performance and Policies: Overview (vol. 1)', *The World Bank, Informal Discussion Papers on Aspects of the Economy of South Africa*.

Fedderke, J. (2006) 'Technology, Human Capital and Growth: Evidence from a Middle Income Country Case Study Applying Dynamic Heterogeneous Panel Analysis', in South African Reserve Bank, Banco de Mexico and The People's Bank of China (eds.) *Economic Growth*, Proceedings of a G20 seminar held in Pretoria, South Africa, on 4–5 August 2005.

Fedderke, J. and P. Vase (2001) 'The Nature of South Africa's Trade Patterns by Economic Sector, and the Extent of Trade Liberalisation During the Course of the 1990's', *South African Journal of Economics*, 69(3): 436–73.

Fedderke, J., C. Kularatne, and M. Mariotti (2007) 'Mark-up Pricing in South African Industry', *Journal of African Economies*, 16(1): 28–69.

Fedderke, J. W., Y. Shin, and P. Vaze (2003) 'Trade and Labor Usage: An Examination of the South African Manufacturing Industry', Mimeo. Available at <http://www.commerce.uct.ac.za/Economics/staff/jfedderke/research.asp>.

Feenstra, R. and G. Hanson (1999) 'The Impact of Outsourcing and High-Technology Capital on Labor: Estimates for the United States, 1979–90', *Quarterly Journal of Economics*, (August): 907–40.

Flatters, F. (2002) 'SADC Rules of Origin: Undermining Regional Free Trade', paper presented at Trade and Industry Policy Strategies Forum, 2002.

Flatters, F. and S. Stern (2006) 'SACU Revenue Sharing: Issues and Options', Queens University, available at <http://qed.econ.queensu.ca/faculty/flatters/writings/ff&ms_sacursf_2006.pdf>.

Gumede, V. (2000) 'Import Demand Elasticities for South Africa: a Cointegration Analysis', *Journal for Studies in Economics and Econometrics*, 24(1): 21–38.

Harding, T. and J. Rattsø (2005) 'The Barrier Model of Productivity Growth: South Africa', *Trade and Industry Policy Strategies Working Paper* 5-2005.

Hodge, J. (2001) 'Examining the Costs of Services Protection in the Developing Economy: The Case of South Africa', in R. Stern (ed.), *Services in the International Economy*, Ann Arbor: University of Michigan Press.

Hoekman, B. (1995) *Tentative First Steps—An Assessment of the Uruguay Round Agreement on Services*. World Bank Policy Research Paper, no. 1455.

Holden, M. (1992) 'The Structure and Incidence of Protection in South Africa', in P. Black and B. Dollery (eds.), *Leading Issues in South African Microeconomics*, Johannesburg: Southern Book Publishers.

Jenkins, C., M. Bleaney, M. Holden, and N. Siwisa (1997) 'A Review of South Africa's Trade Policy', paper presented at the Trade and Industrial Policy Annual Forum, Muldersdrift, September 1997.

Jenkins, R. (2008) 'Trade, Technology and Employment in South Africa', *Journal of Development Studies*, 44(1): 60–79.

Jonsson, G. and A. Subramanian (2000) 'Dynamic Gains from Trade: Evidence from South Africa', *International Monetary Fund Working Paper*, no. 00/45.

Kaplan D. (2003) 'Manufacturing Policy and Performance in South Africa', paper presented at the Trade and Industry Policy Strategies Forum, 2003.

Leamer, E. E. (1996) 'In Search of the Stolper Samuelson Effects on U.S. Wages,' *National Bureau of Economic Research Working Paper*, no. 5427, Cambridge, Mass.

—— (2000) 'What's the Use of Factor Contents?' *Journal of International Economics*, 51(1): 17–49.

Mpalhwa, M. (2007) 'Proposal to Go It Alone on Trade Misreads the Evidence', *Business Day* (7 November).

Rangasamy, J. (2003) 'The Impact of Tariff Liberalisation on the Competitiveness of the South African Manufacturing Sector During the 1990s', Unpublished PhD thesis, University of Pretoria, available at <upetd.up.ac.za/thesis/available/etd-07072004-124524/unrestricted/00front.pdf>.

Rangasamy, L. and C. Harmse (2003) 'The Extent of Trade Liberalisation in the 1990s: Revisited', *South African Journal of Economics*, 71(4): 705–28.

Republic of South Africa (1996) *Growth, Employment and Redistribution: A Macroeconomic Strategy*, Pretoria: South African government printers.

—— (2006) *Accelerated and Shared Growth Initiative of South Africa*, Pretoria: South African government printers.

Rodrik, D. (2006) 'Understanding South Africa's Economic Puzzles', *National Bureau of Economic Research Working Paper*, no. 12565, Cambridge, Mass.

Senhadji, A. (1997) 'Time-Series Estimation of Structural Import Demand Equations: A Cross-Country Analysis', *International Monetary Fund (IMF) Working Paper*, WP/97/132.

Stern, M. and N. Khumalo (2007) 'From Theory to Practise: Getting the Most Out of a Services Agreement With the USA', in P. Draper and N. Khumalo (eds.), *One Size Doesn't Fit All: Deal-breaker Issues in the Failed US-SACU Free Trade Negotiations. South African Institute of International Affairs*, Johannesburg.

Steuart, I. (2005) 'Liberalisation Of Trade in Services in South Africa: the Multilateral Dimension', *Human Science Research Centre Research Paper*.

Thurlow, J. (2007) 'Trade Liberalisation and Pro-Poor Growth in South Africa', *Journal for Studies in Economics and Econometrics*, 31(2): 161–79.

Tsikata, Y. (1999) 'Liberalisation and Trade Performance in South Africa', *World Bank Informal Discussion Papers on Aspects of the South African Economy*, no. 13, The Southern Africa Department, The World Bank.

van Seventer, D.E.N. (2001) 'The Level and Variation of Tariff Rates: An Analysis of Tariff Rates in South Africa', *Trade and Industry Policy Monitor*, 19.

Wood, A. (1994) *North-South Trade, Employment and Inequality*, Oxford: Oxford University Press.

WTO (1998) *Trade Policy Review: Republic of South Africa*, Geneva: World Trade Organisation Secretariat.

—— (2003) *Trade Policy Review: South African Customs Union*, Geneva: World Trade Organisation Secretariat.

7
Capital Formation in South Africa

Johannes W. Fedderke

1. Introduction[1]

Over the past decade capital formation in South Africa has received considerable attention. Given the centrality of investment to improvements in per capita income, and the importance of improved growth if South Africa's considerable developmental challenges are to be realized, the close attention that capital accumulation has received is not surprising.

The structure of growth in South Africa has changed substantially over the past three decades. The evidence from a range of sources is consistent: over the past three decades the pattern of South African growth has switched from being based on factor accumulation, to one based heavily on the efficiency gains encapsulated by total factor productivity based growth. Specifically, the contribution of capital accumulation has been on a steady decline, a pattern that is present both for aggregate output, but also for virtually all major sectors in the economy. Chapter 2 in this book reviews the evidence on the decomposition of output growth through standard growth accounting approaches (Tables 2.4 to 2.8, Chapter 2).

At one level such evidence is reassuring. The switch from factor accumulation to innovation is associated with the maturing of an economy into developed country status. However, the performance of the South African economy remains well below that required to meet the pressing social developmental goals of South Africa. By the early 2000s, South African per capita GDP, even once adjusted for purchasing power parity, was still only US$11,140 compared to US$26,500 in high income countries. The point is reinforced by a comparison

---

[1] Acknowledgements: The author is grateful for comments from Janine Aron and John Muellbauer (Oxford University), and from two anonymous referees.

Capital Formation in South Africa

of South Africa's historical growth performance with that of comparator countries (see Figure 2.2 in Chapter 2). During the 1990s, middle- and low-income countries, sub-Saharan Africa, as well as the world on average, grew faster than did South Africa,[2] and while there has been a recovery, South Africa remains firmly outside the set of fastest growing countries.

One of the reasons for this has been the steadily declining investment rate in South Africa. Figure 7.1 reports South African investment rates against a range of comparators. What is striking is the strong decline in the investment rate, and since the 1980s, South Africa's investment performance has lagged behind sub-Saharan Africa, as well as average performance in poor and middle income countries and the world average.

Fortunately there are signs of significant recovery. In Figure 7.2 we report gross fixed capital formation as a percentage of GDP, broken down by the major sectors of the economy. It is evident is that the long-term decline in the investment rate leading up to 2000, has been reversed, with the ratio climbing from 15 per cent of GDP in the mid 1990s to approximately 22 per cent of GDP

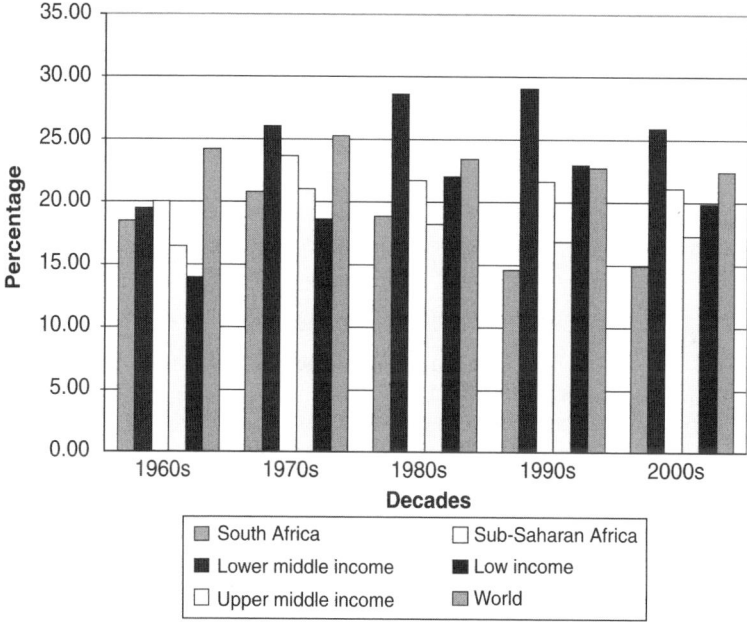

Figure 7.1. Gross capital formation as a percentage of GDP
Source: World Development Indicators, World Bank.

---

[2] Using data from the World Bank's World Development Indicators.

in 2006. Much of this recovery in the investment rate has been contributed by the Manufacturing and Financial sectors, as well as Transport, Storage, and Communications.[3] However, it should be noted that private sector gross fixed capital formation lies below 22 per cent of GDP, at approximately 15 per cent of GDP—though here too there is evidence of a positive trend, with recovery from the mid 1990s level of approximately 10 per cent of GDP.

At the same time the recovery has exacerbated a long-standing structural feature of the South African economy. Except for very brief periods in the 1960s and the early 1980s, South Africa's private sector has not produced sufficient savings to cover its demand for physical capital formation.[4] Since the

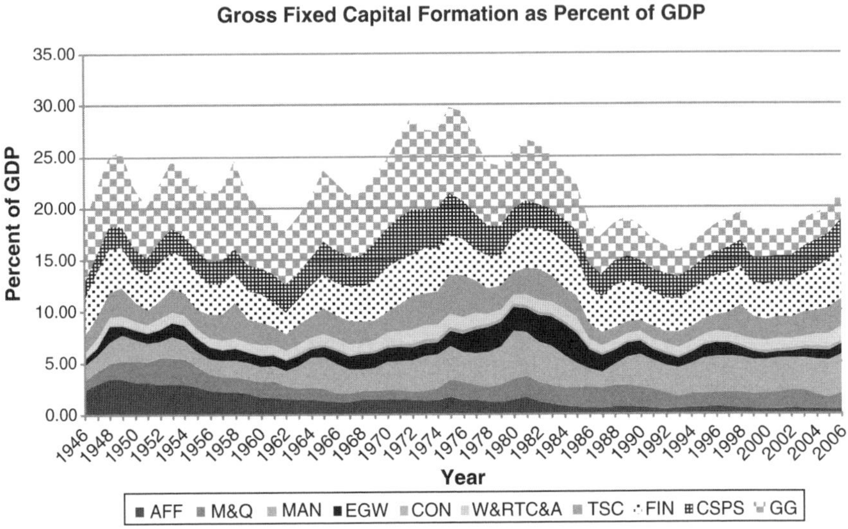

Figure 7.2. Gross capital formation as a percentage of GDP by major economic sector
Source: South African Reserve Bank.
Key: AFF = Agriculture, Forestry & Fishing; M&Q = Mining & Quarrying; MAN = Manufacturing; EGW = Electricity, Gas & Water; W&RTC&A = Wholesale & Retail Trade, Catering & Accommodation; TSC = Transport, Storage & Communication; FIN = Financial Services; CSPS = Community, Social and Personal Services, GG = General Government.

---

[3] A substantial restructuring of capital investment occurred in the 1990s, see Fedderke et al. (2001). The evidence suggested the falling investment rate was related to falling investment of parastatals, and a strong proportional increase in investment in those sectors historically potentially crowded out of capital markets by a strong state presence. Thus, the falling investment rate was not necessarily a sign of failure, but of restructuring of the economy.

[4] For a study of South Africa's personal and corporate saving, see Aron and Muellbauer (2000). Recent empirical work on the determinants of consumption (the obverse of personal saving), taking account of financial liberalization and wealth effects, can be found in Aron and Muellbauer (2008).

mid 1990s the ratio of savings by households and corporates to GDP has fallen dramatically, leaving a substantial gap[5] between the financing requirements of investment in the economy and domestically produced private sector savings, even bearing in mind the increased saving by the government sector after 1994 (see Chapter 4). The implication is that South Africa has been, and remains, reliant on capital inflows in order to finance its physical capital formation.

Under these conditions, understanding investment behaviour and its constraints is important. A substantial body of literature on investment in South Africa has emerged over the past decade, with diverse findings. This paper attempts to provide an assessment of reported findings. What do we know of the determinants of investment? Are the findings in the range of studies consistent with one another, and do a set of common thematic insights emerge for investment? Perhaps most importantly, can we identify the gaps in our knowledge?

In addressing these questions, this chapter considers domestic private physical capital accumulation in section 2, and public capital accumulation in section 3, and it reflects briefly on the likely growth consequences of the evidence reviewed. In section 4, the chapter takes stock of the evidence, placing emphasis on the broader thematic insights that emerge from the relatively diverse set of papers on investment behaviour in South Africa.

2. Domestic private physical capital stock formation

The modern theory of investment expenditure has paid consistent attention to the impact of uncertainty on investment, applied in a dynamic stochastic environment.[6] The key insight is that where the profit function is concave in the stochastic demand drivers,[7] the impact of uncertainty on investment (derived by maximizing the discounted present value of expected profits) is negative. Convexity generates a positive investment response to uncertainty.[8] Where investment faces irreversibility or lumpy adjustment costs, investment will only be undertaken after a return threshold is reached.[9] The implication is that empirical applications of irreversible investment models should control for the impact of uncertainty.[10]

---

[5] The gap is somewhat smaller when considering gross capital formation and gross savings for the economy as a whole (but still measures 7 per cent of GDP).
[6] A comprehensive coverage of the debate can be found in Bond and van Reenen (2007).
[7] Reference is to the demand determinants of profit, which are subject to shocks, and in which profit increases but at a diminishing rate.
[8] See Hartman (1972).
[9] Dixit and Pindyck (1994) is the standard reference, drawing on a sequence of earlier contributions. Under the real options approach, uncertainty generates a reward for waiting, since a rise in uncertainty raises the threshold at which investment will be triggered.
[10] See for example Ferderer (1993), and Guiso and Parigi (1999).

Other determinants of investment are suggested by the potential impact of imperfections in financial markets, the structure of product markets, and macroeconomic policy conditions. These are discussed in detail below. We first examine the determinants of aggregate investment expenditure in South Africa and specifically in the manufacturing industry.

Results from the South African investment literature are summarized in Table 7.1.[11] Several consistent results emerge from the literature. First, standard theoretical priors appear to hold for South Africa. Proxies for the rate of return on capital and the user cost of capital consistently show statistical significance in the expected direction. In all eleven papers in Table 7.1, the rate of return net of the marginal cost of investment features in some form. Returns on investment are proxied by a range of variables. Expected future demand is captured by either sectoral or aggregate output,[12] all but one study employs a proxy for the user cost of capital,[13] and additional cost variables considered are the own price of capital[14] and the real wage of labour.[15]

The South African findings add to international findings in confirming the negative impact of uncertainty on investment. Specifically, the striking finding is that uncertainty exercises a statistically significant and strong effect on investment expenditure in South Africa. Uncertainty unambiguously lowers investment rates both for the aggregate investment rate[16] and for the manufacturing sector.[17] Moreover, the finding emerges across a range of estimation methodologies, with time series cointegration approaches,[18] dynamic heterogeneous panel[19] and non-parametric[20] estimation methodologies.

Both systemic and sectoral uncertainty appear important for investment—though systemic uncertainty has a stronger impact than sectoral uncertainty. The systemic measure of uncertainty measure is proxied by the measure of political instability derived in Fedderke et al. (2001), and is measured as a weighted index of eleven objective indicators of action against political

---

[11] Papers do not appear in any particular order, other than chronological order of first draft.
[12] Only Fielding (1997) does not employ such a measure, since it assumes demand conditions away by relying on an assumption of perfectly competitive markets. The study relies on export prices instead. Mariotti (2002) and Romm (2005) employ a multiple equation framework, such that output does not enter the investment equation directly, but does so in the full cointegrating framework indirectly.
[13] The exception is Fielding (1997).
[14] See Fielding (1997).
[15] See Fielding (1999, 2002).
[16] See Fielding (1997, 2002), Kularatne (2002), Mariotti (2002), Romm (2005), Fedderke and Luiz (2008a).
[17] See Fielding (1999, 2000), Fedderke (2004), Fedderke and Szalontai (2008) and Fedderke and Naumann (2008).
[18] See Fielding (1997, 2002), Kularatne (2002), Mariotti (2002), Romm (2005) and Fedderke and Luiz (2008a).
[19] See Fedderke (2004), Fedderke and Szalontai (2008) and Fedderke and Naumann (2005).
[20] See Fielding (2000).

Table 7.1. Summary of results for determinants of physical capital stock accumulation in South Africa

	Fielding (1997)		Fielding (1999)	Fielding (2000)	Fielding (2002)	Fedderke (2004)	Kularatne (2002)		Mariotti (2002)	Romm (2005)	Fedderke and Szalontai (2008)	Fedderke and Naumann (2005)	Fedderke and Luiz (2008a)
	Nontraded Capital	Traded Capital					Model 1	Model 2					
Type	Single Eq.	Single Eq.	Single Eq.	Nonparametric	Single Eq.	Single Eq.	Mult. Eq.	Mult. Eq.	Mult. Eq.	Mult. Eq.	Single Eq.	Single Eq.	Mult. Eq.
Data	Agg Time Series	Agg Time Series	Manuf. Panel	Manuf. Sector	Agg Time Series	Manuf. Panel	Agg Time Series	Agg Time Series	Agg Time Series	Agg Time Series	Manuf. Panel	Manuf. Panel	Agg Time Series
Output			0.25*	—	0.22*	0.05*		0.21	†	†	0.20*	0.03*	6.16
Own Price	−2.28*	−0.88*		—									
Export Price	0.84	1.69*											
User Cost			−.06*	—	−.09*	−.04*	−.01	−.01	−0.001	−0.002*	−0.09*	−0.005	−0.47
Real Wages			−0.50*	—	−0.51*								
Savings										0.97*			
Sect. Dem. Uncertainty						−0.12*					−0.17*	−0.074*	
User Cost Uncertainty												—	
Macro Instability			1.80*	—	1.53*								
Industrial Action			−1.12*	—	−1.37*								
Systemic Uncertainty	−0.31*	−0.09*		—			−1.25×10⁻⁵	−2.6×10⁻⁶	−0.012	−0.77×10⁻⁵*	−0.01*	−0.092*	−0.21
Cap. Utilization	−1.48*	−0.02		—	−0.21*	0.53*							

(Continued)

Table 7.1. (Continued)

	Fielding (1997)		Fielding (1999)	Fielding (2000)	Fielding (2002)	Fedderke (2004)	Kularatne (2002)		Mariotti (2002)	Romm (2005)	Fedderke and Szalontai (2008)	Fedderke and Naumann (2005)	Fedderke and Luiz (2008a)
	Nontraded Capital	Traded Capital					Model 1	Model 2					
Type	Single Eq.	Single Eq.	Single Eq.	Nonpara metric	Single Eq.	Single Eq.	Mult. Eq.	Mult. Eq.	Mult. Eq.	Mult. Eq.	Single Eq.	Single Eq.	Mult. Eq.
Data	Agg Time Series	Agg Time Series	Manuf. Panel	Manuf. Sector	Agg Time Series	Manuf. Panel	Agg Time Series	Agg Time Series	Agg Time Series	Agg Time Series	Manuf. Panel	Manuf. Panel	Agg Time Series
Ret. Earnings			—	—		0.01							
Openness			—	—		0.05*							
Imports			—	—		−0.67							
Exports			—	—		−50.54*							
TFP			—	—		−0.01							
Skills Ratio			—	—		0.02*							
Public Capital	0.18	0.58*	−0.13	—									
Credit				—			0.32						
Liquidity				—			0.15	0.28		1.61*			
Gini				—							0.76*		
Rosenbluth				—							−0.62*		
Schooling				—					0.73				
Gov. Cons.				—					−0.96			−0.051	
IG12				—					0.16			−1.103*	
Property Rights				—		0.39*							3.18
FREQUENCY	Annual	Annual	Annual	Annual	Annual	Annual	Annual	Annual	Annual	Annual	Annual	Annual	Annual
SAMPLE PERIOD	1946–92	1946–92	1960–93	1960–93	Unclear in paper	1970–97	1954–92	1954–92	1935–92 1947–92	1946–92	1970–96	1970–2001	1954–1992

agitation. The index is illustrated in Figure 7.3, which shows peaks in political instability in the early 1950s, the early and mid 1960s, the mid 1970s, and an extended period of the 1980s.

The relevance of this systemic uncertainty variable is shown in a panel data manufacturing sector study by Fedderke (2004).[21] Figure 7.4 reports the standardized coefficients from the investment function. The results imply that the systemic uncertainty variable dominates not only the sectoral demand uncertainty (measured as a moving average of demand volatility using the standard deviation of sectoral GDP), but all other determinants of investment in South African manufacturing.[22] This finding appears robust since the systemic uncertainty variable is significant and negative in a range of alternative studies of investment in South Africa,[23] both aggregate and sectoral. Nor is the finding of the importance of uncertainty restricted to the aggregate systemic measure of political instability. Alternative measures of uncertainty, covering sectoral

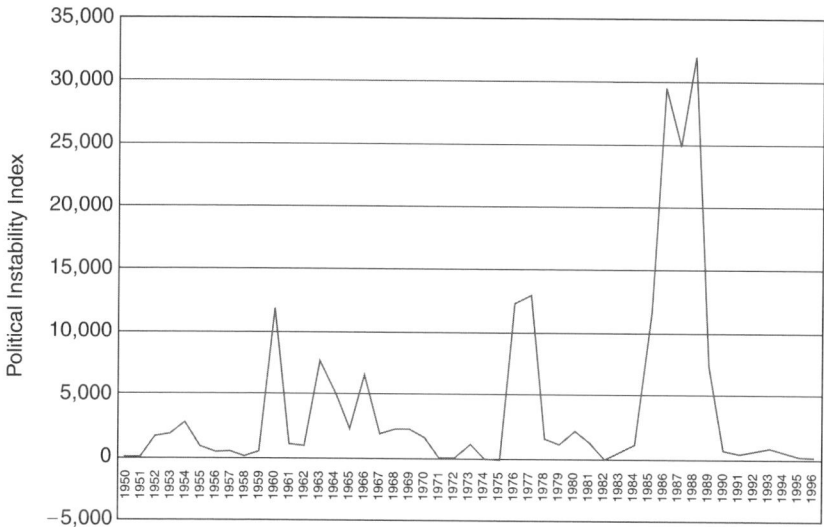

Figure 7.3. Index of systemic uncertainty
Source: Fedderke et al. (2001).

---

[21] While the systemic uncertainty variable is available from 1935, the Fedderke (2004) study uses panel data for the 1970–97 period only, due to limited availability of South African manufacturing data.
[22] This result is a consistent and robust finding regardless of which other variables are controlled for in estimation. For instance, Fedderke (2004) also tested for the impact of credit rationing, openness of the manufacturing sectors to international trade, technological progress, the skills composition of the labour force, the real wage, and government crowd-in.
[23] See Fielding (2002), Kularatne (2002), Mariotti (2002), Romm (2005), Fedderke & Szalontai (2008), Fedderke and Naumann (2008) and Fedderke and Luiz (2008a).

Johannes W. Fedderke

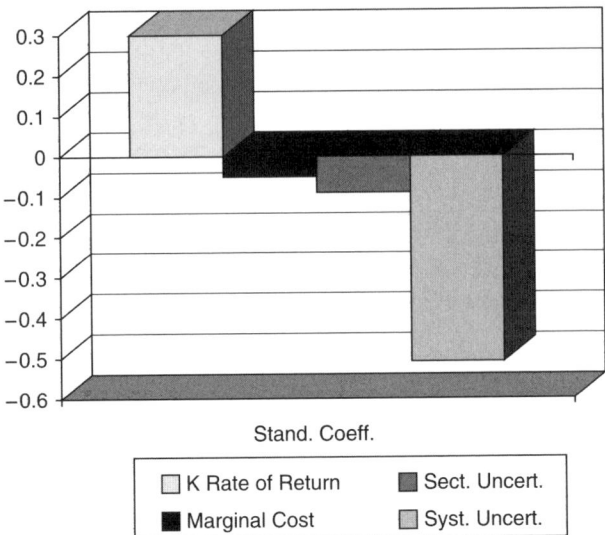

Figure 7.4. Standardized coefficients in the investment relation
Source: Fedderke (2001a).
Key: K Rate of Return denotes the proxy for the expected rate of return on capital; Marginal Cost the user cost of capital; Sect. Uncert. a measure of sectoral demand uncertainty; Syst. Uncert. a measure of systemic uncertainty. Figures are standard deviations, denoting the standard deviation response in the investment rate to a one standard deviation change in the independent variable. All coefficients statistically significant.

demand uncertainty,[24] user cost uncertainty,[25] macroeconomic instability,[26] as well as measures of industrial action[27] also find support in the literature. Thus, while formulations of the uncertainty variable differ, there is overriding confirmation that uncertainty needs to be included in the formulation of South African investment models.[28]

---

[24] This is measured as a moving average of demand volatility, see Fedderke (2004), Fedderke and Naumann (2008), and Fedderke and Szalontai (2008).
[25] This is measured as the variability of past costs of capital, see Fielding (1999, 2002).
[26] This is measured by the spread across the yield curve, see Fielding (1999, 2002).
[27] See Fielding (1997). Measures of industrial action are published by the South African Reserve Bank.
[28] We note that one paper, du Toit and Moolman (2004) does present evidence in favour of a neoclassical investment function. The paper finds that marginal rates of return and cost were equalized in the long run over the 1970–2001 period in South Africa. The paper excluded uncertainty, though it dummied for the sanctions period, and controlled for financial constraints, the user cost of capital and an index of 'international position'. Earlier contributions to investment functions in the neoclassical tradition are given by Pretorius (1998) and Wesso (1995).

Two important implications follow.

First, the impact of uncertainty moderates the finding that the marginal rates of return on and cost of investment (key 'policy handles') are significant determinants of investment. The large, negative impact of uncertainty on investment (see coefficients in Figure 7.4) suggests systemic stability is needed for sustained or increased investment rates in manufacturing industry. This supports the pursuit of stability in the conduct of macroeconomic policy (e.g. an emphasis on price stability) and sustaining a stable political environment.

Moreover, uncertainty raises the threshold rate of return below which investment is unlikely to occur. This implies that any policy intervention designed to stimulate investment expenditure may face constraints where an industry is operating below the threshold rate of return on investment. Therefore, creating a stable and predictable macroeconomic and microeconomic environment, devoid of sudden and arbitrary intervention, is a policy goal that emerges not only because lowering uncertainty gives a direct positive stimulus to investment, but also because it renders other policy levers more effective.

Second, not only is uncertainty important to investment, but the institutional environment appears to influence investment in a number of dimensions, including property rights, political stability, and crime rates. The measure of systemic uncertainty discussed above is purely a measure of political instability. However, the relevant institutional context extends beyond stability of the political environment. Fielding (1999) finds a positive return on a property rights measure.[29] Similarly, Fedderke and Luiz (2008a) affirm the positive impact of proxies for the rate of return on capital, and the negative impact of the user cost of capital and systemic measure of political uncertainty, but find property rights also drive capital accumulation. Not only is there a strong direct positive impact of property rights on investment (with estimated elasticity of 3.18), but the evolution of property rights in South Africa led the measure of political instability. Thus, improving property rights served to lower the level of political instability (with elasticity of −2.49). Extending these findings further, Fedderke and Luiz (2008b) affirm the complex linkages among social, human capital, political and economic dimensions, where human capital accumulation and crime rates particularly influence investment.

The remainder of this section examines in detail three additional structural determinants of investment in South Africa: credit markets, output market structure, and the macroeconomic policy environment. A few other

---

[29] See Fedderke, De Kadt, and Luiz (2001) on the construction of the property rights index.

Johannes W. Fedderke

potential determinants considered in the literature are not covered in this chapter. For instance, there is some evidence that there is positive complementarity between public and private sector capital (i.e. crowd-in, rather than crowd-out),[30] a positive impact of openness measured as exports and imports as a proportion of output,[31] and a complementarity between the skills composition of the labour force[32] or human capital measures[33] and investment in physical capital stock. On the other hand, TFP does not appear to be statistically significantly associated with investment in South African manufacturing.[34]

2.1. The impact of saving, the financial system, and credit rationing

The impact of the savings constraint on investment in physical capital is clearly of significance in South Africa. Within the international growth literature, the role of the financial system in long-term development has received considerable attention. While this line of enquiry is still at a relatively early stage in South Africa, a number of papers have explored the impact of saving, the structure of the financial system in the sense of the interplay of credit markets and the stock market, and credit rationing on investment performance.

The interdependence of saving, investment, and growth in South Africa has been explored by Romm (2005) during 1946 to 1992, using the Johansen vector error correction model (VECM) technique. The saving rate has both a direct effect on growth and an indirect effect through the private investment rate.[35] The elasticity of investment with respect to saving is reported as 1.32. While investment does not directly impact on saving, the model does report a strong feedback effect on saving via an investment impact on output, with a reduced form elasticity which is greater than proportional. The suggestion is thus that saving does respond to the demand for capital. A further implication is that saving does contribute to growth in South Africa, with both a direct and an indirect impact on per capita output. Between the direct elasticity of 0.58, and the indirect elasticity via investment of 0.50, the impact is approximately proportional. Romm also finds a strong impact of the credit rate[36] on

---

[30] See Fielding (1997, 1999), and Fedderke (2001).
[31] See Fedderke (2004)—and see also the positive impact of export prices in Fielding (1997).
[32] See Fedderke (2004).
[33] See Mariotti (2002).
[34] See Fedderke (2004).
[35] Romm does not find a direct impact of output on the investment rate, unlike other papers reported here. However, since the three equation model reports an output impact on saving, and saving in turn impacts on investment, output has a strong (more than proportional) impact on investment, consistent with the other reported papers.
[36] The credit rate is defined as the ratio of the quantity of loans and advances issued by banks to the private sector to GDP.

investment. This could reflect either a credit supply effect or an expectations effect, or both.

The finding of a role of credit markets for investment echoes earlier work by Kularatne (2002) covering the period 1954 to 1992. Exploring the interaction between financial deepening and economic growth,[37] both via the impact of credit extension and liquidity on the stock market, Kularatne finds that both have a positive effect on per capita GDP, but that the impact is indirect, operating via the investment channel rather than on output directly. There are also feedback effects from per capita output to financial deepening. Increased liquidity of the equities market appears to have stimulated investment in physical capital. Credit extension appears to have fuelled the development of the equities markets in South Africa, and only indirectly, through the equities market, the development of capital and output. Specifically, a 1 per cent increase in the ratio of total value of shares traded to GDP increases the investment rate and per capita output by 0.28 per cent and 0.30 per cent, respectively.[38] The effect of a 1 per cent increase in credit extension on per capita GDP and the investment rate is estimated to be an increase of 0.08 per cent and 0.07 per cent, respectively. The two dimensions of financial deepening are thus complementary to one another. Credit extension appears to serve as a means of improving the liquidity of the stock market, rather than increasing investment in physical capital stock directly. This may reflect the historic role of the South African mining houses in raising capital on international markets. The financial deepening variable with a direct real effect, is the measure of stock market liquidity.

One possible explanation for the apparent absence of a direct association between financial intermediation and the real sector may be credit rationing, where firms find it difficult to source working capital from financial intermediaries for investment projects. However, this would be at odds with results reported for the manufacturing sector by Fedderke (2004), where retained earnings were not significantly correlated with investment rates in a panel of three-digit manufacturing sectors. On the other hand, Fielding (2000) reports nonparametric results that are strongly consistent with the presence of credit rationing, particularly for smaller firms. Since the manufacturing sector is dominated by large formal sector firms, and the Kularatne finding is for the economy as a whole, this may account for the divergent results. Generally speaking, the structure of the financial system appears to matter for investment in South Africa.

---

[37] The paper is in the spirit of the wider endogenous growth literature e.g., Levine (1997), Levine and Zervos (1998), and Levine, Loaysa, and Beck (2000). It also employs extensive 'causality' testing.

[38] It remains to be seen, however, whether these parameter estimates are stable when the sample is extended to 2007, given the sharp increases in the value of shares traded to GDP in recent years.

2.2. The impact of market structure

A feature of South African output markets, consistently noted in the literature, is the relatively high levels of concentration (see also Chapter 8).[39] It is of interest whether market structure carries implications for performance, in investment terms and for long-term growth.

Both Fedderke and Szalontai (2008) and Fedderke and Naumann (2008) explore the impact of industry concentration on investment rates in the manufacturing sector, with the latter paper extending the analysis from 1996 to 2001. In Fedderke and Szalontai (2008), estimation is for 1970–96 and produces mixed results—with the sign on the Rosenbluth concentration index being negative, while that on a Gini coefficient of the size distribution of production, is positive. The implication is that while an increase in the inequality of the size distribution of firms raises the investment rate of the manufacturing sectors, a reduction in the number of firms, at any size distribution, lowers the investment rate. One interpretation is that while an increase in the market share controlled by the dominant firms may serve to stimulate investment (perhaps in order to consolidate their dominant market position), as the market becomes less competitive (with a decline in the number of competing firms), the incentive to raise the capital stock declines, and monopolistic practices come to predominate. The results are consistent with the implications of the literature on the behaviour of dominant firms in the presence of a competitive fringe.

An important caveat, however, is that the differential impact of size distribution and numbers of firms is not robust to the extension of the sample period to the post-1996 period of trade and especially capital account liberalization. Fedderke and Naumann (2008) extend the sample period from 1996 to 2001, when both the Gini and the Rosenbluth indexes report negative impacts on the investment rates of manufacturing sectors—though only the Rosenbluth index is statistically significant. Over the full 1970–2001 sample period, industry concentration thus appears to have an unambiguously negative impact on investment rates.[40]

The above findings of the negative influence of industry concentration on investment rates in manufacturing, is consistent with work on productivity growth by Aghion, Braun, and Fedderke (2008). They confirm not only the high and constant mark-ups of price over marginal cost of production (already

---

[39] This is long-standing finding, see for instance Du Plessis (1981), Fourie and Smit (1989), and Fourie (1996). Leach (1992) considers a range of appropriate indexes of concentration, and Fedderke and Szalontai (2008) and Fedderke and Naumann (2008) extend the data series considered.

[40] In Fedderke and Szalontai (2008), the negative impact of concentration rates extends to employment creation also. Unfortunately data limitations prevent a replication of the employment results in Fedderke and Naumann (2008).

observed in Fedderke, Kularatne, and Mariotti (2007) for South Africa's manufacturing industry), but isolate a negative role for price mark-ups on productivity growth. The finding is statistically significant, and robust across three distinct data sets both at industry and firm level, as well as robust to controlling for potential non-linearities and endogeneity. Moreover, it is economically meaningful at a loss of 1.6 to 2.4 percentage points of growth per annum for a 10 per cent increase in the price–cost margin.

In a further extension, Aghion et al. (2008) employ a theoretical framework that controls for the impact of product market competition on output growth, but explicitly allows for both direct and indirect impacts of trade liberalization on productivity growth. Trade liberalization is captured through four measures: effective rates of protection, scheduled tariff rates, export taxes, and a measure of anti-export bias. The indirect effects of trade liberalization operate through both a scale effect, and a differential impact on firms conditional on their distance from the international technological frontier. Empirical results from panel estimations for the South African manufacturing sector over 1970–2004, confirm that pricing power as well as industry concentration are strongly negatively associated with productivity growth. Moreover, the impact of pricing power on productivity growth is strengthened once the impact of trade liberalization is explicitly controlled for.

The highly concentrated nature of output markets and the associated pricing power of firms, thus represent a constraint both to investment and to growth prospects for the South African economy.[41] The two obvious policy responses, of liberalizing the trade regime and of increasing anti-trust activities of the Competition Commission,[42] have made some progress in South Africa, but much remains to be done if the investment climate is to continue to improve (see Chapters 6 and 8, respectively).

2.3. The policy environment

Finally we consider the influence on investment of government stabilization policy (see reviews of policy in Chapters 3 and 4). Debate in South Africa has often emphasized demand side stimulus for long-term growth, and that more expansionary fiscal and monetary policy is an underutilized policy tool in government growth strategies. But there is a counterargument, which is that macroeconomic stability is crucial in creating appropriate levels of the net

---

[41] The empirical results confirming a negative impact of market concentration and pricing power on investment and output growth are based on manufacturing industry data. While results for other sectors may plausibly differ, the prominence of manufacturing growth for the long-term growth prospects of the economy, suggest these issues are of concern for the aggregate economy too.

[42] See the analysis in Fedderke, Kularatne, and Mariotti (2007) on the positive effects of these interventions on price–cost margins.

return on physical capital to render investment attractive to the private sector, but above all it is viewed as crucial in rendering the return less uncertain—see for instance, Aron and Muellbauer (2005). Since the main focus of fiscal and monetary policy is stabilization, in effect the best demand-side policy intervention for the purpose of stimulating growth and investment is to create a stable macroeconomic environment. This latter view is consistent with the finding by Fielding (1997) that macroeconomic stability is positively associated with investment.

Mariotti (2002) investigates the impact of demand side policy on postwar South African growth using government consumption expenditure as a proxy for fiscal policy stance, and the inflation rate as a proxy for monetary policy orientation.[43] The study allows for both direct effects of policy on growth, as well as indirect effects via a stimulus of the investment rate in the economy. The central findings are that government consumption expenditure and inflation both have an unambiguously negative impact on long run per capita GDP, such that the economy moves to a lower steady state. While there is a short-lived temporary increase in growth in response to expansionary demand side policy, the stimulus is not sustainable. But the results also indicate that there is an indirect impact of policy on output via its impact on investment. Finally, the dynamics indicate that the relationship between policy and long-term output as well as investment may be non-linear, implying the presence of an optimal level of government consumption expenditure and inflation. The optimal level of government consumption expenditure is low (below 12 per cent of GDP), as is optimal inflation (below 3 per cent). These findings also confirm a range of international evidence in terms of the direct impact of government consumption expenditure on output.[44]

A study using forecasting models for output growth in South Africa also confirms significant potential growth benefits from fiscal discipline, and an important role for lower real interest rates in promoting growth (Aron and Muellbauer, 2002). High and unstable inflation requires high real interest rates for central banks that 'lean against the wind' to control inflation (see also Chapter 3)

Thus there appear to be poor prospects for demand side stimulus, and that the main channel of influence of macroeconomic policy on investment and growth is through creating a stable and predictable macroeconomic environment. Demand side policy intervention will best serve investment by creating an environment conducive to long run capital accumulation.

---

[43] The study does control for a range of additional variables, including political instability, the user cost of capital, and the impact of human capital investment. See Table 7.1.

[44] Sala-i-Martin, Doppelhofer, and Miller (2004) provides references and a useful robustness check on the result.

3. Domestic public physical capital stock formation

The potential positive complementarity between public and private capital investment has previously been noted. This section focuses specifically on the economic infrastructure formation in South Africa, toward the close of the twentieth century. Provision of public infrastructure in South Africa is largely a political decision, rather than market determined; hence the present section concentrates on the productivity impacts of public capital provision. Moreover, attention is confined to economic infrastructure, rather than social infrastructure, though the latter is briefly remarked on.

The infrastructure–growth relationship in South Africa remains relatively understudied. Only three studies were undertaken prior to 2003, all of those in the mid 1990s. Furthermore, some of the early studies used relatively inappropriate statistical techniques and their findings must be treated with caution.[45] For this reason this section focuses on the more recent studies. These studies can broadly be divided into two categories: those that directly measure the infrastructure–growth relationship; and those that indirectly measure the relationship, by analysing the connection between infrastructure and another determinant of growth.[46] Most studies focus purely on infrastructure developed by parastatals and the government. Private-sector infrastructure is seldom considered.

We begin by noting the decline in infrastructure investment in South Africa during 1970–2000 (also extensively detailed in Perkins, Fedderke, and Luiz, 2005). The South African Reserve Bank (SARB) publishes the public sector economic infrastructure components of both gross fixed capital formation and fixed capital stock (in each case for both general government and public corporations). Figure 7.5 shows indices of these measures, per capita. Both demonstrate a long-term deterioration: from the mid 1970s in the case of investment, and from the mid 1980s in the case of fixed capital stock. Investment per capita fell from R1,268 in 1976 to R356 in 2002 (1995 prices), a collapse of 72 per cent. Investment fell from 8.1 per cent of GDP to 2.4 per cent of GDP, which lies below the international benchmark of approximately

---

[45] Abedian and Van Seventer (1995) and Coetzee and Le Roux (1998) focus on financial measures of public-sector infrastructure in analysing the relationship between infrastructure and growth. The papers find output elasticities between 0.17 and 0.33 and economic rates of return between 0.2 and 0.23. However, they neglect stochastic time trends in both infrastructure stock and output measures. The 1998 Development Bank of Southern Africa *Development Report* also focused on public sector infrastructure stock and made an attempt to account for non-stationarity of the data. Nevertheless none of these studies took into account the possibility of non-linear relationships, indirect relationships or crowd-out effects, used highly aggregated data and did not attempt to explore the direction of causality.

[46] Almost all empirical analysis has focused on economic infrastructure to the exclusion of social infrastructure.

Johannes W. Fedderke

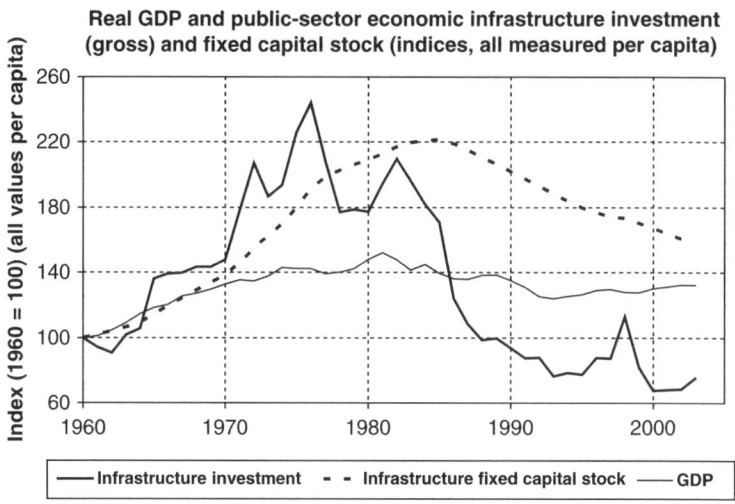

Figure 7.5. Infrastructure investment per capita 1960–2002
Source: Perkins, Fedderke, and Luiz (2005).

3–6 per cent identified by Kessides (1993: p. ix).[47] In 2002, around 70 per cent of public-sector infrastructure investment comprised transport, communication, power, and water. The recovery of infrastructure investment in the 1990s and the subsequent slump were mainly the result of expansion programmes by Telkom and Eskom to extend telephone lines and electricity to under-serviced areas, and the purchase of new aircraft by South African Airways (SARB *Annual Economic Reports*, 1996–2000).

Perkins, Fedderke, and Luiz (2005), was the first of a series of studies attempting to address the estimation challenges of the link between public capital and economic growth. Focusing specifically on the question of causality, while taking into account the time trends in the data, they find that the direction of forcing varied across different infrastructure measures. Aggregate public sector investment and public sector fixed capital stock drive GDP, and roads (total road length, paved road length, number of passenger vehicles) also drive GDP. However, GDP drives ports' freight handling levels and airports' passenger levels; and the direction of forcing is ambiguous for measures of railway, power generation, and telecommunication infrastructure.

---

[47] The decline in infrastructure investment between the mid 1970s and 2002 was part of an overall decline in gross fixed capital formation (GFCF) over the same period. Falling infrastructure investment may also have been a response to overcapacity in certain areas (Merrifield, 2000: 92), especially given the lumpiness of infrastructure investment—see World Bank (1994: 23).

Fedderke, Perkins, and Luiz (2006) develop this result by investigating the relationship between GDP and a range of infrastructure measures between 1875 and 2001. They allow for the possibility of time trends in the data, directly address the issue of causality and explicitly consider both direct and indirect channels of effect. They find that aggregate infrastructure investment and infrastructure stock drive GDP, as do measures of road infrastructure. Telecommunication, port, and airport infrastructure and some railway infrastructure, however, are driven by GDP. The direction of the relationship is ambiguous for electricity generation and some other railway infrastructure. These results are broadly consistent with those of Perkins, Fedderke, and Luiz (2005).

In calculating the magnitude of the relationship between output and infrastructure, Fedderke, Perkins, and Luiz (2006), adopt a multivariate cointegration model that examines the long-term interaction between several variables, allowing for the possibility of ambiguous causal relationships. In this model they include GDP, fixed capital stock, public sector fixed capital stock (a financial measure of infrastructure), total road length, and electricity generation capacity. They find that there is a relationship between infrastructure stock and GDP but that this relationship is indirect, with rising infrastructure stock encouraging investment in fixed capital and thereby boosting GDP. The elasticity of GDP with respect to the total fixed capital stock measure is variable ranging from 0.06 to 0.2[48] and that of fixed capital stock with respect to infrastructure is 1.37. This means that a 1 per cent increase in infrastructure increases fixed capital stock by 1.37 per cent. Furthermore, electricity generation directly effects GDP with an elasticity of 0.2 (i.e. a 1 per cent increase in electricity generation capacity directly increases GDP by 0.2 per cent). Some of these results, however, are not robust to the replacement of total road length by other infrastructure measures. The authors also introduce a control for property rights to test for the role of institutions in the infrastructure–growth relationship. The indirect relationship via fixed capital stock is then maintained and a significant direct positive relationship is also found, with an elasticity of between 0.4 and 0.5.

Having considered the empirical evidence, a number of conclusions can be drawn. The early finding of a positive infrastructure-growth relationship has been borne out by the subsequent application of more sophisticated techniques. However, these later studies have identified two other important features of this relationship. Firstly, while aggregate infrastructure stock and investment appear to drive output, there are feedback effects from output

---

[48] Note that estimation of production function relationships in South Africa faces the difficulty that over the last decades of the twentieth century, investment is distributed I(2), raising a number of important estimation challenges. Fedderke, Perkins, and Luiz (2006) addresses these issues more fully.

to some specific forms of infrastructure. Secondly, much of the relationship appears to be indirect, with expanding infrastructure increasing fixed capital, which in turn increases output. Furthermore, the next subsection demonstrates that there may be a further indirect channel through which the relationship between infrastructure and growth operates.[49]

For these reasons Fedderke and Bogetić (2006) focus their attention on the relationship between infrastructure and productivity, measured by both labour and total factor productivity. Unlike the papers examined above, which employed time-series data on the aggregate economy, Fedderke and Bogetić consider a panel of 24 manufacturing sectors between 1975 and 2000, where the employment data are less unreliable than for the whole economy. They find that aggregate infrastructure stock and investment impact positively on labour productivity, with elasticities of 0.19 and 0.2, respectively. The elasticities are thus higher than those estimated for the economy as a whole. Possible reasons for this might be that infrastructure has a differential impact across distinct sectors of the economy (with manufacturing implicitly more reliant on infrastructure than other sectors), or might be due to the more extensive attempt to account for endogeneity in the Fedderke and Bogetić (2006) study. Aggregate infrastructure investment impacts positively on total factor productivity with an elasticity of 0.04, while aggregate infrastructure stock has no significant relationship with total factor productivity. They also go on to investigate the relationship between infrastructure and productivity for physical measures of particular types of infrastructure. They find that electricity (elasticity 0.05), railways (elasticities between 0.32 and 1.04), air transport (elasticities between 0.05 and 0.25) and particularly road (elasticities between 0.35 and 2.95) infrastructure positively impact on labour productivity. The results for total factor productivity are broadly consistent with an elasticity of 0.04 for electricity, 0.04 for airports and sea ports, 0.07 for telecommunications and elasticities of between 0.03 and 0.18 for railways. While there are some negative and some insignificant infrastructure measures, the picture is overwhelmingly one of a positive relationship between productivity and infrastructure. This in turn suggests a positive relationship between infrastructure and growth. These results, however, are heavily dependent on statistical techniques that control for the possibility of a bicausal relationship between infrastructure and productivity. In the absence of these controls, a substantial number of these measures have insignificant or negative relationships to either or both productivity measures.

One specific policy concern in connection with infrastructure investment arises from the spatial distribution of economic activity in South Africa. A

---

[49] A recent paper by Kularatne (2006) considers both social and economic infrastructure, and their impact on output. He finds no evidence for non-linearity between infrastructure and output, thus discounting the possibility of overinvestment during 1970–2005.

surprising feature of South African manufacturing activity is that it has become spatially less concentrated over time—see Figure 7.6. Fedderke and Wollnik (2007), drawing on predictions from trade and economic geography models, find that high plant-internal scale economies, intensity in the use of human capital and high industry-specific productivity gradients between locations are associated with greater geographical concentration of an industry. Scale economies are the most important pro-concentration force. A greater deviation of labour-intensity from the mean is associated with greater geographical dispersion. Industries with strong inter-firm linkages are also less concentrated. Such linkages are in fact the most important determinant of industry geography.

The low spatial concentration of labour-intensive industries is plausibly a result of legal limitations on migration and tax incentives pursued extensively and under varying degrees of intensity and complexity under apartheid policies. Conversely, the limited success of attempts to control migration meant that apartheid policies failed to curb a supply of labour to the economic centres, limiting the extent of the intended decentralization. Thus the role of labour intensity for locational choice has remained minimal. The low concentration of industries with strong forward linkages may be due to high transportation costs that tie resource beneficiaries and mining suppliers to the locations of resource production, and some consumer goods producers with very high transportation cost to the location of their customers. Table 7.2 summarizes the evidence, stating both the theoretical prior as a sign restriction, and the estimated elasticity to emerge from the empirical results.

In the long run, development will require the deepening and diversification of the manufacturing base of the economy. For most emerging markets, the domestic economy is simply too small to render feasible autonomous trajectories of development. Reliance on export markets is therefore an essential ingredient of long term success. But where industrial structure has been fundamentally shaped by policy intervention that favoured import substitution and the development of large national champions (Chapter 8), domestic market structure may be such that it is dominated by firms sufficiently large to render domestic markets highly concentrated, but insufficiently large to realize the economies of scale that render competitive participation on world markets a readily attractive alternative.

The obvious response to such a scenario is to liberalize the economy, in order to increase competitive pressure on local producers and labour market participants. But we have also noted that for South Africa there is evidence of agglomeration effects through economies of scale, but linkage effects serve to lower the geographical concentration of South African industry. The upshot of this combination of evidence is that while on balance the forces generating improved economies of scale through agglomeration are present, South African manufacturing continues to manifest significant forces that favour dispersion also. Liberalization of the economy may thus not confront a manufacturing

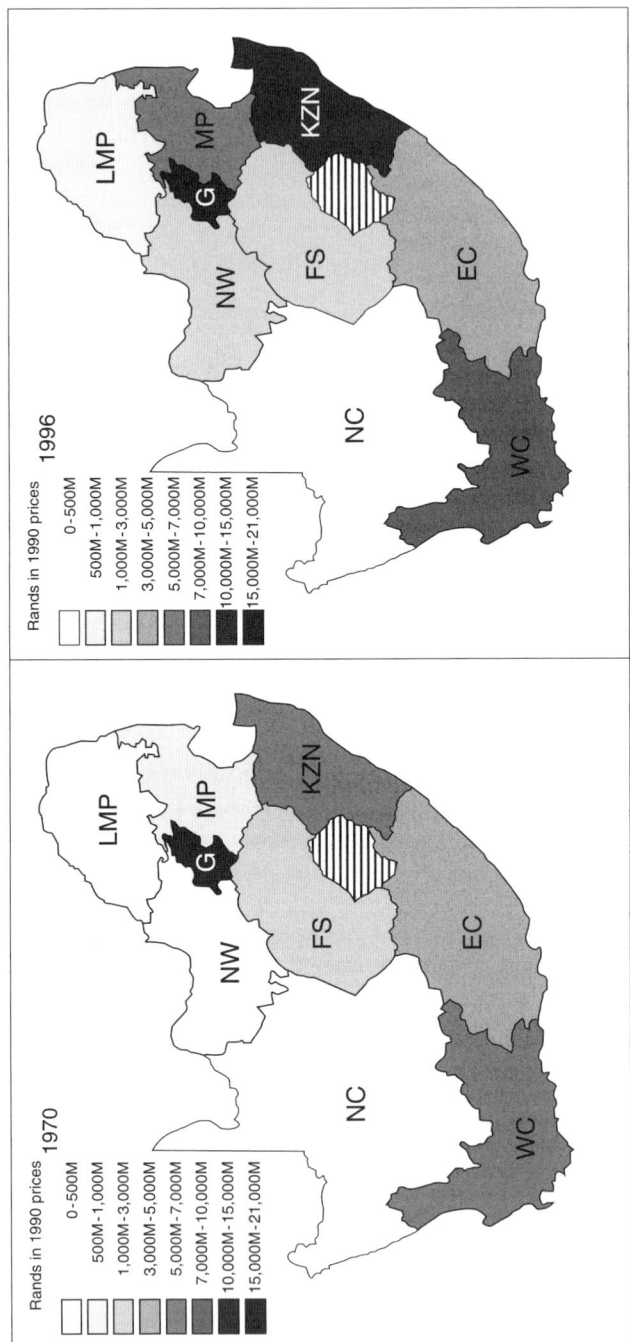

Figure 7.6. Total manufacturing value added by province
Source: Fedderke and Wollnik (2007).
Key: The data exclude the former 'homeland' states. LMP=Limpopo; NW=North-West; G=Gauteng; MP=Mpumalanga; NC=Northern Cape; FS=Free State; KZN=KwaZulu-Natal; WC=Western Cape; EC=Eastern Cape.

Table 7.2. Theoretical priors on elasticities and the empirical findings for South Africa

Theory	Priors and findings	Human capital	Labour intensity	Technology differentials	Scale economies	Industry links
Heckscher–Ohlin	prior	>0	>0			
	actual	+0.09	−0.02			
Ricardian	prior			>0		
	actual			+0.06		
New trade	prior				>0	
	actual				+0.19	
Economic geography	prior	>0			>0	>0
	actual	+0.09			+0.19	−0.63

Source: Fedderke and Wollnik (2007).

Notes: Human capital and Labour intensity capture dispersion of skills intensity and labour intensity about national means; Technology differentials dispersion about national mean labour productivity measures; Scale economies is a measure of the economy of scale of production; Industry links is a measure of the intensity of production in the use of intermediate inputs.

industry that is poised to take advantage of significant economies of scale. Instead, the dispersion and primary commodity reliance of manufacturing in South Africa suggests that liberalization is likely to have a positive impact only if infrastructure investment accompanies the intervention, in order to lower transport and transaction costs.

Edwards and Johnny (2006) report results that are consistent with the hypothesis that improvements in infrastructure positively impact on trade. There is a broad, though not universal, consensus that the relationship between export performance and economic growth is broadly positive (see, for example, Rodrik, 1997). If this is indeed the case, then the results above suggest a further indirect impact of infrastructure on growth. Edwards and Johnny (2006) using firm-level data reveals greater dissatisfaction with transport and communications infrastructure amongst exporting than non-exporting firms, suggesting that infrastructure is limiting firms' ability to export. Further, regression analysis of export performance suggests that total public sector infrastructure stock (in particular, rail-carrying capacity, paved roads and power generation capacity) positively impact export performance and analysis suggests that infrastructure stock drives export performance, rather than vice versa.[50]

Finally, employment generation and skills development may also be key considerations of public sector infrastructure policies—such policies are often

---

[50] Testing for direction of association is by Pesaran, Shin, and Smith bounds testing (Pesaran, Shin, and Smith, 2001).

justified in the language of job creation and skills development, instead of or in addition to that of economic growth. Yet the available empirical evidence in South Africa does not provide significant support for this hypothesis. McCord (2003) finds that the performance of public sector infrastructure projects with respect to skills transfer (and employment generation) has not met the expectations of policy makers, due to the short period of employment and the low-skilled nature of the available work. This suggests a limited or negligible scope for infrastructure to positively impact on economic growth through this channel.

While the evidence thus suggests that infrastructure investment is important for both growth and export performance, note that the evidence makes allowance for neither quality nor cost of infrastructure provision—topics that require further investigation.[51]

4. Taking stock

In this final section we consider three questions. What are the major themes in the literature on South African investment behaviour? Second, what are the immediate prospects for investment in the future, given the evolution of the underlying determinants of investment? Finally, where are the gaps in our knowledge about investment?

A number of important points have emerged. Most fundamentally, economic theory appears to account well for South African investment behaviour. Standard indicators of returns and costs of investment influence investment much as theory predicts they would. For policy makers therefore, raising the net rate of return on investment remains an important means of stimulating investment in fixed capital stock. In this context, the focus of macroeconomic policy in promoting price stability through fiscal discipline and a relatively successful inflation targeting policy framework, has allowed real interest rates to decline in the mid 2000s (see Chapters 3 and 4). Moreover, reform of the tax regime has seen at least some (though very limited) reductions in the corporate tax rate. In these respects, therefore, conditions for investment as predicted by the empirical models considered, have improved since 2000.

A persistent theme has been the fundamental role of uncertainty for investment. Across a range of measures of uncertainty, under alternative estimation methodologies, uncertainty has mattered.[52] What is more, uncertainty measures in South Africa appear to be bound into wider institutional contexts, covering macroeconomic stability and policy certainty, property rights, crime, human capital investment, as well the stability of the political system.

---

[51] This is discussed further in Bogetić and Fedderke (2006a).
[52] This is the case for domestic as well as foreign capital formation, see evidence in Chapter 5.

Output market structure also matters for investment. Trade liberalization and the opening of the economy have made progress in improving the policy environment by lowering the pricing power of domestic industry—see the discussion in Edwards (2005) and Aron and Muellbauer (2007). Similarly, there has been a movement toward more proactive competition policy. Nevertheless, and despite some evidence that market concentration has declined since the liberalization of the economy in 1996,[53] much remains to be done to improve the competitiveness of South African industry (see Chapter 8). Aghion, Braun, and Fedderke (2008) point to levels of pricing power in manufacturing that lies considerably above international comparators.

In terms of public capital, infrastructure investment implies positive productivity gains in South Africa, while the spatial configuration of the economy argues for a heavy emphasis on infrastructure as a means of lowering transport costs. This is likely to be vital not only to realize the productivity gains associated with economies of scale in production, but also in order to access export markets. Government policy has now targeted infrastructure as a priority, and has allocated substantial additional expenditure to it (Chapter 4). However, Bogetić and Fedderke (2006b) show that forecasts for increased demand for electricity and telecommunications alone already generate substantial expenditure requirements for the fiscus—Table 3 illustrates this for a projected growth rate of 3.6 per cent per annum (and a targeted growth rate of 6 per cent approximately doubles the requirement). Thus, meeting the infrastructural demands of the economy will bring renewed attention to borrowing requirements, the interest rate impact, and balance of payments constraints.

Table 7.3. South Africa—Forecast of infrastructure investment needs

	The Current Growth Scenario*, 2003–2010		
	Average Annual Investment Flows		
	In billions of US$	In billions of rand	In per cent of GDP
Power:			
Lower bound	0.29	1.87	0.11
Upper bound	0.52	3.37	0.20
Telecom:	1.98	12.90	0.75
Total (upper bound):	2.50	16.27	0.95

Source: Bogetic and Fedderke (2006b).
Notes: *Average annual growth projection (in %): 3.6 per cent. Source: IMF and World Bank medium-term projection.

---

[53] See Fedderke and Naumann (2008).

Finally, there are some important questions and issues not yet addressed. The most significant of these concerns data. While South Africa is unusual amongst developing countries in having biannual manufacturing census data from 1917 through 1996, after 1996, at precisely the point of most substantial liberalization of the economy, such data collection ceased. Large sample surveys have been collected since 1996, but the release of data has been slow and the frequency of collection too low (twice a decade). Moreover, when data is released, access is limited. As a consequence, research on economic performance has had to rely on data at too high a level of aggregation, making an assessment of the impact of policy changes very difficult. It is high time that reliable and timely data releases at relatively high frequency were resumed.

It is perturbing that with the service sectors of the economy now contributing close to 60 per cent of GDP, there has been very little research in this area. Aggregate studies of investment and those focusing on the manufacturing sector are largely consistent, suggesting that results are likely to be robust to a consideration of the service sectors. Nevertheless the particular nuances and peculiarities of the service sector remain to be more substantively explored.

Unfortunately a similar fate befalls explorations of the interaction between physical capital accumulation, innovation and skills, and human capital investment. This link receives close attention in the modern growth literature, and the changing structure of growth noted in the introduction is suggestive of its importance in South Africa too. At present, only two papers have begun to explore this link, citing evidence which favours Schumpeterian[54] and related Aghion–Howitt type[55] innovation structures. The introduction of substantial R&D incentives by South African policy makers suggests more work is required in this area.

Consideration of the interaction between capital accumulation and performance of the labour market, with its continued high levels of unemployment, as well as with openness and trade performance, are further important research areas.

The substantial improvement in investment from the 1990s into the 2000s is likely to have been associated with improving net rates of return on investment and a lowering of uncertainty faced by investors due to improved institutions and improved macroeconomic stability (see also Chapters 2 to 4). But if South Africa is to realize its desired growth rates of 6 per cent per annum on a sustained basis, more attention will have to be paid to the pricing power of domestic producers, continued improvement in lowering uncertainty faced by investors, better infrastructure services to the private sector, and further liberalization of the economy in order to raise its competitiveness.

---

[54] See Fedderke (2006).
[55] See Aghion, Braun, and Fedderke (2008); Aghion et al. (2008).

References

Abedian, I. and Van Seventer, D., 1995, 'Productivity and Multiplier Analysis of Infrastructure Investment in South Africa: An Econometric Investigation and Preliminary Policy Implications', Mimeo. Pretoria: Ministry of Finance.

Aghion, P., Braun, M., and Fedderke, J. W., 2008, 'Competition and Productivity Growth in South Africa',Economics of Transition, 16(4): 741-68, and *Center for International Development at Harvard Working Paper, no.* 132.

Aghion, P., Fedderke, J. W., Howitt, P., Kularatne, C., and Viegi, N., 2008, 'Testing Creative Destruction in an Opening Economy: The Case of the South African Manufacturing Industries', Mimeo. UCT and Harvard.

Aron, J. and Muellbauer, J., 2000, 'Personal and Corporate Saving in South Africa', *World Bank Economic Review*, 14(3): 509–544.

Aron, J. and Muellbauer, J., 2002, 'Interest rate effects on output: evidence from a GDP forecasting model for South Africa', *IMF Staff Papers* 49 (November, *IMF Annual Research Conference*): 185–213.

Aron, J. and Muellbauer, J., 2005, 'Monetary Policy, Macro-Stability and Growth: South Africa's Recent Experience and Lessons', *World Economics*, 6(4): 123–147, December.

Aron, J., and Muellbauer, J., 2007, 'Inflation Dynamics and Trade Openness: with an application to South Africa', *CSAE Working Paper Series WPC 2007–11*.

Bogetić, Ž. and Fedderke, J. W., 2006a, 'South Africa's Infrastructure Performance: An International Benchmarking Analysis', *Journal of Development Perspectives*, 1(2): 7–31.

Bogetić, Ž. and Fedderke, J. W., 2006b, 'Forecasting Investment Needs in South Africa's Electricity and Telecom Sectors', *South African Journal of Economics*, 74(3): 530–56.

Bond, S. and Van Reenen, J, 2007, Microeconometric models of investment and employment, in Heckman, J.J., and Leamer, E.E. (eds.), *Handbook of Econometrics*. 6A. North Holland, pp. 4417–4498.

Coetzee, Z. and Le Roux, E., 1998, 'Does Public Infrastructure Affect Economic Growth?', presented at the Annual EBM Conference of the National Productivity Institute.

Development Bank of Southern Africa,.1998, 'Infrastructure: A Foundation for Development', *Development Report 1998*. Pretoria: DBSA.

Du Plessis, P. G., 1981, Measuring the Concentration of Economic Power, *Journal for Studies in Economics and Econometrics*, 10: 46–60.

Du Toit, C., and Moolman, E., 2004, 'A Neoclassical Investment Function of the South African Economy', *Economic Modelling*, 21(4): 647–660.

Edwards, L., 2005, 'Has South Africa Liberalised its Trade?', *South African Journal of Economics*, 73(4): 754–775.

Edwards, L. and Johnny, B., 2006, 'South Africa's Export Performance: Determinants of Export Supply', paper presented at the Economic Research Southern Africa Infrastructure Workshop, May 2006.

Fedderke, J. W., 2001, 'Investment in Fixed Capital Stock: Testing for the Impact of Sectoral and Systemic Uncertainty', paper presented at the Royal Economic Society Conference, Durham, April 2001, *Econometric Research Southern Africa Working Paper*, no. 16, University of the Witwatersrand.

——2004, 'Investment in Fixed Capital Stock: Testing for the Impact of Sectoral and Systemic Uncertainty', *Oxford Bulletin of Economics and Statistics,* 66(2): 165–188.

—— 2006, 'Technology, Human Capital and Growth: Evidence from a Middle Income Country Case Study Applying Dynamic Heterogeneous Panel Analysis', in South African Reserve Bank, Banco de Mexico and The People's Bank of China (eds.) *Economic Growth, Proceedings of a G20 seminar held in Pretoria, South Africa, on 4–5 August 2005.*

Fedderke, J. W. and Bogetić, Ž., 2006, 'Infrastructure and Growth in South Africa: Direct and Indirect Productivity Impacts of 19 Infrastructure Measures', *Economic Research Southern Africa Working Paper, no.* 39 and *World Bank Policy Research Working Paper, no.* 3989.

Fedderke, J. W., and Luiz, J. M., 2008a, 'The Political Economy of Institutions, Stability and Investment: A Simultaneous Equation Approach in an Emerging Economy the Case of South Africa. *Journal of Development Studies,* 44(7), 1056–79.

Fedderke, J. W., and Luiz, J. M., 2008b, 'Does Human Generate Social and Institutional Capital? Exploring Evidence from South African Time Series Data', *Oxford Economic Papers,* 60, 649–82.

Fedderke, J. W. and Naumann, D., 2008, 'An Analysis of Industry Concentration in South African Manufacturing, 1972–2001', *Applied Economics,* forthcoming, and *ERSA Working Paper, no.* 26, available at <www.econrsa.org> last accessed 15 September 2008.

Fedderke, J. W. and Szalontai, G., 2008, 'Industry Concentration in South African Manufacturing: Trends and Consequences 1972–96', *Economic Modelling,* forthcoming *World Bank Africa Region Working Paper Series, no.* 96.

Fedderke, J. W., and Wollnik, A., 2007, 'The Spatial Distribution of Manufacturing in South Africa 1970–1996, its Determinants and Policy Implications', *Economic Research Southern Africa Working Paper, no.* 53.

Fedderke, J. W., De Kadt, R., and Luiz, J., 2001, 'Indicators of Political Liberty, Property Rights and Political Instability in South Africa', *International Review of Law and Economics,* 21(1): 103–34.

Fedderke J. W., Kularatne, C., and Mariotti, M., 2007, 'Mark-up Pricing in South African Industry', *Journal of African Economies,* 16(1): 28–69.

Fedderke, J. W., Perkins. P., and Luiz, J. M., 2006, 'Infrastructural Investment in Long-run Economic Growth: South Africa 1875–2001', *World Development,* 34(6): 1037–59.

Fedderke, J. W., Henderson, S., Kayemba, J., Mariotti, M., and Vaze, P., 2001, 'Changing Factor Market Conditions in South Africa: The Capital Market—A Sectoral Description of the Period 1970–1997', *Development Southern Africa,* 18(4): 493–512.

Ferderer, J. P., 1993, 'The Impact of Uncertainty on Aggregate Investment Spending: An Empirical Analysis', *Journal of Money, Credit and Banking,* 25(1): 49–61.

Fielding, D., 1997, 'Aggregate Investment in South Africa: A Model with Implications for Political Reform', *Oxford Bulletin of Economics and Statistics,* 59(3): 349–69.

—— 1999, 'Manufacturing Investment in South Africa: A Time Series Model', *Journal of Development Economics,* 58(2), 405–27.

—— 2000, 'Investment under Credit Rationing and Uncertainty: Evidence from South Africa', *Journal of African Economies,* 9(2): 198–212.

—— 2002, 'Human Rights, Political Instability and Investment in South Africa: A Note', *Journal of Development Economics,* 67(1): 173–80.

Fourie, F. C.v.N., 1996, 'Industrial Concentration Levels and Trends in South Africa: Completing the Picture', *South African Journal of Economics*, 64(1): 97–121.

Fourie, F. C.v.N., and Smit, M. R., 1989, 'Trends in Economic Concentration in South Africa', *South African Journal of Economics*, 57(3): 241–56.

Guiso, L, and Parigi, G., 1999, 'Investment and Demand Uncertainty', *Quarterly Journal of Economics*, 114(1), 185–27.

Hartman, R., 1972, 'The Effects of Price and Cost Uncertainty on Investment', *Journal of Economic Theory*, 5: 258–66.

Kessides, I., 1993, 'The Contributions of Infrastructure to Economic Development', *World Bank Discussion Papers*, no. 213.

Kularatne, C., 2002, 'An Examination of the Impact of Financial Deepening on Long-Run Economic Growth: An Application of a VECM Structure to a Middle-Income Country Context', *South African Journal of Economics*, 70(4): 647–87.

—— 2006, 'Social and Economic Infrastructure Impacts on Economic Growth in South Africa', paper presented at the UCT School of Economics Staff Seminar Series, October 2006.

Leach, D. F., 1992, 'Absolute vs. Relative Concentration in Manufacturing Industry 1972–1985', *South African Journal of Economics*, 60(4): 386–400.

Levine, R., 1997, 'Financial Development and Economic Growth', *Journal of Economic Literature*, 35, 688–726.

Levine, R., and Zervos, S., 1996, 'Stock Market Development and Long-Run Growth', *World Bank Economic Review*, 10(2), 323–40.

—— 1998, 'Stock Markets, Banks and Growth', *American Economic Review*, 88(3): 537–58.

Levine, R., Loayza, N., and Beck, T., 2000, 'Financial Intermediation and Growth: Causality and Causes', *Journal of Monetary Economics*, 46(1): 31–77.

Mariotti, M., 2002, 'An Examination of the Impact of Economic Policy on Long-Run Economic Growth: An Application of a VECM Structure to a Middle-Income Country Context', *South African Journal of Economics*, 70(4): 688–725.

McCord, A., 2003, 'An Overview of Performance and Potential of Public Works Programmes in South Africa', *Centre for Social Science Research Working Paper*, no. 49.

Merrifield, A., 2000, 'Financing of Public Infrastructure Investment in South Africa', in Khosa, M (ed.), 2000, *Infrastructure Mandates for Change 1994–1999*, Pretoria: HSRC Publishers.

Perkins, P., Fedderke, J. W., and Luiz, J. M., 2005, 'An Analysis of Economic Infrastructure Investment in South Africa', *South African Journal of Economics*, 73(2), 211–12.

Pesaran, M. H., Shin, Y., and R. J. Smith, 2001, 'Bounds testing approaches to the analysis of level relationships. *Journal of Applied Econometrics*, 16: 289–326.

Pretorius, C. J., 1998, 'Gross Fixed Investment in the Macroeconometric Model of the Reserve Bank', *SARB Quarterly Bulletin* (March): 35–48.

Rodrik, D., 1997, 'Trade Policy and Economic Performance in Southern Africa', paper prepared for the Swedish Ministry of Foreign Affairs.

Romm, A. T., 2005, 'The Relationship Between Savings and Growth in South Africa: A Time Series Analysis', *South African Journal of Economics*, 73(2): 171–89.

Sala-i-Martin, X., Doppelhofer, G., and Miller, R.I., 2004, 'Determinants of Long-Term Growth: A Bayesian Averaging of Classical Estimates (BACE) Approach', *American Economic Review*, 94(4):813–35.

Wesso, G. R., 1995, 'A Varying Parameter Regression Approach to Investment Modelling in South Africa: Estimation, Stability Testing and Prediction', *Journal for Studies in Economics and Econometrics*, 19(1): 29–50.

World Bank, 1994, *World Development Report 1994: Infrastructure for Development*. New York: Oxford University Press.

8
The Evolution and Impact of Industrial and Competition Policies

Anthony Black and Simon Roberts

1. Introduction[1]

In the run up to the first democratic election in 1994 the South African economy faced a range of serious problems. A key area of weakness was the pattern of industrial development. The manufacturing sector was protected and not very competitive, with many sub-sectors both highly capital intensive and concentrated. Industrial development had been shaped by far-reaching and interventionist policies focused on the strategic concerns of the apartheid government, such as defence and liquid fuels, and the needs of the resource extraction and processing industries. Weak growth and high unemployment were of critical concern. Faced with these difficulties, the new ANC-led government had to formulate strategies to achieve their objectives of reconstruction and development. Industrial development, and more specifically manufacturing, was seen as a key potential growth sector with the ability to be both a source of exports and of employment.

The incoming government had already committed itself to sweeping trade liberalization under the Uruguay round of GATT. The Growth, Employment and Redistribution (GEAR) strategy announced in 1996 entrenched this liberalization programme. An 'outward-oriented stance' designed to pursue 'employment creating international competitiveness' was the central thrust of trade and industrial policy (Republic of South Africa, 1996). Indeed, trade liberalization and international competitiveness have been the consistent themes of policy over the period. These have been accompanied by a wide range of supportive measures for firms

---

[1] Acknowledgements: We are grateful for comments from Janine Aron and Brian Kahn, and an anonymous referee. The views expressed here do not necessarily represent those of the Competition Commission of South Africa.

under the banner of industrial policy, aimed at boosting manufacturing development.

This chapter focuses on industrial policy and performance and on manufacturing industry in particular. We argue that the performance since 1994 has been characterized by the perpetuation from the apartheid years of the superior performance of capital-intensive industries, high levels of concentration and weak competitive rivalry. Industrial policy has been relatively unfocused and in practice has had little impact on the economy's development path, while the privatization and regulation of utilities has also been flawed. We find that competition policy has been relatively more successful, though major challenges remain.

Measured from 1994 to 2005, moderate average growth rates were achieved for South Africa by comparison with similar middle-income countries (Table 8.1). The comparative average performance of exports and investment, and growth in industry and manufacturing value added, have all been relatively poor for this period, although growth rates have improved significantly since 2004 (see Chapter 2). A further concern is the lack of industrial diversification into both more labour demanding and also into more dynamic sectors (Hausmann and Klinger, 2006; Rodrik, 2006; Department of Trade and Industry (DTI), 2007).

We start by reviewing the evolution of policy in section 2. The focus in section 3 is on an assessment of manufacturing performance at the sub-sector level and an analysis of these outcomes. Section 4 specifically focuses on issues of concentration and competition, including the case of privatized and regulated utilities. Section 5 concludes, and draws some implications for the future.

2. A review of industrial, trade, and competition policy and major changes post-1994

At the time of the transition to democracy there was intense debate about the nature of the problem of slow industrial expansion as well as of the policies needed to address this.[2] World Bank analysts characterized the South African economy as a protected and distorted economy in the Latin American model, resulting from apartheid policies compounding an import substituting industrialization strategy (Fallon and Pereira da Silva, 1994; Levy, 1992). According to the Bank, the bias to capital-intensity further resulted from negative real interest rates and the nature of government investment support. The Bank's recommendations to redress this situation were trade liberalization, a reduc-

---

[2] See, for example, Hirsch (2005).

Evolution and Impact of Industrial and Competition Policies

Table 8.1. Economic performance of selected middle income countries, 1994–2005

	South Africa	Hungary	Poland	Turkey	Brazil	Chile	Malaysia	Middle-income countries
Income per capita, 2005 ($)	10 880	16 780	13 370	8 390	8 140	10 920	10 360	7 252
Average annual growth in GDP 1994–2005 (%)	3.3	3.9	4.4	4.4	2.4	4.8	5.1	4.6
Average ratio of GFCF to GDP, 1994–2005 (%)	15.9	22.5	20.3	21.4	19.4	23.1	29.5	24.6
Average growth in industry value added (%)	2.3	5.3	4.8	4.0	2.1	4.0	5.9	5.4
Industrial value added as % of GDP, 2005	26.9	26.5	27.0	19.5	35.6	42.7	51.8	37.1
Average growth in manufacturing value added (%)	2.9	7.2	7.6	5.0	—	3.2	6.7	6.7
Manufacturing value added as % of GDP, 2005	16.5	19.3	16.1	11.5	—	16.1	30.6	21.7
Average growth in total exports (%)	4.6	13.0	11.2	11.4	8.2	7.7	8.0	9.4
Total exports as ratio of GDP, 2005 (%)	27.1	66.4	37.0	27.4	16.8	41.8	123.4	37.9

Source: Calculated from World Bank World Development Indicators

Notes:

[1] All calculations are from constant local currency series, expressed as percentages, except for income per capita.

[2] Income per capita is for 2005, US$, at PPP exchange rates.

[3] Manufacturing value added for Brazil is not available.

[4] Exports are measured in gross output terms, while GDP is based on value added, hence the possibility for Export:GDP ratios in excess of 100 per cent, as for Malaysia.

tion of distortions in factor markets (seen as mainly due to the state) including increased real interest rates, a stable macroeconomic environment, and the 'right' prices to provide an enabling environment to stimulate exports, with a corresponding impetus to the upgrading of skills and technology (Fallon and Pereira da Silva, 1994).

The analysis of the problem put forward by the influential Industrial Strategy Project (ISP) was not that dissimilar although their prescriptions focused much more on 'supply-side' support and industrial policy interventions (Joffe et al., 1995). The ISP was also highly critical of the high degree of concentration and resultant lack of competition in many industrial sectors. Fine and

Rustomjee (1996) offered a somewhat different perspective, arguing that the dominance of the large scale mineral-based industry that comprised South Africa's 'minerals energy complex' should be the starting point for an understanding of industrial development and appropriate industrial policy.

As we shall show, the ISP and World Bank interpretations prevailed in terms of stated policy, although in practice the policies sought to promote a multiplicity of objectives, with international competiveness as a central theme. While objectives included support for non-mineral based sub-sectors and higher value added activities, it was understood that mineral based manufacturing would remain important and should be supported by further beneficiation (Hirsch, 2005: 124).

2.1. The evolution of industrial and trade policy

Some of the key events in the evolution of industrial and competition policy are indicated in Table 8.2. Trade liberalization was also an important element, and is discussed in detail in Chapter 6. Some liberalization had already taken place by the early 1990s. This included a reduction in quantitative controls on imports, the beginnings of tariff reduction and significant privatization. After 1994 the liberalization programme involved removing remaining quantitative restrictions, simplifying the tariff schedule and a significant reduction in average tariff rates. The impact was to reduce effective rates of protection substantially, from a weighted average of 42.4 per cent on manufactured goods in 1989 to 38.1 per cent in 1993 and then to 14.8 per cent in 2003 (Edwards and Lawrence, 2006).

Complementing trade liberalization has been a range of measures to encourage investment, technological improvements and exports, and to support small firms. These have included sector specific adjustment programmes, investment incentives, 'supply-side' incentive programmes, subsidized infrastructure, support measures for skills development and technology, special loan facilities and support programmes for small firms.

The government's concerns about international competitiveness were re-focused on enhancing capabilities in 'knowledge-intensive' activities and advanced technology, with the release in 2002 and 2003 of the *National Research and Development Strategy*, the *Integrated Manufacturing Strategy* and the *Advanced Manufacturing Technology Strategy* (DST, 2002; NACI/DST, 2003; DTI, 2002). These were followed in 2007 by the *National Industrial Policy Framework*, and *Industrial Policy Action Plan* (DTI, 2007). The latter strategies are more targeted by sector, and seek to stimulate diversified activities outside resource-based industries, albeit with identification of a long list of priority sectors and activities.

While there has been no shortage of industrial policy interventions and new programmes, the net impact is far from clear. Together with trade liberalization, it was expected that these measures would counteract the previ-

Evolution and Impact of Industrial and Competition Policies

Table 8.2. A chronology of industrial and competition policy

1989	Board of Trade and Industry publishes 'A Policy and Strategy for the Development and Structural Adjustment of Industry' (outlines interventionist industrial strategy but is never fully adopted)
1991	Introduction of Section 37E of the Income Tax Act (accelerated depreciation for large scale export oriented projects)
	Introduction of Regional Industrial Development Programme (RIDP) (establishment grants and incentives for industrial expansion on a regional basis)
Early 1990s	Introduction of Support Programme of Industry Innovation (SPII) and Technology and Human Resources for Industry Programme (THRIP)
1995	Introduction of Motor Industry Development Programme (MIDP)
1995–6	Establishment of small business support agencies: Centre for Small Business Promotion, Ntsika Enterprise Promotion Agency, Khula Enterprise Finance, and the National Small Business Council
1995–8	Introduction of supply side incentives including Competitiveness Fund (aimed at encouraging competitiveness particularly by small, medium and micro enterprises); Short Term Export Finance Guarantee Facility (aimed at SMME exporters); Life Scheme (low interest financing to export oriented projects through the IDC); Duty Credit Scheme (temporary measure to promote exports by offering import rebate certificates to exporters of clothing and textiles); Sectoral Partnership Fund (to promote groups of firms to collaborate in addressing common problems); Workplace Challenge (to improve productivity by facilitating joint training of workers and managers)
1996	Cancellation of Regional Industrial Development Programme (RIDP)
	Tax holiday scheme introduced
	Spatial Development Initiatives (to coordinate public infrastructure provision with private sector investment on a regional basis)
1998	Competition Act introduced
1999	End of tax holiday scheme
	Establishment of new competition authorities
2002	Announcement of Integrated Manufacturing Strategy with emphasis on knowledge and technology
	Introduction of Strategic Investment Programme (SIP) and Critical Infrastructure Programme
2003	Advanced Manufacturing Technology Strategy
2005	Formation of Small Enterprise Development Agency (SEDA) via the merger of Ntsika and the National Manufacturing Advisory Centre
	Establishment of Apex Fund to support loans to micro-businesses
2007	Announcement of National Industrial Policy Framework and Action Plan

Sources: Department of Trade and Industry (1997); Black (1993); Black and Kahn (2002); Hirsch (2005).

ous government's support for large-scale capital-intensive industries and the legacy of poor productivity, and would facilitate the development of non-traditional manufactured exports (Hanival and Hirsch, 1998; Joffe et al., 1995). However, this has only happened to a limited degree, see section 3. While the stated objective of policy has been to encourage higher value-added activities, labour-intensive activities and smaller firms, in practice the weight of support has continued to be focused on larger scale capital-intensive activities.

2.2. Competition policy, privatization, and regulation

There was broad agreement in 1994 that the South African economy was highly concentrated, especially in terms of the dominance of a very small number of mining based conglomerate groupings (Joffe et al., 1995). High concentration has reinforced the capital and resource-intensive industrial development path, while imperfect competition distorted economic outcomes more widely. Recent studies have pointed to the negative implications resulting from low levels of competition, which have resulted in high price mark-ups, correlated with low productivity growth (Aghion et al., 2006). However, such studies do not provide insight into the nature and implications of competitive rivalry, nor the types of anti-competitive behaviour and arrangements, see section 4.

The dominance of a few large conglomerates, controlled by families through pyramid structures, underpinned the emphasis on competition policy in the *Reconstruction and Development Programme*. South Africa had a Competition Board located within the Department of Trade and Industry, but it was widely perceived as ineffective (Hirsch, 2005). The then Minister of Trade and Industry, Trevor Manuel, proposed a new competition regime soon after the ANC came to power, and threatened the break-up of the conglomerates. Under stiff resistance from big business this initiative stalled. In 1997, the reform of competition policy was reinitiated, drawing from the legislative frameworks of countries such as Canada and Australia. The draft legislation was jointly negotiated by government with representatives of business and organized labour, leading to the new Competition Act of 1998, operative from September 1999.

The Act established two new, independent authorities, the Competition Commission and Competition Tribunal. It also provided for the compulsory pre-merger notification of transactions above a specified amount, expressed in terms of assets and turnover. Other provisions have addressed prohibited horizontal (that is collusive) and vertical arrangements, and the abuse of a dominant position. Evaluation of mergers under the new merger provision dominated the workload in the first five years (Roberts, 2004a). The authorities have increasingly focused on anti-competitive conduct, especially since 2004, with the introduction of a corporate leniency programme for cartels providing a strong incentive for cartel members to break ranks and cooperate with the Competition Commission in exchange for immunity. There have also been a few notable cases of unilateral abuse of dominance, particularly with regard to large firms in steel and chemicals privatized by the apartheid government in 1989 and 1990.

Measures to address the behaviour of large firms are also important in the context of the regulation of utilities. Strategies were devised for the restructuring of state-owned utilities, which covered corporatization and, in some cases, privatization. Regulatory bodies were established to set boundaries to the conduct of these firms, with a rather mixed record (see section 4).

3. Industrial performance—trends and outcomes

Improving a country's industrial competitiveness requires developing improved and diversified production capabilities (Machaka and Roberts, 2003; Imbs and Wacziarg, 2003; Hausmann et al., 2006). It is not necessarily about export performance, per se. For example increasing exports of aluminium, based on cheap electricity and the endowments of coal, is different from improving trade performance in more sophisticated and diversified products such as machinery and equipment. We focus on whether manufacturing has become more diversified, and therefore evaluate in section 3.1. the changing patterns of sectoral performance in terms of value added, international trade, investment, and employment. We draw on data for the twenty-eight main manufacturing sub-sectors, and assess which factors explain the outcomes, including the particular role of industrial policies.

Performance reflects the decisions of firms, and especially large firms. This is especially relevant in South Africa given the high levels of concentration. It matters greatly for industrial performance and competitiveness whether large firms derive profits from the exertion of market power or whether competitive discipline encourages more dynamic strategies to invest in improved production capabilities. Uncompetitive market structures also inhibit the development of capabilities through raising barriers to entry, including in the availability and pricing of complementary services and products. Vibrant local rivalry is an important basis for international competitiveness (Sakakibara and Porter, 2001). We include these considerations in assessing outcomes and industrial policies, before examining the role of competition policy in more detail in section 4.

3.1. An assessment of performance

Compared to the average of middle-income countries, and especially Malaysia and Hungary, the average growth in South African manufacturing value added has been fairly slow when measured from 1994 to 2005 (Table 8.1). However, it is important to distinguish between the transitional period of 1994–9, and the period thereafter, notably with large gains in macro-stability (Chapters 3 and 4). For a discussion on macro-stability and other factors influencing investment, see Chapters 2 and 7.

Figure 8.1 shows overall performance in manufacturing and in Table 8.3 we present sector level manufacturing data on performance in terms of different measures. Manufacturing investment with output contracting (value added) have followed a cyclical pattern with growth from 1994 to 1997, again from 1999 to 2002, and from 2003 to 2007, with investment contracting in 1998 and 2002 (Figure 8.1). Investment improved sharply from 1994 to 1996 and then stagnated for much of the period, with rapid growth again taking place from 2004 and gross domestic fixed investment (GDFI) increasing to 25.7 per cent of value-added

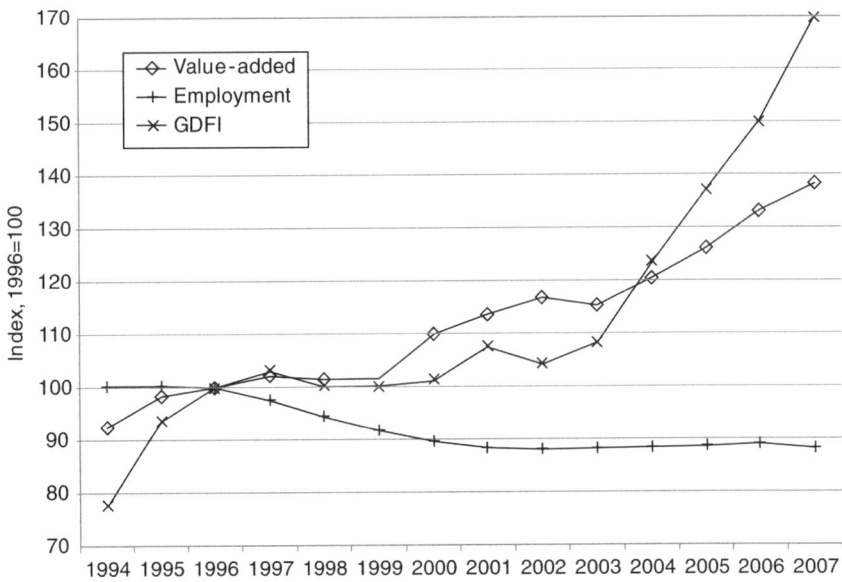

Figure 8.1. Performance of manufacturing, 1994–2007
Source: Calculated from Quantec data

in 2007. Rather than a general improvement in manufacturing investment, the picture is mixed, with high growth in some sectors and contraction in others. The expansion of manufacturing investment in the later period was led by sectors linked to construction and consumer spending, while investment in six sectors declined or remained static from 2002 to 2007.

Formal employment contracted in the second half of the 1990s and the recovery has been slow. While some of the manufacturing job losses reflect outsourcing of services such as catering, cleaning, security, and logistics, the particularly large job losses in absolute terms were in sectors which underwent major restructuring, partly as a result of import liberalization (see Chapters 2, 6, and 11). Electrical machinery, steel, non-metallic minerals, food, textiles, and clothing each shed more than 20,000 jobs over the period 1994 to 2007. Employment in clothing and textiles collectively fell by more than 60,000 jobs, and employment in food products alone decreased by 42,600. The only sectors with significant net gains are machinery and equipment with over 30,000 more jobs in 2007 than in 1994, motor vehicles with a net gain of close to 20,000, and other manufacturing with a net gain of just over 18,000.

The trend towards a reduced share for mining in the economy coupled with trade liberalization might have been expected to herald a new industrial development trajectory, with the growth of more broad-based manufacturing.

Table 8.3. Summary statistics on manufacturing performance, 1994–2007

Sector	Average annual value added growth, % (1994–2007)	Average annual employ-ment growth, % (1994–2007)	Export: output ratio 2006, %	Export: output ratio 1994, %	Import: domestic consum-ption ratio, 2006, %	Import: domestic consump-tion ratio, 1994, %	% semi & unskilled labour, 2007	Capital: labour ratio, 2007 (R'000/employee)	Net export ratio 2007	Average annual export growth, % (1994–2007)	Change in net export ratio (1994 to 2007)
Food	1.6	−1.8	6.3	7.9	10.2	7.7	58	228	−0.34	−3.5	−0.37
Beverages	1.6	−1.5	12.3	7.6	6.3	3.8	58	471	0.22	2.1	−0.07
Tobacco	1.5	−0.2	11.7	3.7	1.7	1.9	64	352	0.48	1.1	0.36
Textiles	−1.5	−3.5	11.3	14.9	26.4	24.5	54	127	−0.53	−8.9	−0.16
Wearing apparel	1.1	−3.0	7.9	8.7	35.5	8.3	50	25	−0.80	−14.7	−0.78
Leather and leather prods	8.1	−2.6	40.3	40.4	35.8	36.7	50	57	−0.02	0.7	−0.09
Footwear	−2.8	−7.0	3.4	4.5	54.1	18.0	46	43	−0.96	−19.6	−0.28
Wood and wood prods	1.7	−0.6	11.4	13.6	12.0	10.8	66	109	−0.03	−3.5	−0.26
Paper and paper prods	4.4	−2.5	15.3	22.4	14.0	14.6	55	604	0.05	−2.8	−0.20
Printing, publishing	0.0	0.9	3.4	2.3	21.4	17.9	32	132	−0.68	1.7	0.14
Coke and refineries	6.8	−1.3	11.9	16.7	12.0	13.0	30	8209	−0.13	−2.7	−0.31
Basic chemicals	4.0	−1.2	33.8	42.3	34.6	46.0	49	3118	−0.03	2.6	0.06
Other chemicals	4.5	0.1	9.3	6.3	22.9	22.3	47	452	−0.59	5.0	0.09
Rubber products	1.9	−2.2	20.5	9.6	37.7	21.8	58	208	−0.55	2.9	−0.06
Plastic products	3.7	0.2	6.1	4.3	13.0	9.8	65	84	−0.35	5.5	0.05
Glass and glass products	4.3	−1.1	8.7	10.5	21.1	18.3	47	350	−0.57	−1.7	−0.25
Non-metallic minerals	0.9	−3.0	8.6	7.7	18.8	10.3	73	444	−0.49	0.5	−0.32

(Continued)

Table 8.3. (Continued)

Sector	Average annual value added growth, % (1994-2007)	Average annual employment growth, % (1994-2007)	Export: output ratio 2006, %	Export: output ratio 1994, %	Import: domestic consumption ratio, 2006, %	Import: domestic consumption ratio, 1994, %	% semi & unskilled labour, 2007	Capital: labour ratio, 2007 (R'000/employee)	Net export ratio 2007	Average annual export growth, % (1994-2007)	Change in net export ratio (1994 to 2007)
Basic iron and steel	5.4	-3.3	51.7	49.0	15.3	11.8	58	702	0.68	3.9	-0.08
Basic non-ferrous	6.6	-0.7	50.8	55.0	36.9	20.6	59	1147	0.31	3.7	-0.22
Metal products	2.4	-0.2	17.0	10.7	18.5	10.5	35	100	-0.22	2.3	-0.02
Machinery and equipment	2.1	2.5	69.7	17.5	85.9	56.3	43	97	-0.48	11.9	0.28
Electrical machinery	3.3	-3.5	12.7	8.5	33.3	32.1	56	97	-0.54	3.2	0.15
TV, radio, and comm.	-2.0	-3.7	49.3	10.1	88.1	59.6	30	202	-0.82	10.0	0.08
Professional equipment	2.6	0.8	59.6	25.5	90.2	73.3	31	108	-0.75	1.7	0.08
Motor vehicles, parts	5.1	1.3	27.1	11.1	42.9	29.9	41	281	-0.20	18.5	0.33
Other transport	1.9	-0.7	32.2	17.3	66.9	44.0	37	201	-0.74	8.6	-0.03
Furniture	9.0	-0.1	29.4	22.1	28.2	5.4	45	35	-0.02	1.0	-0.67
Other manufacturing	1.8	2.7	26.0	20.5	35.2	21.7	48	227	-0.04	3.3	-0.08
Total manufacturing	3.2	-1.0	22.7	16.2	32.1	23.4	50	388	-0.22	4.5	0.03

Source: Quantec Ltd, South Africa

Notes: Value added at factor cost. Employment is formal employment.
X:Q is export to output ratio; M:Cons is imports to domestic consumption ratio (both are for 2006 as this is the latest available data).
Average annual export growth is calculated from constant Rand data.
The net export ratio is calculated as (exports−imports)/(exports+imports).

However, a striking feature since 1994 has been the rapid growth of resource based (and capital-intensive) industries. Growth in these sectors, and in the automotive industry, far outstripped other sectors of manufacturing. The expansion of manufacturing value added at an average annual rate of 3.2 per cent over 1994 to 2007 thus masks very different performances of manufacturing sub-sectors (Table 8.3).

A similar pattern is evident in the composition of merchandise exports. Trade liberalization was followed by rapid growth of international trade in both exports and imports, but exports remain dominated by minerals and resource-intensive manufactured products (Roberts, 2007). Apart from a dip in 1999 and 2000, minerals, basic metals, basic chemicals, and pulp and paper have maintained a share of around 60 per cent of total merchandise exports since 1994. The significant reduction in gold exports has been counterbalanced by increased exports of platinum and other minerals such as iron ore and coal.

The diversification of South Africa's exports has effectively stalled, aside from automotive exports. Edwards and Lawrence (2006) show that non-automotive manufactured exports fell in volume terms by 3.3 per cent per annum from 2000 to 2005. The share of non-traditional exports had expanded from the mid 1980s to the mid 1990s with annual growth rates in excess of 20 per cent in sectors such as motor vehicles, electrical machinery, transport equipment, leather products, beverages, rubber products, printing and publishing, footwear, tobacco and ceramics over the period 1988 to 1996 (Black and Kahn, 2002). However, the base was extremely low for many of these products. Much of this expansion was into Africa, coinciding with political acceptability and the ending of sanctions. Africa's share of South Africa's total exports excluding gold increased from just 9.1 per cent in 1988 to 17.9 per cent in 1996.

The pattern of performance suggests the importance of previous government policies, and 'path dependent' factors, meaning that firms which have developed productive strengths are better able to re-invest and continue to grow. Perhaps the best example of this is the chemicals giant, Sasol, which leads local industry in ongoing R&D spending. The basic chemicals sector which is dominated by Sasol also has the highest investment rates, with GDFI at levels close to or above 50 per cent of value added in the years 2003 to 2007. Investment rates averaging around 40 per cent of value added have also been maintained in the basic iron and steel, non-ferrous metals and coke and petroleum sub-sectors. Such patterns were reinforced by Industrial Development Corporation (IDC) lending in the mid 1990s which went predominantly to large-scale, capital-intensive operations (Roberts, 2004b).

There are important exceptions to the resource-based picture of manufacturing, especially in the performance of motor vehicles, machinery and equipment and smaller sectors such as leather products and furniture. Leather products and furniture have recorded the best performance overall in terms of value added growth, followed by coke and refineries, basic non-ferrous metals, basic iron and steel, and motor vehicles. Each of these sectors had an average annual growth of greater than 5 per cent from 1994 5o 2007. The only sectors with positive employment growth are other manufacturing, machinery and equipment, motor vehicles, professional equipment, printing and publishing, plastic products, and other chemical products.

To assess associations of this performance with patterns of competitiveness we look at both exports and imports. Aside from resource-based sectors, the most export-oriented sectors are machinery and equipment, professional equipment, TV, radio and communications equipment, and leather products each of which export more than one-third of their output. There have also been huge increases in the export orientation of most of these sectors, along with motor vehicles suggesting some diversification. However, it is misleading to look only at exports as these sectors also have the greatest import penetration, with imports in excess of 80 per cent of domestic consumption for the three equipment sectors. This suggests a significant portion of exports is due to re-export of imported products by South African distributors to southern African markets.

Changing patterns of comparative advantage, as revealed in the net export ratio to total trade[3] indicates that only basic iron and steel, tobacco products, basic non-ferrous metals, beverages, and paper and paper products recorded a positive trade balance in 2007. The ratio improved in the case of ten sectors, although some are still in deficit with the biggest improvements in tobacco products, motor vehicles, and machinery and equipment. Tobacco products is one of the few sectors in which nominal tariffs were increased over the 1990s, to 42 per cent in 2001.[4] With low value-added growth over the period it appears as if declining local consumption has led to increased exports, probably into southern African markets.

Disaggregating further is revealing of what underlies trade performance, as many sectors are still highly heterogeneous. This raises questions about the view of Edwards and Lawrence (2006) that improved export performance of (aggregated) non-commodity manufactures especially in 1990 to 2000 is mainly due to import liberalization. As already indicated, automotive exports play a big role here, accounting for 21 per cent of manufactured exports in 2007, followed by machinery and equipment with 10 per cent. But, over half of the latter sector's exports are of centrifuges, filtering and purifying machines for liquids and gases. This category is almost entirely comprised of catalytic converters for motor vehicles, while the machinery export category also includes vehicle engines. These products have benefited handsomely from

---

[3] This is one of the measures of 'revealed comparative advantage' used by Greenaway and Milner (1993).
[4] See Cassim et al. (2002).

the *Motor Industry Development Programme* (MIDP) introduced in 1995, which has assisted exports by allowing exporters to offset import duties (see section 3.2). Of the remainder of machinery exports, mining equipment stands out, accounting for around one-tenth of the total. The capabilities in mining equipment reflect a sustained source of local demand leading to a diverse, sophisticated and internationally integrated supplier industry, providing hi-tech capital equipment, consumables, and support services to the local mining community (Walker and Minnitt, 2006). Key to the development of machinery and equipment as a late-industrializing country is the adoption and adaptation of technologies. Sophisticated capabilities in products such as valves, pumps, and sorting equipment have all involved competition with imported products, links with multinational sources of technology, reverse engineering, and local innovation (Hofmaenner et al., 2004). In other words, exporting has followed rather than led the development of local capabilities.

Leather products and furniture are both identified as recording improved trade performance in the 1990s, coupled with the highest growth rates in value-added from 1994 to 2007 (Table 8.3). There are notable links to the automotive sector here as well. The growth of leather products while footwear underwent massive decline is explained by the market provided for stitched seat leather for the automotive industry, and the incentives under the MIDP. The development of the furniture sector is largely associated with growing local demand, as well as improved exports. In both local and international markets large buyers are crucial, setting standards and exerting monopsony power (Kaplinsky and Manning, 1999; Kaplinsky et al., 2002). As a result, the growth has been due to very large manufacturers, dominated by one multinational (Steinhoff) in particular.[5] Smaller firms have fallen by the wayside, partly explaining the contraction in employment.

Other diversified exports in the 1990s include textiles, other transport equipment, and plastic products. Again, disaggregation reveals insights into the factors at work. Textiles exports are dominated by raw and minimally processed wool. There have also been notable successes in certain engineering textiles, such as parachute fabric and substrate for conveyor belts, both in response to domestic demand—from the defence sector and from heavy industry respectively, under apartheid. This has enabled moves into other products such as airbags and seatbelts for the auto sector (Roberts and Thoburn, 2003).

Exports of other transport products are due to local demand idiosyncrasies aided by the entrepreneurial 'discovery' process in the form of the manufacture

---

[5] Steinhoff identifies its employment in South Africa as being 20,000, more than half the employment of the whole furniture sector (Steinhoff, *Annual Report* 2004).

of luxury yachts, mainly in Cape Town (Bertrand et al., 2004). The impetus to develop the necessary capabilities and skills partly derived from local demand due to the highly skewed income distribution in South Africa, but was also given a stimulus by a tax and foreign exchange loophole which led South Africans to invest in yachts for charter in the Caribbean and similar locations.

Lastly, an important group of products with strong global demand, and high growth rates in successfully industrializing countries is that of plastic products, as developments in materials enable the replacement of metal (Machaka and Roberts, 2003). In South Africa the development of the sector has lagged, but improved production and technological capabilities have enabled growth and innovation in some product areas such as automotive components, swimming pool cleaners, baths and basins, and fruit packaging (Roberts, 2001 and 2006; Mohamed and Roberts, 2005). International relationships enabling the sourcing of machinery, and improvements in technological capabilities, rather than simply exporting, are important for firm performance. The development of the sector has, however, been inhibited by monopoly pricing of material inputs, discussed further in section 4 below.

3.2. Analysis of industrial policy and its impact

It is apparent from the descriptive analysis of manufacturing performance that, aside from the auto sector, the combination of liberalization and incentives largely failed to achieve the improved export performance sought. While trade liberalization changed relative prices faced by firms, rationalized the confused structure of protection, and reduced the bias in favour of the local market, it was not sufficient to develop a broad-based and internationally competitive manufacturing sector. In practice, increased trade has seen the growth of sectors with an existing comparative advantage, due mainly to the resource base and the historical support of government.

The growth of resource-based sectors of manufacturing has been on the back of cheap (coal-based) energy and government support to exploit linkages within the 'minerals-energy complex' (Fine and Rustomjee, 1996). For example, the aluminium production which dominates non-ferrous metals is based entirely on low priced electricity to process imported material inputs. Cheap electricity has been a function not just of abundant coal resources, but also the extraordinary electricity pricing policies (see section 4.3). Massive over investment in electricity capacity in the 1970s and early 1980s by the state owned utility, Eskom, led government to set extremely low tariffs to attract major investment in a series of huge metal processing plants.

Direct state support for basic metals production was further provided in the form of Industrial Development Corporation (IDC) finance for aluminium and stainless steel plants into the 1990s, through state ownership of the main

Evolution and Impact of Industrial and Competition Policies

steel producer until 1989, and in the provision of infrastructure over recent decades (Fine and Rustomjee, 1996). Similarly, the basic chemicals sector is dominated by Sasol, which was initially a state corporation. Its capabilities are derived from huge state financing of its synthetic fuel-from-coal operations which were established for strategic reasons as a result of the sanctions threat (Rustomjee et al., 2007).

The paper and paper products sector is reliant on timber and has historically benefitted from the apartheid government's policies with regard to land and water resources for extensive afforestation. The large paper mills of the two dominant producers, Sappi and Mondi, are also capital and energy intensive. It is notable that South Africa exports around one-third of the pulp produced in the country for processing elsewhere, in addition to net exports of paper (Genesis, 2005).

Moreover, some of the very substantial support programmes provided by government appear to have reinforced rather than altered the industrial development path. An accelerated depreciation allowance under the 37E incentive was given to major resource-based projects in the 1990s such as Columbus Stainless Steel and Saldanha Steel. The *Strategic Industrial Projects* programme provided tax relief equivalent to R7.7bn from 2002 to 2005 for large capital-intensive projects many of which are in basic metals and basic chemicals (including four projects undertaken by Sasol) (Roberts, 2007). Similarly, much of the IDC finance in the second half of the 1990s continued to be oriented to large, capital-intensive, resource-based activities. The IDC only more recently increased the emphasis on employment creation.

The evidence on the other various tax breaks and incentives does not suggest that they have had a significant impact, with the possible exception of the *Small and Medium Enterprise Development Programme* (SMEDP) (Machaka and Roberts, 2006). There are examples of the supply-side programmes supporting diversification in the second half of the 1990s, such as the assistance of the *Support Programme for Industrial Innovation* (SPII) for mining machinery producers in product development (Hofmaenner et al., 2004). However, the overarching picture is of limited diversification in the 1990s in a period when prices of resource-based products such as steel were at long-term lows. Post-2000 this diversification has not been sustained and may even have been reversed.

One industrial policy measure which has had a substantial and direct impact on firm decision-making consistent with diversification from the resource-based trajectory is the MIDP. It was introduced with the objective of restructuring the automotive industry to achieve higher scale production in the face of falling protection.

The MIDP is essentially an import–export complementation programme.[6] By exporting built-up vehicles and components, firms earn Import Rebate

---

[6] See Barnes (2000), Barnes et al. (2004), Black (2001) and Black and Bhanisi (2007).

Credit Certificates (IRCCs) which allow them to offset import duties on automotive products. Over time the credits earned by a unit of exports have been phased down. Tariffs on completely built-up cars have also been reduced from over 100 per cent at the beginning of the 1990s to 29 per cent in 2008. The combination of falling protection and the ability to offset import duties has encouraged local manufacturers to reduce the number of models produced locally and to increase the scale of production.

The MIDP has been contentious as it has been based on the maintenance of relatively high import duties. Critics argue this has a cost to consumers: with full liberalization, including of imports of second-hand cars, the increased car ownership resulting from more affordable cars would have generated jobs in car servicing and repair (see Flatters, 2005). However, protection has been significantly reduced, reducing vehicle prices in real terms, and introducing increased choice into the domestic market. The automotive sector has recorded strong value-added growth and positive employment growth on the back of exports and investment, while the number of locally produced model platforms was rationalized from 42 in the mid 1990s to 21 in 2007 (NAAMSA, 2007). Exports of components have also grown strongly, dominated by catalytic converters, which accounted for more than half of all components exports in 2006, followed by seat leather, tyres, engines, and engine parts (NAAMSA, 2007). The MIDP thus underpins improved export performance across manufacturing, including machinery and equipment, leather products, and rubber products, in which auto components dominate export performance.

The 'moving target' in terms of which firms have to progressively increase exports in order to achieve the same level of duty free imports has induced the major vehicle producers to collectively take steps to improve the competitiveness of suppliers. These linkages have underpinned the growth of the supply chain including industries such as foundries (Phele et al., 2005) and plastics (Dobreva, Mahomed, et al., 2005) where the automotive industry has had a major impact on product development, productivity, and work organization.

By comparison, the emphasis on knowledge-intensive and new technologically-advanced industries in the government's strategies of 2002 and 2003 has yet to yield clear returns. The DTI has sought to develop *Customized Sector Programmes* (CSPs) on a sector by sector basis, but progress in translating these to concrete measures has been woefully slow: only in 2007 were the first two formally approved (for chemicals and clothing & textiles). The CSPs appear to fit a model of partnership between business and government to identify bottlenecks and obstacles to growth, recommended by Hausmann and Klinger (2006). However, they have not translated into coordinated plans that link the actions of different agencies such as the IDC and the Centre for Scientific and Industrial Research (CSIR) with DTI, to deal with problems facing individual sub-sectors. The chemicals industry also suffers from the dominance of the major firms, lobbying strongly through the industry association for

Evolution and Impact of Industrial and Competition Policies

continued protection and government support for capital-intensive upstream operations.

The most striking example of coordination failures within government is in the information and communication industries. While the DTI has prioritized these as the epitome of knowledge-intensive activities, it has been stymied by extremely expensive broadband pricing (Hodge et al., 2007). This is due to the regulatory framework supported by the Department of Communications and the dominance of the incumbent utility (see section 4.3).

While the *National Industrial Policy Framework* (DTI, 2007) has set clear objectives in terms of altering South Africa's trajectory of industrial development to one which is more diversified and labour absorbing, as well as more knowledge-intensive, it is too early to evaluate its impact. We have argued that altering the industrial development trajectory will need concerted action across public institutions. The wide range of priority sectors in the above framework means this will be difficult, while the resources and levers still have to be specified in more detail. Not least is the challenge of addressing the entrenched interests of large firms in the resource-based activities. We now examine how competition policy has fared in this regard.

4. Concentration, Competition, and Privatization

Despite important changes outlined below in section 4.1, the South African economy remains highly concentrated. The five largest conglomerate groupings, led by Anglo American, still controlled 44.6 per cent of the capitalization of the Johannesburg Stock Exchange in 2006 (Table 8.4). The orientation of big business is thus central to South Africa's industrial development trajectory, and an important consideration is whether large firms pursue strategies of rent extraction from a position of established dominance, or through constructive competitive rivalry (see Chandler et al., 1997). Assessing competitive rivalry requires careful analysis of firm behaviour in specific markets, including considering whether dominant firms are insulated from effective competitive discipline, without which initial advantages and even small asymmetries can create long-term economic distortions (Geroski and Jacquemin, 1984).

We argue that the dominant firms have often attained pre-eminence in part through the legacy of state support and protection for heavy industry. This poses particular challenges both for competition policy and industrial policy (Fingleton, 2006). To explore the implications of anti-competitive conduct and how it has been addressed by competition policy, we examine three important sectoral case studies: for steel, chemicals and food in section 4.2.

There are similar challenges with regard to constraining the monopolistic conduct of utilities. We assess the record in section 4.3 on the restructuring and privatization of state owned enterprises in the telecommunications and

Table 8.4. Summary of control of JSE market capitalization (% of total)

	1990	1994	1998	2002	2006
Anglo American Corp	44.2	43.3	17.4	20.2	21.0
Sanlam	13.2	10.5	11.1	6.3	2.3
Liberty Life/Std Bank	2.6	7.2	9.5	6.0	3.5
Rembrandt/Remgro	13.6	13.0	9.0	10.0	7.8
SA Mutual/Old Mutual	10.2	9.7	8.8	12.0	5.5
Anglovaal	2.5	3.6	0.8	—	—
RMB/First Rand	—	0.5	4.8	4.7	3.9
Sasol	—	1.7	2.2	3.8	4.6
SABMiller	—	—	—	4.0	5.7
Top 5 groups collectively	83.8	83.7	55.8	54.5	44.6

Source: McGregors (2007), *Who Owns Whom*.
Notes:
¹ Control is assessed by taking into account the various cross-holdings of shares that exist and may be associated with a relatively small direct shareholding in any given company.
² In 1998, the Anglovaal shareholding was split equally between the Hersov and Menell families.

electricity sectors. Cross-cutting implications for competition policy and regulation are drawn at the end of the section.

4.1. The high concentration of industry

The apparent de-concentration of ownership and control in the South African economy, as measured by control of listed companies, does not imply reduced concentration *within* industries. The unbundled entities of the major conglomerates often still retain their dominant position, and moreover, these changes do not extend across all conglomerates. Anglo American has divested many subsidiaries to focus on its core mining business, but in contrast, Remgro has increased its diversified activities across industry while remaining controlled by the Rupert family.

Alongside unbundling has been a series of mergers to consolidate the operations of conglomerates within sectors. For example, Anglo American has bought various interests in packaging to vertically integrate with its paper manufacturing arm. In minerals it has sought to consolidate its gold and platinum interests and extend into iron ore through the acquisition of Kumba. Similar patterns can be observed in Remgro's acquisitions in food, beverages and healthcare, and on a smaller scale across South African industry.[7]

There has also been a process of internationalization of South African business. This includes the creation of the Billiton group by Gencor (now merged to become BHP-Billiton), the restructuring of Anglo American/De Beers and

---

[7] See Chabane et al. (2006) for a detailed account of the changes in conglomerates' holdings since 1994.

Evolution and Impact of Industrial and Competition Policies

Minorco holdings and the move to London by Anglo American, and the overseas listings of Liberty Life, Old Mutual, South African Breweries (now SAB-Miller) and Sappi. Locally listed companies such as Sasol have secondary overseas listings with very significant equity held by US shareholders, in particular. There have also been major acquisitions of South African firms by foreign multinationals, including the steel company Iscor by Mittal Steel, and Barclays' acquisition of Absa bank.

The dominance of large corporations in many areas of industrial activity perpetuates past patterns, notwithstanding changes in terms of increased internationalization and increasing pressure from government for significant black shareholdings. However, a deeper understanding of the implications of anti-competitive behaviour and market power is gained by sectoral level analysis.

4.2. Competition case studies

The three case-studies assessed are of significant industrial sectors. They support the role for competitive discipline if diversified manufacturing is not to be hindered by supra-competitive pricing of intermediate inputs. Two cases cover important intermediate product groupings in manufacturing, namely steel and basic chemicals, where historically state support and protection have entrenched the dominance of large firms. The main users of these products include key sectors for developing a more sophisticated and diversified industrial base. The third case examines an important industry grouping, food and agricultural products, extensively regulated under apartheid but where the system of controls was swept aside by the new government.

4.2.1. EXCESSIVE PRICING OF STEEL[8]

Mittal Steel South Africa, formerly Iscor, has openly engaged in unilateral price setting of its flat steel products to South African customers, at imputed import parity price levels. This is despite a large net trade surplus and very low production costs. In 2007, in its first ruling on excessive pricing, the Competition Tribunal found Mittal's pricing to be in contravention of the South African Competition Act and imposed a fine of R691.8mn or 5.5 per cent of turnover.[9]

Perhaps the most obvious implication of market power (whether exerted unilaterally or collusively) is in pricing at monopoly levels. Where this is in pricing of intermediate inputs for other industries, not only does it imply reduced consumption of the product in question, but also production by downstream industries. In concentrated upstream sectors such as basic iron

---

[8] See Roberts (2008).   [9] The ruling is being appealed in October 2008.

and steel, non-ferrous metals, and basic chemicals, it is common for firms in South Africa to charge import-parity prices to local buyers for products in which there is, in fact, a large trade surplus. In such cases competition would be expected to yield a price close to the export price received, as an exporting firm would be willing to sell the product at any price above that currently being received for the exported product. Instead, pricing at import parity reflects the firms' market power to act as price setters rather than price takers.

While Iscor was built by the government, following privatization in 1989 it was subject to a liberalized trading environment, with the reduction in import duties from 30 per cent to 5 per cent in 1996. However, the import parity price, calculated by taking the main sources from Eastern Europe and Asia and adding transport costs and port charges implied a price differential of 20 to 30 per cent over the free-on-board export price (see Competition Tribunal, 2007a and 2007b). The price differential over that received by the South African producer for their exported product (the international price less the transport and other costs to the international destination) is typically between 40 and 50 per cent (Roberts, 2008).

Such pricing is effectively a costly transfer from local buyers (generally downstream, more labour-intensive industries) to the upstream industries, especially where material inputs are a significant part of costs. Basic iron and steel comprises 42 per cent of direct and indirect[10] inputs to fabricated metal products (Roberts and Zalk, 2004). In general machinery, the contribution is 25 per cent. In effect, import parity pricing means there is no advantage to downstream industries from this internationally competitive, low production-cost, resource-based industry. This entrenches the capital-intensity of manufactured exports—and basic iron and steel was by far the largest single sector in manufactured exports, accounting for 19 per cent in 2007.

4.2.2. CHEMICALS[11]

The broad chemicals industry grouping includes the production of intermediate goods such as fertilizer, pesticides, explosives, and polymer chemicals, as well as liquid fuels. The development of the chemicals industry in South Africa had two main drivers. The first was market-oriented, with demand from mining and agriculture underpinning the development of ammonia-based fertilizer and explosives, led by Anglo American's subsidiary AECI. The second was the strategic objective of the apartheid state to reduce dependence on imported oil, supporting the development of Sasol as a producer of liquid fuels from coal. Through successive phases of large investments under

---

[10] The indirect contribution includes the steel component in intermediate products.
[11] This section draws on Dobreva, Makrelov, et al. (2005).

state ownership and protection, Sasol has become a major organic chemicals complex.

Following privatization in 1991 and with the trade liberalization in the 1990s, Sasol has continued to invest and expand through acquisitions, representing a case of an infant industry which has 'grown up'. Sasol took sole control of its Polifin joint venture with AECI in 2000 to dominate local polymer manufacturing, and is the sole local producer of ammonia following the closure of AECI's facility at around the same time. Both these moves followed the rejection of a proposed merger between Sasol and AECI by the then Competition Board in 1998—effectively achieving the same level of concentration on a product by product basis as would have been realized by the merger (Competition Board, 1998).

In products such as polypropylene, which accounts for some 51 per cent of direct inputs to plastic product, import parity pricing has been practiced despite a large trade surplus. Given substantial transport costs and a 10 per cent import duty, local plastic product manufacturers pay substantially above the opportunity cost for their key material input

The chemicals industry illustrates the impact of competition law which has blocked some mergers, but had a more limited effect in curbing anti-competitive behaviour. The Competition Tribunal blocked the proposed merger of the liquid fuels interests of Sasol and Engen in 2006 and the acquisition by Sasol of the largest candle manufacturer in 2001. The latter decision was overturned by the Competition Appeal Court, approving a merger that vertically integrated Sasol's local monopoly position in wax. Many mergers in the sector have also been analysed and approved by the competition authorities on the grounds of corporate restructuring, consolidation, and increasing vertical integration. Sasol has been the subject of several complaints, which have not been resolved or against which it has successful appealed. The Competition Tribunal ruled in 2005 that Sasol had abused its dominance in discriminating in the pricing of creosote, a decision which was overturned on appeal. Complaints of abuse of dominance in fertilizer by Sasol and collusion with other producers are scheduled to be heard early in 2009.

4.2.3. FOOD AND AGRICULTURAL PRODUCTS

Competition issues in the food sector demonstrate the scope for tight oligopolies to continue to control markets in their own narrow interest after the state has deregulated. Under apartheid, the prices of most agricultural products were regulated through state-sanctioned control boards under the 1937 Marketing Act, re-promulgated in 1968, to the advantage of white farmers, a key constituency of the government (Bayley, 2000). This was coupled with support for farmers (including protection, subsidized finance, and export subsidies), and a large role for cooperatives in providing inputs and services such as storage, packaging, and processing.

Under the new government the far-reaching liberalization started in the 1980s continued (the one exception being sugar), with the closure of the control boards under the 1996 Marketing of Agricultural Products Act. Large farmer cooperatives, such as OTK in the old Eastern Transvaal, converted themselves into private companies. Prices were set in developing agricultural markets, including the South African Futures Exchange (SAFEX) quoting prices for maize from 1996. As a result, prices have fluctuated considerably, and are generally linked to international prices expressed in import or export parity terms.

The liberalized markets have, however, been dominated by a small number of vertically integrated firms, including former cooperatives and the food interests of major conglomerate groupings. Three regionally focused former cooperatives, OTK/Afgri, Senwes, and Noordwes, dominate grain storage with a 70 per cent share of domestic storage facilities or silos (FPMC, 2003). Of these, OTK/Afgri and Senwes are two of the four major traders of grain on SAFEX and these two companies were estimated to account for more than 30 per cent of the grain traded in 2003/4. Such has been the concentration of traders, that in 2002 a single large trading house, W. J. Morgan, was able to affect the price of maize substantially through speculative activities which may have contravened SAFEX trading rules (FPMC, 2003).

One of the largest former cooperatives, OTK, listed on the JSE and subsequently renamed Afgri, has led the way in vertically and horizontally integrating. In essence it is on both sides of the farming activity, providing finance, seeds and agro-chemicals, and then on the demand side; storage, logistics, purchasing, and milling of crops, together with the manufacturing of animal feed through to interests in broiler chickens that are the major markets for the feed.

While the possibilities for anti-competitive behaviour have frequently been raised (see FPMC, 2003; Competition Tribunal, 2004) no evidence was found until recently. The Food Price Monitoring Committee established by the government to probe food price hikes in 2002, while noting concerns, effectively confirmed an earlier analysis for National Treasury (Vink and Kirsten, 2002) in finding 'no profiteering on these basic foodstuffs [maize] has occurred' (FPMC, 2003: summary report). This was despite evidence of increased milling margins following removal of controls (Traub and Jayne, 2004). However, the three major firms dominating milling of wheat and maize and the production of bread have been colluding to set prices through regular meetings and contact from at least 1994 up to 2007, when the cartel was uncovered by the Competition Commission.[12] Other competition cases are pending relating

---

[12] See proceedings of Competition Tribunal hearing on 28 November, 2007.

Evolution and Impact of Industrial and Competition Policies

to abuse of dominance in grain silos and coordinated conduct and abuse of dominance in milk processing and dairy products.

In effect, notwithstanding liberalization, the major firms have entrenched dominance through vertical integration and increased concentration within specific activities. This raises barriers to entry and has allowed behaviour akin to private regulation, in products such as maize meal and bread, replacing the previous price-setting of the control boards. In addition to harming consumers by supra-competitive pricing, the distorted prices for intermediates impact on food manufacturing, while the barriers to entry negatively influence the dynamism of the whole sector.

4.3. PRIVATIZATION AND REGULATION OF UTILITIES

The incentives and constraints on the behaviour of dominant firms are relevant to utilities in the pricing and provision of services. In 1994, the main providers of telecommunications, electricity, rail, and air transport services were state owned, along with the airports and seaports. The low levels of investment in economic infrastructure, including by such entities, are also crucial to understanding South Africa's growth performance (Chapters 2 and 7).

The ANC government sought to restructure state assets, including privatization where deemed appropriate. At first sight, changes have been small, and largely limited to the privatization of Telkom, the state-owned fixed-line telecommunications provider. The electricity utility Eskom remains state owned, as does the transport company Transnet which is responsible for rail and port services. The privatized South Africa Airways was taken over again by the state when its new owner, Swissair, went into liquidation. However, the main question is not ownership as such, but the changes to the conditions that underpin conduct and performance. These conditions include the objectives and incentive arrangements for senior management set by the shareholder, the monitoring and governance mechanisms, as well as the regulatory framework. This section assesses the record in two cases, those of telecommunications and electricity. The first of these has been the most significant privatization since 1994, while in the second, the state has retained ownership. In each there have been major flaws, underlining the pitfalls of focusing on ownership per se.

4.3.1. TELECOMMUNICATIONS

The case of telecommunications starkly illustrates the problems of poorly designed and implemented privatization. Telkom was effectively privatized through the sale of a 30 per cent stake to a USA/Malaysia consortium under a shareholder contract which bestowed control to the private shareholder. Under the arrangement, Telkom was given a five-year monopoly (1997–2002) in fixed lines in exchange for investing in the roll-out of lines to disadvantaged areas.¹³ The rationale was that the controlling private sector 'Strategic Equity Partner' would bring its joint expertise to bear in turning Telkom's internal efficiency around and at the same time would make investments that were not commercially attractive but important to support broader economic participation and growth.

The scope for abuse of Telkom's pricing power was limited by price cap regulation under the 1996 Telecommunications Act. The price-cap was set for five years, with annual increases set at consumer price inflation less 1.5 percentage points, to ensure strong incentives for efficiency improvements and cost reductions. In addition, the average price-cap allowed for major 'rebalancing' of local, long-distance, and international call charges. This resulted in charges for local calls increasing significantly over the period while international and long-distance charges were reduced. First, the South African Telecommunications Regulatory Agency (SATRA), and later, the Independent Communications Authority of South Africa (ICASA), had regulatory responsibility for telecommunications. While intended to be independent, ICASA has been overruled by the Department of Communications on a number of key issues including the licensing of new operators and the regulation of prices (Melody, 2002).

The outcomes have been mixed, at best. There has been major investment in digitization of the network, and Telkom met the target for roll-out of lines.¹⁴ However, the increase in local call charges prompted the termination of accounts such that the number of lines to households actually fell. The prices of data lines also increased at far above the average price cap, while in most of the world, such prices were reduced (Makhaya and Roberts, 2003). The resultant high prices have been identified as an obstacle to attracting business for outsourcing activities, including call centres, and have led to far lower growth rates of broadband internet usage than expected (Hodge et al., 2007).

The duration of Telkom's monopoly was also extended beyond the *de jure* time period due to problems in licensing a second national operator (SNO). Indeed, while Telkom's de facto monopoly extended until 2008, the SNO is still establishing its infrastructure and has yet to provide effective competitive discipline to Telkom—it has publicly stated that it does not plan to compete head to head with Telkom on price but to focus on particular niches.¹⁵

---

¹³ In the five-year period Telkom was required to provide 2.69 million new working exchange lines to add to the network which amounted to just over 4 million lines in 1996. A specified number of these new lines (1.676 million) were set aside for areas designated as 'under-serviced'. Service conditions were set on a range of criteria such as the time to install new lines, fault rates and response to complaints. Financial penalties were stipulated for failure to meet the targets. Targets were also set in terms of the upgrading of the network, including the digitization of all exchanges (see Makhaya and Roberts, 2003).

¹⁴ The target in one year was missed for which Telkom incurred a penalty (Makhaya and Roberts, 2003).

¹⁵ See Competition Tribunal decision in the Telkom / BCX merger, case number 51LMJun06, paragraph 63.

Evolution and Impact of Industrial and Competition Policies

Moreover, while there has been growth of value added network services, including internet service provision, there are several pending competition cases relating to Telkom abusing its position. These are being delayed by Telkom contesting the jurisdiction of the competition authorities in such matters through the courts.[16] The Competition Act has provisions guarding against the anti-competitive behaviour engaged in by Telkom, but scope for such legal manoeuvring is a constraint on the effectiveness of competition policy.

Another major change since 1994 has been the growth of the mobile phone market: two companies were licensed in the early 1990s, MTN and Vodacom, and a third operator, Cell C was licensed more recently. The growth in mobile services exceeded expectations and, as a result, the regulation of maximum prices which were based on cost recovery on much lower take-up has allowed high mobile phone charges. Competitive rivalry was expected to discipline pricing of these services; however, prices for mobile telephony remain very high by international standards (Hodge et al., 2007). Several cases are pending relating to alleged anti-competitive conduct. However, competition policy is a blunt tool compared to what could be achieved through regulation, given the time required to bring competition cases and potential delays through firms taking legal points.

4.3.2. ELECTRICITY

The approach to electricity restructuring contrasts sharply with telecommunications: yet outcomes too have been poor. Eskom has remained state-owned and has aggressively pursued the roll-out of electricity connections to low income households. Eskom set its own national connection targets in 1992, and then pursued the more ambitious targets set by the RDP.[17] The capital costs for the new connections were subsidized first by Eskom and then directly by the fiscus from the end of the 1990s. In 2002, the government further decided to fund free basic electricity of 50 kWh per month, targeted at low income households. In contrast to the negative impact of high telecommunications prices in deterring investment in user industries, electricity prices are amongst the lowest in the world and have attracted substantial investments in energy-intensive activities.

The electricity restructuring programme has evolved through government reacting to developments—some poorly anticipated. First, the role of government as the owner of Eskom has moved to a more arm's length basis,

---

[16] In 2006 the Competition Commission referred a case brought by an association of Value Added Network Service Providers (SAVA) to the Tribunal. The hearing on jurisdiction was scheduled to be heard in the High Court in April 2008.

[17] The RDP targets of 300,000 new connections per annum for the second half of the 1990s were met and exceeded (Steyn, 2003).

with performance contracts in place for the senior managers and, under corporatization in 2001, Eskom started to pay taxes and dividends to the state (Steyn, 2003). Second, a separate regulatory body (the National Electricity Regulator, NER, later National Energy Regulator of South Africa, NERSA) was established to approve price increases and other performance targets such as continuity of supply. Third, the government planned to separate generation from transmission and distribution. At the level of generation, the intention was to separate and then privatize some of the capacity, and for independent power producers to meet the further need for new capacity; at the distribution level the government intended creating six Regional Electricity Distributors (REDs) from the existing distribution mix of Eskom and municipalities.[18]

The unfortunate outcome has been worsening power outages in 2007 and 2008 due to the increasingly acute shortage of supply capacity. Industrial activity (including mining) has been severely disrupted. With hindsight, this can be attributed to a combination of factors. Under-investment in generation capacity stemmed from the partial privatization of generation, so that government in effect restricted Eskom's plans to build new capacity. When privatization plans were halted, Eskom had to scramble to scale-up its investment in generation. Moreover, there have been delays in the programme to procure privately generated power, even in relation to scaled-down expectations.[19]

A further factor is that electricity prices under the rate of return calculations used by the regulator are set accounting for Eskom's assets at historic cost. Eskom massively over-invested in generation capacity in the 1970s meaning that historic cost significantly under-represents the capital costs for expanding generation, and prices are far below long run marginal cost (Eberhard and Mtepa, 2003). The miscalculation of the necessary incentives for private sector participation was compounded by the lumpiness of such major investments and the planning periods required, given the global investments in generation occurring over the same period.[20]

Maintenance backlogs have also built up at all levels, from generation to transmission and distribution. These include backlogs in municipalities' distribution networks. The backlogs have been exacerbated by the expectation that the Regional Electricity Distributors (REDs) would be taking over the networks. Finally, the constraints on supply have been compounded by the

---

[18] The White Paper on Energy Policy, 1998, set out the steps to be taken, including the expected private participation.

[19] In October 2004, Alec Erwin, the Minister of Public Enterprises, announced that Eskom was authorized to take responsibility for at least 70 per cent of new generation capacity requirements. This still left around 30 per cent of new generation to be procured from the private sources.

[20] Investments in generation, especially in China, have been widely cited as leading to delays in the delivery of the necessary capital equipment, as well as escalating costs.

Evolution and Impact of Industrial and Competition Policies

effects of the incentives governing the performance of Eskom management. An increased focus on short-term financial returns following corporatization meant a strong incentive for management to seek aggressively to cut costs, including through reducing coal stock piles and not undertaking repair and rehabilitation work until absolutely necessary. The greater vulnerability to breakdowns and short-term constraints on coal supply has been blamed for some power outages.

Sub-economic electricity prices have contributed to distortions on the demand-side by favouring large-scale energy-intensive activities. In recent years, Eskom prices have been the lowest of comparator countries by a substantial margin.[21] However, this is only partly due to South Africa's endowment of coal, the source of some 90 per cent of South Africa's electricity. With constraints on exports and significant transport costs, coal has been available to Eskom for much of the last decade at less than one-third of the price in north-west Europe. But, the Eskom electricity prices are much cheaper than even in other coal exporting countries, such as Canada and Australia due to the way in which assets are accounted for in setting prices (Eberhard and Mtepa, 2003).

Finally, as noted in the analysis of manufacturing performance, the prices agreed to supply electricity to large and energy intensive industries such as aluminium smelters are significantly lower than the benchmark prices for industry. In the past this was justified by a large excess generation capacity resulting from the earlier over-investment. However, even with capacity running out, agreements were being reached in 2007 with Alcan for an aluminium smelter, reportedly at an electricity price around US$0.02/kWh or R0.14, compared with average prices R0.18 for other industrial users and R0.45 for households.[22] The severe constraints on South Africa's generation capacity have meant the plans were postponed in mid 2008.

In effect, the electricity pricing structure exacerbates the impact that South Africa's natural resource endowment has on the pattern of trade discussed above. While there have not been any analyses of the country's trade performance which properly take this into account, the reported statistics on the planned Alcan smelter offer a graphic illustration. The R21bn greenfield investment will employ just 800 people, with the product expected to be almost entirely exported in primary form.

---

[21] Based on data collected by NUS Consulting Group, South African prices in 2007 were some 40 per cent lower than those in the next lowest priced country, Canada (*Engineering News* (21 June 2007)). In 2006, South Africa's prices were 23 per cent lower than next lowest (Australia) and more than 60 per cent cheaper than the median of the 14 countries assessed.

[22] See Mathabo Le Roux, *The Weekender* (9–10 February 2008), 'Why the Alcan Deal Does Not Compute'. BHP Billiton's smelters are reported to pay around R0.12/kWh (Lynley Donnelly, *Mail & Guardian* (8–14 February 2008) 'Anatomy of a Catastrophe').

5. Conclusions

Despite the focus of industrial policy on more diversified international competitiveness, the pattern of industrial performance under democracy shows strong continuity: resource-based heavy manufacturing industries have remained the strongest performers during 1994–2007. This suggests the predominance of path dependency, confounding the expectations that reducing apartheid era distortions would encourage a more vibrant and diversified industrial sector. Ironically, this is in part due to ongoing support under democracy for resource-based ventures through tax breaks and IDC finance.

However, part of the explanation also rests with intrinsic obstacles to shifting patterns of specialization. These include the acquisition of relevant skills, expertise, technology and knowledge as well as linkages with ancillary services, inputs and output markets. As observed by Hausmann and Klinger (2007), diversification tends to be into similar types of products or products which require similar sets of production capabilties.

Trade liberalization has tended to reinforce existing patterns of specialization. Moreover, the low levels of competitive rivalry, supra-competitive pricing practices as exemplified by Mittal Steel South Africa, and indications of collusive behaviour in sectors such as food products, all further inhibit the dynamism of industrial development. Without action to ensure more effective competitive discipline on resource-based firms, in particular, they will continue to extract monopoly rents and, given their dominance, shape industrial development. Substantial transport costs, given South Africa's relative isolation from other industrial economies, allows significant scope for anti-competitive mark-ups, even where tariffs on intermediate inputs are reduced to zero, as is the case with steel.

The record of regulation of utilities is one of insufficient attention to the conditions and incentives governing price-setting and other decision-making by large and influential corporations, whether privatized or state owned. This may reflect an over-simplified approach which focuses on changes in ownership and on the need to establish regulatory bodies which are independent in status but not necessarily in effect. Telecommunications and electricity are crucial intermediate inputs for more diversified industrial development. Yet, in telecommunications, high prices and a lack of competitive rivalry extended far beyond the period originally envisaged to allow for the roll-out of the network. In electricity, flaws in the restructuring programme resulted in under-investment in generation and maintenance and distorted prices, especially favouring capital and energy intensive industrial activities. Both telecommunications and electricity illustrate the importance of appropriate pricing policies to avoid outcomes inimical to the labour-absorbing economic growth which is the objective of government policy. In telecommunications, the behaviour of the dominant firm has hindered the growth of employment generation in services, while sub-economic electricity prices, especially to large-scale capital-intensive activities have contributed to a skewed pattern of manufacturing competitiveness.

Competition policy is often viewed as the appropriate remedy to redress abuses by dominant enterprises. The cases analysed above indicate the far-reaching exertion of market power by large firms, unilaterally and in oligopolies through coordinated behaviour. While the new competition authorities have been relatively effective in evaluating mergers, the record is mixed on anti-competitive conduct. The competition authorities' focus is on prosecuting contraventions. Cases are time-consuming and, while competition law provides strong powers for information gathering, analysis and sanction, it is less effective in directly influencing firm behaviour or encouraging new entry. The role of the competition authorities could be strengthened toward achieving greater competitive dynamism and addressing entry barriers, but this will also require industrial policies to play a stronger complementary role.

Such a role includes recognizing the potential levers at the government's disposal for linking incentives to competitive behaviour and supporting new entry. More concerted industrial policies could support growth of diversified and more sophisticated activities, using direct levers as in the MIDP. However, this demands substantially improved analytical capacity on the part of government and better intra-governmental coordination across development finance institutions (e.g. the IDC) and research institutions (e.g. the CSIR), where reasonable institutional capacity already exists. Important too is the requirement for flexible policy, to set and enforce conditionalities in incentive programmes that are temporary in nature and that can be adapted where objectives are not being met.

In recent years two major new stimuli for industrial development have emerged. The first is the planned spending on infrastructure announced by government (see Chapters 2, 4, and 7). For many industries this will provide a demand stimulus after low levels of spending on physical infrastructure for over two decades. The second is recent higher rates of growth and investment in the southern African region, including in minerals extraction and processing where South Africa has established capabilities. Both have been recognized in the government's 2006 Accelerated and Shared Growth Initiative for South Africa (ASGISA). The question is whether well designed policy and effective implementation will allow for the maximum exploitation of these opportunities.

References

Aghion, P., M. Braun, J. Fedderke (2006) 'Competition and Productivity Growth in South Africa', *CID Working Paper*, no. 132, Harvard University

Barnes, J. (2000) 'Changing Lanes: The Political Economy of the South African Automotive Value Chain', *Development Southern Africa*, 17(3): 401–15.

Barnes, J. R. Kaplinsky and M. Morris (2004) 'Industrial Policy in Developing Economies: Developing Dynamic Comparative Advantage in the South African Automobile Sector', *Competition and Change*, 8(2): 153–72.

Bayley, B. (2000) A *Revolution in the Market—The Deregulation of South African Agriculture*. Oxford: Oxford Policy Management.

Bertrand, D., T. Phele, S. Roberts, I. Steuart, M. Taka (2004) 'Western Cape Report on: Metals & Engineering Industries, Including Ship-Building', report for the Western Cape Provincial government, December 2004.

Black, A. (1993) 'The Role of the State in Promoting Industrialisation: Selective Intervention, Trade Orientation and Concessionary Industrial Finance', in M. Lipton and C. Simkins (eds.) *State and Market in Post Apartheid South Africa*. Johannesburg: Witwatersrand University Press.

—— (2001) 'Globalization and Restructuring in the South African Automotive Industry' *Journal of International Development*. 13(6): 779–96.

Black, A. and S. Bhanisi (2007) 'The SA Automotive Industry in a Globalising World— What Has Happened to Imports?', *Trade & Industry Monitor*, 38: 131–52.

Black, A. and S. B. Kahn (2002) 'Growing without Gold? South Africa's Non-Traditional Exports since 1980', in G. Helleiner (ed.) *Non-Traditional Export Promotion in Africa: Experience and Issues*. Basingstoke: Palgrave.

Cassim, R., D. Onyango, D. Van Seventer (2002) 'The State of Trade Policy in South Africa', *Trade and Industrial Policy Strategies Research Paper*.

Chabane, N, A. Goldstein and S. Roberts (2006) 'The Changing Face and Strategies of Big Business in South Africa: Ten Years of Political Democracy', *Industrial and Corporate Change*, 15(3): 549–578.

Chandler, A. Jr., F. Amatori, T. Hikino (eds.) (1997) *Big Business and the Wealth of Nations*. Cambridge: Cambridge University Press.

Competition Board of South Africa (1998) 'Investigation Into the Transaction between SASOL Ltd and AECI Ltd.' *Report*, no. 68, Pretoria: Government Printer.

Competition Tribunal (2004) 'Reasons in the Large Merger between Afgri Operations Ltd and Natal Agricultural Co-operative Ltd', 6 July 2004, <www.comptrib.co.za>

—— (2007a) case number 13/CR/Feb04 *Reasons*.

—— (2007b) case number 13/CR/Feb04 *Remedies*.

Department of Science and Technology (2002) *South Africa's National Research and Development Strategy*.

Department of Trade and Industry (DTI) (1997) *Incentive Schemes*. Pretoria, Department of Trade and Industry.

—— (2002) *Accelerating Growth and Development: The Contribution of the Integrated Manufacturing Strategy*, Pretoria.

—— (2007) *A National Industrial Policy Framework*, Pretoria

Dobreva, R., G. Mahomed, T. Pogue, S. Roberts (2005) 'Developing a Dynamic Plastics Industry Cluster in Ekurhuleni: Report on Firm Interviews and Survey', report commissioned by Ekurhuleni Metro, March 2005.

Dobreva, R., K. Makrelov, C. May, G. Mohamed (2005) 'A Case Study of the Impact of Competition Law and Policy on South Africa's Investment Climate and Competitiveness: the Industrial Chemicals Sector', November 2005, commissioned by the World Bank.

Eberhard, A. and M. Mtepa, (2003). 'Rationale for Restructuring and Regulation of a 'Low-Priced' Public Utility: a Case Study of Eskom in South Africa', *International Journal of Regulation and Governance*, 3(2): 77–102.

Edwards, L. and R. Lawrence (2006) 'South African Trade Policy Matters: Trade Performance and Trade Policy', *CID Working Paper*, no. 135, Harvard University.

Fallon, P. and L. Pereira da Silva (1994) 'South Africa: Economic Performance and Policies' *Informal Discussion Papers on Aspects of the South African Economy*, no. 7, Southern Africa Department. World Bank, Washington.

Fine, B. and Z. Rustomjee (1996). *The Political Economy of South Africa—from Minerals—Energy Complex to Industrialisation*. London: Hurst.

Fingleton, J. (2006), 'Demonopolizing Ireland', in C.-D. Ehlermann and I. Atanasiu (eds.) *European Competition Law Annual, 2003: What is an Abuse of a Dominant Position?*, Oxford: Hart Publishing.

Flatters, F. (2005) 'The Economics of the MIDP and the South African Motor Industry', paper prepared for presentation at TIPS/NEDLAC workshop, Johannesburg, 2 November 2005.

Food Price Monitoring Committee (2003) 'Final Report', Report to the Minister of Agriculture and Land Affairs of Committee established under Section 7 of the Marketing of Agricultural Products Act, <www.nda.gov.za>

Genesis Analytics (2005) 'The Contribution, Costs and Development Opportunities of the Forestry, Timber, Pulp and Paper Industries in South Africa', mimeo.

Geroski, P. and A. Jacquemin (1984) 'Dominant Firms and Their Alleged Decline', *International Journal of Industrial Organisation*, 1.

Greenaway, D. and C. Milner (1993) *Trade and Industrial Policy in Developing Countrie*. London: MacMillan.

Hanival, S. and A. Hirsch (1998) 'Industrial Policy and Programmes in South Africa', *TIPS Forum Paper*, April.

Hausmann, R., J. Hwang and D. Rodrik (2006) 'What You Export Matters', *NBER Working Paper*, 11905, Cambridge Mass.: National Bureau of Economic Research.

Hausmann, R. and B. Klinger (2006) 'South Africa's Export Predicament', *CID Working Paper*, no. 129, Harvard University.

——(2007) 'The Structure of the Product Space and the Evolution of Comparative Advantage', *CID Working Paper*, no. 146, Harvard University.

Hirsch, A. (2005) *Season of Hope—Economic Reform under Mandela and Mbeki*. Durban: UKZN Press.

Hodge, J., S. Truen, B. Cloete, G. Biacuna (2007) 'South African Telecommunications Prices— an Updated International Price Comparison, With Regulatory Recommendations', *Business Leadership South Africa Occasional Paper*, no. 3.

Hofmaenner, A., S. Roberts, G. Steyn (2004) 'Innovation in Resource Based Technology Clusters', Phase One—Project Overview and Synthesis of Findings, HSRC

Imbs, J. and R. Wacziarg (2003) 'Stages of Diversification', *American Economic Review*, 93(1): 63–86

Joffe, A., D. Kaplan, R. Kaplinsky, and D. Lewis (1995) *Improving Manufacturing Performance in South Africa: The Report of the Industrial Strategy Project*. Cape Town: UCT Press

Kaplinsky, R. and C. Manning (1999) 'Concentration, Competition Policy and the Role of Small and Medium Sized Enterprises in South Africa's Industrial Development', *Journal of Development Studies*, 35(1): 139–61.

Kaplinksy R., M. Morris, J. Readman (2002) 'The Globalisation of Product Markets and Immiserizing Growth: Lessons from the South African Furniture Industry', *World Development*, 30(7): 1159–77.

Levy, B. (1992) 'How can South African Manufacturing Efficiently Create Employment? An Analysis of the Impact of Trade and Industrial Policy', Washington DC: World Bank Southern African Department.

Machaka, J. and S. Roberts (2003) 'The DTI's New "Integrated Manufacturing Strategy"? Comparative Industrial Performance, Linkages and Technology', *South African Journal of Economics*, 70(4): 679–704.

—— (2006) 'Addressing the Apartheid Industrial Legacy: Local Economic Development and Industrial Policy in South Africa—the Case of Ekurhuleni', in S. Roberts (ed.) *Sustainable Manufacturing? The Case of South Africa*, Cape Town: Juta Press

Makhaya, G. and S. Roberts (2003) 'Telecommunications in Developing Countries: Reflections from the South African Experience', *Telecommunications Policy*, 27(1–2): 41–59

McGregors (2007), *Who Owns Whom*. Johannesburg: Kluwer.

Melody, W. (2002) 'Assessing Telkom's 2003 Price Increase Proposal: Price Cap Regulation as a Test of Progress in Sa Telecom Reform and E Economic Development', LINK Centre *Policy Research Paper*, no. 2. Johannesburg.

Mohamed, G. and S. Roberts (2005) 'An Analysis of the Technology and Production Capabilities of the South African Plastic Products Sector, and Possible Roles for Government' Conference on Development of Business in Africa: The Role of Networks, Relationships, Industrial Clusters and Innovation Systems, 10–11 March 2005, Johannesburg, Universities of Chalmers and the Witwatersrand

NAAMSA (2007) *Annual Report 2007*, <www.naamsa.co.za>

NACI/DST (2003) *Advanced Manufacturing Technology Strategy*, Pretoria.

Phele, T, S. Roberts and I. Steuart (2005) 'Industrial Strategy and Local Economic Development: the Case of the Foundry Industry in Ekurhuleni Metro', *South African Journal of Economic and Management Sciences*, 8(4).

Republic of South Africa (1996) *Growth, Employment and Redistribution: A Macroeconomic Strategy*. Johannesburg: Government Printer

Roberts, S. (2001) 'Globalisation, Industrial Development and the Plastics Industry in South Africa', *Journal of International Development*, 13: 797–810.

—— (2004a) 'The Role for Competition Policy in Economic Development: the South African Experience' *Development Southern Africa*, 21(1): 227–43.

—— (2004b) 'Investment in South Africa—A Comment on Recent Contributions' *Development Southern Africa*, 21(4): 743–56.

—— (2006) 'Understanding technology and economic development in South African industry: The case of the plastics sector', in W.Blankley, M. Scerri, N. Molotja, I. Saloojee (eds.) *Measuring Innovation in OECD and Non-OECD Countries*, Cape Town: HSRC Press.

—— (2007) 'Patterns of Industrial Performance in South Africa in the First Decade of Democracy—the Continued Influence of Minerals-Based Activities', *Transformation*, 65, 4–34.

—— (2008) 'Assessing Excessive Pricing—The Case of Flat Steel in South Africa', *Journal of Competition Law and Economics* (forthcoming)

Roberts, S. and J. Thoburn (2003) 'Adjusting to Trade Liberalisation: The Case of Firms in the South African Textile Sector', *Journal of African Economies*, 12(1): 67–96,

Roberts, S. and N. Zalk (2004) 'Addressing Market Power in a Small, Isolated, Resource-Based Economy: the Case of Steel in SA', *Trade and Industry Monitor*, 31: 19–25.

Rodrik, D. (2006) 'Understanding South Africa's Economic Puzzles', *CID Working Paper*, no. 130, Harvard University.

Rustomjee, Z., R. Crompton, A. Maule, B. Mehlomakulu, G. Steyn (2007) 'Possible Reforms to the Fiscal Regime Applicable to Windfall Profits in South Africa's Liquid Fuels Sector, With Particular Reference to the Synthetic Fuel Industry', 9 February 2007, report of the Task Team appointed by the Minister of Finance, <www.treasury.gov.za>.

Sakakibara, M. and M.E. Porter (2001) 'Competing at Home to Win Abroad: Evidence from Japanese Industry', *Review of Economics and Statistics*, 83(2): 310–22.

Steyn, G. (2003). 'Administered Prices: Electricity', A report for National Treasury, Pretoria South Africa.

Traub, L. and T. S. Jayne, (2004) 'The Effect of Market Reform on Maize Marketing Margins in South Africa', Michigan State University *International Development Working Paper*, no. 82, <www.aec.msu.edu/agecon/fs2/index.htm>

Vink, N. and J. Kirsten (2002) 'Pricing behaviour in the South African food and agricultural sector', Report commissioned by the National Treasury, June 2002, <www.nda.gov.za>

Walker, M. and R. Minnitt (2006) 'Understanding the Dynamics and Competitiveness of the South African Minerals Inputs Cluster', *Resources Policy*, 31: 12–26.

9

The Macroeconomic Impact of AIDS and ART

Ben Smit and Linette Ellis

1. Introduction[1]

The HIV/AIDS epidemic[2] is one of the most significant developments in South Africa since the political transition in 1994. South Africa currently has the highest number of HIV-positive inhabitants (more than 5 million) in the world and more than 350,000 deaths annually are currently ascribed to AIDS (Dorrington et al., 2006). The economic and social consequences of the increased mortality and morbidity associated with HIV/AIDS include sharp declines in average life expectancy and in the living standards of affected households, sharp increases in the number of orphans, productivity losses which increase production costs, and a slowdown in economic growth (Chapter 2). The adverse social and economic implications of the epidemic clearly required remedial action from the authorities.

Yet, the South African government's responses to the HIV/AIDS epidemic have been controversial and widely criticized at home and abroad.[3] Formally, the African National Congress (ANC) government took office in 1994 with a comprehensive national AIDS plan. However, in a thorough review of South

---

[1] Acknowledgements: The research on which this chapter is based was funded by AusAID, DFID, and USAID and by the UNDP of South Africa. The management and technical assistance was provided by the Joint Economics AIDS and Poverty Programme (JEAPP), which is affiliated to the African Asian Society (AAS). The authors are grateful to Janine Aron, Geeta Kingdon, and Nicoli Nattrass for comments, and an anonymous referee.

[2] HIV is the acronym for the Human Immunodeficiency Virus, while AIDS stands for Acquired Immune Deficiency Syndrome.

[3] One commentator suggests that government policy in South Africa has been 'a sorry tale of missed opportunities, inadequate analysis, bureaucratic failure and political mismanagement' (Nattrass, 2004: 41).

Africa's HIV/AIDS policy from 1994 to 2004, Butler (2005: 593) suggests the plan was 'insufficiently informed by institutional and social realities' and it 'overestimated the economic, and especially human, resources at the disposal of the incoming government'. These problems resulted in a wide-ranging review of the government's HIV/AIDS policy in 1997, and a new AIDS action plan, but no provision for publicly-funded anti-retroviral (ARV) therapies. From 1999, government policy was shrouded in controversy, especially about resistance to the use of ARV's to prevent mother-to-child transmission of HIV, and exacerbated by President Mbeki's critiques of the conventional intellectual foundations of AIDS health policy.[4] In 2000 the government launched a new strategy, the HIV/AIDS/STD Strategic Plan for South Africa 2000-5, though Butler (2005: 595) considered that 'it lacked concrete commitments and time frames and created controversy by evading analysis of ARV options'. The South African government, which has been severely criticized for its slow response to the epidemic, and especially concerning the large-scale provision of ARV's,[5] eventually bowed to public pressure and announced a large-scale anti-retroviral treatment (ART) programme in August 2003 (Nattrass and Geffen, 2005).

This chapter analyses the macroeconomic effects of HIV/AIDS and of the proposed large scale ART programme in South Africa, and considers the prognosis for the future. Although the impact of HIV/AIDS on a country's economic performance is likely to be adverse, the extent of these economic costs is difficult to determine with any reasonable degree of certainty, as attested to by the large diversity in the results of studies (see below). Moreover, although a large-scale ART programme should be beneficial to the HIV-positive members of society and their close relations, it is not necessarily the case that it would be economically beneficial.

The macroeconomic impact of HIV/AIDS in South Africa and of its large-scale ART programme is analysed by means of scenarios for the period 2000-20, using a macro-econometric model. Three alternative scenarios are considered: (i) a no-AIDS counterfactual; (ii) AIDS with certain prevention programmes, but excluding large-scale ART; and, (iii) AIDS with these prevention programmes and a large-scale ART programme (assuming a 50 per cent take-up rate).

The model used to generate the alternative scenarios is an adaptation of the Bureau for Economic Research's (BER) macro-econometric model of the

---

[4] In Butler's view the controversies surrounding HIV/AIDS policies in South Africa may be attributed in part to the co-existence of two competing complexes of policy prescriptions:
an 'immobilization/ biomedical' paradigm that emphasized society-wide mobilization, political will and anti-retroviral (ARV) treatments; and a 'nationalist/ameliorative' paradigm that focused on poverty, individual responsibility, palliative care, traditional medicine and appropriate nutrition (Butler 2005: 492).

[5] See Nattrass (2008) for an exhaustive account of the 'battle' for ART in South Africa.

South African economy, using annual data. The model scenarios focus on the demographic impact of HIV/AIDS and the associated implications for the supply of labour in South Africa. They incorporate several detailed assumptions related to the health care costs of the epidemic, and to various other channels through which HIV/AIDS may impact on the macro economy.[6]

There are several channels through which the epidemic might be expected to have an economic influence. These include the implications of slower growth in the population and labour force on the production and expenditure sides of the economy; direct costs to companies that provide employee benefits such as medical aid and death benefits; indirect costs related to increased absenteeism, lost experience and skills, higher recruitment and training costs, and lower labour productivity; the impact of HIV/AIDS on the demand for health care and welfare spending by government; and, the economic effects of an increase in the number of funerals.

It should be noted upfront that the precision of any projection is dependent on the accuracy of the assumptions. An inherent difficulty in modelling work of this nature is the large number of assumptions required. Some were based on insufficient evidence, which may well compromise the accuracy of the projections. In view of the uncertainties involved with these assumptions, a number of the key economic assumptions were varied in order to test the sensitivity of the model to changes in these assumptions.

The analysis suggests that GDP growth could be 0.5 percentage points lower on average per annum over the period 2000–20 compared to what could have been achieved in the absence of HIV/AIDS.[7] However, the provision of ART with a 50 per cent uptake, could reduce this impact to 0.4 percentage points. The results also show that, on a macroeconomic level, the benefits of providing ART (in terms of economic growth 'saved') clearly outweigh the costs.

The chapter is structured as follows. The next section contains a brief discussion of the demographic impact of the epidemic, with reference to the three scenarios modelled. This is followed in section 3 by a description of the macro-impact analysis, including a brief survey of previous such studies and of the impact of a large-scale ART programme. Section 4 concludes.

---

[6] The demographic analysis was provided by Rob Dorrington and Leigh Johnson (University of Cape Town), the labour force data and projections by Claude van der Merwe (Quantec Research) and the health care costing by Andrew Boulle and Susan Cleary (University of Cape Town).

[7] The results from the sensitivity analysis suggested that the model is not particularly sensitive to changes in any one specific assumption. The combination of the different assumptions tested did influence the magnitude of the impact on certain economic variables, but the direction (i.e. positive or negative effect) remained unchanged. Simulations incorporating the whole range of the potential effects (i.e. overall results from the sensitivity analysis) suggest that the impact on GDP growth could be between −0.41 and −0.55 percentage points on average per annum between 2000 and 2020 in the absence of ART, while real per capita GDP growth could be 0.28 to 0.43 percentage points higher compared to a no-AIDS scenario.

2. The demographic impact of the HIV/AIDS epidemic

The demographic impact of HIV/AIDS and various intervention programmes constitutes the primary input in the analysis of its economic impact. Demographic changes ensue as the epidemic affects the labour force and labour costs, the demand (and supply) of government services and other goods and services, the medical and pharmaceutical sectors, the retirement and funeral industries, and so on. Various sources of demographic impact data for South Africa are available. The analysis below is based on the ASSA 2002 model.[8,9]

The historical data and projections using population and related statistics reveal the staggering impact of the HIV/AIDS epidemic. HIV prevalence in the SA population appears to have increased to 11.2 per cent in 2007 (from 0.1 per cent in 1990), to a total of more than 5 million people. It is furthermore estimated that 11.4 per cent of this HIV-positive population are AIDS-sick, a total of approximately 650,000 people (or 1.4 per cent of the population). The total cumulative number of AIDS deaths was estimated (by mid 2005) at 1.5 million (Dorrington et al., 2004: 18).

The three alternative macroeconomic scenarios presented in Section 3 utilize demographic projections from the ASSA 2002 model for the period 2000–20. These projections are summarized in Table 9.1.

Table 9.1. Impact of HIV/AIDS on SA population (including prevention and treatment): 2000–20

	Population (million)			HIV prevalence (%)		AIDS prevalence (%)		AIDS deaths (nearest '000)	
	No-AIDS	Including AIDS							
		No ART	50% ART	No ART	50% ART	No ART	50% ART	No ART	50% ART
2000	44.3	43.9	44.0	8.25	8.25	0.43	0.43	151	151
2005	47.8	46.2	46.2	10.93	11.00	1.33	1.24	384	346
2010	50.9	47.0	47.5	10.61	11.29	1.84	1.43	490	377
2015	53.9	47.4	48.4	9.83	11.11	1.76	1.51	458	391
2020	56.7	47.9	49.2	9.55	11.00	1.62	1.49	427	392

Source: Actuarial Society of South Africa (ASSA) 2002 AIDS demographic model

[8] The ASSA 2002 AIDS and Demographic model is a model of the AIDS epidemic in South Africa, released in July of 2004 by the Actuarial Society of South Africa (ASSA). A more up to date demographic impact analysis is now available through the ASSA 2003 model (Dorrington et al., 2006). The ASSA 2003 model is structurally similar to the ASSA 2002 model and the results do not differ substantially from that of the ASSA 2002 model.

[9] The prevention and treatment programmes provided for in the ASSA 2002 demographic modelling of the impact of HIV/AIDS consisted of: (i) information and education campaigns, (ii) treatment of sexually transmitted diseases (STDs), (iii) voluntary counselling and testing (VCT), (iv) prevention of mother-to-child transmission (PMTCT), and (v) anti-retroviral treatment (ART). See Dorrington and Johnson (2002).

The first column shows projected population growth under the three scenarios. While the size of the population does not contract in absolute terms, the cumulative growth in the population is limited. It is estimated at only 1.7 million people between 2005 and 2020 in the prevention-only scenario, or 3 million with the inclusion of ART. Expressed alternatively, in the prevention-only scenario the population is projected to be 15.6 per cent smaller by 2020 compared to a no-AIDS scenario; with ART, the projected gap is only 13.3 per cent, i.e. a population 'gain' of 1.3 million people (or 2.3 per cent). In the absence of the HIV/AIDS epidemic, the cumulative growth estimated is close to 9 million. The implied population loss is staggering, albeit smaller than previously predicted.

HIV prevalence, shown in the second column, is projected to increase in the prevention and ART scenario compared to a prevention-only scenario, as ART prolongs the lives of HIV-positive individuals. Excluding ART, HIV prevalence is projected to peak at 11 per cent in 2006, declining thereafter to 9.6 per cent by 2020 as the rate of mortality begins to exceed the rate of HIV incidence. With ART, HIV prevalence peaks at 11.3 per cent (2010), remaining close to this level over the remainder of the projection period. The implication is that by 2005 the HIV/AIDS epidemic in SA had reached a 'stable state', that is, the estimated number of individuals infected with HIV (around 5 million) is expected to remain around this level over the next fifteen years. Whilst the HIV population may be close to a stationary state, we are only beginning to experience the full mortality consequences of such a large HIV-positive population.

The third and fourth columns of Table 9.1 show AIDS prevalence and deaths from AIDS. AIDS prevalence is projected to peak at 1.9 per cent in 2011 (with 872,000 people being AIDS-sick), leading to around 490,000 AIDS deaths per annum in the prevention-only scenario. The introduction of ART reduces peak prevalence to 1.5 per cent (or around 730,000 AIDS-sick individuals) and the annual number of AIDS deaths to around 390,000 (2015–20). This suggests the introduction of ART could reduce the annual number of AIDS deaths by around 100,000 (2008–11), with this 'saving' narrowing to 35,000 by 2020.

3. The macroeconomic impact of HIV/AIDS

The HIV/AIDS epidemic has reached such proportions in many African countries that it may detrimentally affect macroeconomic variables such as economic growth, employment, capital formation, and inflation. Several studies of the possible macroeconomic effects have been conducted for some of the more heavily infected African countries, including South Africa, and a brief survey of the available literature is presented here.[10] Following this, an updated study by the BER in 2005/6 is presented.

3.1. Modelling the macroeconomic impact of HIV/AIDS: A brief survey

During the early 1990s, several studies attempted to quantify the impact of HIV/AIDS on the economic growth rates of African countries with severe epidemics, see Over (1992), Kambou, Devarajan, and Over (1992), Cuddington (1993a and 1993b), Cuddington and Hancock (1994a and 1994b), and Bloom and Mahal (1995). These earlier studies generally relied on relatively simple models, often consisting of no more than a production function, and projected the impact of HIV/AIDS over a fifteen to twenty-five year time frame by comparing 'no-AIDS' and 'AIDS' scenarios. With the exception of the Bloom and Mahal study, these authors typically arrived at the conclusion that the AIDS epidemic would lead to a substantial reduction in overall economic growth and that AIDS could even reduce the growth rate of per capita income, albeit only slightly (Table 9.2).

During 1995–9 there was little quantitative research on the economic impact of AIDS. Research efforts were renewed during 2000/1, resulting in at least five papers on the economic impact of the epidemic. One of these studies, Haacker (2002), follows the approach of Cuddington (1993b) using a neoclassical growth model framework to simulate the impact of HIV/AIDS on per capita incomes in a number of southern African countries. Unfortunately, his results are not easily comparable to the other studies as his methodology did not allow for an explicit analysis of the impact of HIV/AIDS on annual growth rates.[11]

The other studies rely on somewhat more complex, yet quite different analytical models. The Botswana Institute for Development Policy Analysis (BIDPA) built on the work done by Cuddington and constructed an extended Solow type growth model, distinguishing between a formal and an informal sector, as well as between skilled and unskilled labour, to simulate the macroeconomic impact of AIDS on Botswana. BIDPA estimated that the average growth rate in Botswana's GDP could be 1.1 percentage points lower than in a no-AIDS scenario during 1996–2021. However, a sensitivity analysis suggested the decline in GDP growth could range between 0.8 and 1.9 percentage points and GDP per capita could increase or decrease, depending on a number of assumptions.

---

[10] A useful recent survey of literature on the macroeconomic impact of HIV/AIDS is presented in Haacker (2004: ch. 2).

[11] He did, however, conclude that, in the case of an open economy model 'while the evolution of HIV prevalence rates and hence HIV/AIDS-related mortality rates differ across countries, this suggests that the rate of per capita output growth will be between 0.3 and 0.7 percentage points lower than otherwise' (Haacker, 2002: 35).

Table 9.2. Summary of results from previous studies on the macroeconomic impact of AIDS on different African countries

Authors	Country	Projection period	Average differences between year on year growth rates	
			GDP	Per capita GDP
Over (1992)[a]	30 Sub-Saharan countries	1990–2025	−0.56 to −1.08	0.17 to −0.35
	10 Most advanced epidemics		−0.73 to −1.47	0.13 to −0.60
Kambou, Devarajan, and Over (1992)[b]	Cameroon	1987–91	−1.9	NA
Cuddington (1993a)[c]	Tanzania	1985–2010	−0.6 to −0.8	0.0 to −0.2
Cuddington (1993b)[c]	Tanzania	1985–2010	−0.5 to −0.9	0.1 to −0.3
Cuddington and Hancock (1994a)[c]	Malawi	1985–2010	−0.2 to −0.3	0.0 to −0.1
Cuddington and Hancock (1994b)[c]	Malawi	1985–2010	−0.1 to −0.3	0.1 to −0.1
BIDPA (2000)[d]	Botswana	1996–2021	−0.8 to −1.9	0.4 to −0.5
MacFarlan and Sgherri (2001)[e]	Botswana	1999–2010	−3.3 to −4.4	Negative
Quattek (2000)	South Africa	2001–15	−0.3	Positive
Arndt and Lewis (2000)	South Africa	1998–2010	−1.6	Negative
Laubscher et al. (2001)	South Africa	2001–15	−0.33 to −0.63	0.7 to 1.0

Notes:
[a] Fraction of AIDS costs financed from savings varied from 0 per cent to 100 per cent. The distribution of AIDS over three skills categories of labour was varied between fairly downwardly biased to extremely upwardly biased—at the time of this study the thinking was still that skilled labour had higher HIV infection rates than unskilled labour.
[b] Simulation results of the impact of a 10,000 worker reduction per year in each of three different skill categories of labour.
[c] Fraction of AIDS costs financed from savings varied from 0 per cent to 100 per cent. Labour productivity lost per AIDS case varied from 0 per cent to 100 per cent.
[d] Projections depend on assumptions with regard to labour productivity losses, HIV prevalence amongst skilled workers, the rate of growth of the skilled workforce, investment rates, and total factor productivity (TFP) growth.
[e] Projections depend on assumptions with regard to labour productivity losses, the rate of growth of capital inflows and capital accumulation in the formal sector, and TFP growth.

An IMF working paper by MacFarlan and Sgherri (2001) suggests that the AIDS epidemic may have an even more devastating impact on Botswana's economy. Using a broadly similar model to BIDPA, but more pessimistic assumptions about the impact of the epidemic (particularly on savings and investment in Botswana), MacFarlan and Sgherri's simulation results indicate that the average growth rate in Botswana's non-mining GDP could be a massive 3.3 to 4.4 percentage points lower per annum compared to a no-AIDS scenario for 1999–2010. These projections are some of the most pessimistic estimates of the economic impact of HIV/AIDS in an African country to date.

Although the 1990s saw a number of researchers attempting to quantify the impact of HIV/AIDS on other African economies, there was no similar serious attempt for South Africa until the research of ING Barings (Quattek 2000) and Arndt and Lewis (2000).

The ING Barings study was not only the first quantitative research on the economic impact of AIDS in South Africa available in the public domain, but also the first study to use an econometrically estimated, demand-orientated macro-model. Their simulation results indicated that GDP growth could be on average 0.3 percentage points lower between 2001 and 2015 than it would have been in the absence of the AIDS epidemic. Although ING Barings refrains from any statements on the impact of the epidemic on per capita GDP, a comparison of their projections for the decline in the level of GDP, and the decline in the population suggests that per capita GDP will be significantly higher in the AIDS scenario (the decline in the real GDP is substantially less than the decline in the population due to AIDS). Apart from the projections by Cuddington and Hancock for the Malawian economy, this is the least pessimistic view on the impact of HIV/AIDS on an African economy. This may be related to the demand-driven nature of their model, whereby HIV/AIDS induced expenditure stimulates demand and raises economic growth.

Arndt and Lewis simulated the impact of AIDS on the growth prospects of the South African economy using a fourteen-sector computable general equilibrium (CGE) model, similar to that employed in the Cameroonian study by Kambou, Devarajan, and Over. As with Cameroon, the projections by Arndt and Lewis for the South African economy are quite devastating. They project that GDP growth could be as much as 1.6 percentage points per annum lower between 1998 and 2010 compared to what would have been possible without AIDS, and that per capita GDP levels may also decline due to AIDS. The significantly more pessimistic projections by Arndt and Lewis may be due to the type of model that was used. In contrast to the demand-driven macro-econometric model used in the ING Barings study, a CGE model is supply-constrained. It appears that CGE models magnify the adverse impact of declining production (due to lower productivity and a smaller labour force), and declining incomes and savings, on overall economic growth (Parker et al., 2000: 17).[12] Furthermore, they assume an extreme rate of total factor productivity decline (50 per cent), which accounts for roughly a third of their projected GDP growth impact.

In light of the diverging projections of the likely impact of HIV/AIDS on the South African economy by ING Barings and Arndt and Lewis, the Bureau for Economic Research (BER) also conducted a macroeconomic impact analysis in 2001. This was the second published macroeconomic impact study for South Africa based on an econometrically estimated macro-model and the

---

[12] It should be noted, however, that the negative implications for the production potential of the economy is partially countered by the positive labour productivity and capital per worker effects of a decrease in the labour supply.

results suggested a decline of (on average) 0.47 percentage points in economic growth over a fifteen-year period. The projected impact on potential GDP was, however, significantly larger at −1.4 percentage points.[13] The projected impact on per capita GDP was a (positive) 0.9 percentage points per annum (Laubscher et al., 2001).[14]

A more recent study of the impact of HIV/AIDS on economic growth is that of Bell, Devarajan, and Gersbach (2006). In contrast to the earlier studies that were based on Solow-type growth models, CGE models or macro-econometric models, this study is based on an overlapping-generations (OLG) model. The study centres on the impact of HIV/AIDS on human capital formation over the long term (i.e. over generations).[15] The focus of the study is on the effects of the death of one or both parents on their children's ability to accumulate human capital and on the reduction in the returns to investment in the children's education. According to this study, the impact on economic growth (using data on the South African economy), assuming that no remedial action is taken by society, is devastating: income of the average South African family declines from R26,366 in 1990 to R12,901 in 2080 (compared to an increase from R22,335 in 1990 to R94,715 in 2080 in the no-AIDS scenario. The Bell, Devarajan, and Gersbach study also provides for two scenarios where the society does respond to the problem. In these scenarios the average family income increases from R22,536 in 1990 to R45,136 in 2080 and from R22,445 in 1990 to R83,269 in 2080 respectively.

Young (2004) also investigated the impact of AIDS on human capital formation in South Africa using an overlapping generations framework. In contrast to the Bell, Devarajan, and Gersbach study, Young concluded that, while 'AIDS is a humanitarian disaster of millennial proportions...it is not, however, an economic disaster' (Young, 2004: 38).[16]

It is evident that researchers have not reached consensus on the impact of HIV/AIDS on economic growth—estimates of the impact of HIV/AIDS on countries with advanced epidemics range between a reduction of 0.1 and 4.4 percentage points in the average annual GDP growth rate over the next ten to twenty years. Even for South Africa, projections diverge—whereas Arndt and Lewis project that per capita income levels will be lower due to AIDS, the

---

[13] Inasmuch as potential GDP is closer to GDP in the CGE models, it is significant that this rate of decline (1.4 percent) is close to that obtained from the Arndt and Lewis model (1.6 percent).

[14] The results of a sensitivity analysis suggested a range of −0.33 to −0.63 for GDP growth, −1.4 to −1.8 percentage points for potential GDP and 0.7 to 1.0 percentage points for GDP per capita (Laubscher et al., 2001: 40).

[15] Other studies that focus on the human capital impact of HIV/AIDS include Birdsall and Hamoudi (2004) and Ferreira and Pessoa (2003).

[16] It should be noted that an important assumption in Young's model, namely the impact of AIDS on fertility, has been questioned in a study by Sebnem Kalemli-Ozcan (2006).

The Macroeconomic Impact of AIDS and ART

ING Barings study (Quattek, 2000) and the 2001 BER study (Laubscher et al., 2001) suggest that per capita income may rise significantly. It should be noted, however, that the different classes of models reviewed above capture different mechanisms and are therefore not strictly comparable with one another.

3.2. The macroeconomic impact of HIV/AIDS and ART in South Africa—An updated study by the BER

In light of the divergence in previous estimates of the macroeconomic impact of HIV/AIDS in South Africa, and the government's implementation of a large scale ART programme (not in place earlier and hence not modelled in previous studies), the BER decided in 2005/6 to update its earlier macroeconomic impact analysis. The aim was to quantify the economic impact of HIV/AIDS using the latest available demographic projections, with a specific focus on the costs and benefits of HIV prevention and treatment interventions. In what follows, the methodology and assumptions employed by the BER are described, and the results are presented and discussed.

3.2.1. MODELLING METHOD

Modelling the macroeconomic effects of the HIV/AIDS epidemic is a complex exercise. This study approached this problem in the following way. First, the BER's macro-econometric forecasting model (see Box 1) was re-estimated and focused on modelling the impact of HIV/AIDS on the economy. The annual estimation period varied between 1970 and 2004, depending on data availability and other concerns. The analysis was conducted with the aid of three model-based scenarios introduced above, the no-AIDS scenario; AIDS with prevention programmes, but no ART programme ('AIDS–no ART'); and AIDS with prevention programmes and a large scale ART programme with a take-up rate of 50 per cent ('AIDS–50 per cent ART'). Since very few people received ART prior to 2004, the historical period was treated as the 'AIDS–no ART' scenario.

The next step was to identify the key channels for the macroeconomic impact of the epidemic and to adopt a specific set of assumptions for each AIDS impact channel in each AIDS scenario. The AIDS–no ART scenario was treated as the baseline scenario and assumptions were made on AIDS-affected variables in the AIDS–50 per cent ART and no-AIDS scenarios.

Thirdly, a baseline forecast simulation of the economy was constructed with the BER's macro-econometric model under the AIDS–no ART scenario for 2005–20.

Having conducted the baseline AIDS–no ART simulation, the no-AIDS assumptions were 'activated' in the model and the no-AIDS simulation was conducted. The macroeconomic effect of each impact channel was analysed independently, after which all the impact channels were combined in the model for the all-inclusive no-AIDS simulation. Similarly, the AIDS–50 per cent ART assumptions were activated and the AIDS–50 per cent ART simulation was conducted.

> **Box 1** THE BER'S MACROECONOMIC FORECASTING MODEL
>
> The broad structure of BER's model can be described as that of a demand-orientated macro-econometric model. Although the model essentially determines South Africa's gross domestic product (GDP) from the demand side (i.e. GDP is determined as the sum of final consumption expenditure by households, final consumption expenditure by general government, gross fixed capital formation, inventory investment and exports of goods and services, less imports of goods and services), specific supply elements in the form of a measure of potential output and economy-wide capacity utilisation have been included in an attempt to capture the production side of the economy. Capacity utilisation, which is measured as the inverse of the gap between actual and potential output, enters the equations for imports and prices as a variable supply constraint.
>
> The BER's model of the South African economy contains 135 equations, of which 30 are econometrically estimated and 105 are identities and transformations. The E-Views 5 econometric package was employed to estimate the equations and to compile the model. Cointegration techniques were used to estimate the majority of the behavioural equations in the BER's model. These techniques, which are currently used by, inter alia, the SA Reserve Bank and the SA National Treasury to construct macro-econometric models, have several advantages compared to the standard techniques such as Ordinary Least Squares (OLS). The most important advantages are that they provide an answer to the so-called spurious correlation problem and provide for specification of both the long run theory-based relationships between the variables as well as the short-run dynamic relationships.
>
> Historical labour force data (1970 – 2004) per skill category were generated by Dr. Claude van der Merwe of Quantec Research. For econometric modelling purposes, it was decided to differentiate between two skill categories of labour—skilled and unskilled. Given South Africa's high unskilled unemployment rate and the comparatively small reserve pool of skilled people, it is important to differentiate between skilled and unskilled labour. Furthermore, HIV/AIDS prevalence is slightly lower for skilled labour—the labour category with the relatively higher contribution to the country's GDP.

3.2.2. THE ECONOMIC IMPACT CHANNELS OF HIV/AIDS

In modelling the macroeconomic impact of HIV/AIDS in South Africa, the BER considered the following impact channels[17] of the epidemic.

3.2.2.1. *Lower population and labour force due to lower fertility and AIDS deaths*

Firstly and most notably, AIDS slows the growth in the population and the labour force (Chapter 11), with negative implications for both the production potential of the economy and the expenditure side of the economy (e.g. residential investment and consumer spending). A smaller population may also translate into lower government consumption expenditure (e.g. spend-

---

[17] The BER's AIDS impact assumptions are discussed in more detail in the BER's (June 2006) full report: 'The macroeconomic impact of HIV/AIDS under alternative intervention scenarios (with specific reference to ART) on the South African economy'.

ing on welfare, education, health care, safety and security, and pensions) and increased social spending such as on child support grants and old age pensions. In the BER's model, government consumption expenditure is split between government wage expenses (i.e. employment) and other non-wage government spending. In order to account for the impact on government employment of the lower demand for government services due to the smaller population (compared to a no-AIDS scenario) and the difficulty government would experience finding skilled workers to replace AIDS-sick employees, it was assumed that only 75 per cent of government employees lost due to AIDS would be replaced from unemployed or other sources. Furthermore, it was assumed that, in each AIDS scenario, non-wage government consumption expenditure and transfers from government to households would decline by half of the percentage difference in the relevant AIDS population as compared with the no-AIDS population.

3.2.2.2. Higher government health care and welfare expenditure

The second channel of impact concerned the implications of the epidemic for health care and welfare expenditure by the government (see Chapters 4 and 10). Estimates of additional health care costs due to HIV/AIDS were produced by Andrew Boulle and Susan Cleary[18] (BER, 2006: appendix B) for each AIDS scenario (see Table 9.3). Their projections suggest an R11.6bn (R10.8bn) increase in health care costs by 2010 (2019) in the AIDS–no ART scenario and a R15.9bn (R21.5bn) increase in the AIDS–50 per cent ART scenario.[19] However, these projections were based on the assumption that all AIDS victims in need of and accessing primary care would receive treatment in public sector hospitals and clinics. Since we also needed to model private sector health care costs, we assumed that a small percentage (roughly 20 per cent) of HIV/AIDS victims will choose to attend private sector hospitals for treatment and pay for this out of pocket, via their medical aid or receive financial support or health care from their employers. Furthermore, it was assumed that hospital services, HIV care pre-ART and ART would be 50 per cent more expensive in the private sector than in the public sector. In order to account for the budget constraints of the government, it was assumed that the government would finance 50 per cent of the extra health care expenditure by cutting back spending in other departments or within the health department (or HIV/AIDS is simply allowed to crowd out other illnesses in public sector hospitals).[20]

---

[18] School of Public Health and Family Medicine, University of Cape Town.

[19] Although the ART costing analysis conducted by Boulle and Cleary for the BER study does account for potential savings to the public health sector arising from the provision of HAART (e.g. fewer hospital admissions), other studies, such as Nattrass and Geffen (2005) calculated even higher cost savings, suggesting a more positive economic outcome.

[20] Note that the model does not distinguish between the marginal productivity of government and private sector investment.

Table 9.3. HIV/AIDS Health Care Cost Estimates (in Rand)

	AIDS with Prevention Programmes (no ART)			
Service	2005	2010	2015	2019
Programme-level	701,307,735	1,057,502,161	1,086,943,218	1,063,770,884
VCT	153,844,101	139,237,156	138,405,879	138,672,339
HIV care pre-ART	1,294,228,575	2,344,785,761	2,283,052,813	2,147,317,456
Condoms	123,744,000	171,264,086	180,725,000	180,725,000
PMTCT	179,169,354	147,409,531	142,001,600	141,311,917
TB care	403,982,881	729,801,143	709,688,752	667,375,390
Hospital services	3,517,652,043	7,034,116,739	6,831,499,609	6,420,578,497
Grand Total	6,373,928,689	11,624,116,575	11,372,316,870	10,759,751,483
	AIDS with Prevention Programmes and ART (50% scenario)			
Service	2005	2010	2015	2019
Programme-level	793,919,968	1,567,055,660	1,987,019,766	2,102,472,922
VCT	160,905,253	149,986,979	146,772,194	146,430,430
HIV care pre-ART	1,139,602,556	1,282,852,922	1,118,556,427	1,017,831,539
Condoms	123,744,000	171,264,086	180,725,000	180,725,000
PMTCT	179,655,833	149,905,206	144,786,947	143,798,717
TB care	404,703,774	694,487,463	822,372,465	850,765,857
Hospital services	3,382,821,447	5,496,813,594	6,066,578,995	6,171,359,418
Anti-retroviral programme	1,155,731,521	6,398,109,440	9,796,210,292	10,853,537,373
Grand Total	7,341,084,352	15,910,475,350	20,263,022,086	21,466,921,258

Source: Andrew Boulle—Cape Town ARV Costing Model

One of the most tragic consequences of the HIV/AIDS epidemic is the growth in the number of children who have lost one or more parents to AIDS—the number of maternal orphans (under the age of 18) is expected to increase to 2.3 million in 2010 and 2.7 million by 2020 in the absence of ART.[21] A doubling in the number of orphans over the next five years is bound to have a significant impact on social grants such as foster care grants. This analysis explores the impact of providing foster care grants[22] at a constant price cost of R560 per beneficiary per month, with the take-up rate increasing to 20 per cent in 2007.[23] In the AIDS–no ART scenario, this amounts to roughly R2.3bn

---

[21] Projections by Prof. Rob Dorrington, Centre for Actuarial Research, University of Cape Town.

[22] Although HIV/AIDS will likely also impact on the number of people eligible for disability and care dependency grants, these effects proved to be too complex to model in this analysis.

[23] The foster care grant amounted to R560 per beneficiary per month in 2005. It was assumed that the grant amount will increase in line with inflation (but remain unchanged in real terms).

of extra welfare spending on orphans (in constant prices) by the year 2010 and R3.0bn by 2020. The provision of ART could save roughly R0.5bn in foster care grants per year between 2011 and 2020.

3.2.2.3. Direct costs of HIV/AIDS to the private sector

Thirdly, it is expected that HIV/AIDS will lead to increases in direct costs to companies that provide employee benefits such as medical aid and death benefits to their employees. Private sector health care costs related to HIV/AIDS were linked to the number of AIDS-sick individuals receiving treatment in the private sector and it was assumed that private sector health care services for HIV/AIDS would be 50 per cent more expensive than in the public sector.[24] In turn, additional death and disability benefit payments (compared to a *no-AIDS* scenario) were linked to AIDS deaths and it was assumed that an average benefit of three times the annual salary would be paid out in a lump sum to household members left behind. The modelling of the direct costs impact channel also required a complex set of assumptions about the proportion of the increase in employee benefit contributions carried by the employer/employee, the impact on the salaries and wages of skilled vs. unskilled employees (in both the private and public sectors) and how companies and individuals would finance these cost increases (e.g. it was assumed that firms would only be able to pass 30 per cent of their cost increases on to customers via higher prices).

3.2.2.4. Indirect costs of HIV/AIDS to the private sector

Fourthly, AIDS related illnesses and deaths of employees will lead to indirect costs to companies, including costs related to absenteeism, lost experience and skills, recruitment and training costs and lower labour productivity (see Chapters 7, 8, and 12). In this regard, it was assumed that indirect costs of an AIDS sick employee would be equal to the average real wage/salary for his/her skills category (i.e. the indirect costs involved are significantly higher for highly skilled employees) and that 100 per cent of indirect costs would fall on employers. Since virtually all companies will be hit by the indirect cost of HIV/AIDS and companies cannot escape these costs by shifting them onto their employees (as is the case for employee benefit contributions), indirect costs to companies significantly outweigh the direct costs of the epidemic. Regarding the financing of the indirect cost increases, it was assumed that firms would pass 30 per cent of the costs on to its customers through price increases (producer price inflation), while the remainder would be absorbed through a reduction in their operating surpluses (lower company profits).

---

[24] In the AIDS–no ART scenario, private sector health care costs related to HIV/AIDS were estimated to peak at R2.85 billion in 2011, while HIV/AIDS related costs are projected to reach R5.16 billion in 2019 in the AIDS–50 per cent ART scenario.

Furthermore, we assumed a 40 per cent reduction in the productivity of both skilled and unskilled workers who are sick with AIDS, as well as a gradual reduction in the rate of total factor productivity[25] growth to about 63 per cent of what it could have been in 2020 without AIDS.[26] (These assumptions mainly impact on potential GDP in the model.) The assumption on the gradual decline in total factor productivity growth was, inter alia, made to account for the adverse impact of the sharp increase in the number of orphans and the accompanying decline in the quality of labour due to HIV/AIDS (as the loss of parents implies a decline in the transfer of knowledge and skills over generations).

3.2.2.5. Funeral costs

Finally, in order to analyse the impact of HIV/AIDS related funeral expenses on household consumption expenditure and personal savings, average funeral expenses of R5,000 per death was assumed. While higher income households are likely to spend far more, low income households appear to be more vulnerable to HIV/AIDS and have fewer resources to spend on funerals. Based on these assumptions, South Africans are projected to spend approximately R2.3bn more on funeral services in 2010 if no ART is provided. Since personal savings in South Africa are so low, it was assumed that households would finance only 30 per cent of HIV/AIDS related funeral expenses from savings and 70 per cent by cutting back their spending on other consumer products and services.

3.2.3. MAIN RESULTS

In this section the overall results of the modeling exercise for the major macroeconomic variables in the South African economy are presented. The first scenarios that are compared are the no-AIDS and the AIDS Prevention Programme (AIDS–no ART) scenarios. This represents the economic impact of HIV/AIDS on the assumption that current levels of prevention are maintained, but no ART is provided. Secondly, the AIDS Prevention Programme scenario and the AIDS Prevention Programme plus AIDS–50 per cent ART scenarios are compared. These results represent the impact of a large scale ART programme with a 50 per cent take-up rate in South Africa. These results are presented in the form of the relative improvement in macroeconomic conditions resulting from the ART programme.

---

[25] Total factor productivity refers to 'efficiency improvements (or declines) that are not attributable solely to one or the other of the two factor inputs (labour and capital), but rather to their combination in production' (Parker et al., 2000: 17).

[26] In the AIDS–50 per cent ART scenario, the rate of total factor productivity growth was assumed to decline by slightly less—to 69 per cent of the no-AIDS rate by 2020.

The Macroeconomic Impact of AIDS and ART

3.2.3.1. The macroeconomic impact in the absence of an ART programme

The basis of the macroeconomic impact of HIV/AIDS lies first and foremost in the demographic impact, including the labour force implications, and secondly in the direct and indirect costs of combating the disease. However, in understanding the macroeconomic impact, it should be noted that, whilst the population (and labour force) is reduced by 16 per cent (19 per cent), respectively, compared to the no-AIDS scenario by 2020, the decline in economic output, employment and income is substantially less. Firstly, the economic impact is softened by the fact that labour losses can be replaced from unemployed resources, given South Africa's relatively high unemployment rate. Secondly, surviving household incomes would be augmented from insurance payouts and the liquidation/inheritance of the deceased's assets, lessening the impact on spending levels.[27] Thirdly, the flip side of the cost pressures arising from the epidemic is spending in the economy, measured as increases in GDP. For instance, the increased risk benefits borne by companies also represent additional income to employees, eventually translating into increased spending (mainly, but not exclusively), on health care products and services. Also, the increased spending by companies on recruitment and training implies increased levels of economic activity. With this in mind, our projections of the macroeconomic impact of HIV/AIDS are discussed by means of a comparison between the no-AIDS and AIDS–no ART scenarios.

3.2.3.1.1. Growth and employment The impact of HIV/AIDS on output and employment is unambiguously negative. However, the impact appears to manifest gradually. Compared to the no-AIDS scenario, the level of real GDP is projected to be 3.4 per cent lower by 2010 and 8.8 per cent lower by 2020. In average growth rate terms this translates into a loss of growth of 0.46 per cent over the full period 2000–20 (see Table 9.4).

The GDP impact results primarily from the demographic impact and the cost-increasing impact of HIV/AIDS. Since actual GDP is determined as the sum of the various expenditure components, the GDP impact follows from the demographic and cost changes on household and government expenditure, investment and exports. These are discussed in more detail below.

HIV/AIDS also effects the level (and growth) of potential GDP. This effect, which follows from the impact of HIV/AIDS on the labour force, productivity (including multifactor productivity) and the capital stock, is quite pronounced. By 2020 the level of potential GDP is projected to be 20 per cent lower in the AIDS scenario. This implies that the output gap (i.e. the difference

---

[27] It should be noted that the long run impact on economic growth would depend on the extent to which these assets are divided between the financing of capital formation and current spending.

Table 9.4. The impact on real GDP and employment

	Real GDP	Per capita GDP	Potential GDP	Employment	Unemployment rates	
					AIDS	No-AIDS
2000[1]	−0.2	0.5	−0.75	−0.1	27.8	28.3
2004[1]	−0.9	1.8	−3.0	−0.4	27.5	29.4
2010[1]	−3.4	4.7	−9.3	−1.8	21.0	27.2
2020[1]	−8.8	8.0	−20.0	−6.2	8.7	21.0
2000–20[2]	−0.46	0.4	−1.10	−0.31		

Notes:
[1] Percentage differences in constant price levels in the AIDS and no-AIDS scenarios.
[2] Year-on-year average growth rate differentials.

between actual and potential GDP) declines in the AIDS scenario, putting upward pressure on prices and interest rates.

The negative impact on output also implies a reduced demand for labour and thus employment in the AIDS scenario. This effect is aggravated by a decline in the unemployment rate (due to the slowdown in the growth in the labour force[28]), which in turn puts upward pressure on wage rates in both the skilled and unskilled components of the labour market (see Chapter 11, which suggests that reductions in the unemployment rate from 2003 onwards are due to a reduction in the growth of the labour force, attributed partly to the effect of HIV/AIDS). The impact on employment is substantial, but much less than that on the labour force. By 2020, the level of total employment is projected to be 6.2 per cent lower in the AIDS scenario. In growth rate terms, this implies a decline of 0.3 per cent per year.

The much bigger impact of HIV/AIDS on the labour force compared to employment has clear implications for the rate of unemployment. In the AIDS scenario, the unemployment rate is much lower than in the no-AIDS scenario. By 2020, the model projects an unemployment rate of 8.7 per cent in the AIDS scenario, compared to 21 per cent in the no-AIDS scenario.

3.2.3.1.2. Inflation and interest rates The impact on inflation and therefore on interest rates (Chapter 3), is one of the key macroeconomic implications of HIV/AIDS. The simulation results suggest that the inflation rate could increase by 1 per cent (on average over 2000–20) in the AIDS scenario relative to the no-AIDS scenario. As far as interest rates are concerned, the results indicate that the prime overdraft rate could, on average, be 1.6 percentage points higher over the same period (see Table 9.5).

---

[28] By 2020, the total labour force is projected to be 18.8 per cent lower in the AIDS scenario compared to the no-AIDS scenario.

Table 9.5. The impact on inflation and interest rates

	CPIX inflation[3]	PPI inflation[3]	Short-term interest rate[1,4]		Long-term interest rate[2,4]	
			Nominal	Real	Nominal	Real
2000–4	0.50	0.71	0.55	0.06	0.40	−0.10
2005–10	0.92	1.06	1.21	0.29	1.06	0.14
2011–20	1.27	1.43	2.32	1.04	1.60	0.33
2000–20	0.99	1.15	1.58	0.59	1.16	0.17

Notes:
[1] Prime overdraft rate.
[2] Long term government stock rate.
[3] Difference in percentage changes.
[4] Difference in levels.

A number of factors contribute to the upward pressure on inflation in the *AIDS* scenario. Increased contributions by employers to medical and other employee benefit schemes (i.e. direct costs) translate into higher wages, putting upward pressure on product prices as companies strive to ameliorate the impact of these increased costs on their profitability by passing on (at least part of) these cost increases. Higher indirect costs to companies will result in similar price pressures, as will increased pressure on country-wide salary and wage rates (as unemployment rates decline due to the lower labour force growth rates). Finally, the higher inflation outcome may also be ascribed to the narrower output gap in the economy under the AIDS scenario. The gap between potential and actual GDP declines, as the adverse impact of the epidemic on potential output (via the sharp declines in the labour force and productivity) outweighs the negative impact on actual output. This implies an increase in capacity utilization, which puts upward pressure on prices.

The increased levels of interest rates in the AIDS scenario then follow from the increases in inflation, the deterioration in the deficit on the current account of the balance of payments, and in the case of longer-term rates, also the deterioration in the government deficit before borrowing.

3.2.3.1.3. Government finance and the balance of payments Both the government deficit before borrowing and the current account of the balance of payments worsen in the AIDS scenario relative to the no-AIDS scenario. The government budget deficit increases by, on average, 0.75 per cent of GDP over 2000–20. This comes about despite a relatively lower level of real government current expenditure (see Table 9.6) and follows from the relative decline in corporate taxes and the relative increase in government interest payments and direct and indirect employment costs.

In the case of the balance of payments, the relative deterioration in the AIDS scenario is the result of a decline in net exports. This follows from the

Table 9.6. The impact on government finances and the balance of payments

	Government consumption expenditure	Government deficit/GDP		Balance of payments: current account/GDP		Exchange rate (real effective)
		AIDS	no-AIDS	AIDS	no-AIDS	
2000[1]	−0.1	−1.9	−1.3	−4.1	−3.9	0.1
2004[1]	−1.4	0.5	1.4	−4.1	−3.3	−0.1
2010[1]	−4.0	−0.6	0.2	−3.5	−2.4	1.3
2020[1]	−6.3	−1.2	−0.2	−3.2	−1.6	3.5
2000–20[2]	−0.3					0.2

Notes:
[1] Percentage differences in constant price levels in the AIDS and no-AIDS scenarios.
[2] Year-on-year average growth rate differentials.

small (0.2 per cent per annum on average over 2000–20) appreciation in the trade-weighted Rand exchange rate and additional AIDS-related imports.

3.2.3.1.4. Fixed investment and saving The impact of HIV/AIDS on savings, is, as would be expected, negative (see Table 9.7). This follows primarily from the impact of the direct and indirect costs associated with HIV/AIDS on corporate profits and the impact on government savings.

As far as fixed investment is concerned, the impact of HIV/AIDS is clearly negative. This can be ascribed to the relative decline in production levels, relatively higher interest rates, lower corporate profits, and the impact of the lower population (compared to a no-AIDS scenario) on the demand for housing. The impact on total fixed investment over the period 2000–20 is an average relative decline of 0.6 per cent per annum—11 per cent lower in level terms by 2020 under the AIDS scenario. In the case of residential investment, the AIDS scenario reflects a relative decline of 12.3 per cent in its level by 2020.

Table 9.7. The impact on savings and fixed investment

	Residential investment	Private non-residential investment	Total fixed investment	Domestic savings as % of GDP
2000[1]	0.0	−0.6	−0.4	−0.2
2004[1]	−0.8	−2.4	−1.5	−1.0
2010[1]	−3.9	−8.1	−5.0	−1.6
2020[1]	−12.3	−16.2	−11.0	−0.9
2000–20[2]	−0.7	−0.9	−0.6	

Notes:
[1] Percentage differences in constant price levels in the AIDS and no-AIDS scenarios.
[2] Year-on-year average growth rate differentials.

3.2.3.1.5. Final household consumption expenditure The overall impact on household consumption expenditure is negative, as should be expected under conditions where the total population declines by approximately 9 million compared to a no-AIDS scenario. However, measuring the impact is not straightforward, as there are a number of opposing forces at work.

First, the relative decline in the population impacts negatively on the total demand for consumer goods and services. However, the fact that incomes decline by less than the population implies an increase in per capita disposable income, which limits the impact on household consumption expenditure. The relatively lower levels of employment in the AIDS scenario (following from lower levels of production and increases in wage rates) impact negatively on disposable income and therefore also on the demand for consumer goods and services. However, the negative impact on household expenditure as a result of lower disposable income would be mitigated by consumers activating past savings in an attempt to maintain living standards. Finally, the relatively higher interest and inflation rates also impacts negatively on consumer spending.

The impact on overall consumption is a 0.3 per cent reduction in the average growth rate over the twenty-year period—alternatively expressed, the level of consumption expenditure in the AIDS scenario could be 5.2 per cent lower than in the no-AIDS scenario by 2020. With respect to the subcategories of household consumption expenditure, the impact on durable and semi-durable goods is approximately double that on non-durables and services (see Table 9.8). This reflects primarily the extra health care (i.e. non-durable goods and services) spending by households due to HIV/AIDS, as well as the fact that semi-durable and durable goods are more sensitive to interest rate increases than non-durable goods and services.

3.2.3.2. *The macroeconomic impact of the 50 per cent ART programme*

The implementation of a large-scale anti-retroviral treatment programme with a take-up rate of 50 per cent will extend the working lives of many South

Table 9.8. The impact on final household consumption expenditure

	Durable goods	Semi-durable goods	Non-durable goods	Services	Total	Real disposable income
2000[1]	−0.1	−0.1	0	−0.1	0.0	−0.1
2004[1]	−1.1	−0.9	−0.2	0	−0.3	−0.6
2010[1]	−3.7	−3.0	−1.2	−0.8	−1.5	−1.8
2020[1]	−7.9	−7.4	−4.2	−4.1	−5.2	−3.8
2000–20[2]	−0.4	−0.4	−0.2	−0.2	−0.3	−0.2

Notes:
[1] Percentage differences in constant price levels in the AIDS and no-AIDS scenarios.
[2] Year-on-year average growth rate differentials.

Africans and soften the economic consequences of the epidemic. ASSA 2002 model projections showed that the introduction of ART (with 50 per cent uptake) could reduce the number of AIDS deaths by around 100,000 per year between 2008 and 2010. However, since ART is ultimately not a cure for the disease, this 'saving' could narrow to 35,000 per year by 2020. While the provision of ART will ameliorate the impact of the epidemic, the social and economic consequences remain far-reaching and will affect almost every facet of life in South Africa.

In order to measure the macroeconomic impact of the 50 per cent ART programme, the two AIDS scenarios, i.e. one with and the other without the ART programme were compared. The results are presented in Table 9.9 in the form of the relative improvement in the major macroeconomic variables relative to the no-ART scenario.

The results of the analysis suggest that a large-scale ART programme in South Africa could be expected to result in significant economic gains, despite the additional health care costs implied. Whereas the baseline AIDS–no ART projection shows that GDP growth could be 0.46 percentage points lower on average per annum over the period 2000–20, the provision of ART with a 50 per cent uptake could reduce this impact by 0.08 percentage points to 0.38 percentage points. In other words, the ART programme is projected to 'recover' 17 per cent of the costs of AIDS over the period 2000–20 (i.e. 0.08 per cent / 0.46 per cent = 17 per cent). Similarly, the provision of ART will have a positive impact on employment, inflation, interest rates and even the government's budget deficit—employment growth will be higher, while inflation, interest rates and the budget deficit will be lower if ART is provided.

The impact of the ART only really manifests after 2008, as would be expected given the gradual phase in of the government's ART programme between 2004 and 2008. In terms of the GDP impact, by 2010 the level of the real GDP is only 0.9 per cent higher in the *ART* scenario than in the AIDS–no ART scen-

Table 9.9. AIDS no-ART vs. AIDS 50% ART scenarios: 2000–20

	Difference	As % of AIDS 'Cost'
Real GDP growth[1]	0.08	0.08/0.46 = 0.17
Employment growth[1]	0.06	0.06/0.31 = 0.19
CPIX inflation rate[1]	−0.12	−0.12/0.99 = −0.12
Prime interest rate[2]	−0.33	−0.33/1.58 = −0.21
Government deficit (% of GDP)[2]	−0.07	−0.07/0.73 = −0.10

Notes:
[1] Year-on-year average growth rate differentials.
[2] Difference in levels.

ario (see Table 9.10). However, this impact gradually increases to 1.7 per cent by 2020 (from −8.8 per cent in the AIDS–no ART to −7.1 per cent in the AIDS–50 per cent ART scenario). The positive GDP impact follows primarily from the impact of the ART programme on the size and the health of the total population and the labour force—a larger and healthier labour force relative to the AIDS–no ART scenario implies higher labour productivity, lower HIV/AIDS related indirect costs and higher potential output, which translates into lower pressure on capacity utilization and hence, lower inflation and interest rates. Relatively lower interest rates, in turn, stimulate consumer spending and fixed investment, while population-sensitive variables like residential investment also benefit from the higher population.

Tables 9.9 and 9.10 show that, although the government's budget deficit also improves (as a percentage of GDP) if ART is provided, the impact on the budget deficit is not as pronounced compared to the positive effects on employment and overall economic growth. The relatively small improvement can be ascribed to the fact that the public sector will be funding a large proportion of the ART programme.

The benefits of the ART *programme may also be illustrated by comparing the GDP 'gained' relative to the AIDS–no ART* scenario with the total cost (to the private and public sectors) of providing ART. The provision of ART with a 50 per cent uptake is projected to cost South Africa R11.7 billion per year by 2020, while the benefit in terms of economic growth is projected to be R34 billion in 2020. The cumulative cost of ART between 2005 and 2020 is projected to be around R111 billion, while the economic benefit (in terms of GDP 'saved')

Table 9.10. The macroeconomic impact of HIV/AIDS: AIDS–no ART and AIDS–50% ART projections relative to no AIDS scenario

		2005	2010	2020	2000–20
Real GDP[1]	no ART	−1.2	−3.4	−8.8	−0.46 [2]
	50% ART	−1.0	−2.5	−7.1	−0.38 [2]
Employment[1]	no ART	−0.5	−1.8	−6.2	−1.10 [2]
	50% ART	−0.4	−1.3	−4.9	−1.04 [2]
CPIX inflation rate[2]	no ART	0.8	1.0	1.7	0.99
	50% ART	0.6	0.9	1.5	0.87
Prime interest rate[2]	no ART	0.9	1.6	3.2	1.58
	50% ART	0.4	1.1	2.9	1.25
Government deficit as % of GDP[1]	no ART	0.7	0.9	1.0	0.73
	50% ART	0.5	0.7	0.9	0.66

Notes:
[1] Percentage differences in constant price levels in the AIDS and no-AIDS scenarios.
[2] Year-on-year average growth rate differentials.

could be in the region of R290 billion. On a macroeconomic level, the benefits of providing ART therefore far outweigh the costs.

4. Conclusions and future prospects

The results from a number of macroeconomic impact analyses suggest the HIV/AIDS epidemic undoubtedly has a negative impact on economic growth in South Africa. Our literature survey demonstrates that the short-run macro-econometric models that capture the effects of AIDS on labour supply and the demand for health care show a relatively mild impact, whereas medium-term CGE models and long-run overlapping generations models reflect far gloomier prospects for the economy (Table 9.2). All the studies suggest that prevention and treatment can ameliorate the impact.

The BER in 2005/6 updated its earlier analysis of the macroeconomic impact of HIV/AIDS, both to throw light on the considerable divergences in the estimates from other studies, and to assess, for the first time, the implementation of a large scale ART programme by the South African government (not modelled in previous studies). The analysis compared the AIDS–50 per cent ART scenario with two others, a no-AIDS scenario and an AIDS–no ART scenario. The key finding is that on a macroeconomic level, the benefits of providing ART far outweigh the costs. In the BER analysis with ART, the economic impact of the epidemic will manifest gradually— the brunt of the impact of the epidemic will most likely be felt during 2010–20, but, even then, GDP growth will remain positive. The level of GDP will be significantly higher than it is now, while the size of the population could be similar to the current level. Thus, the BER analysis implies that real per capita income will not only be higher in ten to fifteen years time than it is now, but will also be higher compared to a no-AIDS scenario. By contrast, the findings of the Arndt and Lewis (2000) and the Bell et al. (2006) studies are more pessimistic. However, it is important to note that the BER model does not capture the adverse effect of AIDS on human capital formation in the long run as modelled, for example, in overlapping generations models.

Looking ahead it appears that South Africa's HIV/AIDS policies are improving to some extent. The government adopted a new National Strategic Plan for the period 2007–11 in April 2007 (SANAC, 2007). The main objectives of this strategy are the reduction of new HIV infections by 50 per cent in 2011 and the mitigation of the impact of AIDS by expanding access to appropriate treatment, care and support to 80 per cent of all HIV-positive people and their families by 2011. These goals are very ambitious and likely to be constrained by the continuing challenge of sufficient human resources in the health sector and implementation problems. As far as the ART programme is concerned, the government has reported (Republic of South Africa, 2008) that 42 per cent of the estimated 889,000 requiring treatment (i.e. 371,731 patients), received treatment in 2007, 68 per cent of them in the public sector. In the case of the provision of ARV's to reduce the risk of mother-to-child transmission, the percentage of patients receiving treatment increased from 60 in 2006 to 66 in 2007. In the Western Cape Province this percentage stood at 90 in 2007, indicating that the rollout in the rest of South Africa still has some way to go. The geographical distribution of ART services has also improved. By the end of 2007, 362 public health facilities, covering more than 80 per cent of the 254 local municipality and metropolitan councils provided ART services, an increase of 89 from the end of 2006. Finally, the replacement of Mr. Mbeki as South Africa's President in 2009 should result in a more focused, and perhaps more efficient approach to prevention and treatment of HIV and AIDS in South Africa.

References

Actuarial Society of South Africa, 2004. AIDS Demographic Model 2002. [Online] Available at <http://www.actuarialsociety.co.za/aids/content.asp?id=1000000451>

——, July 2004. New AIDS Model Reflects Significant Impact of Interventions. Press Release, [Online] Available at <http://www.actuarialsociety.co.za>

Arndt, C. and Lewis, J. D., August 2000. 'The Macro Implications of HIV/AIDS in South Africa: A Preliminary Assessment'. *South African Journal of Economics*, 68(5): 1–32.

Bell, C., Devarajan, S., and Gersbach, H., 2006. 'The Long-Run Economic Costs of Aids: a Model with an Application to South Africa'. *World Bank Economic Review* 20(1): 55–89.

Birdsall, N. and Hamoudi, A., 2004. 'Aids and the Accumulation and Utilization of Human Capital in Africa', in Haacker (ed.) *The Macroeconomics of HIV/AIDS*, International Monetary Fund, ch. 4, pp 134–66.

Bloom, D. E. and Mahal, A. S., 1995. 'Does the AIDS Epidemic Really Threaten Economic Growth?' *NBER Working Paper*, no. 5148. June.

Botswana Institute for Development Policy Analysis. 2000. *Macroeconomic Impacts of HIV/AIDS Epidemic in Botswana*. Gaborone: BIDPA.

Bureau for Economic Research, June 2006. 'The Macroeconomic Impact of Hiv/Aids under Alternative Intervention Scenarios (With Specific Reference to Art) on the South African Economy'. [Online] Available at: <http://www.ber.ac.za>

Butler, A., 2005. 'South Africa's HIV/AIDS Policy, 1994–2004: How Can It be Explained?' *African Affairs*, 104(417): 591–614.

Cuddington, J. T., 1993a. 'Modelling the Macroeconomic Effects of AIDS with an Application to Tanzania'. *World Bank Economic Review*, 7(2): 173–89.

——1993b. 'Further Results on the Macroeconomic Effects of AIDS: The Dualistic, Labour-Surplus Economy'. *World Bank Economic Review*, 7(3): 403–27.

Cuddington, J. T and Hancock, J. D, 1994a. 'Assessing the Impact of AIDS on the Growth Path of the Malawian Economy'. *Journal of Development Economics*, 43: 363–368.

—— 1994b. 'The Macroeconomic Impact of AIDS in Malawi: A Dualistic, Labour Surplus Economy'. *Journal of African Economies*, 4(1): 1–28.

Cuddington, J. T., Hancock, J. D., and Rogers, C. A., 1994. 'A Dynamic Aggregative Model of the AIDS Epidemic with Possible Policy Interventions'. *Journal of Policy Modelling*, 16(5): 473–96.

Dorrington, R.E. and Johnson, L. F., 2002. 'The Demographic and Epidemiological Impact of Hiv/Aids Treatment and Prevention Programmes: An Evaluation Based on the Assa 2000 Model'. Centre for Actuarial Research, University of Cape Town.

Dorrington, R. E., Johnson, L. F., and Budlender, D., 2004. 'The Demographic Impact of Hiv/Aids in South Africa: National Indicators 2004'. Cape Town: Centre for Actuarial Research, South African Medical Council, Actuarial Society of South Africa.

Dorrington R. E., Johnson L. F., Bradshaw, D., and Daniel, T.-J., 2006. 'The Demographic Impact of HIV/Aids in South Africa: National and Provincial Indicators for 2006'. Centre for Actuarial Research, University of Cape Town.

Ferreira, P. C. and Pessoa, S., 2003. 'The Long-Run Economic Impact of HIV/AIDS'. Rio de Janeiro, Graduate School of Economics, Fundacão Getulio Vargas.

Haacker, M., 2002. 'The Modeling the Macroeconomic Impact of HIV/AIDS'. *IMF Working Paper*, no. 02/195 [Online] Available at: SSRN <http://ssrn.com/abstract=880315>.

—— M. 2004. 'HIV/AIDS: The Impact on the Social Fabric and the Economy, in Haacker M. (ed.), *The Macroeconomics of HIV/AIDS*, International Monetary Fund, ch. 2, pp. 41–95.

Kalemli-Ozcan, S., 2006. 'AIDS, Reversal of the Demographic Transition and Economic Development: Evidence from Africa'. *NBER Working Paper*, no. 12181.

Kambou, G., Devarajan, S., and Over, M., 1992. 'The Economic Impact of AIDS in an African Country: Simulations with a Computable General Equilibrium Model of Cameroon'. *Journal of African Economies* 1(1): 109–30.

Laubscher, P., Smit, B. W., and Visagie, L., September 2001. 'The Macroeconomic Impact of HIV/AIDS in South Africa'. Bureau for Economic Research. *Research Note*, no. 10. University of Stellenbosch.

Macfarlan, M. and Sgherri, S., June 2001. 'The Macroeconomic Impact of HIV/AIDS in Botswana'. *IMF Working Paper*, no. 01/80. Research Department and African Department. [Online]. Available at <http://www.imf.org/>

Nattrass, N., 2004. *The Moral Enemy of AIDS in South Africa*. Cambridge University Press, Cambridge.

—— 2008. 'Aids and the Scientific Governance of Medicine in Post-Apartheid South Africa'. *African Affairs*, 107(427): 157–76.

Nattrass, N. and Geffen, N., 2005. 'The Impact of Reduced Drug Prices on the cost-effectiveness of HAART in South Africa'. *African Journal of AIDS Research*, 4(1): 65–7.

Over, M., 1992. 'The Macroeconomic Impact of AIDS in Sub-Saharan Africa'. The World Bank: Population and Human Resources Department. [Online]. Available at <http://www.iaen.org/files.cgi/335_macro.pdf/>

Parker, W. et al., November 2000. 'The Economic Impact of HIV/AIDS in South Africa and its Implications for Governance: A Literature Review'. Draft for comment compiled by the Centre for AIDS Development, Research and Evaluation (CADRE) on behalf of the Joint Center for Political and Economic Studies and USAID.

Quattek, K., April 2000. 'Economic Impact of AIDS in South Africa: A Dark Cloud on the Horizon'. A study by Wefa SA commissioned by ING Barings, Johannesburg.

Republic of South Africa. 2008. 'Progress Report on Declaration of Commitment on HIV and AIDS', United Nations General Assembly Special Session on HIV and AIDS (UNGASS) [Online]. Available at<http://data.unaids.org/pub/report/2008/South_Africa_2008_country_progress_report_en.pdf>

South African National Aids Council (SANAC). 2007. *HIV and AIDS and STI Strategic Plan for South Africa: 2007–2011*. Pretoria.

Young, A., December 2004. 'The Gift of Dying: the Tragedy of Aids and the Welfare of Future African Generations'. *NBER Working Paper*, no. 10991.

10

A Long-run Perspective on Contemporary Poverty and Inequality Dynamics

Murray Leibbrandt, Ingrid Woolard, and Christopher Woolard

1. Introduction[1]

South Africa has an infamous history of high inequality with an overbearing racial stamp. The issue of inequality has continued to dominate the post-apartheid landscape. There are two indicators of the post-apartheid political economy that have attracted special attention in this regard. The first is whether the evolving post-apartheid economy and especially the policy efforts of the post-apartheid government have been able to lower this inherited inequality. The second is the related question of whether the blunt racial footprint would start to grey under more subtle post-apartheid socio-economic dynamics.

Historically the profiling and measurement of poverty have formed sub-themes of this inequality discussion because of the overt relegation of the non-white majority to the bottom of the income and wealth distributions in the country under apartheid. Showing this to be the case and illuminating the poverty inducing features of apartheid policies were the central tasks of much apartheid era social science.

The next section describes inequality and poverty trends in South Africa over the long run. Census data provide the primary sources for such comparisons. The focus is on aggregate indicators and also on racial shares. In addition,

---

[1] Acknowledgements: Ingrid Woolard gratefully acknowledges support from the UK Economic and Social Research Council (RES-167-25-0076). Murray Leibbrandt gratefully acknowledges support from the U.S. National Institute of Child Health and Human Development (Grants R01HD39788 and R01HD045581), the Fogarty International Center of the U.S. National Institutes of Health (D43TW000657) and the Research Chairs Initiative of the Department of Science and Technology and National Research Foundation.

Contemporary Poverty and Inequality Dynamics

the rural–urban dimension of inequality and poverty is given some attention. The very name apartheid indicates the importance of race-based geography and race-based policy. Although formal policies of spatial separation by race are long gone, a lingering rural–urban legacy remains. From a policy point of view, the inheritance of a huge group of marginalized rural poor has greatly increased the difficulty and the costs of social delivery.

While aggregate descriptions of poverty and inequality provide important context, they do little more than hint at the forces driving socio-economic development and the complex relationship between poverty and inequality. Even under high apartheid with job reservation explicitly widening racial inequality by rationing high-skill and high-wage jobs to whites and low-wage and low-skill jobs to non-whites, in periods of strong economic growth there was dissent about whether this unequal growth path was improving or worsening poverty (Seekings and Nattrass (2005). Two key mechanisms were at issue and still continue to dominate debates over the relationship between inequality and poverty. The first is the employment and remuneration behaviour of the labour market. Strong positive employment and real wage responses to economic growth are the major poverty alleviating mechanisms of the private sector economy. The second mechanism is the fiscal resources that growth puts in the hands of the state for active social policy and poverty alleviation.

This chapter gives serious attention to these two prongs of the redistributionist regimes of the pre- and post-apartheid eras. In an attempt to provide an integrated review of apartheid and post-apartheid inequality trends, section 2 uses census data to provide an empirical summary of inequality trends from 1970 to 2001. Section 3 updates this review through to 2006 by summarizing some of the recent debates around measured changes in poverty and inequality over the last decade. Section 4 presents and discusses a set of inequality decompositions by income source. This provides the backdrop for more detailed discussions of the performance of the post-apartheid labour market in section 5 and the role of social grants in section 6. Section 7 briefly summarizes the major points from the preceding sections and concludes by exploring implications of this empirical analysis for inequality and poverty going forward.

2. A long-run empirical picture of changes in inequality and poverty by race

Few data series allow the presentation of a long-run empirical picture. Leibbrandt et al. (2001) derive a series of estimates of the per capita incomes of the different race groups since 1917 from a range of data sources. These are presented in Table 10.1. Three key points emerge from the two sections of the table. Looking at the top section of the table, it can be seen that average real

Table 10.1. A compilation of estimates of annual per capita personal income by race group in 2000 Rands and relative to white levels, 1917–95

Year	White	Coloured	Indian/Asian	African	Average
	Per capita income in constant 2000 Rands:				
1917	13,069	2,875	2,894	1,184	3,946
1924	13,853	2,770	2,694	1,099	4,137
1936	19,212	3000	4,443	1,462	5,359
1946	26,252	4,280	6,037	2,331	7,556
1956	30,494	5,158	6,668	2,627	8,541
1959	31,640	4,977	5,407	2,435	8,454
1960	31,230	4,977	5,340	2,532	8,378
1970	45,751	7,929	9,248	3,133	11,140
1975	49,877	9,688	12,687	4,289	12,696
1980	48,340	9,238	12,304	4,088	11,818
1987	45,828	9,572	13,823	3,879	10,661
1993	46,486	8,990	19,537	5,073	11,177
1995	48,387	9,668	23,424	6,525	12,572
	Relative per capita personal incomes (% of white level):				
1917	100	22.0	22.1	9.1	30.2
1924	100	20.0	19.4	7.9	29.9
1936	100	15.6	23.1	7.6	27.9
1946	100	16.3	23.0	8.9	28.8
1956	100	16.9	21.9	8.6	28.0
1959	100	15.7	17.1	7.7	26.7
1960	100	15.9	17.1	8.1	26.8
1970	100	17.3	20.2	6.8	24.3
1975	100	19.4	25.4	8.6	25.5
1980	100	19.1	25.5	8.5	24.4
1987	100	20.9	30.2	8.5	23.3
1993	100	19.3	42.0	10.9	24.0
1995	100	20.0	48.4	13.5	26.0

Source: van der Berg (2001) and own calculations.

incomes have been rising for all groups. The mean per capita income of the poorest group—Africans—reached a plausible (in 2000 income terms) poverty line around 1970 and has doubled since. However, as shown later, even today many members of this group are still in poverty. Second, the relative ratios presented in the bottom section of the table show the persistence of stark average income gaps by race over the course of the twentieth century. The fact that these gaps pre-date apartheid indicates that they are the products of a very long-run development trajectory of the South African economy. This is important context to the stubborn persistence of these differences over the post-apartheid period too. Finally, the average ratio in the last column is low and declines over the long run as a result of the fact that the white group is a declining minority of the population with its decline corresponding to an increase in the share of the African population. Thus, aggregate income dynamics in the economy are being increasingly driven by the dynamics within the African group.

Underlying these trends are the analytic issues connecting household level poverty and the growth and employment performance of the labour market. For example, in the high-growth 1960s the African/white income gap actually increased, because skills scarcity, exacerbated by the industrial colour bar, led to a premium being paid on the wages of relatively skilled white workers. In the early 1970s, the shift in economic power and to a lesser degree changing skill profiles narrowed the wage gap and thereby the income gap. Thereafter, the impact on the income gap of the continued narrowing of the wage gap was partly counteracted by growing unemployment amongst those with the least skills and education. Even in the apartheid period, economic growth best translated into a reduction of the inter-group income gap when the racial wage gap narrowed and there was sufficient growth of employment.

An important empirical tradition in tracking longer-run South African inequality and poverty changes has made use of records of personal income collected in the national censuses of 1970, 1991, 1996, and 2001 (McGrath, 1983; Whiteford and McGrath, 1994; Whiteford and Van Seventer, 2000; Leibbrandt et al., 2006; Simkins, 2005). Two important points emerge from this census-based work. First, starting in 1970 through to 2001 inequality as measured by the Gini coefficient was very high by international standards. This illustrates just how high the levels of inequality are that underlie the average figures presented in Table 10.1. Whiteford and Van Seventer (2000) show that national Gini coefficients for the period 1975 to 1996 remained close to 0.68. Leibbrandt et al. (2006) then show that this national inequality remained at least this high in the period 1996–2001. Second, the Gini coefficients by race show widening inequality within each group for each census from 1975 to 2001. From the 1991 census onwards, the Gini coefficients for the African and white groups are, respectively, the highest and lowest of the four race groups.

This picture of rising aggregate inequality and also rising inequality within each race group begs the question of the relative importance of the within-race versus the between race components of inequality. To address this, the South African literature has decomposed total inequality into within-group and between-group contributions. In these decompositions the between-group contribution represents a marker of the importance of race in driving inequality while the within-group contribution represents the extent to which factors other than race are driving inequality.

Measures of the between-group component of inequality in South Africa have always been larger than all available international comparators (Bhorat et al., 2000), a stark marker of apartheid-driven inequality in South Africa. However, all of the census-based empirical work makes a consistent case that between-group inequality declined over the period 1975 to 1996. Clearly, the forces driving a widening inequality within each racial group over the last forty years have been strong enough to increase the overlap between the within-race distributions. Some of the declining between-group inequality is due to the fact that the African share of the population has increased significantly over the period. Between 1970 and 2001 the African population share increased from 70 per cent to 80 per cent. This increased share was matched by the declining shares of the white group which fell from 17 per cent of the population in 1970 to 9 per cent of the population in 2001. Clearly such demographic change gives increasing importance to the intra-African distribution in driving the aggregate distribution.

However, there is more to these changes than shifting population shares. Whiteford and Van Seventer (2000) show that the income share of the African group rose much more strongly than the African population share over this period from a low base of 19.8 per cent in 1970 to 30 per cent in 1991 and 36 per cent in 1996. The coloured and the Indian/Asian shares rise too. These rising shares are matched by the sharply declining income share of the white group. This share decrease from 71 per cent in 1970 to 60 per cent in 1991 and 52 per cent in 1996. These striking changes motivate a need to explore the economic factors driving them.

A further nuance, evident in Leibbrandt et al. (2006), is that the rapid decline in the white income share took place up only until 1996 and then slowed or even stopped in the period to 2001. Support for this picture emerges from an examination of the ratios between mean white per capita income and the mean per capita income of other groups from 1970 to 2001. Census data suggest that the period 1970 to 1996 saw this disparity ratio of African to white mean per capita incomes decrease from 15 to 9. This ratio fell for coloured and Indian/Asian groups too. This is consistent with the evidence presented in Table 10.1. However, the evidence from the 2001 census suggests that this ratio did not fall further for any racial group between 1996 and 2001. Thus, the direction of these changes is not inexorable but rather is the product of actual socio-economic developments in the post-apartheid period.

The national increases in inequality are supported by increased inequality across the rural/urban divide which we do not show here. Rather, we give the rural/urban divide more detailed attention in the poverty analysis that follows. As a bridge to the poverty analysis, Figure 10.1 gives an aggregate snapshot of the change in real per capita incomes in South Africa between 1996 and 2001, with 2001 incomes deflated to their 1996 equivalents for comparability

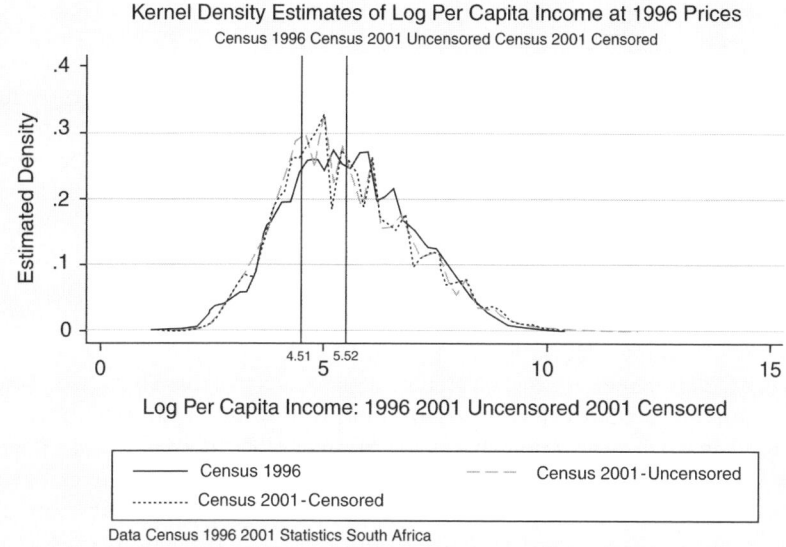

Figure 10.1 A distributional plot of South African incomes in 1996 and 2001

Source: Leibbrandt et al. (2006) calculations using 1996 and 2001 census data, Statistics South Africa.

purposes[2]. There are two plots for 2001. Relative to the 1996 data, the 2001 census provided additional detail on the top end of the distribution by including a number of additional high-income brackets in the question. The figure controls for the impact of this innovation by plotting all of the top-income brackets as they are found in the 2001 data (we call this 'uncensored' data) as well as with the top brackets collapsed into a 1996 equivalent top band ('censored' data). It is clear from the figure that this censoring narrows 2001 inequality.

Even with the censored data, the 2001 plot lies above the 1996 plot at the top end of the income distribution. This suggests that the top end of the 2001 distribution contains a greater share of the population than it did in 1996. Thus, there is some evidence of improved real incomes at the top end. Apart from this group at the top, the 2001 distribution shows a leftward shift, implying decreased real incomes for the rest of the distribution. This is particularly

---

[2] In order to keep the distribution within a narrower range without altering its shape, the graph plots the log of per capita income rather than per capita income itself. When taking logarithms we exclude all of the zero earning households.

pronounced in the middle and lower-middle sections of the distribution, with the situation at the bottom looking largely unchanged. As we have shown above, the net effect of all of these changes is an unambiguous increase in inequality from 1996 to 2001.

The two vertical lines drawn on the figure represent the two poverty lines that we use for the poverty analysis. The lower line is a $2 per day poverty line, which is widely used for international poverty comparisons. The upper poverty line is R250 per person per month (in 1996 Rands), which was first suggested in the poverty-mapping work of Statistics South Africa (2000). The leftward shift of incomes in the middle and lower-middle areas of the 2001 distribution suggests a slight but unambiguous increase in measured poverty between 1996 and 2001. A brief analysis of poverty using the 1996 and 2001 censuses confirms this finding.

At the national level, the key picture is presented in Table 10.2. Two poverty measures are used at the two poverty lines that were introduced above. The first is the headcount ratio—that is the number of the poor as a percentage of the total population at each poverty line. This headcount ratio increases from 1996 to 2001 for both poverty lines. It can be seen that, at the low poverty line ($2 per day/R91 per month) the headcount ratio is 26 per cent in 1996 and 28 per cent in 2001. For the higher poverty line (R250 per month in 1996 Rands)

Table 10.2. Poverty levels in 1996 and 2001 at the national level and by population group

	Headcount	Poverty gap ratio	Headcount	Poverty gap ratio
	1996		2001	
$2 per day				
National	0.26	0.11	0.28	0.11
African	0.34	0.14	0.35	0.14
Coloured	0.10	0.03	0.13	0.04
Indian/Asian	0.03	0.01	0.03	0.01
White	0.01	0.00	0.01	0.00
Urban	0.13	0.05	0.16	0.06
Rural	0.45	0.19	0.46	0.19
R250 (1996) per month				
National	0.50	0.30	0.55	0.32
African	0.62	0.38	0.67	0.39
Coloured	0.34	0.16	0.41	0.19
Indian/Asian	0.11	0.05	0.14	0.06
White	0.03	0.02	0.04	0.02
Urban	0.36	0.17	0.40	0.21
Rural	0.75	0.48	0.79	0.49

Source: Leibbrandt et al. (2006) calculations using 1996 and 2001 census data, Statistics South Africa.

the headcount rises from 50 per cent to 55 per cent. Unlike the headcount ratio, the poverty gap ratio takes some account of the depth of poverty as it is based on the income gap by which poor households fall short of the poverty line. Given this, it need not record the same poverty change as the headcount ratio. In the South African data, however, it does reflect the same increase in measured poverty. For example, using R250 per person per month, the 1996 Census poverty gap ratio is 0.30 and it rises to 0.32 in 2001, reflecting an increase in the depth of poverty. Thus, at both poverty lines, measured poverty increases from 1996 to 2001. Leibbrandt et al. (2006) use poverty dominance techniques to show that this increase in measured poverty is not dependent on the choice of poverty line or the inclusion or exclusion of households with zero reported income.

In addition, Table 10.2 reports poverty rankings by population group in both 1996 and 2001, as well as how poverty changed for each group from 1996 to 2001. The poverty ranking by race is seen to be robust. At any poverty line, Africans are very much poorer than coloureds, who are very much poorer than Indians/Asians, who are poorer than whites. In addition, the table shows that measured poverty increased for Africans, coloureds and Indians/Asians. However, here the choice of poverty line seems to make a difference. There were only small increases in poverty between 1996 and 2001 for Africans and coloureds when measured at the low poverty line ($2 per day) but fairly large increases in poverty for these two groups and the Indian/Asian group when the higher poverty line (R250) is used.

Both the headcount ratio and the poverty gap ratio can be used to generate poverty shares to complement these poverty rates. The African group has been shown to have the highest poverty rates by far in both time periods. When this is combined with this group's dominant population share, the result is an overwhelming set of African poverty shares. Leibbrandt at al. (2006) show that, for the lower $2 per day poverty line, the African share is 95 per cent or higher in both 1996 and 2001. If the higher poverty line is used in the calculation the African share falls to 91 per cent using the headcount ratio and 93 per cent using the poverty gap ratio. This poverty gap ratio statistic reflects the fact that the African poor are over-represented in the poorest of the poor group. In all of these calculations, the coloured poverty share accounts for nearly all of the remaining poverty with 1 per cent of poverty or less being attributed to the other two groups.

We complete our discussion of income poverty by comparing rural and urban poverty. This rural/urban divide cuts across race group to some extent; although the population share of the African group is even higher in rural areas than at the national level. Table 10.2 shows that rural poverty rates are substantially higher than urban poverty rates (regardless of the poverty line chosen). However, poverty rates increased unambiguously in urban areas between censuses. This cannot be unequivocally concluded for rural areas.

This point can be made more sharply by considering the rural and urban poverty shares, although these are not shown in the table. While a much higher proportion of the rural population are poor, the proportion of the poor who are in rural areas is declining. Using the higher poverty line, 38 per cent of the poor were in urban areas in 1996, whereas 44 per cent of the poor were in urban areas in 2001. This is to be expected, given that a significant amount of rural to urban migration occurred over the period.

3. Shades of grey: Debates over recent inequality and poverty trends

In order to give a longer-run perspective on changes in inequality and poverty, the previous section made use of census data going back to 1970. Since 1993, researchers have been able to access information from a number of national sample surveys and have used these to complement census-based analyses and to provide alternative estimates of inequality and poverty. The result is a substantial literature which is very useful in updating the census-based picture to the present. There has been some debate in this literature over the magnitudes of measured inequality and poverty implied by the different surveys and even over whether poverty has increased or decreased over the post-apartheid period.

The inequality picture can be quickly dealt with as all of this work (Simkins, 2005; Fedderke et al., 2003; Hoogeveen and Özler, 2006; van der Berg et al., 2005) supports the picture coming out of the census data; namely that both aggregate inequality and inequality within each race group has continued to increase through the 1990s and into the 2000s. Table 10.3 presents a set of South African Gini coefficients based on expenditure data from the 2004 General Household Survey. They show that South African inequality remains very high by international standards. The results also confirm that the greatest inequality is within the African population and lowest within the white population. The table holds a useful caution. The actual magnitudes of the inequality measures that come from household sample surveys are much lower than the census estimates presented in the previous section and it is inequality

Table 10.3. Gini coefficients by race and location, 2004

	African	Coloured	Indian/Asian	White	Total
Rural	0.43	0.38	—	0.37	0.51
Urban	0.53	0.45	0.43	0.36	0.56
Overall	0.51	0.47	0.43	0.36	0.59

Source: Own calculations on 2004 General Household Survey, Statistics South Africa.

measures such as these expenditure based estimates that are used in order to compare South African inequality in the post 2000 period to other countries.

The poverty trends are more contentious than the inequality trends. It is useful to structure the discussion around two sub-periods; 1994 to 2000 and then the post-2000 period. Regarding the first sub-period a series of studies have found evidence for an increase in poverty over this time (Statistics South Africa, 2002; Hoogeveen and Özler, 2006). Hoogeveen and Özler (2006) estimate that 12.6 million South Africans were living on less than PPP$1 per day in 1995 compared to 14.4 million in 2000 and that 22.9 million South Africans were living on less than PPP$2 per day in 1995 rising to 25.2 million in 2000. The direction of these findings accords with the census based analysis presented earlier. However, the measured increase in poverty is more acute than that found using the census. Simkins (2005) performed analysis on the 1995 and 2000 Income and Expenditure Surveys (IES) as well as the 1996 and 2001 censuses. Using a poverty line set at household income of R800 per month, he finds that poverty worsened slightly over the period, rising from 29 per cent in 1995 to 34 per cent in 2000.

On the other hand, the UNDP (2004), van der Berg and Louw (2004) and van der Berg et al. (2005) find that poverty stabilized or declined over this period. However, none of this work argues for a notable improvement in poverty over this sub-period. The UNDP report that while the extent of poverty appears to have declined slightly, the depth of poverty (measured by the poverty gap) increased, particularly when using lower poverty lines. Van der Berg and Louw (2004) note that current household income as seen in the national accounts rose over the sub-period and that this is inconsistent with the decline in household incomes observed by using the IES 1995 and 2000 survey data. After adjustments to mean incomes for each race group in line with the national accounts and other sources of data, they find that the poverty headcount ratio stabilized or even declined slightly between 1995 and 2000, although the number of people living in poverty increased due to population growth.

Van der Berg et al. (2005) use the same technique with the All Media and Products Survey (AMPS) data in order to extend their analysis to 2004. As shown in Table 10.4 they find that the poverty rate rose between 1993 and 2000 and then fell quite dramatically between 2000 and 2004. At the R250 per capita per month poverty line they estimate that there were 18.5 million poor in 2000 and this fell to 15.4 million in 2004. In addition per capita real incomes of individuals in the poorest two quintiles rose by more than 30 per cent during 2000–2004. While the magnitude of this rise may be debatable, it should be borne in mind that this period coincides with a large increase in social grants. Van der Berg et al. (2005) point out that the total income received by the poorest two quintiles in 2000 amounted to R27 billion and that government subsequently increased its annual social grant payment bill

Table 10.4. Selected indicators of poverty, assuming poverty line of R3,000 per capita per year (in constant 2000 prices)

	1993	2000	2004
Average per capita income (R) in quintile 1	855	866	1,185
Average per capita income (R) in quintile 2	2,162	2,086	2,770
% of population that is poor	40.6	41.3	33.2
Number of poor	16.2m	18.5m	15.4m

Source: van der Berg et al. (2005).

by R22 billion (in constant 2000 Rand terms). Most of these grant payments would have been received by individuals in the bottom two quintiles of the income distribution which provides a strong expectation of some improvement in the incomes of the poor.

The methodology and therefore the findings of the papers by van der Berg and co-authors are contentious. Meth (2006 and 2007) has been most strident in arguing against the methodology and has derived an alternative set of post-2000 poverty estimates using an income variable constructed from the information in the 2004 General Household Survey and the Labour Force Survey. His work supports a finding that the poverty rate has declined between 2000 and 2004 and that this was driven by social grant payments. However, his estimates still place 18 to 20 million South Africans in poverty in 2004. This is a much smaller decline and a less clear sign of success for anti-poverty policies in the post-apartheid era than that shown by van der Berg and co-authors.

In sum, there is something of a consensus around the direction of post-apartheid inequality and poverty trends even if there are disagreements about the precise levels at any point in time. Aggregate inequality has remained stubbornly high and perhaps even increased. This is being driven by increasing intra-race inequality. In the adjustments to South African society accompanying the advent of democracy, such dynamism is not unexpected and not necessarily bad. However, the fact that the post-apartheid society started off with such a high level of inequality certainly adds an ominous note to this trend. Given the skewed distribution of human and physical assets that undergirds these trends, it is unsurprising that there has not been a dramatic improvement in money-metric poverty over the early years of the post-apartheid period. More recent years have witnessed stronger gains against poverty. Indeed, one of the useful features of the interchange between Meth and van der Berg et al. is that it has highlighted the importance of the social grant system as a social safety net in South Africa. The importance of the state old age pension has been recognized from the outset of the post-apartheid period and the demonstrable impact of the child support grant in the last six years is notable. This takes the aggregate empirical picture a little closer to the real application of post-apartheid policy in South Africa. In this spirit, the next section of the paper undertakes a decomposition of income inequality by income sources for the year 2000 in order to re-emphasize the importance of the labour market and social grants in understanding South African inequality.

4. Decomposing inequality

In this section, we begin with a decomposition of the Gini coefficient by income sources. The decomposition highlights those income sources that are dominating the distribution of income. For the purposes of this chapter, we decompose income into remittances, wage income (including self-employment), social assistance ('grants'), and capital income (such as dividends, interest, rent income, imputed rent from residing in own dwelling, and private pensions).

The key aspects of the method can be summarized as follows. If South African society is represented as n households deriving income from K different sources or components, then Shorrocks (1984) shows that the Gini coefficient (G) for the distribution of total income can be derived as:

$$G = \sum_{k=1}^{K} R_k G_k S_k$$

where:
S_k is the share of source k income in total income (i.e. $S_k=\mu_k/\mu$),
G_k is the Gini coefficient measuring the inequality in the distribution of income component k, and
R_k is the Gini correlation of income from source k with total income.[3]
The larger the product of these three components, the greater the contribution of income from source k to total income inequality. While S_k and G_k are always positive and less than one, R_k can fall anywhere on the interval $[-1,1]$. When R_k is less than zero, income from source k is negatively correlated with total income and thus serves to lower the overall Gini measure for the sample.

Table 10.5 presents the results of this decomposition for the total South African sample using the most recent comprehensive income data, namely the 2000 Income and Expenditure Survey (IES). A few illustrative features of the tables will be highlighted. It can be seen that wage income (including self-employment income) has a dominant share of income (72 per cent) but makes

---

[3] R_k is a form of rank correlation coefficient as it measures the extent to which the relationship between Y_k (the income from source k) and the cumulative rank distribution of total income coincides with the relationship between Y_k and its own cumulative rank distribution.

Table 10.5. Decomposition of total national income by income sources, 2000

Income source	Percentage of households receiving income source ($100*P_k$)	Mean monthly income from source (Rands)	Percentage share in total income (S_k)	Gini for income source for households receiving such income (G'_k)	Gini for income source for all households (G_k)	Gini correlation with total income rankings (R_k)	Contribution to Gini coefficient of total income ($S_k G_k R_k$)	Percentage share in overall Gini	Percentage change in Gini for 1% change in component
Remittances	41.1	165.42	5.1	0.605	0.837	0.113	0.005	0.7	−0.044
Capital income	24.9	311.02	9.6	0.795	0.949	0.772	0.070	10.9	0.013
State transfers	24.1	177.85	5.5	0.365	0.847	0.156	0.007	1.1	−0.044
Wage and self-employment income	72.4	2,579.20	79.8	0.640	0.740	0.953	0.562	87.2	0.074
Total		3,233.48	100.0		0.645		0.645	100.0	0.000

Source: Own calculations on 2000 Income and Expenditure Survey, Statistics South Africa.

an even larger contribution to inequality (87 per cent). The reason for this is the high R of 0.95, implying that a household's rank in the distribution of wage income is strongly correlated with that household's rank in the distribution of total income.

As shown by Lerman and Yitzhaki (1994), the Gini coefficient for a particular income source (G_k) is driven by the inequality among those earning income from that source (G_A) and the proportion of households who have positive income from that source (P_k), or, more accurately, *the proportion of households with no access* to a particular income source ($1-P_k$). Thus, it can be seen that:

$$G_{wage} = P_{wage} G_A + (1-P_{wage}) = (0.72)(0.64) + (1-0.72) = 0.46 + 0.28 = 0.74$$

This takes the analysis part of the way to apportioning the 'blame' for Gini inequality into two parts; the inequality amongst earners and the inequality between those with some wage income and those with none. It would appear that more than one-third of what is ostensibly 'wage inequality' is attributable to the 28 per cent of households with zero wage income.

In 2000, state transfers accounted for 6 per cent of income but, according to this analysis, made almost no contribution to inequality. This very low contribution to inequality (of only 1 per cent) arises because of the low correlation ($R = 0.16$) between the rank ordering of remittance income as well as the low Gini coefficient (0.37) for state transfers. In 2000, state transfers were heavily concentrated in the middle of the distribution—access to an Old Age Pension or Disability Grant was sufficient to lift most households out of the bottom quintile, while the means tests for these grants excluded households at the upper end of the income distribution.

The last column of Table 10.5 shows the effects of a 1 per cent increase in a particular income component. It can be seen that a change in state transfers or remittances will decrease the Gini while an increase in wages or capital income will aggravate inequality. The components which increase inequality correlate highly with total income rankings (i.e. R_k is high), which implies that an increase in these sources will primarily benefit the better off and thus raise the Gini.

To better understand the mechanism whereby employment affects inequality, we make use of a second decomposition technique to unpack the earned (i.e. wage and self-employment) income component of household income. We begin by recognizing that household labour market income depends on three factors, namely, the number of 'potential workers' (that is, household members of working age), the number of household members that are actually employed, and the earnings of these workers. Glewwe (1986) uses the log-variance to decompose household earnings into these three components. Employing a slight modification of Glewwe's technique, earnings per capita can be expressed as:

$$\frac{W}{hhsize} = \frac{L_p}{hhsize} \bullet \frac{L_w}{L_p} \bullet \frac{W}{L_w}$$

where W is labour market income from both wage and self-employment (for simplicity we call it merely 'wage income'), *hhsize* is household size, L_p is the potential number of workers (defined here as the number of persons aged 15-64) and L_w is the number of people actually employed.

Taking the natural logarithm of both sides of the equation above and calculating the variance gives:

$$\operatorname{var}\left[\ln\left(\frac{W}{hhsize}\right)\right] = \operatorname{var}\left[\ln\left(\frac{L_p}{hhsize}\right)\right] + \operatorname{var}\left[\ln\left(\frac{L_w}{L_p}\right)\right] + \operatorname{var}\left[\ln\left(\frac{W}{L_w}\right)\right]$$
$$+ 2\times\operatorname{cov}\left[\ln\left(\frac{L_p}{hhsize}\right),\ln\left(\frac{L_w}{L_p}\right)\right] + 2\times\operatorname{cov}\left[\ln\left(\frac{L_p}{hhsize}\right),\ln\left(\frac{W}{L_w}\right)\right]$$
$$+ 2\times\operatorname{cov}\left[\ln\left(\frac{L_w}{L_p}\right),\ln\left(\frac{W}{L_w}\right)\right]$$

The contribution of each of the first three terms on the right-hand-side can be thought of as the contribution of household composition (the number of persons of working age), access to employment and wage inequality, respectively.

Table 10.6 reveals that most of the inequality in shared household earnings is the result of unequal wage incomes, rather than the fraction of household members that are of working age or who are actually working. Nevertheless, joblessness has a significant effect on household wage inequality. This is particularly true in African households. While this decomposition tackles the issue from a different perspective to that of the income source decomposition above, the results support a general conclusion of high wage inequality being a product of a considerable wage dispersion coupled with unequal access to employment opportunities.

5. Poverty and the labour market

Table 10.7 provides a bridge between the above inequality analysis and a poverty analysis by detailing a series of key labour market rates by per capita expenditure quintiles.[4] In the lower quintiles, participation rates are very low and unemployment rates are staggeringly high—taken together, this implies

---

[4] In all tables that make use of quintiles or deciles from the General Household Survey (GHS), we replace household expenditure with household wages + household income from grants if the latter exceeds the former. We do this because household expenditures are grossly under-reported in the GHS (see Meth, 2006).

Table 10.6. Decomposition of shared household earnings

	Variances				Covariances	
	$\ln\left(\dfrac{L_p}{hhsize}\right)$	$\ln\left(\dfrac{L_w}{L_p}\right)$	$\ln\left(\dfrac{W}{L_w}\right)$	$\left[\ln\left(\dfrac{L_p}{hhsize}\right),\ln\left(\dfrac{L_w}{L_p}\right)\right]$	$\left[\ln\left(\dfrac{L_p}{hhsize}\right),\ln\left(\dfrac{W}{L_w}\right)\right]$	$\left[\ln\left(\dfrac{L_w}{L_p}\right),\ln\left(\dfrac{W}{L_w}\right)\right]$
All households	0.146	0.250	1.374	0.023	0.043	0.037
	(7.4%)	(12.6%)	(69.4%)	(2.4%)	(4.4%)	(3.6%)
White	0.113	0.150	1.084	−0.007	−0.010	−0.060
	(9.5%)	(12.6%)	(90.7%)	(−1.2%)	(−1.6%)	(−10.0%)
African	0.155	0.268	1.155	0.034	0.047	0.023
	(8.7%)	(15.0%)	(64.8%)	(3.8%)	(5.2%)	(2.6%)

Source: Own calculations based on September 2006 Labour Force Survey, Statistics South Africa. The percentage contribution to earnings inequality is shown in parentheses.

Table 10.7. Labour market characteristics by quintile

Quintile	Labour force participation rate %	Unemployment rate %	% of adults that are working	Median individual wage of the employed (2006 prices pm) R
1st (bottom)	35	72	10	300
2nd	39	53	19	600
3rd	49	35	32	900
4th	63	17	51	1,200
5th (top)	76	7	71	4,500

Source: Own calculations based on 2006 General Household Survey data. Quintiles contain equal numbers of individuals and are based on per capita expenditure.

extremely low rates of employment among the poor. The table further shows that the average worker in the top quintile earns fifteen times as much as the average worker in the lowest quintile. Thus, the table powerfully demonstrates the relationship between household poverty and the labour market.

In order to better understand the labour market context we go on to discuss the disparate trends in participation, employment and unemployment by race and educational attainment, the unequal burden of unemployment across households and trends in wage income.

Table 10.8 reveals a legacy of the apartheid era in that Africans have worse labour market outcomes than the other groups. Coloured and Indians/Asians also had worse outcomes than whites. In 1995, the labour force participation of Africans was only 45.9 per cent, their employment rate was 36.7 per cent, and their unemployment rate was 20.1 per cent (on the narrow definition, which applies a job-search test). All the other groups have participation rates above 60 per cent and unemployment rates that are substantially lower. The unemployment rate of coloureds was 13.8 per cent, Indians/Asians 9.3 per cent and whites 3.3 per cent. Since 1995, all groups have increased their labour market participation, but they have not increased their employment rates—indeed coloured and Indians/Asians saw slight decreases. All population groups experienced increased unemployment rates (see also Chapter 11, which presents unemployment rates by race over time and probit equations of unemployment in 1995 and 2003). Africans increased participation rates by approximately 10 percentage points from 1995 to 2005 and their unemployment rate increased by about 50 per cent. Coloureds and Indians/Asians increased their participation rates by only about 3 percentage points and yet unemployment rates about doubled. Finally, the unemployment rate for whites, while small, rose by about 50 per cent. Thus, all racial groups are performing worse in terms of employment than they were a decade ago.

Table 10.8. Participation, employment and unemployment by race (%)

Year	African			Coloured		
	Participation	Employment	Unemployment	Participation	Employment	Unemployment
1995	45.9	36.7	20.1	64.2	55.3	13.8
1997	43.5	31.3	28.0	60.8	50.9	16.3
1999	51.1	35.4	30.6	67.1	56.1	16.4
2001	56.1	35.6	36.7	67.2	52.2	22.4
2003	53.6	35.4	34.0	65.8	51.4	21.8
2005	54.2	36.9	31.9	65.4	52.3	20.0

Year	Indian/Asian			White		
	Participation	Employment	Unemployment	Participation	Employment	Unemployment
1995	60.1	54.4	9.3	68.6	66.4	3.3
1997	57.6	51.2	11.1	64.8	61.9	4.6
1999	64.6	53.5	17.3	71.3	67.1	5.9
2001	67.0	53.4	20.3	72.0	66.9	7.0
2003	63.8	52.7	17.4	71.3	67.3	5.5
2005	63.9	52.0	18.7	70.3	66.7	5.1

Source: Own calculations based on 1995, 1997, and 1999 October Household Surveys and September 2001, September 2003, and September 2005 Labour Force Surveys, Statistics South Africa.
Notes: All statistics are for population 15 to 64 years old.

One of the most important distortions of apartheid for South Africa's long-term development path is skewed access to education by race. As it turns out, labour demand patterns have been particularly punitive of this distortion. Since 1970, there has been significant structural change in the demand for labour. The primary sector (agriculture and mining) was shedding labour throughout the period while financial services, wholesale and retail trade and community, social and personal services increased employment (Bhorat et al., 2000). Thus, the sectoral composition of employment changed substantially in South Africa. Agriculture went from 33 per cent of total employment to only 11 per cent, while wholesale and retail trade increased from 9 to 25 per cent, and employment in the financial sector also increased substantially from 3 to 11 per cent.

As can be seen in Table 10.9, this altered the composition of employment in terms of educational attainment, favouring more skilled workers. Displaced workers from agriculture and mining are often unable to relocate to other areas where jobs might be available, so they make up a large share of discouraged workers in rural areas. We return to this changing demand for skills in our conclusion as it has profound implications for every aspect of policy.

Table 10.9. Evolution of relative employment by education level (%)

Education Level	1970	1995	2000	2005
None	38	7	7	5
Some Primary	31	20	24	18
Some Secondary	23	31	30	29
Complete Secondary	6	24	21	29
Tertiary	1	17	18	18

Source: Banerjee et al. (2006), based on Census 1970, October Household Survey 1995 and Labour Force Surveys September 2000 and March 2005.

As members of a household tend to have similar levels of education to each other and they all dwell in places that are well or badly located relative to regional labour markets, there tends to be a strong household pattern to unemployment. Table 10.10 shows that in 2006 slightly over 50 per cent of the unemployed lived in households where someone is employed; another 11 per cent of the unemployed lived in households which received remittances from an absent household member. This is largely related to the migrant labour system created by apartheid era restrictions on movements. Thus about 62 per cent of the unemployed are able to depend on labour income from a present (or absent) household member and about 38 per cent of all unemployed live in households with no connection to the labour market. This disconnection from the labour market for the unemployed has increased over time. In 1993 some 60 per cent of the unemployed lived in a household with a working member, 20 per cent in households with remittances, and only 20 per cent had no connection to the labour market (see Klasen and Woolard, forthcoming).

Table 10.11 presents household-level analysis, showing the distribution of the employed and unemployed among households. The table shows that,

Table 10.10. Labour market connections of unemployed individuals

	1997	2006
	%	%
No-one employed, no remittances, no grants	11.8	13.2
No-one employed, no remittances, grants	17.5	24.7
No-one employed, remittances	21.3	11.2
1 employed	35.8	39.4
2–3 employed	12.6	10.9
4+ employed	0.9	0.6
Total	100.0	100.0

Source: 1997 October Household Survey and September 2006 Labour Force Survey, Statistics South Africa.

Table 10.11. The distribution of the unemployed by the labour market linkages of other household members

	Number of unemployed				
Number of employed	0	1	2–3	4+	Total
No-one employed, no remittances, no grants	3.0	4.0	1.6	0.2	8.8
No-one employed, no remittances, grants	6.8	4.3	4.1	0.5	15.7
No-one employed, remittances	3.1	3.3	1.5	0.1	8.0
1 employed	28.2	13.2	4.1	0.6	46.1
2–3 employed	16.0	3.0	1.5	0.2	20.5
4+ employed	0.6	0.2	0.1	0.0	0.9
Total	57.6	28.0	12.8	1.6	100.0

Source: Own calculations using September 2006 Labour Force Survey, Statistics South Africa.

despite high unemployment, the majority of households (58 per cent) contain no unemployed person.[5] Twenty-eight per cent of households contain one unemployed person, and 13 per cent contain 2 or 3 unemployed members, suggesting that these households are severely burdened by the presence of unemployed members. The table also shows that 24 per cent of households receive neither labour income nor remittances and are thus disconnected from the labour market. Particularly worrying is that about half of the households with 2 or more unemployed members belong to that category of households disconnected from the labour market. Trends over time show that the burden of unemployment has increased on many households. The share of households containing not a single unemployed person has fallen from 70 per cent in 1993 (Klasen and Woolard, forthcoming) to 57 per cent in 2006, and, correspondingly, the shares of households with one, two, three, or more unemployed have all increased significantly in that time period.

The two analyses suggest four findings. First, the unemployed are relatively widely distributed across households, certainly much more widely than in rich countries (Klasen and Woolard, forthcoming). In the South African context, this is particularly surprising given that, due to racial differences in unemployment, white households (and, to a lesser extent, Indian/Asian households) are largely insulated from the burden of unemployment. Indeed, 90 per cent of white and 75 per cent of Indian/Asian households did not contain an unemployed person in 2004. This implies that among African households, the burden of unemployment is particularly widely dispersed, with nearly 50 per cent of households having at least one unemployed person, and quite a few more than one.

---

[5] Given the racial differences in unemployment rates and the near absence of interracial households, most white and Indian/Asian, and a large share of coloured households are among this group of households.

Second, the most important source of resources for the unemployed are labour incomes of other household members, either directly from working household members or indirectly via remittances from absent household members. However, as shown in Table 10.12, the role of remittances as a source of income has decreased over time. Third, the burden of unemployment on the employed and the households hosting them has increased over time. The share of unemployed living in households with no connection to the labour market has markedly increased over time, as has the share of households containing an unemployed person. Lastly, the burden is apportioned unequally. A minority of households, many of which have little connection to the labour market themselves, house a majority of unemployed, while the majority of households are not affected.

How do the unemployed survive in households without labour market connections? Table 10.12 shows that the majority of those households receive social grants (which we discuss later). Thus the public safety net complements the private safety net and plays a large role in the support of the unemployed, despite the fact that the direct beneficiaries of social assistance are the elderly, the disabled, and children.

Our earlier inequality decomposition by income source showed that both the zero-earning households and the inequality of household wage income for those households that have such income are important drivers of overall inequality. We have given attention to the zero-earners above. Now we present some material on wage trends. Fallon (cited in Woolard and Woolard, 2007b) shows that racial earnings disparities declined substantially between 1970 and 1990. Figure 10.2 shows that this rapid convergence did not continue indefinitely. Since the late 1990s, there has been little change in the average ratio of African to white wages. If we use only the Labour Force Surveys (LFS) (which are not entirely comparable with the earlier October Household

Table 10.12. Percentage of households reporting grants as their main source of income and reporting any income from grants, by quintile

Quintile	% of households with grants as main income source					% of households reporting any income from grants					
	2002	2003	2004	2005	2006	1997	2002	2003	2004	2005	2006
1	16.1	16.9	21.4	39.6	47.7	15.9	32.0	31.7	40.2	47.7	69.4
2	31.4	36.1	44.0	49.5	51.0	54.0	55.8	50.9	71.2	73.3	69.9
3	31.1	34.0	42.2	38.1	34.5	46.7	51.6	53.2	67.1	69.1	69.4
4	18.1	19.5	16.7	14.3	16.0	33.8	33.2	34.8	35.8	40.1	45.4
5	4.4	4.2	3.5	2.8	2.5	14.0	11.3	7.9	8.8	10.0	12.0
Total	18.2	19.6	21.5	28.9	30.4	32.9	36.8	32.0	38.6	45.5	55.2

Source: Own calculations using 1997 October Household Survey and 2002, 2003, 2004, 2005, and 2006 General Household Surveys, Statistics South Africa.

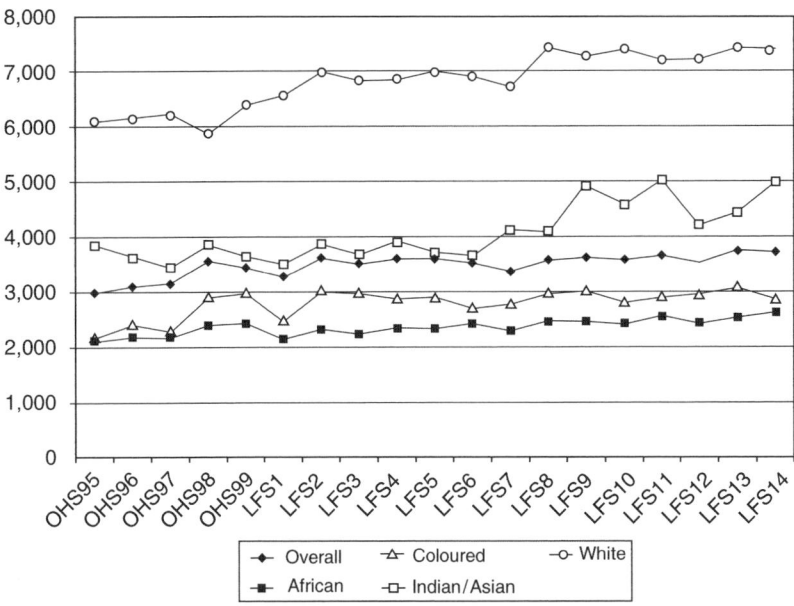

Figure 10.2 Average formal sector monthly earnings (in 2000 prices), by race: 1995–2005

Source: own calculations based on 1995–9 October Houselold Surveys and 2000–5 biannual Labour Force Surveys, Statistics South Africa.

Surveys (OHS)), the average ratio of African to white wages increased from 33 per cent in 2000 to 35 per cent in 2005.

Africans continue to be over-represented in lower skilled occupations where wages have grown more slowly than for higher skilled categories. In Figure 3 we show the average monthly wages of formal sector workers in different skill categories. The skill categories are based on the International Standard Classification of Occupations. Occupational group 1 (legislators, senior officials, and managers, which we refer to using the shorthand term 'managers') cannot be mapped onto a skill category and is thus kept separate. We further distinguish between managers with and without tertiary (i.e. a post-secondary school diploma or degree) qualifications since these are fundamentally different groups. Figure 10.3 shows the marked difference in wages between unskilled and skilled labour even within the formal economy. It also clearly demonstrates that there has been no convergence between the wages of lower versus higher skill categories since the mid 1990s.

It is clear from Figures 10.2 and 10.3 that even if the developments in the 1980s and over the post-apartheid period removed the vestiges of formal wage

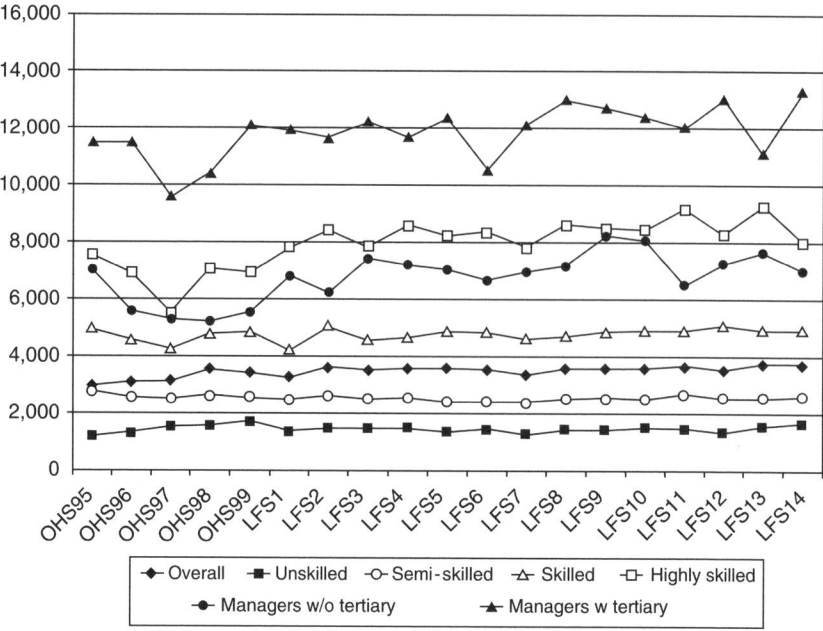

Figure 10.3. Average formal sector monthly earnings (in 2000 prices), by skill level: 1995–2005

Source: Own calculations based on 1995–9 October Household Surveys and 2000–5 biannual Labour Force Surveys, Statistics South Africa.

discrimination by race, lingering differences by race in education and skill levels and difference in the demand for labour by skill continue to ensure stark racial differences in earnings.

6. The impact of social assistance grants in reducing poverty

Our earlier discussions of money-metric poverty and our income source decompositions showed how important grants are for many households in South Africa. The South African social security system is notably well developed for a middle income country (Lund, 1993, van der Berg, 1997 and Case and Deaton, 1998). This fact can be ascribed to the way that the system developed under apartheid as a welfare state for whites and was then expanded under social and political pressure to incorporate other groups (van der Berg, 1997). The major grant types consist of the State Old Age Pension, the Disability Grant and the Child Support Grant. In this section we briefly describe the extent of the coverage of these grants before going on to illustrate their significance in reducing poverty (on the fiscal implications of changes in grant schemes post-transition, see Chapter 4).

The old age pension is available to women at the age of 60 years and to men at the age of 65 years. It is subject to a means test which is based on the income and assets of the applicant plus, if the applicant is married, the income and assets of the spouse. In 2007, the value of the grant was R870 per month which was roughly double the per capita income of the African population. More than 80 per cent of the elderly receive the pension. According to our estimates based on survey data, more than two-thirds of the recipients are women because they go into payment earlier than men and typically live longer.

The disability grant is the other large grant in terms of take-up. It is intended for disabled persons over the age of eighteen but below the age at which they would be eligible for the Old Age Pension. The means test is the same as for the Old Age Pension. The main criterion is that the person should be disabled to the extent that they are unable to support themselves. Permanent grants are awarded to those who are permanently disabled. Temporary grants are awarded for a shorter period, for example six months, to those who are expected to regain the ability to support themselves. Numbers for the disability grant have increased significantly over recent years, partly as a result of the HIV/AIDS pandemic (also see Chapter 9). Just over 1.4 million people currently receive some form of disability grant.

When the Child Support Grant was introduced in April 1998 it was intended to cover the poorest 30 per cent of children under the age of 7 and was means-tested, i.e. the child had to be residing in a household with a household income below a certain threshold. The threshold was set at R800 for children living in urban areas and at R1,100 for those living in rural areas or in informal settlements. In 1999, due to a low take-up rate, the means test was altered from a household based measure to one which considered only the income of the primary caregiver plus that of his/her spouse. Our estimates suggest that this change to the means test meant that more than two-thirds of age-eligible children were eligible for the Child Support Grant in 1999—more than twice as many as the intended 'poorest 30 per cent' that the grant was supposed to reach. We speculate that it was for this reason that the means test has remained unchanged in nominal terms since 1998, despite the fact that the Consumer Price Index rose 55 per cent between April 1998 and December 2007. About half of age-eligible children are currently in receipt of the grant.

The government has increased the age limit for eligibility in recent years. In April 2003 the age limit was raised to 9 years old and a year later this was increased to 11 years. In April 2005 the age limit was raised to fourteen. In January 2009 the age limit will be raised further to 15.

Some aspects of this system were inherited from the pre-democratic era. However, the post-apartheid state has been very active in reforming and adding to this system. There has been a rapid expansion in spending on social assistance over the last few years. While spending on education and health have remained fairly constant in real terms, consolidated expenditure on welfare and social security has increased from R23.6 billion (3.4 per cent of GDP) in 1997/8 to a projected R105.2 billion (4.6 per cent of GDP) in 2008/9 (National Treasury, 2008) By April 2007, 12.0 million people were benefitting from social grants. Of these, 2.2 million were receiving old age pensions, 1.4 million were receiving disability grants, and 7.9 million children were benefitting from child support grants.

Given this extensive reach and the importance of these grants in the budget, it is important to establish that the grants have strong anti-poverty impacts. Table 12 shows the percentage of households that report social grants as their main source of income. Prior to the introduction of the Child Support Grant, the major sources of grant income were the Old Age Pension and the Disability Grant. Because the value of these grants is large, access to either of these grants was sufficient to raise the per capita income of all but the largest households out of the bottom quintile. Consequently, in the 2002 data it can be observed that grants were twice as likely to be the main source of income in the second and third quintile than in the bottom quintile. By 2005, however, the Child Support Grant (of much lower monetary value than the Old Age Pension or Disability Grant) was reaching more than 9 million children in about 5 million households and we observe a substantial number of households in the bottom decile reporting grant income as their main source of income. There was a rapid roll-out of the Child Support Grant from 2000 onwards. Whereas in 1997 just under one-third of households were receiving a grant, by 2006 this percentage had risen to more than half. Most significantly, the percentage of households in the bottom quintile with access to social assistance rose from 16 per cent to 69 per cent between 1997 and 2006.

Table 10.12 tells a broad-brush picture of the significance of social transfers in directly reducing income poverty. Given that social transfers are targeted at the poor and spending on social transfers has grown rapidly in recent years it is unsurprising that these transfers have a direct effect on poverty by channelling cash into poor households. We have, however, not dealt here with the indirect effects of the grants in terms of their role in ameliorating the intergenerational transmission of poverty by permitting poor households to invest in better nutrition, health and education. There are a growing number of both qualitative and quantitative studies (reviewed in Budlender and Woolard, 2006) which demonstrate these indirect effects of the grants.

7. Conclusion

This chapter began by showing that the long-run development trajectory in South Africa has generated a society defined by very high inequality with a strong racial component. Historically this was the result of direct racial privileging in state policy; spanning direct racial interventions in the labour market as well as racial biases in determining where people were allowed to live and in education, health and social services expenditures. The intersections between these policies and a growing private sector economy serve as a prototypical model of inequality-perpetuating growth. Unfortunately such spatial and human capital inequities leave very long-run legacies and these processes are hard to reverse.

As a way of highlighting this central point, we have shown that a number of the overt racial policy prescriptions in the labour market and in spatial and social policy of high apartheid were deracializing in complicated ways for two decades before 1994. This incremental and uneven reform process was responsible for the observed decline in the importance of between-race inequality and the sharply increased importance of within-race inequality for each of South Africa's racial groups that started in the 1970s and has continued through to the present. These powerful forces should not have been expected to disappear at the dawning of democracy and, we have drawn on a number of analyses of post-1993 survey data to show that they have continued to influence our post-apartheid development path.

Clearly, fourteen years of post-apartheid transition has not been not enough time for these factors to work their way out of South African society. South Africa's high aggregate inequality has not fallen. Indeed, going into the future, South Africa's socio-economic dynamics still contain considerable inequality generating momentum despite a post-apartheid policy milieu that has explicitly taken on the task of addressing this legacy. The rest of the conclusions section attempts to look at the implications of this situation looking forward.

A demographic trend that will have a bearing on these dynamics going into the future is the fact that the African group accounts for 80 per cent of the population now and this share is rising. Thus, intra-African inequality and poverty trends are already and will increasingly dominate aggregate inequality and poverty trends. This is not to say that the country's racial footprint has gone. Indeed, we showed earlier that the between-race component of income inequality remains remarkably high by international norms and its decline has slowed since the mid 1990s. Moreover, the bottom deciles of the income distribution and the poverty profile are still dominated by Africans and racial income shares are far from proportionate with population shares. Nonetheless, South Africa's changing population shares imply that a policy focus on race-based redistribution will become increasingly limited in the future as the foundation for further broad-based social development. Rather, it would seem that a more dynamically sustainable direction lies in addressing seriously the increasing inequality within each race group and looking to ensure virtuous linkages in two directions. The first is that between employers of all races and economically active South Africans wanting to supply their labour into the labour market. The second is between the tax revenue being contributed by the employed of all races to the state for use on human capital, social welfare, and direct poverty alleviation interventions.

The forging of virtuous linkages in the labour market is not going to be easy. We have emphasized that the operation of the labour market has made effective policy making much harder for the post-apartheid government. Preceding 1994 there were two key drivers of household inequality; namely, the (rising) share of zero earners (the unemployed) in the labour market and the inequality in labour market earnings for those with jobs. We have shown that both dimensions of this situation have become more acute in the period to the present. This is a pervasive poverty issue. Unemployment is a strong marker of poverty in and of itself and, while a substantial share of the unemployed are connected to some labour market based income support through the wages and remittance income of other household members, these employed and remitters are likely to be the more poorly remunerated earners in households that are at the lower end of the earnings distribution.

Looking ahead, this serves to highlight two key labour market questions. How do people get employed and what determines earnings? In addressing both of these issues the demand-side of the labour market will be central as it will determine the number, type and location of jobs. Strong economic growth is a pre-condition for any job growth. However, the nature of contemporary economic growth has resulted in a shift in labour demand towards higher skilled persons in recent years. Thus, things have become harder for South Africans whose poverty traps them in rural areas with inferior educational opportunities. Self-employment and informal employment have received little attention in this chapter (see Chapter 11 for some discussion). This is not because such employment is unimportant. Indeed, it is clear that such employment will be called on to make a much larger contribution to total employment than it has in the past; especially given the skills twist in formal sector labour demand that we have described.

The contemporary situation is one in which the demand side of the labour market is looking for workers with ever-rising skills and, in particular, with stronger literacy and numeracy skills. State education policy is already crucial and is going to gain even more importance over the coming decades. The post-apartheid government has directed substantial resources at the education system and benefit incidence studies (e.g. van der Berg, 2006) show that these resources are well-targeted at those at the bottom of the income distribution. The impact of this policy is evidenced by rapidly increasing average years of education. These increases have been particularly impressive for Africans with average years rising from about seven years in 1993 to about ten years now (see Chapter 12). However, over the same period, the skill demands in the labour market have seen the returns to education fall for all education levels below complete secondary (twelve years).

Thus, there have been demonstrable policy successes but these have not led to improved outcomes or labour market prospects for any but the best educated young South Africans. Rather there is a rising tide of youth unemployment. Looking forward, government is being asked to put more teachers and school managers in classrooms all over the country, but these teachers and school managers are being required to be better than ever before. This is a tall order but remains central to facilitating the kind of broader based employment generation that is required to undergird the broader socio-economic transformation of South African society.

Poor Africans living in rural areas have borne the brunt of contemporary employment dynamics. That said, it is important to highlight a post-apartheid policy prong that has had a positive impact on rural poverty alleviation; namely, improved service delivery to the rural areas. Perhaps the inequality and poverty review in this chapter has been unfair to these mechanisms and achievements of post-apartheid policy. We have focused on money-metric poverty and inequality and largely ignored a literature (Leibbrandt et al., 2006; Bhorat et al., 2006; and Woolard and Woolard, 2007a) showing substantial improvements in access to services such as housing, water, and electricity over the post-apartheid period. Certainly rural areas have benefitted from many of these services and such improvements, along with the provision of improved roads and infrastructure are important in creating an environment in which the rural poor can better participate in available schooling and labour market opportunities. Thus, in many areas, these achievements offer the rural poor an improved platform for their future livelihood strategies. Improving the quality of life of rural households represents an important return in and of itself. However, a flow of high social returns into the future from these improvements would seem to be conditional on a vibrant labour market in the future.

Another area in which post-apartheid anti-poverty policy deserves credit is in the area of the expansion of social grants. Our discussion of the social grants has shown that the post-apartheid government has increased real expenditures and the budget share of this system. Moreover, these grants are well targeted at the poor. Indeed, the roll-out of the child support grant was seen to be a major reason for the fall in poverty since 2000.

In the light of the success of these grants, there are many that argue that the social grant system should be extended to focus directly on the rural unemployed who remain uncovered by other grants. However, it is important not to forget that the contemporary context is one of a massive post-2000 expansion of the grant's system. Further expansion in the future has to confront the issue of fiscal sustainability (see Chapter 4). Economic growth has supported the growth in the grants system and the high returns in terms of social well-being have justified this expenditure. The country confronts a tougher growth milieu over the medium term and this will place the existing system under strain. Clearly, the over-riding goal of economic and social policy has to be the assimilation of many more of the unemployed into the labour market and thus a positive employment environment is the key parameter for sustainable social transformation into the future.

References

Banerjee, A., Galiani, S., Levinsohn, J., and Woolard, I. (2006) 'Why Has Unemployment Risen in the New South Africa?' *CID Working Paper* 134. Harvard University.

Bhorat, H., Leibbrandt, M., and Woolard, I. (2000) 'Understanding Contemporary Household Inequality in South Africa', *Studies in Economics and Econometrics*, 24(3): 31–52.

Bhorat, H., Naidoo, P., and van der Westhuizen, C. (2006) 'Shifts in Non-income Welfare in South Africa, 1993–2004'. DPRU conference paper. 18–20 October, Johannesburg.

Budlender, D. and Woolard, I. (2006) 'The Impact of the South African Child Support and Old Age Grants on Children's Schooling and Work'. Study prepared for: International Programme on the Elimination of Child Labour International Labour Office.

Case, A. and Deaton, A. (1998) 'Large Cash Transfers to the Elderly in South Africa'. *Economic Journal*, 108: 1330–61.

Fedderke, J. W., Manga, J., and Pirouz, F. (2003) 'Challenging Cassandra: Household and Per Capita Household Income Distribution in the October Household Surveys 1995–1999: Income and Expenditure Surveys 1995 and 2000 and the Labour Force Survey 2000'. Unpublished mimeograph, University of the Witwatersrand.

Glewwe, P. (1986) 'The Distribution of Income in Sri Lanka in 1969–70 and 1980–81: A Decomposition Analysis'. *Journal of Development Economics*, 24: 255–74.

Hoogeveen, J. G. and Özler, B (2006). 'Poverty And Inequality in Post-Apartheid South Africa: 1995–2000'. In Bhorat, H. and Kanbur, R. *Poverty and Policy in Post-Apartheid South Africa.* Cape Town: HSRC Press.

Klasen S. and Woolard, I. (forthcoming) 'Surviving unemployment without state support: unemployment and household formation in South Africa. *Journal of African Economies.*

Leibbrandt, M., van der Berg, S., and Bhorat, H. (2001) 'Introduction'. In Bhorat, H., Leibbrandt, M., Maziya, M., Van der Berg, S. and Woolard, I. (eds.) *Fighting Poverty: Labour Markets and Inequality in South Africa.* Cape Town: UCT Press. pp. 1–20.

Leibbrandt, M., Poswell, L., Naidoo, P., and Welch, M. (2006) 'Measuring Recent Changes in South African Inequality and Poverty Using 1996 and 2001 Census Data'. In Bhorat, H. and Kanbur, R. (eds) *Poverty and Policy in Post-Apartheid South Africa.* Pretoria: HSRC Press.

Lerman, R., and Yitzhaki, S. (1994). 'Effect of Marginal Changes in Income Sources on U.S. Income Inequality'. *Public Finance Quarterly*, 22(4): 403–17.

Lund, F. J. (1993) 'State Social Benefits in South Africa'. *International Social Security Review* 46(1): 5–25

McGrath, M. D. (1983) 'Inequality in the Size Distribution of Personal Income in South Africa in Selected Years Over the Period from 1945 to 1980'. Unpublished PhD Dissertation, University of Natal Durban.

Meth, C. (2006) 'What Was the Poverty Headcount in 2004 and How Does It Compare to Recent Estimates by van der Berg et al?' *SALDRU Working Paper* 01/2006. School of Economics, University of Cape Town.

——(2007) 'Flogging a Dead Horse: Attempts by van der Berg et al to Measure Changes in Poverty and Inequality', *SALDRU Working Paper* 09/2007.

National Treasury (2008). *Budget Review 2008*. Pretoria: Government Printer.

Seekings, J. and Nattrass, N. (2005) *Class, Race and Inequality in South Africa*. New Haven: Yale University Press.

Shorrocks, A. F.(1984) 'Inequality Decomposition by Population Subgroups', *Econometrica*, 52:1369–88.

Simkins, C. (2005) 'What Happened to the Distribution of Income in South Africa between 1995 and 2001?' Unpublished paper. University of the Witwatersrand.

Statistics South Africa (1995) *Income and Expenditure Survey 1995*. Pretoria: Statistics South Africa.

——(2002) *Earning and Spending in South Africa. Selected Findings and Comparisons from the Income and Expenditure Surveys of October 1995 and October 2000*. Pretoria: Statistics South Africa.

United Nations Development Program (2004) *South Africa Human Development Report 2003: The Challenge of Sustainable Development*. UNDP South Africa: Oxford University Press.

van der Berg, S. (1997) 'South African Social Security under Apartheid and Beyond'. *Development Southern Africa*, 14(4): 481–503.

van der Berg, S. (2001) 'Trends in Racial Fiscal Incidence in South Africa'. *South African Journal of Economics*, 69(2): 243–68

van der Berg, S. (2006) 'Public Spending and the Poor in the Transition to Democracy'. In Bhorat, H. and Kanbur, R. 2006 *Poverty and Policy in Post-Apartheid South Africa*. Pretoria: HSRC.

van der Berg, S. and Louw M. (2004) 'Changing Patterns of South African Income Distribution: Towards Time Series Estimates of Distribution and Poverty'. *South African Journal of Economics*, 72(3): 546–72.

van der Berg, S., Burger, R., Burger, R., Louw, M., and Yu, D. (2005) 'Trends in Poverty and Inequality since the Political Transition'. A report prepared for the Office of the President. Department of Economics, University of Stellenbosch.

van der Berg, S., Louw, M., and Yu, D. (2008) 'Post-Transition Poverty Trends Based on an Alternative Data Source'. *South African Journal of Economics*, 76(1).

van der Merwe, T (1996) 'Bestaansbeveiliging: 'n Ekonomiese perspektief'. D.Litt. et Phil. Thesis. Pretoria: University of South Africa (UNISA).

Whiteford, A. and McGrath, M. (1994) *Distribution of Income in South Africa*. Pretoria: Human Sciences Research Council.

Whiteford, A. and Van Seventer, D. (2000) 'South Africa's Changing Income Distribution in the 1990s', *Journal of Studies in Economics and Econometrics*, 24(3): 7–30.

Woolard, I. and Woolard, C. (2007a) The Social and Human Development Context. In Kraak, A. (ed.) *Human Resources Development Review: Education, Employment and Skills in South Africa*. Pretoria: Human Sciences Research Council Press.

——(2007b) *Earnings Inequality in South Africa* 1995–2003. Pretoria: HSRC Press. ISBN 978-0796921734.

11

Unemployment: South Africa's Achilles' Heel

Geeta Kingdon and John Knight

1. Introduction[1]

At the time of democratization, 57 per cent of South African households reported the provision of jobs to be one of the three most important things the government could do for them (SALDRU, 1993). This reflected the high levels of joblessness in South Africa already existing at that time. This chapter examines the trends in unemployment since then and seeks to explain them. The issue is important because developments in the labour market and in the extent of joblessness may well hold the key to South African prosperity or penury. It is from the labour market that the income benefits from growing labour scarcity, or the threat to social and political stability from growing unemployment and underemployment, could emerge. Moreover, the South African labour market is of wider interest because its high unemployment, sharp labour market segmentation, and low non-farm informal sector employment make it an international outlier.

Our primary concern in this chapter is with unemployment and the informal employment that often disguises unemployment. However, in order to understand these phenomena it is necessary to take a broader view and to examine a range of labour market variables and relationships. We make use of the official representative household surveys that span the period of democracy. The earliest such annual survey is the October Household Survey 1995 (OHS95) and our end-date for most purposes is provided by the Labour Force Survey, September

---

[1] Acknowledgements: This chapter is a revised and extended version of Kingdon and Knight (2007). We are grateful to Rulof Burger for advice and assistance in updating the material, and to Haroon Bhorat, Daniela Casale, Stephan Klasen, Murray Leibbrandt, Nicoli Nattrass, and Dori Posel for comments. The views and opinions expressed are those of the authors alone.

2003 (LFS03). We consider the period after 2003 (LFS03—LFS07) separately. Comparisons over time are complicated by subtle changes in questions, definitions and sampling, and by reweighting in the light of new census data.[2] This hazard is somewhat diminished because the purpose of the chapter is not to examine year-to-year changes but to take a long-run view of labour market trends.

In its starkest terms, the issue is depicted in Table 11.1. The problem is that the economy is unable to absorb productively all the current labour force or all the increment to the labour force. In the near-decade after the advent of democracy (1995–2003), the narrow labour force grew by 4.6 million and the broad labour force (including the non-searching unemployed) by 6.3 million (by 4.2 and 4.8 per cent per annum, respectively). By contrast, over the same period, wage employment rose by only 1.3 million (1.8 per cent per annum), self-employment grew by 0.7 million (5.1 per cent per annum), and narrow and broad unemployment grew by 2.6 and 4.3 million respectively (both above 9 per cent per annum). Over that period the unemployment rate rose from 17 to 28 per cent on the narrow definition and from 29 to 42 per cent on the broad definition. South Africa thus has one of the highest rates of unemployment in the world even on the official narrow (but, as we shall explain, potentially misleading) definition.

The growing divergence between labour supply and demand inevitably had a depressing effect on market-determined real wages. However, the wage sector, and in particular the formal wage sector, was relatively protected, so pushing

Table 11.1. Summary of labour market outcomes, 1995–2003

	1995 OHS	2003 LFS	Change 1995–2003	
			000s	% p.a.
Labour force, narrow (000)	11,628	16,192	4,564	4.2
Labour force, broad (000)	13,667	19,954	6,287	4.8
Wage employment (000)	8,231	9,509	1,278	1.8
Self employment (000)	1,421	2,111	690	5.1
Unemployment, narrow (000)	1,976	4,570	2,584	11.0
Unemployment, broad (000)	4,015	8,332	4,317	9.6
Unemployment rate, narrow (%)	17	28	11	—
Unemployment rate, broad (%)	29	42	13	—
Real earnings in wage employment, 2000 prices	3,191	2,805	−386	−1.6
Real earnings in self employment, 2000 prices	6,866	2,610	−4,256	−11.4

Source: Tables 11.5 and 11.6.

---

[2] Such problems of the surveys are discussed in Bhorat (2002), Casale and Posel (2002), Devey et al., (2003), and Klasen and Woolard (1999).

the burden of adjustment onto the self-employment sector, especially that part of it which had relatively free entry. Whereas real wages fell by 1.6 per cent per annum over the period 1995–2003 (and formal sector real wages by 0.5 per cent per annum over the period 1997–2003), self-employment incomes fell dramatically in real terms, by 11.4 per cent per annum (and informal sector real wages by 7.8 per cent per annum over those six years). The growth of large parts of the informal sector—with underemployed people eking out a living—is a sign of labour market failure rather than of success.

The theoretical framework suggested by the evidence is that of a two-sector model characterized by labour market segmentation. The formal sector wage is set exogenously at a level above the market-clearing wage and the residual labour force is distributed between informal sector employment and unemployment. We must set this picture against the view that, given enough competition, the labour market will clear at the natural rate of unemployment, voluntarily chosen, and so unemployment should not go on rising and rising. Why has it risen? The superficial answer is labour market rigidities—whether they are due to trade unions, or bargaining councils, or profit-maximizing interventions by employers (the efficiency wage and labour turnover arguments as to why wages may be set above the market-clearing levels). In reality, however, it is the sheer speed of divergence between the growth of the labour force and the growth of formal sector employment (the divergence over the period 1997–2003 being nearly 4 per cent per annum) that is the underlying cause. This puts great strain on the necessary downward wage adjustment process and inevitably meets resistance. Nevertheless, the wage rigidities of the formal sector exacerbate the problem by narrowing the segment of the labour market on which the burden of adjustment is placed. Given constraints on the opportunities for profitable informal sector activities, the result has been rising unemployment.

Our general argument is that the rise in unemployment is best explained by the rapid growth in the labour force relative to the growth of formal sector employment, as a result of which the burgeoning residual labour force was absorbed either into the informal sector, which might disguise unemployment, or into open unemployment. Accordingly, we examine the growth of each of these variables in more detail: in section 2 the labour force, in section 3 formal sector employment, and in section 4 informal sector employment. Our main topic, unemployment, is covered in section 5. Section 6 updates the analysis by examining the period 2003–7 and poses the question: has a turning point now been reached? Section 7 concludes.

2. Labour force growth

The South African labour force has grown remarkably rapidly: over 4 per cent per annum is extremely unusual in international terms (Table 11.2). There

Table 11.2. South African population of working age, not economically active, labour force, and labour force participation rate, 1995–2003

	1995 OHS	2003 LFS	Change 1995–2003	
			000s	% p.a.
Population 15–65 (000)	24,232	29,917	5,685	2.7
Narrow measure				
Labour force (000)	11,628	16,192	5,464	4.2
Not economically active (000)	12,604	13,725	1,121	1.1
Labour force participation rate (%)	48	54	6	—
Broad measure				
Labour force (000)	13,667	19,954	6,287	4.8
Not economically active (000)	10,565	9,963	–602	–0.7
Labour force participation rate (%)	56	67	11	—

Source: Table 11.6.
Note: Labour force participation rate = (labour force)/(working age population).

are three possible explanations: in-migration, rapid natural increase in the number of working-age people, and increased labour force participation. In-migration is difficult to quantify as much of it is informal or illegal. Only part of the explanation is a rapid rate of increase in the adult population, whether due to natural increase or net in-migration. We see that this grew by 2.7 per cent per annum over the period 1995–2003 whereas the labour force grew by 4.2 per cent per annum on the narrow definition of unemployment and by 4.8 per cent on the broad definition. The labour force participation rate rose from 48 to 54 per cent (narrow) and from 56 to 67 per cent (broad). We cannot rule out the possibility that labour force growth is exaggerated by changing definitions, changing coverage, or sampling errors. Nevertheless, the labour force appears to have grown at a daunting pace.

Table 11.3 shows that the growth of the labour force has been the greatest among the African population group. The female participation rate rose by fully 15 percentage points and the male rate by over 5 percentage points in a mere eight-year period.[3] The increase in participation rates is due partly to the

---

[3] The Labour Force Surveys made a greater effort to capture informal work than did the previous October Household Surveys. Thus, some persons who worked very informally and who may previously have been classified as out of the labour force may now have counted as labour force participants. However, such a change would not lead to an increase in unemployment. The fact that unemployment rose so much suggests that the increase in labour force participation rates is not mainly due to the better capture of informal work. Moreover, as much as 13 of the 15 percentage point increase in the female participation rate occurred before the introduction of the LFS (Casale and Posel, 2002).

Table 11.3. Labour force participation rates (%), 1995–2003

	Males			Females			Total		
	1995	2003	Change % points	1995	2003	Change % points	1995	2003	Change % points
African	59.9	69.2	9.3	44.3	63.1	18.8	51.8	65.9	14.1
Coloured	72.1	75.7	3.6	55.4	64.8	9.4	63.5	69.8	6.3
Indian	75.7	77.3	1.6	39.2	51.9	12.7	57.2	64.3	7.1
White	72.1	79.8	7.7	47.9	61.5	13.6	59.9	70.4	10.5
All	65.9	71.1	5.2	47.8	62.8	15.0	56.4	66.7	10.3

Source: October Household Survey, 1995; Labour Force Survey, 2003.

lifting of apartheid restrictions on movement to urban areas and the new possibilities of employment that this was perceived to open. The better occupational attainment then possible for non-white groups and for women (partly due to employment equity legislation) is likely to have raised the expected returns to their employment. Educational levels have risen (as documented in more detail in Chapter 12) and participation rates typically increase with educational level, particularly so for women. The significantly greater increase in the female than the male participation rate appears to be due to a decline in women's access to male income on account of increased unemployment among males, the HIV epidemic creating more single parent households, and increased incidence of female headship resulting from changes in household structure.[4]

3. Formal sector employment

A distinction can be made between the formal sector (comprising firms that are formally registered) and the (unregistered) informal sector. The insider–outsider theory of labour economists is helpful here: formal sector employees can be regarded as 'insiders', and residual workers, comprising those in the informal sector (which serves as a residual labour 'sponge') and the unemployed, as 'outsiders'. South African insiders fall within the scope of the industrial relations regulations, including recognition of trade unions and collective bargaining, the right to strike, protection against dismissal, and minimum standards concerning hours of normal and overtime work, minimum wages,

---

[4] Casale and Posel (2002) show that, between 1995 and 2002, the percentage of working-age women living with at least one employed male in the household fell from 53 to 44 per cent, the incidence of female headship increased from 28 to 34 per cent, and the percentage of women reported to be married fell from 40 to 35 per cent.

and minimum leave provisions. There is provision for exemptions, generally granted on the basis of small scale and inability to pay. The informal sector workers fall outside the labour regulation system, and generally receive much lower income. The simple ratio of monthly income per worker of the formal to the informal sector in 2003 was 3.4 to 1 (Table 11.5); Kingdon and Knight (2004a) report that in 1993 this ratio was 3.5 to 1 but that after standardizing for the different average personal characteristics of workers in formal and informal sectors, the formal-informal earnings gap fell by between 50 and 64 per cent depending on whether OLS (ordinary least squares) or selectivity corrected earnings functions were used, i.e. the ratio was roughly halved, to about 1.75 to 1. Inevitably, in some respects, the two groups have conflicting interests and are in competition with each other.

The formal sector in South Africa possesses the characteristics of a middle-income country, whereas the informal sector has those of a poor, less developed country. Like other middle-income countries, especially those with a mineral economy, the formal sector has a comparative advantage in natural resource-intensive, or capital-intensive, or skill-intensive manufacturing. It cannot compete with the East Asian economies in low-wage unskilled-labour-intensive manufacturing. Moreover, any successful labour-intensive manufacturing by the informal or small-scale sector, leading to its growth, is likely to lead to its formalization.

There are two sources of information on formal sector employment: one based on the OHS and LFS household surveys, and the other based on the enumeration of employees in enterprise surveys. Both are prone to be inaccurate. The former can suffer from sampling error and the need to adjust figures periodically in the light of new population census estimates[5]. The latter suffer from non-reporting and may miss casual employees of registered enterprises. Table 11.4 shows formal sector non-agricultural employment in 1997 (the earliest year for which comparable figures are available) and for 2003. It is based on OHS and LFS sources. Formal sector employment increased by 702,000, implying an annual average rate of growth of 1.6 per cent. This figure

---

[5] Labour market data in South African household surveys are not without problems. Data collected in the early post-apartheid period are problematic for various reasons such as differing sampling, non-coverage of former 'homelands' in some surveys, small samples, etc. Moreover, comparability over time is undermined both by changing questions between the various surveys particularly as between the October Household Survey (OHS) and Labour Force Survey (LFS), and by changes in the way employment and unemployment are derived from the questions in the different surveys. The definition of the 'informal sector' also changed in 1997. Further, population estimates change at every census so that when the weights are revised in each 5-year period, recent statistics require re-estimation with the revised weights, and sometimes such revisions make a non-trivial difference to some statistics. Lastly, labour market data display some inexplicable large fluctuations from year to year. The figures presented here are thus not necessarily an accurate reflection of specific labour market numbers but rather a description of broad labour market trends.

is probably more accurate than the one obtained from the enterprise surveys, which capture employment only in the large- and medium-size businesses and show a fall in employment over that period. To some extent the trends were the result of structural changes in the economy: the long run decline of mining with its high labour-intensity, the trend towards capital-intensive and skill-intensive activities, and the capital- and skill-using nature of technical progress in various industries (Alleyne and Subramanian, 2001; Seekings et al., 2004). Employment in the informal sector grew more rapidly than in the formal sector, by 1,088,000, equal to 8.4 per cent per annum, but from a much smaller base. Similar results are obtained by comparing wage employment and self-employment over the period 1995–2003. Wage employment grew by 839,000, or by 1.3 per cent per annum. Self-employment grew more, and faster: by 991,000, or by 11.2 per cent per annum (again, from a smaller base). Agricultural employment—less accurately recorded, especially in subsistence agriculture—is shown separately; it rose very slowly. Overall, total employment increased by almost 2 million jobs, i.e. by 2.3 per cent per annum, over the eight years. However, we see that the formal and wage-employing sectors grew disappointingly[6], and that they lost ground to the lower-paying informal and self-employment sectors which, in their free-entry segments, served as a residual sponge.

Table 11.4. Formal and informal sector employment, wage- and self-employment, and total employment, 1995, 1997 and 2003 (000s)

	1995 OHS	1997 OHS	2003 LFS	Change 000	Change % p.a.
Non-agricultural					
Formal		6,839	7,541	702	1.6
Informal		1,750	2,838	1,088	8.4
Wage employment	7,845		8,684	839	1.3
Self employment	703		1,694	991	11.2
Agricultural	944		1,010	66	0.8
Total	9,631		11,579	1,948	2.3

Source: Casale et al. (2004), table 1.
Notes: For 2003, the authors use the March round of the Labour Force Study data. Estimates for 1995 and 1997 are weighted using the 1996 population weights and for 2003 using the 2001 population weights. Domestic service work is treated as informal sector wage employment.

[6] Although largely overlapping, wage employment does not equate with formal sector employment, nor self-employment with informal sector employment. For instance, casually employed workers may report themselves as working for a VAT-registered employer and thus count in the surveys as formal sector workers (Muller and Esselar, 2004).

Table 11.5. Real earnings (Formal and informal sector; wage and self-employment; and total) 1995, 1997, and 2003

				Percentage change			
				Total		Per annum	
	1995	1997	2003	1995–2003	1997–2003	1995–2003	1997–2003
Non-agricultural							
Formal		3,339	3,241		−2.9		−0.5
Informal		1,523	941		−38.2		−7.7
Large scale formal*				15.4	10.8	1.8	1.7
Wage employment	3,190		2,805	−12.1		−1.6	
Self employment	6,866		2,610	−62.0		−11.4	
Agricultural	690		608	−11.9		−1.6	
Total	3,014		2,360	−21.7		−3.0	

Source: Adapted from Casale et al. (2004: table 3)
Note: * from Annual Survey of Employment and Earnings.

Table 11.5 shows how real earnings behaved over the relevant period. We see that the real earnings of wage employees fell only slowly (by 1.6 per cent per annum) and those of formal sector workers even more gently (by 0.5 per cent per annum). In fact, the formal sector fall was confined to small employers: the data obtained from VAT-registered firms (effectively large and medium size employers) show a rise of 1.7 per cent per annum. We return to Table 11.5 for the analysis of the informal sector in section 5.

Collective bargaining appears to produce 'real wage resistance'. Kingdon et al. (2006) show that the union wage premium increased in South Africa between 1993 and 1999: even though unionized workers' wage fell a little in real terms, non-unionized wages fell more sharply. Thus, unionized workers are more insulated than non-unionized workers from the wage-depressing effect of labour market competition. This is consistent with another form of wage inflexibility noted by Kingdon and Knight (2006b). They examined the sensitivity of wages to unemployment across space by estimating 'wage curves' across neighbourhoods in South Africa, using the SALDRU 1993 survey. Whereas union wages were found to be unresponsive, non-union wages were sensitive, negatively, to variations in local unemployment rates.

It is apparent from Table 11.5, and also from estimated earnings functions, that much of the formal sector pays well above the level of competitively determined market wages. Do these relatively high wages adversely affect the level of employment in the formal sector? The wage-employment elasticity—the proportionate fall in employment that occurs in response to a unit proportionate rise in the wage rate—is therefore an important issue. It has attracted considerable research attention. A World Bank study (Fallon and Lucas, 1998) showed a long run weighted mean wage-employment elasticity for black workers in the formal sector of –0.71 (after three years, when adjustment was likely to be complete). This implies that a 10 per cent increase in the wage rate results, in due course, in a 7 per cent decrease in black employment. Other researchers (Bowles and Heinz,1996; Bhorat and Leibbrandt, 1998; Fields et al.,1999) have produced similar results.

The implication of these studies is that there is indeed a difficult policy trade-off between wages and employment. The 'real wage resistance' shown within the formal sector over the last decade has had a harmful effect on employment. However, it is also clear from the estimated elasticities that greater wage flexibility would have been unable to prevent the rise in unemployment. The problem is essentially the dynamic one of inadequate growth of formal sector labour demand in relation to the growth of labour supply. Those unable to find employment in the formal sector either remain in unemployment or enter informal sector employment.

4. Informal sector employment

Being the residual economic sector into which workers can in principle move, the informal sector can be predicted to have two features. First, it should have increased rapidly in response to the growing divergence between labour supply and formal sector labour demand. Secondly, its free-entry parts should contain a good deal of underemployment and poverty.

The informal sector, as defined by Statistics South Africa (StatsSA), absorbed a mere 16 per cent of the labour force in 1997. Although the figures are unreliable (Devey et al., 2002), the informal sector shows growth in recent years, with the proportion rising to 19 per cent in 2002. South Africa nevertheless remains an international outlier in the size of its informal sector. With the unemployment rate (on the narrow definition, for comparability) then 29 per cent, its ratio of informal sector non-agricultural employment to unemployment was a mere 0.7. By contrast, the averages for Sub-Saharan Africa, Latin America and Asia are 4.7, 7.0, and 11.9 respectively (Kingdon and Knight, 2004a, table 1, drawn from Charmes, 2000). It is possible that the definition of the informal sector used in South Africa is narrower than in other countries. StatsSA includes as 'informal worker' persons in own-account activities and those working for employers who are not VAT-registered. However, some employees of VAT-registered firms might also be informal in the sense that they are not well protected from market forces. Defining formal employees as only those receiving good treatment from employers (paid leave, pension rights, and unemployment insurance) or, failing that information, a formal contract, Posel (private correspondence) produced a formal/informal employment split of 41 to 59 per cent, to be compared with the StatsSA split of 72 to 28 per cent for LFS03. However, even with this adjustment, South Africa would still be an outlier: informal sector workers would still constitute only 34 per cent of the 2003 labour force, and the ratio of informal employment to *narrow* unemployment would be 34 : 28, i.e. 1.2 and to *broad* unemployment 34 : 42, i.e. 0.8.

It is argued in section 5 below that the bulk of unemployment is involuntary rather than voluntary, and that informal sector workers have both higher income and higher subjective well-being than do the unemployed. The implication is that unemployed workers should want to enter the informal sector. If they fail to do so, the implication is that there are barriers to entry. What are these barriers? There is a paucity of evidence on whether the informal sector is a free-entry sector. In a survey of 500 informal sector operators in the Johannesburg area in 1999, respondents listed crime, lack of access to credit, lack of access to infrastructure and services, and need for training as the top four constraints on their businesses. Chandra et al.(2002: 26, 30) find that the informal sector operators had required substantial start-up capital (averaging over 2.5 times the average monthly earnings in the sample). New small businesses have to rely on their own financial resources: there was very little access to formal or even informal credit. The 1999 survey suggests that government support continued to be inadequate, particularly in relation to crime prevention, investment in infrastructure, and the provision of credit and training facilities (Chandra et al., 2003: 18, 20, 44–5; table A2). 30 per cent of the informal businesses had been victims of crime in the previous year, but the number of respondents expressing concern was double that figure. The Johannesburg survey found that 81 per cent of all informal sector operators (and 90 per cent of the self-employed non-employers within that group) had never received any business assistance or training. The lack of training reflected the high cost: the few owners who had been trained had paid on average three times the average monthly earnings of the sample for their training. Sixty per cent of the operators did not have access to the 'small business support centres' that had been established by central and local government. Xaba et al. (2002: 25) argue that the South African government's avowed support for small, medium and micro enterprises (SMMEs) is concentrated on the formal sector and neglects the informal sector. However, such problems exist in most developing countries and do not explain why the South African informal sector is relatively so small.

One thing that might distinguish South Africa is the degree of effectiveness with which labour regulations are enforced. Labour market institutions such as Bargaining Councils and Wage Boards set sectoral minimum wages and stipulate working conditions in many industries, and these are applied to all firms in the industry and region, irrespective of size, *via* the 'extension' provision. There are serious penalties for flouting the agreements of these institutions (Moll, 1996; Nattrass, 2000). Such provisions impose a burden of high labour costs on small firms and it is likely that they do seriously inhibit the entry and growth of such firms. This is one explanation for the large average size of firms in South Africa.

These institutional features may inhibit small firms but they should not inhibit individual entrepreneurship, i.e., owner-operators. The lack of African self-employment is partly a legacy of apartheid. The apartheid system had repressed the informal activities of black South Africans through such restrictive legislation as the Group Areas Act, harsh licensing, strict zoning regulations, and effective detection and prosecution of offenders. Bouts of slum clearance and other periodic attacks on the illegal spaces within which informal enterprise thrived, served to rid South African cities of informal sector niches that were construed as hazardous to public health and stereotyped as unsightly and unsanitary (Rogerson, 1992). Although these restrictions have been progressively lifted since the mid 1980s, there were lingering licensing controls and restrictive bye-laws in many urban centres in the late 1990s. Moreover, repression and disempowerment of Africans under apartheid would have inhibited the development of entrepreneurial and social skills and of relevant social networks. These factors are important for confidence in entering the self-employed sector and for success in it.

Several authors note that many activities in the so-called informal sector of developing countries are highly stratified, requiring skills, experience and contacts, with identifiable barriers to entry. For example, petty trading often has highly structured labour and product markets with considerable costs of entry. Banerjee (1986) found that even in urban India, with its large self-employment sector, entry is not easy. Even when skill and capital are not required, entry can be difficult because of the presence of cohesive networks which exercise control over location and zone of operation. Support for these ideas also comes from Latin America. For instance, Maloney (1999, 2002) argues that informal sector workers tend to be older and to enter from the formal sector after they have accumulated knowledge, capital and contacts, and that lack of experience and capital are barriers to entry that deter participation in the informal sector. If such barriers are greater in South Africa, this might help to explain why the South African informal sector is so small.

There is considerable scope for the further development of a productive informal sector—comprising medium- and small-scale enterprises (SMMEs). These have the advantage of often being more labour-intensive than large scale enterprises, and of promoting black economic empowerment. The existing policy support to SMMEs in South Africa has focused on the provision of finance and facilities. However, while finance removes one obstacle, the SMME sector faces another, probably more important, obstacle to its development, namely unfair competition. The extension provision, which requires each Bargaining Council agreement about minimum wages and working conditions to be extended to all employers in the industry and area, puts SMMEs at a disadvantage, with crippling labour market burdens. Removing this provision would provide a boost to the development of the productive part of the self-employment sector in South Africa.

Informal sector non-agricultural employment grew rapidly in recent years—informal sector employment rose by 8.4 per cent and (overlapping) self-employment by 11.2 per cent per annum, though from a small base (Table 11.4). This was mainly due to the residual labour force crowding into activities such as petty trading and crafts, which are relatively free to enter. Support comes from Table 11.5: in the non-agricultural sector, real earnings in informal employment fell by 7.7 per cent and in self-employment by no less than 11.4 per cent per annum. Part of the recorded increase in employment and of the decrease in real earnings in the informal sector is the result of the attempt made in the LFS to extend the coverage of the informal sector to more marginal economic activities. For the most part, however, the burgeoning of informal activities in the sample surveys should be taken as evidence of the expansion of that part of the informal sector which is relatively easy for the unskilled to enter, and thus as a sign of economic failure rather than success.

5. Unemployment

5.1. The definition of unemployment

In South Africa two different concepts of unemployment are used routinely: the strict (narrow) and the expanded (broad) definition. The narrow definition applies a job-search test whereas the broad definition accepts as unemployed those who did not search for work in a four-week reference period but who report being available for work and say they would accept the offer of a suitable job. In 1998 the narrow concept was declared the 'official' definition of unemployment and it is now the one generally used. Yet it has been argued that the broad measure of unemployment is a more accurate reflection of joblessness than the narrow measure in South African conditions.

Kingdon and Knight (2006a), investigating the issue, use three new approaches to test whether, in conditions of high unemployment, the searching and non-searching unemployed states are distinct. They find, firstly, that in South Africa the non-searching unemployed are, on average, significantly more deprived than the searching. The fact that they are not better-off casts doubt on the interpretation based on tastes (lack of desire for employment) and favours the interpretation that active search is discouraged (low prospective returns to search). This view is supported by evidence from a job-search logit model, which suggests that search is hampered by poverty, by the cost of job-search from remote rural areas (almost uniquely in the world, South Africa has a higher rural than urban unemployment rate), and by high local unemployment. Secondly, the non-searching unemployed are not any happier than the searching unemployed: their unemployment depresses their subjective well-being to the same extent as is the case for the searching unemployed. Thirdly, evidence on the wage-unemployment relationship indicates that local wage determination takes non-searching workers into account as genuine labour force participants. The searching and the non-searching unemployed are very close in terms of potential labour supply. These findings indicate that lack of search is due to discouragement and to constraints such as poverty. The de-emphasis of the broad measure in policy circles may be because even narrowly measured unemployment is a large enough problem in itself, or because the searching unemployed are viewed as more deserving of policy concern.

5.2 The nature of unemployment

The high level of joblessness begs the question: why do the mass of the unemployed not join the informal sector, as in most other developing and middle-income countries? If the informal sector is an open-entry sector then, in principle, persons not entering it may be considered voluntarily unemployed. The dominant view of unemployment in developing countries is indeed that much open unemployment is due to search and is voluntary (Harris and Todaro, 1970), i.e. people choose to remain jobless while they search for a good job. If search for a formal sector job from the unemployed state is more efficient than from informal employment, those able to afford unemployment remain openly unemployed and engage in search. However, the poor cannot afford it. Thus, if most unemployment in the economy is of the voluntary search variety, the relationship between unemployment and household income is likely to be positive because the well-off will choose search unemployment but the poor will enter informal sector employment.

Kingdon and Knight (2004a) find little support for the idea that South Africans choose to be unemployed. The unemployed are, on average, substantially worse off than the informally employed—both in terms of income and expenditure and in terms of a range of indicators of well-being. This contradicts the search, or luxury, unemployment interpretation, whereby higher income raises the incentive to remain searching and reduces the incentive to obtain informal employment. Moreover, they find that the unemployed are substantially and significantly less happy than informally employed people, suggesting that their unemployment is not due to choice. Finally, the average duration of uncompleted spells of unemployment (2.2 years) is too long to sustain a person in search unemployment. The fact that the unemployed are significantly poorer and unhappier than the informally employed suggests that the failure of unemployed people to enter self employment is due to some barriers to entry into the informal sector.

Several papers have examined the labour supply response of adults in South African households that receive state old age pensions, pensions being an important source of income in many poor households. While Bertrand et al. (2003) find that pension income is associated with reduced labour supply of prime-age members of the household, Posel et al. (2006), using the same data and methods but widening the definition of the household to include non-resident members, find that the pension is positively associated with labour supply. They conclude that pension income facilitates the migration of household members to places of employment. Moreover, Edmonds et al.(2005) find that when an older woman becomes eligible for a pension, there is a fall in the number of co-resident women in their thirties. Thus, the pension enables the household to send out members to search for, and possibly find, employment. These results are consistent with the findings and interpretation of Kingdon and Knight (2006a) that unwillingness to search reflects a privately rational decision based on the perception of the benefits of searching in relation to the costs, and the ability to fund the search activity. Overall, the research on pensions does not provide support for the view that non-labour income encourages voluntary unemployment or withdrawal from the labour force. The fact that prime-age males tend to attach themselves to households in receipt of pension income (Klasen and Woolard, 2000) may simply reflect a propensity for endogenous household formation in conditions of hardship and involuntary unemployment.

It is arguable that some workers would be willing to accept a job only at an unrealistically high wage, and that this would suggest that they are voluntarily unemployed. Nattrass and Walker (2005) examine the proposition that the unemployed price themselves out of employment by requiring high wages, i.e. that their 'reservation wages' exceed the wages on offer. In a study of a working class area of Cape Town they find that workers' reservation wages are not out of line with the wages that they are predicted to earn on the basis of their characteristics: the ratio of reservation wages to predicted wages averaged 0.85 for unemployed persons and it exceeded 1.0 for only 1.3 per cent of them. This is further evidence against the view that unemployment is voluntary.

5.3. Is high unemployment a mirage?

Commenting on the official estimate of narrow unemployment, which then exceeded four million (giving an unemployment rate of 27 per cent), President Mbeki (2005) has stated that 'this is such a large number of people that nobody could possibly have missed the millions that would be in the streets and village paths 'actively looking for work' in all likely places of employment. It therefore seems quite unlikely that the StatsSA figure is correct'. A possible explanation is that 'employment' is underestimated, for instance because it excludes irregular or illegal work. In fact, a very broad definition of employment is used. The LFS03 asked all household members aged 15 or over whether in the last seven days, even for only one hour, they did any of a wide range of activities, including running any kind of business, working for a wage, even as a domestic worker and even in kind, helping unpaid in a household business, working on the household land or food garden, looking after livestock, etc. An affirmative answer to any of these questions was taken as employment.

On the contrary, it can be argued that narrow unemployment is underestimated, both because some of the workers recorded as employed are under-employed and because StatsSA's definition of search is too restrictive. First, according to the LFS03, 4 per cent of employed workers worked for no more than ten hours a week, and 10 per cent worked for no more than twenty-five hours a week. Secondly, in both the OHS and LFS the unemployed are asked whether they have taken any action to look for work in the relevant period, and only if the answer is yes are they asked about the method. A common method of job search is to wait to be called by friends or relatives: a respondent who does not regard this as 'action to find work' will not be asked about the method, and will be classified as a non-searcher. The existence of very high unemployment cannot be doubted, even if many of the unemployed are not publicly and visibly searching much of the time.

5.4. Unemployment, employment, and gender

Table 11.6 shows the increase in unemployment rates from 1995 to 2003. On the broad definition, which includes the 'discouraged workers', the unemployment rate rose from 29 per cent to 42 per cent, an increase of more than 12 percentage points. On the narrow definition, it rose by 11 percentage points, from 17 per cent to 28 per cent. Thus the extent of both searching and non-searching unemployment rose similarly: the problem is not only due to growth in the number of non-searchers.

The broad unemployment rate rose more for men (from 23 to 36 per cent) than for women (from 38 to 48 per cent). This differential rise (by 3 percentage points) is striking given that the labour force participation rate increased far more for women than for men. It is to be explained by the fact that, of the 1.97 million increase in the total number of employees, no fewer than 1.43 million were women (Table 11.6). Thus the remarkable increase in female labour force participation was at least in part a response to perceived new opportunities for employment. Assisted by the employment equity legislation, women were able to increase their share of (combined farm and non-farm) wage employment, from 35 per cent in 1995 to 44 per cent in 2003. Indeed, for men all net new employment during that period was in self-employment and none

Table 11.6. Unemployment and employment, by alternative definitions and by gender

	1995 (OHS)			2003 (LFS)			1995–2003 (change)		
	men	women	total	men	women	total	men	women	total
Broad unemployment									
Rate %	22.5	38.0	29.4	35.7	47.8	41.8	13.2	9.8	12.4
'000	1,710	2,305	4,015	3,529	4,753	8,332	1,869	2,448	4,317
Share %	42.6	57.4	100.0	43.0	57.0	100.0	43.3	56.7	100.0
Narrow unemployment									
Rate %	13.0	22.6	17.0	25.4	31.5	28.2	12.4	8.9	11.2
'000	879	1,097	1,976	2,187	2,382	4,570	1,309	1,285	2,594
Share %	44.5	55.5	100.0	47.9	52.1	100.0	50.5	49.5	100.0
Total Employment									
'000	5,892	3,760	9,652	6,436	5,187	11,622	544	1,427	1,970
Share %	61.0	39.0	100.0	55.4	44.6	100.0	27.6	72.4	100.0
Wage employment									
'000	5,379	2,852	8,231	5,302	4,207	95,09	–77	1,355	1,278
Share %	65.4	34.6	100.0	55.8	44.2	100.0	–6.0	106.0	100.0
Self employment									
'000	513	908	1,421	1,134	977	2,111	621	69	690
Share %	36.1	63.9	100.0	53.7	46.3	100.0	90.0	10.0	100.0

Source: October Household Survey, 1995; Labour Force Survey, September 2003.
Note: Agricultural workers are included in wage employment.

in wage employment. Women maintained their share of total unemployment over the eight years, at 57 per cent of the total.

5.5. Changes in the incidence of unemployment

Although the absolute level of unemployment may be determined largely by macroeconomic forces, it is nevertheless relevant to know the characteristics of the workers who end up unemployed. Table 11.7 presents, for both 1995 and 2003, the actual proportions of people in various categories who are unemployed, the coefficient on each characteristic in an estimated probit equation predicting unemployment as opposed to employment, and the marginal effect of that characteristic. For instance, we learn from the first row that 36.9 per cent of African workers were unemployed in 1995, that the incidence of unemployment was significantly higher than for whites, and that, holding all other observed characteristics constant, Africans had a higher probability of being unemployed than whites, of 29.6 per cent. The actual increase in the

Table 11.7. Binary probits predicting unemployment, 1995 and 2003

	1995 (OHS)			2003 (LFS)			1995–2003 (change)	
	U rate	marginal effect		U rate	marginal effect		U rate change % point	marginal effect
Race								
African	36.9	0.296	**	48.8	0.361		11.9	6.5
Coloured	22.2	0.211	**	29.4	0.275	**	7.2	6.4
Indian	13.2	0.076	**	20.7	0.163	**	7.5	8.7
White (base)	5.3	—		7.6	—		2.3	—
Gender								
Male	22.5	−0.144	**	35.7	−0.129	**	13.2	1.5
Female (base)	38.0	—		47.8	—		9.7	—
Education								
None (base)	35.0	—		33.8	—		−1.2	—
Primary	36.3	−0.001		44.7	0.057	**	8.4	5.8
Junior	32.8	0.005		47.4	0.068	**	14.6	6.3
Secondary	27.3	−0.047	**	44.9	0.030	**	17.6	7.7
Higher	6.0	−0.225	**	13.0	−0.211	**	7.0	1.4
Age								
16–20 years	59.4	0.450	**	76.7	0.476	**	17.3	2.6
21–25 years	45.8	0.305	**	66.2	0.386	**	20.4	8.1
26–35 years	30.4	0.118	**	43.1	0.174	**	12.7	5.6
36–45 years (base)	20.6	—		28.3	—		7.7	—
46–55 years	17.6	−0.028	**	23.4	−0.056	**	5.8	−2.8
56–64 years	11.9	−0.089	**	15.8	−0.124	**	3.9	−3.5
Region								
Rural (base)	37.9	—		49.7	0.018	**	11.8	−3.5
Urban	24.1	0.053	**	36.8	—		12.7	—

Notes: The dependent variable is being broadly unemployed, with the alternative as being employed.
** represents significance at the 1% level.

African unemployment rate (11.9 percentage points) represented a 9.6 percentage point increase over the white rate. This was due partly (3.1 percentage points) to the white possession of different average characteristics and partly (6.5 percentage points) to the pure effect of race or of unobserved characteristics correlated with race.

In 1995 possession of secondary and of higher education provided strong protection against unemployment: they reduced the chances of unemployment by 4.7 and 22.5 percentage points respectively vis-à-vis those with no education. However, by 2003 secondary education actually raised the relative probability of unemployment, by 3.0 percentage points. Relative to those without education, the chances of unemployment of workers with primary, junior, and secondary education had all increased by some 6–8 percentage points. Although the actual unemployment rate of graduates from higher education rose from 6.0 to 13.0 per cent over the eight years, the standardized increase (given that the unemployment rate of the tiny group without education fell by 1.2 per cent) was a mere 0.2 per cent.

Given that the omitted category in the dummy variable analysis is the age group 36–45, we see that, in both years, there is a monotonic fall in the standardized probability of unemployment as age increases. Moreover, relative to the reference group, between 1995 and 2003 the probability of unemployment rose for those aged 35 and under, and fell for those aged 46 and over. The problem of unemployment is worst for the young, and has become more so. Whereas older workers are often incumbents whose jobs are protected by firm-specific human capital or by legislation, new entrants to the labour market bear the brunt of labour market competition. Province dummies are included but not shown. Over the eight years the unemployment rate rose most rapidly in Gauteng, probably reflecting its attraction to rural-urban migrants. Relative to Gauteng, the standardized unemployment rate fell in almost all of the other provinces.

5.6. Changes in the duration of unemployment

There are effectively no panel data available on labour force participants in South Africa. While the Labour Force Surveys were intended to provide a rotating panel, the person identifiers are not coded in such a way that they can enable the user to achieve reliable matching of individuals from one round to another (Hertz, 2005). Consequently, there are no satisfactory data on unemployment duration in South Africa. What is available is the length of uncompleted spells of unemployment of those currently narrowly unemployed. While they understate the true duration of unemployment, uncompleted spells are suggestive. However, even this information is deficient: the data are in categorized rather than continuous form and the categories are not sensibly distributed (for more analysis see Kingdon and Knight, 2004b). We merely note that the percentage of persons whose uncompleted duration of unemployment was greater than three years rose by 4.6 percentage points between 1995 and 2003, from 32.5 to 37.1 per cent of the total. The growth of long term unemployment meant that the unemployment problem was exacerbated in this additional dimension.

6. Has unemployment turned the corner?

Table 11.8 reproduces roughly the same evidence as Tables 11.1 and 11.2 for the subsequent four years, 2003–7. The shorter the period being considered, the more susceptible is the recorded trend to measurement error in the

Table 11.8. Summary of labour market outcomes, 2003—7

	Sept. 2003	Sept. 2007	Change Sept. 2003—Sept. 2007	
			Absolute	% p.a.
Population 15–65 (000)	28,938	30,413	1,475	1.3
Men	13,997	14,682	685	1.2
Women	14,941	15,708	767	1.3
Labour force participation rate, broad measure (%)	68	68	0	—
Men	73	73	0	—
Women	63	63	0	—
Labour force, narrow (000)	15,858	17,178	1,320	2.0
Labour force, broad (000)	19,631	20,603	972	1.2
Men	10,166	10,684	518	1.3
Women	9,465	9,919	454	1.2
Total employment (000)	11,424	13,234	1,810	3.7
Unemployment, narrow (000)	4,434	3,945	−489	−2.9
Unemployment, broad (000)	8.208	7,370	−838	−2.7
Unemployment rate, narrow (%)	28	23	−5	—
Unemployment rate, broad (%)	42	36	−6	—
Real earnings in formal employment	2,865	3,349	484	4.0
Real earnings in informal employment	619	868	249	8.8
Real earnings in informal self-employment	1,052	1,140	88	2.0

Source: Labour Force Survey, September 2003 (taken from StatsSA, 2005, Revised Estimates); Labour Force Survey, September 2007 (taken from StatsSA, 2008).

Note: This table uses Statistics South Africa's *revised* estimates for Labour Force Survey of September 2003, taken from the historical series of revised estimates (StatsSA, 2005) i.e. revised to reflect the new population estimates released in February 2005. Thus, the labour market numbers for September 2003 in this table differ somewhat from those presented in earlier tables. Real earnings are shown in 2000 prices. Observations with zero earnings or earnings over R200,000 a month are excluded.

end-years. Nevertheless, there are sharp contrasts with the previous eight years. Unemployment actually declined, and the unemployment rate fell by 6 percentage points, to 36 per cent, on the broad measure and by 5 percentage points, to 23 per cent, on the narrow measure. Has unemployment turned the corner? In order to judge whether this is a sustainable new trend we need to understand the reasons for the change.

In the earlier period (1995–2003, shown in Tables 1 and 2), the annual growth of total employment (wage- plus self-employment) averaged 2.3 per cent. With GDP growth at 5 per cent per annum over the four years 2003–7[7], total employment grew by 3.7 per cent per annum—i.e. 1.4 percentage points faster than in the previous period. The growth rate of adult population, now

---

[7] Chapter 2 in this volume identifies macroeconomic stability, the commodity price boom and increase in capital flows as the major factors behind this improved economic growth rate in the recent past.

1.3 per cent per annum, was also down by 1.4 percentage points. By contrast, the annual average growth rates of the broad and narrow labour force were 1.2 and 2.0 per cent, i.e. down by no less than 3.6 and 2.2 percentage points respectively. The table shows that broad unemployment rate (36 per cent in 2007) had fallen by 6 percentage points over the four years and the narrow rate (23 per cent) by 5 points. The fall in unemployment came more from the supply side than from the demand side. But that raises the question: is it plausible that labour force growth could have decelerated so rapidly?

Far from providing an explanation, one recent development would have increased the labour force and exacerbated the unemployment problem. Over the 2000s, there has been a growing influx of Zimbabweans as economic conditions in that country have deteriorated and its people have had increasingly to rely for survival on foreign remittances. Insofar as many of the arrivals are illegal, they are unlikely to be much represented in household surveys or population censuses, so that their growing presence is not reflected in the recorded labour force. Nevertheless, they will have intensified the competition for jobs and thus raised unemployment among South Africans. If there are at least a million Zimbabwean workers now present, as some commentators have suggested, this influx serves to offset over half of the growth of total employment (1.8 million) over the period 2003–7. The recorded fall in unemployment over that period is thus even more remarkable.

Wage behaviour can be both cause and consequence of changes in labour supply and demand. According to the Labour Force Surveys, between 2003 and 2007 the real mean earnings of formal employees rose annually by 4.0 per cent, those of informal employees by 8.8 per cent, and those of the informal self-employed by 2.0 per cent (Table 8). The continued rise of formal sector wages in the face of high unemployment no doubt reflects wage bargaining. The rise of informal sector incomes is more difficult to explain: it might reflect either labour market tightening or improved qualifications as the educated trickled down into lesser jobs. For instance, the proportion of unskilled workers without secondary education fell from 53 per cent in 2003 to 42 per cent in 2007.[8]

The sharp fall in the growth of the adult population raises doubt about the accuracy both of the labour force survey statistics and of the extrapolations from the six-monthly sample surveys to national figures. Nevertheless, it is likely that there was indeed a slowdown in the growth of the labour force in very recent years and that it was at least partly due to the spread of HIV/AIDS. Looking to the future, it is necessary to consider the likely effect of the HIV/AIDS epidemic. By way of illustration, we draw on the results of a particular study (Quattek, 2000). For the population as a whole, HIV infection rates were forecast to peak at 17 per cent in 2006 and AIDS-related deaths about 5 years

---

[8] Chapter 12 provides detailed analysis of the quantity and quality of education in post-apartheid South Africa.

later, when the AIDS mortality rate will be 1.8 per cent. However, the peak HIV infection rate will be higher for economically active people, at 26 per cent. In the absence of AIDS, the growth of the labour force would be 1.9 per cent per annum over the decade 2003–2013, but in the AIDS-inclusive scenario it is forecast to be 1.1 per cent per annum. Because the rate of growth of the economy is sure to be adversely affected in various complex ways by the epidemic, we cannot simply subtract the projected slower growth of the labour force in order to measure the effect on unemployment. Any projection would have to be based on numerous untestable assumptions. The study by Quattek (2000), which projects employment growth as slower by 1.2 per cent per annum over the decade 2003–2013 on account of the disease, and unemployment to be 9.2 percentage points lower than it would otherwise be in 2013, suggests the possible orders of magnitude. Similarly, Smit and Ellis (2008, table 4), in this volume, estimate that by 2010 the employment level will be 1.8 per cent lower in the HIV/AIDS than in the non-HIV/AIDS scenario and the narrow unemployment rate 6.2 percentage points lower, the corresponding figures for 2020 being 6.2 per cent and 12.3 percentage points respectively. However, Nattrass (2003) cautions that the various models of the impact of HIV/AIDS in South Africa lead to differing or even conflicting predictions for the labour market.

7. Conclusions

The legacy of history continues to have long term effects on the labour market. Economic stagnation in the two decades before democracy, the extreme economic inequality, and the development of a powerful trade union movement, all continue to have their impact today. Since it took office, the ANC government has had little political and economic room to manoeuvre in its economic policies (Gelb, 2004). The two basic policy choices were: what points on the trade-off between economic efficiency and social equity, and between long and short run benefits, to choose? The government has resisted the calls of populism and has tended to stress efficiency and long term considerations in most areas of economic policy (such as trade liberalization, deregulation, and the encouragement of the private sector) that underlie its general macroeconomic strategy—the GEAR. Nevertheless, the labour market outcomes of this set of policies have been unsuccessful. That raises the broad question: to what extent are the general economic policies and to what extent are labour market policies to blame for this? Our argument is that the two are intertwined: labour market policies can have adverse effects in themselves but they can also reduce the effectiveness of the GEAR policies.

There is potential for an economy to enter a virtuous circle of economic growth or get caught in a vicious circle of relative stagnation. During the democratic period South Africa has been on a knife-edge: the economy could go either way. Although the improving long run world prospects for primary commodities are tilting the balance favourably, the danger remains that low business confidence and inadequate investment make things worse in the labour market, which in turn by various processes of cumulative causation feeds through into self-fulfilling pessimism about the economy. Despite the relative success of the economy in various other dimensions, unemployment remains South Africa's Achilles' Heel.

In explaining the rise in unemployment and its possible cures, we placed our emphasis on the slow growth of the economy, and thus slow growth in the demand for labour relative to the rapidly growing supply, and the need above all else to pursue economic policies to help raise the economic growth rate. The rapid divergence in the supply and demand for labour until the early 2000s placed a great burden of adjustment on the labour market, which would put a great strain on even the most flexible of labour markets. In fact, it appears that major segments of the South African labour market are not flexible. This imposes an excessive burden on the more flexible segments, the result of which has been rising unemployment.

The system of labour market governance that has been put in place over the first decade of democracy has been built on consensus and co-operation. However, it has involved largely government, formal sector employees, and employers. Another party, potentially affected but not adequately represented in developing the consensus on governance, is the growing number of informal sector poor and the unemployed poor. The system embodied in the various pieces of legislation—such as the Labour Relations Act of 1995, the Basic Conditions of Employment Act of 1997, and the Employment Equity Act of 1999—establishes a framework which would be appropriate, indeed admirable, in a fully employed economy with little labour market segmentation. It is arguably less appropriate in South African conditions of unemployment and extreme labour market segmentation. The danger is that in protecting the rights of formal sector workers, the legislation and its implementation harms the interests of those outside the formal sector. Well-intentioned labour laws can have unfortunate unintended labour market consequences. In particular, they may discourage employment (a static effect) and discourage investment (a dynamic effect). It is an uncomfortable fact that a government which espouses trade liberalization must be prepared when necessary to espouse also a good degree of labour market liberalization.

The measurement of potential ill-effects of labour legislation is difficult, and well-established research results on this issue are not yet available. It is certainly the case, however, that many employers complain about various constraints on their decisions such as the legal and procedural requirements with respect to hiring and firing of workers, the extent of union power to raise wages or disrupt production, the extension of bargaining agreements, and the 'hassle factor' arising from the labour relations legislation. While it is natural for survey respondents to stress the importance of things they dislike, complaints of this sort should not be ignored. If acted upon, these complaints can result in hiring fewer workers, substituting capital for labour, diverting managerial resources from the main task, depressing business optimism and discouraging investment. In this way the inflexibilities of the labour market may exacerbate not only income inequalities but also the underlying problem of inadequate employment creation. It is true that efficient managers can be expected to try to circumvent the problems that they perceive, for instance by hiring casual workers and employing sub-contactors. This behaviour can reduce the problems but not remove them.

It is beyond the scope of this paper to examine the many determinants of poverty including the effects on poverty of trends in the labour market (see Chapter 10 for a discussion on these issues). Nevertheless, the evidence is consistent with our view that the remarkable increase in unemployment in both open and disguised form, and the associated fall in real earnings in the less protected parts of the labour market, have raised the number of households in poverty. For instance, between 1995 and 2003 the average real earnings of all workers fell by 22 per cent (Table 11.5). While the magnitudes of the estimates differ, there is a general consensus that poverty rose over the post-apartheid period. This is reflected in a number of studies using different surveys, questions, levels of aggregation, time periods, and methods (Hoogeveen and Özler, 2004; Casale et. al., 2004; Leibbrandt et al., 2005; van de Ruit and May, 2003; Meth and Dias, 2004; van der Berg and Louw, 2003; Leibbrandt et al., current volume).

There is empirical evidence that crime has increased in South Africa at the same time as unemployment has risen (SAPS, 2004; Masuku, 2003). For instance, the SAPS website shows that between 1994/5 and 2003/4 reported common robbery was up by 193 per cent and reported burglary of residential premises by 29 per cent. The rise in unemployment and in poverty may force more people into illegal ways of getting income. A World Bank survey of 600 firms in Durban in 2002/3 (Devey et al., 2003) found that crime and theft were listed as the biggest constraint on firm growth. This might produce another vicious circle: a higher crime rate can reduce prospective profits, sap business confidence, and lead to a brain drain. Economic growth, and thus the labour market outturn, can therefore suffer.

The South African government has produced two main types of active labour market policy: public works programmes, and skill development programmes. These are examined in Kingdon and Knight (2007). The lack of systematic evaluation makes judgment difficult, but the authors reached the conclusion that neither type of policy intervention has substantially reduced unemployment. Impact evaluation studies inevitably have methodological limitations. For instance, do the programmes create employment or merely redistribute it? Nevertheless, well conducted evaluation studies would assist policy design, especially if an expansion of active labour market policies is envisaged.

The main policy conclusions emerging from the paper are three-fold. Firstly, if labour market statistics are to be used effectively for policy purposes, their deficiencies and problems need to be addressed by means of thorough interaction among StatsSA, policy-makers, and independent researchers. Despite the statistical progress of the last decade, the lack of appropriate data hinders the analysis of important issues that impinge on unemployment.[9] Secondly, labour market regulations require reconsideration, giving greater weight to the concerns of employers and investors, and also to the interests of those—the unemployed and informally employed poor—who are beyond the reach of the labour institutions but can be hurt by them nevertheless. For instance, the removal of the provision for the extension of Bargaining Council agreements to all (including small) employers might well promote the SMME sector by removing the burden of high labour costs on small firms. Lastly but most importantly, it is crucial to pursue a set of policies that promote the rate of economic growth. Government should bear constantly in mind the growth implications of all its policies—whether these are general economic policies, or labour market policies, or even policies on international relations (such as those on relations with Zimbabwe), crime or health (e.g. on HIV/AIDS).

The fall in the unemployment rate over the period 2003–7 raises the possibility that unemployment has turned the corner. The reason for the fall can be traced partly to the faster growth of employment in recent years but mainly to the slower growth of the adult population and of the labour force. This in turn is likely to be the result of the spread of HIV/AIDS among the population. Being highly sensitive to periodic revisions, the various labour market indicators are not sufficiently consistent for us to be confident that the new trend will continue into the future. In any case, no comfort can be drawn if one great scourge is merely being replaced by another.

References

Alleyne, T. and Subramanian, A. (2001) 'What Does South Africa's Pattern of Trade Say about its Labor Market?', *IMF Working Paper*, no. 01/148, October.

Banerjee, B. (1986) *Rural to Urban Migration and the Urban Labour Market: A Case Study of Delhi*, Bombay: Himalaya Publishing House.

---

[9] For instance, at present we know little about entry into, exit from, and duration of unemployment: these and many other issues are best analysed by means of a panel survey. The questions about job search, and their sequencing, can lead to too restrictive a definition of search. There are no reliable data on reservation wages. Discrepancies from one (six-monthly) Labour Force Survey to another raise doubts about the reliability of the survey or of the extrapolation from sample to the national figures.

Bertrand, M., Mullainathan, S., and Miller, D. (2003) 'Public Policy and Extended Families: Evidence from Pensions in South Africa', *World Bank Economic Review*, 17(1): 27–50.

Bhorat, H. (2002) 'Employment and Unemployment Trends in Post-Apartheid South Africa', paper prepared for the Presidency 10-Year Cabinet Review Process, 2nd Draft.

Bhorat, H. and Leibbrandt, M. (1998) 'Estimates of Wage-Employment Elasticities for South Africa', unpublished.

Bowles, S. and Heinz, J. (1996) 'Wages and Jobs in the South African Economy: an Econometric Investigation', Department of Economics, University of Massachusetts.

Casale, D. and Posel, D. (2002) 'The Continued Feminisation of the Labour Force in South Africa: An Analysis of Recent Data and Trends.' *South African Journal of Economics*, 70(1): 156–84.

Casale, D., Muller, C., and Posel, D. (2004) 'Two Million Net New Jobs: A Reconsideration of the Rise in Employment in South Africa, 1995–2003', *South African Journal of Economics*, 72(5): 978–1002.

Chandra, V., Nganou, J., and Noel, C. (2002) 'Constraints to Growth in Johannesburg's Black Informal Sector: Evidence from the 1999 Informal Sector Survey'. *World Bank Report*, no. 24449-ZA, June.

Charmes, J. (2000) 'Informal Sector, Poverty and Gender: A Review of Empirical Evidence'. Background paper for World Development Report 2001. Centre of Economics and Ethics for Environment and Development, University of Versailles-St Quentin en Yvelines.

Devey, R., Skinner, C., and Valodia, I. (2002) 'The Informal Economy in South Africa: Who, Where, What and How Much?'. Paper presented to the DPRU Conference on Labour Markets and Poverty in South Africa, Johannesburg, 22–4 October, 2002.

Devey R., Valodia I., Rajaratnam B., and Velia M. (2003) 'Constraints to Growth and Employment: Evidence from the Greater Durban Metropolitan Area'. Trade and Industry Policy Secretariat (TIPS) and Development Policy Research Unit (DPRU) Conference, Pretoria.

Edmonds, E., Mammen, K., and Miller, D. (2005) 'Rearranging the Family? Household Composition Response to Large Pension Receipts', *Journal of Human Resources*, 40(1): 186–207.

Fallon, P. and Lucas, R. (1998) 'South Africa: Labor Markets, Adjustment, and Inequalities', *Discussion Paper*, no. 12, Informal Discussion Papers on Aspects of the Economy of South Africa, Southern Africa Department, World Bank, Washington D.C.

Fields, G., Leibbrandt, M., and Wakefield, J. (1999) 'Key Labour Market Elasticities in South Africa', report commissioned by the South African Department of Finance.

Gelb, Stephen (2004) 'Inequality in South Africa: Nature Causes and Responses', The Edge Institute, Johannesburg.

Harris, J. and Todaro, M. (1970) 'Migration, Unemployment, and Development: A Two-Sector Analysis'. *American Economic Review*, 60(1): 126–42.

Hertz, T. (2005) 'The Effect of Minimum Wages on the Employment and Earnings of South Africa's Domestic Service Workers', *Upjohn Institute Working Paper* 05-120. American University, August.

Hoogeveen, J. and Özler, B. (2004) 'Not Separate, Not Equal: Poverty and Inequality in Post-Apartheid South Africa', World Bank mimeo, presented to the NEUDC Conference, Montreal, October.

Kingdon, G. and Knight, J. (2004a) 'Unemployment in South Africa: The Nature of the Beast', *World Development*, 32(3): 391–408.

Kingdon, G. and Knight, J. (2004b) 'Race and the Incidence of Unemployment in South Africa', *Review of Development Economics*, 8(3): 198–222.

Kingdon, G. and Knight, J. (2006a) 'The Measurement of Unemployment when Unemployment is High', *Labour Economics*, 13(3): 291–315.

Kingdon, G. and Knight, J. (2006b) 'How Flexible are Wages in Response to Local Unemployment in South Africa?', *Industrial and Labor Relations Review*, 59(3): 471–95.

Kingdon, G. and Knight, J. (2007) 'Unemployment in South Africa, 1995–2003: Causes, Problems and Policies', *Journal of African Economies*, 16(3): 813–48.

Kingdon, G., J. Sandefur, and F. Teal (2006) 'Labour Market Flexibility, Wages and Incomes in Sub-Saharan Africa in the 1990s', *African Development Review*, 18(3).

Klasen, S. and I. Woolard (1999) 'Levels, Trends, and Consistency of Employment and Unemployment Figures in South Africa,' *Development Southern Africa*, 16: 3–36.

—— (2000) 'Surviving Unemployment Without State Support: Unemployment and Household Formation in South Africa', *IZA Discussion Paper*, no. 237, Institute for the Study of Labor, Cologne, Germany.

Leibbrandt, M., Levinsohn, J. and McCrary, J. (2005) 'Incomes in South Africa Since the Fall of Apartheid', draft mimeo, May. University of Cape Town and University of Michigan.

Maloney, W. (1999) 'Does Informality Imply Segmentation in Urban Labor Markets? Evidence from Sectoral Transitions in Mexico'. *World Bank Economic Review*, 13: 275–2.

—— (2002) 'Informality Revisited'. Mimeo, World Bank.

Masuku, S. (2003) 'For Better and for Worse: South African Crime Trends in 2002', *South Africa Crime Quarterly*, 3 (March)

Mbeki, T. (2005) 'DRC: Forward Ever, Backward Never!: Letter from the President', *ANC Today*, 5(20) 20–6 May.

Meth, C. (2005) 'Unemployment for Beginners: Being a Catalogue of some of the Pitfalls and Pleasures of Do-it-yourself Interpreter may Encounter in the Official Statistics', *New Agenda*, 19, Third Quarter.

Meth, C. and Dias, R. (2004) 'Increases in Poverty in South Africa: 1999–2002', *Development Southern Africa*, 21(1): 59–86.

Moll, P. (1996) 'Compulsory Centralisation of Collective Bargaining in South Africa', *American Economic Review*, 86(2): 326–9.

Muller, C. and Esselar, J. (2004) 'Documenting the informalisation of working South Africa: Evidence from national household surveys, 1997–2001', *Journal of Interdisciplinary Economics*, 15: 229–249.

Nattrass, N. (2000) 'Inequality, Unemployment and Wage-Setting Institutions in South Africa', *Studies in Economics and Econometrics*, 24(3): 129–42.

—— (2003) 'Aids, Economic Growth and Distribution in South Africa', *South African Journal of Economics,* 71(3): 428–54.

Nattrass, N. and Walker, R. (2005) 'Unemployment and Reservation Wages in Working Class Cape Town', *South African Journal of Economics,* 73(3):498–509.

Posel, D., Fairburn, J., and Lund, F. (2006) 'Labour Migration and Households: A Reconsideration of the Effects of the Social Pension on Labour Supply in South Africa', *Economic Modelling,* 23(4): 836–53.

Quattek, K. (2000) 'The Economic Impact of Aids in South Africa: a Dark Cloud on the Horizon', *Konrad Adenauer Stiftung Occasional Paper*, Johannesburg, June 2000.

Rogerson, C. M. (1992) 'The Absorptive Capacity of the Informal Sector in the South African City'. In D. M. Smith, *The Apartheid City and Beyond*, London: Routledge.

SALDRU (1993) Survey under 'Project for Statistics on Living Standards and Development', South African Labour and Development Research Unit, Cape Town.

SAPS (2004) 'Crime Statistics per Category', South African Police Services, <http://www.saps.gov.za/statistics/reports/crimestats/2004/crime_stats.htm>.

Smit, B. and Ellis, L. (2008) 'The Macroeconomic Impact of Aids and Art in South Africa', in Aron, Kahn, and Kingdon (eds.) *South African Economic Policy Under Democracy*, Oxford University Press.

Seekings, J., M. Leibbrandt and N. Nattrass (2004) 'Income inequality after apartheid', *CSSR Working Paper*, no. 75, Centre for Social Science Research, University of Cape Town.

StatsSA (2004) *'Labour Force Survey*, September 2003', Statistical release P0210. Statistics South Africa. March.

—— (2005) *'Labour Force Survey*, September 2000 to March 2005, Historical Series of Revised Estimates', *Statistical release* P0210. Statistics South Africa. September 2005.

—— (2008) *'Labour Force Survey*, September 2007', *Statistical release* P0210. Statistics South Africa. March.

van der Berg, S. (2001) 'Education and Skills Constraint', extract from a talk delivered to a conference of the Bureau for Economic Research, Cape Town, November.

van der Berg, S. & Louw, M., (2003) 'Changing Patterns of South African Income Distribution: Towards Time Series Estimates of Distribution and Poverty', paper to the Conference of the Economic Society of South Africa, Stellenbosch, 17–19 September, 2003.

van de Ruit, C., and May, J. (2003) 'Triangulating Qualitative and Quantitative Approaches to the Measurement of Poverty: a Case Study in the Limpopo Province, South Africa', *IDS Bulletin*, 34(4):21–33.

Xaba, J., Horn, P., and Motala, S. (2002) 'The Informal Sector in Sub-Saharan Africa'. *ILO Working Paper on the Informal Economy*, Employment Sector, ILO, Geneva.

12

The Persistence of Inequalities in Education

Servaas van der Berg

1. Introduction[1]

One enduring manifestation of South African inequality is in the field of education, which Simkins (1998: 4) refers to as one of apartheid's 'footprints in the sand of poverty and inequality'. Although South African inequality is strongly rooted in the labour market (Chapter 10 in this volume confirms this in an analysis of factors contributing to income inequality), labour market race discrimination may have declined more compared to other factors that contribute to inequality, such as education, location, and household size and composition. Burger and Jafta (2006) find little evidence of reduced labour market inequality between race groups in post-apartheid labour market datasets, except for new entrants to the labour market and at the upper end of the wage distribution. However, they point to the importance of variations in educational quality that may account for much of the residual earnings differentials usually ascribed to labour market discrimination. This accentuates the importance of education (in both quantitative and qualitative terms) in the long run generation or reduction of inequality.

Given large-scale educational inequality along racial lines, it is no wonder the new government placed much attention on education, which is perceived to be the vehicle for transforming a greatly unequal society into a more egalitarian one. This is the objective against which educational progress in South Africa is now measured. For this reason, and because school education acts as constraint on expanding the supply of tertiary education and training, the focus of this chapter is on school education.

---

[1] Acknowledgements: This chapter is a revised and extended version of Van der Berg (2007).

This chapter provides an overview of the educational situation in South Africa a decade after the political transition, with the focus on its economic dimensions. This overview often draws on the author's own previous work, with the empirical contribution confined to a production function analysis of educational outcomes. An important question is whether changes since the transition have substantially ameliorated the role of race in education. As comparative inter-temporal data are scarce, this chapter analyses recent educational outcomes to show that race, and the race-based former school systems, still remain the most pervasive determinants of educational outcomes.

Section 2 addresses the South African educational context, in terms of inequality in educational attainment and quality. An overview of educational inequality in sub-section 2.1 shows that quantitative educational *attainment* differentials have been substantially reduced, but sub-section 2.2 shows that *quality* differentials are enduring. Sub-section 2.3 touches on sources of inequality other than race, including evidence of growing educational stratification amongst blacks. Section 3 analyses school performance and its determinants, using regression analysis, and section 4 provides a brief economic perspective on school education policy. Section 5 concludes.

A case will be made that the school system still largely fails in enhancing upward mobility of poor children in the labour market, inter alia because of the continued weak performance of many black schools. The empirical analysis will show that racial composition of a school—as proxy for former school department—remains a major determinant of matriculation pass rates. The conclusion points to enduring socio-economic and racial differentials in school outcomes, but also cautions against seeking the solution mainly through resource shifts. For as Hanushek (2002a: 3–4) has remarked:

Eager to improve quality and unable to do it directly, government policy typically moves to what is thought to be the next best thing—providing added resources to schools. Broad evidence from the experience in the United States and the rest of the world suggests that this is an ineffective way to improve quality.

The empirical analysis in this chapter fully supports this perspective: for resource inputs to improve educational quality may first require some other conditions for quality education to be met, e.g. well-functioning school and education management, and effective quality control systems. The conclusions are alarming in that they show that quality differentials between schools are large and enduring, that despite fiscal resource shifts there has been little reduction in these differentials, and that there are major impediments to overcoming these qualitative differences in school performance. In the light of the growing acknowledgment of the importance of education quality for economic growth (Hanushek and Woessmann, 2007), this is a major concern.

2. The education and skills context

2.1. Educational attainment

The legacy of apartheid education, with racially segregated schools and under-resourcing of schools for blacks, is still evident in large educational differentials between whites and blacks. A perhaps even greater impact was on educational *quality* differentials, as will be discussed in sub-section 2.2. Race remains the main correlate of both education quality and quantity, but race and class are to some extent conflated despite growing socio-economic cleavages within the black population.

Census data showed that quantitative educational attainment differentials by race (in mean years of education completed) had been substantially reduced even during the apartheid era (Louw, van der Berg, and Yu, 2008). The black cohort born in 1920 had on average attained 7.2 fewer years of education than whites, the 1950 cohort 6.0 years less, the 1960 cohort 4.9 years less, the 1970 cohort 3.6 and the 1980 cohort 2.3 years less. There were still large differentials in mean attainment by race and urban versus rural location, but gender differences were quite small.

High levels of educational inequality had historically given rise to large earnings inequalities, but inequality in educational attainment has declined both within and between race groups. Investigating two cohorts thirty years apart, the 25–29 and 55–59 year cohorts respectively in 2002, mean educational attainment level rose and the coefficient of variation declined, whilst the variance declined even amongst blacks.[2] Despite apartheid, black educational attainment grew apace in the 1970s and 1980s, although growth levelled off somewhat in the 1990s. Up to age 15 there is now almost universal school enrolment, but there is a noticeable drop

---

[2] Lam (1999) discussed the significance of this finding. As the earnings function literature shows that earnings are log-linearly related to educational attainment, even a reduction in mean-invariant measures of educational inequality—such as the coefficient of variation—does not guarantee a reduction in earnings inequality if the variance increases with constant returns to education. If the logarithm of earnings of worker i is

$$\log y_i = \alpha + \beta S_i + u_i$$

(y_i is earnings, S_i schooling, u_i residual uncorrelated with schooling), then
$\text{var}(\log y_i) = \beta^2 \text{var}(S_i) + \text{var}(u_i)$

Thus earnings inequality (variance of log-earnings) is a linear function of variance in schooling. If schooling inequality is measured by the coefficient of variation $CV = \sigma/\mu$ (standard deviation divided by mean), which is mean-invariant, then *greater earnings inequality is possible despite reduced schooling inequality.*

Lam showed that in Brazil the standard deviation for schooling indeed rose less than the mean for cohorts born 1925 to 1950. Thus, although the *coefficient of variation* declined, lower schooling inequality did not reduce high earnings inequality as the *variance* of schooling attainment rose. This was unlike the case in South Africa.

out of the school system at the upper secondary level, reflecting the fact that many who reach matric are poorly prepared for this sole externally set 'hurdle' in the school system.

Whilst the white population has educational levels almost similar to those for developed countries, backlogs still plague other groups. By 1996 altogether 70 per cent of whites above age 26 had completed matric or more; almost 15 per cent had a degree. In comparison, only 19 per cent of blacks over 26 years had completed matric or more, and only 1.4 per cent had graduated. For younger cohorts of blacks the educational lag behind whites had narrowed considerably. There is a dramatically higher proportion (36.2 per cent) with at least matric amongst the black cohort aged 26–30, but the number of university graduates had not yet shown such improvement, in part because poor school quality limited university access.

In 1970, only 43,000 people matriculated; in 1990, 191,000 did, and in 2005, 347,000 did. The growth rate of matriculants of 7.8 per cent per year in the period 1970 to 1990 thus dropped to a still respectable 4.1 per cent per year in the next fifteen years. However, the annual rate did slow in the immediate post-transition period and only recovered recently, as Figure 12.1 shows—some of this improvement in pass rates resulted from a reduction in the number of candidates due to restrictions introduced on over-age children in the school system. The performance in terms of endorsements or university exemptions (a level of performance usually required to gain access to university studies)

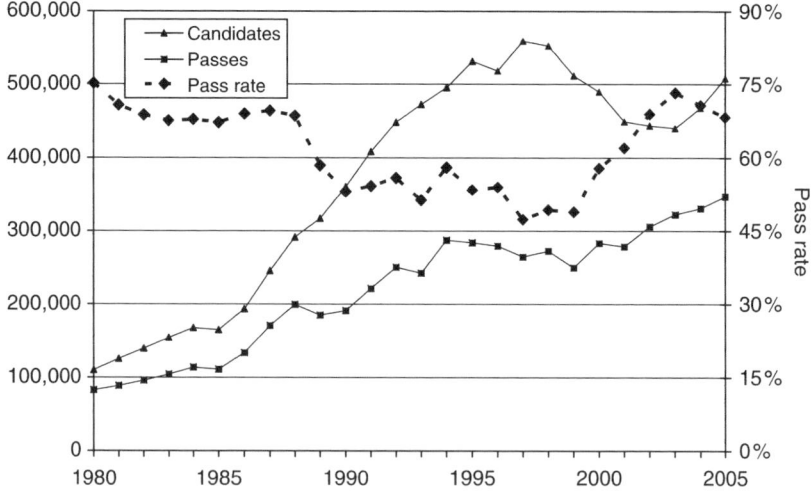

Figure 12.1. Matric candidates, passes and pass rate, 1980 to 2005

Source: SA Institute of Race Relations 2001, 156 for earlier data; Department of National Education, website for data from 2001

had not improved as much. The 16,000 endorsements obtained in 1970 grew at 6.7 per cent per year to 60,000 in 1990, but thereafter growth decelerated to a paltry 2.4 per cent per year to arrive at almost 87,000 exemptions in 2005.

2.2 Educational quality

Many black pupils now attend formerly white schools,[3] whilst amongst formerly black schools there is great variation in *quality*. South African schools generally perform at an even lower level than most of their African counterparts, despite greater South African resources, less acute poverty, and more educated parents. International tests show that at a much earlier stage than matric South African students have already fallen far behind their contemporaries in many other countries. Promotion to higher grades appears to be relatively easy, thus educational attainment (years of education completed) may exaggerate progress in cognitive levels mastered.

Taylor et al. (2003: 41) summarized some evidence on educational quality as follows: 'Studies conducted in South Africa from 1998 to 2002 suggest that learners' scores are far below what is expected at all levels of the schooling system, both in relation to other countries (including other developing countries) and in relation to the expectations of the South African curriculum.' This view is supported by a growing body of evidence:

- The 1993 Statistics for Living Standards and Development household survey showed severe quality problems in large parts of the education system (Fuller, Pillay, and Sirur, 1995; van der Berg, Wood, and Le Roux, 2001). Blacks aged 13–18 had reached 78–86 per cent of the years of education attained by whites, but their literacy scores were 50–63 per cent and their numeracy scores only 36–47 per cent of white levels. Case and Deaton's (1999: table 8) regression results indicated that the average cognitive backlog experienced by black teenagers aged 13–18 would have required ten years of schooling to bring them on par with their white counterparts.
- The 1995 MLA (Monitoring Learning Achievement) study found that South African Grade 4 pupils' numeracy score of 30 per cent was by far the lowest of twelve participating African countries. In literacy, South Africa outperformed only 3 of the 12 countries.

---

[3] Data for 1997 for 7 provinces (all but Mpumalanga and Eastern Cape) showed that, even so soon after the transition, about 22 000, or 5.4 per cent, of the 400 000 pupils in 'mainly white' schools (those with more than 70 per cent white pupils) were blacks, whilst in "mixed" schools (where no race group constituted more than 70 per cent of pupils), 197 000 out of 488 000 (40.3 per cent) were black, and 104 000 (21.3 per cent) white. Nevertheless, most black pupils (95.8 per cent) were still in predominantly black schools. In 2003, 93.2 per cent of black matric candidates were in schools where most matriculants were black. Some of these schools, however, could formerly have been schools restricted to other race groups.

- South Africa's performance on the Grade 6 education evaluation test conducted by the Southern African Consortium for Monitoring Educational Quality in 2000 (SACMEQ II) placed it in the bottom half of the fourteen participating countries on both Reading and Mathematics (see Table 12.1). South Africa's high standard deviation indicated large inequality in performance; the intraclass correlation coefficient, rho (the proportion of variance between individuals that occurred *between* rather than *within* schools) was also extremely high (van der Berg 2007). A government report (South Africa, Department of Education, 2003a: 102) noted the weak South African performance despite much higher expenditure per pupil. Surprisingly also, despite its greater fiscal resources (Chapter 4), South Africa lagged many countries in the region in availability of textbooks in the classroom, particularly in Mathematics.

- In the 2003 Trends in International Mathematics and Science Study (TIMSS), South African Grade 8 students scored 264 for Mathematics compared to the average of 467 for all fifty-three participating countries, and 244 for Science, compared to the international average of 474 (Reddy, 2006). This was no improvement on the 1999 scores (see Table 12.2). South Africa

Table 12.1. Mean score and scores of poor (low SES) and rich (high SES) pupils on SACMEQ II Grade 6 reading and mathematics tests by country (arranged by mean scores in each test)

READING (arranged by mean score)				MATHEMATICS (arranged by mean score)			
	Low SES	High SES	MEAN		Low SES	High SES	MEAN
Seychelles	561.8	594.4	582.0	Mauritius	550.0	607.7	584.6
Kenya	525.3	577.5	546.5	Kenya	546.9	587.1	563.3
Tanzania	528.8	575.2	545.9	Seychelles	532.4	567.8	554.3
Mauritius	508.3	555.1	536.4	Mozambique	527.5	532.6	530.0
Swaziland	519.1	541.0	529.6	Tanzania	509.0	545.5	522.4
Botswana	502.5	543.6	521.1	Swaziland	511.3	522.2	516.5
Mozambique	510.5	523.0	516.7	Botswana	498.9	529.8	512.9
South Africa	440.2	543.6	493.3	Uganda	496.3	519.2	506.3
Uganda	472.3	495.5	482.4	South Africa	446.8	524.3	486.3
Zanzibar	468.1	492.2	478.2	Zanzibar	474.0	483.9	478.1
Lesotho	449.2	454.5	451.2	Lesotho	448.6	444.9	447.2
Namibia	421.5	486.1	448.8	Zambia	425.5	444.8	435.2
Zambia	423.6	456.5	440.1	Malawi	428.2	442.2	432.9
Malawi	422.9	440.7	428.9	Namibia	408.7	461.3	430.9
SACMEQ Average			500.0	SACMEQ Average			500.0

Source: Indicators on SACMEQ website. Available online at <http://www.sacmeq.org/indicate.htm>.
Note: SES refers to socio-economic status, measured here using a proxy for affluence based on answers on household possessions obtained from the pupil questionnaire.

Table 12.2. Mathematics and Science scores in TIMSS Grade 8 tests in comparative perspective, 1999 and 2003

	Mathematics		Science	
	1999	2003	1999	2003
International average*	487	467	488	474
South Africa:				
Country average	275	264	243	244
Former white schools	—	456	—	468
Former black schools	—	227	—	200

Source: Reddy, 2006: 20–1, 34–5
* Note: International sample changed between surveys

maintained its bottom rank, below all five other participating African countries (Egypt, Tunisia, Morocco, Botswana, and Ghana, though South Africa slightly outperforms Ghana in Science (Human Sciences Research Council 2005; Taylor et al., 2003). Whilst former white schools performed just below the international average, the scores in former black schools were only half as much in Mathematics and even worse in Science.

- The 2003 Systemic Evaluation of 54,000 Grade 3 pupils indicated serious shortcomings in education quality. For life skills and listening comprehension, mean scores were 54 per cent and 69 per cent (as against a norm of 50 per cent regarded as the lowest acceptable performance at this grade), but for reading comprehension the average score was only 38 per cent and for numeracy 30 per cent (South Africa, Department of Education, 2003b: pp. viii–ix). Here too there were great inequalities.

- In the 2006 PIRLS (Progress in International Reading Literacy Study) in which Grade 4 pupils were tested in reading, mainly in their home language, South Africa performed worst of the 40 participating countries. The South African mean score of 302 was almost 2 standard deviations below the international mean score (the international mean was calibrated to be 500, and the standard deviation 100). (Twist, Schagen, and Hodgson 2007)

Figure 12.2 shows lowess (locally weighted) regressions for pupil mathematics scores against socio-economic status (SES) for South Africa and for thirteen other African countries combined in SACMEQ II. Apart from at the top of the SES distribution, South African pupils under-perform compared to their equally poor counterparts, despite more favourable pupil/teacher ratios, teacher qualifications, and availability of textbook.

Table 12.3 shows that the number of candidates who took Mathematics at the Higher Grade almost halved between 1997 and 2001, and the pass rate increased from one-third to 56 per cent. Worryingly, however, only 15.5 per cent of black candidates passed this exam—in all, only just over 3,000 pupils.

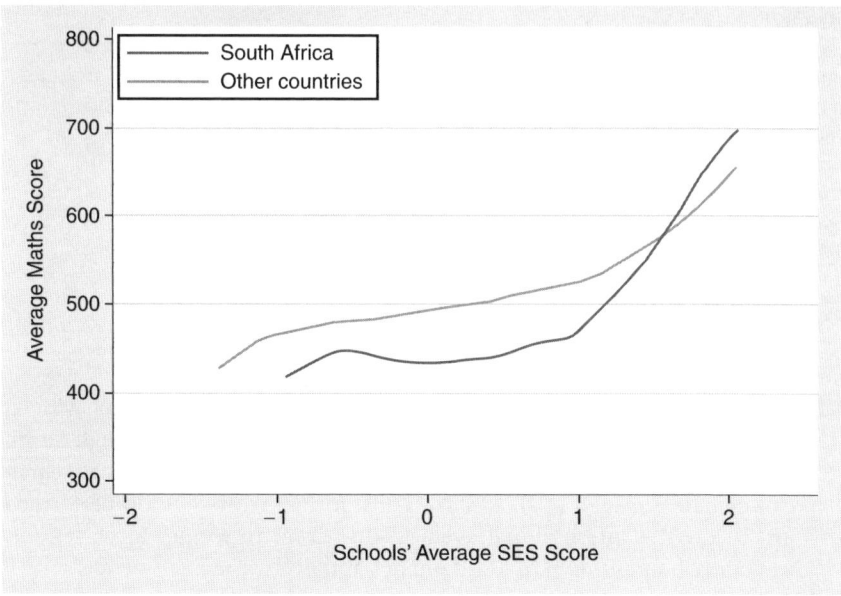

Figure 12.2. Lowess regression on school mean maths score by mean SES level of school, South Africa vs. other countries

Source: Own calculations based on SACMEQ data

Note: SES score derived from principal component analysis of assets

As a good performance in Higher Grade Mathematics is required for entry into university studies in Science, Engineering, Medicine, and Commerce, this is particularly alarming from the perspective of the skills constraint and black access to skilled positions. Even at Standard Grade, the success rate for blacks of 23 per cent was below the national average of 32 per cent. Only 4.6 per cent of all matriculants passed Mathematics at the Higher Grade in 2002. The performance of black students in Physical Science was as perturbing. Only 27 per cent of all matric candidates passed Mathematics at some level in 2002, and just 22 per cent passed Physical Science. This poor performance was despite the compensation of 5 per cent per subject (marks are multiplied by a factor of 1.05) to candidates whose home language is neither Afrikaans nor English (Fatti, 2006: 56).[4] A contributory factor was that only 50 per cent and 42 per cent of all teachers teaching Mathematics and Science respectively had studied these subjects beyond secondary-school level (Edusource, 1999: 5).

---

[4] Language policy in schools is currently strongly debated in South Africa. Official policy is presently mother tongue instruction up to Grade 4, but many educationists favour postponing the switch to English medium instruction, so that students can first be better grounded in their home language.

Table 12.3. Higher and standard grade matriculation passes in Mathematics and Physical Science for all pupils and black pupils

	Higher Grade				Standard Grade				Higher plus Standard Grade	
	Wrote	Pass	% of candidates	% of all matriculants	Wrote	Pass	% of candidates	% of all matriculants	Pass	% of all matriculants
Mathematics:										
1997	68,500	22,800	33.3	4.1	184,200	66,900	36.3	12.0	89,700	16.0
1998	60,300	20,300	33.7	3.7	219,400	68,600	31.3	12.4	88,900	16.1
1999	50,100	19,900	39.7	3.9	231,200	82,200	35.6	16.1	102,100	20.0
2000	38,520	19,327	50.2	3.9	245,497	79,631	32.4	16.3	98,958	20.2
2001	34,870	19,504	55.9	4.3	229,075	72,301	31.6	16.1	91,805	20.4
2002	—	20,528	—	4.6	—	101,289	—	22.8	121,817	27.4
2000: Blacks	20,243	3,128	15.5	—	180,202	41,540	23.1	—	44,668	—
Physical Science:										
1997	76,100	27,000	35.5	4.8	65,200	35,200	54.0	6.3	62,200	11.1
1998	73,300	26,700	36.4	4.8	83,800	43,200	51.6	7.8	69,900	12.6
1999	66,500	24,200	36.4	4.7	93,500	44,000	47.1	8.6	68,200	13.3
2000	55,699	23,344	41.9	4.8	107,486	54,884	51.1	11.2	78,228	16.0
2001	48,996	24,280	49.6	5.4	104,851	45,314	43.2	10.1	69,594	15.5
2002	—	24,888	—	5.6	—	70,763	—	15.9	95,651	21.6
2000: Blacks	33,657	5,136	15.3	—	77,680	32,874	42.3	—	38,010	—

Source: South Africa, Dept of Education, 2001b. *National Strategy for Mathematics, Science and Technology in general and further education and training*. Pretoria: June, table 1, p. 8 and table 2, p. 12; South Africa, Department of Education, 2001c. *Preliminary Report: 2001 Senior Certificate Examination*. Pretoria, Spreadsheet Total(1); and South Africa, National Treasury, 2003. *Intergovernmental Fiscal Review 2003*, Pretoria, tables 4.18 and 4.19

Table 12.4. Matric-aged cohort and matriculation results in public schools by race, 2003

	Black	Coloured	Indian	White	Total	Black share
Matric-aged cohort	819,700	76,400	21,800	66,900	984,800	83%
Pass matric	229,871	27,988	15,673	45,883	323,057	71%
Maths passes	96,949	10,424	9,971	29,387	148,582	65%
Endorsements	42,310	5,523	8,988	24,000	82,265	51%
Higher Grade Maths passes	9,669	1,494	3,945	11,942	27,671	35%
Higher Grade Maths D symbol (50%) or better	3,768	884	2,749	8,969	16,822	22%
A-aggregate mark	833	405	1,871	6,503	9,929	8%

Source: Own calculations from matriculation data obtained from Department of Education

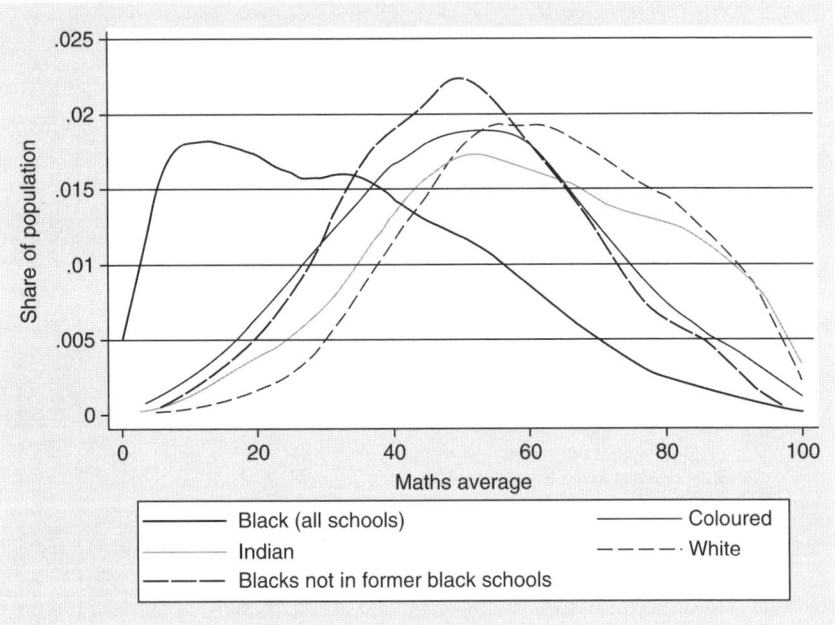

Figure 12.3. Density curves for Higher Grade Maths percentage mark by race, 2003
Source: Own calculations from matriculation data obtained from Department of Education

In 2003, matric passes constituted 28 per cent of the 19-year-old cohort amongst blacks and 68 per cent amongst whites (Table 12.4). Almost one in ten of the white cohort achieved a matric A-aggregate in public schools, versus just more than one in a thousand of the black cohort. Moreover, almost half of these A-achieving black candidates attended schools where blacks were not in the majority in the matric class, probably indicating that these were former white or Indian schools. Figure 12.3 shows the results in Higher Grade Mathematics by race group. This was already a select group, as few black pupils entered for Higher Grade Mathematics. The results of black candidates in mainly black schools generally were dismal: the mode lay well below the 20 per cent mark. In contrast, black students outside mainly black schools also performed much better and not much different from other groups. However, this was a relatively select group within the black population: they were usually more urban and often came from a higher socio-economic background.

2.3. Other educational inequalities

Differential quality of school education is a major cause of unequal labour market earnings. In some Latin American countries, where private education offers an important route to quality education, 'individuals from the lower deciles receive a primary education whose quality (measured in terms of income generation capacity) is 35 percent lower than that of the next decile above' (Inter-American Development Bank, 1998: 54). Growing inequality of educational attainment amongst blacks contributes to increasing stratification within black society. Figure 12.4 shows that children from the top two black deciles progressed considerably better through the school system than their poorer counterparts, and only at about age 15 started lagging behind whites.

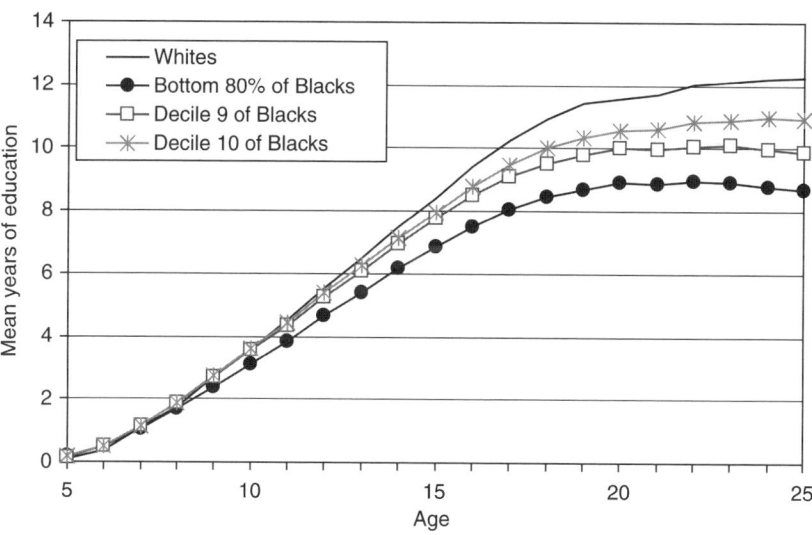

Figure 12.4. Years of education by age, race, and income group, Census 2001
Source: Derived from Census 2001

Children of more educated parents progress better in school and they also fare better in the labour market once they leave school. Data from the 2001 census show that even for children who had matriculated, having a parent who had also matriculated virtually doubled own earnings, whilst for children with tertiary education, earnings were only 40 per cent higher in cases where parents had matriculated. Parent education translated into higher earnings for children, whether through the quality of education, some other non-observed aspect of human capital transmitted from parents to children, or parent social networks.

3. Analysing school performance using a school-level dataset

3.1. Inequalities in school outcomes

Post-transition performance in numbers of pupils with matric passes or with endorsements for university studies has not been particularly good. Despite more resources for historically black schools, output of the school system barely kept pace with population growth. Weak matriculation performance is particularly severe in the poorest provinces, which benefited most from resource shifts.

Table 12.5 illustrates uneven school level performance. This is based on racial composition and school fees (a measure of socio-economic status) in 1997, linked to the matriculation results for the years 1999 and 2000. A school was identified with a particular race group if more than 70 per cent of pupils in 1997 were drawn from that race group. There were massive differentials between the poorest and the richest schools (average pass rate of 44 per cent versus 97 per cent), and between predominantly black and predominantly white schools (43 per cent versus 97 per cent). To put this into historical context, in 1994 the black pass rate had been 49 per cent as against the 97 per cent of whites. Thus there had seemingly been no improvement in pass rates in black schools in the first few years of the new dispensation, despite large resource shifts, whilst mainly white schools accommodated far more black pupils than before. However, mobility does not explain the failure to improve pass rates in predominantly black schools, since 96 per cent of black pupils were still in historically black schools (which constituted some 80 per cent of the total school population).

Whilst pass rates in more affluent schools were almost uniformly high, predominantly black schools performed abysmally, with most recording pass rates in the range 20–60 per cent or even lower (Table 12.6). In contrast, only 3 out of 179 mainly white schools had pass rates below 80 per cent. Amongst poor mainly black schools that charged school fees of less than R30 per annum, the best performing quartile had a pass rate of 68 per cent, against the 18 per

Table 12.5. Number of schools, mean and standard deviation of average matriculation pass rates in sample by school fee group, 'race type' and province, 1999/2000*

	Number of schools	Mean %	Standard deviation %
Total sample:	2,768	55.5	27.3
School fee group:			
<R20	651	43.9	23.4
R20-R49	1,177	47.8	22.2
R50-R99	496	54.1	22.2
R100-R199	82	69.7	23.2
R200-R999	243	91.9	15.0
R1000+	119	97.2	8.6
School 'race type':			
>70% Black	2,106	43.3	20.3
>70% Coloured	138	75.5	14.2
>70% Indian	42	80.5	12.3
>70% White	179	97.3	3.8
Mixed	206	79.0	21.5
Race not specified	97	91.8	13.9
Province:			
Limpopo	1,002	43.9	20.2
Free State	289	49.1	29.5
Kwazulu-Natal	784	55.7	25.5
Gauteng	367	62.2	29.5
Northern Cape	87	66.2	25.6
Western Cape	239	81.8	19.7

Source: Own calculations from Department of Education datasets.
*Note: Examination data relate to the average pass rates for 1999 and 2000; school fees and racial composition relate to 1997. The racial composition or socio-economic status of some schools may have changed between 1997 and 2000.

cent of the worst quartile, despite similar socio-economic status and legacies of inadequate teaching resources. The difference therefore probably should be sought in the functioning of schools and/or in the unobserved characteristics of students, since more motivated students may have chosen to attend schools which functioned better, i.e. school quality and student unobserved characteristics may have been jointly determined. However, as geographical impediments limited mobility, differences in school functioning may be the dominant factor. Evidence presented later shows little indication of systematic mobility in response to quality differentials.

3.2. Explaining school performance

A production function approach is now applied to this dataset to analyse school performance (see Hanushek (2002b) and Filmer and Pritchett (1999)

Table 12.6. Frequency distribution of schools by 'race type' and pass rate range, 1999–2000

Range of average pass rate by school (%)	Black	Coloured	Indian	White	Mixed	Race unspe-cified	Total
Below 20	207				3	1	211
20–39	743	3			11	1	758
40–59	668	23	2		33	5	731
60–79	342	57	16	3	45	11	474
80–100	146	55	24	176	114	79	594
Total	2,106	138	42	179	206	97	2,768
Below 20	9.8%	0.0%	0.0%	0.0%	1.5%	1.0%	7.6%
20–39	35.3%	2.2%	0.0%	0.0%	5.3%	1.0%	27.4%
40–59	31.7%	16.7%	4.8%	0.0%	16.0%	5.2%	26.4%
60–79	16.2%	41.3%	38.1%	1.7%	21.8%	11.3%	17.1%
80–100	6.9%	39.9%	57.1%	98.3%	55.3%	81.4%	21.5%
Total	100%	100%	100%	100%	100%	100%	100%

Source: Own calculations from Department of Education datasets.
*Note: Examination data relate to the average pass rates for 1999 and 2000; racial composition relates to 1997.

for good overviews of this approach). Essentially such an approach tries to measure statistically the relationship between educational inputs and outputs, after controlling for other explanatory factors such as socio-economic status.

The data consisted of matriculation pass rates for 1999 and 2000, matched to data for seven provinces on 1997 school resources and racial composition. The only output measure available was the aggregate pass rate of the schools. No data matching was possible for the North West province. The sample of almost 2,800 covered about half of all schools, matriculation candidates and matriculation passes nationally, and represented about 70 per cent of the total in the six provinces covered. Thus the results applied to a fairly but not fully representative sample of about half of all schools and matriculation candidates.

The examination data set contained pass rates for 1999 and 2000, and the number of candidates who entered the examination in 2000. The correlation between the pass rates for 1999 and 2000 (r = 0.85) indicated a large measure of stability in pass rates at the school level. The *average* pass rate over the two years was used as performance measure to reduce the effect of year-to-year variations, and the number of candidates in each school who wrote exams in 2000 was used to weight each observation (school). This was the dependent variable. The 1997 racial composition of schools provides a fair approximation of the racial composition of each school's matric class in 1999 and 2000, and 1997 educational resources and school fees (average actual fees paid) were taken as a crude proxy for these variables over the high school career. Apartheid-era resource differentials between schools had not yet been eliminated in 1997, so that the data captured a variety of experiences. Teacher resources were measured by pupil/teacher ratio, average teacher salaries (a function of their qualifications and experience), or a combination of these two, viz. average teacher costs per pupil. Racial composition of schools was used as a proxy for former race departments. Mobility between schools meant that the racial composition of schools may have been endogenous, if mobility occurred in response to school quality. However, as there was limited mobility of members of other groups to former black schools, most former black schools were easily identified.

The data are summarized in Table 12.7. A priori, one would have expected matriculation pass rates to improve with higher school fees, a lower pupil/teacher ratio, higher teacher salaries, fewer black pupils, and in historically better-endowed provinces. Regression results were broadly consistent with these expectations. Regression 1 in Table 12.8 shows that matriculation pass rates of schools were associated with pupil socio-economic background as measured by school fees, teaching resources (pupil/teacher ratio and average teacher salary), provincial location, and the race category of schools. The Western Cape and Kwazulu-Natal performed significantly better than similar schools in Limpopo, the reference province. All other variables were highly significant and their signs as expected. A full log-transformation did not improve the fit. The coefficient of determination was high for a cross-sectional regression of this nature where the dependent variable, pass rates, reflects little differentiation at the upper end. Tests showed the results to be insensitive to the presence of outliers.

The coefficient of the dummy for mainly white schools indicated that, *holding constant the level of school fees, pupil/teacher ratios, teacher salary level*

Table 12.7. Descriptive statistics: Schools from six provinces

	Matric pass rate %	Fees per pupil (R)	Pupils per teacher	Average teacher salary (R)
Black schools (n= 2106)				
Mean	43	49	33.7	82,720
Std dev	20	118	9.9	7,498
Other schools (n=662)*				
Mean	85	545	27.1	97,574
Std dev	17	679	5.2	5,747
All schools (n=2768)				
Mean	56	194	31.7	87,084
Std dev	27	443	9.3	9,756

Note: *179 mainly white schools, 179 mixed schools, 138 mainly coloured, 42 mainly Indian, and 97 schools for which race composition was unknown

Table 12.8. Regressions of matriculation pass rates by school in six provinces, 1999–2000 (t-values shown below coefficients)

Dependent variable: Pass rate (average 1999 and 2000)	Regression 1: All schools	Regression 2: Mainly black schools	Regression 3: Other schools
School fees per student (R100 per annum)	3.685	10.501	2.846
	(13.92)**	(9.27)**	(13.85)**
Square of school fees per student (R100 per annum)	−0.107	−0.513	−0.075
	(10.55)**	(4.86)**	(9.99)**
Student/teacher ratio	−0.127	−0.085	−0.312
	(2.87)**	(1.90)	(2.56)**
Average teacher salary (R'000 per month)	5.012	4.474	8.445
	(6.05)**	(4.43)**	(5.83)**
Mainly coloured school (dummy)	22.833		
	(11.53)**		
Mainly Indian school (dummy	24.162		
	(8.94)**		
Mixed school (dummy)	17.672		
	(9.16)**		
Mainly white school (dummy)	24.632		
	(11.45)**		
Race unspecified (dummy)	26.222		
	(10.49)**		
Kwazulu-Natal (dummy)	5.568	4.528	3.023
	(4.90)**	(3.47)**	(0.77)
Free State (dummy)	−1.873	−2.004	5.359
	(1.21)	(1.14)	(1.36)
Northern Cape (dummy)	2.537	3.929	5.506
	(1.28)	(1.23)	(1.30)
Gauteng (dummy)	−1.486	−0.713	.497
	(1.21)	(0.48)	(0.13)
Western Cape (dummy)	7.174	3.630	11.866
	(3.71)**	(1.00)	(3.11)**
Constant	10.172	10.025	9.721
	(1.65)	(1.36)	(0.79)
Observations	2770	2106	664
R^2	0.58	0.12	0.49

Note: Robust t-statistics in parentheses
* indicates .05 level of significance
** indicates .01 level of significance

The Persistence of Inequalities in Education

and province, a school containing mainly white pupils had a matriculation pass rate 25 percentage points higher than a similar mainly black school (the reference category). Therefore, a large part of the 54 percentage points difference between black and white schools could not be explained away by school fees, educational resources and province—and even these factors were highly correlated with race. Despite home background differences between students attending mainly black and mainly white schools that could not be fully controlled for, this finding was highly disturbing, that a large part of the educational system was still unable to overcome the ravages of apartheid education. It appeared that the reason should be sought in the poor ability of many schools to convert school resources into educational outcomes, perhaps related to dysfunctional management structures.

Replacing the pupil/teacher ratio and the teacher salary by a single combined variable, the teacher cost per pupil,[5] or using a log specification for school fees left other coefficients relatively unaffected, suggesting that the model was not greatly affected by the particular specification. Non-linear specifications of the pupil/teacher ratio variable did not improve the fit.

However, the bi-modal distribution of school pass rates signified two underlying data generation processes rather than a single one. These processes may be better understood if they were modelled separately, thus the initial sample was split into two groups, viz. mainly black schools versus other schools. The results could be summarized as follows:

- School fees and educational resources had a significantly positive association with matriculation pass rates in both regressions, and again this effect declined with rising school fees.
- Surprisingly, the responsiveness of school pass rates to school fee levels was larger in black schools than in other schools.
- The coefficient on the pupil/teacher ratio was statistically insignificant in mainly black schools, where high pupil/teacher ratio historically had been particularly detrimental. These results may explain why, *on their own*, teacher resource shifts to blacks schools may have had limited impact in improving overall educational performance. The correlation coefficient of –0.06 between the 1999–2000 matriculation results and the pupil/teacher ratio for black schools in 1997 (when apartheid-era differentials had not yet been fully eliminated) meant that less than 4 per cent of the variation in matriculation pass rates amongst black schools could be explained by the pupil/teacher ratio.

---

[5] The coefficient per one rand of school fees was five times as large as that for teacher cost per pupil. This implied that school fees did more than only augment fiscal resources, possibly because school fees were spent more effectively than other school expenditures (being controlled by school governing bodies, who were closer to schools' real needs), or because school fees were a good proxy for economic status.

- The coefficient of determination of 0.12 for Regression 2 indicated that the model left the large variation in pass rates in black schools around a low mean largely unexplained. In striking contrast, 48 per cent of the smaller variation in matric results in other schools was explained by these few explanatory variables.
- Kwazulu-Natal's black schools fared significantly better than expected, whilst for other schools the Western Cape significantly outperformed other provinces.

Thus race or associated factors still constituted a major determinant of differential matriculation pass rates. These results also imply that the 'success' of the first regression in 'explaining' variation in matriculation results was in part artificial, because race composition (presumably reflecting former department) blurred the effects of other explanatory variables on school performance and ignored the two different data generating processes at work. The question then arises: which school characteristics were captured by race composition? In South African education policy circles, such differences are often ascribed to the management culture in schools of the various former racial departments. For instance, the inefficiency in converting inputs into outputs in many former black schools can be seen as a form of managerial inefficiency that dates back to the apartheid era and that educational reforms since the transition may not yet have overcome. Amongst blacks schools, the quarter that exceeded the total sample's average pass rate of 56 per cent had only slightly better pupil/teacher ratios (32.5 as against 34.0), slightly better remunerated teachers (R83,900 versus R82,387), and slightly better socio-economic status (low school fees of R92 versus R36 per annum) than their weaker performing counterparts. Thus performance above and below average in black schools could not be explained by differences in resources and only to a limited extent by differences in socio-economic status.

To supplement the above analysis, a regression tree methodology was also applied. The method selects a point that splits the data into two sets (or nodes in a tree) so as to give the greatest possible separation between high values and low values of the dependent variable for these sub-sets of the data. This procedure is repeated for each of the two nodes, thus a binary split is made on each node, with stopping rules (e.g. a minimum number of cases per node) determining when the splitting process should stop. This methodology was applied to the pass rate to ascertain which predictor values played a role. The results largely confirm those from the regressions. School race type was found to be the first differentiating factor. The pupil/teacher ratio never emerged as a predictor variable, not even amongst predominantly black schools. Higher school fees were a better predictor of improved pass rates than were more teachers. Regression tree analysis thus confirmed that race still played a strong role, whilst number of teachers was not an important predictor of school performance.

Unobserved characteristics such as motivation or mobility of more able students to better schools may have influenced some of these findings. However, the small magnitude of physical mobility signified that this was unlikely to provide a major explanation. A Western Cape study showed that mobility was not systematic even in urban areas. Changes in enrolment in 2000 and in 2001 were virtually uncorrelated (r = .07), and many schools experienced large enrolment increases in 2000, followed by enrolment losses in 2001, or vice versa (van der Berg and Achterbosch 2001: 13). In the absence of information to parents and students about school quality, this lack of systematic mobility is not surprising.

Other studies on school production functions in South Africa are relatively scarce. The findings presented above accord with those of Crouch and Mabogoane (1996), who showed that much of the variation in school performance could not be explained by input variables or by controls for socio-economic status. Although Fiske and Ladd interpreted their findings differently, their regression (Fiske and Ladd, 2004: 250, Appendix Table B) implied that a large reduction of the Western Cape pupil/teacher ratio, from 35 to 25, would have improved the matric pass rate by only 5 percentage points, if teacher quality was left unchanged. This was swamped by dummies for the former racial departments: compared to former white schools, the negative impact on the pass rate of a school having been part of the former black department was 29 percentage points, and 12 percentage points in the case of the former coloured department. Using *quality* of Western Cape matric results rather than only pass rates leads to broadly similar conclusions (van der Berg and Burger, 2002), that resources alone leave much unexplained that is captured by dummies for former department. But this still leaves the mystery of how to interpret the former department dummy.

Both Gustafsson (2007) and van der Berg (2007) used hierarchical linear models (HLM, also known as multi-level models) on 2001 SACMEQ data. This richer dataset allowed controls for home background variables (socio-economic status, parent education, books at home, and whether the child lived with the parents), but Gustafsson (2007) notes how little (7 per cent) of within school variance in results is explained by these factors. Socio-economic status seemed to have a limited impact on pupil performance except for the richest schools. Pupil/teacher ratios had at best a mild influence—although he found some evidence of non-linear effects that showed that very high class sizes may be particularly detrimental. Some other school level resources (textbooks and school facilities) influenced learning, but all inputs together accounted for only a small part of the between school variance in results.

Production functions thus appear to be consistent with a perspective that teacher resources may only play a stronger role in improving school performance in poorer schools *if certain efficiency conditions are met*. This may imply that, at the margin, resources may only matter conditionally. The policy implication is that additional fiscal resources *by themselves* may make only a limited contribution to improving educational performance. Better school management is probably most important, while availability of good teachers remains a binding constraint. Getting more qualified teachers and better management into poor schools is more than only a fiscal problem. Issues of location (urban/rural and city/township), language, race, and union opposition to salary differentiation all play a role, and teacher training is slow to yield results.

4. An economic perspective on school education policy

Faced with an educational system ravaged by apartheid, the new government tackled a number of tasks simultaneously: reunification of the education system; deracialisation of schools; curricula; and the highly contentious introduction of outcomes-based education. Efforts aimed at more equitable access to quality schooling included shifts in the allocation of education expenditure; infrastructure investments, notably the construction and repair of school buildings; and a primary school nutrition programme reaching about 5 million school children.

South Africa allocates a large share of its national resources to public education—its public education spending ratio of 6 per cent of GDP is high by world standards. Moreover, school education spending increased relatively rapidly immediately after the transition. Substantial further increases of fiscal resources for education do not seem viable. But larger *financial* flows to education did not cause a commensurate increase in *real* resources for schools, as fiscal resource shifts were overshadowed by salary increases for teachers (in part to eliminate apartheid-era discrimination in teacher salaries). In contrast to international experience, teacher salaries outpaced the growth of per capita GDP so that the relative burden of teacher salaries (measured as a fraction of per capita GDP) increased.[6] But even before the transition, Donaldson, (1992: 147) had noted that:

> the constraint at work ... is not (only) finance, but the limited real resources available to the economy. Competent teachers, nurses, doctors and community workers are scarce, as is the capacity to produce books, medical supplies, and building materials. So the growth and improved distribution of social services must be viewed as the growth and

---

[6] Lee and Barro (1997: 17–18) provide some international evidence of the relative decline of teachers' salaries:

The ratios of estimated real salaries of primary school teachers to per capita GDP have typically declined over time; from 1965 to 1990, the value dropped from 2.5 to 2.2 in the OECD, from 4.9 to 3.6 in the overall group of developing countries, and from 7.4 to 1.7 in the (centrally planned economies).

improved distribution of the inputs required for delivering these services. Chapter 4 refers to the increased fiscal allocations to education. However, improving teacher qualifications and school management in poorly functioning schools is not merely a fiscal problem but a complex social problem involving dimensions such as location (rural vs urban), language, race and union objections to salary differentiation among teachers.

Inter- and intra-provincial fiscal redistribution after the transition targeted education spending much better at the poor (see van der Berg, 2000). An analysis of Western Cape data showed that the limited remaining fiscal inequalities between schools largely resulted from differences in qualifications and experience of teachers (Fiske and Ladd, 2004: 124, table 6-6). Table 12.9 shows complete equalization of the pupil/teacher ratio in Western Cape schools by 2002, across former departments and also by school poverty quintile (arranged by economic status of their neighbourhood), but with major differentials in teacher quality. Nationally, teachers paid by the state increased from 24 to 31 per 1,000 students in formerly black schools, and decreased from 59 to 31 in formerly white schools. Private funding allowed richer schools to supplement teaching resources from parental fees; formerly white schools on average had another 12 teachers per 1,000 students paid for by parents through the school governing body, thus overall there was a reduction in teacher numbers from 59 to 43 per 1,000 pupils in formerly white schools. Surprisingly, however, these large changes had little effect on relative performance in these two groups of schools.

This massive shift in teacher resources took place without major conflict and flight of the more affluent into private schools. The 3 per cent of children in private schools remains small compared with almost one-third in many Latin American countries, which face similar equity and quality problems. Retaining most children in public schools also prevented the flight of scarce qualified teachers to private schools. An important decision here was to continue to allow schools to charge school fees, which allowed more affluent communities to supplement school resources.

Despite the fiscal resource shifts, there were still stark differences in teacher qualifications between more and less privileged schools, e.g. almost 30 teachers with a REQV of 14 or above—the supposed minimum desired qualification for secondary schools, viz. four years of post-matric education—per 1,000 pupils in formerly white schools versus only 21 in former black schools (see notes to Table 12.9 for definition of REQV). The absence of enough qualified teachers remains one of the most intractable problems in overcoming apartheid legacies, as this limits the potential impact of resource shifts to poorer schools. For a good overview of the teacher supply issue in the presence also of AIDS, see Simkins (2002).

Personnel spending is very dominant, thus even a small shift towards non-personnel spending would considerably improve availability of complementary classroom resources. These may in any event provide the highest

Table 12.9. Some indicators of performance, resources and teacher qualifications by former department and poverty quintile, Western Cape 2002

	DET	HOR	HOD	CED	Q1	Q2	Q3	Q4	Q5	Total
Number writing matric	5415	17 363	296	12 550	7 229	7 091	7 181	7 040	7 083	35624
Matric aggregate	823	919	1 097	1 289	844	891	997	1 192	1 264	1 037
Matric aggregate (%)	39	44	52	61	40	42	47	57	60	49
Pass rate (%)	68	83	94	99	71	81	88	94	97	86
School fees p.a. (R)	122	221	340	2,369	129	244	424	1,623	2,576	1,033
Poverty rate (%)	47	31	28	18	47	38	29	22	14	29
REQV Index	13.91	14.09	14.14	14.51	13.95	14.05	14.18	14.40	14.48	14.21
Teachers per 1,000 pupils by qualification of teachers										
REQV17	0.09	0.17	0.14	0.81	0.12	0.24	0.17	0.76	0.66	0.39
REQV16	0.95	1.60	2.24	3.35	1.08	1.29	2.06	2.96	3.24	2.12
REQV15	5.49	5.49	6.64	8.03	5.47	5.00	6.28	7.21	8.03	6.39
REQV14	14.07	15.86	16.70	17.37	14.57	16.70	15.89	16.54	16.97	16.13
REQV13	8.54	6.07	3.82	1.26	8.13	6.31	4.81	2.84	1.48	4.73
REQV12	0.43	0.14	0.00	0.03	0.36	0.11	0.08	0.13	0.04	0.14
REQV11	0.01	0.03	0.00	0.00	0.02	0.00	0.05	0.01	0.01	0.02
REQV10	0.19	0.06	0.86	0.05	0.14	0.10	0.08	0.03	0.05	0.08
Qualifications unknown	0.65	0.56	0.62	0.50	0.61	0.55	0.49	0.53	0.58	0.55
Total: REQV 14 or higher	20.00	23.12	25.72	29.56	21.24	23.23	24.4	27.47	28.9	25.03
Total: Publicly appointed teachers	30.41	29.98	31.01	31.40	30.50	30.31	29.91	31.00	31.07	30.55
Teachers appointed by School Governing Bodies from own resources	0.07	1.12	0.99	11.61	0.21	1.26	2.58	7.85	11.52	4.66
Total: All teachers	30.48	31.10	32.00	43.01	30.71	31.57	32.49	38.85	42.59	35.21

Notes: DET (Dept of Education and Training), HOR (House of Representatives), HOD (House of Delegates) and CED (Cape Education Department). These were the former departments dealing with blacks, coloureds, Indian and whites respectively in the apartheid era in the Western Cape.

Q1 to Q5 are the poverty quintiles of schools, derived from the socio-economic status of the area surrounding the schools.

REQV10 is a qualification of matric or equivalent; each additional unit increase implies one more year of tertiary education, with REQV17 being a doctorate or equivalent.

marginal return to further investment, as Filmer and Pritchett (1999) argued. Jansen (2005:75) also contends that textbooks may be particularly useful in empowering both pupils and weak teachers:

> Textbooks serve two functions in developing countries. First, they provide learners with substantive learning content to complement and even compensate for the weak knowledge base of teachers. Second ... textbooks provide under-qualified or less than competent teachers with reliable and accessible learning content to guide, inform and even correct their teaching. The combination of incompetent teachers and the non-availability of textbooks holds dire consequences for teacher preparation and student achievement.

After the transition, teacher unions used their strong bargaining power to raise real salaries substantially, crowding out other educational spending. From 1995/6 to 1997/8, personnel expenditure increased by 20 per cent in real terms, while non-personnel expenditure declined by 17 per cent (South Africa, Budget Office, 1998: 27). Thus increased non-personnel spending appears warranted. However, the clearest need now is to utilize existing resources better. This was already partly acknowledged by 1996 with the launch of the COLTS (Culture of Learning, Teaching, and Service) campaign: 'the first more or less official recognition of the fact that efficiency and work effort problems, rather than funding by itself, were at the heart of the problems in the education sector' (South Africa, Budget Office, 1998: 35).

School level inefficiencies often result from a principal-agent problem. Outputs of the educational system are extremely complex to monitor, as is teacher effort (input). The educational authorities did attempt to shift monitoring to the parent community as the final 'principal', but this was hard where parents themselves had little formal education. One avenue for addressing a principal-agent problem is through providing more information. The education authorities have a paucity of information for decision making. Identifying under-performing schools in order to take remedial action requires understanding school performance. Educational policy improvements need evidence on what works and what does not, and '(d)eveloping such evidence means that regular high quality information about student outcomes must be generated.' (Hanushek, 2003: F94) The Department of Education acknowledged this in a recent report and consequently undertook to:

- Invest in a system that integrates existing performance data from schools and produces performance scores specific to the country, provinces, sub-provincial units down to the district/circuit, and poverty quintiles....
- Research input-output trends in South African schools (as part of the research into production functions) and in other, similar schooling systems in order to arrive at normative scores that can be used to gauge the performance success of schools with varying levels of resourcing, and varying levels of socio-economic disadvantage.

- Produce comprehensive and user-friendly statistics for public consumption that will allow comparisons between provinces and districts/circuits in terms of learner performance. Both absolute scores and scores that factor out socio-economic variations should be provided. Normative scores that will allow the public to assess where the schooling system is functioning best, and worst, should also be made available. Public dissemination of this information will be aimed at producing constructive debate and pressures, and will begin during 2004.

(South Africa, Department of Education 2003a)

This would certainly increase openness and information. Teachers, schools and education departments currently have limited accountability to parents and communities for ensuring education quality, whilst parents and society have little information about the effectiveness of specific schools. Systematic availability of such information would increase pressures for weaker schools to bring their performance more closely into line with better-performing schools. The poor information is illustrated by the fact that not even matriculation results have hitherto been analysed properly in a multivariate framework by the education authorities. Literacy and numeracy levels are already far below expectations at early ages, where there is hardly any measurement of quality: According to Moloi (2005), most pupils at Grade 6 level performed at Grade 3 level or worse in Mathematics tests. So the problem may require intervention much before matric. But evaluating the appropriateness of alternative interventions requires proper investigation of the data, and the availability of such data.

5. Conclusion and a look ahead

Improving black education is crucial to reducing the racial unemployment and earnings gaps (Chapter 11 examines the relationship between education and unemployment). Educational access is now almost universal and racial gaps in educational attainment (years of education completed) have also been substantially reduced. The major cause for concern now lies in severe problems with the quality of education of many schools. Only limited scope remains for additional resource outlays or resource shifts to redress this. Moreover, the evidence presented supports the view that providing more resources to poor schools has thus far improved educational performance but little.

Robust economic growth may reduce poverty and racial inequality in coming decades (see Chapter 2 on growth). But from the perspective of distribution—and even as a growth factor itself—an improvement in the quality of education of South Africa's poor is likely to be highly rewarding. This requires urgent attention to the functioning of poorly performing schools, to permit continued upward mobility of the largest part of the workforce as well as to support sustained economic growth. It helps that demographic pressures on the schools system have largely abated; fertility decline has sharply reduced growth of the school-age population, and there is already almost universal access, thus there is scope for concentrating both resources and policy largely on quality improvement. But unfortunately educational change is usually a slow process and its effects on the labour market take even longer to show.

Government policy and discussion presently seem to be focused on changing teacher incentives, strengthening existing management, and incrementally distancing itself from the controversial outcomes-based education that had been introduced against strong opposition in the 1990s. The first two of these have strong economic dimensions.

Regarding incentives, a new wage policy was negotiated and accepted in the first half of 2008, intended to increase the attractiveness of teaching as a career. However, it will take a long period to fully implement and will therefore require time before it could have a noticeable effect on the quality of new teachers entering the profession. In the long negotiations teacher unions considerably watered down the principle of performance based pay that the government tried to introduce, thus this is unlikely to have a major effect on teacher incentives and performance in practice.

More promising appears to be strengthening accountability systems for school teachers and principals. Such accountability structures are, however, difficult to put in place in a generally poorly managed system, particularly where there is already strong provider capture. Principals of poor schools have little discretionary resources and often do not regard performance management as a central part of their duties. Thus, schools lacking strong parental inputs—often in poorer communities—face little pressure to improve student performance. Economists favour provision of more information as a response to information asymmetries associated with principal-agent relationships. Such asymmetries are definitely present in many poor schools—surveys show that parents express unjustifiably high levels of satisfaction with schools, despite poor academic performance, as the inadequacy of such performance is usually not known to parents. A simple way of providing information would be to test children nationally at different levels in the school system and to make such test scores available to parents. Information provided in a form that enables parents to judge how their children are performing relative to norms, or relative to schools serving similar socio-economic communities (perhaps neighbouring schools) would empower parents relative to principals and teachers. Such feedback to the community will increase pressure on and competition between schools. The Minister of Education has already asked for an expansion of the existing systemic evaluation testing to more grades (formerly confined to national testing in only one grade every year), which is a step in the right direction. But the education authorities still only see this as a diagnostic tool for identifying systemic weaknesses rather than as a way of reducing the information asymmetry on educational performance that lies at the heart of the principal-agent problem and producer capture of the benefits of the education system. Unsurprisingly, union opposition against moves in this direction is also strong.

Perhaps the greatest hope for improvement in school education comes from the growing recognition of its weak performance. International evaluations have contributed much to this. At the political level, national and even some provincial policymakers appear to have a new sense of urgency in dealing with poor efficiency of schools. Reports in the media, which early in the transition focused much on the undoubted achievements in improving resource equity and on curriculum issues, have in recent years become increasingly critical. The middle class are voting with their feet, leaving weaker schools in droves for either former Model C (largely white) or private schools. Ironically, most children of teachers in poorer or weaker schools attend Model C schools. But this option is only open to a relatively small group of parents—many lack the information or the resources to elect to take this route, and the relatively few well-performing schools cannot accommodate all who want a good education. So pressure will continue to grow in the wider community to address the inefficiency and weak performance of the bulk of the school system. The recognition has also come amongst many policymakers that resources are not the main issue, but rather the efficiency with which resources are applied. Growing criticism of the commitments and qualities of part of the teaching corps will also increase pressure on the system to perform.

References

Burger, Rulof and Jafta, Rachel. 2006. 'Returns to Race: Labour Market Discrimination in Post-Apartheid South Africa'. Working Papers 04/2006. Stellenbosch University, Department of Economics. Accessed 20 Sept. 2007 at <http://stbweb02.stb.sun.ac.za/economics/3.Research/2.Working%20Papers.php>

Case, Anne and Deaton, Angus. 1999. 'School Inputs and Educational Outcomes in South Africa'. *Quarterly Journal of Economics*, 114(3): 1047–84

Crouch, Luis and Mabogoane, T. 1998. 'When the Residuals Matter More Than the Coefficients: An Educational Perspective'. *Studies in Economics and Econometrics*, 22(2): 1–14.

Donaldson, Andrew 1992. 'Restructuring social services'. In R. Schrire (ed.), *Wealth or Poverty? Critical choices for South Africa*. Oxford

University Press: Cape Town

Edusource. 1999. *Edusource Data News 24*. Johannesburg: Education Foundation. March.

Fatti, L. Paul. 2006. 'The Statistical Adjustment of Matric Marks'. In: Vijay Reddy (ed.). *Marking matric: Colloquium proceedings*. Human Sciences Research Council, Pretoria. February: 45–57

Filmer, Deon and Pritchett, Lant. 1999. 'What Education Production Functions Really Show: A Positive Theory of Education Expenditures'. *Economics of Education Review* 18(2): 223–39

Fiske, Edward B. and Ladd, Helen F. 2004. *Elusive Equity: Education Reform in Post-Apartheid South Africa*. Washington, D.C.: Brookings.

Fuller, Bruce; Pillay, Pundy; Sirur, Neeta. 1995. 'Literacy Trends in South Africa: Expanding Education While Reinforcing Unequal Achievement?' Mimeo. Saldru: University of Cape Town

Gustafsson, Martin. 2007. 'Using the Hierarchical Linear Model to Understand School Production in South Africa'. *South African Journal of Economics* 75(1): 84–98.

Hanushek, Eric A. 2002a. *The long-run importance of school quality*. NBER Working Paper 9071. Cambridge, Mass.: National Bureau of Economic Research

Hanushek, Eric A. 2002b. *Publicly Provided Education*. NBER Working Paper. Cambridge, Mass.: National Bureau of Economic Research.

Hanushek, Eric A. 2003. *The Failure of Input-Based Schooling Policies*. NBER Working Paper 9040. *Economic Journal*, 113 (485), February: F64–F98

Hanushek, Eric A. and Woessmann, Ludger. 2007. *The Role of School Improvement In Economic Development*. NBER Working Paper. Cambridge, Mass.: National Bureau of Economic Research.

Inter-American Development Bank (IADB). 1998. *Facing up to Inequality in Latin America*. Economic and Social Progress in Latin America 1998–1999 Report. Washington, D.C.: Johns Hopkins University Press

Jansen, Jonathan. 2005. 'Educationally Essential: Teachers, Textbooks and Time'. In: S. Brown (ed.). 2005. *Conflict and Governance. Transformation Audit*. Cape Town: Institute for Justice and Reconciliation. 71–5.

Lam, David, 1999. 'Generating Extreme Inequality: Schooling, Earnings, and Intergenerational Transmission of Human Capital in South Africa and Brazil'. *Research Report* 99-439. Ann Arbor: Population Studies Center, University of Michigan.

Lee, Jong-Wha and Barro, Robert J. 1997. 'Schooling Quality in a Cross Section of Countries'. *NBER Working Paper* 6198. Cambridge, Mass.: National Bureau of Economic Research.

Londoño, Juan Luis. 1996. *Poverty, Inequality, and Human Capital Development in Latin America, 1950–2025*. World Bank Latin American and Caribbean Studies: Viewpoints. Washington, D.C.: World Bank

Louw, Megan; van der Berg, Servaas: Yu, Derek. 2007. 'Convergence of a kind: educational attainment and inter-generational social mobility in South Africa'. *South African Journal of Economics*, 75(3): 548–571.

Moloi, Meshack Q. 2005. 'Mathematics Achievement in South Africa: A Comparison of the Official Curriculum with Pupil Performance in the SACMEQ II Project'. Paper to SACMEQ International Invitational Conference, 28–30 September 2005. International Institute for Educational Planning, Unesco, Paris.

Reddy, Vijay. 2006. *Mathematics and Science Achievement at South African Schools in TIMSS 2003*. Pretoria: Human Sciences Research Council.

SACMEQ (Southern Africa Consortium for Monitoring Educational Quality). 2002. *Cross-National Comparisons*. Paper presented to MINEDAF VIII. Dar-es-Salaam: SACMEQ.

Simkins, Charles. 1998. *On the Durability of South African Inequality*. Input paper for Macarthur Network on Inequality and Poverty, Princeton University. Mimeo. Johannesburg: University of the Witwatersrand. December.

—— 2002. *The Jagged Tear: Human Capital, Education, and AIDS in South Africa, 2002–2010*. CDE Focus 7. Johannesburg: Centre for Development and Enterprise.

South Africa, Budget Office. 1998. *1998 Medium Term Expenditure Review: Education.* Pretoria: Department of Finance.

South Africa, Department of Education. 2003a. *Report to the Minister: Review of the Financing, Resourcing and Costs of Education in Public Schools.* 3 March. Pretoria: Department of Education.

——2003b. *Systemic Evaluation 2003: Foundation Phase: Mainstream.* Pretoria: Department of Education.

South African Institute of Race Relations. 2001. *South African Survey 2000/01.* Braamfontein: SAIRR.

Taylor, N., Muller, J., and Vinjevold, P. 2003. *Getting Schools Working.* Cape Town: Pearson Education.

Twist, L., Schagen, I. and Hodgson, C. 2007. *Readers and Reading: the National Report for England 2006*, PIRLS: Progress in International Reading Literacy Study. Slough: National Foundation for Educational Research.

van der Berg, Servaas. 2000. *An Analysis of Fiscal Incidence of Social Spending in South Africa, 1993–97.* Report to the Department of Finance, Pretoria and funded by Deutsche Gesellschaft für Technische Zusammenarbeit. Stellenbosch: Mimeo.

——2007. 'Apartheid's Enduring Legacy: Inequalities in Education'. *Journal for African Economies*, 16(5): 849–80

——2008. 'How Effective are poor schools? Poverty and Educational Outcomes in South Africa'. *Studies in Educational Evaluation*, 34(3): 145–154.

van der Berg, Servaas and Achterbosch, Thom. 2001. *School Education in the Western Cape: Matching Supply to Demand.* Report for the Western Cape Education Department. Stellenbosch: April. 23pp.

van der Berg, Servaas and Burger, Ronelle. 2002. 'Education and Socio-Economic Differentials: A Study of School Performance in the Western Cape'. *South African Journal of Economics*, 71(3): 496–522.

van der Berg, Servaas; Wood, Louise, and Le Roux, Neil. 2002. 'Differentiation in Black Education'. *Development Southern Africa*, 19(2): 289–306.

Index

Abedian, I. 92, 197
Absa Bank 229
Accelerated and Shared Growth Initiative for SA (AsgiSA) 3, 10–11, 14, 17–18, 22–4, 51–2, 84, 177, 239
accountability 61, 83
Achterbosch, T. 345
acquisitions 137
Actuarial Society of South Africa (ASSA) 247
administration reform 96–7
AECI 230, 231
Afgri 232
Agénor, P. R. 47
Aghion, P. 42, 43, 194, 195, 205, 206, 216
Agüero, J. M. 111
Ahmed, F. 82, 125, 126, 127
AIDS *see* HIV/AIDS
Ajam, T. 8, 9, 112
Albuquerque, R. 126
Alcan 237
Alesina, A. 113
Alfaro, L. 137
All Media and Products Survey (AMPS) 279
Alleyne, T. 306
Allsopp, C. 113
ANC 5–6, 16, 18–19, 23–5, 52, 59, 74, 211, 233, 244, 320
Anglo American plc 77, 129, 135, 138, 227, 228, 229, 230
anti-competitive conduct 227
anti-retroviral treatment (ART) 22, 245, 246, 264–6
Aoki, K. 65
apartheid 1–6, 13, 19, 20, 34, 50, 93–4, 106, 169, 201, 212, 216, 230, 272–8, 286–8, 295, 304, 310, 329, 343–7
Ardagna, S. 113
Argentina 34, 35, 36, 142
ARMSCOR 4, 5
Arndt, C. 49, 251, 252, 266
Aron, J. 2, 8–9, 18, 36, 45–6, 58, 61, 63–8, 74, 80, 84, 87, 106–7, 112, 153, 166, 174, 184, 196, 205

Arora, V. 14, 38, 44, 173
Arvanitis, A. 127
Aten, B. 34
Auditor General 94
Australia 81, 139, 140, 142, 216
Australian Reserve Bank 75, 84
automotive industry 222–3, 225–6

Bahmani-Oskooee, M. 167
balance of payments 10, 261–2
Baldwin, R. E. 171
Ballim, G. 68
Banerjee, A. 37, 48, 49, 288
Banerjee, B. 310
Bank of England 66, 86
Barclays Bank 135, 229
Barker, F. S. 49
Barnes, J. 225
Barro, R. J. 36, 346
Barth, M. 64
Basic Income Grant 115
Bayley, B. 231
Bean, C. 64
Beck, T. 193
Bell, C. 252, 266
Bell, T. 151, 153, 155, 163, 177
Belli, P. 155, 156, 173
Bernanke, B. 60
Bernhardsen, T. 67
Bertrand, M. 313
Bertrand, D. 224
Bhanisi, S. 225
Bhorat, H. 48, 49, 297, 301, 308
BHP-Billiton 138, 228
Bhundia, A. 14, 44, 77, 173
Bill of Rights 95
Birdsall, N. 252
Black, A. 137, 215, 221, 225
Black, P. 19, 104
Bleaney, M. F. 46
BLNS countries 158
Bloom, D. E. 249
Blundell, R. 42
Bogetić, Z. 9, 47, 107, 200, 204, 205
Bond, S. 185

355

Index

Bond Exchange (BESA) 130
bond market 129–32, 131–2
Bosworth, B. 36, 37
Botha, P. W., President 155
Botswana 158, 249–50, 333
Botswana Institute for Development Policy Analysis (BIDPA) 249
Boulle, A. 246, 255, 257
Bowles, S. 308
Braun, M. 194, 205, 206
Brazil 36, 81, 329
Breton, A. 108
budget:
 deficit 3, 7, 98–101, 261, 264–5
 indicators 97–101
 projections 104–5
 reform 95–6
Budget Council 96
Bureau for Economic Research (BER)
 macro-econometric model 245–6, 251–2, 253–66
Burger, R. P. 48, 49, 327, 345
Butler, A. 245

Caballero, R. 76, 84
Calitz, E. 92, 96, 97, 101
Calvo, G. A. 147
Cameroon 251
Campa, J. M. 84
Canada 139, 140, 216
capital:
 accumulation 44–7
 contribution to growth 39–53
 costs of 45, 186, 190, 191
 formation 184
 human 42, 192, 252
 international flows 31–2, 47, 70, 122, 185
 liberalization 11–12
 public sector 9, 198–200
 see also investment
capital account liberalization 8, 118, 121, 137, 194
Casale, D. 177, 301, 303, 304, 306, 307, 322
Case, A. 111, 292, 331
Cassim, R. 159, 222
Cavallo, E. A. 147
Cell C 235
censuses 270–1, 273, 278
CGE models 22
Chabane, N. 228
Chandler, A. 227
Chandra, V. 309
Charmes, J. 308
chemicals 225, 226–7, 230–1
Child Support Grant 280, 292–4
Chile 81, 87, 121–2, 141, 142
China 84, 158

Chirinko, R. S. 44, 46
Cleary, S. 246, 255
Coetzee, Z. 197
Collins, S. M. 36, 37
Columbus Stainless Steel 225
competition 19–20, 42, 195
Competition Commission 195, 216, 232
competition policy 216, 239
Competition Tribunal 216, 229, 231
Competition Board 216, 231
competitiveness 5, 211, 214
concentration 227, 228–9
conglomerates 2
Constitution 7, 93–5, 108
construction 30
Cosatu 6
counter-cyclical policy 8, 104
Cowan, K. 130, 131
CPIX (consumer price index) 59–60, 63, 74–80, 102, 261, 264–5
credibility 18, 58, 61, 65–70, 106–7, 113
credit 65, 193
crime 309, 322
Crouch, L. 345
crowding-in 192
Cuddington, J. T. 249, 251
Culture of Learning, Teaching, and Service (COLTS) 349
currency 75, 77–8, 82
 crisis 14, 71, 74–5, 22, 97, 121
 see also rand
current account deficits 85, 145, 147
Customized Sector Programmes (CSPs) 226
customs revenue 158
cyclically adjusted fiscal measures 93, 100–1, 114

Dahlquist, M. 142
Daniels, R. 174
data:
 census 270–1, 273, 278
 errors 78–80
 firm-level 166
 fiscal 96
 labour market 305
 manufacturing 206
 quality 87
 unemployment 313–14
Davis, E. P. 120
De Beers 77, 129, 135, 138, 228
de Jager, S. 64
De Kadt, R. 191
De Kock, G. 59–60, 72
De Kock Commission 61
De Wet, G. L. 28
Deaton, A. 111, 292, 331

356

Index

debt
 crisis 71, 132, 153, 155
 domestic 3, 105–6, 130
 foreign 5, 12, 84, 105, 119, 124, 55
 household 86
 management 105–6
 rescheduling agreement 70
DeLong, J. B. 33
demand side policy 196
Demirguc-Kunt, A. 45
democratic elections 5, 14, 151
demographic factors 13, 247–8, 295, 303, 319, 350–1
Department of Trade and Industry (DTI) 159, 226, 227
 Competition Board 216, 231
 National Industrial Policy Framework (NIPF) 152, 177, 227
Devarajan, S. 249, 251, 252
Devey, R. 301, 308, 322
Dias, R. 322
Disability Grant 283, 292–4
Dixit, A. K. 42, 45, 46, 185
Dobreva, R. 226, 230
Dollar, D. 49
Donaldson, A. 346
Doppelhofer, G. 196
Dorrington, R. E. 244, 246, 247, 256
Dowrick, S. 33
du Plessis, P. G. 194
du Plessis, S. A. 15, 28, 61
du Toit, C. 45, 190
Dunne, P. 171, 172
Duty Credit Certificates 160, 166

earnings 307, 311, 329
 see also wages
Eastern Cape 110
Eberhard, A. 236, 237
economic activity, spatial distribution 200–1, 202, 205
economic growth 25
 and AIDS 21–2
 constraints 23
 determinants 13
 rates 13–14
Edmonds, E. 313
education 2, 3, 4, 9, 53, 304
 attainment 34–5, 328, 329–31
 drop outs 329–30
 and earnings 329
 inputs and outputs 20–1, 328, 338, 340
 international comparisons 333–4
 motivation 345
 performance analysis 339–46
 policy 296–7, 351
 private 337
 public 346
 quality 107, 112, 328, 331–7
 racial inequality 21, 327–8, 329, 344
 and socio-economic status 345
 Systemic Evaluation 333
 see also schools; teachers
Edwards, L. 11, 15, 43, 49, 51, 151–2, 155, 157, 159, 160, 162–6, 168–72, 174, 175, 176, 177, 178, 203, 205, 214, 221–2
Egypt 11, 333
Eichengreen, B. 121
Eijffinger, S. 65, 66
Elbadawi, I. 70, 74
electricity 52, 80, 205, 224, 235–8
Ellis, L. 22, 320
emerging equity portfolios 132–4
employment 223
 by category 310
 formal 304–9, 305–6
 and gender 314–15
 growth 48–50, 222
 and HIV/AIDS epidemic 259–60
 informal 296, 300, 302, 308–11
 and openness 169–73
 restructuring 11
 sectoral composition 287
 trends 305–6, 314–15
 see also labour; self-employment
endorsements 330–1
enterprise surveys 305
equities, foreign investment in 127–9
equity finance 80–1
equity indices 128–9
equity portfolios 10, 141–5
Erwin, Alec 236
Eskom 4, 9, 52, 198, 224, 233, 235–7
Essalar, J. 306
European Free Trade Association (EFTA) 151, 158
European Union (EU) 151, 152, 155, 158–9, 162–3
Evenett, S. 155, 169
exchange controls 2
 liberalization of 119–23, 124
 transactions, costs of 144
exchange rate 83, 84
 dual 119–20
 policy 9–11, 68–72
 stability 23–4
 volatility 72
expectations 64, 67, 121
Export Development Assistance scheme 153
export ratio 222
exports 4
 growth of 156, 221
 manufacturing share 36
 tax 168–9

357

Index

external balance sheet:
  and macroeconomic policy 145
  sustainability in 134, 141
external reform 121–2

factor accumulation 37
factor inputs 36
factor prices 50
factor returns 169–70
Fallon, P. 48, 153, 212, 213, 290, 308
fan-chart 73
Farrell, G. 81
Faruqee, H. 142
Fedderke, J. W. 9, 18, 37–9, 41–50, 107, 122, 126–7, 159, 163, 169–71, 173, 175, 184, 186, 191–5, 197–201, 203–6, 278
federalism theory 111
Feenstra, R. 170
Feinstein, C. H. 33, 34
Ferderer, J. P. 185
Fernández-Arias, E. 11, 126, 136, 137
Ferreira, P. C. 252
fertility 35–6
Fielding, D. 46–7, 107, 186, 189–93, 196
Fields, G. 308
Filmer, D. 339, 349
Financial and Fiscal Commission 94, 96
financial markets 186
financial sector 31
financial structure 44–5
Fine, B. 213, 224, 225
Fingleton, J. 227
fiscal:
  decentralization 108–12
  framework 121
  impulse 103–4
  prudence 7
  reform 95–7
fiscal policy 3, 8–9, 204
  consolidation 7, 58, 98–9, 104, 106, 231
  credibility 8, 97
  in the Constitution 93–5
  performance of 97–107
  transparency 8, 10
Fiske, E. B. 345, 347
Flatters, F. 158, 159, 226
food and agricultural products 231–3
Food Price Monitoring Committee 232
food prices 78, 80, 83
Forbes, K. J. 121
foreign assets 24, 119–22, 124–5, 140–6
foreign direct investment (FDI) 10–11, 125–6
  factors influencing 127
  liberalized 123
  low 134–7
  stock of 136
  versus portfolio investment 136–7, 139–41

foreign liabilities 145–6
foreign reserves 84, 145
foreign trade *see* trade
Forward Rate Agreement (FRA) 68
Fourie, F. C.v.N. 194
Frankel, J. A. 18, 51, 147
free trade agreements (FTA) 151
French, K. R. 142
Fuller, B. 331
furniture 223

Geffen, N. 245, 255
Gelb, S. 137, 320
General Agreement in Services (GATS) 176
General Agreement on Tariffs and Trade (GATT) 11, 162
  Uruguay round 151, 156, 211
General Export Incentive Scheme (GEIS) 156
General Household
  Survey 280, 284
Geraats, P. 65, 66
Geroski, P. 227
Gersbach, H. 252
Ghana 333
Gidlow, R. M. 61
Glewwe, P. 283
globalization 92–3
Goldberg, L. S. 84
gold price 68, 77, 153–5
Goldstein, I. 126, 136
Goodhart, C. A. E. 66
government:
  bonds 81–2
  deficits 126
  finance 261–2, 265
  see also local government; provincial government
governance 3, 16, 92–3, 142, 233, 321
Grandes, M. 82
Greenaway, D. 222
Groenewegen, P. D. 108
growth 36, 58–9, 106–7, 126
  and competition 195
  historical 183
  and HIV/AIDS epidemic 259–60
  and investment 1992–3
  prospects for 50–3
  and public capital 198–200
  trends 29–32
growth accounting 32, 33–9
Growth, Equality, and Redistribution (GEAR) 6, 7, 11, 12, 22, 95, 99, 113, 156, 211, 320
Guidotti, P. E. 147
Guiso, L. 185
Gumede, V. 167
Gustafsson, M. 345

Index

Haacker, M. 249
Habermeier, K. 121
Hamilton, L. 34
Hamoudi, A. 252
Hancock, J. D. 249, 251
Hanival, S. 215
Hanson, G. 170
Hanushek, E. A. 328, 339, 349
Harding, T. 174
Harmse, C. 159, 163
Harris, J. 312
Hartman, R. 185
Hausmann, R. 11, 23, 51, 52, 126, 136, 137, 212, 217, 226, 238
health and welfare 2, 9
  government expenditure 255–6
  private sector costs 256–8
Heinz, J. 308
Hertz, T. 317
Heston, A. 34
Hirsch, A. 5–6, 212, 214, 215, 216
HIV/AIDS epidemic 4, 16, 244–67
  demographic impact 247–8
  effect of ART 259–64, 264–6
  funeral costs 258
  and government finance 261–2, 265
  and growth 21–2, 259–60
  health and welfare costs 255–8
  and household consumption 263–4
  National Strategy Plan 266–7
  population and labour force 254–5, 259–60, 319–20
HIV/AIDS impact studies:
  assumptions 246
  Bureau for Economic Research (BER) macro-econometric model 245–6, 251–2, 253–66, 266
  general equilibrium model 251
  ING Barings study 251
  overlapping-generations model 252
  sensitivity analysis 246
  survey 249–53
HIV/AIDS/STD Strategic Plan (2000–5) 245
Hodge, J. S. 176, 227, 234, 235
Hodgson, C. 333
Hodrick Prescott filter 101
Hoekman, B. 176
Hofmaenner, A. 223, 225
Holden, M. 155, 163, 177
home bias 25, 119, 141–7, 160, 164–8, 195
homelands 92–3, 109, 305
Hoogeveen, J. G. 278, 279, 322
Horton, M. 101, 103, 104, 106
house prices 64–5, 74, 86

household:
  consumption 263–4
  income 283–4, 285
housing 9
  costs 74
  market 86–7
human capital 42, 192, 252
Hungary 217
Hunter, R. 112

Imbs, J. 217
imports 153, 155, 212, 221
income 2
  household 283–4, 285
  sources decomposed 281–4
Income and Expenditure Survey (IES) 281
Income Tax Act 97
Independent Communications Authority of South Africa (ICASA) 234
India 11, 84, 158, 310
industrial action 190
Industrial Development Corporation (IDC) 221, 224, 225
industrial diversification 212
industrial policy 19–20, 24, 212, 214–15
industry, export-oriented 222
Industry Strategy Project (ISP) 213, 214
inequality 36
  long-run trends 271–5
  rural/urban divide 274
  sample surveys 278–9
  under apartheid 270
  wage 283
  within-group 12, 273–4
  within-race 295
inflation 58–9, 126, 196
  causes of 78
  expectations 67
  forecast errors 73–4
  and HIV/AIDS epidemic 260–1
  hurts the poor 85
  and openness 174–5
inflation targeting 7, 83, 106, 113, 145
  interest rates under 80–2
  introduction of 9–10, 58–9, 61–4
  under Mboweni 76–80
  see also interest rate; monetary policy
information asymmetries 349, 351
information and communications industries 227
infrastructure 47, 52
  economic 197
  investment in 18–19, 107
  and productivity 200
  spending on 239
  and trade 203
ING Barings study 251

359

Index

innovation 42
insider-outside theory 304
institutional reform 99
interest rates 51, 58–9, 83
   and HIV/AIDS epidemic 260–1
   predictability 67–8
   real 196
   volatility 9
   see also inflation targeting; monetary policy
Intergovernmental Fiscal Relations Act (1997) 96
International Federation of Accountants 96
International Liquidity Position (ILP) 70
International Monetary Fund (IMF) 11, 14
International Panel 23, 51–2, 84
International Public Sector Accounting Standards 96
internationalization 228
internet service providers 235
investment 15
   and credit markets 193
   decisions 46–7
   declining rate 183
   determinants of 185–6, 187–8
   and growth 192–3
   and HIV/AIDS epidemic 262–3
   in infrastructure 18–19, 107
   and institutional environment 191
   and market structure 194–5
   neoclassical function 190
   non-tradable sectors 18–19
   private sector 18, 31, 47
   public 47
   returns on 186
   and saving 192–3
   spillovers 40–1
   trends 30–2
   and uncertainty 107, 185–91, 204
   see also capital
investors:
   institutional 120, 122–3, 139, 143–4
   resident and non-resident 121
Iraq war 79
irreversibility 46
ISCOR 4, 5, 229–30
Ishii, S. 121
Israel 142

Jafta, R. 327
Jansen, J. 349
Jansen, Z. 81
Japan 142, 169
Jaquemin, A. 227
Jayne, T. S. 232
Jenkins, C. 151, 153
Jenkins, R. 171, 173
job creation 203–4
job losses 218

Joffe, A. 213, 215, 216
Johannesburg Stock Exchange (JSE) 127, 128, 129, 144, 227, 228, 232
Johnny, B. 203
Johnson, L. F. 246, 247
Jonsson, G. 44, 50, 173, 175
Judson, R. 65

Kahn, B. 70, 71, 75, 81122, 130, 215, 221
Kalemli-Ozcan, S. 252
Kambou, G. 249, 251
Kaplan, D. 160
Kaplan, E. 121
Kaplinsky, R. 223
Katz Commission 96
Kershoff, G. 67
Keys, Finance Minister 5
Kho, B.-C. 142
Khumalo, N. 176
Kingdon, G. 16, 17, 48, 305, 307, 308, 311, 312, 313, 322
Kirsten, J. 232
Klasen, S. 16, 48, 288, 289, 301, 313
Klinger, B. 212, 226, 238
Kloster, A. 67
Knight, J. 16, 17, 48, 305, 307, 308, 311, 312, 313, 322
knowledge-intensive industry 214, 226–7
Kopits, G. 97
Kraay, A. 49
Kularatne, C. 45, 46, 186, 189, 193, 195, 200
Kumba 228
KwaZulu-Natal 110, 341, 344

labour 37
   contribution to growth 39–53
   costs 256–8
   legislation 4, 16–17
   regulation 304–5, 309–10, 311, 321, 323
   see also employment; migration
labour force:
   growth 302–4
   and HIV/AIDS 254–5, 259–60, 319–20
   participation rate 286, 303, 304
Labour Force Survey (LFS) 280, 290, 300, 305, 314, 319
labour market 15–17, 271
   data 301, 305
   decisions 46–7
   demand side 296
   inflexible 16–17
   policies 320–2
   and poverty 273, 284–92
   rigidities 16, 17, 24, 49–50, 286, 300, 302, 321–3, 327–8
   rural 297
   segmentation 302, 321

Index

Ladd, H. F. 345, 347
Lam, D. 329
language policy 334
Laubscher, P. 29, 49, 252, 253
Lawrence, R. Z. 51, 152, 163–5, 168–9, 176, 178, 214, 221–2
Le Roux, M. 237
Le Roux, E. 197
Le Roux, N. 331
Leach, D. F. 194
Leamer, E. E. 170, 171
Leape, J. 10, 11, 69, 71, 75, 144
leather 223
Lee, J.-W. 346
Lehmann, A. 137
Leibbrandt, M. 13, 271, 273–7, 297, 308, 322
Leiderman, L. 63
Lerman, R. 283
Lesotho 158
Levine, R. 45, 193
Levy, B. 212
Lewis, D. 49
Lewis, J. D. 251, 252, 266
Lewis, K. 142
liberalization 4, 6, 20, 201
  gradual 120, 121–2, 137
Liberty Life 229
Limpopo 110
liquid asset ratio-based system 61
liquidity 44–5, 70, 77
literacy 33–4
Liu, F. J. 107, 122, 126
Liu, W. 47
Loaysa, N. 193
local government 95, 108, 114
  see also provincial government
Loots, E. 48
Louw, M. 279, 322, 329
Lucas, R. J. 41, 48, 308
Luiz, J. M. 46, 47, 186, 189, 191, 197–9
Lund, F. J. 292

Mabogoane, T. 345
McCarthy, J. 77
McCord, A. 204
MacFarlan, M. 250
McGrath, M. D. 273
McGregors 228
Machaka, J. 217, 224, 225
Mackenzie, G. A. 113
macroeconomic policy 145
macroeconomic stability 6, 8, 190
Maddison, A. 34
Mahadeva, L. 66
Mahal, A. S. 249
Mahomed, T. 226
Makhaya, G. 234

Makrelov, K. 230
Malawi 251
Malaysia 11, 36, 217
Maloney, W. 310
Manning, C. 223
Manuel, Trevor 9, 216
manufacturing 2, 4, 30, 212
  base 201–2
  data 206
  diversification 217
  exports 36
  performance 217–24
  policy impacts 224–7
Mariotti, M. 46, 186, 189, 192, 195, 196
Marketing Act 231
Marketing of Agricultural Products Act (1996) 232
Masuku, S. 322
matriculation 330, 335–6, 340
May 322
Mbeki, T. President 245, 313
Mboweni, central bank governor 59–60, 66, 70, 71, 76–80
Medium Term Budget Policy Statement (MTBPS) 96
Medium-Term Expenditure Framework (MTEF) 96, 99, 111
Melody, W. 234
Meltzer, A. H. 104
MERCOSUR 151, 158
mergers 216, 228, 231
Merrifield, A. 198
Meth, C. 280, 284, 322
Mexico 34, 35, 36
migration 16, 201, 288, 303, 319
Miller, R. I. 196
Milner, C. 222
mineral-based industry 214
minerals-energy complex 224
mining 4, 216, 218
mining equipment 223
Minnitt, R. 223
Minorco 229
Mittal Steel 229
mobile phones 235
mobility:
  between schools 341, 345
  social 328
Mocke, B. A. 122
Mohamed, G. 224
Moll, P. 310
Moll, T. 33
Moloi, M. Q. 350
Momoniat, I. 108
monetary policy 3, 5, 7, 9–11
  design 61–4
  performance 72–82

361

Index

monetary policy (*continued*)
  transmission 64–5
  transparency 3, 7–10, 58, 61, 65–71, 82, 97, 136
  see also inflation targeting; interest rate
Monetary Policy Committee (MPC) 61–2, 66
monetary target 61
Money Bills 93
Monitoring Learning Achievement (MLA) 331
Montiel, P. 126
Moolman, E. 45, 68, 190
Morocco 333
Morris, M. 177
Morris, S. 66
Most Favoured Nation (MFN) 11, 152
  tariffs 157, 162, 176
Motor Industry Development Programme (MIDP) 160, 163, 166, 223, 225–6, 239
Mpahlwa, M. 177
Mpumalanga 110
Mtepa, M. 236
MTN 235
Muellbauer, J. 2, 9, 18, 36, 45–6, 58, 61, 63, 65–8, 74, 80, 84, 86–7, 106–7, 153, 166, 174, 184, 196, 205
Muller, C. 306
multinationals 144, 229
  re-domiciling of 123, 138, 139, 140
Municipal Finance Management Act (2003) 96
Musgrave, R.A. and P. B. 111
Myburgh Commission 77, 82

Namibia 158
National Electricity Regulator (NER) 236
National Energy Regulator of South Africa (NERSA) 236
National Industrial Policy Framework 152, 177, 227
National Strategy Plan 22
National Treasury 23, 51, 63, 94, 110–12, 254, 294
Nationalist government 4, 13–14
nationalization 5
Nattrass, J. 4
Nattrass, N. 22, 48–9, 244–5, 255, 271, 310, 313, 320
Naumann, D. 186, 189, 190, 194, 205
net borrowing requirement 105–6
net open foreign exchange position (NOFP) 9, 70–1, 76–7, 82, 84
Netherlands 144
New Zealand 142
Nickell, S. 42, 46
Nigeria 35
Niroomand, F. 167
Noordwes 232

North West 110
Norway 87, 142

Obstfeld, M. 70, 75, 85
October Household Survey (OHS) 290–1, 300, 305
Old Age Pension 280, 283
Old Mutual 229
Oosthuizen, M. 48, 49
Orphanides, A. 65
orphans 256
OTK 232
output gap 102–4
outward investment 137–45
Over, M. 249, 251
Özler, B. 278, 279, 322

Pact government 4
Parigi, G. 185
Parker, W. 251, 258
Pauw, K. 49
Pereira da Silva, L. 153, 212, 213
Perkins, P. 107, 197–9
Pesaran, M. Y. 43, 203
Pessoa, S. 252
petty trading 310
Phele, T. 226
Pillay, P. 331
Pindyck, R. S. 45, 46, 185
plastic products 224
Plenderleith, Ian 66
policy transparency 61, 65–6, 83
Polifin 231
political instability 191
Polokwane 25
population *see* demographic factors
Porter, M. E. 217
portfolio investment 123, 125
  equity 10, 141–5
  factors influencing 127
  outward 137–8
  versus FDI 136–7, 139–41
Posel, D. 301, 303, 304, 309, 313
Poterba, J. M. 142
poverty 12–13, 322
  gap 277
  headcount ratio 276–7
  household 273
  and inequality 271
  and the labour market 273, 284–92
  long-run trends 274–8
  measurement 270
  rankings 277
  rural/urban divide 277–8
  sample surveys 279–80
Power, M. 80

362

Index

predictability 61, 67–8, 83, 106
Pretorius, C. J. 190
prices:
  electricity 236–7
  energy 83
  factor 50
  food 78, 80, 83
  house 64–5, 74, 86
  mark-up 175, 194–5, 216
  and openness 174–5
  steel 229–30
primary sector 30
Prinsloo, J. W. 140, 144
Pritchett, L. 339, 349
privatization 6, 216, 233–7
product market imperfections 43
productivity:
  contribution to growth 39–53
  and infrastructure 200
  see also total factor productivity (TFP)
Progress in International Reading Literacy Study 333
property rights 191
provincial governments 98
  budget gaming 109–10
  equitable share grant 108
  expenditure and revenue 94–5
  future of 112, 114
  micro-service delivery 113–14
  rollovers 110
  see also local government
prudential regulation 12, 25, 122–5, 143, 147
Public Finance Management Act (1999) 95–6, 99
public works programmes 17, 322
pupil/teacher ratios 341, 344, 345

quantitative restrictions (QRs) 153
Quattek, K. 251, 253, 319, 320

Ramey, V. 64
rand:
  commercial 121
  financial 69, 119, 121, 128
  see also currency
Rangasamy, J. 159, 163, 167
Rao, A. 108
Rattsø, J. 174
Razin, A. 126, 136
Rebate Credit Certificates (IRCCs) 225–6
Reconstruction and Development Programme (RDP) 6, 7, 12, 95, 98, 216, 235
Reddy, V. 332
redistribution 5, 13, 82, 104, 113, 295, 347
Regional Electricity Distributors (REDs) 236

regulation 216, 233–7
  framework 121, 122–3
  utilities 19–20, 216, 233–7, 238
Reinhart, C. 126
Remgro 228
remittances 290
rental measurement error 74
Reserve Bank of New Zealand 66
resource-based industry 221, 224, 238
retirement financing reform 111–12
  see also State Old Age Pension
Ricci, L. 77
Richard, S. F. 104
risk:
  political 126
  premium 2, 6, 18, 36, 81
  sovereign 81–2
Roberts, S. 19, 216–17, 221, 223–5, 229, 230, 234
Rodrik, D. 29, 36, 87, 121, 171, 212
Roeger, W. 43
Rogerson, C. M. 310
Romer, P. M. 40
Romm, A. T. 107, 127, 186, 189, 192
Rothenburg, A. D. 147
Rustomjee, Z. 214, 224, 225

SABMiller 138
Sakakibara, M. 217
Sala-i-Martin, X. 196
Saldanha Steel 225
sanctions 1–5, 14, 69, 74, 136, 155, 167–9, 221, 225
Sappi 229
Sarno, L. 126
SASOL 4, 5, 221, 225, 229, 231
savings:
  and HIV/AIDS epidemic 262–3
  and investment 1992–3
  private sector 52, 184–5
  public 52, 85–6
scale economies 201
Schagen, I. 333
Scherer, F. 42
Schoeman, N. J. 104
schools:
  accountability 351
  demographic pressures on 350–1
  management 344, 346
  monitoring 349–50
  outcome inequality 338–9
  private 347
  racial composition 341
  teacher cost/pupil 343
  see also education; teachers
Sector Education Training Authorities (SETAS) 17

Index

Seekings, J. 271, 306
self-employment 296, 302, 306, 310
Senhadji, A. 167
Senwes 232
service sector 206
Sgherri, S. 250
Shah, A. 108
Shin, H. 66
Shin, Y. 203
Siebrits, F. K. 96, 97, 101
Simkins, C. 273, 278, 279, 327, 347
Singh, N. 108
Sirur, N. 331
skills 9, 14, 26, 37, 49, 192, 203–4, 213–4, 238, 273, 296, 329
skills training 17, 203–4, 322
Smal, M. M. 63, 64, 66, 72, 73
small businesses 309–11
Small and Medium Enterprise Development Programme (SMEDP) 225
Smit, B. 22, 320 15, 28, 49, 122
Smit, M. R. 194
Smith, R. J. 203
social grants 110, 280, 290, 292–4, 297
social policy 271
social security reform 111–12
social services 114
social stratification 337
South Africa Development Community (SADC) 151, 152, 158–9, 162
South Africa Foundation 6
South African Airways 198, 233
South African Breweries 229
South African Futures Exchange (SAFEX) 232
South African Reserve Bank Act 7
South African Reserve Bank (SARB) 9, 14, 61, 79, 174, 197
  forecast errors 72–4, 79
  in foreign exchange markets 70, 84
  and inflation targeting 23, 63, 66
  policy objectives 74
  role 85
  view of monetary policy transmission 64–5
South African Revenue Services (SARS) 7, 8, 96–7, 103, 108
South African Social Security Agency 111
South African Telecommunications Regulatory Agency (SATRA) 234
Southern African Customs Union (SACU) 157–9, 176, 177
Southern and Eastern Africa Consortium for Monitoring Educational Quality (SACMEQ) 35, 332
Southern and Eastern African Consortium for Monitoring Educational Quality stabilization policy 195–6

Stals, C. 7, 59–60, 66, 70, 71, 72, 74–6
Standard and Poors 133–4
Standing, G. 48
State Old Age Pension 292–4, 313
state transfers 13, 280, 283, 292–4
Project Statistics for Living Standards and Development (PSLSD) 331
Statistics South Africa (StatsSA) 78–80, 308, 309, 314, 323
steel 229–30
Steinhoff 223
Stern, M. 176
Stern, S. 158
Sterne, G. 66
Steuart, I. 176
Steyn, G. 235
Stiglitz, J. E. 42
Stolper-Samuelson theorem 169–70
Stopford, J. 74
Strategic Industrial Projects 225
structural adjustment
  programmes 156
Subramanian, A. 44, 50, 173, 175, 306
Summers, R. 34
Svensson, L. E. O. 63, 66, 85
Swanepoel, J. A. 104
Swanson, E. T. 68
Swaziland 158
Sweden 142, 144, 155
Swissair 233
Switzerland 144
Symansky, S. 97
Szalontai, G. 186, 189, 190, 194

tariffs:
  anti-export bias 164–6
  database 166
  nominal 168–9
  reform 11
  structure 15, 160–2, 176, 178
tax:
  on exports 168–9
  incentives 201
  policy 96–7
  property and land 86
  reform 8, 99, 101
Taylor, J. 61
Taylor, M. P. 126
Taylor, N. 331, 333
teachers:
  qualifications 347
  salaries 346, 349
  unions 21
  see also education; schools
technological change 172–3
technology 214, 226–7
telecommunications 205, 233–7, 238

364

Index

Telecommunications Act (1996) 234
Telkom 135, 198, 233–7
Tenreyro, S. 85
terms of trade 87
tertiary sector 29–30
Tesar, L. L. 142
textbooks 349
textiles 223
Thoburn, J. 223
Thomas, L. 10, 11, 69, 135, 137, 144
Thurlow, J. 175
Todaro, M. 312
total factor productivity (TFP) 192
  explaining 40–4
  and growth 15, 36–9, 50
  Schumpeterian 41, 42
  and trade openness 173–4
  see also productivity
trade:
  effective protection 163–4, 168–9
  and infrastructure 203
  liberalization 11, 15, 19, 49, 195, 205, 212, 214, 238
  nominal protection 160–3
  openness 44, 50–1, 166–75, 192
  preferential agreements 151, 152, 157–9, 178
  reform 152, 153–6
  sanctions 1, 2, 3, 5
  volume of 166–9
Trade, Development and Cooperation Agreement (TDCA) 159
trade policy 24
  chronology 214–15
  future of 176–8
trade unions 6, 21, 307
training costs 309
transactions costs 144
Transnet 4, 9
transparency 8, 61, 65–6, 83, 97, 106
transport costs 238
Traub, L. 232
Trends in International Mathematics and Science Study 332
Tsikata, Y. 166, 168
Tunisia 333
Twist, L. 333

uncertainty 18, 46, 50–1, 65
  impact of 191
  and investment 107, 185–91, 204
  reduced 113
  sectoral 186, 189–90
  systemic 186, 189
  user cost 190
UNDP report 279

unemployment 308
  characteristics of 315–17
  data accuracy 313–14
  definition 311–12
  duration 317
  and gender 314–15
  and HIV/AIDS epidemic 259–60
  involuntary 309, 312–13
  and the labour market 15–17, 25
  policy effects on 320, 323
  and poverty 13, 284, 286, 296
  trends 4, 314–15, 318–19
  within households 288–90
United Kingdom 65, 81, 86, 144
United States 33, 81, 86, 142, 144, 155, 158, 169, 328
utilities 227–8
  regulation 19–20, 216, 233–7, 238
  see also electricity

Value Added Network Service Providers (SAVA) 235
Value Added Tax (VAT) 101
Van de Ruit, C. 322
Van de Winkel, T. 175
Van der Berg, S. 20, 35, 42, 92, 107, 272, 278–80, 292, 296, 322, 329, 311–2, 345, 347
Van der Merwe, C. 246, 254
Van der Merwe, E. 58, 61, 72
Van Reenen, J. 185
Van Ryneweld, P. 114
Van Seventer, D. 159, 197, 273, 274
VAR model 77, 78
Vase, P. 159, 163
Venezuela 34, 35, 36
Vines, D. 113
Vink, N. 232
Visagie, L. 49
Vodacom 235
volatility 83

Wacziarg, R. 217
wage-employment 306, 307
wages 319
  income from 13, 281
  inequality 283
  real 48–9, 170–1
  setting of 64
  trends 170–1, 290–2
  see also earnings
Waldmeier, P. 5
Walker, M. 223
Walker, R. 313
Walters, S. S. 140, 144
Warnock, F. E. 147
water, access to 36

365

Index

Werner, I. M. 142
Wesso, G. R. 126
Western Cape 341, 344, 347
Whiteford, A. 273, 274
Williamson, J. 121
Woessmann, L. 328
Wollnik, A. 201, 203
Wood, A. 172
Wood, L. 331
Woolard, C. 297
Woolard, I. 16, 48, 49, 288, 289, 297, 301, 313
World Bank 212, 214
World Trade Organization (WTO) 11, 156
  Doha round 176

Xaba, J. 309

yachts 224
Yitzhaki, S. 283
Young, A. 252
Yu, D. 49, 329

Zalk, N. 230
Zervos, S. 193
Zimbabwe 16, 82, 319
Zuma, Jacob 52